Butterworths Student Statutes

Public Law

Professor Maurice Sunkin, LLM (Lon)
Barrister
Head of the Department of Law
at the University of Essex

Gavin Phillipson, BA, LLM (Cantab)
Solicitor
Lecturer in Public Law
at the University of Essex

Butterworths
London, Edinburgh, Dublin
1998

United Kingdom	Butterworths, a Division of Reed Elsevier (UK) Ltd, Halsbury House, 35 Chancery Lane, LONDON WC2A 1EL and 4 Hill Street, EDINBURGH EH2 3JZ
Australia	Butterworths, a Division of Reed International Books Australia Pty Ltd, CHATSWOOD, New South Wales
Canada	Butterworths Canada Ltd, MARKHAM, Ontario
Hong Kong	Butterworths Asia (Hong Kong), HONG KONG
India	Butterworths India, NEW DELHI
Ireland	Butterworths (Ireland) Ltd, DUBLIN
Malaysia	Malayan Law Journal Sdn Bhd, KUALA LUMPUR
New Zealand	Butterworths of New Zealand Ltd, WELLINGTON
Singapore	Butterworths Asia, SINGAPORE
South Africa	Butterworths Publishers (Pty) Ltd, DURBAN
USA	Lexis Law Publishing, CHARLOTTESVILLE, Virginia

A CIP catalogue record for this book is available from the British Library.

ISBN 0 406 98140 X

Printed in Great Britain by Redwood Books, Trowbridge, Wiltshire

Preface

As a glance through this book will emphatically confirm, there is a burgeoning output of legislation of importance to students of public law. The contents list of this book reveals that 43 of the selected statutes were passed within the present decade. Given the quantity of this legislation we have inevitably had to be selective in our choice of statutory material for inclusion in this book. This has meant that at times we have drawn what may look like arbitrary lines in the sand. However, our selection has been guided by some broad principles.

First, we have ensured that we reflect fully the recent increase in legislative activity in this field. Therefore this book includes the most significant public law legislation enacted during the first year of the Labour Government, including the Northern Ireland (Assembly) Act 1998, the Data Protection Act 1998 and the amendments made by the Criminal Justice (Terrorism and Conspiracy) Act 1998. In addition the relevant provisions of the Human Rights Act 1998 are included. We have also included a number of significant provisions from the final period of the Conservative Government, notably the Disability Discrimination Act 1995, the Civil Procedure Act 1997 (which provides the basic framework required to introduce the Woolf reforms on civil justice) and the Protection from Harassment Act 1997.

Secondly, we have recognised the crucial role played in the modern constitution by quasi-legislative and non-legislative provisions by including key parts of the Codes of Practice and Notes for Guidance made under PACE as well as extracts from the Code of Practice on Access to Government Information and from the Ministerial Code.

Thirdly, we have included a greater range of international materials than is usually found in similar books. Some of these (the EC and EU Treaties and the Equal Treatment Directive) function also as substantive, indeed, overriding, principles of domestic law. The European Convention on Human Rights is important to both international and national jurisdictions. The other international materials are included for comparative purposes: thus the reader will find not only the Amendments to the Constitution of the United States of America, but also extracts from The Canadian Charter of Rights and Freedoms, and from the widely admired Constitution of the Republic of South Africa. As the UK constitution moves more closely to resemble constitutions of other liberal democracies—a process which will accelerate with the promised Freedom of Information Act as well as the Scotland Act—we believe that such international comparisons will become increasingly valuable and important to enable a proper analysis and evaluation of the changing UK constitutional order to be made. We would like to acknowledge with great gratitude and admiration the meticulous care and efficiency with which the Primary Sources Department at Butterworths has carried out the task of turning our list of suggestions into the finished product, pointing out and correcting errors and inconsistencies in the course of the book's preparation. Any remaining errors remain the editors' sole responsibility—other than those made by Parliament itself!

Maurice Sunkin
Gavin Phillipson

October 1998

Contents

PART I
UK LEGISLATION

(MAGNA CARTA) (1215)

The GREAT CHARTER of the LIBERTIES of ENGLAND, and of the LIBERTIES of the FOREST—

NOTES
The Great Charter of 1215 was confirmed, with some changes in wording and in numbering of sections, on a number of occasions. The text below is based on the 1297 version (25 Edw 1).

Chapter 1 Confirmation of Liberties

First, we have granted to God, and by this our present charter have confirmed, for us and our heirs for ever, that the church of England shall be free, and shall have all her whole rights and liberties inviolable. We have granted also, and given to all the freemen of our realm, for us and our heirs for ever, these liberties underwritten, to have and to hold to them and their heirs, of us and our heirs for ever.

Chapter 9 Liberties of London, etc

The city of London shall have all the old liberties and customs [which it hath been used to have]. Moreover we will and grant that all other cities, boroughs, towns, and the barons of the five ports, and all other ports, shall have all their liberties and free customs.

Chapter 29 Imprisonment, etc contrary to law

No freeman shall be taken or imprisoned, or be disseised of his freehold, or liberties, or free customs, or be outlawed, or exiled, or any other wise destroyed; nor will we not pass upon him, nor [condemn him,[1]] but by lawful judgment of his peers, or by the law of the land. We will sell to no man, we will not deny or defer to any man either justice or right.

NOTES
[1] deal with him.

TREASON ACT 1351

(c 2)

NOTES
This Act was given its short title by the Short Titles Act 1896.

Declaration what offences shall be adjudged treason

Item, whereas divers opinions have been before this time [in what case treason shall be said, and in what not;[1]] the King, at the request of the lords and of the commons, hath made a declaration in the manner as hereafter followeth, that is to say; when a man doth compass or imagine the death of our lord the King, or of our lady his [Queen[2]] or of their eldest son and heir; or if a man do violate the King's [companion,[2]] or the King's eldest daughter unmarried, or the wife[3] the King's eldest son and heir; or if a man do levy war against our lord the King in his realm, or be adherent to the King's enemies in his realm, giving to them aid and comfort in the realm, or elsewhere, and thereof be [probably[4]] attainted of open deed by [the people[5]] of their condition: . . . and if a man slea the chancellor, treasurer, or the King's justices of the one bench or the other, justices in eyre, or justices of assise, and all other justices assigned to hear and determine, being in their places, doing their offices: and it is to be understood, that in the cases above rehearsed, [that[6]] ought to be judged treason which extends to our lord the King, and his royal majesty: . . .

1 That case should be adjudged treason, and what not;

2 wife

3 of

4 proveably *Ms Tr* 2

5 people

6 it

NOTES

First words omitted repealed by the Forgery Act 1830, s 31, and by 2 & 3 Will 4 c 34 (1831–2), s 1.

Second words omitted repealed by 9 Geo 4 c 31, s 1; 10 Geo 4 c 34, s 1; the Escheat (Procedure) Act 1887, Schedule; the SLR Act 1948; the Criminal Law Act 1967, s 10(2), Sch 3, Pt I; and the Criminal Law Act (Northern Ireland) 1967, Sch 2, Pt I.

BILL OF RIGHTS (1688)

(c 2)

An Act declaring the Rights and Liberties of the Subject and Setleing the Succession of the Crowne

NOTES

This Act was given its short title by the Short Titles Act 1896.

. . . . .

The subject's Rights—And thereupon the said lords spirituall and temporall and commons pursuant to their respective letters and elections being now assembled in a full and free representative of this nation takeing into their most serious consideration the best meanes for attaining the ends aforesaid doe in the first place (as their auncestors in like case have usually done) for the vindicating and asserting their auntient rights and liberties, declare

NOTES

Words omitted outside the scope of this work.

[1] Suspending power—That the pretended power of suspending of laws or the execution of laws by regall authority without consent of Parlyament is illegall.

Late dispensing power—That the pretended power of dispensing with laws or the execution of laws by regall authoritie as it hath beene assumed and exercised of late is illegall.

Ecclesiastical courts illegal—That the commission for erecting the late court of commissioners for ecclesiasticall causes and all other commissions and courts of like nature are illegal and pernicious.

Levying money—That levying money for or to the use of the Crowne by [pretence] of prerogative without grant of Parlyament for longer time or in other manner than the same is or shall be granted is illegal.

Right to petition—That it is the right of the subjects to petition the King and all commitments and prosecutions for such petitioning are illegal.

Standing army—That the raising or keeping a standing army within the kingdome in time of peace unlesse it be with consent of Parlyament is against law.

Subject's arms—That the subjects which are protestants may have arms for their defence suitable to their conditions and as allowed by law.

Freedom of election—That election of members of Parlyament ought to be free.

Freedom of speech—That the freedome of speech and debates or proceedings in Parlyament ought not to be impeached or questioned in any court or place out of Parlyament.

Excessive bail—That excessive baile ought not to be required nor excessive fines imposed nor cruell and unusuall punishments inflicted.

Juries—That jurors ought to be duly impannelled and returned . . .

Grants of forfeitures—That all grants and promises of fines and forfeitures of particular persons before conviction are illegal and void.

Frequent Parliaments—And that for redresse of all grievances and for the amending strengthening and preserving of the lawes Parlyaments ought to be held frequently.

The said right claimed, tender of the crown, regal power exercised, limitation of the crown, new oaths of allegiance, etc—And they doe claime demand and insist upon all and singular the premises as their undoubted rights and liberties and that noe declarations judgements doeings or proceedings to the prejudice of the people in any of the said premisses ought in any wise to be drawne hereafter into consequence or example. . . . The said lords spirituall and temporall and commons assembled at Westminster doe resolve that William and Mary Prince and Princesse of Orange be and be declared King and Queene of England France and Ireland and the dominions thereunto belonging . . . And that the oathes hereafter mentioned be taken by all persons of whome the oathes of allegiance and supremacy might be required by law instead of them and that the said oathes of allegiance and supremacy be abrogated.

. . . . .

NOTES

Words omitted outside the scope of this work.

ACT OF SETTLEMENT (1700)

(c 2)

An Act for the further Limitation of the Crown and better securing the Rights and Liberties of the Subject

NOTES

This Act was given its short title by the Short Titles Act 1896.

1 The Princess Sophia, Electress and Duchess dowager of Hanover, daughter of the late Queen of Bohemia, daughter of King James the First, to inherit after the King and the Princess Anne, in default of issue of the said princess and his Majesty, respectively; and the heirs of her body, being protestants

the most excellent Princess Sophia Electress and Dutchess dowager of Hanover daughter of the most excellent Princess Elizabeth late Queen of Bohemia daughter of our late sovereign lord King James the First of happy memory be and is hereby declared to be the next in succession in the protestant line to the imperiall crown and dignity of the [said[1]] realms of England France and Ireland with the dominions and territories thereunto belonging after his Majesty and the Princess Ann of Denmark and in default of issue of the said Princess Ann and of his Majesty respectively and that from and after the deceases of his said Majesty our now soveriegn lord and of her royall Highness the Princess Ann of Denmark and for default of issue of the said Princess Ann and of his Majesty respectively the crown and regall government of the said kingdoms of England France and Ireland and of the dominions thereunto belonging with the royall state and dignity of the said realms and all honours stiles titles regalities prerogatives powers jurisdictions and authorities to the same belonging and appertaining shall be remain and continue to the said most excellent Princess Sophia and the heirs of her body being protestants And thereunto the said lords spirituall and temporall and commons shall and will in the name of all the people of this realm most humbly and faithfully submitt themselves their heirs and posterities and do faithfully promise that after the deceases of his Majesty and her royall Highness and the failure of the heirs of their respective bodies to stand to maintain and defend the said Princess Sophia and the heirs of her body being [protestants[1]] according to the limitation and succession of the crown in this Act specified and contained to the utmost of their powers with their lives and estates against all persons whatsoever that shall attempt any thing to the contrary.

NOTES

[1] Interlined on the roll.

---

2 The persons inheritable by this Act, holding communion with the church of Rome, incapacitated as by the former Act; to take the oath at their coronation, according to Stat 1 W & M c 6

Provided always and it is hereby enacted that all and every person and persons who shall or may take or inherit the said crown by vertue of the limitation of this present Act and is are or shall be reconciled to or shall hold communion with the see or church of Rome or shall profess the popish religion or shall marry a papist shall be subject to such incapacities as in such case or cases are by the said recited Act provided enacted and established. And that every King and Queen of this realm who shall come to and succeed in the imperiall crown of this kingdom by vertue of this Act shall have the coronation oath administered to him her or them at their respective coronations according to the Act of Parliament made in the first year of the reign of his Majesty and the said late Queen Mary intituled An Act for establishing the coronation oath and shall make subscribe and repeat the declaration in the Act first above recited mentioned or referred to in the manner and form thereby prescribed.

NOTES

Declaration: form of declaration is now that prescribed by the Accession Declaration Act 1910, Schedule, and reads as follows:

I [*here insert the name of the Sovereign*] do solemnly and sincerely in the presence of God profess, testify, and declare that I am a faithful Protestant, and that I will, according to the true intent of the enactments which secure the Protestant succession to the Throne of my Realm, uphold and maintain the said enactments to the best of my powers according to law.

3 Further provisions for securing the religions, laws, and liberties of these realms

And whereas it is requisite and necessary that some further provision be made for securing our religion laws and liberties from and after the death of his Majesty and the Princess Ann of Denmark . . . Be it enacted by the Kings most excellent Majesty by and with the advice and consent of the lords spirituall and temporall and commons in Parliament and by the authority of the same

That whosoever shall hereafter come to the possession of this crown shall joyn in communion with the Church of England as by law established

That in case the crown and imperiall dignity of this realm shall hereafter come to any person not being a native of this kingdom of England this nation be not obliged to ingage in any warr for the defence of any dominions or territories which do not belong to the crown of England without the consent of Parliament

. . . . .

That after the said limitation shall take effect as aforesaid no person born out of the kingdoms of England Scotland or Ireland or the dominions thereunto belonging (although he be . . . made a denizen (except such as [are] born of English parents) shall be capable to be of the privy councill or a member of either House of Parliament or to enjoy any office or place of trust either civill or military or to have any grant of lands tenements or hereditaments from the Crown to himself or to any other or others in trust for him.

. . . . .

That no pardon under the great seal of England be pleadable to an impeachment by the commons in Parliament.

NOTES

Words omitted in first place outside the scope of this work.

Words omitted in second place repealed by 1 Geo 1 stat 2 c 51 (1714–16) and 4 & 5 Anne c 20 (1705), s 27.

Words omitted in third place repealed by the Status of Aliens Act 1914, s 28, Sch 3.

Words omitted in fourth place repealed by 4 & 5 Anne c 20 (1705), s 28, the Statute Law Revision and Civil Procedure Act 1881, and, as to Northern Ireland, by the SLR Act 1950.

[1] Interlined on the roll.

4 The laws and statutes of the realm confirmed

And whereas the laws of England are the birthright of the people thereof and all the Kings and Queens who shall ascend the throne of this realm ought to administer the government of the same according to the said laws and all their officers and ministers ought to serve them respectively according to the same The said lords spirituall and temporall and commons do therefore further humbly pray that all the laws and statutes of this realm for securing the established religion and the rights and liberties of the people thereof and all other laws and statutes of the same now in force may be ratified and confirmed And the same are by his Majesty by and with the advice and consent of the said lords spirituall and temporall and commons and by authority of the same ratified and confirmed accordingly.

UNION WITH SCOTLAND ACT 1706

(c 11)

An Act for an Union of the Two Kingdoms of England and Scotland

NOTES

This Act was given its short title by the Short Titles Act 1896.

ARTICLE I

The kingdoms united; . . . —That the two kingdoms of England and Scotland shall upon the first day of May which shall be in the year one thousand seven hundred and [sever[1]] and for ever after be united into one kingdom by the name of Great Britain . . .

NOTES

Words omitted outside the scope of this work.

[1] Seven.

ARTICLE II

Succession to the monarchy—That the succession to the monarchy of the United Kingdom of Great Britain and of the dominions thereto belonging after her most sacred Majesty and in default of issue of her Majesty be remain and continue to the most excellent Princess Sophia Electoress and Dutchess dowager of Hanover and the heirs of her body being protestants upon whom the crown of England is settled by an Act of Parliament made in England in the twelfth year of the reign of his late Majesty King William the Third . . . And that all papists and persons marrying papists shall be excluded from and for ever incapable to inherit possess or enjoy the imperial crown of Great Britain and the dominions thereunto belonging or any part thereof and in every such case the crown and government shall from time to time descend to and be enjoyed by such person being a protestant as should have inherited and enjoyed the same in case such papist or person marrying a papist was naturally dead according to the provision for the descent of the crown of England made by another Act of Parliament in England in the first year of the reign of their late Majesties King William and Queen Mary intituled An Act declaring the rights and liberties of the subject and settling the succession of the crown.

ARTICLE III

Parliament—That the United Kingdom of Great Britain be represented by one and the same Parliament to be stiled the Parliament of Great Britain.

ARTICLE IIII

Trade and navigation and other rights—That all the subjects of the United Kingdom of Great Britain shall from and after the union have full freedom and intercourse of trade and navigation to and from any port or place within the said United Kingdom and the dominions and plantations thereunto belonging and that there be a communication of all other rights privileges and advantages which do or may belong to the subjects of either kingdom except where it is otherwise expressly agreed in these articles.

ARTICLE VI

Regulations of trade, duties, etc—That all parts of the United Kingdom for ever from and after the union shall have the same allowances encouragements and drawbacks and be under the same prohibitions restrictions and regulations of trade and liable to the same customs and duties on import and export and that the allowances encouragements and drawbacks prohibitions restrictions and regulations of trade and the customs and duties on import and export settled in England when the union commences shall from and after the union take place throughout the whole United Kingdom . . .

NOTES

Words omitted in first place outside the scope of this work.

Words omitted in second place repealed by the SLR Act 1948, by the SL(R) Act 1973, and by virtue of the partial repeal of s 4 by the SLR Act 1867.

ARTICLE VII

Excise—That all parts of the United Kingdom be for ever from and after the union liable to the same excises upon all exciseable liquors . . .

NOTES

Words omitted repealed by the SLR Act 1948.

ARTICLE XVI

Coin—That from and after the union the coin shall be of the same standard and value throughout the United Kingdom as now in England . . .

NOTES

Words omitted repealed by virtue of the partial repeal of s 4 by the SLR Act 1867.

ARTICLE XVIII

Laws concerning public rights; private rights—That the laws concerning regulation of trade customs and such excises to which Scotland is by virtue of this treaty to be liable be the same in Scotland from and after the union as in England and that all other laws in use within the kingdom of Scotland do after the union and notwithstanding thereof remain in the same force as before (except such as are contrary to or inconsistent with this treaty) but alterable by the Parliament of Great Britain with this difference betwixt the laws concerning publick right policy and civil government and those which concern private right [that the laws which concern publick right[1]] policy and civil government may be made the same throughout the whole United Kingdom. But that no alteration be made in laws which concern private right except for evident utility of the subjects within Scotland

NOTES

[1] Interlined on the roll.

ARTICLE XIX

Court of Session; Writers to the signet admitted lords of session; Court of Justiciary; Other Courts; Causes in Scotland not cognizable in courts in Westminster Hall—That the Court of Session or colledge of justice do after the union and notwithstanding thereof remain in all time coming within Scotland as it is now constituted by the laws of that kingdom and with the same authority and privileges as before the union subject nevertheless to such regulations for the better administration of justice as shall be made by the Parliament of Great Britain and that hereafter none shall be named by Her Majesty or her royal successors to be ordinary lords of session but such who have served in the colledge of justice as advocates or principal clerks of session for the space of five years or as writers to the signet for the space of ten years with this provision that no writer to the signet be capable to be admitted a lord of the session unless he undergo a private and publick tryal on the civil law before the faculty of advocates and be found by them qualified for the said office two years before he be named to be a lord of the session yet so as the qualifications made or to be made for capacitating persons to be named ordinary lords of session may be altered by the Parliament of Great Britain And that the Court of Justiciary do also after the union and notwithstanding thereof remain in all time coming within Scotland as it is now constituted by the laws of that kingdom and with the same authority and privileges as before the union subject nevertheless to such regulations as shall be made by the Parliament of Great Britain and without prejudice of other rights of justiciary . . . And that the heretable rights of admiralty and vice admiralties in Scotland be reserved to the respective proprietors as rights of property subject nevertheless as to the manner of exercising such heretable rights to such regulations and alterations as shall be thought proper to be made by the Parliament of Great Britain And that all other courts now being within the kingdom of Scotland do remain but subject to alterations by the Parliament of Great Britain and that all inferiour courts within the said limits do remain subordinate as they are now to the supreme courts of justice within the same in all time coming And that no causes in Scotland be cognoscible by the courts of Chancery Queen's Bench Common Pleas or any other court in Westminster Hall and that the said courts or any other of the like nature after the union shall have no power to cognosce review or alter the acts or sentences of the judicatures within Scotland or stop the execution of the same . . .

NOTES

Words omitted in first place repealed by the SL(R) Act 1973.

Other words omitted repealed by virtue of the partial repeal of s 4 by the SLR Act 1867, and by the SLR Act 1948.

ARTICLE XX

Heritable offices, etc—That all heretable offices superiorities heretable jurisdictions offices for life and jurisdictions for life be reserved to the owners thereof as rights of property in the same manner as they are now enjoyed by the laws of Scotland notwithstanding this treaty.

ARTICLE XXI

Royal Burghs—That the rights and privileges of the royal burghs in Scotland as they now are do remain entire after the union and notwithstanding thereof.

ARTICLE XXV

Laws inconsistent with the articles, void—That all laws and statutes in either kingdom so far as they are contrary to or inconsistent with the terms of these articles or any of them shall from and after the union cease and become void and shall be so declared to be by the respective Parliaments of the said kingdoms.

As by the said articles of union ratified and approved by the said Act of Parliament of Scotland relation [being thereunto[1]] had may appear.

NOTES

[1] Thereunto being.

5 Cap 8 ante, and the said Act of Parliament of Scotland to be observed as fundamental conditions of the said union; and the said articles and Acts of Parliament to continue the union

And it is hereby further enacted by the authority aforesaid that the said Act passed in this present session of Parliament intituled An Act for securing the Church of England as by law established and all and every the matters and things therein contained and also the said Act of Parliament of Scotland intituled Act for securing the Protestant religion and Presbyterian Church government with the establishment in the said Act contained be and shall for ever be held and adjudged to be and observed as fundamental and essential conditions of the said union and shall in all times coming be taken to be and are hereby declared to be essential and fundamental parts of the said articles and union and the said articles of union so as aforesaid ratified approved and confirmed by Act of Parliament of Scotland and by this present Act and the said Act passed in this present session of Parliament intituled an Act for securing the Church of England as by law established and also the said Act passed in the Parliament of Scotland intituled Act for securing the Protestant religion and Presbyterian Church government are hereby enacted and ordained to be and continue in all times coming the complete and intire union of the two kingdoms of England and Scotland.

PARLIAMENTARY PAPERS ACT 1840

(c 9)

An Act to give summary Protection to Persons employed in the Publication of Parliamentary Papers

[14 April 1840]

NOTES

This Act was given its short title by the Short Titles Act 1896.

[1] Proceedings, criminal or civil, against persons for publication of papers printed by order of Parliament to be stayed upon delivery of a certificate and affidavit to the effect that such publication is by order of either House of Parliament

. . . It shall and may be lawful for any person or persons who now is or are, or hereafter shall be, a defendant or defendants in any civil or criminal proceeding commenced or prosecuted in any manner soever, for or on account or in respect of the publication of any such report, paper, votes, or proceedings by such person or persons, or by his, her, or their servant or servants, by or under the authority of either House of Parliament, to bring before the court in which such proceeding shall have been or shall be so commenced or prosecuted, or before any judge of the same (if one of the superior courts at Westminster), first giving twenty-four hours notice of his intention so to do to the prosecutor or plaintiff in such proceeding, a certificate under the hand of the lord high chancellor of Great Britain, or the lord keeper of the great seal, or of the speaker of the House of Lords, for the time being, or of the clerk of the Parliaments, or of the speaker of the House of Commons, or of the clerk of the same house, stating that the report, paper, votes, or proceedings, as the case may be, in respect whereof such civil or criminal proceeding shall have been commenced or prosecuted, was published by such person or persons, or by his, her, or their servant or servants, by order or under the authority of the House of Lords or of the House of Commons, as the case may be, together with an affidavit verifying such certificate; and such court or judge shall thereupon immediately stay such civil or criminal proceeding, and the same, and every writ or process issued therein, shall be and shall be deemed and taken to be finally put an end to, determined, and superseded by virtue of this Act.

NOTES

Words omitted repealed by the SLR (No 2) Act 1890.

2 Proceedings to be stayed when commenced in respect of a copy of an authenticated report, etc

. . . In case of any civil or criminal proceeding hereafter to be commenced or prosecuted for or on account or in respect of the publication of any copy of such report, paper, votes, or proceedings, it shall be lawful for the defendant or defendants at any stage of the proceedings to lay before the court or judge such report, paper, votes, or proceedings, and such copy, with an affidavit verifying such report, paper, votes, or proceedings, and the correctness of such copy, and the court or judge shall immediately stay such civil or criminal proceeding, and the same, and every writ or process issued therein, shall be and shall be deemed and taken to be finally put an end to, determined, and superseded by virtue of this Act.

NOTES

Words omitted repealed by the SLR (No 2) Act 1888.

3 In proceedings for printing any extract or abstract of a paper, it may be shown that such extract was bona fide made

. . . It shall be lawful in any civil or criminal proceeding to be commenced or prosecuted for printing any extract from or abstract of such report, paper, votes, or proceedings, to give in evidence . . . such report, paper, votes, or proceedings, and to show that such extract or abstract was published bona fide and without malice; and if such shall be the opinion of the jury, a verdict of not guilty shall be entered for the defendant or defendants.

NOTES

Words omitted repealed by the SLR (No 2) Act 1888, and by the SLR Act 1958.

4 Act not to affect the privileges of Parliament

Provided always . . . that nothing herein contained shall be deemed or taken, or held or construed, directly or indirectly, by implication or otherwise, to affect the privileges of Parliament in any manner whatsoever.

NOTES

Words omitted repealed by the SLR (No 2) Act 1888.

PARLIAMENT ACT 1911

(c 13)

An Act to make provision with respect to the powers of the House of Lords in relation to those of the House of Commons, and to limit the duration of Parliament

[18 August 1911]

Preamble

Whereas it is expedient that provision should be made for regulating the relations between the two Houses of Parliament:

And whereas it is intended to substitute for the House of Lords as it at present exists a Second Chamber constituted on a popular instead of hereditary basis, but such substitution cannot be immediately brought into operation:

And whereas provision will require hereafter to be made by Parliament in a measure effecting such substitution for limiting and defining the powers of the new Second Chamber, but it is expedient to make such provision as in this Act appears for restricting the existing powers of the House of Lords:

1 Powers of House of Lords as to Money Bills

(1) If a Money Bill, having been passed by the House of Commons, and sent up to the House of Lords at least one month before the end of the session, is not passed by the House of Lords without amendment within one month after it is so sent up to that House, the Bill shall, unless the House of Commons direct to the contrary, be presented to His Majesty and become an Act of Parliament on the Royal Assent being signified, notwithstanding that the House of Lords have not consented to the Bill.

(2) A Money Bill means a Public Bill which in the opinion of the Speaker of the House of Commons contains only provisions dealing with all or any of the following subjects, namely, the imposition, repeal, remission, alteration, or regulation of taxation; the imposition for the payment of debt or other financial purposes of charges on the Consolidated Fund, [the National Loans Fund] or on money provided by Parliament, or the variation or repeal of any such charges; supply; the appropriation, receipt, custody, issue or audit of accounts of public money; the raising or guarantee of any loan or the repayment thereof; or subordinate matters incidental to those subjects or any of them. In this subsection the expressions "taxation", "public money", and "loan" respectively do not include any taxation, money, or loan raised by local authorities or bodies for local purposes.

(3) There shall be endorsed on every Money Bill when it is sent up to the House of Lords and when it is presented to His Majesty for assent the certificate of the Speaker of the House of Commons signed by him that it is a Money Bill. Before giving his certificate, the Speaker shall consult, if practicable, two members to be appointed from the Chairmen's Panel at the beginning of each Session by the Committee of Selection.

NOTES

Sub-s (2): words in square brackets inserted by the National Loans Act 1968, s 1(5).

2 Restriction of the powers of the House of Lords as to Bills other than Money Bills

(1) If any Public Bill (other than a Money Bill or a Bill containing any provision to extend the maximum duration of Parliament beyond five years) is passed by the House of Commons [in two successive sessions] (whether of the same Parliament or not), and, having been sent up to the House of Lords at least one month before the end of the session, is rejected by the House of Lords in each of those sessions, that Bill shall, on its rejection [for the second time] by the House of Lords, unless the House of Commons direct to the contrary, be presented to His Majesty and become an Act of Parliament on the Royal Assent being signified thereto, notwithstanding that the House of Lords have not consented to the Bill: Provided that this provision shall not take effect unless [one year has elapsed] between the date of the second reading in the first of those sessions of the Bill in the House of Commons and the date on which it passes the House of Commons [in the second of those sessions].

(2) When a Bill is presented to His Majesty for assent in pursuance of the provisions of this section, there shall be endorsed on the Bill the certificate of the Speaker of the House of Commons signed by him that the provisions of this section have been duly complied with.

(3) A Bill shall be deemed to be rejected by the House of Lords if it is not passed by the House of Lords either without amendment or with such amendments only as may be agreed to by both Houses.

(4) A Bill shall be deemed to be the same Bill as a former Bill sent up to the House of Lords in the preceding session if, when it is sent up to the House of Lords, it is identical with the former Bill or contains only such alterations as are certified by the Speaker of the House of Commons to be necessary owing to the time which has elapsed since the date of the former Bill, or to represent any amendments which have been made by the House of Lords in the former Bill in the preceding session, and any amendments which are certified by the Speaker to have been made by the House of Lords [in the second session] and agreed to by the House of Commons shall be inserted in the Bill as presented for Royal Assent in pursuance of this section:

Provided that the House of Commons may, if they think fit, on the passage of such a Bill through the House [in the second session], suggest any further amendments without inserting the amendments in the Bill, and any such suggested amendments shall be considered by the House of Lords, and, if agreed to by that House, shall be treated as amendments made by the House of Lords and agreed to by the House of Commons; but the exercise of this power by the House of Commons shall not affect the operation of this section in the event of the Bill being rejected by the House of Lords.

NOTES

Sub-ss (1), (4): words in square brackets substituted by the Parliament Act 1949, s 1, as from beginning of session in which Bill for that Act originated.

3 Certificate of Speaker

Any certificate of the Speaker of the House of Commons given under this Act shall be conclusive for all purposes, and shall not be questioned in any court of law.

4 Enacting words

(1) In every Bill presented to His Majesty under the preceding provisions of this Act, the words of enactment shall be as follows, that is to say:—

"Be it enacted by the King's most Excellent Majesty, by and with the advice and consent of the Commons in this present Parliament assembled, in accordance with the provisions of [the Parliament Acts 1911 and 1949], and by authority of the same, as follows."

(2) Any alteration of a Bill necessary to give effect to this section shall not be deemed to be an amendment of the Bill.

NOTES

Words in square brackets substituted by the Parliament Act 1949, s 2(2).

---

5 Provisional Order Bills excluded

In this Act the expression "Public Bill" does not include any Bill for confirming a Provisional Order.

6 Saving for existing rights and privileges of the House of Commons

Nothing in this Act shall diminish or qualify the existing rights and privileges of the House of Commons.

8 Short title

This Act may be cited as the Parliament Act 1911.

OFFICIAL SECRETS ACT 1911

(c 28)

An Act to re-enact the Official Secrets Act 1889, with Amendments

[22 August 1911]

1 Penalties for spying

(1) If any person for any purpose prejudicial to the safety or interests of the State—

(a) approaches [inspects, passes over] or is in the neighbourhood of, or enters any prohibited place within the meaning of this Act; or

(b) makes any sketch, plan, model, or note which is calculated to be or might be or is intended to be directly or indirectly useful to an enemy; or

(c) obtains, [collects, records, or publishes,] or communicates to any other person [any secret official code word or pass word, or] any sketch, plan, model, article, or note, or other document or information which is calculated to be or might be or is intended to be directly or indirectly useful to an enemy;

he shall be guilty of felony . . .

(2) On a prosecution under this section, it shall not be necessary to show that the accused person was guilty of any particular act tending to show a purpose prejudicial to the safety or interests of the State, and, notwithstanding that no such act is proved

against him, he may be convicted if, from the circumstances of the case, or his conduct, or his known character as proved, it appears that his purpose was a purpose prejudicial to the safety or interests of the State; and if any sketch, plan, model, article, note, document, or information relating to or used in any prohibited place within the meaning of this Act, or anything in such a place [or any secret official code word or pass word], is made, obtained, [collected, recorded, published], or communicated by any person other than a person acting under lawful authority, it shall be deemed to have been made, obtained, [collected, recorded, published] or communicated for a purpose prejudicial to the safety or interests of the State unless the contrary is proved.

NOTES

Words in square brackets inserted, and words omitted repealed, by the Official Secrets Act 1920, ss 10, 11(2), Schs 1, 2.

3 Definition of prohibited place

For the purposes of this Act, the expression "prohibited place" means—

[(a) any work of defence, arsenal, naval or air force establishment or station, factory, dockyard, mine, minefield, camp, ship, or aircraft belonging to or occupied by or on behalf of His Majesty, or any telegraph, telephone, wireless or signal station, or office so belonging or occupied, and any place belonging to or occupied by or on behalf of His Majesty and used for the purpose of building, repairing, making, or storing any munitions of war, or any sketches, plans, models, or documents relating thereto, or for the purpose of getting any metals, oil, or minerals of use in time of war];

(b) any place not belonging to His Majesty where any [munitions of war], or any [sketches, models, plans] or documents relating thereto, are being made, repaired, [gotten] or stored under contract with, or with any person on behalf of, His Majesty, or otherwise on behalf of His Majesty; and

(c) any place belonging to [or used for the purposes of] His Majesty which is for the time being declared [by order of a Secretary of State] to be a prohibited place for the purposes of this section on the ground that information with respect thereto, or damage thereto, would be useful to an enemy; and

(d) any railway, road, way, or channel, or other means of communication by land or water (including any works or structures being part thereof or connected therewith), or any place used for gas, water, or electricity works or other works for purposes of a public character, or any place where any [munitions of war], or any [sketches, models, plans] or documents relating thereto, are being made, repaired, or stored otherwise than on behalf of His Majesty, which is for the time being declared [by order of a Secretary of State] to be a prohibited place for the purposes of this section, on the ground that information with respect thereto, or the destruction or obstruction thereof, or interference therewith, would be useful to an enemy.

NOTES

Words in square brackets substituted or inserted by the Official Secrets Act 1920, s 10, Sch 1.

6 Power of arrest

Any person who is found committing an offence under this Act . . . or who is reasonably suspected of having committed, or having attempted to commit, or being about to commit, such an offence, may be apprehended and detained . . .

NOTES

Words omitted repealed by the Criminal Law Act 1967, s 10(2), Sch 3, Pt III.

8 Restriction on prosecution

A prosecution for an offence under this Act shall not be instituted except by or with the consent of the Attorney-General:

. . . . .

NOTES

Words omitted repealed by the Criminal Jurisdiction Act 1975, s 14(5), Sch 6, Pt I.

9 Search warrants

(1) If a justice of the peace is satisfied by information on oath that there is reasonable ground for suspecting that an offence under this Act has been or is about to be committed, he may grant a search warrant authorising any constable . . . to enter at any time any premises or place named in the warrant, if necessary, by force, and to search the premises or place and every person found therein, and to seize any sketch, plan, model, article, note, or document, or anything of a like nature or anything which is evidence of an offence under this Act having been or being about to be committed, which he may find on the premises or place or on any such person, and with regard to or in connexion with which he has reasonable ground for suspecting that an offence under this Act has been or is about to be committed.

(2) Where it appears to a superintendent of police that the case is one of great emergency and that in the interests of the State immediate action is necessary, he may by a written order under his hand give to any constable the like authority as may be given by the warrant of a justice under this section.

NOTES

Sub-s (1): words omitted repealed by the Police and Criminal Evidence Act 1984, ss 119(2), 120, Sch 7, Pt I.

10 Extent of Act and place of trial of offence

(1) This Act shall apply to all acts which are offences under this Act when committed in any part of His Majesty's dominions, or when committed by British officers or subjects elsewhere.

(2)–(4) . . .

NOTES

Sub-ss (2)–(4): outside the scope of this work.

13 Short title

(1) This Act may be cited as the Official Secrets Act 1911.

(2) . . .

NOTES

Sub-s (2): repealed by the SLR Act 1927.

EMERGENCY POWERS ACT 1920

(c 55)

An Act to make exceptional provision for the Protection of the Community in cases of Emergency
[29 October 1920]

1 Issue of proclamations of emergency

(1) If at any time it appears to His Majesty that [there have occurred, or are about to occur, events of such a nature] as to be calculated, by interfering with the supply and distribution of food, water, fuel, or light, or with the means of locomotion, to deprive the community, or any substantial portion of the community, of the essentials of life, His Majesty may, by proclamation (hereinafter referred to as a proclamation of emergency), declare that a state of emergency exists.

No such proclamation shall be in force for more than one month, without prejudice to the issue of another proclamation at or before the end of that period.

(2) Where a proclamation of emergency has been made the occasion thereof shall forthwith be communicated to Parliament, and, if Parliament is then separated by such adjournment or prorogation as will not expire within five days, a proclamation shall be issued for the meeting of Parliament within five days, and Parliament shall accordingly meet and sit upon the day appointed by that proclamation, and shall continue to sit and act in like manner as if it had stood adjourned or prorogued to the same day.

NOTES

Sub-s (1): words in square brackets substituted by the Emergency Powers Act 1964, s 1.

2 Emergency regulations

(1) Where a proclamation of emergency has been made, and so long as the proclamation is in force, it shall be lawful for His Majesty in Council, by Order, to make regulations for securing the essentials of life to the community, and those regulations may confer or impose on a Secretary of State or other Government department, or any other persons in His Majesty's service or acting on His Majesty's behalf, such powers and duties as His Majesty may deem necessary for the preservation of the peace, for securing and regulating the supply and distribution of food, water, fuel, light, and other necessities, for maintaining the means of transit or locomotion, and for any other purposes essential to the public safety and the life of the community, and may make such provisions incidental to the powers aforesaid as may appear to His Majesty to be required for making the exercise of those powers effective:

Provided that nothing in this Act shall be construed to authorise the making of any regulations imposing any form of compulsory military service or industrial conscription:

Provided also that no such regulation shall make it an offence for any person or persons to take part in a strike, or peacefully to persuade any other person or persons to take part in a strike.

(2) Any regulations so made shall be laid before Parliament as soon as may be after they are made, and shall not continue in force after the expiration of seven days from the time when they are so laid unless a resolution is passed by both Houses providing for the continuance thereof.

(3) The regulations may provide for the trial, by courts of summary jurisdiction, of persons guilty of offences against the regulations; so, however, that the maximum penalty which may be inflicted for any offence against any such regulations shall be imprisonment with or without hard labour for a term of three months, or a fine [not exceeding level 5 on the standard scale, . . . , or not exceeding a lesser amount], or both such imprisonment and fine, together with the forfeiture of any goods or money in respect of which the offence has been committed: Provided that no such regulations shall alter any existing procedure in criminal cases, or confer any right to punish by fine or imprisonment without trial.

(4), (5) . . .

NOTES

Sub-s (3): words in square brackets substituted by the Criminal Justice Act 1982, s 41; words omitted repealed by the SL(R) Act 1993.

Sub-ss (4), (5): outside the scope of this work.

3 Short title and application

(1) This Act may be cited as the Emergency Powers Act 1920.

(2) This Act shall not apply to Ireland.

OFFICIAL SECRETS ACT 1920

(c 75)

An Act to amend the Official Secrets Act 1911

[23 December 1920]

1 Unauthorised use of uniforms; falsification of reports, forgery, personation, and false documents

(1) If any person for the purpose of gaining admission, or of assisting any other person to gain admission, to a prohibited place, within the meaning of the Official Secrets Act 1911 (hereinafter referred to as "the principal Act"), or for any other purpose prejudicial to the safety or interests of the State within the meaning of the said Act—

(a) uses or wears, without lawful authority, any naval, military, air-force, police, or other official uniform, or any uniform so nearly resembling the same as to be calculated to deceive, or falsely represents himself to be a person who is or has been entitled to use or wear any such uniform; or

(b) orally, or in writing in any declaration or application, or in any document signed by him or on his behalf, knowingly makes or connives at the making of any false statement or any omission; or

(c) . . . tampers with any passport or any naval, military, air-force, police, or official pass, permit, certificate, licence, or other document of a similar character (hereinafter in this section referred to as an official document), . . . or has in his possession any . . . forged, altered, or irregular official document; or

(d) personates, or falsely represents himself to be a person holding, or in the employment of a person holding office under His Majesty, or to be or not to be a person to whom an official document or secret official code word or pass word has been duly issued or communicated, or with intent to obtain an official document, secret official code word or pass word, whether for himself or any other person, knowingly makes any false statement; or

(e) uses, or has in his possession or under his control, without the authority of the Government Department or the authority concerned, any die, seal, or stamp of or belonging to, or used, made or provided by any Government Department, or by any diplomatic, naval, military, or air force authority appointed by or acting under the authority of His Majesty, or any die, seal or stamp so nearly resembling any such die, seal or stamp as to be calculated to deceive, or counterfeits any such die, seal or stamp, or uses, or has in his possession, or under his control, any such counterfeited die, seal or stamp;

he shall be guilty of a misdemeanour.

(2) If any person—

(a) retains for any purpose prejudicial to the safety or interests of the State any official document, whether or not completed or issued for use, when he has no right to retain it, or when it is contrary to his duty to retain it, or fails to comply with any directions issued by any Government Department or any person authorised by such department with regard to the return or disposal thereof; or

(b) allows any other person to have possession of any official document issued for his use alone, or communicates any secret official code word or pass word so issued, or, without lawful authority or excuse, has in his possession any official document or secret official code word or pass word issued for the use of some person other than himself, or on obtaining possession of any official document by finding or otherwise, neglects or fails to restore it to the person or authority by whom or for whose use it was issued, or to a police constable; or

(c) without lawful authority or excuse, manufactures or sells, or has in his possession for sale any such die, seal or stamp as aforesaid;

he shall be guilty of a misdemeanour.

(3) In the case of any prosecution under this section involving the proof of a purpose prejudicial to the safety or interests of the State, subsection (2) of section one of the principal Act shall apply in like manner as it applies to prosecutions under that section.

NOTES

Sub-s (1): words omitted from para (c) repealed by the Forgery and Counterfeiting Act 1981, s 30, Schedule, Pt I; accordingly, word "forgery" in marginal note no longer has any effect.

[6 Duty of giving information as to commission of offences

(1) Where a chief officer of police is satisfied that there is reasonable ground for suspecting that an offence under section one of the principal Act has been committed and for believing that any person is able to furnish information as to the offence or suspected offence, he may apply to a Secretary of State for permission to exercise the powers conferred by this subsection and, if such permission is granted, he may authorise a superintendent of police, or any police officer not below the rank of inspector, to require the person believed to be able to furnish information to give any information in his power relating to the offence or suspected offence, and, if so required and on tender of his reasonable expenses, to attend at such reasonable time and place as may be specified by the superintendent or other officer; and if a person

required in pursuance of such an authorisation to give information, or to attend as aforesaid, fails to comply with any such requirement or knowingly gives false information, he shall be guilty of a misdemeanour.

(2) Where a chief officer of police has reasonable grounds to believe that the case is one of great emergency and that in the interest of the State immediate action is necessary, he may exercise the powers conferred by the last foregoing subsection without applying for or being granted the permission of a Secretary of State, but if he does so shall forthwith report the circumstances to the Secretary of State.

(3) References in this section to a chief officer of police shall be construed as including references to any other officer of police expressly authorised by a chief officer of police to act on his behalf for the purposes of this section when by reason of illness, absence, or other cause he is unable to do so.]

NOTES

Substituted by the Official Secrets Act 1939, s 1.

---

7 Attempts, incitements, etc

Any person who attempts to commit any offence under the principal Act or this Act, or solicits or incites or endeavours to persuade another person to commit an offence, or aids or abets and does any act preparatory to the commission of an offence under the principal Act or this Act, shall be guilty of a felony or a misdemeanour or a summary offence according as the offence in question is a felony, a misdemeanour or a summary offence, and on conviction shall be liable to the same punishment, and to be proceeded against in the same manner, as if he had committed the offence.

8 Provisions as to trial and punishment of offences

(1) Any person who is guilty of a felony under the principal Act or this Act shall be liable to penal servitude for a term of not less than three years and not exceeding fourteen years.

(2) Any person who is guilty of a misdemeanour under the principal Act or this Act shall be liable on conviction on indictment to imprisonment with or without hard labour, for a term not exceeding two years, or, on conviction under the Summary Jurisdiction Acts, to imprisonment, with or without hard labour, for a term not exceeding three months or to a fine not exceeding [the prescribed sum], or both such imprisonment and fine:

Provided that no misdemeanour under the principal Act or this Act shall be dealt with summarily except with the consent of the Attorney General.

(3) For the purposes of the trial of a person for an offence under the principal Act or this Act, the offence shall be deemed to have been committed either at the place in which the same actually was committed, or at any place in the United Kingdom in which the offender may be found.

(4) In addition and without prejudice to any powers which a court may possess to order the exclusion of the public from any proceedings if, in the course of proceedings before a court against any person for an offence under the principal Act or this Act or the proceedings on appeal, or in the course of the trial of a person for felony or misdemeanour under the principal Act or this Act, application is made by the prosecution, on the ground that the publication of any evidence to be given or of any statement to be made in the course of the proceedings would be prejudicial to

the national safety, that all or any portion of the public shall be excluded during any part of the hearing, the court may make an order to that effect, but the passing of sentence shall in any case take place in public.

(5) Where the person guilty of an offence under the principal Act or this Act is a company or corporation, every director and officer of the company or corporation shall be guilty of the like offence unless he proves that the act or omission constituting the offence took place without his knowledge or consent.

NOTES

Sub-s (2): reference to "the prescribed sum" substituted by virtue of the Magistrates' Courts Act 1980, s 32(2).

11 Short title, construction, and repeal

(1) This Act may be cited as the Official Secrets Act 1920, and shall be construed as one with the principal Act, and the principal Act and this Act may be cited together as the Official Secrets Acts 1911 and 1920.

Provided that—

(a) . . . ; and

(b) . . .

[(1A) For the purposes of this Act as it extends to Northern Ireland, the expression "chief officer of police" means a superintendent or chief superintendent of the Royal Ulster Constabulary.]

(2), (3) . . .

NOTES

Sub-s (1): para (a) repealed by the SL(R) Act 1993, s 1(1), Sch 1, Pt I; para (b) outside the scope of this work.

Sub-s (1A): inserted by the SL(R) Act 1993, s 1(2), Sch 2, para 21.

Sub-s (2): repealed by the SLR Act 1927.

Sub-s (3): repealed by the SL(R) Act 1993, s 1(1), Sch 1, Pt I.

STATUTE OF WESTMINSTER 1931

(c 4)

An Act to give effect to certain resolutions passed by Imperial Conferences held in the years 1926 and 1930

[11 December 1931]

1 Meaning of "Dominion" in this Act

In this Act the expression "Dominion" means any of the following Dominions, that is to say, the Dominion of Canada, the Commonwealth of Australia, the Dominion of New Zealand, . . . the Irish Free State and Newfoundland.

NOTES

Words omitted repealed by the South Africa Act 1962, s 2(3), Sch 5.

2 Validity of laws made by Parliament of a Dominion

(1) The Colonial Laws Validity Act 1865 shall not apply to any law made after the commencement of this Act by the Parliament of a Dominion.

(2) No law and no provision of any law made after the commencement of this Act by the Parliament of a Dominion shall be void or inoperative on the ground that it is repugnant to the law of England, or to the provisions of any existing or future Act of Parliament of the United Kingdom, or to any order, rule or regulation made under any such Act, and the powers of the Parliament of a Dominion shall include the power to repeal or amend any such Act, order, rule or regulation in so far as the same is part of the law of the Dominion.

3 Power of Parliament of Dominion to legislate extra-territorially

It is hereby declared and enacted that the Parliament of a Dominion has full power to make laws having extra-territorial operation.

4 Parliament of United Kingdom not to legislate for Dominion except by consent

No Act of Parliament of the United Kingdom passed after the commencement of this Act shall extend, or be deemed to extend, to a Dominion as part of the law of that Dominion unless it is expressly declared in that Act that that Dominion has requested, and consented to, the enactment thereof.

NOTES

Repealed, in relation to Canada, by the Canada Act 1982, s 1, Sch B, s 53, Schedule, item 17 and, in relation to Australia, by the Australia Act 1986, s 12.

8 Saving for Constitution Acts of Australia and New Zealand

Nothing in this Act shall be deemed to confer any power to repeal or alter the Constitution or the Constitution Act of the Commonwealth of Australia or the Constitution Act of the Dominion of New Zealand otherwise than in accordance with the law existing before the commencement of this Act.

9 Saving with respect to States of Australia

(1) Nothing in this Act shall be deemed to authorise the Parliament of the Commonwealth of Australia to make laws on any matter within the authority of the States of Australia, not being a matter within the authority of the Parliament or Government of the Commonwealth of Australia.

(2), (3) . . .

NOTES

Sub-ss (2), (3): repealed by the Australia Act 1986, s 12.

12 Short title

This Act may be cited as the Statute of Westminster 1931.

PUBLIC ORDER ACT 1936

(c 6)

An Act to prohibit the wearing of uniforms in connection with political objects and the maintenance by private persons of associations of military or similar character; and to make further provision for the preservation of public order on the occasion of public processions and meetings and in public places

[18 December 1936]

1 Prohibition of uniforms in connection with political objects

(1) Subject as hereinafter provided, any person who in any public place or at any public meeting wears uniform signifying his association with any political organisation or with the promotion of any political object shall be guilty of an offence:

Provided that, if the chief officer of police is satisfied that the wearing of any such uniform as aforesaid on any ceremonial, anniversary, or other special occasion will not be likely to involve risk of public disorder, he may, with the consent of a Secretary of State, by order permit the wearing of such uniform on that occasion either absolutely or subject to such conditions as may be specified in the order.

(2) Where any person is charged before any court with an offence under this section, no further proceedings in respect thereof shall be taken against him without the consent of the Attorney-General [except such as are authorised by [section 6 of the Prosecution of Offences Act 1979]] so, however, that if that person is remanded in custody he shall, after the expiration of a period of eight days from the date on which he was so remanded, be entitled to be [released on bail] without sureties unless within that period the Attorney-General has consented to such further proceedings as aforesaid.

NOTES

Sub-s (2): words in first (outer) pair of square brackets substituted by the Criminal Jurisdiction Act 1975, s 14(4), Sch 5, para 1; words in second (inner) pair of square brackets substituted by the Prosecution of Offences Act 1979, s 11(1), Sch 1; words in third pair of square brackets substituted by the Bail Act 1976, s 12, Sch 2, para 10.

2 Prohibition of quasi-military organisations

(1) If the members or adherents of any association of persons, whether incorporated or not, are—

(a) organised or trained or equipped for the purpose of enabling them to be employed in usurping the functions of the police or of the armed forces of the Crown; or

(b) organised and trained or organised and equipped either for the purpose of enabling them to be employed for the use or display of physical force in promoting any political object, or in such manner as to arouse reasonable apprehension that they are organised and either trained or equipped for that purpose;

then any person who takes part in the control or management of the association, or in so organising or training as aforesaid any members or adherents thereof, shall be guilty of an offence under this section:

Provided that in any proceedings against a person charged with the offence of taking part in the control or management of such an association as aforesaid it shall be a defence to that charge to prove that he neither consented to nor connived at the organisation, training, or equipment of members or adherents of the association in contravention of the provisions of this section.

(2) No prosecution shall be instituted under this section without the consent of the Attorney-General.

(3) If upon application being made by the Attorney-General it appears to the High Court that any association is an association of which members or adherents are organised, trained, or equipped in contravention of the provisions of this section, the Court may make such order as appears necessary to prevent any disposition without the leave of the Court of property held by or for the association and in accordance with rules of court may direct an inquiry and report to be made as to any such property as aforesaid and as to the affairs of the association and make such further orders as appear to the Court to be just and equitable for the application of such property in or towards the discharge of the liabilities of the association lawfully incurred before the date of the application or since that date with the approval of the Court, in or towards the repayment of moneys to persons who became subscribers or contributors to the association in good faith and without knowledge of any such contravention as aforesaid, and in or towards any costs incurred in connection with any such inquiry and report as aforesaid or in winding-up or dissolving the association, and may order that any property which is not directed by the Court to be so applied as aforesaid shall be forfeited to the Crown.

(4) In any criminal or civil proceedings under this section proof of things done or of words written, spoken or published (whether or not in the presence of any party to the proceedings) by any person taking part in the control or management of an association or in organising, training or equipping members or adherents of an association shall be admissible as evidence of the purposes for which, or the manner in which, members or adherents of the association (whether those persons or others) were organised, or trained, or equipped.

(5) If a judge of the High Court is satisfied by information on oath that there is reasonable ground for suspecting that an offence under this section has been committed, and that evidence of the commission thereof is to be found at any premises or place specified in the information, he may, on an application made by an officer of police of a rank not lower than that of inspector, grant a search warrant authorising any such officer as aforesaid named in the warrant together with any other persons named in the warrant and any other officers of police to enter the premises or place at any time within one month from the date of the warrant, if necessary by force, and to search the premises or place and every person found therein, and to seize anything found on the premises or place or on any such person which the officer has reasonable ground for suspecting to be evidence of the commission of such an offence as aforesaid:

Provided that no woman shall, in pursuance of a warrant issued under this subsection, be searched except by a woman.

(6) Nothing in this section shall be construed as prohibiting the employment of a reasonable number of persons as stewards to assist in the preservation of order at any public meeting held upon private premises, or the making of arrangements for that purpose or the instruction of the persons to be so employed in their lawful duties as such stewards, or their being furnished with badges or other distinguishing signs.

7 Enforcement

(1) Any person who commits an offence under section two of this Act shall be liable on summary conviction to imprisonment for a term not exceeding six months or to a fine not exceeding [the prescribed sum], or to both such imprisonment and fine, or, on conviction on indictment, to imprisonment for a term not exceeding two years or to a fine . . . or to both such imprisonment and fine.

(2) Any person guilty of [any offence under this Act other than an offence under section 2 . . .] shall be liable on summary conviction to imprisonment for a term not exceeding three months or to a fine not exceeding [level 4 on the standard scale], or to both such imprisonment and fine.

(3) A constable may without warrant arrest any person reasonably suspected by him to be committing an offence under section one . . . of this Act.

NOTES

Sub-s (1): reference to "the prescribed sum" substituted by virtue of the Magistrates' Courts Act 1980, s 32(2); words "not exceeding five hundred pounds" omitted by virtue of the Criminal Law Act 1977, s 32(1) post.

Sub-s (2): words in first pair of square brackets substituted by the Public Order Act 1963, s 1(2); words omitted repealed by the Public Order Act 1986, s 40(3), Sch 3; reference to "level 4 on the standard scale" substituted by virtue of the Criminal Justice Act 1982, ss 38, 46 (maximum fine previously increased from £50 to £500 by the Criminal Law Act 1977, s 31(1), Sch 6).

Sub-s (3): words omitted repealed by the Public Order Act 1986, s 40(3), Sch 3.

9 Interpretation, etc

(1) In this Act the following expressions have the meanings hereby respectively assigned to them, that is to say:—

. . . . .

"Meeting" means a meeting held for the purpose of the discussion of matters of public interest or for the purpose of the expression of views on such matters;

"Private premises" means premises to which the public have access (whether on payment or otherwise) only by permission of the owner, occupier, or lessee of the premises;

"Public meeting" includes any meeting in a public place and any meeting which the public or any section thereof are permitted to attend, whether on payment or otherwise;

["Public place" includes any highway and any other premises or place to which at the material time the public have or are permitted to have access, whether on payment or otherwise;]

. . . . .

(2)–(4) . . .

NOTES

Sub-s (1): definition "Chief officer of police" repealed by the Police Act 1964, s 64(3), Sch 10; definition "Public procession" repealed by the Public Order Act 1986, s 40(3), Sch 3; definition "Public place" substituted by the Criminal Justice Act 1972, s 33; definition "Recognised corps" outside the scope of this work.

Sub-s (2): repealed by the Law Officers Act 1997, s 3(2), Schedule.

Sub-ss (3), (4): outside the scope of this work.

10 Short title and extent

(1) This Act may be cited as the Public Order Act 1936.

(2) This Act shall not extend to Northern Ireland.

(3) . . .

NOTES

Sub-s (3): repealed by the SLR Act 1950.

REGENCY ACT 1937

(c 16)

An Act to make provision for a Regency in the event of the Sovereign being on His Accession under the age of eighteen years, and in the event of the incapacity of the Sovereign through illness, and for the performance of certain of the royal functions in the name and on behalf of the Sovereign in certain other events; to repeal the Lords Justices Act 1837; and for purposes connected with the matters aforesaid

[19 March 1937]

NOTES

By the Regency Act 1953, s 4(1), the following Acts may be cited together by the collective title Regency Acts 1937 to 1953: the Regency Act 1937, the Regency Act 1943 and the Regency Act 1953.

1 Regency while the Sovereign is under eighteen

(1) If the Sovereign is, at His Accession, under the age of eighteen years, then, until He attains that age, the royal functions shall be performed in the name and on behalf of the Sovereign by a Regent.

(2) . . .

NOTES

Sub-s (2): outside the scope of this work.

2 Regency during total incapacity of the Sovereign

(1) If the following persons or any three or more of them, that is to say, the wife or husband of the Sovereign, the Lord Chancellor, the Speaker of the House of Commons, the Lord Chief Justice of England, and the Master of the Rolls, declare in writing that they are satisfied by evidence which shall include the evidence of physicians that the Sovereign is by reason of infirmity of mind or body incapable for the time being of performing the royal functions or that they are satisfied by evidence that the Sovereign is for some definite cause not available for the performance of those functions, then, until it is declared in like manner that His Majesty has so far recovered His health as to warrant His resumption of the royal functions or has become available for the performance thereof, as the case may be, those functions shall be performed in the name and on behalf of the Sovereign by a Regent.

(2) A declaration under this section shall be made to the Privy Council and communicated to the Governments of His Majesty's Dominions and to the Government of India.

3 The Regent

(1) If a Regency becomes necessary under this Act, the Regent shall be that person who, excluding any persons disqualified under this section, is next in the line of succession to the Crown.

(2) A person shall be disqualified from becoming or being Regent, if he is not a British subject of full age and domiciled in some part of the United Kingdom, or is a person who would, under section two of the Act of Settlement, be incapable of inheriting, possessing, and enjoying the Crown; and section three of the Act of Settlement shall apply in the case of a Regent as it applies in the case of a Sovereign.

(3) If any person who would at the commencement of a Regency have become Regent but for the fact that he was not then of full age becomes of full age during the Regency, he shall, if he is not otherwise disqualified under this section, thereupon become Regent instead of the person who has theretofore been Regent.

(4), (5) . . .

NOTES
Sub-ss (4), (5): outside the scope of this work.

4 Oaths to be taken by, and limitations of power of, Regent

(1) The Regent shall, before he acts in or enters upon his office, take and subscribe before the Privy Council the oaths set out in the Schedule to this Act, and the Privy Council are empowered and required to administer those oaths and to enter them in the Council Books.

(2) The Regent shall not have power to assent to any Bill for changing the order of succession to the Crown or for repealing or altering an Act of the fifth year of the reign of Queen Anne made in Scotland entitled "An Act for Securing the Protestant Religion and Presbyterian Church Government".

8 Short title and interpretation

(1) This Act may be cited as the Regency Act 1937.

(2) In this Act, save as otherwise expressly provided, the expression "royal functions" includes all powers and authorities belonging to the Crown, whether prerogative or statutory, together with the receiving of any homage required to be done to His Majesty.

BANK OF ENGLAND ACT 1946

(c 27)

An Act to bring the capital stock of the Bank of England into public ownership and bring the Bank under public control, to make provision with respect to the relations between the Treasury, the Bank of England and other banks and for purposes connected with the matters aforesaid

[14 February 1946]

4 Treasury directions to the Bank and relations of the Bank with other banks

(1) The Treasury may from time to time give such directions to the Bank as, after consultation with the Governor of the Bank, they think necessary in the public interest[, except in relation to monetary policy].

(2) . . .

(3) The Bank, if they think it necessary in the public interest, may request information from and make recommendations to bankers, and may, if so authorised by the Treasury, issue directions to any banker for the purpose of securing that effect is given to any such request or recommendation:

Provided that:—

(a) no such request or recommendations shall be made with respect to the affairs of any particular customer of a banker; and

(b) before authorising the issue of any such directions the Treasury shall give the banker concerned, or such person as appears to them to represent him, an opportunity of making representations with respect thereto.

(4), (5) . . .

(6) In this section the expression "banker" means any such person carrying on a banking undertaking as may be declared by order of the Treasury to be a banker for the purposes of this section.

(7) Any order made under the last foregoing subsection may be varied or revoked by a subsequent order.

(8) . . .

NOTES

Sub-s (1): words in square brackets added by the Bank of England Act 1998, s 10.

Sub-s (2): repealed by the Bank of England Act 1998, s 43, Sch 9.

Sub-ss (4), (5): repealed by the Official Secrets Act 1989, s 16(4), Sch 2.

Sub-s (8): repealed by the Statute Law Revision Act 1950.

6 Short title

This Act may be cited as the Bank of England Act 1946.

STATUTORY INSTRUMENTS ACT 1946

(c 36)

An Act to repeal the Rules Publication Act 1893 and to make further provision as to the instruments by which statutory powers to make orders, rules, regulations and other subordinate legislation are exercised

[26 March 1946]

1 Definition of "Statutory Instrument"

(1) Where by this Act or any Act passed after the commencement of this Act power to make, confirm or approve orders, rules, regulations or other subordinate legislation is conferred on His Majesty in Council or on any Minister of the Crown then, if the power is expressed—

(a) in the case of a power conferred on His Majesty, to be exercisable by Order in Council;

(b) in the case of a power conferred on a Minister of the Crown, to be exercisable by statutory instrument,

any document by which that power is exercised shall be known as a "statutory instrument" and the provisions of this Act shall apply thereto accordingly.

(2) Where by any Act passed before the commencement of this Act power to make statutory rules within the meaning of the Rules Publication Act 1893 was conferred

on any rule-making authority within the meaning of that Act, any document by which that power is exercised after the commencement of this Act shall, save as is otherwise provided by regulations made under this Act, be known as a "statutory instrument" and the provisions of this Act shall apply thereto accordingly.

2 Numbering, printing, publication and citation

(1) Immediately after the making of any statutory instrument, it shall be sent to the King's printer of Acts of Parliament and numbered in accordance with regulations made under this Act, and except in such cases as may be provided by any Act passed after the commencement of this Act or prescribed by regulations made under this Act, copies thereof shall as soon as possible be printed and sold by [or under the authority of] the King's printer of Acts of Parliament.

(2) Any statutory instrument may, without prejudice to any other mode of citation, be cited by the number given to it in accordance with the provisions of this section, and the calendar year.

NOTES

Sub-s (1): words in square brackets inserted by the Statutory Instruments (Production and Sale) Act 1996, s 1(1)(a).

3 Supplementary provisions as to publication

(1) Regulations made for the purposes of this Act shall make provision for the publication by His Majesty's Stationery Office of lists showing the date upon which every statutory instrument printed and sold by [or under the authority of] the King's printer of Acts of Parliament was first issued by [or under the authority of] that office; and in any legal proceedings a copy of any list so published . . . shall be received in evidence as a true copy, and an entry therein shall be conclusive evidence of the date on which any statutory instrument was first issued by [or under the authority of] His Majesty's Stationery Office.

(2) In any proceedings against any person for an offence consisting of a contravention of any such statutory instrument, it shall be a defence to prove that the instrument had not been issued by [or under the authority of] His Majesty's Stationery Office at the date of the alleged contravention unless it is proved that at that date reasonable steps had been taken for the purpose of bringing the purport of the instrument to the notice of the public, or of persons likely to be affected by it, or of the person charged.

(3) Save as therein otherwise expressly provided, nothing in this section shall affect any enactment or rule of law relating to the time at which any statutory instrument comes into operation.

NOTES

Sub-s (1): words in square brackets inserted, and words omitted repealed, by the Statutory Instruments (Production and Sale) Act 1996, s 1(1).

Sub-s (2): words in square brackets inserted by the Statutory Instruments (Production and Sale) Act 1996, s 1.

4 Statutory instruments which are required to be laid before Parliament

(1) Where by this Act or any Act passed after the commencement of this Act any statutory instrument is required to be laid before Parliament after being made, a copy of the instrument shall be laid before each House of Parliament and, subject as hereinafter provided, shall be so laid before the instrument comes into operation:

Provided that if it is essential that any such instrument should come into operation before copies thereof can be so laid as aforesaid, the instrument may be made so as to come into operation before it has been so laid; and where any statutory instrument comes into operation before it is laid before Parliament, notification shall forthwith be sent to the Lord Chancellor and to the Speaker of the House of Commons drawing attention to the fact that copies of the instrument have yet to be laid before Parliament and explaining why such copies were not so laid before the instrument came into operation.

(2) Every copy of any such statutory instrument sold by [or under the authority of] the King's printer of Acts of Parliament shall bear on the face thereof—

(a) a statement showing the date on which the statutory instrument came or will come into operation; and

(b) either a statement showing the date on which copies thereof were laid before Parliament or a statement that such copies are to be laid before Parliament.

(3) . . .

NOTES

Sub-s (2): words in square brackets inserted by the Statutory Instruments (Production and Sale) Act 1996, s 1(1)(a).

Sub-s (3): outside the scope of this work.

5 Statutory instruments which are subject to annulment by resolution of either House of Parliament

(1) Where by this Act or any Act passed after the commencement of this Act, it is provided that any statutory instrument shall be subject to annulment in pursuance of resolution of either House of Parliament, the instrument shall be laid before Parliament after being made and the provisions of the last foregoing section shall apply thereto accordingly, and if either House, within the period of forty days beginning with the day on which a copy thereof is laid before it, resolves that an Address be presented to His Majesty praying that the instrument be annulled, no further proceedings shall be taken thereunder after the date of the resolution, and His Majesty may by Order in Council revoke the instrument, so, however, that any such resolution and revocation shall be without prejudice to the validity of anything previously done under the instrument or to the making of a new statutory instrument.

(2) . . .

NOTES

Sub-s (2): outside the scope of this work.

6 Statutory instruments of which drafts are to be laid before Parliament

(1) Where by this Act or any Act passed after the commencement of this Act it is provided that a draft of any statutory instrument shall be laid before Parliament, but the Act does not prohibit the making of the instrument without the approval of Parliament, then, in the case of an Order in Council the draft shall not be submitted to His Majesty in Council, and in any other case, the statutory instrument shall not be made, until after the expiration of a period of forty days beginning with the day on which a copy of the draft is laid before each House of Parliament, or, if such copies are laid on different days, with the later of the two days, and if within that

period either House resolves that the draft be not submitted to His Majesty or that the statutory instrument be not made, as the case may be, no further proceedings shall be taken thereon, but without prejudice to the laying before Parliament of a new draft.

(2) . . .

NOTES

Sub-s (2): outside the scope of this work.

10 Commencement of Act

(1) This Act shall come into operation on such date as His Majesty may by Order in Council appoint:

Provided that, without prejudice to the provisions of [section 13 of the Interpretation Act 1978], the last foregoing section and, in relation to any Order in Council made thereunder, the provisions of sections six and seven of this Act shall come into operation on the passing of this Act.

(2) . . .

NOTES

Sub-s (1): words in square brackets substituted by virtue of the Interpretation Act 1978, s 25(2).
Sub-s (2): repealed by the Statute Law (Repeals) Act 1977, s 1(1), Sch 1, Pt XIX.

13 Short title and extent

(1) This Act may be cited as the Statutory Instruments Act 1946.

(2) This Act shall apply to any statutory instrument made by His Majesty in Council or by any Minister of the Crown (not being a rule-making authority within the meaning of the Rules Publication Act (Northern Ireland) 1925) in so far as it extends to Northern Ireland, but except as aforesaid this Act shall not extend to Northern Ireland.

CROWN PROCEEDINGS ACT 1947

(c 44)

An Act to amend the law relating to the civil liabilities and rights of the Crown and to civil proceedings by and against the Crown, to amend the law relating to the civil liabilities of persons other than the Crown in certain cases involving the affairs or property of the Crown, and for purposes connected with the matters aforesaid

[31 July 1947]

PART I
SUBSTANTIVE LAW

1 Right to sue the Crown

Where any person has a claim against the Crown after the commencement of this Act, and, if this Act had not been passed, the claim might have been enforced, subject to the grant of His Majesty's fiat, by petition of right, or might have been enforced by a proceeding provided by any statutory provision repealed by this Act, then, subject to the provisions of this Act, the claim may be enforced as of right, and without the fiat of His Majesty, by proceedings taken against the Crown for that purpose in accordance with the provisions of this Act.

2 Liability of the Crown in tort

(1) Subject to the provisions of this Act, the Crown shall be subject to all those liabilities in tort to which, if it were a private person of full age and capacity, it would be subject:—

- (a) in respect of torts committed by its servants or agents;
- (b) in respect of any breach of those duties which a person owes to his servants or agents at common law by reason of being their employer; and
- (c) in respect of any breach of the duties attaching at common law to the ownership, occupation, possession or control of property:

Provided that no proceedings shall lie against the Crown by virtue of paragraph (a) of this subsection in respect of any act or omission of a servant or agent of the Crown unless the act or omission would apart from the provisions of this Act have given rise to a cause of action in tort against that servant or agent or his estate.

(2) Where the Crown is bound by a statutory duty which is binding also upon persons other than the Crown and its officers, then, subject to the provisions of this Act, the Crown shall, in respect of a failure to comply with that duty, be subject to all those liabilities in tort (if any) to which it would be so subject if it were a private person of full age and capacity.

(3) Where any functions are conferred or imposed upon an officer of the Crown as such either by any rule of the common law or by statute, and that officer commits a tort while performing or purporting to perform those functions, the liabilities of the Crown in respect of the tort shall be such as they would have been if those functions had been conferred or imposed solely by virtue of instructions lawfully given by the Crown.

(4) Any enactment which negatives or limits the amount of the liability of any Government department or officer of the Crown in respect of any tort committed by that department or officer shall, in the case of proceedings against the Crown under this section in respect of a tort committed by that department or officer, apply in relation to the Crown as it would have applied in relation to that department or officer if the proceedings against the Crown had been proceedings against that department or officer.

(5) No proceedings shall lie against the Crown by virtue of this section in respect of anything done or omitted to be done by any person while discharging or purporting to discharge any responsibilities of a judicial nature vested in him, or any responsibilities which he has in connection with the execution of judicial process.

(6) No proceedings shall lie against the Crown by virtue of this section in respect of any act, neglect or default of any officer of the Crown, unless that officer has been directly or indirectly appointed by the Crown and was at the material time paid in respect of his duties as an officer of the Crown wholly out of the Consolidated Fund

of the United Kingdom, moneys provided by Parliament, . . . , or any other Fund certified by the Treasury for the purposes of this subsection or was at the material time holding an office in respect of which the Treasury certify that the holder thereof would normally be so paid.

NOTES

Sub-s (6): words omitted repealed by the SL(R) Act 1981.

10 Provisions relating to the armed forces

(1) Nothing done or omitted to be done by a member of the armed forces of the Crown while on duty as such shall subject either him or the Crown to liability in tort for causing the death of another person, or for causing personal injury to another person, in so far as the death or personal injury is due to anything suffered by that other person while he is a member of the armed forces of the Crown if—

- *(a) at the time when that thing is suffered by that other person, he is either on duty as a member of the armed forces of the Crown or is, though not on duty as such, on any land, premises, ship, aircraft or vehicle for the time being used for the purposes of the armed forces of the Crown; and*
- *(b) [the Secretary of State] certifies that his suffering that thing has been or will be treated as attributable to service for the purposes of entitlement to an award under the Royal Warrant, Order in Council or Order of His Majesty relating to the disablement or death of members of the force of which he is a member:*

Provided that this subsection shall not exempt a member of the said forces from liability in tort in any case in which the court is satisfied that the act or omission was not connected with the execution of his duties as a member of those forces.

(2) No proceedings in tort shall lie against the Crown for death or personal injury due to anything suffered by a member of the armed forces of the Crown if—

- *(a) that thing is suffered by him in consequence of the nature or condition of any such land, premises, ship, aircraft or vehicle as aforesaid, or in consequence of the nature or condition of any equipment or supplies used for the purposes of those forces; and*
- *(b) [the Secretary of State] certifies as mentioned in the preceding subsection;*

nor shall any act or omission of an officer of the Crown subject him to liability in tort for death or personal injury, in so far as the death or personal injury is due to anything suffered by a member of the armed forces of the Crown being a thing as to which the conditions aforesaid are satisfied.

(3) . . . a Secretary of State, if satisfied that it is the fact:—

- *(a) that a person was or was not on any particular occasion on duty as a member of the armed forces of the Crown; or*
- *(b) that at any particular time any land, premises, ship, aircraft, vehicle, equipment or supplies was or was not, or were or were not, used for the purposes of the said forces;*

may issue a certificate certifying that to be the fact; and any such certificate shall, for the purposes of this section, be conclusive as to the fact which it certifies.

NOTES

Section repealed by the Crown Proceedings (Armed Forces) Act 1987, s 1, except in relation to anything suffered by a person in consequence of an act or omission committed before 15 May 1987. At any time after that date, the Secretary of State may revive this section by order made under s 2 of the 1987 Act.

Sub-ss (1), (2): in para (b) of both subsections, references to Secretary of State substituted by the Transfer of Functions (Ministry of Pensions) Order 1953, SI 1953/1198, the Ministry of Social Security Act 1966, s 2(3) and the Secretary of State for Social Services Order 1968, SI 1968/1699.

Sub-s (3): words omitted repealed with a saving by the Defence (Transfer of Functions) (No 1) Order 1964, SI 1964/488, art 2, Sch 1, Pt II.

11 Saving in respect of acts done under prerogative and statutory powers

(1) Nothing in Part I of this Act shall extinguish or abridge any powers or authorities which, if this Act had not been passed, would have been exercisable by virtue of the prerogative of the Crown, or any powers or authorities conferred on the Crown by any statute, and, in particular, nothing in the said Part I shall extinguish or abridge any powers or authorities exercisable by the Crown, whether in time of peace or of war, for the purpose of the defence of the realm or of training, or maintaining the efficiency of, any of the armed forces of the Crown.

(2) Where in any proceedings under this Act it is material to determine whether anything was properly done or omitted to be done in the exercise of the prerogative of the Crown, . . . a Secretary of State may, if satisfied that the act or omission was necessary for any such purpose as is mentioned in the last preceding subsection, issue a certificate to the effect that the act or omission was necessary for that purpose; and the certificate shall, in those proceedings, be conclusive as to the matter so certified.

NOTES

Sub-s (2): words omitted repealed with a saving by the Defence (Transfer of Functions) (No 1) Order 1964, SI 1964/488, art 2, Sch 1, Pt II.

PART II
JURISDICTION AND PROCEDURE

General

17 Parties to proceedings

(1) [The Minister for the Civil Service] shall publish a list specifying the several Government departments which are authorised departments for the purposes of this Act, and the name and address for service of the person who is, or is acting for the purposes of this Act as, the solicitor for each such department, and may from time to time amend or vary the said list.

. . . . .

(2) Civil proceedings by the Crown may be instituted either by an authorised Government department in its own name, whether that department was or was not at the commencement of this Act authorised to sue, or by the Attorney General.

(3) Civil proceedings against the Crown shall be instituted against the appropriate authorised Government department, or, if none of the authorised Government departments is appropriate or the person instituting the proceedings has any reasonable doubt whether any and if so which of those departments is appropriate, against the Attorney General.

(4), (5) . . .

NOTES

Sub-s (1): words in square brackets substituted by the Minister for the Civil Service Order 1968, SI 1968/1656, art 3(2), consequent on the transfer of functions of the Treasury to that Minister by art 2(2) of, and the Schedule to, the Order; words omitted outside the scope of this work.

Sub-ss (4), (5): outside the scope of this work.

21 Nature of relief

(1) In any civil proceedings by or against the Crown the court shall, subject to the provisions of this Act, have power to make all such orders as it has power to make in proceedings between subjects, and otherwise to give such appropriate relief as the case may require:

Provided that:—

(a) where in any proceedings against the Crown any such relief is sought as might in proceedings between subjects be granted by way of injunction or specific performance, the court shall not grant an injunction or make an order for specific performance, but may in lieu thereof make an order declaratory of the rights of the parties; and

(b) in any proceedings against the Crown for the recovery of land or other property the court shall not make an order for the recovery of the land or the delivery of the property, but may in lieu thereof make an order declaring that the plaintiff is entitled as against the Crown to the land or property or to the possession thereof.

(2) The court shall not in any civil proceedings grant any injunction or make any order against an officer of the Crown if the effect of granting the injunction or making the order would be to give any relief against the Crown which could not have been obtained in proceedings against the Crown.

PART III
JUDGMENTS AND EXECUTION

25 Satisfaction of orders against the Crown

(1) Where in any civil proceedings by or against the Crown, or in any proceedings on the Crown side of the King's Bench Division, or in connection with any arbitration to which the Crown is a party, any order (including an order for costs) is made by any court in favour of any person against the Crown or against a Government department or against an officer of the Crown as such, the proper officer of the court shall, on an application in that behalf made by or on behalf of that person at any time after the expiration of twenty-one days from the date of the order . . . issue to that person a certificate in the prescribed form containing particulars of the order:

. . . . .

(2) . . .

(3) If the order provides for the payment of any money by way of damages or otherwise, or of any costs, the certificate shall state the amount so payable, and the appropriate Government department shall, subject as hereinafter provided, pay to the person entitled or to his solicitor the amount appearing by the certificate to be due to him together with the interest, if any, lawfully due thereon:

. . . . .

(4) Save as aforesaid no execution or attachment or process in the nature thereof shall be issued out of any court for enforcing payment by the Crown of any such money or costs as aforesaid, and no person shall be individually liable under any order for the payment by the Crown, or any Government department, or any officer of the Crown as such, of any such money or costs.

(5) . . .

NOTES

Sub-ss (1), (3): words omitted outside the scope of this work.

Sub-s (2): outside the scope of this work.

Sub-s (5): repealed by the SL(R) Act 1993, subject to s 1(2) of, and Sch 2, Pt II, para 27 to, that Act, in relation to Northern Ireland.

PART IV
MISCELLANEOUS AND SUPPLEMENTAL

Miscellaneous

28 Discovery

(1) Subject to and in accordance with rules of court and county court rules:—

(a) in any civil proceedings in the High Court or a county court to which the Crown is a party, the Crown may be required by the court to make discovery of documents and produce documents for inspection; and

(b) in any such proceedings as aforesaid, the Crown may be required by the court to answer interrogatories:

Provided that this section shall be without prejudice to any rule of law which authorises or requires the withholding of any document or the refusal to answer any question on the ground that the disclosure of the document or the answering of the question would be injurious to the public interest.

Any order of the court made under the powers conferred by paragraph (b) of this subsection shall direct by what officer of the Crown the interrogatories are to be answered.

(2) Without prejudice to the proviso to the preceding subsection, any rules made for the purposes of this section shall be such as to secure that the existence of a document will not be disclosed if, in the opinion of a Minister of the Crown, it would be injurious to the public interest to disclose the existence thereof.

31 Application to the Crown of certain statutory provisions

(1) This Act shall not prejudice the right of the Crown to take advantage of the provisions of an Act of Parliament although not named therein; and it is hereby declared that in any civil proceedings against the Crown the provisions of any Act of Parliament which could, if the proceedings were between subjects, be relied upon by the defendant as a defence to the proceedings, whether in whole or in part, or otherwise, may, subject to any express provision to the contrary, be so relied upon by the Crown.

(2) . . .

NOTES

Sub-s (2): outside the scope of this work.

Supplemental

38 Interpretation

(1) . . .

(2) In this Act, except in so far as the context otherwise requires or it is otherwise expressly provided, the following expressions have the meanings hereby respectively assigned to them, that is to say:—

. . . . .

"Civil proceedings" includes proceedings in the High Court or the county court for the recovery of fines or penalties, but does not include proceedings on the Crown side of the King's Bench Division;

. . . . .

"Officer", in relation to the Crown, includes any servant of His Majesty, and accordingly (but without prejudice to the generality of the foregoing provision) includes a Minister of the Crown;

. . . . .

(3)–(6) . . .

NOTES

Sub-ss (1), (3), (4), (6): outside the scope of this work.

Sub-s (2): definitions omitted outside the scope of this work.

Sub-s (5): repealed by the Armed Forces Act 1981, s 28(2), Sch 5, Pt I.

40 Savings

(1) Nothing in this Act shall apply to proceedings by or against, or authorise proceedings in tort to be brought against, His Majesty in His private capacity.

(2)–(5) . . .

NOTES

Sub-s (2): paras (a)–(d), (f)–(h) outside the scope of this work; para (e) repealed by the Highways (Miscellaneous Provisions) Act 1961, ss 1(6), (8), 17(3).

Sub-ss (3)–(5): outside the scope of this work.

PART VI
EXTENT, COMMENCEMENT, SHORT TITLE, ETC

52 Extent of Act

Subject to the provisions hereinafter contained with respect to Northern Ireland, this Act shall not affect the law enforced in courts elsewhere than in England and Scotland, or the procedure in any such courts.

53 Provisions as to Northern Ireland

(1) His Majesty may by Order in Council provide for extending this Act to Northern Ireland with such additions, exceptions and modifications as appear to His Majesty to be expedient.

(2)–(7) . . .

NOTES

Sub-ss (2)–(5), (7): outside the scope of this work.

Sub-s (6): repealed by the Northern Ireland Constitution Act 1973, s 41(1), Sch 6, Pt I.

54 Short title and commencement

(1) This Act may be cited as the Crown Proceedings Act 1947.

(2) . . .

NOTES

Sub-s (2): repealed by the SLR Act 1950.

POST OFFICE ACT 1953

(c 36)

An Act to consolidate certain enactments relating to the Post Office with corrections and improvements made under the Consolidation of Enactments (Procedure) Act 1949

[31 July 1953]

General provisions as to transmission of postal packets

11 Prohibition on sending by post of certain articles

(1) A person shall not send or attempt to send or procure to be sent a postal packet which—

(a) save as [the Post Office] may either generally or in any particular case allow, encloses any explosive, dangerous, noxious or deleterious substance, any filth, any sharp instrument not properly protected, any noxious living creature, or any creature, article or thing whatsoever which is likely to injure either other postal packets in course of conveyance or [a person engaged in the business of the Post Office]; or

(b) encloses any indecent or obscene print, painting, photograph, lithograph, engraving, cinematograph film, book, card or written communication, or any indecent or obscene article whether similar to the above or not; or

(c) has on the packet, or on the cover thereof, any words, marks or designs which are grossly offensive or of an indecent or obscene character.

(2) If any person acts in contravention of the foregoing subsection, he shall be liable on summary conviction to a fine not exceeding [the prescribed sum] or on conviction on indictment to imprisonment for a term not exceeding twelve months.

(3) . . .

(4) The [detention by the Post Office] of any postal packet on the grounds of a contravention of this section or of [any provisions of a scheme made under section 28 of the Post Office Act 1969] shall not exempt the sender thereof from any proceedings which might have been taken if the packet had been delivered in due course of post.

NOTES

Sub-s (1): words in square brackets substituted by virtue of the Post Office Act 1969, ss 76, 88, 139, Sch 4, paras 1, 2(3)(a).

Sub-s (2): reference to "the prescribed sum" substituted by virtue of the Magistrates' Courts Act 1980, s 32(2).

Sub-s (3): repealed by the Post Office Act 1969, s 141, Sch 11, Pt II.

Sub-s (4): words in square brackets substituted by virtue of the Post Office Act 1969, ss 76, 88, 139, Sch 4, paras 1, 2(3)(b).

General offences

58 Opening or delaying of postal packets by officers of the Post Office

(1) If any [person engaged in the business of the Post Office], contrary to his duty, opens, or procures or suffers to be opened, any postal packet in course of transmission by post, or wilfully detains or delays, or procures or suffers to be detained or delayed, any such postal packet, he shall be guilty of a misdemeanour and be liable to imprisonment [for a term not exceeding two years] or to a fine, or to both:

Provided that nothing in this section shall extend to the opening, detaining or delaying of a postal packet returned for want of a true direction, or returned by reason that the person to whom it is directed has refused it, or has refused or neglected to pay the postage thereof, or that the packet cannot for any other reason be delivered, or to the opening, detaining or delaying of a postal packet under the authority of this Act or in obedience to [a warrant issued by the Secretary of State under section 2 of the Interception of Communications Act 1985].

(2) . . .

NOTES

Sub-s (1): words in first pair of square brackets substituted by virtue of the Post Office Act 1969, ss 76, 88, 139, Sch 4, paras 1, 2(1) post; words in second pair of square brackets substituted by the Theft Act 1968, s 33(1), Sch 2, Pt I, paras 1, 6; words in third pair of square brackets substituted by the Interception of Communications Act 1985, s 11(2).

Sub-s (2): outside the scope of this work.

Miscellaneous and general

92 Short title

(1) This Act may be cited as the Post Office Act 1953.

(2) This Act shall come into force one month after the passing thereof.

LIFE PEERAGES ACT 1958

(c 21)

An Act to make provision for the creation of life peerages carrying the right to sit and vote in the House of Lords

[30 April 1958]

1 Power to create life peerages carrying right to sit in the House of Lords

(1) Without prejudice to Her Majesty's powers as to the appointment of Lords of Appeal in Ordinary, Her Majesty shall have power by letters patent to confer

on any person a peerage for life having the incidents specified in subsection (2) of this section.

(2) A peerage conferred under this section shall, during the life of the person on whom it is conferred, entitle him—

(a) to rank as a baron under such style as may be appointed by the letters patent; and

(b) subject to subsection (4) of this section, to receive writs of summons to attend the House of Lords and sit and vote therein accordingly,

and shall expire on his death.

(3) A life peerage may be conferred under this section on a woman.

(4) Nothing in this section shall enable any person to receive a writ of summons to attend the House of Lords, or to sit and vote in that House, at any time when disqualified therefor by law.

2 Short title

This Act may be cited as the Life Peerages Act 1958.

PUBLIC RECORDS ACT 1958

(c 51)

An Act to make new provision with respect to public records and the Public Record Office, and for connected purposes

[23 July 1958]

1 General responsibility of the Lord Chancellor for public records

(1) The direction of the Public Record Office shall be transferred from the Master of the Rolls to the Lord Chancellor, and the Lord Chancellor shall be generally responsible for the execution of this Act and shall supervise the care and preservation of public records.

(2) There shall be an Advisory Council on Public Records to advise the Lord Chancellor on matters concerning public records in general and, in particular, on those aspects of the work of the Public Record Office which affect members of the public who make use of the facilities provided by the Public Record Office.

The Master of the Rolls shall be chairman of the said Council and the remaining members of the Council shall be appointed by the Lord Chancellor on such terms as he may specify.

(3) The Lord Chancellor shall in every year lay before both Houses of Parliament a report on the work of the Public Record Office, which shall include any report made to him by the Advisory Council on Public Records.

3 Selection and preservation of public records

(1) It shall be the duty of every person responsible for public records of any description which are not in the Public Record Office or a place of deposit appointed by the Lord Chancellor under this Act to make arrangements for the selection of those records which ought to be permanently preserved and for their safe-keeping.

(2) Every person shall perform his duties under this section under the guidance of the Keeper of Public Records and the said Keeper shall be responsible for co-ordinating and supervising all action taken under this section.

(3) All public records created before the year sixteen hundred and sixty shall be included among those selected for permanent preservation.

(4) Public records selected for permanent preservation under this section shall be transferred not later than thirty years after their creation either to the Public Record Office or to such other place of deposit appointed by the Lord Chancellor under this Act as the Lord Chancellor may direct:

Provided that any records may be retained after the said period if, in the opinion of the person who is responsible for them, they are required for administrative purposes or ought to be retained for any other special reason and, where that person is not the Lord Chancellor, the Lord Chancellor has been informed of the facts and given his approval.

(5) . . .

(6) Public records which, following the arrangements made in pursuance of this section, have been rejected as not required for permanent preservation shall be destroyed or, subject, in the case of records for which some person other than the Lord Chancellor is responsible, to the approval of the Lord Chancellor, disposed of in any other way.

(7) Any question as to the person whose duty it is to make arrangements under this section with respect to any class of public records shall be referred to the Lord Chancellor for his decision.

(8) . . .

NOTES

Sub-ss (5), (8): outside the scope of this work.

5 Access to public records

(1) Public records in the Public Record Office, other than those to which members of the public had access before their transfer to the Public Record Office, shall not be available for public inspection [until the expiration of the period of thirty years beginning with the first day of January in the year next after that in which they were created, or such other period], either longer or shorter, as the Lord Chancellor may, with the approval, or at the request, of the Minister or other person, if any, who appears to him to be primarily concerned, for the time being prescribe as respects any particular class of public records.

(2) Without prejudice to the generality of the foregoing subsection, if it appears to the person responsible for any public records which have been selected by him under section three of this Act for permanent preservation that they contain information which was obtained from members of the public under such conditions that the opening of those records to the public after the period determined under the foregoing subsection would or might constitute a breach of good faith on the part of the Government or on the part of the persons who obtained the information, he shall inform the Lord Chancellor accordingly and those records shall not be available in the

Public Record Office for public inspection even after the expiration of the said period except in such circumstances and subject to such conditions, if any, as the Lord Chancellor and that person may approve, or, if the Lord Chancellor and that person think fit, after the expiration of such further period as they may approve.

(3)–(5) . . .

NOTES

Sub-s (1): words in square brackets substituted by the Public Records Act 1967, s 1.

Sub-ss (3)–(5): outside the scope of this work.

10 Interpretation

(1) In this Act "public records" has the meaning assigned to it by the First Schedule to this Act and "records" includes not only written records but records conveying information by any other means whatsoever.

(2) Where records created at different dates are for administrative purposes kept together in one file or other assembly all the records in that file or other assembly shall be treated for the purposes of this Act as having been created when the latest of those records was created.

12 Northern Ireland

(1) It shall be lawful for any government department or other body or person having the custody of any public records relating exclusively or mainly to Northern Ireland to transmit those records to the Public Record Office of Northern Ireland.

(2) . . .

NOTES

Sub-s (2): repealed by the Northern Ireland Constitution Act 1973, s 41(1), Sch 6, Pt I.

13 Short title, repeals and commencement

(1) This Act may be cited as the Public Records Act 1958.

(2) . . .

(3) This Act shall come into force on the first day of January, nineteen hundred and fifty-nine.

NOTES

Sub-s (2): repealed by the SL(R) Act 1974.

FIRST SCHEDULE

Section 10

DEFINITION OF PUBLIC RECORDS

1. The provisions of this Schedule shall have effect for determining what are public records for the purposes of this Act.

Departmental records

2.—(1) Subject to the provisions of this paragraph, administrative and departmental records belonging to Her Majesty, whether in the United Kingdom or elsewhere, in right of Her Majesty's Government in the United Kingdom and, in particular,—

(a) records of, or held in, any department of Her Majesty's Government in the United Kingdom, or

(b) records of any office, commission or other body or establishment whatsoever under Her Majesty's Government in the United Kingdom,

shall be public records.

(2) Sub-paragraph (1) of this paragraph shall not apply—

(a) . . .

(b) to registers, or certified copies of entries in registers, being registers or certified copies kept or deposited in the General Register Office under or in pursuance of any enactment, whether past or future, which provides for the registration of births, deaths, marriages or adoptions, or

(c) except so far as provided by paragraph 4 of this Schedule, to records of the Duchy of Lancaster, or

(d) to records of the office of the Public Trustee relating to individual trusts.

3–8. . . .

NOTES

Paras 2(2)(a), 3–8: outside the scope of this work.

OBSCENE PUBLICATIONS ACT 1959

(c 66)

An Act to amend the law relating to the publication of obscene matter; to provide for the protection of literature; and to strengthen the law concerning pornography

[29 July 1959]

1 Test of obscenity

(1) For the purposes of this Act an article shall be deemed to be obscene if its effect or (where the article comprises two or more distinct items) the effect of any one of its items is, if taken as a whole, such as to tend to deprave and corrupt persons who are likely, having regard to all relevant circumstances, to read, see or hear the matter contained or embodied in it.

(2) In this Act "article" means any description of article containing or embodying matter to be read or looked at or both, any sound record, and any film or other record of a picture or pictures.

(3) For the purposes of this Act a person publishes an article who—

(a) distributes, circulates, sells, lets on hire, gives, or lends it, or who offers it for sale or for letting on hire; or

(b) in the case of an article containing or embodying matter to be looked at or a record, shows, plays or projects it[, or, where the matter is data stored electronically, transmits that data.]

. . .

[(4) For the purposes of this Act a person also publishes an article to the extent that any matter recorded on it is included by him in a programme included in a programme service.

(5) Where the inclusion of any matter in a programme so included would, if that matter were recorded matter, constitute the publication of an obscene article for the purposes of this Act by virtue of subsection (4) above, this Act shall have effect in relation to the inclusion of that matter in that programme as if it were recorded matter.

(6) In this section "programme" and "programme service" have the same meaning as in the Broadcasting Act 1990.]

NOTES

Sub-s (3): words in square brackets in para (b) added by the Criminal Justice and Public Order Act 1994, s 168(1), Sch 9, para 3; proviso repealed by the Broadcasting Act 1990, ss 162(1)(a), 203(3), Sch 21.

Sub-ss (4)–(6): added by the Broadcasting Act 1990, s 162(1)(b).

2 Prohibition of publication of obscene matter

(1) Subject as hereinafter provided, any person who, whether for gain or not, publishes an obscene article [or who has an obscene article for publication for gain (whether gain to himself or gain to another)] shall be liable—

- (a) on summary conviction to a fine not exceeding [the prescribed sum] or to imprisonment for a term not exceeding six months;
- (b) on conviction on indictment to a fine or to imprisonment for a term not exceeding three years or both.

(2) . . .

(3) A prosecution . . . for an offence against this section shall not be commenced more than two years after the commission of the offence.

[(3A) Proceedings for an offence under this section shall not be instituted except by or with the consent of the Director of Public Prosecutions in any case where the article in question is a moving picture film of a width of not less than sixteen millimetres and the relevant publication or the only other publication which followed or could reasonably have been expected to follow from the relevant publication took place or (as the case may be) was to take place in the course of a [film exhibition]; and in this subsection "the relevant publication" means—

- (a) in the case of any proceedings under this section for publishing an obscene article, the publication in respect of which the defendant would be charged if the proceedings were brought; and
- (b) in the case of any proceedings under this section for having an obscene article for publication for gain, the publication which, if the proceedings were brought, the defendant would be alleged to have had in contemplation.]

(4) A person publishing an article shall not be proceeded against for an offence at common law consisting of the publication of any matter contained or embodied in the article where it is of the essence of the offence that the matter is obscene.

[(4A) Without prejudice to subsection (4) above, a person shall not be proceeded against for an offence at common law—

- (a) in respect of a [film exhibition] or anything said or done in the course of a [film exhibition], where it is of the essence of the common law offence that the exhibition or, as the case may be, what was said or done was obscene, indecent, offensive, disgusting or injurious to morality; or
- (b) in respect of an agreement to give a [film exhibition] or to cause anything to be said or done in the course of such an exhibition where the common law offence consists of conspiring to corrupt public morals or to do any act contrary to public morals or decency.]

(5) A person shall not be convicted of an offence against this section if he proves that he had not examined the article in respect of which he is charged and had no reasonable cause to suspect that it was such that his publication of it would make him liable to be convicted of an offence against this section.

(6) In any proceedings against a person under this section the question whether an article is obscene shall be determined without regard to any publication by another person unless it could reasonably have been expected that the publication by the other person would follow from publication by the person charged.

[(7) In this section "film exhibition" has the same meaning as in the Cinemas Act 1985.]

NOTES

Sub-s (1): words in square brackets inserted by the Obscene Publications Act 1964, s 1(1); reference to "the prescribed sum" substituted by virtue of the Magistrates' Courts Act 1980, s 32(2).

Sub-s (2): repealed by the Criminal Law Act 1977, s 65(5), Sch 13.

Sub-s (3) words omitted repealed by the Criminal Law Act 1977, s 65(5), Sch 13.

Sub-s (3A): inserted by the Criminal Law Act 1977, ss 53(2); words in square brackets substituted by the Cinemas Act 1985, s 24(1), Sch 2, para 6(1), (2).

Sub-s (4A): inserted by the Criminal Law Act 1977, ss 53(3); words in square brackets substituted by the Cinemas Act 1985, s 24(1), Sch 2, para 6(1), (2).

Sub-s (7): substituted by the Cinemas Act 1985, s 24(1), Sch 2, para 6(1), (3).

3 Powers of search and seizure

(1) If a justice of the peace is satisfied by information on oath that there is reasonable ground for suspecting that, in any premises in the petty sessions area for which he acts, or on any stall or vehicle in that area, being premises or a stall or vehicle specified in the information, obscene articles are, or are from time to time, kept for publication for gain, the justice may issue a warrant under his hand empowering any constable to enter (if need be by force) and search the premises, or to search the stall or vehicle, . . . , and to seize and remove any articles found therein or thereon which the constable has reason to believe to be obscene articles and to be kept for publication for gain.

(2) A warrant under the foregoing subsection shall, if any obscene articles are seized under the warrant, also empower the seizure and removal of any documents found in the premises or, as the case may be, on the stall or vehicle which relate to a trade or business carried on at the premises or from the stall or vehicle.

(3) [Subject to subsection (3A) of this section] any articles seized under subsection (1) of this section shall be brought before a justice of the peace acting for the same petty sessions area as the justice who issued the warrant, and the justice before whom the articles are brought may thereupon issue a summons to the occupier of the premises or, as the case may be, the user of the stall or vehicle to appear on a day specified in the summons before a magistrates' court for that petty sessions area to show cause why the articles or any of them should not be forfeited; and if the court is satisfied, as respects any of the articles, that at the time when they were seized they were obscene articles kept for publication for gain, the court shall order those articles to be forfeited:

Provided that if the person summoned does not appear, the court shall not make an order unless service of the summons is proved.

[Provided also that this subsection does not apply in relation to any article seized under subsection (1) of this section which is returned to the occupier of the premises or, as the case may be, to the user of the stall or vehicle in or on which it was found.]

[(3A) Without prejudice to the duty of a court to make an order for the forfeiture of an article where section 1(4) of the Obscene Publications Act 1964 applies (orders made on conviction), in a case where by virtue of subsection (3A) of section 2 of this Act proceedings under the said section 2 for having an article for publication for gain could not be instituted except by or with the consent of the Director of Public Prosecutions, no order for the forfeiture of the article shall be made under this section unless the warrant under which the article was seized was issued on an information laid by or on behalf of the Director of Public Prosecutions.]

(4) In addition to the person summoned, any other person being the owner, author or maker of any of the articles brought before the court, or any other person through whose hands they had passed before being seized, shall be entitled to appear before the court on the day specified in the summons to show cause why they should not be forfeited.

(5) Where an order is made under this section for the forfeiture of any articles, any person who appeared, or was entitled to appear, to show cause against the making of the order may appeal to [the Crown Court]; and no such order shall take effect until the expiration of [the period within which notice of appeal to the Crown Court may be given against the order,] or, if before the expiration thereof notice of appeal is duly given or application is made for the statement of a case for the opinion of the High Court, until the final determination or abandonment of the proceedings on the appeal or case.

(6) If as respects any articles brought before it the court does not order forfeiture, the court may if it thinks fit order the person on whose information the warrant for the seizure of the articles was issued to pay such costs as the court thinks reasonable to any person who has appeared before the court to show cause why those articles should not be forfeited; and costs ordered to be paid under this subsection shall be enforceable as a civil debt.

(7) For the purposes of this section the question whether an article is obscene shall be determined on the assumption that copies of it would be published in any manner likely having regard to the circumstances in which it was found, but in no other manner.

(8) . . .

NOTES

Sub-s (1): words omitted repealed by the Police and Criminal Evidence Act 1984, s 119(2), Sch 7, Pt I.

Sub-s (3): words in square brackets and second proviso inserted by the Criminal Law Act 1977, ss 53(5), 65(4), Sch 12.

Sub-s (3A): inserted by the Criminal Law Act 1977, s 53(5).

Sub-s (5): words in square brackets substituted by the Courts Act 1971, s 56(2), Sch 8, para 37, Sch 9, Pt I.

Sub-s (8): outside the scope of this work.

4 Defence of public good

(1) [Subject to subsection (1A) of this section] a person shall not be convicted of an offence against section two of this Act, and an order for forfeiture shall not be made under the foregoing section, if it is proved that publication of the article in question is justified as being for the public good on the ground that it is in the interests of science, literature, art or learning, or of other objects of general concern.

[(1A) Subsection (1) of this section shall not apply where the article in question is a moving picture film or soundtrack, but—

(a) a person shall not be convicted of an offence against section 2 of this Act in relation to any such film or soundtrack, and

(b) an order for forfeiture of any such film or soundtrack shall not be made under section 3 of this Act,

if it is proved that publication of the film or soundtrack is justified as being for the public good on the ground that it is in the interests of drama, opera, ballet or any other art, or of literature or learning.]

(2) It is hereby declared that the opinion of experts as to the literary, artistic, scientific or other merits of an article may be admitted in any proceedings under this Act either to establish or to negative the said ground.

[(3) In this section "moving picture soundtrack" means any sound record designed for playing with a moving picture film, whether incorporated with the film or not.]

NOTES

Sub-s (1): words in square brackets inserted by the Criminal Law Act 1977, s 53(6).

Sub-s (1A): inserted by the Criminal Law Act 1977, s 53(6).

Sub-s (3): added by the Criminal Law Act 1977, s 53(7).

5 Citation, commencement and extent

(1) This Act may be cited as the Obscene Publications Act 1959.

(2) This Act shall come into operation on the expiration of one month beginning with the date of the passing thereof.

(3) This Act shall not extend to Scotland or to Northern Ireland.

ADMINISTRATION OF JUSTICE ACT 1960

(c 65)

An Act to make further provision for appeals to the House of Lords in criminal cases; to amend the law relating to contempt of court, habeas corpus and certiorari; and for purposes connected with the matters aforesaid

[27 October 1960]

Contempt of court, habeas corpus and certiorari

12 Publication of information relating to proceedings in private

(1) The publication of information relating to proceedings before any court sitting in private shall not of itself be contempt of court except in the following cases, that is to say—

[(a) where the proceedings—

(i) relate to the exercise of the inherent jurisdiction of the High Court with respect to minors;

(ii) are brought under the Children Act 1989; or

(iii) otherwise relate wholly or mainly to the maintenance or upbringing of a minor;]

(b) where the proceedings are brought under Part VIII of the Mental Health Act 1959, or under any provision of that Act authorising an application or reference to be made to a Mental Health Review Tribunal or to a county court;

(c) where the court sits in private for reasons of national security during that part of the proceedings about which the information in question is published;

(d) where the information relates to a secret process, discovery or invention which is in issue in the proceedings;

(e) where the court (having power to do so) expressly prohibits the publication of all information relating to the proceedings or of information of the description which is published.

(2) Without prejudice to the foregoing subsection, the publication of the text or a summary of the whole or part of an order made by a court sitting in private shall not of itself be contempt of court except where the court (having power to do so) expressly prohibits the publication.

(3) In this section references to a court include references to a judge and to a tribunal and to any person exercising the functions of a court, a judge or a tribunal; and references to a court sitting in private include references to a court sitting in camera or in chambers.

(4) Nothing in this section shall be construed as implying that any publication is punishable as contempt of court which would not be so punishable apart from this section.

NOTES

Sub-s (1): para (a) substituted by the Children Act 1989, s 108(5), Sch 13, para 14.

13 Appeal in cases of contempt of court

(1) Subject to the provisions of this section, an appeal shall lie under this section from any order or decision of a court in the exercise of jurisdiction to punish for contempt of court (including criminal contempt); and in relation to any such order or decision the provisions of this section shall have effect in substitution for any other enactment relating to appeals in civil or criminal proceedings.

(2) An appeal under this section shall lie in any case at the instance of the defendant and, in the case of an application for committal or attachment, at the instance of the applicant; and the appeal shall lie—

(a) from an order or decision of any inferior court not referred to in the next following paragraph, to a Divisional Court of the High Court;

(b) from an order or decision of a county court or any other inferior court from which appeals generally lie to the Court of Appeal, and from an order or decision, . . . of a single judge of the High Court, or of any court having the powers of the High Court or of a judge of that court, to the Court of Appeal;

[(bb) from an order or decision of the Crown Court to the Court of Appeal;]

(c) from an order or decision of a Divisional Court or the Court of Appeal (including a decision of either of those courts on an appeal under this section), and from an order or decision of the Court of Criminal Appeal or the Courts-Martial Appeal Court, to the House of Lords.

(3) The court to which an appeal is brought under this section may reverse or vary the order or decision of the court below, and make such other order as may be just; and without prejudice to the inherent powers of any court referred to in subsection (2) of this section, provision may be made by rules of court for authorising the release on bail of an appellant under this section.

(4)–(6) . . .

NOTES

Sub-s (2): words omitted from para (b) repealed, and para (bb) inserted, by the Courts Act 1971, s 56(1), (4), Sch 8, Pt II, para 40(1), Sch 11, Pt II.

Sub-ss (4)–(6): outside the scope of this work.

Supplementary

20 Short title and extent

(1) This Act may be cited as the Administration of Justice Act 1960.

(2) . . .

NOTES

Sub-s (2): outside the scope of this work.

PUBLIC BODIES (ADMISSION TO MEETINGS) ACT 1960

(c 67)

An Act to provide for the admission of representatives of the press and other members of the public to the meetings of certain bodies exercising public functions

[27 October 1960]

1 Admission of public to meetings of local authorities and other bodies

(1) Subject to subsection (2) below, any meeting of a . . . body exercising public functions, being [a body] to which this Act applies, shall be open to the public.

(2) A body may, by resolution, exclude the public from a meeting (whether during the whole or part of the proceedings) whenever publicity would be prejudicial to the public interest by reason of the confidential nature of the business to be transacted or for other special reasons stated in the resolution and arising from the nature of that business or of the proceedings; and where such a resolution is passed, this Act shall not require the meeting to be open to the public during proceedings to which the resolution applies.

(3) A body may under subsection (2) above treat the need to receive or consider recommendations or advice from sources other than members, committees or sub-committees of the body as a special reason why publicity would be prejudicial to the public interest, without regard to the subject or purport of the recommendations or advice; but the making by this subsection of express provision for that case shall not be taken to restrict the generality of subsection (2) above in relation to other cases (including in particular cases where the report of a committee or sub-committee of the body is of a confidential nature).

(4)–(7) . . .

(8) The provisions of this section shall be without prejudice to any power of exclusion to suppress or prevent disorderly conduct or other misbehaviour at a meeting.

NOTES

Sub-s (1): words omitted repealed, and words in square brackets substituted, by the Local Government (Access to Information) Act 1985, s 3, Sch 2, para 4(2), Sch 3.

Sub-ss (4)–(7): outside the scope of this work.

3 Short title, repeal, extent and commencement

(1) This Act may be cited as the Public Bodies (Admission to Meetings) Act 1960.

(2) . . .

(3) This Act shall not extend to Northern Ireland.

(4) This Act shall come into force on the first day of June, nineteen hundred and sixty-one.

NOTES

Sub-s (2): outside the scope of this work.

OBSCENE PUBLICATIONS ACT 1964

(c 74)

An Act to strengthen the law for preventing the publication for gain of obscene matter and the publication of things intended for the production of obscene matter

[31 July 1964]

1 Obscene articles intended for publication for gain

(1) . . .

(2) For the purpose of any proceedings for an offence against the said section 2 a person shall be deemed to have an article for publication for gain if with a view to such publication he has the article in his ownership, possession or control.

(3) In proceedings brought against a person under the said section 2 for having an obscene article for publication for gain the following provisions shall apply in place of subsections (5) and (6) of that section, that is to say,—

(a) he shall not be convicted of that offence if he proves that he had not examined the article and had no reasonable cause to suspect that it was such that his having it would make him liable to be convicted of an offence against that section; and

(b) the question whether the article is obscene shall be determined by reference to such publication for gain of the article as in the circumstances it may reasonably be inferred he had in contemplation and to any further publication that could reasonably be expected to follow from it, but not to any other publication.

(4) Where articles are seized under section 3 of the Obscene Publications Act 1959 (which provides for the seizure and forfeiture of obscene articles kept for publication for gain), and a person is convicted under section 2 of that Act of having them for publication for gain, the court on his conviction shall order the forfeiture of those articles:

Provided that an order made by virtue of this subsection (including an order so made on appeal) shall not take effect until the expiration of the ordinary time within which an appeal in the matter of the proceedings in which the order was made may be instituted or, where such an appeal is duly instituted, until the appeal is finally decided or abandoned; . . .

(5) . . .

NOTES

Sub-s (1) amends the Obscene Publications Act 1959, s 2(1).

Sub-s (4): words omitted outside the scope of this work.

Sub-s (5): outside the scope of this work.

3 Citation, commencement and extent

(1) This Act may be cited as the Obscene Publications Act 1964, and this Act and the Obscene Publications Act 1959 may be cited together as the Obscene Publications Acts 1959 and 1964.

(2) This Act shall come into operation on the expiration of one month beginning with the date of the passing thereof.

(3) This Act shall not extend to Scotland or to Northern Ireland.

WAR DAMAGE ACT 1965

(c 18)

An Act to abolish rights at common law to compensation in respect of damage to, or destruction of, property effected by, or on the authority of, the Crown during, or in contemplation of the outbreak of, war

[2 June 1965]

1 Abolition of rights at common law to compensation for certain damage to, or destruction of, property

(1) No person shall be entitled at common law to receive from the Crown compensation in respect of damage to, or destruction of, property caused (whether before or after the passing of this Act, within or outside the United Kingdom) by acts lawfully done by, or on the authority of, the Crown during, or in contemplation of the outbreak of, a war in which the Sovereign was, or is, engaged.

(2) . . .

NOTES

Sub-s (2): repealed by the SL(R) Act 1995.

2 Short title

This Act may be cited as the War Damage Act 1965.

PARLIAMENTARY COMMISSIONER ACT 1967

(c 13)

An Act to make provision for the appointment and functions of a Parliamentary Commissioner for the investigation of administrative action taken on behalf of the Crown, and for purposes connected therewith

[22 March 1967]

The Parliamentary Commissioner for Administration

1 Appointment and tenure of office

(1) For the purpose of conducting investigations in accordance with the following provisions of this Act there shall be appointed a Commissioner, to be known as the Parliamentary Commissioner for Administration.

(2) Her Majesty may by Letters Patent from time to time appoint a person to be the Commissioner, and any person so appointed shall (subject to [subsections (3) and (3A)] of this section) hold office during good behaviour.

(3) A person appointed to be the Commissioner may be relieved of office by Her Majesty at his own request, or may be removed from office by Her Majesty in consequence of Addresses from both Houses of Parliament, and shall in any case vacate office on completing the year of service in which he attains the age of sixty-five years.

[(3A) Her Majesty may declare the office of Commissioner to have been vacated if satisfied that the person appointed to be the Commissioner is incapable for medical reasons—

(a) of performing duties of his office; and
(b) of requesting to be relieved of it.]

(4), (5) . . .

NOTES

Sub-s (2): words in square brackets substituted by the Parliamentary and Health Service Commissioners Act 1987, s 2(1)(a).

Sub-s (3A): inserted by the Parliamentary and Health Service Commissioners Act 1987, s 2(1)(b).

Sub-s (4): repealed by the House of Commons Disqualification Act 1975, s 10(2), Sch 3 and the Northern Ireland Assembly Disqualification Act 1975, s 5(2), Sch 3, Pt I.

Sub-s (5): repealed by the Tribunals and Inquiries Act 1971, s 18(2), Sch 4, Pt I.

3 Administrative provisions

(1) The Commissioner may appoint such officers as he may determine with the approval of the Treasury as to numbers and conditions of service.

(2), (3) . . .

NOTES

Sub-ss (2), (3): outside the scope of this work.

Investigation by the Commissioner

[4 Departments etc subject to investigation

(1) Subject to the provisions of this section and to the notes contained in Schedule 2 to this Act, this Act applies to the government departments, corporations and unincorporated bodies listed in that Schedule; and references in this Act to an authority to which this Act applies are references to any such corporation or body.

(2) Her Majesty may by Order in Council amend Schedule 2 to this Act by the alteration of any entry or note, the removal of any entry or note or the insertion of any additional entry or note.

(3) An Order in Council may only insert an entry if—

(a) it relates—

(i) to a government department; or

(ii) to a corporation or body whose functions are exercised on behalf of the Crown; or

(b) it relates to a corporation or body—

(i) which is established by virtue of Her Majesty's prerogative or by an Act of Parliament or on Order in Council or order made under an Act of Parliament or which is established in any other way by a Minister of the Crown in his capacity as a Minister or by a government department;

(ii) at least half of whose revenues derive directly from money provided by Parliament, a levy authorised by an enactment, a fee or charge of any other description so authorised or more than one of those sources; and

(iii) which is wholly or partly constituted by appointment made by Her Majesty or a Minister of the Crown or government department.

(4) No entry shall be made in respect of a corporation or body whose sole activity is, or whose main activities are, included among the activities specified in subsection (5) below.

(5) The activities mentioned in subsection (4) above are—

(a) the provision of education, or the provision of training otherwise than under the Industrial Training Act 1982;

(b) the development of curricula, the conduct of examinations or the validation of educational courses;

(c) the control of entry to any profession or the regulation of the conduct of members of any profession;

(d) the investigation of complaints by members of the public regarding the actions of any person or body, or the supervision or review of such investigations or of steps taken following them.

(6) No entry shall be made in respect of a corporation or body operating in an exclusively or predominantly commercial manner or a corporation carrying on under national ownership an industry or undertaking or part of an industry or undertaking.

(7) Any statutory instrument made by virtue of this section shall be subject to annulment in pursuance of a resolution of either House of Parliament.

(8) . . .]

NOTES

Substituted by the Parliamentary and Health Service Commissioners Act 1987, s 1(1).

Sub-s (8): outside the scope of this work.

5 Matters subject to investigation

(1) Subject to the provisions of this section, the Commissioner may investigate any action taken by or on behalf of a government department or other authority to which this Act applies, being action taken in the exercise of administrative functions of that department or authority, in any case where—

(a) a written complaint is duly made to a member of the House of Commons by a member of the public who claims to have sustained injustice in consequence of maladministration in connection with the action so taken; and

(b) the complaint is referred to the Commissioner, with the consent of the person who made it, by a member of that House with a request to conduct an investigation thereon.

(2) Except as hereinafter provided, the Commissioner shall not conduct an investigation under this Act in respect of any of the following matters, that is to say—

(a) any action in respect of which the person aggrieved has or had a right of appeal, reference or review to or before a tribunal constituted by or under any enactment or by virtue of Her Majesty's prerogative;

(b) any action in respect of which the person aggrieved has or had a remedy by way of proceedings in any court of law:

Provided that the Commissioner may conduct an investigation notwithstanding that the person aggrieved has or had such a right or remedy if satisfied that in the particular circumstances it is not reasonable to expect him to resort or have resorted to it.

(3) Without prejudice to subsection (2) of this section, the Commissioner shall not conduct an investigation under this Act in respect of any such action or matter as is described in Schedule 3 to this Act.

(4) Her Majesty may by Order in Council amend the said Schedule 3 so as to exclude from the provisions of that Schedule such actions or matters as may be described in the Order; and any statutory instrument made by virtue of this subsection shall be subject to annulment in pursuance of a resolution of either House of Parliament.

(5) In determining whether to initiate, continue or discontinue an investigation under this Act, the Commissioner shall, subject to the foregoing provisions of this section, act in accordance with his own discretion; and any question whether a complaint is duly made under this Act shall be determined by the Commissioner.

[(6) For the purposes of this section, administrative functions exercisable by any person appointed by the Lord Chancellor as a member of the administrative staff of any court or tribunal shall be taken to be administrative functions of the Lord Chancellor's Department or, in Northern Ireland, of the Northern Ireland Court Service.]

(7)–(9) . . .

NOTES

Sub-s (6): added by the Courts and Legal Services Act 1990, s 110(1).

Sub-ss (7)–(9): outside the scope of this work.

6 Provisions relating to complaints

(1) A complaint under this Act may be made by any individual, or by any body of persons whether incorporated or not, not being—

(a) a local authority or other authority or body constituted for purposes of the public service or of local government or for the purposes of carrying on under national ownership any industry or undertaking or part of an industry or undertaking;

(b) any other authority or body whose members are appointed by Her Majesty or any Minister of the Crown or government department, or whose revenues consist wholly or mainly of moneys provided by Parliament.

(2) Where the person by whom a complaint might have been made under the foregoing provisions of this Act has died or is for any reason unable to act for himself, the complaint may be made by his personal representative or by a member of his family or other individual suitable to represent him; but except as aforesaid a complaint shall not be entertained under this Act unless made by the person aggrieved himself.

(3) A complaint shall not be entertained under this Act unless it is made to a member of the House of Commons not later than twelve months from the day on which the person aggrieved first had notice of the matters alleged in the complaint; but the Commissioner may conduct an investigation pursuant to a complaint not made within that period if he considers that there are special circumstances which make it proper to do so.

(4) [Except as provided in subsection (5) below] a complaint shall not be entertained under this Act unless the person aggrieved is resident in the United Kingdom (or, if he is dead, was so resident at the time of his death) or the complaint relates to action taken in relation to him while he was present in the United Kingdom or on an installation in a designated area within the meaning of the Continental Shelf Act 1964 or on a ship registered in the United Kingdom or an aircraft so registered, or in relation to rights or obligations which accrued or arose in the United Kingdom or on such an installation, ship or aircraft.

[(5) A complaint may be entertained under this Act in circumstances not falling within subsection (4) above where—

(a) the complaint relates to action taken in any country or territory outside the United Kingdom by an officer (not being an honorary consular officer) in the exercise of a consular function on behalf of the Government of the United Kingdom; and

(b) the person aggrieved is a citizen of the United Kingdom and Colonies who, under section 2 of the Immigration Act 1971, has the right of abode in the United Kingdom.]

NOTES

Sub-s (4): words in square brackets inserted by the Parliamentary Commissioner (Consular Complaints) Act 1981, s 1.

Sub-s (5): added by the Parliamentary Commissioner (Consular Complaints) Act 1981, s 1.

7 Procedure in respect of investigations

(1) Where the Commissioner proposes to conduct an investigation pursuant to a complaint under this Act, he shall afford to the principal officer of the department or authority concerned, and to any person who is alleged in the complaint to have taken or authorised the action complained of, an opportunity to comment on any allegations contained in the complaint.

(2) Every such investigation shall be conducted in private, but except as aforesaid the procedure for conducting an investigation shall be such as the Commissioner considers appropriate in the circumstances of the case; and without prejudice to the generality of the foregoing provision the Commissioner may obtain information from such persons and in such manner, and make such inquiries, as he thinks fit, and may determine whether any person may be represented, by counsel or solicitor or otherwise, in the investigation.

(3) . . .

(4) The conduct of an investigation under this Act shall not affect any action taken by the department or authority concerned, or any power or duty of that department or authority to take further action with respect to any matters subject to the investigation; but where the person aggrieved has been removed from the United Kingdom under any Order in force under the Aliens Restriction Acts 1914 and 1919 or under the Commonwealth Immigrants Act 1962, he shall, if the Commissioner so directs, be permitted to re-enter and remain in the United Kingdom, subject to such conditions as the Secretary of State may direct, for the purposes of the investigation.

NOTES

Sub-s (3): outside the scope of this work.

Sub-s (4): words in square brackets inserted by the Parliamentary Commissioner (Consular Complaints) Act 1981, s 1.

8 Evidence

(1) For the purposes of an investigation under this Act the Commissioner may require any Minister, officer or member of the department or authority concerned or any other person who in his opinion is able to furnish information or produce documents relevant to the investigation to furnish any such information or produce any such document.

(2) For the purposes of any such investigation the Commissioner shall have the same powers as the Court in respect of the attendance and examination of witnesses (including the administration of oaths or affirmations and the examination of witnesses abroad) and in respect of the production of documents.

(3) No obligation to maintain secrecy or other restriction upon the disclosure of information obtained by or furnished to persons in Her Majesty's service, whether imposed by any enactment or by any rule of law, shall apply to the disclosure of information for the purposes of an investigation under this Act; and the Crown shall not be entitled in relation to any such investigation to any such privilege in respect of the production of documents or the giving of evidence as is allowed by law in legal proceedings.

(4) No person shall be required or authorised by virtue of this Act to furnish any information or answer any question relating to proceedings of the Cabinet or of any committee of the Cabinet or to produce so much of any document as relates to such proceedings; and for the purposes of this subsection a certificate issued by the Secretary of the Cabinet with the approval of the Prime Minister and certifying that any information, question, document or part of a document so relates shall be conclusive.

(5) Subject to subsection (3) of this section, no person shall be compelled for the purposes of an investigation under this Act to give any evidence or produce any document which he could not be compelled to give or produce in [civil] proceedings before the Court.

NOTES

Sub-s (5): word in square brackets inserted by the Civil Evidence Act 1968, s 17(1)(b).

9 Obstruction and contempt

(1) If any person without lawful excuse obstructs the Commissioner or any officer of the Commissioner in the performance of his functions under this Act, or is guilty of any act or omission in relation to any investigation under this Act which, if that investigation were a proceeding in the Court, would constitute contempt of court, the Commissioner may certify the offence to the Court.

(2) Where an offence is certified under this section, the Court may inquire into the matter and, after hearing any witnesses who may be produced against or on behalf of the person charged with the offence, and after hearing any statement that may be offered in defence, deal with him in any manner in which the Court could deal with him if he had committed the like offence in relation to the Court.

(3) Nothing in this section shall be construed as applying to the taking of any such action as is mentioned in subsection (4) of section 7 of this Act.

10 Reports by Commissioner

(1) In any case where the Commissioner conducts an investigation under this Act or decides not to conduct such an investigation, he shall send to the member of the House of Commons by whom the request for investigation was made (or if he is no longer a member of that House, to such member of that House as the Commissioner thinks appropriate) a report of the results of the investigation or, as the case may be, a statement of his reasons for not conducting an investigation.

(2) In any case where the Commissioner conducts an investigation under this Act, he shall also send a report of the results of the investigation to the principal officer of the department or authority concerned and to any other person who is alleged in the relevant complaint to have taken or authorised the action complained of.

(3) If, after conducting an investigation under this Act, it appears to the Commissioner that injustice has been caused to the person aggrieved in consequence of maladministration and that the injustice has not been, or will not be, remedied, he may, if he thinks fit, lay before each House of Parliament a special report upon the case.

(4) The Commissioner shall annually lay before each House of Parliament a general report on the performance of his functions under this Act and may from time to time lay before each House of Parliament such other reports with respect to those functions as he thinks fit.

(5) For the purposes of the law of defamation, any such publication as is hereinafter mentioned shall be absolutely privileged, that is to say—

(a) the publication of any matter by the Commissioner in making a report to either House of Parliament for the purposes of this Act;

(b) the publication of any matter by a member of the House of Commons in communicating with the Commissioner or his officers for those purposes or by the Commissioner or his officers in communicating with such a member for those purposes;

(c) the publication by such a member to the person by whom a complaint was made under this Act of a report or statement sent to the member in respect of the complaint in pursuance of section (1) of this section;

(d) the publication by the Commissioner to such a person as is mentioned in subsection (2) of this section of a report to that person in pursuance of that subsection.

11 Provision for secrecy of information

(1) . . .

(2) Information obtained by the Commissioner or his officers in the course of or for the purposes of an investigation under this Act shall not be disclosed except—

(a) for the purposes of the investigation and of any report to be made thereon under this Act;

(b) for the purposes of any proceedings for an offence under [the Official Secrets Acts 1911 to 1989] alleged to have been committed in respect of information obtained by the Commissioner or any of his officers by virtue of this Act or for an offence of perjury alleged to have been committed in the course of an investigation under this Act or for the purposes of an inquiry with a view to the taking of such proceedings; or

(c) for the purposes of any proceedings under section 9 of this Act;

and the Commissioner and his officers shall not be called upon to give evidence in any proceedings (other than such proceedings as aforesaid) of matters coming to his or their knowledge in the course of an investigation under this Act.

[(2A) Where the Commissioner also holds office as a Health Service Commissioner and a person initiates a complaint to him in his capacity as such a Commissioner which relates partly to a matter with respect to which that person has previously initiated a complaint under this Act, or subsequently initiates such a complaint, information obtained by the Commissioner or his officers in the course of or for the purposes of investigating the complaint under this Act may be disclosed for the purposes of his carrying out his functions in relation to the other complaint.]

(3) A Minister of the Crown may give notice in writing to the Commissioner, with respect to any document or information specified in the notice, or any class of documents or information so specified, that in the opinion of the Minister the disclosure of that document or information, or of documents or information of that class, would be prejudicial to the safety of the State or otherwise contrary to the public interest; and where such a notice is given nothing in this Act shall be construed as authorising or requiring the Commissioner or any officer of the Commissioner to communicate to any person or for any purpose any document or information specified in the notice, or any document or information of a class so specified.

(4) The references in this section to a Minister of the Crown include references to the Commissioners of Customs and Excise and the Commissioners of Inland Revenue.

NOTES

Sub-s (1): repealed by the Official Secrets Act 1989, s 16(4), Sch 2.

Sub-s (2): words in square brackets substituted by the Official Secrets Act 1989, s 16(3), Sch 1, para 1(a).

Sub-s (2A): inserted by the Parliamentary and Health Service Commissioners Act 1987, s 4(1).

Supplemental

12 Interpretation

(1), (2) . . .

(3) It is hereby declared that nothing in this Act authorises or requires the Commissioner to question the merits of a decision taken without maladministration by a government department or other authority in the exercise of a discretion vested in that department or authority.

NOTES

Sub-ss (1), (2): outside the scope of this work.

13 Application to Northern Ireland

(1) Subject to the provisions of this section, this Act extends to Northern Ireland.

(2) Nothing in this section shall be construed as authorising the inclusion among the departments and authorities to which this Act applies of any department of the Government of Northern Ireland, or any authority [or body] established by or with the authority of the Parliament of Northern Ireland; but this Act shall apply to any such department [authority or body], in relation to any action taken by them as agent for a department or authority to which this Act applies, as it applies to the last-mentioned department or authority.

(3) In section 6 of this Act the references to a Minister of the Crown or government department and to Parliament shall include references to a Minister or department of the Government of Northern Ireland and to the Parliament of Northern Ireland.

(4) In section 8 of this Act the references to the Cabinet shall include references to the [Northern Ireland Executive], and in relation to [that Executive] for the reference to the Prime Minister there shall be substituted a reference to the Prime Minister of Northern Ireland.

NOTES

Sub-s (2): words in square brackets substituted by the Parliamentary and Health Service Commissioners Act 1987, s 1(3)(a).

Sub-s (4): words in square brackets substituted by the Northern Ireland (Modification of Enactments—No 1) Order 1973, SI 1973/2163, art 14(1), Sch 5, para 18.

14 Short title and commencement

(1) This Act may be cited as the Parliamentary Commissioner Act 1967.

(2) This Act shall come into force on such date as Her Majesty may by Order in Council appoint.

(3) A complaint under this Act may be made in respect of matters [whenever arising]; and for the purposes of subsection (3) of section 6 of this Act any time elapsing between the date of the passing and the date of the commencement of this Act (but not any time before the first of those dates) shall be disregarded.

NOTES

Sub-s (3): words in square brackets substituted by the Parliamentary and Health Service Commissioners Act 1987, s 1(3)(b).

[SCHEDULE 2

Section 4

DEPARTMENTS ETC SUBJECT TO INVESTIGATION

Advisory, Conciliation and Arbitration Service.

Agricultural wages committees.

Ministry of Agriculture, Fisheries and Food.

Arts Council of England.
Arts Council of Great Britain.
Arts Council of Wales (Cyngor Celfyddydau Cymru).
Scottish Arts Council.
British Council.
British Library Board.
Building Societies Commission.
Bwrdd yr Iaith Gymraeg (Welsh Language Board).
Certification Officer.
Charity Commission.
Civil Service Commission.
Coal Authority.
Co-operative Development Agency.
Countryside Commission.
Countryside Council for Wales.
Crafts Council.
Crofters Commission.
Crown Estate Office.
Department for Culture, Media and Sport.
Customs and Excise.
Data Protection Registrar.
Deer Commission for Scotland.
Ministry of Defence.
Department for International Development
Development Commission.
Education Assets Board.
Central Bureau for Educational Visits and Exchanges.
Office of the Director General of Electricity Supply.
The Department for Education and Employment.
The Department of the Environment, Transport and the Regions.
English Sports Council.
Environment Agency.
Equal Opportunities Commission.
Export Credits Guarantee Department.
Office of the Director General of Fair Trading.
British Film Institute.
Foreign and Commonwealth Office.
Forestry Commission.
Friendly Societies Commission.
Registry of Friendly Societies.
Office of the Director General of Gas Supply.
Health and Safety Commission.
Health and Safety Executive.
Department of Health.
Historic Buildings and Monuments Commission for England.

Home Office.

Horserace Betting Levy Board.

Housing Corporation.

Housing for Wales.

Human Fertilisation and Embryology Authority.

Central Office of Information.

Inland Revenue.

The International Rail Regulator.

Intervention Board for Agricultural Produce.

Land Registry.

Legal Aid Board.

The following general lighthouse authorities—

(a) the Corporation of the Trinity House of Deptford Strond;

(b) the Commissioners of Northern Lighthouses.

Local Government Commission for England.

The Lord Chancellor's Department.

Lord President of the Council's Office.

Medical Practices Committee.

Scottish Medical Practices Committee.

Museums and Galleries Commission.

National Debt Office.

Trustees of the National Heritage Memorial Fund.

Office of the Director General of the National Lottery.

Department for National Savings.

The Office for National Statistics.

Nature Conservancy Council for England.

Commission for the New Towns.

Development corporations for new towns.

Northern Ireland Court Service.

Northern Ireland Office.

Occupational Pensions Board.

The Occupational Pensions Regulatory Authority.

Ordnance Survey.

The Director of Passenger Rail Franchising.

The Pensions Compensation Board.

Police Information Technology Organisation;

Office of the Commissioner for Protection Against Unlawful Industrial Action.

Registrar of Public Lending Right.

Public Record Office.

Office of Public Service

Commission for Racial Equality.

The Rail Regulator.

Department of the Registers of Scotland.

General Register Office, Scotland.

Biotechnology and Biological Sciences Research Council.

Economic and Social Research Council.

Engineering and Physical Sciences Research Council.
Medical Research Council.
Natural Environment Research Council.
Particle Physics and Astronomy Research Council.
Council for the Central Laboratory of the Research Councils.
Residuary Bodies.
Office of the Commissioner for the Rights of Trade Union Members.
Royal Mint.
Office of Her Majesty's Chief Inspector of Schools in England.
Office of Her Majesty's Chief Inspector of Schools in Wales.
Scottish Courts Administration.
Scottish Environment Protection Agency.
Scottish Homes.
Scottish Legal Aid Board.
Scottish Natural Heritage.
Scottish Office.
Scottish Record Office.
Council for Small Industries in Rural Areas.
Department of Social Security.
Central Council for Education and Training in Social Work.
Sports Council.
Scottish Sports Council.
Sports Council for Wales.
The Staff Commission for Wales (Comisiwn Staff Cymru).
Stationery Office.
Office of the Director General of Telecommunication.
English Tourist Board.
Scottish Tourist Board.
Wales Tourist Board.
Board of Trade.
Department of Trade and Industry.
Traffic Director for London.
Agricultural Training Board.
Clothing and Allied Products Industry Training Board.
Construction Industry Training Board.
Engineering Industry Training Board.
Hotel and Catering Industry Training Board.
Plastics Processing Industry Training Board.
Road Transport Industry Training Board.
Treasury.
Treasury Solicitor.
United Kingdom Ecolabelling Board.
United Kingdom Sports Council.
Urban development corporations.
Urban Regeneration Agency.
Development Board for Rural Wales.

Office of the Director General of Water Services.

Welsh Office.

NOTES

Substituted by the Parliamentary and Health Service Commissioners Act 1987, s 1(2), Sch 1.

Printed as amended as at 21 July 1998; entries omitted outside the scope of this work.

Prospective amendments: entry 'Data Protection Registrar' substituted by entry 'Data Protection Commissioner' by the Data Protection Act 1998, s 74(1), Sch 15, para 2; entry 'Office of the Director General of the National Lottery' repealed and entry 'National Lottery Commission' inserted by the National Lottery Act 1998, ss 1(5), 26, Sch 1, Pt III, para 9, Sch 5, Pt I; in the entry 'Urban development corporations' the words 'established for urban development areas wholly in England' added by the Government of Wales Act 1998, s 125, Sch 12, para 9(a).

Notes omitted at end of Schedule outside the scope of this work.

SCHEDULE 3

Section 5

MATTERS NOT SUBJECT TO INVESTIGATION

1. Action taken in matters certified by a Secretary of State or other Minister of the Crown to affect relations or dealings between the Government of the United Kingdom and any other Government or any international organisation of States or Governments.

2. Action taken, in any country or territory outside the United Kingdom, by or on behalf of any officer representing or acting under the authority of Her Majesty in respect of the United Kingdom, or any other officer of the Government of the United Kingdom [other than action which is taken by an officer (not being an honorary consular officer) in the exercise of a consular function on behalf of the Government of the United Kingdom . . .].

3. Action taken in connection with the administration of the government of any country or territory outside the United Kingdom which forms part of Her Majesty's dominions or in which Her Majesty has jurisdiction.

4. Action taken by the Secretary of State under the Extradition Act 1870[, the Fugitive Offenders Act 1967 or the Extradition Act 1989].

5. Action taken by or with the authority of the Secretary of State for the purposes of investigating crime or of protecting the security of the State, including action so taken with respect to passports.

6. The commencement or conduct of civil or criminal proceedings before any court of law in the United Kingdom, of proceedings at any place under the Naval Discipline Act 1957, the Army Act 1955 or the Air Force Act 1955, or of proceedings before any international court or tribunal.

[6A. Action taken by any person appointed by the Lord Chancellor as a member of the administrative staff of any court or tribunal, so far as that action is taken at the direction, or on the authority (whether express or implied), of any person acting in a judicial capacity or in his capacity as a member of the tribunal.]

[6B.—(1) Action taken by any member of the administrative staff of a relevant tribunal, so far as that action is taken at the direction, or on the authority (whether express or implied), of any person acting in his capacity as a member of the tribunal.

(2) In this paragraph, "relevant tribunal" has the meaning given by section 5(8) of this Act.]

[6C. Action taken by any person appointed under section 5(3)(c) of the Criminal Injuries Compensation Act 1995, so far as that action is taken at the direction, or on the authority (whether express or implied), of any person acting in his capacity as an adjudicator appointed under section 5 of that Act to determine appeals.]

7. Any exercise of the prerogative of mercy or of the power of a Secretary of State to make a reference in respect of any person to . . . the High Court of Justiciary or the Courts-Martial Appeal Court.

8. Action taken on behalf of the Minister of Health or the Secretary of State by a [[Health Authority, a Special Health Authority] [except the Rampton Hospital Review Board] [. . . the Rampton Hospital Board,] [the Broadmoor Hospital Board or the Moss Side and Park Lane Hospitals Board,] . . . a Health Board or the Common Services Agency for the Scottish Health Service [by the Dental Practice Board or the Scottish Dental Practice Board]], or by the Public Health Laboratory Service Board.

9. Action taken in matters relating to contractual or other commercial transactions, whether within the United Kingdom or elsewhere, being transactions of a government department or authority to which this Act applies or of any such authority or body as is mentioned in paragraph (a) or (b) of subsection (1) of section 6 of this Act and not being transactions for or relating to—

(a) the acquisition of land compulsorily or in circumstances in which it could be acquired compulsorily;

(b) the disposal as surplus of land acquired compulsorily or in such circumstances as aforesaid.

10.—[(1)] Action taken in respect of appointments or removals, pay, discipline, superannuation or other personnel matters, in relation to—

(a) service in any of the armed forces of the Crown, including reserve and auxiliary and cadet forces;

(b) service in any office or employment under the Crown or under any authority [to which this Act applies]; or

(c) service in any office or employment, or under any contract for services, in respect of which power to take action, or to determine or approve the action to be taken, in such matters is vested in Her Majesty, any Minister of the Crown or any such authority as aforesaid.

[(2) Sub-paragraph (1)(c) above shall not apply to any action (not otherwise excluded from investigation by this Schedule) which is taken by the Secretary of State in connection with—

(a) the provision of information relating to the terms and conditions of any employment covered by an agreement entered into by him under section 12(1) of the Overseas Development and Co-operation Act 1980 or

(b) the provision of any allowance, grant or supplement or any benefit (other than those relating to superannuation) arising from the designation of any person in accordance with such an agreement.]

11. The grant of honours, awards or privileges within the gift of the Crown, including the grant of Royal Charters.

NOTES

Para 2: words in square brackets added by the Parliamentary Commissioner Order 1979, SI 1979/915; words omitted repealed by the Parliamentary Commissioner (No 2) Order 1988, SI 1988/1985.

Para 4: words in square brackets substituted by the Extradition Act 1989, s 36(1).

Para 6A: inserted by the Courts and Legal Services Act 1990, s 110(2).

Para 6B: inserted by the Parliamentary Commissioner Act 1994, s 1(2).

Para 6C: inserted by the Criminal Injuries Compensation Act 1995, s 10(2).

Para 7: words omitted repealed by the Criminal Appeal Act 1995, s 29(2), Sch 3.

Para 8: words in first (outer) pair of square brackets substituted by the National Health Service Reorganisation Act 1973, ss 57, 58, Sch 4, para 109; words in second (inner) pair of square brackets substituted, and words omitted in second place repealed, by the Health Authorities Act 1995, ss 2(1), 5(1), 8, Sch 1, Pt III, para 93, partly as from 1 April 1996; words in third (inner) pair of square brackets inserted by the Parliamentary Commissioner Order 1981, SI 1981/736; words in fourth (inner pair) of square brackets inserted by the Parliamentary Commissioner Order 1986, SI 1986/1168; words omitted in first place repealed, and words in fifth (inner) pair of square brackets inserted, by the Parliamentary Commissioner Order 1987, SI 1987/661; words in sixth (inner) pair of square brackets inserted by the Health Service Commissioners Act 1993, s 20(1), Sch 2, para 2.

Para 10: original renumbered 10(1) and new sub-para (2) added by the Parliamentary Commissioner Order 1983, SI 1983/1707; words in square brackets in sub-para (1)(b) substituted by the Parliamentary and Health Service Commissioners Act 1987, s 1(3)(c).

CRIMINAL LAW ACT 1967

(c 58)

An Act to amend the law of England and Wales by abolishing the division of crimes into felonies and misdemeanours and to amend and simplify the law in respect of matters arising from or related to that division or the abolition of it; to do away (within or without England and Wales) with certain obsolete crimes together with the torts of maintenance and champerty; and for purposes connected therewith

[21 July 1967]

PART I
FELONY AND MISDEMEANOUR

3 Use of force in making arrest, etc

(1) A person may use such force as is reasonable in the circumstances in the prevention of crime, or in effecting or assisting in the lawful arrest of offenders or suspected offenders or of persons unlawfully at large.

(2) Subsection (1) above shall replace the rules of the common law on the question when force used for a purpose mentioned in the subsection is justified by that purpose.

11 Extent of Part I, and provision for Northern Ireland

(1) Subject to subsections (2) to (4) below, this Part of this Act shall not extend to . . . Northern Ireland.

(2)–(4) . . .

NOTES

Words omitted from subs-s (1), and whole of sub-ss (2)–(4), outside the scope of this work.

PART III
SUPPLEMENTARY

15 Short title

This Act may be cited as the Criminal Law Act 1967.

THEATRES ACT 1968

(c 54)

An Act to abolish censorship of the theatre and to amend the law in respect of theatres and theatrical performances

[26 July 1968]

Abolition of censorship of the theatre

1 Abolition of censorship of the theatre

(1) The Theatres Act 1843 is hereby repealed; and none of the powers which were exercisable thereunder by the Lord Chamberlain of Her Majesty's Household shall be exercisable by or on behalf of Her Majesty by virtue of Her royal prerogative.

(2) In granting, renewing or transferring any licence under this Act for the use of any premises for the public performance of plays or in varying any of the terms, conditions or restrictions on or subject to which any such licence is held, the licensing authority shall not have power to impose any term, condition or restriction as to the nature of the plays which may be performed under the licence or as to the manner of performing plays thereunder:

Provided that nothing in this subsection shall prevent a licensing authority from imposing any term, condition or restriction which they consider necessary in the interests of physical safety or health or any condition regulating or prohibiting the giving of an exhibition, demonstration or performance of hypnotism within the meaning of the Hypnotism Act 1952.

Provisions with respect to performances of plays

2 Prohibition of presentation of obscene performances of plays

(1) For the purposes of this section a performance of a play shall be deemed to be obscene if, taken as a whole, its effect was such as to tend to deprave and corrupt persons who were likely, having regard to all relevant circumstances, to attend it.

(2) Subject to sections 3 and 7 of this Act, if an obscene performance of a play is given, whether in public or private, any person who (whether for gain or not) presented or directed that performance shall be liable—

- (a) on summary conviction, to a fine not exceeding [the prescribed sum] or to imprisonment for a term not exceeding six months;
- (b) on conviction on indictment, to a fine or to imprisonment for a term not exceeding three years, or both.

(3) A prosecution on indictment for an offence under this section shall not be commenced more than two years after the commission of the offence.

(4) No person shall be proceeded against in respect of a performance of a play or anything said or done in the course of a performance—

- (a) for an offence at common law where it is of the essence of the offence that the performance or, as the case may be, what was said or done was obscene, indecent, offensive, disgusting or injurious to morality; or
- (b), (c) . . .

and no person shall be proceeded against for an offence at common law of conspiring to corrupt public morals, or to do any act contrary to public morals or decency, in respect of an agreement to present or give a performance of a play, or to cause anything to be said or done in the course of such a performance.

NOTES

Sub-s (2): reference to "the prescribed sum" substituted by virtue of the Magistrates' Courts Act 1980, s 32(2).

Sub-s (4): para (b) repealed by the Indecent Displays (Control) Act 1981, s 5(2), Schedule; para (c) repealed by the Civic Government (Scotland) Act 1982, s 137, Sch 4.

3 Defence of public good

(1) A person shall not be convicted of an offence under section 2 of this Act if it is proved that the giving of the performance in question was justified as being for the

public good on the ground that it was in the interests of drama, opera, ballet or any other art, or of literature or learning.

(2) It is hereby declared that the opinion of experts as to the artistic, literary or other merits of a performance of a play may be admitted in any proceedings for an offence under section 2 of this Act either to establish or negative the said ground.

4 Amendment of law of defamation

(1) For the purposes of the law of libel and slander (including the law of criminal libel so far as it relates to the publication of defamatory matter) the publication of words in the course of a performance of a play shall, subject to section 7 of this Act, be treated as publication in permanent form.

(2)–(4) . . .

NOTES

Sub-ss (2)–(4): outside the scope of this work.

6 Provocation of breach of peace by means of public performance of a play

(1) Subject to section 7 of this Act, if there is given a public performance of a play involving the use of threatening, abusive or insulting words or behaviour, any person who (whether for gain or not) presented or directed that performance shall be guilty of an offence under this section if—

(a) he did so with intent to provoke a breach of the peace; or

(b) the performance, taken as a whole, was likely to occasion a breach of the peace.

(2) A person guilty of an offence under this section shall be liable [on summary conviction to a fine not exceeding [level 5 on the standard scale] or to imprisonment for a term not exceeding six months or to both].

NOTES

Sub-s (2): words in first (outer) pair of square brackets substituted by the Criminal Law Act 1977, ss 15, 30, Sch 1; reference to level 5 on the standard scale substituted by virtue of the Criminal Justice Act 1982, s 46.

7 Exceptions for performances given in certain circumstances

(1) Nothing in sections 2 to 4 of this Act shall apply in relation to a performance of a play given on a domestic occasion in a private dwelling.

(2) Nothing in sections 2 to 6 of this Act shall apply in relation to a performance of a play given solely or primarily for one or more of the following purposes, that is to say—

(a) rehearsal; or

(b) to enable—

(i) a record or cinematograph film to be made from or by means of the performance; or

(ii) the performance to be broadcast; or

[(iii) the performance to be included in a programme service (within the meaning of the Broadcasting Act 1990) other than a sound or television broadcasting service;]

but in any proceedings for an offence under section 2, . . . or 6 of this Act alleged to have been committed in respect of a performance of a play or an offence at common law alleged to have been committed in England and Wales by the publication of defamatory matter in the course of a performance of a play, if it is proved that the performance was attended by persons other than persons directly connected with the giving of the performance or the doing in relation thereto of any of the things mentioned in paragraph (b) above, the performance shall be taken not to have been given solely or primarily for one or more of the said purposes unless the contrary is shown.

(3) In this section—

"broadcast" means broadcast by wireless telegraphy (within the meaning of the Wireless Telegraphy Act 1949), whether by way of sound broadcasting or television;

"cinematograph film" means any print, negative, tape or other article on which a performance of a play or any part of such a performance is recorded for the purposes of visual reproduction;

"record" means any record or similar contrivance for reproducing sound, including the sound-track of a cinematograph film;

. . . . .

NOTES

Sub-s (2): para (b)(iii) substituted by the Broadcasting Act 1990, s 203(1), Sch 20, para 13; figure omitted repealed by the Public Order Act 1986, s 40(3), Sch 3.

Sub-s (3): words omitted repealed by the Cable and Broadcasting Act 1984, s 57, Sch 5, para 21, Sch 6.

8 Restriction on institution of proceedings

Proceedings for an offence under section 2, . . . or 6 of this Act or an offence at common law committed by the publication of defamatory matter in the course of a performance of a play shall not be instituted in England and Wales except by or with the consent of the Attorney-General.

NOTES

Figure omitted repealed by the Public Order Act 1986, s 40(3), Sch 3.

Miscellaneous and general

20 Short title, commencement, extent . . .

(1) This Act may be cited as the Theatres Act 1968.

(2) The provisions of this Act mentioned in subsection (3) below shall come into force on the passing of this Act, and the other provisions of this Act shall come into force on the expiration of a period of two months beginning with the date on which this Act is passed; . . .

(3) The provisions of this Act referred to in subsection (2) above are the following—

(a) sections 1(2) . . . and this section;

(b), (c) . . .

(4) This Act does not extend to Northern Ireland.

(5) . . .

NOTES

Words omitted from provision title, sub-ss (2), (3), and the whole of sub-s (5), outside the scope of this work.

FOREIGN COMPENSATION ACT 1969

(c 20)

An Act to make provision with respect to certain property (including the proceeds thereof and any income or other property accruing therefrom) of persons formerly resident or carrying on business in Estonia, Latvia, Lithuania or a part of Czechoslovakia, Finland, Poland or Rumania which has been ceded to the Union of Soviet Socialist Republics, and to amend the Foreign Compensation Act 1950

[16 May 1969]

3 Determinations of the Foreign Compensation Commission and appeals against such determinations

(1) The Foreign Compensation Commission shall have power to determine any question as to the construction or interpretation of any provision of an Order in Council under section 3 of the Foreign Compensation Act 1950 with respect to claims falling to be determined by them.

(2) Subject to subsection (4) below, the Commission shall, if so required by a person mentioned in subsection (6) below who is aggrieved by any determination of the Commission on any question of law relating to the jurisdiction of the Commission or on any question mentioned in subsection (1) above, state and sign a case for the decision of the Court of Appeal.

(3) In this section "determination" includes a determination which under rules under section 4(2) of the Foreign Compensation Act 1950 (rules of procedure) is a provisional determination, and anything which purports to be a determination.

(4) . . .

(5) Any person mentioned in subsection (6) below may, with a view to requiring the Commission to state and sign a case under this section, request the Commission to furnish a written statement of the reasons for any determination of theirs, but the Commission shall not be obliged to state the reasons for any determination unless it is given on a claim in which a question mentioned in subsection (2) above arises.

(6) The persons who may make a request under subsection (5) above or a requirement under subsection (2) above in relation to any claim are the claimant and any person appointed by the Commission to represent the interests of any fund out of which the claim would, if allowed, be met.

(7) . . .

(8) Notwithstanding anything in section 3 of the Appellate Jurisdiction Act 1876 (right of appeal to the House of Lords from decisions of the Court of Appeal), no appeal shall lie to the House of Lords from a decision of the Court of Appeal on an appeal under this section.

(9) Except as provided by subsection (2) above and subsection (10) below, no determination by the Commission on any claim made to them under the Foreign Compensation Act 1950 shall be called in question in any court of law.

(10) Subsection (9) above shall not affect any right of any person to bring proceedings questioning any determination of the Commission on the ground that it is contrary to natural justice.

(11), (12) . . .

NOTES

Sub-ss (4), (7): outside the scope of this work.

Sub-ss (11), (12): repealed by the SL(R) Act 1989.

5 Short title

This Act may be cited as the Foreign Compensation Act 1969.

COURTS ACT 1971

(c 23)

An Act to make further provision as respects the Supreme Court and county courts, judges and juries, to establish a Crown Court as part of the Supreme Court to try indictments and exercise certain other jurisdiction, to abolish courts of assize and certain other courts and to deal with their jurisdiction and other consequential matters, and to amend in other respects the law about courts and court proceedings

[12 May 1971]

PART III
JUDGES

17 Retirement, removal and disqualifications of Circuit judges

(1)–(3) . . .

(4) The Lord Chancellor may, if he thinks fit, remove a Circuit judge from office on the ground of incapacity or misbehaviour.

(5), (6) . . .

NOTES

Sub-s (1): outside the scope of this work.

Sub-ss (2), (3): repealed by the Judicial Pensions and Retirement Act 1993, ss 26(10), 31(4), Sch 6, para 8(1), (3), (4), Sch 9.

Sub-s (5): repealed by the House of Commons Disqualification Act 1975, s 10(2), Sch 3, and the Northern Ireland Assembly Disqualification Act 1975, s 5(2), Sch 3, Part I.

Sub-s (6): repealed by the Courts and Legal Services Act 1990, s 125(7), Sch 20.

PART VI
MISCELLANEOUS AND SUPPLEMENTAL

Supplemental

59 Short title, commencement and extent

(1) This Act may be cited as the Courts Act 1971.

(2)–(7) . . .

NOTES

Sub-ss (2)–(7): outside the scope of this work.

MISUSE OF DRUGS ACT 1971

(c 38)

An Act to make new provision with respect to dangerous or otherwise harmful drugs and related matters, and for purposes connected therewith

[27 May 1971]

Law enforcement and punishment of offences

23 Powers to search and obtain evidence

(1) A constable or other person authorised in that behalf by a general or special order of the Secretary of State (or in Northern Ireland either of the Secretary of State or the Ministry of Home Affairs for Northern Ireland) shall, for the purposes of the execution of this Act, have power to enter the premises of a person carrying on business as a producer or supplier of any controlled drugs and to demand the production of, and to inspect, any books or documents relating to dealings in any such drugs and to inspect any stocks of any such drugs.

(2) If a constable has reasonable grounds to suspect that any person is in possession of a controlled drug in contravention of this Act or of any regulations made thereunder, the constable may—

- (a) search that person, and detain him for the purpose of searching him;
- (b) search any vehicle or vessel in which the constable suspects that the drug may be found, and for that purpose require the person in control of the vehicle or vessel to stop it;
- (c) seize and detain, for the purposes of proceedings under this Act, anything found in the course of the search which appears to the constable to be evidence of an offence under this Act.

In this subsection "vessel" includes a hovercraft within the meaning of the Hovercraft Act 1968; and nothing in this subsection shall prejudice any power of search or any power to seize or detain property which exercisable by a constable apart from this subsection.

(3) If a justice of the peace (or in Scotland a justice of the peace, a magistrate or a sheriff) is satisfied by information on oath that there is reasonable ground for suspecting—

- (a) that any controlled drugs are, in contravention of this Act or of any regulations made thereunder, in the possession of a person on any premises; or
- (b) that a document directly or indirectly relating to, or connected with, a transaction or dealing which was, or an intended transaction or dealing which would if carried out be, an offence under this Act, or in the case of a transaction or dealing carried out or intended to be carried out in a place

outside the United Kingdom, an offence against the provisions of a corresponding law in force in that place, is in the possession of a person on any premises,

he may grant a warrant authorising any constable acting for the police area in which the premises are situated at any time or times within one month from the date of the warrant, to enter, if need be by force, the premises named in the warrant, and to search the premises and any persons found therein and, if there is reasonable ground for suspecting that an offence under this Act has been committed in relation to any controlled drugs found on the premises or in the possession of any such persons, or that a document so found is such a document as is mentioned in paragraph (b) above, to seize and detain those drugs or that document, as the case may be.

[(3A) The powers conferred by subsection (1) above shall be exercised also for the purposes of the execution of Part II of the Criminal Justice (International Co-operation) Act 1990 [or section 49 of the Drug Trafficking Act 1994] [or Article 47 of the Proceeds of Crime (Northern Ireland) Order 1996] and subsection (3) above (excluding paragraph (a)) shall apply also to offences under section 12 or 13 of that Act [of 1990], taking references in those provisions to controlled drugs as references to scheduled substances within the meaning of that Part.]

(4) A person commits an offence if he—

(a) intentionally obstructs a person in the exercise of his powers under this section; or

(b) conceals from a person acting in the exercise of his powers under subsection (1) above any such books, documents, stocks or drugs as are mentioned in that subsection; or

(c) without reasonable excuse (proof of which shall lie on him) fails to produce any such books or documents as are so mentioned where their production is demanded by a person in the exercise of his powers under that subsection.

(5) In its application to Northern Ireland subsection (3) above shall have effect as if the words "acting for the police area in which the premises are situated" were omitted.

NOTES

Sub-s (3A): inserted by the Criminal Justice (International Co-operation) Act 1990, s 23(1), (4); words in first and third pairs of square brackets inserted by the Drug Trafficking Act 1994, s 65(1), Sch 1, para 4; words in second pair of square brackets inserted by the Proceeds of Crime (Northern Ireland) Order 1996, SI 1996/1299, art 57(1), Sch 3, para 2.

Miscellaneous and supplementary provisions

40 Short title, extent and commencement

(1) This Act may be cited as the Misuse of Drugs Act 1971.

(2) This Act extends to Northern Ireland.

(3) This Act shall come into operation on such day as the Secretary of State may by order made by statutory instrument appoint, and different dates may be appointed under this subsection for different purposes.

IMMIGRATION ACT 1971

(c 77)

An Act to amend and replace the present immigration laws, to make certain related changes in the citizenship law and enable help to be given to those wishing to return abroad, and for purposes connected therewith

[28 October 1971]

PART I
REGULATION OF ENTRY INTO AND STAY IN UNITED KINGDOM

1 General principles

(1) All those who are in this Act expressed to have the right of abode in the United Kingdom shall be free to live in, and to come and go into and from, the United Kingdom without let or hindrance except such as may be required under and in accordance with this Act to enable their right to be established or as may be otherwise lawfully imposed on any person.

(2) Those not having that right may live, work and settle in the United Kingdom by permission and subject to such regulation and control of their entry into, stay in and departure from the United Kingdom as is imposed by this Act; and indefinite leave to enter or remain in the United Kingdom shall, by virtue of this provision be treated as having been given under this Act to those in the United Kingdom at its coming into force, if they are then settled there (and not exempt under this Act from the provisions relating to leave to enter or remain).

(3) Arrival in and departure from the United Kingdom on a local journey from or to any of the Islands (that is to say, the Channel Islands and Isle of Man) or the Republic of Ireland shall not be subject to control under this Act, nor shall a person require leave to enter the United Kingdom on so arriving, except in so far as any of those places is for any purpose excluded from this subsection under the powers conferred by this Act; and in this Act the United Kingdom and those places, or such of them as are not so excluded, are collectively referred to as "the common travel area".

(4) The rules laid down by the Secretary of State as to the practice to be followed in the administration of this Act for regulating the entry into and stay in the United Kingdom of persons not having the right of abode shall include provision for admitting (in such cases and subject to such restrictions as may be provided by the rules, and subject or not to conditions as to length of stay or otherwise) persons coming for the purpose of taking employment, or for purposes of study, or as visitors, or as dependants of persons lawfully in or entering the United Kingdom.

(5) . . .

NOTES

Sub-s (5): repealed by the Immigration Act 1988, s 1.

[2 Statement of right of abode in United Kingdom

(1) A person is under this Act to have the right of abode in the United Kingdom if—

(a) he is a British citizen; or
(b) he is a Commonwealth citizen who—
   (i) immediately before the commencement of the British Nationality Act 1981 was a Commonwealth citizen having the right of abode in the United Kingdom by virtue of section 2(1)(d) or section 2(2) of this Act as then in force; and
   (ii) has not ceased to be a Commonwealth citizen in the meanwhile.

(2) In relation to Commonwealth citizens who have the right of abode in the United Kingdom by virtue of subsection (1)(b) above, this Act, except this section and [section 5(2)], shall apply as if they were British citizens; and in this Act (except as aforesaid) "British citizen" shall be construed accordingly.]

NOTES
Substituted by the British Nationality Act 1981, s 39(1), (2).
Sub-s (2): words in square brackets substituted by the Immigration Act 1988, s 3(3).

3 General provisions for regulation and control

(1) Except as otherwise provided by or under this Act, where a person is not [a British citizen]—
(a) he shall not enter the United Kingdom unless given leave to do so in accordance with this Act;
(b) he may be given leave to enter the United Kingdom (or, when already there, leave to remain in the United Kingdom) either for a limited or for an indefinite period;
[(c) if he is given limited leave to enter or remain in the United Kingdom, it may be given subject to all or any of the following conditions, namely—
   (i) a condition restricting his employment or occupation in the United Kingdom;
   (ii) a condition requiring him to maintain and accommodate himself, and any dependants of his, without recourse to public funds; and
   (iii) a condition requiring him to register with the police.]

(2) The Secretary of State shall from time to time (and as soon as may be) lay before Parliament statements of the rules, or of any changes in the rules, laid down by him as to the practice to be followed in the administration of this Act for regulating the entry into and stay in the United Kingdom of persons required by this Act to have leave to enter, including any rules as to the period for which leave is to be given and the conditions to be attached in different circumstances; and section 1(4) above shall not be taken to require uniform provision to be made by the rules as regards admission of persons for a purpose or in a capacity specified in section 1(4) (and in particular, for this as well as other purposes of this Act, account may be taken of citizenship or nationality).

If a statement laid before either House of Parliament under this subsection is disapproved by a resolution of that House passed within the period of forty days beginning with the date of laying (and exclusive of any period during which Parliament is dissolved or prorogued or during which both Houses are adjourned for more than four days), then the Secretary of State shall as soon as may be make such changes or further changes in the rules as appear to him to be required in the circumstances, so that the statement of those changes be laid before Parliament at latest by the end of the period of forty days beginning with the date of the resolution (but exclusive as aforesaid).

(3) In the case of a limited leave to enter or remain in the United Kingdom,—

(a) a person's leave may be varied, whether by restricting, enlarging or removing the limit on its duration, or by adding, varying or revoking conditions, but if the limit on its duration is removed, any conditions attached to the leave shall cease to apply; and

(b) the limitation on and any conditions attached to a person's leave [(whether imposed originally or on a variation) shall], if not superseded, apply also to any subsequent leave he may obtain after an absence from the United Kingdom within the period limited for the duration of the earlier leave.

(4) A person's leave to enter or remain in the United Kingdom shall lapse on his going to a country or territory outside the common travel area (whether or not he lands there), unless within the period for which he had leave he returns to the United Kingdom in circumstances in which he is not required to obtain leave to enter; but, if he does so return, his previous leave (and any limitation on it or conditions attached to it) shall continue to apply.

(5) A person who is not [a British citizen] shall be liable to deportation from the United Kingdom—

(a) if, having only a limited leave to enter or remain, he does not observe a condition attached to the leave or remains beyond the time limited by the leave; or

[(aa) if he has obtained leave to remain by deception; or]

(b) if the Secretary of State deems his deportation to be conducive to the public good; or

(c) if another person to whose family he belongs is or has been ordered to be deported.

(6) Without prejudice to the operation of subsection (5) above, a person who is not [a British citizen] shall also be liable to deportation from the United Kingdom if, after he has attained the age of seventeen, he is convicted of an offence for which he is punishable with imprisonment and on his conviction is recommended for deportation by a court empowered by this Act to do so.

(7) Where it appears to Her Majesty proper so to do by reason of restrictions or conditions imposed on [British citizens, British Dependent Territories citizens or British Overseas citizens] when leaving or seeking to leave any country or the territory subject to the government of any country, Her Majesty may by Order in Council make provision for prohibiting persons who are nationals or citizens of that country and are not [British citizens] from embarking in the United Kingdom, or from doing so elsewhere than at a port of exit, or for imposing restrictions or conditions on them when embarking or about to embark in the United Kingdom; and Her Majesty may also make provision by Order in Council to enable those who are not [British citizens] to be, in such cases as may be prescribed by the Order, prohibited in the interests of safety from so embarking on a ship or aircraft specified or indicated in the prohibition.

Any Order in Council under this subsection shall be subject to annulment in pursuance of a resolution of either House of Parliament.

(8) When any question arises under this Act whether or not a person is [a British citizen], or is entitled to any exemption under this Act, it shall lie on the person asserting it to prove that he is.

[(9) A person seeking to enter the United Kingdom and claiming to have the right of abode there shall prove that he has that right by means of either—

(a) a United Kingdom passport describing him as a British citizen or as a citizen of the United Kingdom and Colonies having the right of abode in the United Kingdom; or

(b) a certificate of entitlement issued by or on behalf of the Government of the United Kingdom certifying that he has such a right of abode.]

NOTES

Sub-s (1): words in first pair of square brackets substituted by the British Nationality Act 1981, s 39(1), (6), Sch 4, para 2(a); para (c) substituted by the Asylum and Immigration Act 1996, s 12(1), Sch 2, para 1(1).

Sub-s (3): words in square brackets substituted by the Immigration Act 1988, s 10, Schedule, para 1.

Sub-s (5): words in first pair of square brackets substituted by the British Nationality Act 1981, s 39(1), (6), Sch 4, para 2(a); para (aa) inserted by the Asylum and Immigration Act 1996, s 12(1), Sch 2, para 1(2).

Sub-s (6): words in square brackets substituted by the British Nationality Act 1981, s 39(1), (6), Sch 4, para 2(a).

Sub-s (7): words in square brackets substituted by the British Nationality Act 1981, s 39(1), (6), Sch 4, paras 2(b), 4.

Sub-s (8): words in square brackets substituted by the British Nationality Act 1981, s 39(1), (6), Sch 4, para 2(a).

Sub-s (9): substituted for existing sub-ss (9), (9A) by the Immigration Act 1988, s 3(1).

Modification: modified, in relation to France and the United Kingdom, by the Channel Tunnel (International Arrangements) Order 1993, SI 1993/1813, art 7(1), Sch 4, para 1(2); modified, in relation to its application to frontier controls between the United Kingdom, France and Belgium, by the Channel Tunnel (Miscellaneous Provisions) Order 1994, SI 1994/1405, art 7.

6 Recommendations by court for deportation

(1) Where under section 3(6) above a person convicted of an offence is liable to deportation on the recommendation of a court, he may be recommended for deportation by any court having power to sentence him for the offence unless the court commits him to be sentenced or further dealt with for that offence by another court:

. . . . .

(2), (3) . . .

(4) Notwithstanding any rule of practice restricting the matters which ought to be taken into account in dealing with an offender who is sentenced to imprisonment, a recommendation for deportation may be made in respect of an offender who is sentenced to imprisonment for life.

(5) Where a court recommends or purports to recommend a person for deportation, the validity of the recommendation shall not be called in question except on an appeal against the recommendation or against the conviction on which it is made; but—

(a) . . . the recommendation shall be treated as a sentence for the purpose of any enactment providing an appeal against sentence; . . .

(b) . . .

(6) A deportation order shall not be made on the recommendation of a court so long as an appeal or further appeal is pending against the recommendation or against the conviction on which it was made; . . .

(7) . . .

NOTES

Sub-ss (1), (6): words omitted outside the scope of this work.

Sub-ss (2), (3), (7): outside the scope of this work.

Sub-s (5): words omitted repealed by the Criminal Justice (Scotland) Act 1980, s 83(3), Sch 8, and the Criminal Justice Act 1982, ss 77, 78, Sch 15, para 15, Sch 16.

7 Exemption from deportation for certain existing residents

(1) Notwithstanding anything in section 3(5) or (6) above but subject to the provisions of this section, a Commonwealth citizen or citizen of the Republic of Ireland who was such a citizen at the coming into force of this Act and was then ordinarily resident in the United Kingdom—

- (a) shall not be liable to deportation under section 3(5)(b) if at the time of the Secretary of State's decision he had at all times since the coming into force of this Act been ordinarily resident in the United Kingdom and Islands; and
- (b) shall not be liable to deportation under section 3(5)(a), (b) or (c) if at the time of the Secretary of State's decision he had for the last five years been ordinarily resident in the United Kingdom and Islands; and
- (c) shall not on conviction of an offence be recommended for deportation under section 3(6) if at the time of the conviction he had for the last five years been ordinarily resident in the United Kingdom and Islands.

(2) A person who has at any time become ordinarily resident in the United Kingdom or in any of the Islands shall not be treated for the purposes of this section as having ceased to be so by reason only of his having remained there in breach of the immigration laws.

(3) The "last five years" before the material time under subsection (1)(b) or (c) above is to be taken as a period amounting in total to five years exclusive of any time during which the person claiming exemption under this section was undergoing imprisonment or detention by virtue of a sentence passed for an offence on a conviction in the United Kingdom and Islands, and the period for which he was imprisoned or detained by virtue of the sentence amounted to six months or more.

(4), (5) . . .

NOTES

Sub-ss (4), (5): outside the scope of this work.

PART II
APPEALS

The appellate authorities

12 Immigration Appeal Tribunal and adjudicators

The Immigration Appeal Tribunal and adjudicators provided for by the Immigration Appeals Act 1969 shall continue for purposes of this Act, and—

- [(a) members of the Tribunal and adjudicators shall be appointed by the Lord Chancellor; and
- (b) Schedule 5 to this Act shall have effect in relation to the adjudicators and the Tribunal.]

NOTES

Paras (a), (b): substituted by the Transfer of Functions (Immigration Appeals) Order 1987, SI 1987/465, art 3(1), (2).

Appeals to adjudicator or Tribunal in first instance

13 Appeals against exclusion from United Kingdom

(1) Subject to the provisions of this Part of this Act, a person who is refused leave to enter the United Kingdom under this Act may appeal to an adjudicator against the decision that he requires leave or against the refusal.

(2) Subject to the provisions of this Part of this Act, a person who, on an application duly made, is refused a [certificate of entitlement] or may appeal to an adjudicator against the refusal.

(3) [A person shall not be entitled to appeal, on the ground that he has a right of abode in the United Kingdom, against a decision that he requires leave to enter the United Kingdom unless he holds such a passport or certificate as is mentioned in section 3(9) above;] and a person shall not be entitled to appeal against a refusal of leave to enter so long as he is in the United Kingdom, unless he was refused leave at a port of entry and at a time when he held a current entry clearance or was a person named in a current work permit.

[(3A) A person who seeks to enter the United Kingdom—

- (a) as a visitor, or
- (b) in order to follow a course of study of not more than six months duration for which he has been accepted, or
- (c) with the intention of studying but without having been accepted for any course of study, or
- (d) as a dependant of a person within paragraph (a), (b) or (c) above,

shall not be entitled to appeal against a refusal of an entry clearance and shall not be entitled to appeal against a refusal of leave to enter unless he held a current entry clearance at the time of the refusal.

(3AA) The Secretary of State shall appoint a person, not being an officer of his, to monitor, in such manner as the Secretary of State may determine, refusals of entry clearance in cases where there is, by virtue of subsection (3A) above, no right of appeal; and the person so appointed shall make an annual report on the discharge of his functions to the Secretary of State who shall lay a copy of it before each House of Parliament.

(3AB) The Secretary of State may pay to a person appointed under subsection (3AA) above such fees and allowances as he may with the approval of the Treasury determine.]

[(3B) A person shall not be entitled to appeal against a refusal of an entry clearance if the refusal is on the ground that—

- (a) he or any person whose dependant he is does not hold a relevant document which is required by the immigration rules; or
- (b) he or any person whose dependant he is does not satisfy a requirement of the immigration rules as to age or nationality or citizenship; or
- (c) he or any person whose dependant he is seeks entry for a period exceeding that permitted by the immigration rules;

and a person shall not be entitled to appeal against a refusal of leave to enter if the refusal is on any of those grounds.

(3C) For the purposes of subsection (3B)(a) above, the following are "relevant documents"—

- (a) entry clearances;

(b) passports or other identity documents; and

(c) work permits.]

(4) An appeal against a refusal of leave to enter shall be dismissed by the adjudicator if he is satisfied that the appellant was at the time of the refusal an illegal entrant, and an appeal against a refusal of an entry clearance shall be dismissed by the adjudicator if he is satisfied that a deportation order was at the time of the refusal in force in respect of the appellant.

(5) A person shall not be entitled to appeal against a refusal of leave to enter, or against a refusal of an entry clearance, if the Secretary of State certifies that directions have been given by the Secretary of State (and not by a person acting under his authority) for the appellant not to be given entry to the United Kingdom on the ground that his exclusion is conducive to the public good, or if the leave to enter or entry clearance was refused in obedience to any such directions.

NOTES

Sub-s (2): words in square brackets substituted by the British Nationality Act 1981, s 39(1), (6), Sch 4, para 3(1).

Sub-s (3): words in square brackets substituted by the Immigration Act 1988, s 3(2).

Sub-ss (3A), (3AA), (3AB): inserted by the Asylum and Immigration Appeals Act 1993, s 10, except in relation to refusals made before 26 July 1993.

Sub-ss (3B), (3C): inserted by the Asylum and Immigration Appeals Act 1993, s 11(1), except in relation to refusals made before 26 July 1993.

Modification: modified, in relation to France and the United Kingdom, by the Channel Tunnel (International Arrangements) Order 1993, SI 1993/1813, art 7(1), Sch 4, para 1(6); modified, in relation to its application to frontier controls between the United Kingdom, France and Belgium, by the Channel Tunnel (Miscellaneous Provisions) Order 1994, SI 1994/1405, art 7.

14 Appeals against conditions

(1) Subject to the provisions of this Part of this Act, a person who has a limited leave under this Act to enter or remain in the United Kingdom may appeal to an adjudicator against any variation of the leave (whether as regards duration or conditions), or against any refusal to vary it; and a variation shall not take effect so long as an appeal is pending under this subsection against the variation, nor shall an appellant be required to leave the United Kingdom by reason of the expiration of his leave so long as his appeal is pending under this subsection against a refusal to enlarge or remove the limit on the duration of the leave.

(2), (2ZA) . . .

[(2A) A person shall not be entitled to appeal under subsection (1) above against any refusal to vary his leave if the refusal is on the ground that—

(a) a relevant document which is required by the immigration rules has not been issued; or

(b) the person or a person whose dependant he is does not satisfy a requirement of the immigration rules as to age or nationality or citizenship; or

(c) the variation would result in the duration of the person's leave exceeding what is permitted by the immigration rules; or

(d) any fee required by or under any enactment has not been paid.

(2B) For the purposes of subsection (2A)(a) above, the following are relevant documents—

(a) entry clearances;

(b) passports or other identity documents; and

[(c) work permits, or equivalent documents issued after entry.]]

(3) A person shall not be entitled to appeal under subsection (1) above against any variation of his leave which reduces its duration, or against any refusal to enlarge or remove the limit on its duration, if the Secretary of State certifies that the appellant's departure from the United Kingdom would be conducive to the public good, as being in the interests of national security or of the relations between the United Kingdom and any other country or for other reasons of a political nature, or the decision questioned by the appeal was taken on that ground by the Secretary of State (and not by a person acting under his authority).

(4) A person shall not be entitled to appeal under subsection (1) above against any variation made by statutory instrument, or against any refusal of the Secretary of State to make a statutory instrument.

(5) . . .

NOTES

Sub-ss (2), (2ZA), (5): outside the scope of this work.

Sub-s (2A): inserted by the Asylum and Immigration Appeals Act 1993, s 11(2), except in relation to refusals made before 26 July 1993.

Sub-s (2B): inserted by the Asylum and Immigration Appeals Act 1993, s 11(2), except in relation to refusals made before 26 July 1993; para (c) substituted by the Asylum and Immigration Act 1996, s 12(1), Sch 2, para 3(2).

15 Appeals in respect of deportation orders

(1) Subject to the provisions of this Part of this Act, a person may appeal to an adjudicator against—

(a) a decision of the Secretary of State to make a deportation order against him by virtue of section 3(5) above; or

(b) a refusal by the Secretary of State to revoke a deportation order made against him.

(2) A deportation order shall not be made against a person by virtue of section 3(5) above so long as an appeal may be brought against the decision to make it nor, if such an appeal is duly brought, so long as the appeal is pending; . . .

(3) A person shall not be entitled to appeal against a decision to make a deportation order against him if the ground of the decision was that his deportation is conducive to the public good as being in the interests of national security or of the relations between the United Kingdom and any other country or for other reasons of a political nature.

(4) A person shall not be entitled to appeal under this section against a refusal to revoke a deportation order, if the Secretary of State certifies that the appellant's exclusion from the United Kingdom is conducive to the public good or if revocation was refused on that ground by the Secretary of State (and not by a person acting under his authority).

(5) A person shall not be entitled to appeal under this section against a refusal to revoke a deportation order so long as he is in the United Kingdom, whether because he has not complied with the requirement to leave or because he has contravened the prohibition on entering.

(6) . . .

(7) An appeal under this section shall be to the Appeal Tribunal in the first instance, instead of to an adjudicator, if—

(a) it is an appeal against a decision to make a deportation order and the ground of the decision was that the deportation of the appellant is conducive to the public good; or

(b) it is an appeal against a decision to make a deportation order against a person as belonging to the family of another person, or an appeal against a refusal to revoke a deportation order so made; or

(c) there is pending a related appeal to which paragraph (b) above applies.

(8), (9) . . .

NOTES

Sub-s (2): words omitted outside the scope of this work.

Sub-ss (6), (8), (9): outside the scope of this work.

17 Appeals against removal on objection to destination

(1) Subject to the provisions of this Part of this Act, where directions are given under this Act for a person's removal from the United Kingdom either—

(a) on his being refused leave to enter; or

(b) on a deportation order being made against him; or

(c) on his having entered the United Kingdom in breach of a deportation order;

he may appeal to an adjudicator against the directions on the ground that he ought to be removed (if at all) to a different country or territory specified by him.

(2) Where a person appeals under section 13(1) above on being refused leave to enter the United Kingdom, and either—

(a) before he does so, directions have been given for his removal from the United Kingdom to any country or territory; or

(b) before or after he does so, the Secretary of State or an immigration officer serves on him notice that any directions which may be given for his removal by virtue of the refusal will be for his removal to a country or territory or one of several countries or territories specified in the notice;

then he may on that appeal object to the country or territory to which he would be removed in pursuance of the directions, or to that specified in the notice (or to one or more of those specified), and claim that he ought to be removed (if at all) to a different country or territory specified by him.

(3) Where a person appeals under section 15 above against a decision to make a deportation order against him, and before or after he does so the Secretary of State serves on him notice that any directions which may be given for his removal by virtue of the deportation order will be for his removal to a country or territory or one of several countries or territories specified in the notice, then he may on that appeal object to the country or territory specified in the notice (or to one or more of those specified), and claim that he ought to be removed (if at all) to a different country or territory specified by him.

(4) Where by virtue of subsection (2) or (3) above a person is able to object to a country or territory on an appeal under section 13(1) or 15, and either he does not object to it on that appeal or his objection to it on that appeal is not sustained, then he shall not be entitled to appeal under this section against any directions subsequently given by virtue of the refusal or order in question, if their effect will be his removal to that country or territory.

(5) . . .

NOTES

Sub-s (5): outside the scope of this work.

19 Determination of appeals by adjudicators

(1) Subject to sections 13(4) and 16(4) above, and to any restriction on the grounds of appeal, an adjudicator on an appeal to him under this Part of this Act—

(a) shall allow the appeal if he considers—

(i) that the decision or action against which the appeal is brought was not in accordance with the law or with any immigration rules applicable to the case; or

(ii) where the decision or action involved the exercise of a discretion by the Secretary of State or an officer, that the discretion should have been exercised differently; and

(b) in any other case, shall dismiss the appeal.

(2) For the purposes of subsection (1)(a) above the adjudicator may review any determination of a question of fact on which the decision or action was based; and for the purposes of subsection (1)(a)(ii) no decision or action which is in accordance with the immigration rules shall be treated as having involved the exercise of a discretion by the Secretary of State by reason only of the fact that he has been requested by or on behalf of the appellant to depart, or to authorise an officer to depart, from the rules and has refused to do so.

(3) Where an appeal is allowed, the adjudicator shall give such directions for giving effect to the determination as the adjudicator thinks requisite, . . .

NOTES

Sub-s (3): words omitted outside the scope of this work.

Modification: this section has effect as if the Asylum and Immigration Appeals Act 1993, s 8, were contained in this Part: see the Asylum and Immigration Appeals Act 1993, s 8(6), Sch 2.

This section has effect as if the Asylum and Immigration Act 1996, s 3, were contained in this Part: see the Asylum and Immigration Act 1996, s 3(4).

Appeals from adjudicator to Tribunal, and review of decisions

20 Appeal to Tribunal from determination of adjudicator

(1) Subject to any requirement of rules of procedure as to leave to appeal, any party to an appeal to an adjudicator may, if dissatisfied with his determination thereon, appeal to the Appeal Tribunal, and the Tribunal may affirm the determination or make any other determination which could have been made by the adjudicator.

(2), (3) . . .

NOTES

Sub-ss (2), (3): words omitted outside the scope of this work.

Modification: this section has effect as if the Asylum and Immigration Appeals Act 1993, s 8, were contained in this Part: see the Asylum and Immigration Appeals Act 1993, s 8(6), Sch 2.

PART III
CRIMINAL PROCEEDINGS

24 Illegal entry and similar offences

(1) A person who is not [a British citizen] shall be guilty of an offence punishable on summary conviction with a fine of not more than [[level 5] on the standard scale] or with imprisonment for not more than six months, or with both, in any of the following cases:—

(a) if contrary to this Act he knowingly enters the United Kingdom in breach of a deportation order or without leave;

[(aa) if, by means which include deception by him, he obtains or seeks to obtain leave to enter or remain in the United Kingdom;]

(b) if, having only a limited leave to enter or remain in the United Kingdom, he knowingly either—

(i) remains beyond the time limited by the leave; or

(ii) fails to observe a condition of the leave;

(c) if, having lawfully entered the United Kingdom without leave by virtue of section 8(1) above, he remains without leave beyond the time allowed by section 8(1);

(d) if, without reasonable excuse, he fails to comply with any requirement imposed on him under Schedule 2 to this Act to report to a medical officer of health, or to attend, or submit to a test or examination, as required by such an officer;

(e) if, without reasonable excuse, he fails to observe any restriction imposed on him under Schedule 2 or 3 to this Act as to residence[, as to his employment or occupation] or as to reporting to the police or to an immigration officer;

(f) if he disembarks in the United Kingdom from a ship or aircraft after being placed on board under Schedule 2 or 3 to this Act with a view to his removal from the United Kingdom;

(g) if he embarks in contravention of a restriction imposed by or under an Order in Council under section 3(7) of this Act.

[(1A) A person commits an offence under subsection (1)(b)(i) above on the day when he first knows that the time limited by his leave has expired and continues to commit it throughout any period during which he is in the United Kingdom thereafter; but a person shall not be prosecuted under that provision more than once in respect of the same limited leave.]

(2) A constable or immigration officer may arrest without warrant anyone who has, or whom he, with reasonable cause, suspects to have, committed or attempted to commit an offence under this section other than an offence under subsection (1)(d) above.

(3), (4) . . .

NOTES

Sub-s (1): words in first pair of square brackets substituted by the British Nationality Act 1981, s 39(1), (6), Sch 4, para 2(a); words in second (outer) pair of square brackets substituted by virtue of the Criminal Justice Act 1982, ss 37, 38, 46; words in third (inner) square brackets substituted by the Asylum and Immigration Act 1996, s 6; para (aa) inserted by the Asylum and Immigration Act 1996, s 4; words in square brackets in para (e) inserted by the Immigration Act 1988, s 10, Schedule, para 10(3), (4).

Sub-s (1A): inserted by the Immigration Act 1988, s 6(1), except in relation to person whose leave expired before 10 July 1988.

Sub-ss (3), (4): outside the scope of this work.

Modification: modified, in relation to France and the United Kingdom, by the Channel Tunnel (International Arrangements) Order 1993, SI 1993/1813, art 7(1), Sch 4, para 1(7); modified, in relation to its application to frontier controls between the United Kingdom, France and Belgium, by the Channel Tunnel (Miscellaneous Provisions) Order 1994, SI 1994/1405, art 7.

PART IV
SUPPLEMENTARY

33 Interpretation

(1) For purposes of this Act, except in so far as the context otherwise requires—

. . . . .

["entrant" means a person entering or seeking to enter the United Kingdom and "illegal entrant" means a person—

(a) unlawfully entering or seeking to enter in breach of a deportation order or of the immigration laws, or

(b) entering or seeking to enter by means which include deception by another person,

and includes also a person who has entered as mentioned in paragraph (a) or (b) above;]

"entry clearance" means a visa, entry certificate or other document which, in accordance with the immigration rules, is to be taken as evidence [or the requisite evidence] of a person's eligibility, though not [a British citizen], for entry into the United Kingdom (but does not include a work permit);

. . . . .

"immigration rules" means the rules for the time being laid down as mentioned in section 3(2) above;

. . . . .

"work permit" means a permit indicating, in accordance with the immigration rules, that a person named in it is eligible, though not [a British citizen], for entry into the United Kingdom for the purpose of taking employment.

(2) It is hereby declared that, except as otherwise provided in this Act, a person is not to be treated for the purposes of any provision of this Act as ordinarily resident in the United Kingdom or in any of the Islands at a time when he is there in breach of the immigration laws.

(2A), (3), (4) . . .

(5) This Act shall not be taken to supersede or impair any power exercisable by Her Majesty in relation to aliens by virtue of Her prerogative.

NOTES

Sub-s (1): in definition "work permit", words in square brackets substituted by the British Nationality Act 1981, s 39(1), (6), Sch 4, para 2(a); definitions "entrant" and "illegal entrant" substituted by the Asylum and Immigration Act 1996, s 12(1), Sch 2, para 4(1); in definition "entry clearance", words in first pair of square brackets inserted by the Immigration Act 1988, s 10, Schedule, para 5, words in second pair of square brackets substituted by the British Nationality Act 1981, s 39(1), (6), Sch 4, para 2(a); definitions omitted repealed by the Channel Tunnel (International Arrangements) Order 1993, SI 1993/1813, art 9, Sch 6 or outside the scope of this work.

Sub-ss (2A), (3), (4): outside the scope of this work.

Modification: modified, in relation to France and the United Kingdom, by the Channel Tunnel (International Arrangements) Order 1993, SI 1993/1813, art 7(1), Sch 4, para 1(10); modified, in relation to its application to frontier controls between the United Kingdom, France and Belgium, by the Channel Tunnel (Miscellaneous Provisions) Order 1994, SI 1994/1405, art 7.

35 Commencement, and interim provisions

(1) Except as otherwise provided by this Act, Parts I to III of this Act shall come into force on such day as the Secretary of State may appoint by order made by statutory instrument; and references to the coming into force of this Act shall be construed as references to the beginning of the day so appointed

(2)–(5) . . .

NOTES

Sub-s (2): outside the scope of this work.

Sub-ss (3)–(5): repealed by the SL(R) Act 1986.

37 Short title and extent

(1) This Act may be cited as the Immigration Act 1971.

(2) It is hereby declared that this Act extends to Northern Ireland, and (without prejudice to any provision of Schedule 1 to this Act as to the extent of that Schedule) where an enactment repealed by this Act extends outside the United Kingdom, the repeal shall be of like extent.

EUROPEAN COMMUNITIES ACT 1972

(c 68)

An Act to make provision in connection with the enlargement of the European Communities to include the United Kingdom, together with (for certain purposes) the Channel Islands, the Isle of Man and Gibraltar

[17 October 1972]

PART I
GENERAL PROVISIONS

1 Short title and interpretation

(1) This Act may be cited as the European Communities Act 1972.

(2) In this Act . . . —

'the Communities' means the European Economic Community, the European Coal and Steel Community and the European Atomic Energy Community;

'the Treaties' or 'the Community Treaties' means, subject to subsection (3) below, the pre-accession treaties, that is to say, those described in Part I of Schedule 1 to this Act, taken with—

(a) the treaty relating to the accession of the United Kingdom to the European Economic Community and to the European Atomic Energy Community, signed at Brussels on the 22nd January 1972; and

(b) the decision, of the same date, of the Council of the European Communities relating to the accession of the United Kingdom to the European Coal and Steel Community; [and

(c) the treaty relating to the accession of the Hellenic Republic to the European Economic Community and to the European Atomic Energy Community, signed at Athens on 28th May 1979; and
(d) the decision, of 24th May 1979, of the Council relating to the accession of the Hellenic Republic to the European Coal and Steel Community;] [and
(e) the decisions of the Council of 7th May 1985, 24th June 1988, and 31st October 1994, on the Communities' system of own resources; and][
(g) the treaty relating to the accession of the Kingdom of Spain and the Portuguese Republic to the European Economic Community and to the European Atomic Energy Community, signed at Lisbon and Madrid on 12th June 1985; and
(h) the decision, of 11th June 1985, of the Council relating to the accession of the Kingdom of Spain and the Portuguese Republic to the European Coal and Steel Community;] [and
(j) the following provisions of the Single European Act signed at Luxembourg and The Hague on 17th and 28th February 1986, namely Title II (amendment of the treaties establishing the Communities) and, so far as they relate to any of the Communities or any Community institution, the preamble and Titles I (common provisions) and IV (general and final provisions);] [and
(k) Titles II, III and IV of the Treaty on European Union signed at Maastricht on 7th February 1992, together with the other provisions of the Treaty so far as they relate to those Titles, and the Protocols adopted at Maastricht on that date and annexed to the Treaty establishing the European Community with the exception of the Protocol on Social Policy on page 117 of Cm 1934] [and
(l) the decision, of 1st February 1993, of the Council amending the Act concerning the election of the representatives of the European Parliament by direct universal suffrage annexed to Council Decision 76/787/ECSC, EEC, Euratom of 20th September 1976] [and
(m) the Agreement on the European Economic Area signed at Oporto on 2nd May 1992 together with the Protocol adjusting that Agreement signed at Brussels on 17th March 1993] [and
(n) the treaty concerning the accession of the Kingdom of Norway, the Republic of Austria, the Republic of Finland and the Kingdom of Sweden to the European Union, signed at Corfu on 24th June 1994;]

and any other treaty entered into by any of the Communities, with or without any of the member States, or entered into, as a treaty ancillary to any of the Treaties, by the United Kingdom;

[and

(o) the following provisions of the Treaty signed at Amsterdam on 2nd October 1997 amending the Treaty on European Union, the Treaties establishing the European Communities and certain related Acts—
  (i) Articles 2 to 9,
  (ii) Article 12, and
  (iii) the other provisions of the Treaty so far as they relate to those Articles,

and the Protocols adopted on that occasion other than the Protocol on Article J.7 of the Treaty on European Union]

and any expression defined in Schedule 1 to this Act has the meaning there given to it.

(3) If Her Majesty by Order in Council declares that a treaty specified in the Order is to be regarded as one of the Community Treaties as herein defined, the Order shall be conclusive that it is to be so regarded; but a treaty entered into by the United Kingdom after the 22nd January 1972, other than a pre-accession treaty to which the United Kingdom accedes on terms settled on or before that date, shall not be so regarded unless it is so specified, nor be so specified unless a draft of the Order in Council has been approved by resolution of each House of Parliament.

(4) For purposes of subsections (2) and (3) above, 'treaty' includes any international agreement, and any protocol or annex to a treaty or international agreement.

NOTES

Sub-s (2): words omitted repealed by the Interpretation Act 1978, s 25(1), Sch 3; in definitions 'the Treaties' or the 'Community Treaties', paras (c), (d) added by the European Communities (Greek Accession) Act 1979, s 1, para (e) originally added together with para (f), by the European Communities (Finance) Act 1985, s 1, substituted for paras (e), (f), by the European Communities (Finance) Act 1995, s 1, paras (g), (h) added by the European Communities (Spanish and Portuguese Accession) Act 1985, s 1, para (j) added by the European Communities (Amendment) Act 1986, s 1, para (k) added by the European Communities (Amendment) Act 1993, s 1(1), para (l) added by the European Parliamentary Elections Act 1993, s 3(2), para (m) added by the European Economic Area Act 1993, s 1, para (n) added by the European Union (Accessions) Act 1994, s 1, and para (o) added by the European Communities (Amendment) Act 1998, s 1.

No UK legislation has been passed to reflect the fact that Norway did not join the EC.

2 General implementation of Treaties

(1) All such rights, powers, liabilities, obligations and restrictions from time to time created or arising by or under the Treaties, and all such remedies and procedures from time to time provided for by or under the Treaties, as in accordance with the Treaties are without further enactment to be given legal effect or used in the United Kingdom shall be recognised and available in law, and be enforced, allowed and followed accordingly; and the expression 'enforceable Community right' and similar expressions shall be read as referring to one to which this subsection applies.

(2) Subject to Schedule 2 to this Act, at any time after its passing Her Majesty may by Order in Council, and any designated Minister or department may by regulations, make provision—

(a) for the purpose of implementing any Community obligation of the United Kingdom, or enabling any such obligation to be implemented, or of enabling any rights enjoyed or to be enjoyed by the United Kingdom under or by virtue of the Treaties to be exercised; or

(b) for the purpose of dealing with matters arising out of or related to any such obligation or rights or the coming into force, or the operation from time to time, of subsection (1) above;

and in the exercise of any statutory power or duty, including any power to give directions or to legislate by means of orders, rules, regulations or other subordinate instrument, the person entrusted with the power or duty may have regard to the objects of the Communities and to any such obligation or rights as aforesaid.

In this subsection 'designated Minister or department' means such Minister of the Crown or government department as may from time to time be designated by Order in Council in relation to any matter or for any purpose, but subject to such restrictions or conditions (if any) as may be specified by the Order in Council.

(3) There shall be charged on and issued out of the Consolidated Fund or, if so determined by the Treasury, the National Loans Fund the amounts required to meet

any Community obligation to make payments to any of the Communities or member States, or any Community obligation in respect of contributions to the capital or reserves of the European Investment Bank or in respect of loans to the Bank, or to redeem any notes or obligations issued or created in respect of any such Community obligation; and, except as otherwise provided by or under any enactment,—

(a) any other expenses incurred under or by virtue of the Treaties or this Act by any Minister of the Crown or government department may be paid out of moneys provided by Parliament; and

(b) any sums received under or by virtue of the Treaties or this Act by any Minister of the Crown or government department, save for such sums as may be required for disbursements permitted by any other enactment, shall be paid into the Consolidated Fund or, if so determined by the Treasury, the National Loans Fund.

(4) The provision that may be made under subsection (2) above includes, subject to Schedule 2 to this Act, any such provision (of any such extent) as might be made by Act of Parliament, and any enactment passed or to be passed, other than one contained in this Part of this Act, shall be construed and have effect subject to the foregoing provisions of this section; but, except as may be provided by any Act passed after this Act, Schedule 2 shall have effect in connection with the powers conferred by this and the following sections of this Act to make Orders in Council and regulations.

(5), (6) . . .

NOTES

Sub-ss (5), (6): outside the scope of this work.

3 Decisions on, and proof of, Treaties and Community instruments, etc

(1) For the purposes of all legal proceedings any question as to the meaning or effect of any of the Treaties, or as to the validity, meaning or effect of any Community instrument, shall be treated as a question of law (and, if not referred to the European Court, be for determination as such in accordance with the principles laid down by and any relevant [decision of the European Court or any court attached thereto)].

(2) Judicial notice shall be taken of the Treaties, of the Official Journal of the Communities and of any decision of, or expression of opinion by, the European Court [or any court attached thereto] on any such question as aforesaid; and the Official Journal shall be admissible as evidence of any instrument or other act thereby communicated of any of the Communities or of any Community institution.

(3)–(5) . . .

NOTES

Sub-ss (1), (2): words in square brackets substituted or added by the European Communities (Amendment) Act 1986, s 2.

Sub-ss (3)–(5): outside the scope of this work.

SCHEDULE 2

Section 2

PROVISIONS AS TO SUBORDINATE LEGISLATION

1.—(1) The powers conferred by section 2(2) of this Act to make provision for the purposes mentioned in section 2(2)(a) and (b) shall not include power—

(a) to make any provision imposing or increasing taxation; or

(b) to make any provision taking effect from a date earlier than that of the making of the instrument containing the provision; or

(c) to confer any power to legislate by means of orders, rules, regulations or other subordinate instrument, other than rules of procedure for any court or tribunal; or

(d) to create any new criminal offence punishable with imprisonment for more than two years or punishable on summary conviction with imprisonment for more than three months or with a fine of more than [level 5 on the standard scale] (if not calculated on a daily basis) or with a fine of more than [£100 a day].

(2) Sub-paragraph (1)(c) above shall not be taken to preclude the modification of a power to legislate conferred otherwise than under section 2(2), or the extension of any such power to purposes of the like nature as those for which it was conferred; and a power to give directions as to matters of administration is not to be regarded as a power to legislate within the meaning of sub-paragraph (1)(c).

2.—(1) Subject to paragraph 3 below, where a provision contained in any section of this Act confers power to make regulations (otherwise than by modification or extension of an existing power), the power shall be exercisable by statutory instrument.

(2) Any statutory instrument containing an Order in Council or regulations made in the exercise of a power so conferred, if made without a draft having been approved by resolution of each House of Parliament, shall be subject to annulment in pursuance of a resolution of either House.

3–5. . . .

NOTES

Para 1: first-mentioned maximum fine increased and converted to a level on the standard scale by the Criminal Justice Act 1982, ss 37, 40, 46; words in second pair of square brackets substituted by the Criminal Law Act 1977, ss 32(3), 65(10).

Paras 3–5: outside the scope of this work.

LOCAL GOVERNMENT ACT 1972

(c 70)

An Act to make provision with respect to local government and the functions of local authorities in England and Wales; to amend Part II of the Transport Act 1968; to confer rights of appeal in respect of decisions relating to licences under the Home Counties (Music and Dancing) Licensing Act 1926; to make further provision with respect to magistrates' courts committees; to abolish certain inferior courts of record; and for connected purposes

[26 October 1972]

PART V
GENERAL PROVISIONS AS TO MEMBERS AND PROCEEDINGS OF LOCAL AUTHORITIES

Restrictions on voting

94 Disability of members of authorities for voting on account of interest in contracts, etc

(1) Subject to the provisions of section 97 below, if a member of a local authority has any pecuniary interest, direct or indirect, in any contract, proposed contract or other matter, and is present at a meeting of the local authority at which the contract

or other matter is the subject of consideration, he shall at the meeting and as soon as practicable after its commencement disclose the fact and shall not take part in the consideration or discussion of the contract or other matter or vote on any question with respect to it.

(2) If any person fails to comply with the provisions of subsection (1) above he shall for each offence be liable on summary conviction to a fine not exceeding [level 4 on the standard scale] unless he proves that he did not know that the contract, proposed contract or other matter in which he had a pecuniary interest was the subject of consideration at that meeting.

(3) A prosecution for an offence under this section shall not be instituted except by or on behalf of the Director of Public Prosecutions.

(4), (5) . . .

NOTES

Sub-s (2): reference to "level 4 on the standard scale" substituted by virtue of the Criminal Justice Act 1982, ss 38, 46.

Sub-ss (4), (5): outside the scope of this work.

95 Pecuniary interests for purposes of section 94

(1) For the purposes of section 94 above a person shall be treated, subject to the following provisions of this section and to section 97 below, as having indirectly a pecuniary interest in a contract, proposed contract or other matter, if—

- (a) he or any nominee of his is a member of a company or other body with which the contract was made or is proposed to be made or which has a direct pecuniary interest in the other matter under consideration; or
- (b) he is a partner, or is in the employment, of a person with whom the contract was made or is proposed to be made or who has a direct pecuniary interest in the other matter under consideration.

(2) Subsection (1) above does not apply to membership of or employment under any public body, and a member of a company or other body shall not by reason only of his membership be treated as having an interest in any contract, proposed contract or other matter if he has no beneficial interest in any securities of that company or other body.

(3) In the case of married persons living together the interest of one spouse shall, if known to the other, be deemed for the purpose of section 94 above to be also an interest of the other.

96 General notices and recording of disclosures for purposes of section 94

(1) A general notice given in writing to the proper officer of the authority by a member thereof to the effect that he or his spouse is a member or in the employment of a specified company or other body, or that he or his spouse is a partner or in the employment of a specified person, or that he or his spouse is the tenant of any premises owned by the authority, shall, unless and until the notice is withdrawn, be deemed to be a sufficient disclosure of his interest in any contract, proposed contract or other matter relating to that company or other body or to that person or to those premises which may be the subject of consideration after the date of the notice.

(2) The proper officer of the authority shall record in a book to be kept for the purpose particulars of any disclosure made under section 94 above and of any notice given under this section, and the book shall be open at all reasonable hours to the inspection of any member of the local authority.

[PART VA
ACCESS TO MEETINGS AND DOCUMENTS OF CERTAIN AUTHORITIES, COMMITTEES AND SUB-COMMITTEES

100A Admission to meetings of principal councils

(1) A meeting of a principal council shall be open to the public except to the extent that they are excluded (whether during the whole or part of the proceedings) under subsection (2) below or by resolution under subsection (4) below.

(2) The public shall be excluded from a meeting of a principal council during an item of business whenever it is likely, in view of the nature of the business to be transacted or the nature of the proceedings, that, if members of the public were present during that item, confidential information would be disclosed to them in breach of the obligation of confidence; and nothing in this Part shall be taken to authorise or require the disclosure of confidential information in breach of the obligation of confidence.

(3) For the purposes of subsection (2) above, "confidential information" means—

(a) information furnished to the council by a Government department upon terms (however expressed) which forbid the disclosure of the information to the public; and

(b) information the disclosure of which to the public is prohibited by or under any enactment or by the order of a court;

and, in either case, the reference to the obligation of confidence is to be construed accordingly.

(4) A principal council may by resolution exclude the public from a meeting during an item of business whenever it is likely, in view of the nature of the business to be transacted or the nature of the proceedings, that if members of the public were present during that item there would be disclosure to them of exempt information, as defined in section 100I below.

(5) A resolution under subsection (4) above shall—

(a) identify the proceedings, or the part of the proceedings, to which it applies, and

(b) state the description, in terms of Schedule 12A to this Act, of the exempt information giving rise to the exclusion of the public,

and where such a resolution is passed this section does not require the meeting to be open to the public during proceedings to which the resolution applies.

(6) The following provisions shall apply in relation to a meeting of a principal council, that is to say—

(a) public notice of the time and place of the meeting shall be given by posting it at the offices of the council three clear days at least before the meeting or, if the meeting is convened at shorter notice, then at the time it is convened;

(b) while the meeting is open to the public, the council shall not have power to exclude members of the public from the meeting; and

(c) while the meeting is open to the public, duly accredited representatives of newspapers attending the meeting for the purpose of reporting the proceedings for those newspapers shall, so far as practicable, be afforded reasonable facilities for taking their report and, unless the meeting is held in premises not belonging to the council or not on the telephone, for telephoning the report at their own expense.

(7) Nothing in this section shall require a principal council to permit the taking of photographs of any proceedings, or the use of any means to enable persons not present to see or hear any proceedings (whether at the time or later), or the making of any oral report on any proceedings as they take place.

(8) This section is without prejudice to any power of exclusion to suppress or prevent disorderly conduct or other misbehaviour at a meeting.]

NOTES

Inserted by the Local Government (Access to Information) Act 1985, s 1(1).

[100B Access to agenda and connected reports

(1) Copies of the agenda for a meeting of a principal council and, subject to subsection (2) below, copies of any report for the meeting shall be open to inspection by members of the public at the offices of the council in accordance with subsection (3) below.

(2) If the proper officer thinks fit, there may be excluded from the copies of reports provided in pursuance of subsection (1) above the whole of any report which, or any part which, relates only to items during which, in his opinion, the meeting is likely not to be open to the public.

(3) Any document which is required by subsection (1) above to be open to inspection shall be so open at least three clear days before the meeting, except that—

- (a) where the meeting is convened at shorter notice, the copies of the agenda and reports shall be open to inspection from the time the meeting is convened, and
- (b) where an item is added to an agenda copies of which are open to inspection by the public, copies of the item (or of the revised agenda), and the copies of any report for the meeting relating to the item, shall be open to inspection from the time the item is added to the agenda;

but nothing in this subsection requires copies of any agenda, item or report to be open to inspection by the public until copies are available to members of the council.

(4) An item of business may not be considered at a meeting of a principal council unless either—

- (a) a copy of the agenda including the item (or a copy of the item) is open to inspection by members of the public in pursuance of subsection (1) above for at least three clear days before the meeting or, where the meeting is convened at shorter notice, from the time the meeting is convened; or
- (b) by reason of special circumstances, which shall be specified in the minutes, the chairman of the meeting is of the opinion that the item should be considered at the meeting as a matter of urgency.

(5) Where by virtue of subsection (2) above the whole or any part of a report for a meeting is not open to inspection by the public under subsection (1) above—

- (a) every copy of the report or of the part shall be marked "Not for publication"; and

(b) there shall be stated on every copy of the whole or any part of the report the description, in terms of Schedule 12A to this Act, of the exempt information by virtue of which the council are likely to exclude the public during the item to which the report relates.

(6)–(8) . . .]

NOTES

Inserted by the Local Government (Access to Information) Act 1985, s 1(1).

Sub-ss (6)–(8): outside the scope of this work.

[100C Inspection of minutes and other documents after meetings

(1) After a meeting of a principal council the following documents shall be open to inspection by members of the public at the offices of the council until the expiration of the period of six years beginning with the date of the meeting, namely—

(a) the minutes, or a copy of the minutes, of the meeting, excluding so much of the minutes of proceedings during which the meeting was not open to the public as discloses exempt information;

(b) where applicable, a summary under subsection (2) below;

(c) a copy of the agenda for the meeting; and

(d) a copy of so much of any report for the meeting as relates to any item during which the meeting was open to the public.

(2) Where, in consequence of the exclusion of parts of the minutes which disclose exempt information, the document open to inspection under subsection (1)(a) above does not provide members of the public with a reasonably fair and coherent record of the whole or part of the proceedings, the proper officer shall make a written summary of the proceedings or the part, as the case may be, which provides such a record without disclosing the exempt information.]

NOTES

Inserted by the Local Government (Access to Information) Act 1985, s 1(1).

[100D Inspection of background papers

(1) Subject, in the case of section 100C(1), to subsection (2) below, if and so long as copies of the whole or part of a report for a meeting of a principal council are required by section 100B(1) or 100C(1) above to be open to inspection by members of the public—

(a) copies of a list, compiled by the proper officer, of the background papers for the report or the part of the report, and

(b) at least one copy of each of the documents included in that list,

shall also be open to their inspection at the offices of the council.

(2) Subsection (1) above does not require a copy of the list, or of any document included in the list, to be open to inspection after the expiration of the period of four years beginning with the date of the meeting.

(3)–(5) . . .]

NOTES

Inserted by the Local Government (Access to Information) Act 1985, s 1(1).

Sub-ss (3)–(5): outside the scope of this work.

[100E Application to committees and sub-committees

(1) Sections 100A to 100D above shall apply in relation to a committee or sub-committee of a principal council as they apply in relation to a principal council.

(2)–(4). . .]

NOTES

Inserted by the Local Government (Access to Information) Act 1985, s 1(1).

Sub-ss (2)–(4): outside the scope of this work.

[100G Principal councils to publish additional information

(1) A principal council shall maintain a register stating—

(a) the name and address of every member of the council for the time being and the ward or division which he represents; and

(b) the name and address of every member of each committee or sub-committee of the council for the time being.

(2) A principal council shall maintain a list—

(a) specifying those powers of the council which, for the time being, are exercisable from time to time by officers of the council in pursuance of arrangements made under this Act or any other enactment for their discharge by those officers; and

(b) stating the title of the officer by whom each of the powers so specified is for the time being so exercisable;

but this subsection does not require a power to be specified in the list if the arrangements for its discharge by the officer are made for a specified period not exceeding six months.

(3) There shall be kept at the offices of every principal council a written summary of the rights—

(a) to attend meetings of a principal council and of committees and sub-committees of a principal council, and

(b) to inspect and copy documents and to be furnished with documents,

which are for the time being conferred by this Part, Part XI below and such other enactments as the Secretary of State by order specifies.

(4) The register maintained under subsection (1) above, the list maintained under subsection (2) above and the summary kept under subsection (3) above shall be open to inspection by the public at the offices of the council.]

NOTES

Inserted by the Local Government (Access to Information) Act 1985, s 1(1).

Sub-s (1): para (b) substituted by the Local Government and Housing Act 1989, s 194(1), Sch 11, para 24, as from a day to be appointed, as follows—

"(b) in respect of every committee or sub-committee of the council—

(i) the members of the council who are members of the committee or sub-committee or who are entitled, in accordance with any standing orders relating to the committee or sub-committee, to speak at its meetings or any of them;

(ii) the name and address of every other person who is a member of the committee or sub-committee or who is entitled, in accordance with any standing orders relating to the committee or sub-committee, to speak at its meetings or any of them otherwise than in the capacity of an officer of the council; and

(iii) the functions in relation to the committee or sub-committee of every person falling within sub-paragraph (i) above who is not a member of the committee or sub-committee and of every person falling within sub-paragraph (ii) above".

PART VI
DISCHARGE OF FUNCTIONS

101 Arrangements for discharge of functions by local authorities

(1) Subject to any express provision contained in this Act or any Act passed after this Act, a local authority may arrange for the discharge of any of their functions—

(a) by a committee, a sub-committee or an officer of the authority; or

(b) by any other local authority.

(2) Where by virtue of this section any functions of a local authority may be discharged by a committee of theirs, then, unless the local authority otherwise direct, the committee may arrange for the discharge of any of those functions by a sub-committee or an officer of the authority and where by virtue of this section any functions of a local authority may be discharged by a sub-committee of the authority, then, unless the local authority or the committee otherwise direct, the sub-committee may arrange for the discharge of any of those functions by an officer of the authority.

(3)–(5) . . .

(6) A local authority's functions with respect to levying, or issuing a precept for, a rate *or borrowing money* shall be discharged only by the authority.

(7)–(14) . . .

NOTES

Sub-ss (3)–(5), (7)–(10A), (12)–(14): outside the scope of this work.

Sub-s (6): words in italics repealed by the Local Government and Housing Act 1989, s 45(5), which was brought into force on 16 January 1990, and also by s 194(4), of, Sch 12, Pt II to, that Act, which repeal was brought into force on 1 April 1990 in relation to bodies mentioned in s 39(1)(a)–(j) of, or prescribed by regulations made under s 39(3) of, the 1989 Act (Local Government and Housing Act 1989 (Commencement No 5 and Transitional Provisions) Order 1990, SI 1990/431, art 4, Sch 1, para 1), those words being otherwise repealed as from a day to be appointed under s 195(2) of that Act.

Sub-s (11): repealed by the Local Government Act 1985, s 102(2), Sch 17.

PART XI
GENERAL PROVISIONS AS TO LOCAL AUTHORITIES

Legal proceedings

222 Power of local authorities to prosecute or defend legal proceedings

(1) Where a local authority consider it expedient for the promotion or protection of the interests of the inhabitants of their area—

(a) they may prosecute or defend or appear in any legal proceedings and, in the case of civil proceedings, may institute them in their own name, and

(b) they may, in their own name, make representations in the interests of the inhabitants at any public inquiry held by or on behalf of any Minister or public body under any enactment.

(2) In this section "local authority" includes the Common Council.

Byelaws

235 Power of councils to make byelaws for good rule and government and suppression of nuisances

(1) The council of a district [the council of a principal area in Wales] and the council of a London borough may make byelaws for the good rule and government of the whole or any part of the district [principal area] or borough, as the case may be, and for the prevention and suppression of nuisances therein.

(2) The confirming authority in relation to byelaws made under this section shall be the Secretary of State.

(3) Byelaws shall not be made under this section for any purpose as respects any area if provision for that purpose as respects that area is made by, or is or may be made under, any other enactment.

NOTES

Sub-s (1): words in square brackets inserted by the Local Government (Wales) Act 1994, s 66(5), Sch 15, paras 1, 49.

General

273 Commencement

(1) The provisions of this Act to which this subsection applies shall, except so far as brought into force earlier by an order under subsection (2) below, come into force on 1st April 1974.

(2) The Secretary of State may by order appoint an earlier date for the coming into force of any provision to which subsection (1) above applies and different days may be appointed under this subsection for different purposes and, in particular, different days may be so appointed for the coming into force of the same provision in different areas.

(3)–(10). . .

NOTES

Sub-ss (3)–(10): outside the scope of this work.

274 Short title and extent

(1) This Act may be cited as the Local Government Act 1972.

(2) Except for . . . paragraph 35 of Schedule 29 to this Act . . . this Act shall not extend to Scotland.

(3) . . . this Act shall not extend to Northern Ireland.

NOTES

Sub-ss (2), (3): words omitted repealed by the House of Commons Disqualification Act 1975, s 10(2), Sch 3, and the Northern Ireland Assembly Disqualification Act 1975, s 5(2), Sch 3, Pt I.

[SCHEDULE 12A
ACCESS TO INFORMATION: EXEMPT INFORMATION

PART I
DESCRIPTIONS OF EXEMPT INFORMATION

1. Information relating to a particular employee, former employee or applicant to become an employee of, or a particular office-holder, former office-holder or applicant to become an office-holder under, the authority.

2. Information relating to a particular employee, former employee or applicant to become an employee of, or a particular officer, former officer or applicant to become an officer appointed by—
   (a) a magistrates' court committee, within the meaning of [section 27 of the Justices of the Peace Act 1997]; or
   (b) a probation committee [within the meaning of the Probation Service Act 1993].

3. Information relating to any particular occupier or former occupier of, or applicant for, accommodation provided by or at the expense of the authority.

4. Information relating to any particular applicant for, or recipient or former recipient of, any service provided by the authority.

5. Information relating to any particular applicant for, or recipient or former recipient of, any financial assistance provided by the authority.

6. Information relating to the adoption, care, fostering or education of any particular child.

7. Information relating to the financial or business affairs of any particular person (other than the authority).

8. The amount of any expenditure proposed to be incurred by the authority under any particular contract for the acquisition of property or the supply of goods or services.

9. Any terms proposed or to be proposed by or to the authority in the course of negotiations for a contract for the acquisition or disposal of property or the supply of goods or services.

10. The identity of the authority (as well as of any other person, by virtue of paragraph 7 above) as the person offering any particular tender for a contract for the supply of goods or services.

11. Information relating to any consultations or negotiations, or contemplated consultations or negotiations, in connection with any labour relations matter arising between the authority or a Minister of the Crown and employees of, or office-holders under, the authority.

12. Any instructions to counsel and any opinion of counsel (whether or not in connection with any proceedings) and any advice received, information obtained or action to be taken in connection with—
   (a) any legal proceedings by or against the authority, or
   (b) the determination of any matter affecting the authority,

(whether, in either case, proceedings have been commenced or are in contemplation).

13. Information which, if disclosed to the public, would reveal that the authority proposes—
   (a) to give under any enactment a notice under or by virtue of which requirements are imposed on a person; or
   (b) to make an order or direction under any enactment.

14. Any action taken or to be taken in connection with the prevention, investigation or prosecution of crime.

15. The identity of a protected informant.]

NOTES

Inserted by the Local Government (Access to Information) Act 1985, s 1(2), Sch 1, Pt I.

Para 2: words in square brackets in sub-para (a) substituted by the Justices of the Peace Act 1997, s 73(2), Sch 5, para 11; words in square brackets in sub-para (b) substituted by the Probation Service Act 1993, s 32(2), Sch 3, para 4.

NORTHERN IRELAND CONSTITUTION ACT 1973

(c 36)

An Act to make new provision for the government of Northern Ireland

[18 July 1973]

PART I
PRELIMINARY

Status of Northern Ireland

1 Status of Northern Ireland as part of United Kingdom

It is hereby declared that Northern Ireland remains part of Her Majesty's dominions and of the United Kingdom, and it is hereby affirmed that in no event will Northern Ireland or any part of it cease to be part of Her Majesty's dominions and of the United Kingdom without the consent of the majority of the people of Northern Ireland voting in a poll held for the purposes of this section in accordance with Schedule 1 to this Act.

PART V
MISCELLANEOUS AND SUPPLEMENTARY

43 Short title, interpretation and commencement

(1) This Act may be cited as the Northern Ireland Constitution Act 1973.

(2)–(6) . . .

NOTES

Sub-ss (2)–(6): outside the scope of this work.

LOCAL GOVERNMENT ACT 1974

(c 7)

An Act to make further provision, in relation to England and Wales, . . . to provide for the establishment of Commissions for the investigation of administrative action taken by or on behalf of local and other authorities; . . . [8 February 1974]

PART III
LOCAL GOVERNMENT ADMINISTRATION

23 The Commissions for Local Administration

(1) For the purpose of conducting investigations in accordance with this Part of this Act, there shall be—

(a) a body of commissioners to be known as the Commission for Local Administration in England, and

(b) a body consisting of two or more commissioners to be known as the Commission for Local Administration in Wales,

[but each of the Commissions may include persons appointed to act as advisers, not exceeding the number appointed to conduct investigations].

(2) The Parliamentary Commissioner shall be a member of each of the Commissions.

(3) In the following provisions of this Part of this Act the expression "Local Commissioner" means a person, other than the Parliamentary Commissioner [or an advisory member], who is a member of one of the Commissions.

(4) Appointments to the office of . . . Commissioner shall be made by Her Majesty on the recommendation of the Secretary of State after consultation with the [such persons as appear to the Secretary of State to represent authorities in England or, as the case may be, authorities in Wales to which this Part of this Act applies], and a person so appointed shall, subject to subsection (6) below, hold office during good behaviour.

(5) . . . Commissioners may be appointed to serve either as full-time commissioners or as part-time commissioners.

(6) A . . . Commissioner may be relieved of office by Her Majesty at his own request or may be removed from office by Her Majesty on grounds of incapacity or misbehaviour, and shall in any case vacate office on completing the year of service in which he attains the age of sixty-five years.

(7) The Secretary of State shall designate two of the Local Commissioners for England as chairman and vice-chairman respectively of the Commission for Local Administration in England and, in the event of there being more than one Local Commissioner for Wales, shall designate one of them as chairman of the Commission for Local Administration in Wales.

(8) The Commission for Local Administration in England shall divide England into areas and shall provide, in relation to each area, for one or more of the Local Commissioners to be responsible for the area; and where the Commission for Local Administration in Wales consist of more than one Local Commissioner they may, if they think fit, act in a similar way in Wales.

A Local Commissioner may, by virtue of this subsection, be made responsible for more than one area.

(9)–(13) . . .

NOTES

Sub-s (1): words in square brackets added by the Local Government and Housing Act 1989, s 22(1), (2).

Sub-s (3): words in square brackets inserted by the Local Government and Housing Act 1989, s 22(1), (3).

Sub-s (4): words in square brackets substituted by the Local Government and Housing Act 1989, s 194(1), (4), Sch 11, para 37; word "the" before amendment in that subsection should have been removed.

Sub-ss (4)–(6): words omitted repealed by the Local Government and Housing Act 1989, s 22(1), (4), Sch 12, Pt II.

Sub-ss (9)–(13): outside the scope of this work.

25 Authorities subject to investigation

(1) This Part of this Act applies to [the following authorities]—

(a) any local authority,

[(aa) the Land Authority for Wales . . .],

[(ab) a National Park authority;]

(b) any joint board the constituent authorities of which are all local authorities,

[(ba) the Commission for the New Towns,

(bb) any development corporation established for the purposes of a new town,
(bc) the Development Board for Rural Wales,
(bd) any urban development corporation established by an order under section 135 of the Local Government, Planning and Land Act 1980,]
[(be) any housing action trust established under Part III of the Housing Act 1988]
[(bf) the Urban Regeneration Agency;]
[(c) any joint authority established by Part IV of the Local Government Act 1985;
[(ca) any police authority established under [section 3 of the Police Act 1996];]
[(caa) the Service Authority for the National Crime Squad;]
(cb) . . . ; and]
[(d) in relation to the flood defence functions of the Environment Agency, within the meaning of the Water Resources Act 1991, the Environment Agency and any regional flood defence committee.]

(2) Her Majesty may by Order in Council provide that this Part of this Act shall also apply, subject to any modifications or exceptions specified in the Order, to any authority specified in the Order, being an authority which is established by or under an Act of Parliament, and which has power to levy a rate, or to issue a precept.

(3)–(5) . . .

NOTES

Sub-s (1): words in first pair of square brackets inserted by the Local Government Act 1988, s 29, Sch 3, para 4; para (aa) inserted by the Community Land Act 1975, s 58(2), Sch 10, para 9(1) and words omitted therefrom repealed by the Local Government, Planning and Land Act 1980, ss 110, 194, Sch 22, para 14, Sch 34, Pt XI; para (ab) inserted by the Environment Act 1995, s 63(5), Sch 7, para 18(1); paras (ba), (bb), (bc), (bd) inserted by the Local Government Act 1988, s 29, Sch 3, para 4; para (be) inserted by the Housing Act 1988, s 140(1), Sch 17, Pt I, para 19; para (bf) inserted by the Leasehold Reform, Housing and Urban Development Act 1993, s 187(1), Sch 21, para 6(1); paras (c), (ca), (cb) substituted for original para (c) by the Local Government Act 1985, s 84, Sch 14, Pt II, para 51(a); para (ca) again substituted by the Police and Magistrates' Courts Act 1994, s 43, Sch 4, Pt I, para 16, and words in square brackets therein substituted by the Police Act 1996, s 103(1), Sch 7, Pt I, para 1(1), (2)(j); para (caa) inserted by the Police Act 1997, s 88, Sch 6, para 11; para (cb) repealed by the Education Reform Act 1988, s 237(2), Sch 13, Pt I; para (d) substituted by the Environment Act 1995, s 120(1), Sch 22, para 18, subject to savings in s 120(2) of, and Sch 23, Pt I, para 12 to, that Act.

Sub-ss (3)–(5): outside the scope of this work.

26 Matters subject to investigation

(1) Subject to the provisions of this Part of this Act where a written complaint is made by or on behalf of a member of the public who claims to have sustained injustice in consequence of maladministration in connection with action taken by or on behalf of an authority to which this Part of this Act applies, being action taken in the exercise of administrative functions of that authority, a Local Commissioner may investigate that complaint.

(2) A complaint shall not be entertained under this Part of this Act unless [it is made in writing to the Local Commissioner specifying the action alleged to constitute maladministration or]—

(a) it is made in writing to a member of the authority, or of any other authority concerned, specifying the action alleged to constitute maladministration, and
(b) it is referred to the Local Commissioner, with the consent of the person aggrieved, or of a person acting on his behalf, by that member, or by any

other person who is a member of any authority concerned, with a request to investigate the complaint.

(3) If the Local Commissioner is satisfied that any member of any authority concerned has been requested to refer the complaint to a Local Commissioner, and has not done so, the Local Commissioner may, if he thinks fit, dispense with the requirements in subsection (2)(b) above.

(4) A complaint shall not be entertained unless it was made to [the Local Commissioner or] a member of any authority concerned within twelve months from the day on which the person aggrieved first had notice of the matters alleged in the complaint, but a Local Commissioner may conduct an investigation pursuant to a complaint not made within that period if he considers that [it is reasonable] to do so.

(5) Before proceeding to investigate a complaint, a Local Commissioner shall satisfy himself that the complaint has been brought, by or on behalf of the person aggrieved, to the notice of the authority to which the complaint relates and that that authority has been afforded a reasonable opportunity to investigate, and reply to, the complaint.

(6) A Local Commissioner shall not conduct an investigation under this Part of this Act in respect of any of the following matters, that is to say,—

(a) any action in respect of which the person aggrieved has or had a right of appeal, reference or review to or before a tribunal constituted by or under any enactment;

(b) any action in respect of which the person aggrieved has or had a right of appeal to a Minister of the Crown; or

(c) any action in respect of which the person aggrieved has or had a remedy by way of proceedings in any court of law:

Provided that a Local Commissioner may conduct an investigation notwithstanding the existence of such a right or remedy if satisfied that in the particular circumstances it is not reasonable to expect the person aggrieved to resort or have resorted to it.

(7) A Local Commissioner shall not conduct an investigation in respect of any action which in his opinion affects all or most of the inhabitants of the [following areas—

[(aa) where the complaint relates to a National Park authority, the area of the Park for which it is such an authority;]

(a) where the complaint relates to the Commission for the New Towns, the area of the new town or towns to which the complaint relates;

(b) where the complaint relates to the Development Board for Rural Wales, the area in Wales for which the Board is for the time being responsible;

[(ba) where the complaint relates to the Urban Regeneration Agency, any designated area within the meaning of Part III of the Leasehold Reform, Housing and Urban Development Act 1993;]

(c) in any other case, the area of the authority concerned].

(8) Without prejudice to the preceding provisions of this section, a Local Commissioner shall not conduct an investigation under this Part of this Act in respect of any such action or matter as is described in Schedule 5 to this Act.

(9) Her Majesty may by Order in Council amend the said Schedule 5 so as to [add to or exclude from the provisions of that Schedule (as it has effect for the time being)] such actions or matters as may be described in the Order; and any Order made by virtue of this subsection shall be subject to annulment in pursuance of a resolution of either House of Parliament.

(10) In determining whether to initiate, continue or discontinue an investigation, a Local Commissioner shall, subject to the preceding provisions of this section, act at discretion; and any question whether a complaint is duly made under this Part of this Act shall be determined by the Local Commissioner.

(11)–(13) . . .

NOTES

Sub-s (2): words in square brackets inserted by the Local Government Act 1988, s 29, Sch 3, para 5(1), (2).

Sub-s (4): words in first pair of square brackets inserted, and words in second pair of square brackets substituted, by the Local Government Act 1988, s 29, Sch 3, para 5(1), (3), (7).

Sub-s (7): words in first (outer) pair of square brackets substituted by the Local Government Act 1988, s 29, Sch 3, para 5(1), (4); para (aa) inserted by the Environment Act 1995, s 63(5), Sch 7, para 18(2); para (ba) inserted by the Leasehold Reform, Housing and Urban Development Act 1993, s 187(1), Sch 21, para 6(2).

Sub-s (9): words in square brackets substituted by the Local Government Act 1988, s 29, Sch 3, para 5(1), (5).

Sub-ss (11)–(13): outside the scope of this work.

27 Provisions relating to complaints

(1) A complaint under this Part of this Act may be made by any individual, or by any body of persons whether incorporated or not, not being—

(a) a local authority or other authority or body constituted for purposes of the public service or of local government, or for the purposes of carrying on under national ownership any industry or undertaking or part of an industry or undertaking;

(b) any other authority or body whose members are appointed by Her Majesty or any Minister of the Crown or government department, or whose revenues consist wholly or mainly of moneys provided by Parliament.

(2) . . .

NOTES

Sub-s (2): outside the scope of this work.

28 Procedure in respect of investigations

(1) Where a Local Commissioner proposes to conduct an investigation pursuant to a complaint, he shall afford to the authority concerned, and to any person who is alleged in the complaint to have taken or authorised the action complained of, an opportunity to comment on any allegations contained in the complaint.

(2) Every such investigation shall be conducted in private, but except as aforesaid the procedure for conducting an investigation shall be such as the Local Commissioner considers appropriate in the circumstances of the case; and without prejudice to the generality of the preceding provision the Local Commissioner may obtain information from such persons and in such manner, and make such inquiries, as he thinks fit, and may determine whether any person may be represented (by counsel or solicitor or otherwise) in the investigation.

(3) . . .

(4) The conduct of an investigation under this Part of this Act shall not affect any action taken by the authority concerned, or any power or duty of that authority to take further action with respect to any matters subject to the investigation.

NOTES

Sub-s (3): outside the scope of this work.

29 Investigations: further provisions

(1) For the purposes of an investigation under this Part of this Act a Local Commissioner may require any member or officer of the authority concerned, or any other person who in his opinion is able to furnish information or produce documents relevant to the investigation, to furnish any such information or produce any such documents.

(2) For the purposes of any such investigation a Local Commissioner shall have the same powers as the High Court in respect of the attendance and examination of witnesses, and in respect of the production of documents.

(3) A Local Commissioner may, under subsection (1) above, require any person to furnish information concerning communications between the authority concerned and any Government department, or to produce any correspondence or other documents forming part of any such written communications.

(4) No obligation to maintain secrecy or other restriction upon the disclosure of information obtained by or furnished to persons in Her Majesty's service, whether imposed by any enactment or by any rule of law, shall apply to the disclosure of information in accordance with subsection (3) above; and where that subsection applies the Crown shall not be entitled to any such privilege in respect of the production of documents or the giving of evidence as is allowed by law in legal proceedings.

(5)–(10) . . .

NOTES

Sub-ss (5)–(10): outside the scope of this work.

30 Reports on investigations

(1) In any case where a Local Commissioner conducts an investigation, or decides not to conduct an investigation, he shall send a report of the results of the investigation, or as the case may be a statement of his reasons for not conducting an investigation—

- (a) to the person, if any, who referred the complaint to the Local Commissioner in accordance with section 26(2) above, and
- (b) to the complainant, and
- (c) to the authority concerned, and to any other authority or person who is alleged in the complaint to have taken or authorised the action complained of.

(2), (2A) . . .

(3) Apart from identifying the authority or authorities concerned the report shall not[, except where subsection (3A) below applies,]—

- (a) mention the name of any person, or
- (b) contain any particulars which, in the opinion of the Local Commissioner, are likely to identify any person and can be omitted without impairing the effectiveness of the report,

unless, after taking into account the public interest as well as the interests of the complainant and of persons other than the complainant, the Local Commissioner considers it necessary to mention the name of that person or to include in the report any such particulars.

[(3A) Where the Local Commissioner is of the opinion—

(a) that action constituting maladministration was taken which involved a member of the authority concerned, and

(b) that the member's conduct constituted a breach of the National Code of Local Government Conduct,

then, unless the Local Commissioner is satisfied that it would be unjust to do so, the report shall name the member and give particulars of the breach.]

(4) Subject to the provisions of subsection (7) below, the authority concerned shall for a period of three weeks make copies of the report available for inspection by the public without charge at all reasonable hours at one or more of their offices; and any person shall be entitled to take copies of, or extracts from, the report when so made available.

[(4A) Subject to subsection (7) below, the authority concerned shall supply a copy of the report to any person on request if he pays such charge as the authority may reasonably require.]

(5) Not later than [two weeks] after the report is received by the authority concerned, the proper officer of the authority shall give public notice, by advertisement in newspapers and such other ways as appear to him appropriate, that [copies of the report will be available as provided by subsections (4) and (4A)] above, and shall specify the date, being a date [not more than one week after public notice is first given], from which the period of three weeks will begin.

(6) . . .

(7) The Local Commissioner may, if he thinks fit after taking into account the public interest as well as the interests of the complainant and of persons other than the complainant, direct that a report specified in the direction shall not be subject to the provisions of subsections (4)[, (4A) and (5) above].

NOTES

Sub-ss (2), (2A), (6): outside the scope of this work.

Sub-s (3): words in square brackets inserted by the Local Government and Housing Act 1989, s 32(1)(a).

Sub-s (3A): inserted by the Local Government and Housing Act 1989, s 32(1)(b).

Sub-s (4A): inserted by the Local Government Act 1988, s 29, Sch 3, para 6(1), (2).

Sub-s (5): words in square brackets substituted by the Local Government Act 1988, s 29, Sch 3, para 6(1), (3).

Sub-s (7): words in square brackets substituted by the Local Government Act 1988, s 29, Sch 3, para 6(1), (4).

31 Reports on investigations: further provisions

[(1) This section applies where a Local Commissioner reports that injustice has been caused to a person aggrieved in consequence of maladministration.

(2) The report shall be laid before the authority concerned and it shall be the duty of that authority to consider the report and, within the period of three months beginning with the date on which they received the report, or such longer period as the Local Commissioner may agree in writing, to notify the Local Commissioner of the action which the authority have taken or propose to take.

(2A) If the Local Commissioner—

(a) does not receive the notification required by subsection (2) above within the period allowed by or under that subsection, or

(b) is not satisfied with the action which the authority concerned have taken or propose to take, or

(c) does not within a period of three months beginning with the end of the period so allowed, or such longer period as the Local Commissioner may agree in writing, receive confirmation from the authority concerned that they have taken action, as proposed, to the satisfaction of the Local Commissioner,

he shall make a further report setting out those facts and making recommendations.

(2B) Those recommendations are such recommendations as the Local Commissioner thinks fit to make with respect to action which, in his opinion, the authority concerned should take to remedy the injustice to the person aggrieved and to prevent similar injustice being caused in the future.

(2C) Section 30 above, with any necessary modifications, and subsection (2) above shall apply to a report under subsection (2A) above as they apply to a report under that section.

(2D) If the Local Commissioner—

(a) does not receive the notification required by subsection (2) above as applied by subsection (2C) above within the period allowed by or under that subsection or is satisfied before the period allowed by that subsection has expired that the authority concerned have decided to take no action, or

(b) is not satisfied with the action which the authority concerned have taken or propose to take, or

(c) does not within a period of three months beginning with the end of the period allowed by or under subsection (2) above as applied by subsection (2C) above, or such longer period as the Local Commissioner may agree in writing, receive confirmation from the authority concerned that they have taken action, as proposed, to the satisfaction of the Local Commissioner,

he may, by notice to the authority, require them to arrange for a statement to be published in accordance with subsections (2E) and (2F) below.

(2E) The statement referred to in subsection (2D) above is a statement, in such form as the authority concerned and the Local Commissioner may agree, consisting of—

(a) details of any action recommended by the Local Commissioner in his further report which the authority have not taken;

(b) such supporting material as the Local Commissioner may require; and

(c) if the authority so require, a statement of the reasons for their having taken no action on, or not the action recommended in, the report.

(2F) The requirements for the publication of the statement are that—

(a) publication shall be in any two editions within a fortnight of a newspaper circulating in the area of the authority agreed with the Local Commissioner or, in default of agreement, nominated by him; and

(b) publication in the first such edition shall be arranged for the earliest practicable date.

(2G) If the authority concerned—

(a) fail to arrange for the publication of the statement in accordance with subsections (2E) and (2F) above, or

(b) are unable, within the period of one month beginning with the date on which they received the notice under subsection (2D) above, or such longer period as the Local Commissioner may agree in writing, to agree with the Local Commissioner the form of the statement to be published,

the Local Commissioner shall arrange for such a statement as is mentioned in subsection (2E) above to be published in any two editions within a fortnight of a newspaper circulating within the authority's area.

(2H) The authority concerned shall reimburse the Commission on demand any reasonable expenses incurred by the Local Commissioner in performing his duty under subsection (2G) above.]

[(3) In any case where—

(a) a report is laid before an authority under subsection [(2) or (2C)] above, and

(b) on consideration of the report, it appears to the authority that a payment should be made to, or some other benefit should be provided for, a person who has suffered injustice in consequence of maladministration [to which the report relates],

the authority may incur such expenditure as appears to them to be appropriate in making such a payment or providing such a benefit.]

NOTES

Sub-ss (1)–(2H): substituted for sub-ss (1)–(2A) (as inserted in the case of sub-s (2A) by the Local Government Act 1988, s 29, Sch 3, para 7) by the Local Government and Housing Act 1989, s 26.

Sub-s (3): added by the Local Government Act 1978, s 1; words in square brackets in para (a) substituted by the Local Government and Housing Act 1989, s 194(1), Sch 11, para 39; words in square brackets in para (b) substituted by the Local Government Act 1988, s 29, Sch 3, para 7.

34 Interpretation of Part III

(1), (2) . . .

(3) It is hereby declared that nothing in this Part of this Act authorises or requires a Local Commissioner to question the merits of a decision taken without maladministration by an authority in the exercise of a discretion vested in that authority.

NOTES

Sub-ss (1), (2): outside the scope of this work.

PART IV
MISCELLANEOUS AND GENERAL

43 Short title, commencement, construction, application and extent

(1) This Act may be cited as the Local Government Act 1974.

(2)–(5) . . .

(6) . . . this Act shall not extend to Scotland or to Northern Ireland.

NOTES

Sub-ss (2)–(5): outside the scope of this work.

Sub-s (6): words omitted repealed by the House of Commons Disqualification Act 1975, s 10(2), Sch 3, and the Northern Ireland Assembly Disqualification Act 1975, s 5(2), Sch 3.

SCHEDULE 5

Section 26

MATTERS NOT SUBJECT TO INVESTIGATION

1. The commencement or conduct of civil or criminal proceedings before any court of law.

2. Action taken by any [police] authority in connection with the investigation or prevention of crime.

3.—(1) Action taken in matters relating to contractual or other commercial transactions of any authority to which Part III of this Act applies, including transactions falling within sub-paragraph (2) below but excluding transactions falling within sub-paragraph (3) below.

(2) The transactions mentioned in sub-paragraph (1) above as included in the matters which, by virtue of that sub-paragraph, are not subject to investigation are all transactions of an authority to which Part III of this Act applies relating to the operation of public passenger transport, the carrying on of a dock or harbour undertaking, the provision of entertainment, or the provision and operation of industrial establishments and of markets [other than transactions relating to the grant, renewal or revocation of a licence to occupy a pitch or stall in a fair or market, or the attachment of any condition to such a licence].

(3) The transactions mentioned in sub-paragraph (1) above as not included in those matters are—

- (a) transactions for or relating to the acquisition or disposal of land [or the provision of moorings (not being moorings provided in connection with a dock or harbour undertaking)]; and
- (b) all transactions (not being transactions falling within sub-paragraph (2) above) in the discharge of functions exercisable under any public general Act, other than those required for the procurement of the goods and services necessary to discharge those functions.

4. Action taken in respect of appointments or removals, pay, discipline, superannuation or other personnel matters.

5.—(1) Any action taken by a local education authority in the exercise of functions under [section 370 of the Education Act 1996 or section 17 of the Education (No 2) Act 1986] (secular instruction in county schools and in voluntary schools).

(2) Any action concerning—

- (a) the giving of instruction, whether secular or religious, or
- (b) conduct, curriculum, internal organisation, management or discipline, [in any school or other educational establishment maintained by the authority].

[6. Action taken by an authority mentioned in section 25(1)(ba), (bb) or (bc) of this Act which is not action in connection with functions in relation to housing.

7. Action taken by an authority mentioned in section 25(1)(bd) of this Act which is not action in connection with functions in relation to town and country planning.]

[8. Action taken by the Urban Regeneration Agency which is not action in connection with functions in relation to town and country planning.]

NOTES

Para 2: word in square brackets inserted by the Local Government Administration (Matters Subject to Investigation) Order 1988, SI 1988/242.

Para 3: words in square brackets in sub-paras (2), (3) inserted by the Local Government Administration (Matters Subject to Investigation) Order 1993, SI 1993/940.

Para 5: words in square brackets in sub-para (1) (as inserted in part by the Education (No 2) Act 1986, s 67(4), Sch 4, para 5) substituted by the Education Act 1996, s 582(1), Sch 37, Pt I, para 29; words in square brackets in sub-para (2) substituted by the Education Reform Act 1988, s 237(1), Sch 12, Pt III, para 71.

Paras 6, 7: added by the Local Government Act 1988, s 29, Sch 3, para 10.

Para 8: added by the Leasehold Reform, Housing and Urban Development Act 1993, s 187(1), Sch 21, para 6(3).

NORTHERN IRELAND ACT 1974

(c 28)

An Act to provide for the dissolution of the existing Northern Ireland Assembly and its prorogation until dissolution; to make temporary provision for the government of Northern Ireland; to provide for the election and holding of a Constitutional Convention in Northern Ireland; and for purposes connected with those matters

[17 July 1974]

1 Dissolution and prorogation of existing Assembly and temporary provision for government of Northern Ireland

(1) Her Majesty may by Order in Council dissolve the Assembly elected under the Northern Ireland Assembly Act 1973; and subsection (7) of section 27 of the Northern Ireland Constitution Act 1973 (power to appoint day for new elections etc) shall have effect on the dissolution of that Assembly under this section as if it had been dissolved by Her Majesty under subsection (5) of that section.

(2) . . .

(3) The provisions of Schedule 1 to this Act shall have effect with respect to the exercise of legislative, executive and other functions in relation to Northern Ireland during the interim period specified by or under subsection (4) below.

(4) The interim period shall be the period of one year beginning with the passing of this Act but the Secretary of State may by order direct that it shall continue until a date after, or end on a date earlier than, the date on which it would otherwise expire (whether by virtue of this subsection or of a previous order thereunder).

(5) No order under subsection (4) above shall provide for the interim period to continue until a date more than one year after the date on which it would otherwise expire.

(6) The power to make an order under subsection (4) above shall be exercisable by statutory instrument; and no order shall be made under that subsection unless a draft of it has been approved by resolution of each House of Parliament.

NOTES

Sub-s (2): repealed by the Northern Ireland Act 1982, s 7(3), Sch 3.

2 Short title

This Act may be cited as the Northern Ireland Act 1974.

SCHEDULE 1

Section 1(3)

TEMPORARY PROVISION FOR GOVERNMENT OF NORTHERN IRELAND

Legislative functions

1.—(1) During the interim period—

(a) no Measure shall be passed by the Assembly; and

(b) Her Majesty may by Order in Council make laws for Northern Ireland and, in particular, provision for any matter for which the Constitution Act authorises or requires provision to be made by Measure. (2)No recommendation shall be made to Her Majesty to make any Order in Council under this paragraph containing a provision in relation to which the Secretary of State would be precluded by section 5(1) of the Constitution Act from giving his consent if it were contained in a proposed Measure.

(3) The power to make an Order in Council under this paragraph includes power to vary or revoke a previous Order made thereunder.

(4) No recommendation shall be made to Her Majesty to make an Order in Council under this paragraph unless either—

(a) a draft of the Order has been approved by resolution of each House of Parliament; or

(b) the Order declares that it has been made to appear to Her Majesty that by reason of urgency the Order requires to be made without a draft having been so approved.

(5) Any Order in Council under this paragraph, other than an Order of which a draft has been approved by resolution of each House of Parliament, shall be laid before Parliament after being made and, if at the end of the period of forty days after the date on which it is made the Order has not been approved by resolution of each House, shall then cease to have effect (but without prejudice to anything previously done under the Order or to the making of a new Order).

(6) In reckoning the period mentioned in sub-paragraph (5) above no account shall be taken of any time during which Parliament is dissolved or prorogued or during which both Houses are adjourned for more than four days.

(7) References to Measures in any enactment or instrument (whether passed or made before or after the passing of this Act) shall, so far as the context permits, be deemed to include references to Orders in Council under this paragraph.

(8) Orders in Council under this paragraph may be omitted from any annual edition of statutory instruments required to be prepared under regulations made by virtue of section 8 of the Statutory Instruments Act 1946.

2–6. . . .

NOTES

Paras 2–6: outside the scope of this work.

HOUSE OF COMMONS DISQUALIFICATION ACT 1975

(c 24)

An Act to consolidate certain enactments relating to disqualification for membership of the House of Commons

[8 May 1975]

1 Disqualification of holders of certain offices and places

(1) Subject to the provisions of this Act, a person is disqualified for membership of the House of Commons who for the time being—

(a) holds any of the judicial offices specified in Part I of Schedule 1 to this Act;

(b) is employed in the civil service of the Crown, whether in an established capacity or not, and whether for the whole or part of his time;

(c) is a member of any of the regular armed forces of the Crown or the Ulster Defence Regiment;

(d) is a member of any police force maintained by a police authority;

[(da) is a member of the National Criminal Intelligence Service or the National Crime Squad;]

(e) is a member of the legislature of any country or territory outside the Commonwealth; or

(f) holds any office described in Part II or Part III of Schedule 1.

(2), (3) . . .

(4) Except as provided by this Act, a person shall not be disqualified for membership of the House of Commons by reason of his holding an office or place of profit under the Crown or any other office or place; and a person shall not be disqualified for appointment to or for holding any office or place by reason of his being a member of that House.

NOTES

Sub-s (1): para (da) inserted by the Police Act 1997, s 134(1), Sch 9, para 29(2).

Sub-ss (2), (3): outside the scope of this work.

2 Ministerial offices

(1) Not more than ninety-five persons being the holders of offices specified in Schedule 2 to this Act (in this section referred to as Ministerial offices) shall be entitled to sit and vote in the House of Commons at any one time.

(2) If at any time the number of members of the House of Commons who are holders of Ministerial offices exceeds the number entitled to sit and vote in that House under subsection (1) above, none except any who were both members of that House and holders of Ministerial offices before the excess occurred shall sit or vote therein until the number has been reduced, by death, resignation or otherwise, to the number entitled to sit and vote as aforesaid.

(3) A person holding a Ministerial office is not disqualified by this Act by reason of any office held by him ex officio as the holder of that Ministerial office.

4 Stewardship of Chiltern Hundreds, etc

For the purposes of the provisions of this Act relating to the vacation of the seat of a member of the House of Commons who becomes disqualified by this Act for membership of that House, the office of steward or bailiff of Her Majesty's three Chiltern Hundreds of Stoke, Desborough and Burnham, or of the Manor of Northstead, shall be treated as included among the offices described in Part III of Schedule 1 to this Act.

5 Power to amend Schedule 1

(1) If at any time it is resolved by the House of Commons that Schedule 1 to this Act be amended, whether by the addition or omission of any office or the removal of any office from one Part of the Schedule to another, or by altering the description of any office specified therein, Her Majesty may by Order in Council amend that Schedule accordingly.

(2) A copy of this Act as from time to time amended by Order in Council under this section or by or under any other enactment shall be prepared and certified by the Clerk of the Parliaments and deposited with the rolls of Parliament; and all copies of this Act thereafter to be printed by Her Majesty's printer shall be printed in accordance with the copy so certified.

6 Effects of disqualification and provision for relief

(1) Subject to any order made by the House of Commons under this section,—

(a) if any person disqualified by this Act for membership of that House, or for membership for a particular constituency, is elected as a member of that House, or as a member for that constituency, as the case may be, his election shall be void; and

(b) if any person being a member of that House becomes disqualified by this Act for membership, or for membership for the constituency for which he is sitting, his seat shall be vacated.

(2) If, in a case falling or alleged to fall within subsection (1) above, it appears to the House of Commons that the grounds of disqualification or alleged disqualification under this Act which subsisted or arose at the material time have been removed, and that it is otherwise proper so to do, that House may by order direct that any such disqualification incurred on those grounds at that time shall be disregarded for the purposes of this section.

(3) No order under subsection (2) above shall affect the proceedings on any election petition or any determination of an election court, and this subsection shall have effect subject to the provisions of section 144(7) of the Representation of the People Act 1983 (making of an order by the House of Commons when informed of a certificate and any report of an election court).

(4) In any case where [by virtue of the Recess Elections Act 1975] the Speaker of the House of Commons would be required to issue during a recess of that House a warrant for a new writ for election of a member, in the room of a member becoming disqualified by this Act, he may, if it appears to him that an opportunity should be given to that House to consider the making of an order under subsection (2) above, defer the issue of his warrant pending the determination of that House.

NOTES

Sub-s (4): words in square brackets substituted by the Recess Elections Act 1975, s 5(3).

7 Jurisdiction of Privy Council as to disqualification

(1) Any person who claims that a person purporting to be a member of the House of Commons is disqualified by this Act, or has been so disqualified at any time since his election, may apply to Her Majesty in Council, in accordance with such rules as Her Majesty in Council may prescribe, for a declaration to that effect.

(2) Section 3 of the Judicial Committee Act 1833 (reference to the Judicial Committee of the Privy Council of appeals to Her Majesty in Council) shall apply to any application under this section as it applies to an appeal to Her Majesty in Council from a court.

(3)–(5) . . .

NOTES

Sub-ss (3)–(5): outside the scope of this work.

11 Short title and extent

(1) This Act may be cited as the House of Commons Disqualification Act 1975.

(2) This Act extends to Northern Ireland.

SCHEDULE 1

Sections 1, 4, 5

OFFICES DISQUALIFYING FOR MEMBERSHIP

PART II
BODIES OF WHICH ALL MEMBERS ARE DISQUALIFIED

The Authorised Conveyancing Practitioners Board.

The British Coal Corporation.

The British Railways Board.

British Shipbuilders.

The British Steel Corporation.

The British Waterways Board.

The Broadcasting Standards Commission.

The Building Societies Commission.

Bwrdd yr Iaith Gymraeg (Welsh Language Board).

The Central Electricity Generating Board.

The Channel Four Television Corporation.

The Citizen's Charter Advisory Panel.

The Civil Aviation Authority.

The Civil Service Arbitration Tribunal.

The Coal Authority.

The Commission for Local Administration in England.

The Commission for Local Administration in Wales.

The Commission for Local Authority Accounts in Scotland.

The Commission for Racial Equality.

The Council of the Advisory, Conciliation and Arbitration Service.

The Council on Tribunals.

The Criminal Cases Review Commission.

The Criminal Injuries Compensation Board.

The Crown Estate Commissioners.

The Data Protection Tribunal.

The Development Commission.

A Development Corporation within the meaning of the New Towns Act 1981 or the New Towns (Scotland) Act 1968.

The Disability Living Allowance Advisory Board.

The Electricity Council.

The Employment Appeal Tribunal.

The Environment Agency.

The Equal Opportunities Commission.

The Football Licensing Authority.

The Foreign Compensation Commission.

The Gaming Board for Great Britain.

The Health and Safety Executive.

The Housing Corporation.

The Human Fertilisation and Embryology Authority.

The Immigration Appeal Tribunal.

The Independent Broadcasting Authority.

The Independent Commission for Police Complaints for Northern Ireland.

The Independent Television Commission.

The Industrial Injuries Advisory Council.

The Labour Relations Agency.

The Lands Tribunal.

The Law Commission.

The Local Government Boundary Commission for Scotland.

The Local Government Boundary Commission for Wales.

The Local Government Commission for England.

The Lord Chancellor's Advisory Committee on Legal Education and Conduct.

The Meat and Livestock Commission.

A Mental Health Review Tribunal constituted or having effect as if constituted under the Mental Health Act 1983.

The Monopolies and Mergers Commission.

A National Broadcasting Council.

The National Disability Council.

The National Radiological Protection Board.

The Parades Commission for Northern Ireland.

The Parole Board.

A Pensions Appeal Tribunal.

The Police Complaints Authority.

The Post Office.

The Restrictive Practices Court.

The Review Board for Government Contracts.

The Scottish Criminal Cases Review Commission.

Scottish Enterprise.

The Scottish Environment Protection Agency.

The Social Security Advisory Committee.

The Transport Tribunal.

The Tribunal established under section 9 of the Intelligence Services Act 1994.

The Tribunal established under the Interception of Communications Act 1985.

The Tribunal established under the Security Service Act 1989.

The United Kingdom Atomic Energy Authority.

The Urban Regeneration Agency.

The Welsh Development Agency.

NOTES

Printed as amended as at 1 August 1998; entries omitted outside the scope of this work.

Prospective amendments: entry 'The Low Pay Commission appointed under section 8(a) of the National Minimum Wage Act 1998' inserted by the National Minimum Wage Act 1998, s 8, Sch 1, para 5; entry 'The National Lottery Commission' inserted by the National Lottery Act 1998, s 1(5), Sch 1, para 10(a); entry 'The Youth Justice Board for England and Wales' inserted by the Crime and Disorder Act 1998, s 41(11), Sch 2, para 6.

PART III
OTHER DISQUALIFYING OFFICES

Additional Commissioner of the Commission for Racial Equality.

Additional Commissioner of the Equal Opportunities Commission.

Additional Commissioner of the Equal Opportunities Commission for Northern Ireland.

Adjudicator appointed under section 5 of the Criminal Injuries Compensation Act 1995.

Adjudicator appointed for the purposes of the Immigration Act 1971.

Adjudicator for the Inland Revenue, Customs and Excise and the Contributions Agency.

Ambassador or Permanent Representative to an international organisation representing Her Majesty's Government in the United Kingdom.

Assistant Commissioner appointed under Part IV of the Local Government Act 1972.

Attorney General of the Duchy of Lancaster.

Auditor of the Civil List.

Boundary Commissioner or assistant Commissioner appointed under Schedule 1 to the Parliamentary Constituencies Act 1986.

Chairman or Director-General of the British Council.

Regional or other full-time chairman of a child support appeal tribunal established under section 21 of the Child Support Act 1991.

Full-time Chairman of Child Support Appeal Tribunals for Northern Ireland.

Chairman or Deputy Chairman of the Civil Service Appeal Board.

Chairman of a consumers' committee appointed under section 2 of the Electricity Act 1989.

Chairman of a customer service committee maintained under section 28 of the Water Industry Act 1991.

Chairman or Vice-Chairman of the English Sports Council.

Chairman or Deputy Chairman of the Financial Reporting Council.

Chairman of Food from Britain.

Chairman or any director of the Further Education Development Agency.

Chairman of the Gas Consumers' Council.

Chairman or any member, not being also an employee, of any Health Authority or Special Health Authority which is a relevant authority for the purposes of paragraph 9(1) of Schedule 5 to the National Health Service Act 1977.

Chairman of the Health and Safety Commission.

Chairman of the Inland Waterways Amenity Advisory Council.

Chairman of Investors in People UK.

Chairman of the Joint Nature Conservation Committee.

Chairman of the Legal Aid Board.

Chairman or Deputy Chairman of the National Consumer Council.

Chairman or non-executive member of a National Health Service trust established under the National Health Service and Community Care Act 1990 or the National Health Service (Scotland) Act 1978.

Chairman of the National Lottery Charities Board and any chairman of a committee of that Board.

Chairman of the National Research Development Corporation.

Chairman, Deputy Chairman or Chief Executive of the Natural Environment Research Council.

Chairman of the New Opportunities Fund and, if in receipt of remuneration, any other member of that Fund.

Chairman of a rail users' consultative committee, appointed under section 2 of the Railways Act 1993.

A regional or other full-time Chairman of Social Security Appeal Tribunals, Medical Appeal Tribunals and Disability Appeal Tribunals.

A full-time chairman of Social Security Appeal Tribunals, Medical Appeal Tribunals and Disability Appeal Tribunals for Northern Ireland.

Chairman of the Standing Advisory Commission on Human Rights constituted under section 20 of the Northern Ireland Constitution Act 1973.

Chairman of the United Kingdom Sports Council.

Chief Adjudication Officer appointed under section 39 of the Social Security Administration Act 1992.

Chief Child Support Officer appointed under section 13(3) of the Child Support Act 1991.

Chief Electoral Officer for Northern Ireland or any whole time officer appointed under section 14A(1) of the Electoral Law Act (Northern Ireland) 1962.

Civil Service Commissioner

Civil Service Commissioner for Northern Ireland.

The Commissioner for Local Administration in Scotland.

Commissioner or Assistant Commissioner appointed under section 50(1) or (2) of, or Schedule 4 to, the Local Government Act (Northern Ireland) 1972.

Commissioner or Assistant Commissioner of Police of the Metropolis.

Commissioner of the City of London Police.

Commissioner for Protection Against Unlawful Industrial Action.

Commissioner for Public Appointments.

Commissioner for Public Appointments for Northern Ireland.

Commissioner for the Rights of Trade Union Members.

Commons Commissioner.

Comptroller and Auditor General.

Comptroller and Auditor General for Northern Ireland.

Controller of Audit appointed under section 97(4) of the Local Government (Scotland) Act 1973.

Controller of Audit appointed under paragraph 7(1) of Schedule 3 to the Local Government Finance Act 1982.

Crown Solicitor for Northern Ireland.

The Data Protection Registrar.

Director of the British Aerospace Public Limited Company appointed subject to the approval of a Minister or government department.

Director of British Nuclear Fuels plc.

Director of Caledonian MacBrayne Limited.

Director of Citybus Limited.

Director of a company for the time being holding an appointment under Chapter I of Part II of the Water Industry Act 1991 or of such a company's holding company, being a director nominated or appointed by a Minister of the Crown or by a person acting on behalf of the Crown.

Director of any company in receipt of financial assistance under the Local Employment Act 1972, Part II of the Industry Act 1972 or Part III or section 13 of the Industrial Development Act 1982, being a director nominated by a Minister of the Crown or government department.

Director of a company—

(a) which, within the meaning of Part II of the Railways Act 1993, is a successor company wholly owned by the Crown, or

(b) which, within the meaning of that Act, is wholly owned by the Director of Passenger Rail Franchising,

being a director nominated or appointed by a Minister of the Crown, the Director of Passenger Rail Franchising or any other person acting on behalf of the Crown.

Director nominated by the Secretary of State of any company in respect of which an undertaking to make advances has been given by the Secretary of State under section 2 of the Highlands and Islands Shipping Services Act 1960 and is for the time being in force.

Director of Flexibus Limited.

Director of International Military Services Limited.

Director of Northern Ireland Railways Company Limited.

Director of Nuclear Electric plc.

The Director of Passenger Rail Franchising.

Director, or Deputy Director, of Public Prosecutions for Northern Ireland.

Director of a publicly owned successor company (within the meaning of the Atomic Energy Authority Act 1995).

Director appointed at a salary of Remploy Limited.

Director of Scottish Nuclear Limited.

Director of the successor company (within the meaning of the Crown Agents Act 1995) being a director nominated or appointed by a Minister of the Crown or by a person acting on behalf of the Crown.

Director General of Electricity Supply.

Director General of Electricity Supply for Northern Ireland.

Director General of Fair Trading.

Director General of Gas for Northern Ireland.

Director General of Gas Supply.

Director General of the National Economic Development Office.

Director General of the National Lottery.

Director General of Telecommunications.

Director General of Water Services.

District Judge appointed under section 6 of the County Courts Act 1984.

Governor of the British Broadcasting Corporation.

Governor, Deputy Governor or Director of the Bank of England.

Governor, Medical Officer or other officer or member of the staff of a prison to which the Prison Act (Northern Ireland) 1953 applies.

Health Service Commissioner for England.

Health Service Commissioner for Scotland.

Health Service Commissioner for Wales.

Her Majesty's Chief Inspector of Schools in England.

Her Majesty's Chief Inspector of Schools in Wales.

High Commissioner representing Her Majesty's Government in the United Kingdom.

Independent Assessor of Military Complaints Procedures in Northern Ireland.

Independent Commissioner, or Deputy Commissioner, for the Holding Centres in Northern Ireland.

The International Rail Regulator

Judge Advocate General, Vice Judge Advocate General, Assistant Judge Advocate General or Deputy Judge Advocate.

The Legal Services Ombudsman.

Any member of the Audit Commission for Local Authorities and the National Health Service in England and Wales in receipt of remuneration.

Any member in receipt of remuneration of the British Tourist Authority, the English Tourist Board, the Scottish Tourist Board or the Wales Tourist Board.

Any member of the Countryside Commission in receipt of remuneration.

Any member of the Financial Services Tribunal in receipt of remuneration.

Any member of the Funding Agency for Schools in receipt of remuneration.

Any member of the Further Education Funding Council for England in receipt of remuneration.

Any member of the Higher Education Funding Council for England in receipt of remuneration.

Member appointed by the Secretary of State of the Horserace Betting Levy Board.

Any member, in receipt of remuneration, of a housing action trust (within the meaning of Part III of the Housing Act 1988).

Member of the Legal Aid Board.

Member of the Local Enterprise Development Unit.

Member of a Medical Appeal Tribunal appointed under section 50 of the Social Security Administration Act 1992.

Any member of the Mental Health Act Commission in receipt of remuneration.

Member of the staff of the National Audit Office.

Any member of the Nature Conservancy Council for England or the Countryside Council for Wales in receipt of remuneration.

Member of the staff of the Northern Ireland Audit Office.

Member of a panel of chairmen for Child Support Appeal Tribunals for Northern Ireland appointed under paragraph 3(2)(a) of Schedule 3 to the Child Support (Northern Ireland) Order 1991.

Member of a panel of persons appointed to act as chairman or other members of industrial tribunals in Northern Ireland.

Any member of the Qualifications and Curriculum Authority constituted under section 21 of the Education Act 1997 in receipt of remuneration.

Member of the panel of chairmen for Social Security Appeal Tribunals, Medical Appeal Tribunals and Disability Appeal Tribunals for Northern Ireland appointed under section 49(1)(c) of the Social Security Administration (Northern Ireland) Act 1992.

Member of a panel appointed under section 6 of the Tribunals and Inquiries Act 1992 of persons to act as chairmen of Child Support Appeal Tribunals.

Member of a panel appointed under section 6 of the Tribunals and Inquiries Act 1992 of persons to act as chairmen of Social Security Appeal Tribunals, Medical Appeal Tribunals and Disability Appeal Tribunals.

Member of a panel of persons who may be appointed to serve on a Vaccine Damage Tribunal.

Any member, in receipt of remuneration, of an urban development corporation (within the meaning of Part XVI of the Local Government, Planning and Land Act 1980).

Northern Ireland Commissioner for Complaints.

Northern Ireland Commissioner for Protection Against Unlawful Industrial Action.

Northern Ireland Commissioner for the Rights of Trade Union Members.

Northern Ireland Parliamentary Commissioner for Administration.

Officer or servant employed under the Commissioner of Police of the Metropolis or the Receiver for the Metropolitan Police District.

Officer or servant of the Crown Estate Commissioners.

Officer of the Supreme Court being the holder of any office listed in any Part of Schedule 2 to the Supreme Court Act 1981 or a district judge of the High Court.

Parliamentary Commissioner for Administration.

Pensions Ombudsman.

Person appointed under section 3(1) of the Local Government and Housing Act 1989 to carry out functions relating to the political restriction of posts under local authorities, within the meaning of Part I of that Act.

Person appointed to hear and determine appeals under the Trade Marks Act 1994.

Person holding a politically restricted post, within the meaning of Part I of the Local Government and Housing Act 1989, under a local authority, within the meaning of that Part, or a National Park authority.

President of the Employment Tribunals (England and Wales), President of the Employment Tribunals (Scotland), or member of a panel of persons appointed to act as chairmen or other members of industrial tribunals.

President of Social Security Appeal Tribunals, Medical Appeal Tribunals and Disability Appeal Tribunals.

President of Social Security Appeal Tribunals, Medical Appeal Tribunals and Disability Appeal Tribunals for Northern Ireland.

President of the Special Educational Needs Tribunal, or member of a panel of persons appointed to act as chairman or other member of that Tribunal.

President or Vice-President of Value Added Tax Tribunals or full-time chairman of value added tax tribunals.

The Rail Regulator.

Registrar of the Privy Council.

Registration Officer appointed under section 8(2) or (3) of the Representation of the People Act 1983.

Rent officer appointed in pursuance of a scheme under section 63 of the Rent Act 1977.

Returning Officer under section 25(1) of the Representation of the People Act 1983 and any Deputy Returning Officer appointed by him.

Scottish legal services ombudsman appointed under section 34 of the Law Reform (Miscellaneous Provisions) (Scotland) Act 1990.

Social fund Commissioner.

Social fund Commissioner in Northern Ireland.

Solicitor in Scotland to any department of Her Majesty's Government in the United Kingdom.

Standing Counsel to any department of Her Majesty's Government in the United Kingdom.

NOTES

Printed as amended as at 1 August 1998; entries omitted outside the scope of this work.

Prospective amendments: entry 'The Data Protection Registrar' substituted by entry 'The Data Protection Commissioner' by the Data Protection Act 1998, s 74(1), Sch 15, para 5(2); entry 'Any member of the General Teaching Council for England in receipt of remuneration' inserted by the Teaching and Higher Education Act 1998, s 44(1), Sch 3, para 3; entry 'Member of a panel of persons appointed under section 6 of the Social Security Act 1998' inserted by the Social Security Act 1998, s 86(1), Sch 7, para 4(3); entry 'The Police Ombudsman for Northern Ireland' inserted by the Police (Northern Ireland) Act 1998, s 74 Sch 4, para 8; entry 'President of appeal tribunals (within the meaning of Chapter I of Part I of the Social Security Act 1998) appointed under section 5 of that Act' inserted by the Social Security Act 1998, s 86(1), Sch 7, para 4(3); entry 'Sentence Review Commissioner' inserted by the Northern Ireland (Sentences) Act 1998, s 1, Sch 1, para 7.

MINISTERS OF THE CROWN ACT 1975

(c 26)

An Act to consolidate the enactments relating to the redistribution of functions between Ministers of the Crown, the alteration of the style and title of such Ministers and certain other provisions about such Ministers

[8 May 1975]

1 Power by Order in Council to transfer functions of Ministers

(1) Her Majesty may by Order in Council—

(a) provide for the transfer to any Minister of the Crown of any functions previously exercisable by another Minister of the Crown;

(b) provide for the dissolution of the government department in the charge of any Minister of the Crown and the transfer to or distribution among such other Minister or Ministers of the Crown as may be specified in the Order of any functions previously exercisable by the Minister in charge of that department;

(c) direct that functions of any Minister of the Crown shall be exercisable concurrently with another Minister of the Crown, or shall cease to be so exercisable.

(2) An Order in Council under this section may contain such incidental, consequential and supplemental provisions as may be necessary or expedient for the purpose of giving full effect to the Order, including provisions—

(a) for the transfer of any property, rights and liabilities held, enjoyed or incurred by any Minister of the Crown in connection with any functions transferred or distributed;

(b) for the carrying on and completion by or under the authority of the Minister to whom any functions are transferred of anything commenced by or under the authority of a minister of the Crown before the date when the Order takes effect;

(c) for such adaptations of the enactments relating to any functions transferred as may be necessary to enable them to be exercised by the Minister to whom they are transferred and his officers;

(d) for making in the enactments regulating the number of offices in respect of which salaries may be paid or in section 2 of, and Schedule 2 to, the House of Commons Disqualification Act 1975 (which regulate the number of office holders who may be elected, and sit and vote, as members of the House of Commons), such modifications as may be expedient by reason of any transfer of functions or dissolution of a Department effected by the Order;

(e) for the substitution of the Minister to whom functions are transferred for any other Minister of the Crown in any instrument, contract, or legal proceedings made or commenced before the date when the Order takes effect.

(3) No modifications shall be made by virtue of paragraph (d) of subsection (2) above, in any of the enactments mentioned in that paragraph, so as to increase the amount of any salary which may be paid, or the aggregate number of persons to whom salaries may be paid, under those enactments or the aggregate number of persons capable thereunder of sitting and voting as Members of the House of Commons.

(4) Where by any Order made under this section provision is made for the transfer of functions in respect of which any Minister may sue or be sued by virtue of any enactment, the Order shall make any provision which may be required for enabling the Minister to whom those functions are transferred to sue or be sued in like manner.

(5) A certificate issued by a Minister of the Crown that any property vested in any other Minister immediately before an Order under this section takes effect has been transferred by virtue of the Order to the Minister issuing the certificate shall be conclusive evidence of the transfer.

4 Change of title of Ministers

If Her Majesty is pleased by Order in Council to direct that any change shall be made in the style and title of a Minister of the Crown, the Order may contain provisions substituting the new style and title—

(a) in the enactments (including those mentioned in section 1 (2) (d) above) relating to the Minister;

(b) in any instrument, contract, or legal proceedings made or commenced before the date when the Order takes effect.

5 Supplementary provisions as to Orders

(1) No Order in Council which provides for the dissolution of a government department shall be made under this Act unless, after copies of the draft thereof have been laid before Parliament, each House presents an Address to Her Majesty praying that the Order be made.

(2) An Order in Council under this Act, not being an Order made in pursuance of such an Address as aforesaid, shall be laid before Parliament and shall be subject to annulment in pursuance of a resolution of either House of Parliament.

(3), (4) . . .

(5) Nothing in this Act shall prejudice any power exercisable by virtue of the prerogative of the Crown in relation to the functions of Ministers of the Crown.

(6) . . .

NOTES

Sub-ss (3), (4), (6): outside the scope of this work.

9 Short title and extent

(1) This Act may be cited as the Ministers of the Crown Act 1975.

(2) This Act extends to Northern Ireland.

SEX DISCRIMINATION ACT 1975

(c 65)

An Act to render unlawful certain kinds of sex discrimination and discrimination on the ground of marriage, and establish a Commission with the function of working towards the elimination of such discrimination and promoting equality of opportunity between men and women generally; and for related purposes [12 November 1975]

PART I
DISCRIMINATION TO WHICH ACT APPLIES

1 Sex discrimination against women

(1) A person discriminates against a woman in any circumstances relevant for the purposes of any provision of this Act if—

(a) on the ground of her sex he treats her less favourably than he treats or would treat a man, or
(b) he applies to her a requirement or condition which he applies or would apply equally to a man but—
 (i) which is such that the proportion of women who can comply with it is considerably smaller than the proportion of men who can comply with it, and
 (ii) which he cannot show to be justifiable irrespective of the sex of the person to whom it is applied, and
 (iii) which is to her detriment because she cannot comply with it.

(2) If a person treats or would treat a man differently according to the man's marital status, his treatment of a woman is for the purposes of subsection (1)(a) to be compared to his treatment of a man having the like marital status.

2 Sex discrimination against men

(1) Section 1, and the provisions of Parts II and III relating to sex discrimination against women, are to be read as applying equally to the treatment of men, and for that purpose shall have effect with such modifications as are requisite.

(2) In the application of subsection (1) no account shall be taken of special treatment afforded to women in connection with pregnancy or childbirth.

PART III
DISCRIMINATION IN OTHER FIELDS

Education

22 Discrimination by bodies in charge of educational establishments

It is unlawful, in relation to an educational establishment falling within column 1 of the following table, for a person indicated in relation to the establishment in column 2 (the "responsible body") to discriminate against a woman—
(a) in the terms on which it offers to admit her to the establishment as a pupil, or
(b) by refusing or deliberately omitting to accept an application for her admission to the establishment as a pupil, or
(c) where she is a pupil of the establishment—
 (i) in the way it affords her access to any benefits, facilities or services, or by refusing or deliberately omitting to afford her access to them, or
 (ii) by excluding her from the establishment or subjecting her to any other detriment.

TABLE

Establishment	*Responsible body*
ENGLAND AND WALES	
1 Educational establishment maintained by a local education authority.	Local education authority or . . . *governors*, according to which of them has the function in question.

Establishment	*Responsible body*
2 Independent school not being a special school.	Proprietor.
3 Special school not maintained by a local education authority.	Proprietor.
[3A Grant-maintained school.	*Governing body.]*
[3B Institution within the further education sector (within the meaning of section 91(3) of the Further and Higher Education Act 1992).	Governing body.]
4 University.	Governing body.
[4A Institution, other than a university, within the higher education sector (within the meaning of section 91(5) of the Further and Higher Education Act 1992).	Governing body.]
5 Establishment (not falling within paragraphs 1 [to 4A]) providing full-time or part-time education, being an establishment designated under 24(1).	Governing body.

. . . . .

NOTES

Table, para 1: words omitted repealed by the Education Act 1980, s 1(3), Sch 1, para 27; word in italics substituted by words "governing body", by the School Standards and Framework Act 1998, s 140(1), Sch 30, para 5, as from a day to be appointed.

Table, para 3A: inserted by the Education Reform Act 1988, s 237(1), Sch 12, Pt I, para 15; repealed by the School Standards and Framework Act 1998, s 140(3), Sch 31, as from a day to be appointed.

Table, para 3B: inserted by the Further and Higher Education Act 1992, s 93(1), Sch 8, Pt II, paras 75, 76(1), (2).

Table, para 4A: inserted by the Education Reform Act 1988, s 237(1), Sch 12, Pt III, para 72, further substituted by the Further and Higher Education Act 1992, s 93(1), Sch 8, Pt II, paras 75, 76(1), (3).

Table, para 5: words in square brackets substituted by the Further and Higher Education Act 1992, s 93(1), Sch 8, Pt II, paras 75, 76(1), (4).

Other words omitted from Table: outside the scope of this work.

26 Exception for single-sex establishments

(1) Section 22(a) and (b) and 25 do not apply to the admission of pupils to any establishment (a "single-sex establishment") which admits pupils of one sex only, or which would be taken to admit pupils of one sex only if there were disregarded pupils of the opposite sex—

(a) whose admission is exceptional, or

(b) whose numbers are comparatively small and whose admission is confined to particular courses of instruction or teaching classes.

(2)–(4) . . .

NOTES

Sub-ss (2)–(4): outside the scope of this work.

Goods, facilities, services and premises

29 Discrimination in provision of goods, facilities or services

(1) It is unlawful for any person concerned with the provision (for payment or not) of goods, facilities or services to the public or a section of the public to discriminate against a woman who seeks to obtain or use those goods, facilities or services—

(a) by refusing or deliberately omitting to provide her with any of them, or

(b) by refusing or deliberately omitting to provide her with goods, facilities or services of the like quality, in the like manner and on the like terms as are normal in his case in relation to male members of the public or (where she belongs to a section of the public) to male members of that section.

(2), (3) . . .

NOTES

Sub-ss (2), (3): outside the scope of this work.

30 Discrimination in disposal or management of premises

(1) It is unlawful for a person, in relation to premises in Great Britain of which he has power to dispose, to discriminate against a women—

(a) in the terms on which he offers her those premises, or

(b) by refusing her application for those premises, or

(c) in his treatment of her in relation to any list of persons in need of premises of that description.

(2) It is unlawful for a person, in relation to premises managed by him, to discriminate against a woman occupying the premises—

(a) in the way he affords her access to any benefits or facilities, or by refusing or deliberately omitting to afford her access to them, or

(b) by evicting her, or subjecting her to any other detriment.

(3) Subsection (1) does not apply to a person who owns an estate or interest in the premises and wholly occupies them unless he uses the services of an estate agent for the purposes of the disposal of the premises, or publishes or causes to be published an advertisement in connection with the disposal.

33 Exception for political parties

(1) This section applies to a political party if—

(a) it has as its main object, or one of its main objects, the promotion of parliamentary candidatures for the Parliament of the United Kingdom, or

(b) it is an affiliate of, or has as an affiliate, or has similar formal links with, a political party within paragraph *(a)*.

(2) Nothing in section 29(1) shall be construed as affecting any special provision for persons of one sex only in the constitution, organisation or administration of the political party.

(3) Nothing in section 29(1) shall render unlawful an act done in order to give effect to such a special provision.

PART IV
OTHER UNLAWFUL ACTS

37 Discriminatory practices

(1) In this section "discriminatory practice" means the application of a requirement or condition which results in an act of discrimination which is unlawful by virtue of any provision of Part II or III taken with section 1(1)(b) or 3(1)(b) or which would be likely to result in such an act of discrimination if the persons to whom it is applied were not all of one sex.

(2) A person acts in contravention of this section if and so long as—

(a) he applies a discriminatory practice, or

(b) he operates practices or other arrangements which in any circumstances would call for the application by him of a discriminatory practice.

(3) Proceedings in respect of a contravention of this section shall be brought only by the Commission in accordance with sections 67 to 71 of this Act.

38 Discriminatory advertisements

(1) It is unlawful to publish or cause to be published an advertisement which indicates, or might reasonably be understood as indicating, an intention by a person to do any act which is or might be unlawful by virtue of Part II or III.

(2) Subsection (1) does not apply to an advertisement if the intended act would not in fact be unlawful.

(3) For the purposes of subsection (1), use of a job description with a sexual connotation (such as "waiter", "salesgirl", "postman" or "stewardess") shall be taken to indicate an intention to discriminate, unless the advertisement contains an indication to the contrary.

(4) The publisher of an advertisement made unlawful by subsection (1) shall not be subject to any liability under that subsection in respect of the publication of the advertisement if he proves—

(a) that the advertisement was published in reliance on a statement made to him by the person who caused it to be published to the effect that, by reason of the operation of subsection (2), the publication would not be unlawful, and

(b) that it was reasonable for him to rely on the statement.

(5) A person who knowingly or recklessly makes a statement such as is referred to in subsection (4) which in a material respect is false or misleading commits an offence, and shall be liable on summary conviction to a fine not exceeding [level 5 on the standard scale].

NOTES

Sub-s (5): maximum fine increased and converted to a level on the standard scale by the Criminal Justice Act 1982, ss 37, 38, 46.

39 Instructions to discriminate

It is unlawful for a person—

(a) who has authority over another person, or

(b) in accordance with whose wishes that other person is accustomed to act, to instruct him to do any act which is unlawful by virtue of Part II or III, or procure or attempt to procure the doing by him of any such act.

40 Pressure to discriminate

(1) It is unlawful to induce, or attempt to induce, a person to do any act which contravenes Part II or III by—

(a) providing or offering to provide him with any benefit, or

(b) subjecting or threatening to subject him to any detriment.

(2) An offer or threat is not prevented from falling within subsection (1) because it is not made directly to the person in question, if it is made in such a way that he is likely to hear of it.

41 Liability of employers and principals

(1) Anything done by a person in the course of his employment shall be treated for the purposes of this Act as done by his employer as well as by him, whether or not it was done with the employer's knowledge or approval.

(2) Anything done by a person as agent for another person with the authority (whether express or implied, and whether precedent or subsequent) of that other person shall be treated for the purposes of this Act as done by that other person as well as by him.

(3) In proceedings brought under this Act against any person in respect of an act alleged to have been done by an employee of his it shall be a defence for that person to prove that he took such steps as were reasonably practicable to prevent the employee from doing that act, or from doing in the course of his employment acts of that description.

NOTES

Modification: modified, in relation to governing bodies with delegated budgets, by the Education (Modification of Enactments Relating to Employment) Order 1998, SI 1998/218, art 3, Schedule.

42 Aiding unlawful acts

(1) A person who knowingly aids another person to do an act made unlawful by this Act shall be treated for the purposes of this Act as himself doing an unlawful act of the like description.

(2) For the purposes of subsection (1) an employee or agent for whose act the employer or principal is liable under section 41 (or would be so liable but for section 41(3)) shall be deemed to aid the doing of the act by the employer or principal.

(3) A person does not under this section knowingly aid another to do an unlawful act if—

(a) he acts in reliance on a statement made to him by that other person that, by reason of any provision of this Act, the act which he aids would not be unlawful, and

(b) it is reasonable for him to rely on the statement.

(4) A person who knowingly or recklessly makes a statement such as is referred to in subsection (3)(a) which in a material respect is false or misleading commits an offence, and shall be liable on summary conviction to a fine not exceeding [level 5 on the standard scale].

NOTES

Sub-s (4): maximum fine increased and converted to a level on the standard scale by the Criminal Justice Act 1982, ss 37, 38, 46.

PART V
GENERAL EXCEPTIONS FROM PARTS II TO IV

44 Sport etc

Nothing in Parts II to IV shall, in relation to any sport, game or other activity of a competitive nature where the physical strength, stamina or physique of the average woman puts her at a disadvantage to the average man, render unlawful any act related to the participation of a person as a competitor in events involving that activity which are confined to competitors of one sex.

45 Insurance

Nothing in Parts II to IV shall render unlawful the treatment of a person in relation to an annuity, life assurance policy, accident insurance policy, or similar matter involving the assessment of risk, where the treatment—

(a) was effected by reference to actuarial or other data from a source on which it was reasonable to rely, and

(b) was reasonable having regard to the data and any other relevant factors.

46 Communal accommodation

(1) In this section "communal accommodation" means residential accommodation which includes dormitories or other shared sleeping accommodation which for reasons of privacy or decency should be used by men only, or by women only (but which may include some shared sleeping accommodation for men, and some for women, or some ordinary sleeping accommodation).

(2) In this section "communal accommodation" also includes residential accommodation all or part of which should be used by men only, or by women only, because of the nature of the sanitary facilities serving the accommodation.

(3) Nothing in Part II or III shall render unlawful sex discrimination in the admission of persons to communal accommodation if the accommodation is managed in a way which, given the exigencies of the situation, comes as near as may be to fair and equitable treatment of men and women.

(4) In applying subsection (3) account shall be taken of—

(a) whether and how far it is reasonable to expect that the accommodation should be altered or extended, or that further alternative accommodation should be provided; and

(b) the frequency of the demand or need for use of the accommodation by men as compared with women.

(5) Nothing in Part II or III shall render unlawful sex discrimination against a woman, or against a man, as respects the provision of any benefit, facility or service if—

(a) the benefit, facility or service cannot properly and effectively be provided except for those using communal accommodation, and

(b) in the relevant circumstances the woman or, as the case may be, the man could lawfully be refused the use of the accommodation by virtue of subsection (3).

(6) Neither subsection (3) nor subsection (5) is a defence to an act of sex discrimination under Part II unless such arrangements as are reasonably practicable are made to compensate for the detriment caused by the discrimination; but in considering under subsection (5)(b) whether the use of communal accommodation could lawfully be refused (in a case based on Part II), it shall be assumed that the requirements of this subsection have been complied with as respects subsection (3).

(7) Section 25 shall not apply to sex discrimination within subsection (3) or (5).

(8) This section is without prejudice to the generality of section 35(1)(c).

47 Discriminatory training by certain bodies

(1) Nothing in Parts II to IV shall render unlawful any act done in relation to particular work by [any person] in, or in connection with—

- (a) affording women only, or men only, access to facilities for training which would help to fit them for that work, or
- (b) encouraging women only, or men only, to take advantage of opportunities for doing that work,

where [it reasonably appears to that person] that at any time within the 12 months immediately preceding the doing of the act there were no persons of the sex in question doing that work in Great Britain, or the number of persons of that sex doing the work in Great Britain was comparatively small.

(2)–(4) . . .

NOTES

Sub-ss (1): words in square brackets substituted by the Sex Discrimination Act 1986, s 4(1)–(3).
Sub-ss (2)–(4): outside the scope of this work.

48 Other discriminatory training etc

(1) Nothing in Parts II to IV shall render unlawful any act done by an employer in relation to particular work in his employment, being an act done in, or in connection with,—

- (a) affording his female employees only, or his male employees only, access to facilities for training which would help to fit them for that work, or
- (b) encouraging women only, or men only, to take advantage of opportunities for doing that work,

where at any time within the twelve months immediately preceding the doing of the act there were no persons of the sex in question among those doing that work or the number of persons of that sex doing the work was comparatively small.

(2) Nothing in section 12 shall render unlawful any act done by an organisation to which that section applies in, or in connection with,—

- (a) affording female members of the organisation only, or male members of the organisation only, access to facilities for training which would help to fit them for holding a post of any kind in the organisation, or
- (b) encouraging female members only, or male members only, to take advantage of opportunities for holding such posts in the organisation,

where at any time within the twelve months immediately preceding the doing of the act there were no persons of the sex in question among persons holding such posts in the organisation or the number of persons of that sex holding such posts was comparatively small.

(3) Nothing in Parts II to IV shall render unlawful any act done by an organisation to which section 12 applies in, or in connection with, encouraging women only, or men only, to become members of the organisation where at any time within the twelve months immediately preceding the doing of the act there were no persons of the sex in question among those members or the number of persons of that sex among the members was comparatively small.

49 Trade unions etc: elective bodies

(1) If an organisation to which section 12 applies comprises a body the membership of which is wholly or mainly elected, nothing in section 12 shall render unlawful provision which ensures that a minimum number of persons of one sex are members of the body—

(a) by reserving seats on the body for persons of that sex, or

(b) by making extra seats on the body available (by election or co-option or otherwise) for persons of that sex on occasions when the number of persons of that sex in the other seats is below the minimum,

where in the opinion of the organisation the provision is in the circumstances needed to secure a reasonable lower limit to the number of members of that sex serving on the body; and nothing in Parts II to IV shall render unlawful any act done in order to give effect to such a provision.

(2) This section shall not be taken as making lawful—

(a) discrimination in the arrangements for determining the persons entitled to vote in an election of members of the body, or otherwise to choose the persons to serve on the body, or

(b) discrimination in any arrangements concerning membership of the organisation itself.

[51 Acts done for purposes of protection of women

(1) Nothing in the following provisions, namely—

(a) Part II,

(b) Part III so far as it applies to vocational training, or

(c) Part IV so far as it has effect in relation to the provisions mentioned in paragraphs (a) and (b),

shall render unlawful any act done by a person in relation to a woman if—

(i) it was necessary for that person to do it in order to comply with a requirement of an existing statutory provision concerning the protection of women, or

(ii) it was necessary for that person to do it in order to comply with a requirement of a relevant statutory provision (within the meaning of Part I of the Health and Safety at Work etc Act 1974) and it was done by that person for the purpose of the protection of the woman in question (or of any class of women that included that woman).

(2) In subsection (1)—

(a) the reference in paragraph (i) of that subsection to an existing statutory provision concerning the protection of women is a reference to any such provision having effect for the purpose of protecting women as regards—

(i) pregnancy or maternity, or

(ii) other circumstances giving rise to risks specifically affecting women,

whether the provision relates only to such protection or to the protection of any other class of persons as well; and

(b) the reference in paragraph (ii) of that subsection to the protection of a particular woman or class of women is a reference to the protection of that woman or those women as regards any circumstances falling within paragraph (a)(i) or (ii) above.

(3) In this section "existing statutory provision" means (subject to subsection (4)) any provision of—

(a) an Act passed before this Act, or

(b) an instrument approved or made by or under such an Act (including one approved or made after the passing of this Act).

(4) Where an Act passed after this Act re-enacts (with or without modification) a provision of an Act passed before this Act, that provision as re-enacted shall be treated for the purposes of subsection (3) as if it continued to be contained in an Act passed before this Act.]

NOTES

Substituted with savings, together with s 51A, for s 51 as originally enacted and amended, by the Employment Act 1989, ss 3(1), (3), 29(6), Sch 9, para 1.

[51A Acts done under statutory authority to be exempt from certain provisions of Part III

(1) Nothing in—

(a) the relevant provisions of Part III, or

(b) Part IV so far as it has effect in relation to those provisions,

shall render unlawful any act done by a person if it was necessary for that person to do it in order to comply with a requirement of an existing statutory provision within the meaning of section 51.

(2) In subsection (1) "the relevant provisions of Part III" means the provisions of that Part except so far as they apply to vocational training.]

NOTES

Substituted with savings, together with new s 51, for s 51 as originally enacted and amended, by the Employment Act 1989, ss 3(3), 29(6), Sch 9.

52 Acts safeguarding national security

(1) Nothing in Parts II to IV shall render unlawful an act done for the purpose of safeguarding national security.

(2) A certificate purporting to be signed by or on behalf of a Minister of the Crown and certifying that an act specified in the certificate was done for the purpose of safeguarding national security shall be conclusive evidence that it was done for that purpose.

(3) A document purporting to be a certificate such as is mentioned in subsection (2) shall be received in evidence and, unless the contrary is proved, shall be deemed to be such a certificate.

NOTES

The Sex Discrimination (Amendment) Order 1988, SI 1988/249, art 2, provides that sub-ss (2), (3) shall "cease to have effect in relation to the determination of the question whether any act is rendered unlawful by virtue of Part II of that Act, or by Part III of that Act as it applies to vocational training, or by Part IV of that Act taken with Part II or with Part III as it so applies".

PART VIII
SUPPLEMENTAL

87 Short title and extent

(1) This Act may be cited as the Sex Discrimination Act 1975.

(2) This Act . . . does not extend to Northern Ireland.

NOTES

Sub-s (2): words omitted outside the scope of this work.

RACE RELATIONS ACT 1976

(c 74)

An Act to make fresh provision with respect to discrimination on racial grounds and relations between people of different racial groups; and to make in the Sex Discrimination Act 1975 amendments for bringing provisions in that Act relating to its administration and enforcement into conformity with the corresponding provisions in this Act

[22 November 1976]

PART I
DISCRIMINATION TO WHICH ACT APPLIES

1 Racial discrimination

(1) A person discriminates against another in any circumstances relevant for the purposes of any provision of this Act if—

(a) on racial grounds he treats that other less favourably than he treats or would treat other persons; or

(b) he applies to that other a requirement or condition which he applies or would apply equally to persons not of the same racial group as that other but—

(i) which is such that the proportion of persons of the same racial group as that other who can comply with it is considerably smaller than the proportion of persons not of that racial group who can comply with it; and

(ii) which he cannot show to be justifiable irrespective of the colour, race, nationality or ethnic or national origins of the person to whom it is applied; and

(iii) which is to the detriment of that other because he cannot comply with it.

(2) It is hereby declared that, for the purposes of this Act, segregating a person from other persons on racial grounds is treating him less favourably than they are treated.

3 Meaning of "racial grounds", "racial group" etc

(1) In this Act, unless the context otherwise requires—

"racial grounds" means any of the following grounds, namely colour, race nationality or ethnic or national origins;

"racial group" means a group of persons defined by reference to colour, race, nationality or ethnic or national origins, and references to a person's racial group refer to any racial group into which he falls.

(2) The fact that a racial group comprises two or more distinct racial groups does not prevent it from constituting a particular racial group for the purposes of this Act.

(3) In this Act—

(a) references to discrimination refer to any discrimination falling within section 1 or 2; and

(b) references to racial discrimination refer to any discrimination falling within section 1,

and related expressions shall be construed accordingly.

(4) A comparison of the case of a person of a particular racial group with that of a person not of that group under section 1(1) must be such that the relevant circumstances in the one case are the same, or not materially different, in the other.

PART III
DISCRIMINATION IN OTHER FIELDS

Education

17 Discrimination by bodies in charge of educational establishments

NOTES

The provisions of this section correspond to those in the Sex Discrimination Act 1975, s 22.

18 Other discrimination by local education authorities

(1) It is unlawful for a local education authority, in carrying out such of its functions under [the Education Acts] as do not fall under section 17, to do any act which constitutes racial discrimination.

(2) . . .

NOTES

Sub-s (1): words in square brackets substituted by the Education Act 1996, s 582(1), Sch 37, para 39.

Sub-s (2): outside the scope of this work.

[18A Discrimination by Further Education and Higher Education Funding Councils

It is unlawful for the Further Education Funding Council for England, the Further Education Funding Council for Wales, the Higher Education Funding Council for England or the Higher Education Funding Council for Wales in carrying out their functions under [the Education Acts], to do any act which constitutes racial discrimination.]

NOTES

Inserted by the Further and Higher Education Act 1992, s 93(1), Sch 8, Pt II, paras 84, 87.

Words in square brackets substituted by the Education Act 1996, s 582(1), Sch 37, para 40.

[18C Discrimination by Funding Agency for Schools or Schools Funding Council for Wales

It is unlawful for the Funding Agency for Schools or the Schools Funding Council for Wales in carrying out their functions imposed by or under the Education Acts to do any act which constitutes racial discrimination.]

NOTES

Inserted by the Education Act 1993, s 307(1), Sch 19, para 65; substituted by the Education Act 1996, s 582(1), Sch 37, para 41; repealed by the School Standards and Framework Act 1998, s 140(3), Sch 31, as from a day to be appointed.

[18D Discrimination by Teacher Training Agency

It is unlawful for the Teacher Training Agency in carrying out their functions under Part I of the Education Act 1994 to do any act which constitutes racial discrimination.]

NOTES

Inserted by the Education Act 1994, s 24, Sch 2, para 6(1), (3).

19 General duty in public sector of education

(1) Without prejudice to its obligation to comply with any other provision of this Act, a body to which this subsection applies shall be under a general duty to secure that facilities for education provided by it, and any ancillary benefits or services, are provided without racial discrimination.

(2)–(5) . . .

(6) Subsection (1) applies to—

- (a) local education authorities in England and Wales;
- (b) . . .
- (c) any other body which is a responsible body in relation to—
  - (i) an establishment falling within paragraph 1, 3 [*3A*] [3B] [. . .] of the table in section 17;
  - (ii) an establishment designated under section 24 (1) of the Sex Discrimination Act 1975 as falling within paragraph . . . (c) of section 24(2) of that Act;
  - (iii) an establishment designated under the said section 24(1) as falling within paragraph (b) of the said section 24(2) where the grants in question are payable under [section 485 of the Education Act 1996].
- [(d) the Further Education Funding Council for England and the Further Education Funding Council for Wales.]
- *[(e) the Funding Agency for Schools and the Schools Funding Council for Wales.]*
- [(f) the Teacher Training Agency.]

NOTES

Sub-ss (2)–(5): outside the scope of this work.

Sub-s (6): para (b) outside the scope of this work; in para (c)(i), figure in first pair of square brackets inserted by the Education Reform Act 1988, s 237(1), Sch 12, Pt I, para 19 and repealed by the School Standards and Framework Act 1998, s 140(3), Sch 31, as from a day to be appointed, figure in second pair of square brackets inserted by the Education Reform Act 1988, s 237(1), Sch 12, Pt III, para 79, substituted by the Further and Higher Education Act 1992, s 93(1), Sch 8, Pt II, paras 84, 88(1)(a), and words omitted outside the scope of this work; in para (c)(ii), words omitted repealed by the Education Reform Act 1988, s 237, Sch 12, Pt III, para 79, Sch 13, Pt II; in para (c)(iii), words in square brackets substituted by the Education Act 1996, s 582(1), Sch 37, para 42(1)(a), (4)(a); para (d) inserted by the Further and Higher Education Act 1992, s 93(1), Sch 8, Pt II, paras 84, 88(1)(b); para (e) inserted by the Education Act 1993, s 307(1), Sch 19, para 66(b), continued in force by the Education Act 1996, s 582(1), Sch 37, para 42(1)(b), (4)(b) and repealed by the School Standards and Framework Act 1998, s 140(3), Sch 31, as from a day to be appointed; para (f) inserted by the Education Act 1994, s 24, Sch 2, para 6(4)(b).

[*Planning*

19A Discrimination by planning authorities

(1) It is unlawful for a planning authority to discriminate against a person carrying out their planning functions.

(2) In this section "planning authority" means—
- (a) in England and Wales, a county, [county borough,] district or London borough council, [the Broads Authority] [a National Park authority or] a joint planning board, . . . , and
- (b) . . . ,

and includes an urban development corporation and a body having functions (whether as an enterprise zone authority or a body invited to prepare a scheme) under Schedule 32 to the Local Government, Planning and Land Act 1980.

(3) In this section "planning functions" means—
- (a) in England and Wales, functions under [the Town and Country Planning Act 1990, the Planning (Listed Buildings and Conservation Areas) Act 1990 and the Planning (Hazardous Substances) Act 1990], and such other functions as may be prescribed, and
- (b) . . . ,

and includes, in relation to an urban development corporation, planning functions under Part XVI of the Local Government, Planning and Land Act 1980 and, in relation to an enterprise zone authority or body invited to prepare an enterprise zone scheme, functions under Part XVIII of that Act.]

NOTES

Inserted by the Housing and Planning Act 1986, s 55.

Sub-s (2): in para (a), words in first pair of square brackets inserted by the Local Government (Wales) Act 1994, s 66(6), Sch 16, para 52, words in second pair of square brackets inserted by the Norfolk and Suffolk Broads Act 1988, s 2(5), (6), Sch 3, Pt I, para 29, words in third pair of square brackets inserted, and words omitted repealed, by the Environment Act 1995, ss 78, 120(3), Sch 10, para 15(1), Sch 24; para (b) outside the scope of this work.

Sub-s (3): in para (a), words in square brackets substituted by the Planning (Consequential Provisions) Act 1990, s 4, Sch 2, para 36; para (b) outside the scope of this work.

Goods, facilities, services and premises

20 Discrimination in provision of goods, facilities or services

(1) It is unlawful for any person concerned with the provision (for payment or not) of goods, facilities or services to the public or a section of the public to discriminate against a person who seeks to obtain or use those goods, facilities or services—
- (a) by refusing or deliberately omitting to provide him with any of them; or
- (b) by refusing or deliberately omitting to provide him with goods, facilities or services of the like quality, in the like manner and on the like terms as are normal in the first-mentioned person's case in relation to other members of the public or (where the person so seeking belongs to a section of the public) to other members of that section.

(2) The following are examples of the facilities and services mentioned in subsection (1)—
- (a) access to and use of any place which members of the public are permitted to enter;

(b) accommodation in a hotel, boarding house or other similar establishment;
(c) facilities by way of banking or insurance or for grants, loans, credit or finance;
(d) facilities for education;
(e) facilities for entertainment, recreation or refreshment;
(f) facilities for transport or travel;
(g) the services of any profession or trade, or any local or other public authority.

21 Discrimination in disposal or management of premises

NOTES

The provisions of this section correspond to those in the Sex Discrimination Act 1975, s 30.

22 Exception from ss 20(1) and 21: small dwellings

(1) Sections 20(1) and 21 do not apply to the provision by a person of accommodation in any premises, or the disposal of premises by him, if—

(a) that person or a near relative of his ("the relevant occupier") resides, and intends to continue to reside, on the premises; and
(b) there is on the premises, in addition to the accommodation occupied by the relevant occupier, accommodation (not being storage accommodation or means of access) shared by the relevant occupier with other persons residing on the premises who are not members of his household; and
(c) the premises are small premises.

(2) Premises shall be treated for the purposes of this section as small premises if—

(a) in the case of premises comprising residential accommodation for one or more households (under separate letting or similar agreements) in addition to the accommodation occupied by the relevant occupier, there is not normally residential accommodation for more than two such households and only the relevant occupier and any member of his household reside in the accommodation occupied by him;
(b) in the case of premises not falling within paragraph (a), there is not normally residential accommodation on the premises for more than six persons in addition to the relevant occupier and any members of his household.

23 Further exceptions from ss 20(1) and 21

(1) Sections 20(1) and 21 do not apply—

(a) to discrimination which is rendered unlawful by any provision of Part II or section 17 or 18; or
(b) to discrimination which would be rendered unlawful by any provision of Part II but for any of the following provisions, namely sections 4(3), 5(1)(b), 6, 7(4), 9 and 14(4).

(2) Section 20 (1) does not apply to anything done by a person as a participant in arrangements under which he (for reward or not) takes into his home, and treats as if they were members of his family, children, elderly persons, or persons requiring a special degree of care and attention.

PART VI
GENERAL EXCEPTIONS FROM PARTS II TO IV

35 Special needs of racial groups in regard to education, training or welfare

Nothing in Parts II to IV shall render unlawful any act done in affording persons of a particular racial group access to facilities or services to meet the special needs of persons of that group in regard to their education, training or welfare, or any ancillary benefits.

NOTES

The provisions of this Part correspond to those in the Sex Discrimination Act 1975, ss 44–52.

PART VII
THE COMMISSION FOR RACIAL EQUALITY

General

43 Establishment and duties of Commission

(1) There shall be a body of Commissioners named the Commission for Racial Equality consisting of at least eight but not more than fifteen individuals each appointed by the Secretary of State on a full-time or part-time basis, which shall have the following duties—

- (a) to work towards the elimination of discrimination;
- (b) to promote equality of opportunity, and good relations, between persons of different racial groups generally; and
- (c) to keep under review the working of this Act and, when they are so required by the Secretary of State or otherwise think it necessary, draw up and submit to the Secretary of State proposals for amending it.

(2) The Secretary of State shall appoint—

- (a) one of the Commissioners to be chairman of the Commission; and
- (b) either one or more of the Commissioners (as the Secretary of State thinks fit) to be deputy chairman or deputy chairmen of the Commission.

(3) The Secretary of State may by order amend subsection (1) so far as it regulates the number of Commissioners.

(4) Schedule 1 shall have effect with respect to the Commission.

(5) The Race Relations Board and the Community Relations Commission are hereby abolished.

44 Assistance to organisations

(1) The Commission may give financial or other assistance to any organisation appearing to the Commission to be concerned with the promotion of equality of opportunity, and good relations, between persons of different racial groups, but shall not give any such financial assistance out of money provided (through the Secretary of State) by Parliament except with the approval of the Secretary of State given with the consent of the Treasury.

(2) . . .

NOTES

Sub-s (2): outside the scope of this work.

45 Research and education

(1) The Commission may undertake or assist (financially or otherwise) the undertaking by other persons of any research, and any educational activities, which appear to the Commission necessary or expedient for the purposes of section 43(1).

(2) The Commission may make charges for educational or other facilities or services made available by them.

46 Annual reports

(1) As soon as practicable after the end of each calendar year the Commission shall make to the Secretary of State a report on their activities during the year (an "annual report").

(2) Each annual report shall include a general survey of developments, during the period to which it relates, in respect of matters falling within the scope of the Commission's functions.

(3) The Secretary of State shall lay a copy of every annual report before each House of Parliament, and shall cause the report to be published.

Codes of practice

47 Codes of practice

(1) The Commission may issue codes of practice containing such practical guidance as the Commission think fit for [all or any] of the following purposes, namely—

(a) the elimination of discrimination in the field of employment;

(b) the promotion of equality of opportunity in that field between persons of different racial groups;

[(c) the elimination of discrimination in the field of housing . . . ;

(d) the promotion of equality of opportunity in the field of . . . housing between persons of different racial groups].

(2)–(11) . . .

NOTES

Sub-s (1): words in first pair of square brackets substituted, and paras (c), (d) added, by the Housing Act 1988, s 137(1), (2); words omitted repealed by the Local Government and Housing Act 1989, ss 180, 194(4), Sch 12, Pt II.

Sub-ss (2)–(11): outside the scope of this work.

Investigations

48 Power to conduct formal investigations

(1) Without prejudice to their general power to do anything requisite for the performance of their duties under section 43(1), the Commission may if they think fit, and shall if required by the Secretary of State, conduct a formal investigation for any purpose connected with the carrying out of those duties.

(2), (3) . . .

NOTES

Sub-ss (2), (3): outside the scope of this work.

50 Power to obtain information

(1) For the purposes of a formal investigation the Commission, by a notice in the prescribed form served on him in the prescribed manner—

(a) may require any person to furnish such written information as may be described in the notice, and may specify the time at which, and the manner and form in which, the information is to be furnished;

(b) may require any person to attend at such time and place as is specified in the notice and give oral information about, and produce all documents in his possession or control relating to, any matter specified in the notice.

(2) Except as provided by section 60, a notice shall be served under subsection (1) only where—

(a) service of the notice was authorised by an order made by the Secretary of State; or

(b) the terms of reference of the investigation state that the Commission believe that a person named in them may have done or may be doing acts of all or any of the following descriptions—

(i) unlawful discriminatory acts;

(ii) contraventions of section 28; and

(iii) contraventions of sections 29, 30 or 31,

and confine the investigation to those acts.

(3) A notice under subsection (1) shall not require a person—

(a) to give information, or produce any documents, which he could not be compelled to give in evidence, or produce, in civil proceedings before the High Court or the Court of Session; or

(b) to attend at any place unless the necessary expenses of his journey to and from that place are paid or tendered to him.

(4) If a person fails to comply with a notice served on him under subsection (1) or the Commission have reasonable cause to believe that he intends not to comply with it, the Commission may apply to a county court or, in Scotland, a sheriff court for an order requiring him to comply with it or with such directions for the like purpose as may be contained in the order.

(5) [Section 55 of the County Courts Act 1984] (penalty for neglecting witness summons) shall apply to failure without reasonable excuse to comply with an order of a county court under subsection (4) as it applies in the cases provided in the [said section 55]; and paragraph 73 of Schedule 1 to the Sheriff Courts (Scotland) Act 1907 (power of sheriff to grant second diligence for compelling the attendance of witnesses or havers) shall apply to an order of a sheriff court under subsection (4) as it applies in proceedings in the sheriff court.

(6) A person commits an offence if he—

(a) wilfully alters, suppresses, conceals or destroys a document which he has been required by a notice or order under this section to produce; or

(b) in complying with such a notice or order, knowingly or recklessly makes any statement which is false in a material particular,

and shall be liable on summary conviction to a fine not exceeding [level 5 on the standard scale].

(7) Proceedings for an offence under subsection (6) may (without prejudice to any jurisdiction exercisable apart from this subsection) be instituted—

(a) against any person at any place at which he has an office or other place of business;

(b) against an individual at any place where he resides, or at which he is for the time being.

NOTES

Sub-s (5): words in square brackets substituted by the County Courts Act 1984, s 148(1), Sch 2, Pt V, para 61.

Sub-s (6): maximum fine increased and converted to a level on the standard scale by the Criminal Justice Act 1982, ss 37, 38, 46.

51 Recommendations and reports on formal investigations

(1) If in the light of any of their findings in a formal investigation it appears to the Commission necessary or expedient, whether during the course of the investigation or after its conclusion—

(a) to make to any person, with a view to promoting equality of opportunity between persons of different racial groups who are affected by any of his activities, recommendations for changes in his policies or procedures, or as to any other matters; or

(b) to make to the Secretary of State any recommendations, whether for changes in the law or otherwise,

the Commission shall make those recommendations accordingly.

(2) The Commission shall prepare a report of their findings in any formal investigation conducted by them.

(3) If the formal investigation is one required by the Secretary of State—

(a) the Commission shall deliver the report to the Secretary of State; and

(b) the Secretary of State shall cause the report to be published,

and, unless required by the Secretary of State, the Commission shall not publish the report.

(4) If the formal investigation is not one required by the Secretary of State, the Commission shall either publish the report, or make it available for inspection in accordance with subsection (5).

(5) Where under subsection (4) a report is to be made available for inspection, any person shall be entitled, on payment of such fee (if any) as may be determined by the Commission—

(a) to inspect the report during ordinary office hours and take copies of all or any part of the report; or

(b) to obtain from the Commission a copy, certified by the Commission to be correct, of the report.

(6) . . .

(7) The Commission shall give general notice of the place or places where, and the times when, reports may be inspected under subsection (5).

NOTES

Sub-s (6): outside the scope of this work.

52 Restriction on disclosure of information

(1) No information given to the Commission by any person ("the informant") in connection with a formal investigation shall be disclosed by the Commission, or by any person who is or has been a Commissioner, additional Commissioner or employee of the Commission, except—

(a) on the order of any court; or

(b) with the informant's consent; or

(c) in the form of a summary or other general statement published by the Commission which does not identify the informant or any other person to whom the information relates; or

(d) in a report of the investigation published by the Commission or made available for inspection under section 51(5); or

(e) to the Commissioners, additional Commissioners or employees of the Commission, or, so far as may be necessary for the proper performance of the functions of the Commission, to other persons; or

(f) for the purpose of any civil proceedings under this Act to which the Commission are a party, or any criminal proceedings.

(2) Any person who discloses information in contravention of subsection (1) commits an offence and shall be liable on summary conviction to a fine not exceeding [level 5 on the standard scale].

(3) In preparing any report for publication or for inspection the Commission shall exclude, so far as is consistent with their duties and the object of the report, any matter which relates to the private affairs of any individual or the business interests of any person where the publication of that matter might, in the opinion of the Commission, prejudicially affect that individual or person.

NOTES

Sub-s (2): maximum fine increased and converted to a level on the standard scale by the Criminal Justice Act 1982, ss 37, 38, 46.

PART X
SUPPLEMENTAL

71 Local authorities: general statutory duty

[(1)] Without prejudice to their obligation to comply with any other provision of this Act, it shall be the duty of every local authority to make appropriate arrangements with a view to securing that their various functions are carried out with due regard to the need—

(a) to eliminate unlawful racial discrimination; and

(b) to promote equality of opportunity and good relations, between persons of different racial groups[;

and in this section "local authority" includes . . . [a police authority established under [section 3 of the Police Act 1996][, the Service Authority for the National Criminal Intelligence Service, the Service Authority for the National Crime Squad] and] a joint authority established by Part IV of the Local Government Act 1985.]

[The Broads Authority [and every National Park Authority] shall be treated as a local authority for the purposes of this section.]

(2) . . .

NOTES

Section renumbered as sub-s (1), and sub-s (2) added, by the Local Government etc (Scotland) Act 1994, s 180(1), Sch 13, para 108, as from 1 April 1996.

Sub-s (1): words in first (outer) pair of square brackets added by the Local Government Act 1985, s 84, Sch 14, Pt II, para 54; words omitted repealed by the Education Reform Act 1988, s 237(2), Sch 13, Pt I; words in second (inner) pair of square brackets inserted by the Police and Magistrates' Courts Act 1994, s 43, Sch 4, Pt II, para 51; words in third (inner) pair of square brackets substituted by the Police Act 1996, s 103, Sch 7, para 1(2)(l), as from 22 August 1996; words in fourth (inner) pair of square brackets inserted by the Police Act 1997, s 134(1), Sch 9, para 36; words in fifth (outer) pair of square brackets added by the Norfolk and Suffolk Broads Act 1988, s 21, Sch 6, para 16; words in sixth (inner) pair of square brackets inserted by the Environment Act 1995, s 78, Sch 10, para 15(2), as from 19 September 1995.

Sub-s (2):outside the scope of this work.

Modification: modified by the Waste Regulation and Disposal (Authorities) Order 1985, SI 1985/1884, art 10, Sch 3.

80 Short title and extent

(1) This Act may be cited as the Race Relations Act 1976.

(2) This Act, except so far as it amends or repeals any provision of the House of Commons Disqualification Act 1975 or the Northern Ireland Assembly Disqualification Act 1975, does not extend to Northern Ireland.

EUROPEAN PARLIAMENTARY ELECTIONS ACT 1978

(c 10)

An Act to make provision for and in connection with the election of representatives to the European Parliament, and to prevent any treaty providing for any increase in the powers of the European Parliament from being ratified by the United Kingdom unless approved by Act of Parliament

[5 May 1978]

1 Election of representatives to the European Parliament

The representatives of the people of the United Kingdom in the European Parliament ... shall be elected in accordance with this Act.

NOTES

Words omitted repealed by the European Communities (Amendment) Act 1986, s 4(3), Schedule.

2 Number of representatives

The number of representatives to the European Parliament to be elected in the United Kingdom shall be [87]; and of those representatives—

(a) [71] shall be elected in England;
(b) . . .
(c) [5] shall be elected in Wales; and
(d) 3 shall be elected in Northern Ireland.

NOTES

Figures in square brackets substituted by the European Parliamentary Elections Act 1993, s 1(1).

Para (b): outside the scope of this work.

3 Method of election

European Parliamentary elections shall be held and conducted in accordance with the provisions of Schedule 1 to this Act (with Schedule 2) under the simple majority system (for Great Britain) and the single transferable vote system (for Northern Ireland).

4 Double voting

(1) Without prejudice to any enactment relating to voting offences as applied by regulations under this Act to elections of representatives to the European Parliament held in the United Kingdom, a person shall be guilty of an offence if, on any occasion when under Article 9 elections to the European Parliament are held in all the member States, he votes otherwise than as a proxy more than once in those elections, whether in the United Kingdom or elsewhere.

(2) . . .

NOTES

Sub-s (2): outside the scope of this work.

6 Parliamentary approval of treaties increasing European Parliament's powers

(1) No treaty which provides for any increase in the powers of the European Parliament shall be ratified by the United Kingdom unless it has been approved by an Act of Parliament.

(2) In this section "treaty" includes any international agreement, and any protocol or annex to a treaty or international agreement.

9 Citation etc

(1) This Act may be cited as the European Parliamentary Elections Act 1978.

(2) Any power to make orders or regulations conferred by this Act shall be exercisable by statutory instrument; and any power to make an order under any provision of this Act includes power to vary or revoke a previous order made under that provision.

SCHEDULES

SCHEDULE 1

Section 3

SIMPLE MAJORITY SYSTEM (FOR GREAT BRITAIN) WITH STV (FOR NORTHERN IRELAND)

European Parliamentary constituencies

1.—(1) Representatives to the European Parliament shall be elected in Great Britain for the European Parliamentary constituencies for the time being specified in an Order in Council under Schedule 2 to this Act, and in Northern Ireland for a single European Parliamentary constituency comprising the whole of Northern Ireland; and there shall be—

(a) one representative for each such constituency in Great Britain; and

(b) three representatives for the European Parliamentary constituency of Northern Ireland.

(2) There shall be a total of [85] European Parliamentary constituencies, of which—
- (a) [71] shall be in England;
- (b) . . .
- (c) [5] shall be in Wales;
- (d) 1 shall be that of Northern Ireland.

NOTES

Figures in square brackets in sub-para (2) substituted by the European Parliamentary Elections Act 1993, s 1(2); sub-para (2)(b) outside the scope of this work.

European Parliamentary elections

2.—(1) The persons entitled to vote as electors at a European Parliamentary election in any particular European Parliamentary constituency shall be—
- (a) those who, on the day appointed under paragraph 3 below for the election, would be entitled to vote as electors at a parliamentary election in a parliamentary constituency wholly or partly comprised in the European Parliamentary constituency (excluding any person not registered in the register of parliamentary electors at an address within the European Parliamentary constituency); and
- (b) peers who, on that day, would be entitled to vote at a local government election in an electoral area wholly or partly comprised in the European Parliamentary constituency (excluding any peer not registered at an address within the European Parliamentary constituency for the purposes of local government elections).

(2) In a European Parliamentary election in the constituency of Northern Ireland each vote shall be a single transferable vote, that is to say a vote—
- (a) capable of being given so as to indicate the voter's order of preference for the candidates for election as representatives for the constituency; and
- (b) capable of being transferred to the next choice—
  - (i) when the vote is not required to give a prior choice the necessary quota of votes; or
  - (ii) when, owing to the deficiency in the number of votes given for a prior choice, that choice is eliminated from the list of candidates.

(3) Subject to the provisions of this and the following paragraph, the Secretary of State may by regulations make provision—
- (a) as to the conduct of European Parliamentary elections (including the registration of electors and the limitation of candidates' election expenses); and
- (b) as to the questioning of such an election and the consequences of irregularities.

(4) . . .

(5) Section [26] of the Welsh Language Act [1993] (power to prescribe Welsh version) shall apply in relation to regulations under this paragraph as it applies in relation to [Acts of Parliament].

(6) No regulations shall be made under this paragraph unless a draft thereof has been laid before Parliament and approved by a resolution of each House of Parliament.

NOTES

Sub-para (4): outside the scope of this work.

Sub-para (5): words in square brackets substituted by the Welsh Language Act 1993, s 35(3).

Times of elections

3.—(1) Each general election of representatives to the European Parliament shall be held on a day appointed by order of the Secretary of State.

(2) Subject to sub-paragraph (4) below, where, a European Parliamentary election having been held in any particular European Parliamentary constituency, the seat of a representative to the European Parliament is or falls vacant, a by-election shall be held to fill the vacancy.

(3) A by-election in pursuance of sub-paragraph (2) above shall be held on a day appointed by order of the Secretary of State, being a day not later than six months after the occurrence of either of the following events, namely—

- (a) notification of the vacancy by the European Parliament under Article 12(2); or
- (b) declaration of the vacancy by the Secretary of State.

(4) A by-election need not be held if the latest date for holding it would fall on or after the relevant Thursday (that is to say the Thursday with which the next period for holding elections to the European Parliament in all the member States would begin in accordance with Article 10(2) in the absence of any determination by the Council thereunder).

(5) A statutory instrument made under this paragraph shall be laid before Parliament after being made.

4. . . .

Disqualification for office of representative to European Parliament

5.—(1) Subject to sub-paragraph (3) below, and without prejudice to Article 6(1) (incompatibility of office of representative with certain offices in or connected with Community institutions), a person is disqualified for the office of representative to the European Parliament if—

- (a) he is disqualified, whether under the House of Commons Disqualification Act 1975 or otherwise, for membership of the House of Commons; or
- (b) he is a Lord of Appeal in Ordinary.

(2) A person is disqualified for the office of representative to the European Parliament for a particular European Parliamentary constituency if he is under section 1(2) of the House of Commons Disqualification Act 1975 disqualified for membership of the House of Commons for any particular parliamentary constituency wholly or partly comprised in that European Parliamentary constituency.

[(2A) A citizen of the Union, determined in accordance with article 8.1 of the Treaty establishing the European Community (as amended by Title II of the Treaty on European Union), who is not a Commonwealth citizen or a citizen of the Republic of Ireland is disqualified under this paragraph for the office of representative to the European Parliament if he is disqualified for that office through a criminal law or civil law decision under the law of the Member State of which he is a national.

(2B) In sub-paragraph (2A) above "a criminal law or civil law decision" has the same meaning as it has in the directive of the Council of the European Communities No 93/109/EC.]

(3) A person is not disqualified for office as a representative to the European Parliament by reason only—

- (a) that he is a peer, whether of the United Kingdom, Great Britain, England or Scotland; or
- (b) that he has been ordained or is a minister of any religious denomination; or
- (c) that he holds an office mentioned in section 4 of the House of Commons Disqualification Act 1975 (stewardship of Chiltern Hundreds etc); or
- (d) that he holds any of the offices for the time being described in Part II or Part III of Schedule 1 to the House of Commons Disqualification Act 1975 which are for the time being designated in an order by the Secretary of State as non-disqualifying offices in relation to the European Parliament [or
- (e) that he is disqualified under section 3 of the Act of Settlement (disqualification for membership of either House of Parliament of persons born out of the Kingdoms of England, Scotland or Ireland or the dominions thereunto belonging except those who are Commonwealth citizens or citizens of the Republic of Ireland), provided that he is a citizen of the Union, determined in accordance with article 8.1 of the Treaty establishing the European Community (as amended by Title II of the Treaty on European Union), who is resident in the United Kingdom.]

(4) If any person disqualified under this paragraph for the office of representative to the European Parliament, or for the office of representative to the European Parliament for a particular European Parliamentary constituency, is elected as a representative to the European Parliament or as a representative for that constituency, as the case may be, his election shall be void.

(5) If a representative to the European Parliament becomes disqualified under this paragraph for the office of representative to the European Parliament or for the office of representative to the European Parliament for the European Parliamentary constituency for which he was elected, his seat shall be vacated.

(6) A statutory instrument made under this paragraph shall be subject to annulment in pursuance of a resolution of either House of Parliament.

NOTES

Para 4: outside the scope of this work.

Para 5: sub-paras (2A), (2B) inserted, and sub-para (3)(e) and word "or" preceding it added, by the European Parliamentary Elections (Changes to the Franchise and Qualification of Representatives) Regulations 1994, SI 1994/342, reg 3.

Judicial proceedings as to disqualification under paragraph 5

6.—(1) Any person who claims that a person purporting to hold office as a representative to the European Parliament is disqualified or was disqualified at the time of, or at any time since, his election may apply to the court for a declaration or, as the case may be, declarator to that effect, and the decision of the court on the application shall be final.

(2)–(4) . . .

(5) The court for the purposes of this paragraph is the High Court, the Court of Session or the High Court of Justice in Northern Ireland according as the European Parliamentary constituency to which the application relates is in England and Wales, or Scotland, or Northern Ireland; and in this paragraph "disqualified" means disqualified under paragraph 5 above for the office of representative to the European Parliament (whether generally or in relation to a particular European Parliamentary constituency).

NOTES

Sub-paras (2)–(4): outside the scope of this work.

SCHEDULE 2

Section 3, Sch 1, para 1

EUROPEAN PARLIAMENTARY CONSTITUENCIES IN GREAT BRITAIN

PART I

Reports of Boundary Commission and Orders in Council

[1. If—

(a) an Order in Council has been made under [the 1986 Act] giving effect, with or without modifications, to the recommendations contained in a report submitted to the Secretary of State under [section 3(1)] of that Act by the Boundary Commission for any part of Great Britain; or

(b) the Boundary Commission for any part of Great Britain have submitted a report to the Secretary of State under [section 3(1)] stating that, in the opinion of the Commission, no alteration is required to be made in the parliamentary constituencies into which that part of Great Britain is divided;

the Boundary Commission shall thereupon proceed to consider the representation in the European Parliament of the part of Great Britain with which they are concerned and shall as soon as may be after that time submit to the Secretary of State a supplementary report in accordance with paragraph 2 below.]

2. [The supplementary report which the Boundary Commission for any part of Great Britain is required under paragraph 1 above to submit to the Secretary of State shall be a] report either—

(a) showing the European Parliamentary constituencies into which they recommend that that part of Great Britain should be divided in order to give effect to the provisions of paragraph 1(2) of Schedule 1 to this Act and Part II of this Schedule; or

(b) stating that, in the opinion of the Commission, no alteration is required to be made in the European Parliamentary constituencies in that part of Great Britain in order to give effect to those provisions.

[3. If—

(a) an Order in Council has been made under [the 1986 Act] giving effect, with or without modifications, to recommendations for the alteration of any particular parliamentary constituency or constituencies contained in a report submitted to the Secretary of State under [section 3(3)] of that Act by the Boundary Commission for any part of Great Britain; and

(b) the result of the alterations in parliamentary constituencies made by the Order is that paragraph 9 below is no longer complied with in relation to one or more of the European Parliamentary constituencies into which that part of Great Britain is divided;

the Boundary Commission shall thereupon proceed to consider in what manner the European Parliamentary constituency or constituencies affected should be altered in order that paragraph 9 be complied with and shall as soon as may be after that time submit to the Secretary of State a supplementary report showing the alterations which they recommend should be made in the European Parliamentary constituency or constituencies for that purpose.]

[4. A supplementary report of a Boundary Commission under this Schedule showing the European Parliamentary constituencies into which they recommend that any area should be divided shall state, as respects each European Parliamentary constituency, the name by which they recommend that it should be known.

4A.—(1) Where the Boundary Commission for any part of Great Britain intend to consider making a supplementary report under this Schedule, they shall, by notice in writing, inform the Secretary of State accordingly, and a copy of the notice shall be published—

(a) in a case where it was given by the Boundary Commission for England or the Boundary Commission for Wales, in the London Gazette, . . .

(b) . . .

(2) As soon as may be after a Boundary Commission have submitted a supplementary report to the Secretary of State under this Schedule, he shall lay the report before Parliament together, except in a case where the report states that no alteration is required to be made in respect of the part of Great Britain with which the Commission are concerned, with the draft of an Order in Council for giving effect, whether with or without modifications, to the recommendations contained in the report.

4B.—(1) The draft of any Order in Council laid before Parliament by the Secretary of State under this Schedule for giving effect, whether with or without modifications, to the recommendations contained in a supplementary report of a Boundary Commission may make provision for any matters which appear to him to be incidental to, or consequential on, the recommendations.

(2) Where any such draft gives effect to any such recommendations with modifications, the Secretary of State shall lay before Parliament together with the draft a statement of the reasons for the modifications.

(3) If any such draft is approved by resolution of each House of Parliament, the Secretary of State shall submit it to Her Majesty in Council.

(4) If a motion for the approval of any such draft is rejected by either House of Parliament or withdrawn by leave of the House, the Secretary of State may amend the draft and lay the amended draft before Parliament, and if the draft as so amended is approved by resolution of each House of Parliament, the Secretary of State shall submit it to Her Majesty in Council.

(5) Where the draft of an Order in Council is submitted to Her Majesty in Council under this Schedule, Her Majesty in Council may make an Order in terms of the draft which (subject to paragraph 8 below) shall come into force on such date as may be specified in the Order and shall have effect notwithstanding anything in any enactment.

(6) The validity of any Order in Council purporting to be made under this Schedule and reciting that a draft of the Order has been approved by resolution of each House of Parliament shall not be called in question in any legal proceedings whatsoever.]

5.—(1) Where a Boundary Commission have provisionally determined to make recommendations with respect to any European Parliamentary constituency, they shall publish a notice under this paragraph in such manner as they think best calculated to bring it to the attention of those concerned.

(2) A notice under this paragraph relating to a European Parliamentary constituency shall state—

- (a) the effect of the proposed recommendations with respect to that constituency and (except where the proposed recommendations do not involve any alteration in that European Parliamentary constituency) that copies of the recommendations are open to inspection at one or more specified places within each parliamentary constituency included in that European Parliamentary constituency; and
- (b) that representations with respect to the proposed recommendations may be made to the Commission within one month after the first publication of the notice,

and the Commission shall take into consideration any representations duly made in accordance with any such notice.

(3) . . .

[5A.—(1) A Boundary Commission may, if they think fit, cause a local inquiry to be held in respect of any European Parliamentary constituency or constituencies.

(2) Where on the publication of the notice under paragraph 5 above of a recommendation of a Boundary Commission for the alteration of any European Parliamentary constituencies, the Commission receive any representation objecting to the proposed recommendation from an interested authority or from a body of electors numbering five hundred or more, the Commission shall not make the recommendation unless, since the publication of the notice a local inquiry has been held in respect of the European Parliamentary constituencies.

(3) Where a local inquiry was held in respect of the European Parliamentary constituencies before the publication of the notice mentioned in sub-paragraph (2) above, that sub-paragraph shall not apply if the Commission, after considering the matters discussed at the local inquiry, the nature of the representations received on the publication of the notice and any other relevant circumstances, are of opinion that a further local inquiry would not be justified.

(4) In sub-paragraph (2) above, "interested authority" and "elector" respectively means, in relation to any recommendation, a local authority whose area is wholly or partly comprised in the European Parliamentary constituencies affected by the recommendation, and an elector for any of those European Parliamentary constituencies; and for this purpose "local authority" means—

(a) in England . . . , the council of a county, London borough or district,

[(aa) in Wales, the council of a county or county borough;] and

(b) . . .]

6, 7. . . .

8.—(1) An Order in Council under [this Schedule] shall apply to the first general election of representatives to the European Parliament held after the Order comes into force and (subject to any further Order in Council) to any subsequent European Parliamentary election, but shall not affect any earlier election.

(2) The validity of a European Parliamentary election held in a European Parliamentary constituency consisting of an area determined by an Order in Council made under [this Schedule], being an Order which applied to that election, shall not be affected by any alteration made in any parliamentary constituency since the making of that Order.

NOTES

Para 1: substituted by the European Parliamentary Elections Act 1981, s 1(1); words in square brackets in sub-paras (a), (b) substituted by the Parliamentary Constituencies Act 1986, s 7, Sch 3, para 5(1), (2).

Para 2: words in square brackets substituted by the European Parliamentary Elections Act 1981, s 1(2).

Para 3: substituted by the European Parliamentary Elections Act 1981, s 1(3); words in square brackets in sub-para (a) substituted by the Parliamentary Constituencies Act 1986, s 7, Sch 3, para 5(1), (3).

Paras 4, 4A, 4B substituted for original para 4 by the Parliamentary Constituencies Act 1986, s 7, Sch 3, para 5(1), (4).

Para 4A: sub-para (1)(b) outside the scope of this work.

Para 5: sub-para (3) outside the scope of this work.

Para 5A: inserted by the Parliamentary Constituencies Act 1986, s 7, Sch 3, para 5(1), (6); words omitted from sub-para (4)(a) repealed, and sub-para (4)(aa) inserted, by the Local Government (Wales) Act 1994, s 66(6), (8), Sch 16, para 54(2), Sch 18; sub-para (4)(b) outside the scope of this work.

Paras 6, 7: outside the scope of this work.

Para 8: words in square brackets substituted by the Parliamentary Constituencies Act 1986, s 7, Sch 3, para 5(1), (9).

PART II

Division of Great Britain into European Parliamentary Constituencies

9. In Great Britain—
(a) each European Parliamentary constituency shall consist of an area that includes two or more parliamentary constituencies; and
(b) no parliamentary constituency shall be included partly in one European Parliamentary constituency and partly in another.

10. The electorate of any European Parliamentary constituency in Great Britain shall be as near the electoral quota as is reasonably practicable having regard, where appropriate, to special geographical considerations.

PART III

Interpretation

11. In this Schedule—
["the 1986 Act" means the Parliamentary Constituencies Act 1986];
"Boundary Commission" means a Boundary Commission [provided for by the 1986 Act] other than the Boundary Commission for Northern Ireland.

12. In Part II of this Schedule and this paragraph in their application to a part of Great Britain for which there is a Boundary Commission—
"electoral quota" means the number obtained by dividing the electorate of that part of Great Britain by the number of European Parliamentary constituencies specified for that part in paragraph 1(2) of Schedule 1 to this Act;
"electorate" means—
(a) in relation to a European Parliamentary constituency, the number of persons whose names appear on the relevant registers for that European Parliamentary constituency in force on the enumeration date;

(b) in relation to that part of Great Britain, the number of persons whose names appear on the relevant registers for that part of Great Britain in force on the enumeration date;

. . . . .

"the relevant registers" means the following registers under the Representation of the People Acts, namely—

(a) in relation to a European Parliamentary constituency, the registers of parliamentary electors to be used at a European Parliamentary election in that European Parliamentary constituency;

(b) in relation to that part of Great Britain, the registers of parliamentary electors for the parliamentary constituencies in that part.

NOTES

Para 11: words in square brackets substituted by the Parliamentary Constituencies Act 1986, s 7, Sch 3, para 5(1), (10).

Para 12: definition "enumeration date" omitted outside the scope of this work.

SUPPRESSION OF TERRORISM ACT 1978

(c 26)

An Act to give effect to the European Convention on the Suppression of Terrorism; to amend the law relating to the extradition of criminals and the obtaining of evidence for criminal proceedings outside the United Kingdom; to confer jurisdiction in respect of certain offences committed outside the United Kingdom; and for connected purposes

[30 June 1978]

1 Cases in which certain offences are not to be regarded as of a political character

(1) This section applies to any offence of which a person is accused or has been convicted outside the United Kingdom if the act constituting the offence, or the equivalent act, would, if it took place in any part of the United Kingdom or, in the case of an extra-territorial offence, in corresponding circumstances outside the United Kingdom, constitute one of the offences listed in Schedule 1 to this Act.

(2) For the purposes mentioned in subsection (3) below—

(a) no offence to which this section applies shall be regarded as an offence of a political character; and

(b) no proceedings in respect of an offence to which this section applies shall be regarded as a criminal matter of a political character or as criminal proceedings of a political character.

(3) Those purposes are—

(a), (b) . . .

(c) the purposes of the Backing of Warrants (Republic of Ireland) Act 1965 in relation to any warrant issued in the Republic of Ireland to which this paragraph applies by virtue of an order under subsection (4) below; . . .

(d) . . .

(4), (5) . . .

NOTES

Sub-s (3): paras (a), (b) repealed by the Extradition Act 1989, s 37(1), Sch 2; para (d), together with word "and" immediately preceding it, repealed by the Criminal Justice (International Co-operation) Act 1990, s 31(3), Sch 5.

Sub-ss (4), (5): outside the scope of this work.

4 Jurisdiction in respect of offences committed outside United Kingdom

(1) If a person, whether a citizen of the United Kingdom and Colonies or not, does in a convention country any act which, if he had done it in a part of the United Kingdom, would have made him guilty in that part of the United Kingdom of—

- (a) an offence mentioned in paragraph 1, 2, 4, 5, 10, 11, [11B,] 12, 13, 14 or 15 of Schedule 1 to this Act; or
- (b) an offence of attempting to commit any offence so mentioned,

he shall, in that part of the United Kingdom, be guilty of the offence or offences aforesaid of which the act would have made him guilty if he had done it there.

(2) . . .

(3) If a person who is a national of a convention country but not a citizen of the United Kingdom and Colonies does outside the United Kingdom and that convention country any act which makes him in that convention country guilty of an offence and which, if he had been a citizen of the United Kingdom and Colonies, would have made him in any part of the United Kingdom guilty of an offence mentioned in paragraph 1, 2 or 13 of Schedule 1 to this Act, he shall, in any part of the United Kingdom, be guilty of the offence or offences aforesaid of which the act would have made him guilty if he had been such a citizen.

(4) Proceedings for an offence which [(disregarding the provisions of the Internationally Protected Persons Act 1978[, the Nuclear Material (Offences) Act 1983 and the United Nations Personnel Act 1997])] would not be an offence apart from this section shall not be instituted—

- (a) in Northern Ireland, except by or with the consent of the Attorney General for Northern Ireland; or
- (b) in England and Wales, except by or with the consent of the Attorney General;

and references to a consent provision in Article 7(3) to (5) of the Prosecution of Offences (Northern Ireland) Order 1972 (which relates to consents to prosecutions) shall include so much of this subsection as precedes paragraph (b).

(5), (6) . . .

(7) For the purposes of this section any act done—

- (a) on board a ship registered in a convention country, being an act which, if the ship had been registered in the United Kingdom, would have constituted an offence within the jurisdiction of the Admiralty; or
- (b) on board an aircraft registered in a convention country while the aircraft is in flight elsewhere than in or over that country; or
- (c) on board a hovercraft registered in a convention country while the hovercraft is in journey elsewhere than in or over that country,

shall be treated as done in that convention country; [and subsection (4) of section 92 of the Civil Aviation Act 1982 (definition of "in flight" or, as applied to hovercraft, "in journey") shall apply for the purposes of this subsection as it applies for the purposes of that section].

NOTES

Sub-s (1): figure in square brackets inserted by the Child Abduction Act 1984, s 11(4).

Sub-ss (2), (6): repealed by the Internationally Protected Persons Act 1978, s 5(4).

Sub-s (4): words in first (outer) pair of square brackets inserted by the Internationally Protected Persons Act 1978, s 5(4); words in second (inner) pair of square brackets substituted by the United Nations Personnel Act 1997, s 7, Schedule, para 3.

Sub-s (5): outside the scope of this work.

Sub-s (7): words in square brackets substituted by the Civil Aviation Act 1982, s 109, Sch 15, para 21.

5 Power to apply provisions of Act to non-convention countries

(1) In the case of any country which, not being a convention country, is either—

(a) a designated Commonwealth country within the meaning of the [Extradition Act 1989]; or

(b) a foreign state with which there is in force an arrangement of the kind described in section 2 of the Extradition Act 1870 [or in the Extradition Act 1989] with respect to the surrender to that state of fugitive criminals; or

[(c) a colony,]

the Secretary of State may by order direct—

(i) in the case of a country within paragraph (a) or (b) above, that all or any of the provisions [to which this paragraph applies] shall apply in relation to that country (subject to such exceptions, if any, as may be specified in the order) as they apply in relation to a convention country; or

(ii) in the case of a country within paragraph (c) above, that the provisions of section 4 above shall so apply in relation to that country;

and while such an order is in force in the case of any country, the provisions in question shall apply in relation to it accordingly.

[(1A) Subsection (1)(i) above applies—

(a) to the provisions of this Act which would, apart from this section, apply only in relation to convention countries; and

(b) to section 24(1) and (2) of the Extradition Act 1989.]

(2) The Secretary of State may, at any time when the Republic of Ireland is not a convention country, by order direct that section 4 above shall apply in relation to the Republic as if it were a convention country; and while such an order is in force, that section shall apply in relation to the Republic accordingly.

(3) An order under subsection (2) above shall, unless previously revoked, cease to have effect if the Republic of Ireland subsequently becomes a convention country.

NOTES

Sub-s (1): words in first, third and fourth pairs of square brackets substituted, and words in second pair of square brackets inserted, by the Extradition Act 1989, s 36(4)–(7).

Sub-s (1A): inserted by the Extradition Act 1989, s 36(8).

9 Short title, repeals and commencement

(1) This Act may be cited as the Suppression of Terrorism Act 1978.

(2) . . .

(3) This Act shall come into force on such day as the Secretary of State may by order appoint, and different days may be so appointed for different purposes.

NOTES

Sub-s (2): outside the scope of this work.

SCHEDULE 1

Sections 1, 4

LIST OF OFFENCES

Common law offences

1. Murder.

2. Manslaughter or culpable homicide.

3. Rape.

4. Kidnapping, abduction or plagium.

5. False imprisonment.

6. Assault occasioning actual bodily harm or causing injury.

7. Wilful fire-raising.

Offences against the person

8. An offence under any of the following provisions of the Offences against the Person Act 1861—

[(za) section 4 (soliciting etc to commit murder);]

(a) section 18 (wounding with intent to cause grievous bodily harm);

(b) section 20 (causing grievous bodily harm);

(c) section 21 (attempting to choke etc in order to commit or assist in the committing of any indictable offence);

(d) section 22 (using chloroform etc to commit or assist in the committing of any indictable offence);

(e) section 23 (maliciously administering poison etc so as to endanger life or inflict grievous bodily harm);

(f) section 24 (maliciously administering poison etc with intent to injure etc);

(g) section 48 (rape).

9. An offence under section 1 of the Sexual Offences Act 1956 (rape).

[9A. The offence of torture under section 134 of the Criminal Justice Act 1988.]

Abduction

10. An offence under any of the following provisions of the Offences against the Person Act 1861—

(a) section 55 (abduction of unmarried girl under 16);

(b) section 56 (child-stealing or receiving stolen child).

11. An offence under section 20 of the Sexual Offences Act 1956 (abduction of unmarried girl under 16).

[*Taking of hostages*

11A. An offence under the Taking of Hostages Act 1982.]

[11B. An offence under section 2 of the Child Abduction Act 1984 (abduction of child by person other than parent etc) or any corresponding provision in force in Northern Ireland.]

Explosives

12. An offence under any of the following provisions of the Offences against the Person Act 1861—

(a) section 28 (causing bodily injury by gunpowder);

(b) section 29 (causing gunpowder to explode etc with intent to do grievous bodily harm).
(c) section 30 (placing gunpowder near a building etc with intent to cause bodily injury).

13. An offence under any of the following provisions of the Explosive Substances Act 1883—
(a) section 2 (causing explosion likely to endanger life or property);
(b) section 3 (doing any act with intent to cause such an explosion, conspiring to cause such an explosion, or making or possessing explosive with intent to endanger life or property).

[Nuclear material

13A. An offence under any provision of the Nuclear Material (Offences) Act 1983.]

Firearms

14. The following offences under the Firearms Act 1968—
(a) an offence under section 16 (possession of firearm with intent to injure);
(b) an offence under subsection (1) of section 17 (use of firearm or imitation firearm to resist arrest) involving the use or attempted use of a firearm within the meaning of that section.

15. The following offences under the [Firearms (Northern Ireland) Order 1981]
(a) an offence under [Article 17] consisting of a person's having in his possession any firearm or ammunition (within the meaning of [that Article]) with intent by means thereof to endanger life, or to enable another person by means thereof to endanger life;
(b) an offence under [paragraph (1) of Article 18] (use of firearm or imitation firearm to resist arrest) involving the use or attempted use of a firearm within the meaning of [that Article].

Offences against property

16. An offence under section 1(2) of the Criminal Damage Act 1971 (destroying or damaging property intending to endanger life or being reckless as to danger to life).

17. An offence under Article 3(2) of the Criminal Damage (Northern Ireland) Order 1977 (destroying or damaging property intending to endanger life or being reckless as to danger to life).

Offences in relation to aircraft

[18. An offence under Part I of the Aviation Security Act 1982 (other than an offence under section 4 or 7 of that Act).]

[18A. An offence under section 1 of the Aviation and Maritime Security Act 1990.

Offences relating to ships and fixed platforms

18B. An offence under Part II of the Aviation and Maritime Security Act 1990 (other than an offence under section 15 of that Act).]

[Offences relating to Channel Tunnel trains and the tunnel system

18C. An offence under Part II of the Channel Tunnel (Security) Order 1994 No 570.]

[Financing terrorism

19A. An offence under Part III of the Prevention of Terrorism (Temporary Provisions) Act 1989.]

Attempts

20. An offence of attempting to commit any offence mentioned in a preceding paragraph of this Schedule.

[*Conspiracy*

21. An offence of conspiring to commit any offence mentioned in a preceding paragraph of this Schedule.]

NOTES

Para 8: sub-para (za) inserted by the Criminal Justice Act 1988, s 22(1), (2).

Para 9A: inserted by the Criminal Justice Act 1988, s 22(1), (3).

Para 11A: inserted by the Taking of Hostages Act 1982, s 3(2).

Para 11B: inserted by the Child Abduction Act 1984, s 11(4).

Para 13A: inserted by the Criminal Justice Act 1988, s 22(1), (4).

Para 15: words in square brackets substituted by the Firearms (Northern Ireland) Order 1981, SI 1981/155, art 61(1), Sch 4, para 5.

Para 18: substituted for existing paras 18, 19 by the Aviation Security Act 1982, s 40, Sch 2, para 7.

Paras 18A, 18B: inserted by the Aviation and Maritime Security Act 1990, s 53(1), Sch 3, para 6.

Para 18C: inserted by the Channel Tunnel (Security) Order 1994, SI 1994/570, art 38, Sch 3, para 2.

Para 19A: inserted by the Prevention of Terrorism (Temporary Provisions) Act 1989, s 25(1), Sch 8, para 4.

Para 21: inserted by the Criminal Justice Act 1988, s 22(1), (5).

JUSTICES OF THE PEACE ACT 1979

(c 55)

(NOTE)

NOTES

This Act has been consolidated and repealed by the Justices of the Peace Act 1997. In particular, the provisions of s 6 of the 1979 Act (appointment and removal of justices of the peace) are now to be found in s 5 of the 1997 Act, and the provisions of s 30A of the 1979 Act, as inserted by the Police and Magistrates' Courts Act 1994, s 78 (independence of justices' clerk and staff in relation to legal functions), are now to be found in s 48 of the 1997 Act. Both ss 5 and 48 of the 1997 Act are reproduced in this work.

MAGISTRATES' COURTS ACT 1980

(c 43)

An Act to consolidate certain enactments relating to the jurisdiction of, and the practice and procedure before, magistrates' courts and the functions of justices' clerks, and to matters connected therewith, with amendments to give effect to recommendations of the Law Commission

[1 August 1980]

PART VI
RECOGNIZANCES

Recognizances to keep the peace or be of good behaviour

115 Binding over to keep the peace or be of good behaviour

(1) The power of a magistrates' court on the complaint of any person to adjudge any other person to enter into a recognizance, with or without sureties, to keep the

peace or to be of good behaviour towards the complainant shall be exercised by order on complaint.

(2) . . .

(3) If any person ordered by a magistrates' court under subsection (1) above to enter into a recognizance, with or without sureties, to keep the peace or to be of good behaviour fails to comply with the order, the court may commit him to custody for a period not exceeding 6 months or until he sooner complies with the order.

NOTES

Sub-s (2): outside the scope of this work.

PART VII
MISCELLANEOUS AND SUPPLEMENTARY

Repeals, short title, etc

155 Short title, extent and commencement

(1) This Act may be cited as the Magistrates' Courts Act 1980.

(2)–(5) . . .

(6) . . . , this Act extends to England and Wales only.

(7) This Act shall come into force on such date as the Secretary of State may appoint by order made by statutory instrument.

NOTES

Sub-ss (2)–(5): outside the scope of this work.
Sub-s (6): words omitted outside the scope of this work.

HIGHWAYS ACT 1980

(c 66)

An Act to consolidate the Highways Acts 1959 to 1971 and related enactments, with amendments to give effect to recommendations of the Law Commission

[13 November 1980]

PART IX
LAWFUL AND UNLAWFUL INTERFERENCE WITH HIGHWAYS AND STREETS

Obstruction of highways and streets

137 Penalty for wilful obstruction

(1) If a person, without lawful authority or excuse, in any way wilfully obstructs the free passage along a highway he is guilty of an offence and liable to a fine not exceeding [level 3 on the standard scale].

(2) . . .

NOTES

Sub-s (1): reference to "level 3 on the standard scale" substituted by virtue of the Criminal Justice Act 1982, ss 37, 38, 46.

Sub-s (2): repealed by the Police and Criminal Evidence Act 1984, ss 26(1), 119, Sch 7, Pt I.

PART XIV
MISCELLANEOUS AND SUPPLEMENTARY PROVISIONS

Savings, etc

345 Short title, commencement and extent

(1) This Act may be cited as the Highways Act 1980.

(2) This Act shall come into force on 1st January 1981.

(3) This Act . . . extends to England and Wales only.

NOTES

Sub-s (3): words omitted outside the scope of this work.

INDECENT DISPLAYS (CONTROL) ACT 1981

(C 42)

An Act to make fresh provision with respect to the public display of indecent matter; and for purposes connected therewith

[27 July 1981]

1 Indecent displays

(1) If any indecent matter is publicly displayed the person making the display and any person causing or permitting the display to be made shall be guilty of an offence.

(2) Any matter which is displayed in or so as to be visible from any public place shall, for the purposes of this section, be deemed to be publicly displayed.

(3) In subsection (2) above, "public place", in relation to the display of any matter, means any place to which the public have or are permitted to have access (whether on payment or otherwise) while that matter is displayed except—

(a) a place to which the public are permitted to have access only on payment which is or includes payment for that display; or

(b) a shop or any part of a shop to which the public can only gain access by passing beyond an adequate warning notice;

but the exclusions contained in paragraphs (a) and (b) above shall only apply where persons under the age of 18 years are not permitted to enter while the display in question is continuing.

(4) Nothing in this section applies in relation to any matter—

[(a) included by any person in a television broadcasting service or other television programme service (within the meaning of the Broadcasting Act 1990);]
(b) included in the display of an art gallery or museum and visible only from within the gallery or museum; or
(c) displayed by or with the authority of, and visible only from within a building occupied by, the Crown or any local authority; or
(d) included in a performance of a play (within the meaning of the Theatres Act 1968); or
[(e) included in a film exhibition as defined in the Cinemas Act 1985—
(i) given in a place which as regards that exhibition is required to be licensed under section 1 of that Act or by virtue only of section 5, 7 or 8 of that Act is not required to be so licensed; or
(ii) which is an exhibition to which section 6 of that Act applies given by an exempted organisation as defined by subsection (6) of that section].

(5) In this section "matter" includes anything capable of being displayed, except that it does not include an actual human body or any part thereof; and in determining for the purpose of this section whether any displayed matter is indecent—
(a) there shall be disregarded any part of that matter which is not exposed to view; and
(b) account may be taken of the effect of juxtaposing one thing with another.

(6) A warning notice shall not be adequate for the purposes of this section unless it complies with the following requirements—
(a) The warning notice must contain the following words, and no others—
"WARNING
Persons passing beyond this notice will find material on display which they may consider indecent. No admittance to persons under 18 years of age."
(b) The word "WARNING" must appear as a heading.
(c) No pictures or other matter shall appear on the notice.
(d) The notice must be so situated that no one could reasonably gain access to the shop or part of the shop in question without being aware of the notice and it must be easily legible by any person gaining such access.

NOTES
Sub-s (4): para (a) substituted by the Broadcasting Act 1990, s 203(1), Sch 20, para 30; para (e) substituted by the Cinemas Act 1985, s 24(1), Sch 2, para 13.

---

2 Powers of arrest, seizure and entry

(1) . . .

(2) A constable may seize any article which he has reasonable grounds for believing to be or to contain indecent matter and to have been used in the commission of an offence under this Act.

(3) In England and Wales, a justice of the peace if satisfied on information on oath that there are reasonable grounds for suspecting that an offence under this Act has been or is being committed on any premises and, in Scotland, a sheriff or justice of the peace on being so satisfied on evidence on oath, may issue a warrant authorising any constable to enter the premises specified in the information or, as the case may be, evidence (if need be by force) . . . to seize any article which the constable has reasonable grounds for believing to be or to contain indecent matter and to have been used in the commission of an offence under this Act.

NOTES

Sub-s (1): repealed by the Police and Criminal Evidence Act 1984, ss 26(1), 119(2), Sch 7, Pt I.

Sub-s (3): words omitted repealed by the Police and Criminal Evidence Act 1984, ss 26(1), 119(2), Sch 7, Pt I.

4 Penalties

(1) In England and Wales, any person guilty of an offence under this Act shall be liable—

(a) on summary conviction, to a fine not exceeding the statutory maximum; or

(b) on conviction on indictment, to imprisonment for a term not exceeding two years or a fine or both.

(2), (3) . . .

NOTES

Sub-s (2): outside the scope of this work.

Sub-s (3): repealed by the SL(R) Act 1993.

5 Short title, repeal, extent and commencement

(1) This Act may be cited as the Indecent Displays (Control) Act 1981.

(2) . . .

(3) This Act does not extend to Northern Ireland.

(4) . . .

(5) This Act shall come into force at the expiration of a period of three months, beginning with the day on which this Act is passed.

NOTES

Sub-ss (2), (4): outside the scope of this work.

CONTEMPT OF COURT ACT 1981

(C 49)

An Act to amend the law relating to contempt of court and related matters

[27 July 1981]

Strict liability

1 The strict liability rule

In this Act "the strict liability rule" means the rule of law whereby conduct may be treated as a contempt of court as tending to interfere with the course of justice in particular legal proceedings regardless of intent to do so.

2 Limitation of scope of strict liability

(1) The strict liability rule applies only in relation to publications, and for this purpose "publication" includes any speech, writing, [programme included in a

programme service] or other communication in whatever form, which is addressed to the public at large or any section of the public.

(2) The strict liability rule applies only to a publication which creates a substantial risk that the course of justice in the proceedings in question will be seriously impeded or prejudiced.

(3) The strict liability rule applies to a publication only if the proceedings in question are active within the meaning of this section at the time of the publication.

(4) Schedule 1 applies for determining the times at which proceedings are to be treated as active within the meaning of this section.

[(5) In this section "programme service" has the same meaning as in the Broadcasting Act 1990.]

NOTES

Sub-s (1): words in square brackets substituted by the Broadcasting Act 1990, s 203(1), Sch 20, para 31(1)(a).

Sub-s (5): inserted by the Broadcasting Act 1990, s 203(1), Sch 20, para 31(1)(b).

3 Defence of innocent publication or distribution

(1) A person is not guilty of contempt of court under the strict liability rule as the publisher of any matter to which that rule applies if at the time of publication (having taken all reasonable care) he does not know and has no reason to suspect that relevant proceedings are active.

(2) A person is not guilty of contempt of court under the strict liability rule as the distributor of a publication containing any such matter if at the time of distribution (having taken all reasonable care) he does not know that it contains such matter and has no reason to suspect that it is likely to do so.

(3) The burden of proof of any fact tending to establish a defence afforded by this section to any person lies upon that person.

(4) . . .

NOTES

Sub-s (4): repeals the Administration of Justice Act 1960, s 11.

4 Contemporary reports of proceedings

(1) Subject to this section a person is not guilty of contempt of court under the strict liability rule in respect of a fair and accurate report of legal proceedings held in public, published contemporaneously and in good faith.

(2) In any such proceedings the court may, where it appears to be necessary for avoiding a substantial risk of prejudice to the administration of justice in those proceedings, or in any other proceedings pending or imminent, order that the publication of any report of the proceedings, or any part of the proceedings, be postponed for such period as the court thinks necessary for that purpose.

[(2A) Where in proceedings for any offence which is an administration of justice offence for the purposes of section 54 of the Criminal Procedure and Investigations

Act 1996 (acquittal tainted by an administration of justice offence) it appears to the court that there is a possibility that (by virtue of that section) proceedings may be taken against a person for an offence of which he has been acquitted, subsection (2) of this section shall apply as if those proceedings were pending or imminent.]

(3), (4) . . .

NOTES

Sub-s (2A): inserted by the Criminal Procedure and Investigations Act 1996, s 57(3).
Sub-s (3): outside the scope of this work.
Sub-s (4): repeals the Magistrates' Courts Act 1980, s 8(9).

5 Discussion of public affairs

A publication made as or as part of a discussion in good faith of public affairs or other matters of general public interest is not to be treated as a contempt of court under the strict liability rule if the risk of impediment or prejudice to particular legal proceedings is merely incidental to the discussion.

6 Savings

Nothing in the foregoing provisions of this Act—

(a) prejudices any defence available at common law to a charge of contempt of court under the strict liability rule;
(b) implies that any publication is punishable as contempt of court under that rule which would not be so punishable apart from those provisions;
(c) restricts liability for contempt of court in respect of conduct intended to impede or prejudice the administration of justice.

7 Consent required for institution of proceedings

Proceedings for a contempt of court under the strict liability rule (other than Scottish proceedings) shall not be instituted except by or with the consent of the Attorney General or on the motion of a court having jurisdiction to deal with it.

Other aspects of law and procedure

8 Confidentiality of jury's deliberations

(1) Subject to subsection (2) below, it is a contempt of court to obtain, disclose or solicit any particulars of statements made, opinions expressed, arguments advanced or votes cast by members of a jury in the course of their deliberations in any legal proceedings.

(2) This section does not apply to any disclosure of any particulars—

(a) in the proceedings in question for the purpose of enabling the jury to arrive at their verdict, or in connection with the delivery of that verdict, or
(b) in evidence in any subsequent proceedings for an offence alleged to have been committed in relation to the jury in the first mentioned proceedings,

or to the publication of any particulars so disclosed.

(3) Proceedings for a contempt of court under this section (other than Scottish proceedings) shall not be instituted except by or with the consent of the Attorney General or on the motion of a court having jurisdiction to deal with it.

9 Use of tape recorders

(1) Subject to subsection (4) below, it is a contempt of court—

(a) to use in court, or bring into court for use, any tape recorder or other instrument for recording sound, except with the leave of the court;

(b) to publish a recording of legal proceedings made by means of any such instrument, or any recording derived directly or indirectly from it, by playing it in the hearing of the public or any section of the public, or to dispose of it or any recording so derived, with a view to such publication;

(c) to use any such recording in contravention of any conditions of leave granted under paragraph (a).

(2) Leave under paragraph (a) of subsection (1) may be granted or refused at the discretion of the court, and if granted may be granted subject to such conditions as the court thinks proper with respect to the use of any recording made pursuant to the leave; and where leave has been granted the court may at the like discretion withdraw or amend it either generally or in relation to any particular part of the proceedings.

(3) Without prejudice to any other power to deal with an act of contempt under paragraph (a) of subsection (1), the court may order the instrument, or any recording made with it, or both, to be forfeited; and any object so forfeited shall (unless the court otherwise determines on application by a person appearing to be the owner) be sold or otherwise disposed of in such manner as the court may direct.

(4) This section does not apply to the making or use of sound recordings for purposes of official transcripts of proceedings.

10 Sources of information

No court may require a person to disclose, nor is any person guilty of contempt of court for refusing to disclose, the source of information contained in a publication for which he is responsible, unless it be established to the satisfaction of the court that disclosure is necessary in the interests of justice or national security or for the prevention of disorder or crime.

11 Publication of matters exempted from disclosure in court

In any case where a court (having power to do so) allows a name or other matter to be withheld from the public in proceedings before the court, the court may give such directions prohibiting the publication of that name or matter in connection with the proceedings as appear to the court to be necessary for the purpose for which it was so withheld.

12 Offences of contempt of magistrates' courts

(1) A magistrates' court has jurisdiction under this section to deal with any person who—

(a) wilfully insults the justice or justices, any witness before or officer of the court or any solicitor or counsel having business in the court, during his or their sitting or attendance in court or in going to or returning from the court; or

(b) wilfully interrupts the proceedings of the court or otherwise misbehaves in court.

(2) In any such case the court may order any officer of the court, or any constable, to take the offender into custody and detain him until the rising of the court; and the court may, if it thinks fit, commit the offender to custody for a specified period not exceeding one month or impose on him a fine not exceeding [£2,500], or both.

(2A)–(5) . . .

NOTES

Sub-s (2): sum in square brackets substituted by the Criminal Justice Act 1991, s 17(3), Sch 4, Pt I.

Sub-ss (2A), (4), (5): outside the scope of this work.

Sub-s (3): repealed by the Criminal Justice Act 1982, s 78, Sch 16.

Modification: reference in sub-s (2) to "any officer of the court" modified by the Criminal Justice Act 1991, s 100, Sch 11, para 29.

Penalties for contempt and kindred offences

14 Proceedings in England and Wales

(1) In any case where a court has power to commit a person to prison for contempt of court and (apart from this provision) no limitation applies to the period of committal, the committal shall (without prejudice to the power of the court to order his earlier discharge) be for a fixed term, and that term shall not on any occasion exceed two years in the case of committal by a superior court, or one month in the case of committal by an inferior court.

(2) In any case where an inferior court has power to fine a person for contempt of court and (apart from this provision) no limit applies to the amount of the fine, the fine shall not on any occasion exceed [£2,500].

(2A)–(5) . . .

NOTES

Sub-s (2): sum in square brackets substituted by the Criminal Justice Act 1991, s 17(3), Sch 4, Pt I, and substituted in relation to Northern Ireland by the Criminal Justice (Northern Ireland) Order 1994, SI 1994/2795, art 3(5), Sch 1.

Sub-ss (2A), (4), (4A), (5): outside the scope of this work.

Sub-s (3): repealed by the Criminal Justice Act 1982, s 78, Sch 16.

Supplemental

21 Short title, commencement and extent

(1) This Act may be cited as the Contempt of Court Act 1981.

(2)–(4) . . .

(5) This Act, except sections 15 and 17 and Schedules 2 and 3, extends to Northern Ireland.

NOTES

Sub-ss (2)–(4): outside the scope of this work.

SUPREME COURT ACT 1981

(C 54)

An Act to consolidate with amendments the Supreme Court of Judicature (Consolidation) Act 1925 and other enactments relating to the Supreme Court in England and Wales and the administration of justice therein; to repeal certain obsolete or unnecessary enactments so relating; to amend Part VIII of the Mental Health Act 1959, the Courts-Martial (Appeals) Act 1968, the Arbitration Act 1979 and the law relating to county courts; and for connected purposes

[28 July 1981]

PART I
CONSTITUTION OF SUPREME COURT

The Supreme Court

1 The Supreme Court

(1) The Supreme Court of England and Wales shall consist of the Court of Appeal, the High Court of Justice and the Crown Court, each having such jurisdiction as is conferred on it by or under this or any other Act.

(2) The Lord Chancellor shall be president of the Supreme Court.

The High Court

4 The High Court

(1) The High Court shall consist of—

(a) the Lord Chancellor;
(b) the Lord Chief Justice;
(c) the President of the Family Division;
(d) the Vice-Chancellor;
[(dd)the Senior Presiding Judge]; and
(e) not more than [ninety-eight] puisne judges of that court.

(2) The puisne judges of the High Court shall be styled "Justices of the High Court".

(3) All the judges of the High Court shall, except where this Act expressly provides otherwise, have in all respects equal power, authority and jurisdiction.

(4)–(6) . . .

NOTES

Sub-s (1): para (dd) inserted by the Courts and Legal Services Act 1990, s 72(6)(a); words in square brackets in para (e) substituted by the Maximum Number of Judges (No 2) Order 1993, SI 1993/1255, art 2.

Sub-ss (4)–(6): outside the scope of this work.

Other provisions

10 Appointment of judges of Supreme Court

(1) Whenever the office of Lord Chief Justice, Master of the Rolls, President of the Family Division or Vice-Chancellor is vacant, Her Majesty may by letters patent appoint a qualified person to that office.

(2) Subject to the limits on numbers for the time being imposed by sections 2(1) and 4(1), Her Majesty may from time to time by letters patent appoint qualified persons as Lords Justices of Appeal or as puisne judges of the High Court.

(3) No person shall be qualified for appointment—
- (a) as Lord Chief Justice, Master of the Rolls, President of the Family Division or Vice-Chancellor, unless he is qualified for appointment as a Lord Justice of Appeal or is a judge of the Court of Appeal;
- (b) as a Lord Justice of Appeal, [unless—
  - (i) he has a 10 year High Court qualification within the meaning of section 71 of the Courts and Legal Services Act 1990; or
  - (ii) he is a judge of the High Court;] or
- (c) as a puisne judge of the High Court, [unless—
  - (i) he has a 10 year High Court qualification, within the meaning of section 71 of the Courts and Legal Services Act 1990; or
  - (ii) he is a Circuit judge who has held that office for at least 2 years].

(4) Every person appointed to an office mentioned in subsection (1) or as a Lord Justice of Appeal or puisne judge of the High Court shall, as soon as may be after his acceptance of office, take the oath of allegiance and the judicial oath, as set out in the Promissory Oaths Act 1868, in the presence of the Lord Chancellor.

NOTES

Sub-s (3): words in square brackets substituted by the Courts and Legal Services Act 1990, s 71(1).

11 Tenure of office of judges of Supreme Court

(1) This section applies to the office of any judge of the Supreme Court except the Lord Chancellor.

(2) A person appointed to an office to which this section applies shall vacate it on the day on which he attains the age of [seventy] years unless by virtue of this section he has ceased to hold it before then.

(3) A person appointed to an office to which this section applies shall hold that office during good behaviour, subject to a power of removal by Her Majesty on an address presented to Her by both Houses of Parliament.

(4)–(6) . . .

(7) A person who holds an office to which this section applies may at any time resign it by giving the Lord Chancellor notice in writing to that effect.

(8) The Lord Chancellor, if satisfied by means of a medical certificate that a person holding an office to which this section applies—
- (a) is disabled by permanent infirmity from the performance of the duties of his office; and
- (b) is for the time being incapacitated from resigning his office,

may, subject to subsection (9), by instrument under his hand declare that person's office to have been vacated; and the instrument shall have the like effect for all purposes as if that person had on the date of the instrument resigned his office.

(9) A declaration under subsection (8) with respect to a person shall be of no effect unless it is made—
- (a) in the case of any of the Lord Chief Justice, the Master of the Rolls, the President of the Family Division and the Vice-Chancellor, with the concurrence of two others of them;

(b) in the case of a Lord Justice of Appeal, with the concurrence of the Master of the Rolls;

(c) in the case of a puisne judge of any Division of the High Court, with the concurrence of the senior judge of that Division.

(10) . . .

NOTES

Sub-s (2): word in square brackets substituted by the Judicial Pensions and Retirement Act 1993, s 26(10), Sch 6, para 4; for savings see ss 26(11), 27, Sch 7 thereof.

Sub-ss (4)–(6): outside the scope of this work.

Sub-s (10): repealed by the SL(R) Act 1989.

12 Salaries etc of judges of Supreme Court

(1) Subject to subsections (2) and (3), there shall be paid to judges of the Supreme Court, other than the Lord Chancellor, such salaries as may be determined by the Lord Chancellor with the concurrence of the Minister for the Civil Service.

(2) Until otherwise determined under this section, there shall be paid to the judges mentioned in subsection (1) the same salaries as at the commencement of this Act.

(3) Any salary payable under this section may be increased, but not reduced, by a determination or further determination under this section.

(4)–(7) . . .

NOTES

Sub-s (4): repealed by the Courts and Legal Services Act 1990, ss 84, 125(7), Sch 20.

Sub-ss (5)–(7): outside the scope of this work.

PART II
JURISDICTION

THE HIGH COURT

General jurisdiction

19 General jurisdiction

(1) The High Court shall be a superior court of record.

(2) Subject to the provisions of this Act, there shall be exercisable by the High Court—

(a) all such jurisdiction (whether civil or criminal) as is conferred on it by this or any other Act; and

(b) all such other jurisdiction (whether civil or criminal) as was exercisable by it immediately before the commencement of this Act (including jurisdiction conferred on a judge of the High Court by any statutory provision).

(3) Any jurisdiction of the High Court shall be exercised only by a single judge of that court, except in so far as it is—

(a) by or by virtue of rules of court or any other statutory provision required to be exercised by a divisional court; or

(b) by rules of court made exercisable by a master, registrar or other officer of the court, or by any other person.

(4) . . .

NOTES

Sub-s (4): outside the scope of this work.

Other particular fields of jurisdiction

29 Orders of mandamus, prohibition and certiorari

(1) The High Court shall have jurisdiction to make orders of mandamus, prohibition and certiorari in those classes of cases in which it had power to do so immediately before the commencement of this Act.

(2) Every such order shall be final, subject to any right of appeal therefrom.

(3) In relation to the jurisdiction of the Crown Court, other than its jurisdiction in matters relating to trial on indictment, the High Court shall have all such jurisdiction to make orders of mandamus, prohibition or certiorari as the High Court possesses in relation to the jurisdiction of an inferior court.

(4) The power of the High Court under any enactment to require justices of the peace or a judge or officer of a county court to do any act relating to the duties of their respective offices, or to require a magistrates' court to state a case for the opinion of the High Court, in any case where the High Court formerly had by virtue of any enactment jurisdiction to make a rule absolute, or an order, for any of those purposes, shall be exercisable by order of mandamus.

(5) In any enactment—

(a) references to a writ of mandamus, of prohibition or of certiorari shall be read as references to the corresponding order; and

(b) references to the issue or award of any such writ shall be read as references to the making of the corresponding order.

31 Application for judicial review

(1) An application to the High Court for one or more of the following forms of relief, namely—

(a) an order of mandamus, prohibition or certiorari;

(b) a declaration or injunction under subsection (2); or

(c) an injunction under section 30 restraining a person not entitled to do so from acting in an office to which that section applies,

shall be made in accordance with rules of court by a procedure to be known as an application for judicial review.

(2) A declaration may be made or an injunction granted under this subsection in any case where an application for judicial review, seeking that relief, has been made and the High Court considers that, having regard to—

(a) the nature of the matters in respect of which relief may be granted by orders of mandamus, prohibition or certiorari;

(b) the nature of the persons and bodies against whom relief may be granted by such orders; and

(c) all the circumstances of the case,

it would be just and convenient for the declaration to be made or of the injunction to be granted, as the case may be.

(3) No application for judicial review shall be made unless the leave of the High Court has been obtained in accordance with rules of court; and the court shall not grant leave to make such an application unless it considers that the applicant has a sufficient interest in the matter to which the application relates.

(4) On an application for judicial review the High Court may award damages to the applicant if—

(a) he has joined with his application a claim for damages arising from any matter to which the application relates; and

(b) the court is satisfied that, if the claim had been made in an action begun by the applicant at the time of making his application, he would have been awarded damages.

(5) If, on an application for judicial review seeking an order of certiorari, the High Court quashes the decision to which the application relates, the High Court may remit the matter to the court, tribunal or authority concerned, with a direction to reconsider it and reach a decision in accordance with the findings of the High Court.

(6) Where the High Court considers that there has been undue delay in making an application for judicial review, the court may refuse to grant—

(a) leave for the making of the application; or

(b) any relief sought on the application,

if it considers that the granting of the relief sought would be likely to cause substantial hardship to, or substantially prejudice the rights of, any person or would be detrimental to good administration.

(7) Subsection (6) is without prejudice to any enactment or rule of court which has the effect of limiting the time within which an application for judicial review may be made.

NOTES

For RSC Ord 53, see p 10.

PART VI
MISCELLANEOUS AND SUPPLEMENTARY

Supplementary

153 Citation, commencement and extent

(1) This Act may be cited as the Supreme Court Act 1981.

(2) This Act, . . . shall come into force on 1st January 1982; and references to the commencement of this Act shall be construed as references to the beginning of that day.

(3)–(5) . . .

NOTES

Words omitted from sub-s (2), and sub-ss (3)–(5): outside the scope of this work.

RULES OF THE SUPREME COURT (REVISION) 1965

(SI 1965/1776)

Made: 30 September 1965.

Authority: Supreme Court of Judicature (Consolidation) Act 1925, s 99 (see now the Supreme Court Act 1981, s 84).

[DIVISIONAL COURTS, COURT OF APPEAL, ETC

ORDER 53

APPLICATIONS FOR JUDICIAL REVIEW

Order 53, r 1 Cases appropriate for application for judicial review

(1) An application for—

(a) an order of mandamus, prohibition or certiorari, or

(b) an injunction under [section 30 of the Act] restraining a person from acting in any office in which he is not entitled to act,

shall be made by way of an application for judicial review in accordance with the provisions of this Order.

(2) An application for a declaration or an injunction (not being an injunction mentioned in paragraph (1)(b)) may be made by way of an application for judicial review, and on such an application the Court may grant the declaration or injunction claimed if it considers that, having regard to—

(a) the nature of the matters in respect of which relief may be granted by way of an order of mandamus, prohibition or certiorari,

(b) the nature of the persons and bodies against whom relief may be granted by way of such an order, and

(c) all the circumstances of the case,

it would be just and convenient for the declaration or injunction to be granted on an application for judicial review.]

NOTES

Substituted, together with rr 2, 3, 5–14 and the preceding heading, by SI 1977/1955, r 5.

Para (1): words in square brackets in sub-para (b) substituted by SI 1982/1111, r 115, Schedule.

[Order 53, r 2 Joinder of claims for relief

On an application for judicial review any relief mentioned in rule 1(1) or (2) may be claimed as an alternative or in addition to any other relief so mentioned if it arises out of or relates to or is connected with the same matter.]

NOTES

Substituted as noted to Order 53, r 1.

[Order 53, r 3 Grant of leave to apply for judicial review

(1) No application for judicial review shall be made unless the leave of the Court has been obtained in accordance with this rule.

[(2) An application for leave must be made ex parte to a judge by filing in the Crown Office—

(a) a notice in Form No 86A containing a statement of

(i) the name and description of the applicant,

(ii) the relief sought and the grounds upon which it is sought,

(iii) the name and address of the applicant's solicitors (if any), and

(iv) the applicant's address for service; and

(b) an affidavit verifying the facts relied on.

(3) The judge may determine the application without a hearing, unless a hearing is requested in the notice of application, and need not sit in open court; in any case, the Crown Office shall serve a copy of the judge's order on the applicant.

(4) Where the application for leave is refused by the judge, or is granted on terms, the applicant may renew it by applying—

(a) in any criminal cause or matter, to a Divisional Court of the Queen's Bench Division;

(b) in any other case, to a single judge sitting in open court or, if the Court so directs, to a Divisional Court of the Queen's Bench Division;

Provided that no application for leave may be renewed in any non-criminal cause or matter in which the judge has refused leave under paragraph (3) after a hearing.

(5) In order to renew his application for leave the applicant must, within 10 days of being served with notice of the judge's refusal, lodge in the Crown Office notice of his intention in Form No 86B.]

[(6)] Without prejudice to its powers under Order 20, rule 8, the Court hearing an application for leave may allow the applicant's statement to be amended, whether by specifying different or additional grounds or relief or otherwise, on such terms, if any, as it thinks fit.

[(7)] The Court shall not grant leave unless it considers that the applicant has a sufficient interest in the matter to which the application relates.

[(8)] Where leave is sought to apply for an order of certiorari to remove for the purpose of its being quashed any judgment, order, conviction or other proceeding which is subject to appeal and a time is limited for the bringing of the appeal, the Court may adjourn the application for leave until the appeal is determined or the time for appealing has expired.

[(9)] If the Courts grants leave, it may impose such terms as to costs and as to giving security as it thinks fit.

(10) Where leave to apply for judicial review is granted, then—

(a) if the relief sought is an order of prohibition or certiorari and the Court so directs, the grant shall operate as a stay of the proceedings to which the application relates until the determination of the application or until the Court otherwise orders;

(b) if any other relief is sought, the Court may at any time grant in the proceedings such interim relief as could be granted in an action begun by writ.]

NOTES

Substituted as noted to Order 53, r 1.

Paras (2)–(5): substituted, for existing paras (2), (3), by SI 1980/2000, r 2(1).

Paras (6)–(9): originally paras (4)–(7), renumbered as paras (6)–(9) and paras (8), (9) revoked by SI 1980/2000, r 2(2).

[Order 53, r 4 Delay in applying for relief

(1) [An application for leave to apply for judicial review] shall be made promptly and in any event within three months from the date when grounds for the application first arose unless the Court considers that there is good reason for extending the period within which the application shall be made.

(2) Where the relief sought is an order of certiorari in respect of any judgment, order, conviction or other proceeding, the date when grounds for the application first arose shall be taken to be the date of that judgment, order, conviction or proceeding.

(3) Paragraph (1) is without prejudice to any statutory provision which has the effect of limiting the time within which an application for judicial review may be made.]

NOTES

Substituted by SI 1980/2000, r 3.

Para (1): words in square brackets substituted by SI 1987/1423, r 63, Schedule.

Order 53, r 5 Mode of applying for judicial review

[(1) In any criminal cause or matter where leave has been granted to make an application for judicial review, the application shall be made by originating motion to a Divisional Court of the Queen's Bench Division.

(2) In any other such cause or matter, the application shall be made by originating motion to a judge sitting in open court, unless the Court directs that it shall be made—

(a) by originating summons to a judge in chambers; or
(b) by originating motion to a Divisional Court of the Queen's Bench Division.

Any direction under sub-paragraph (a) shall be without prejudice to the judge's powers under Order 32, rule 13.]

(3) The notice of motion or summons must be served on all persons directly affected and where it relates to any proceedings in or before a court and the object of the application is either to compel the court or an officer of the court to do any act in relation to the proceedings or to quash them or any order made therein, the notice or summons must also be served on the clerk or registrar of the court and, where any objection to the conduct of the judge is to be made, on the judge.

(4) Unless the Court granting leave has otherwise directed, there must be at least 10 days between the service of the notice of motion or summons and . . . the hearing.

(5) A motion must be entered for hearing within 14 days after the grant of leave.

(6), (7) . . .

NOTES

Substituted as noted to Order 53, r 1.

Paras (1), (2): substituted by SI 1980/2000, r 4(1).

Para (4): words omitted revoked by SI 1980/2000, r 4(2).

Paras (6), (7): outside the scope of this work.

[Order 53, r 6 Statements and affidavits

(1) Copies of the statement in support of an application for leave under rule 3 must be served with the notice of motion or summons and, subject to paragraph (2), no grounds shall be relied upon or any relief sought at the hearing except the grounds and relief set out in the statement.

[(2) The Court may on the hearing of the motion or summons allow the applicant to amend his statement, whether by specifying different or additional grounds or relief or otherwise, on such terms, if any, as it thinks fit and may allow further affidavits to be used by him.]

(3) Where the applicant intends to ask to be allowed to amend his statement or to use further affidavits, he shall give notice of his intention and of any proposed amendment to every other party.

(4), (5) . . .

NOTES

Substituted as noted to Order 53, r 1.
Para (2): substituted by SI 1992/1907, r 11.
Paras (4), (5): outside the scope of this work.

[Order 53, r 7 Claim for damages

(1) On an application for judicial review the Court may, subject to paragraph (2), award damages to the applicant if—

(a) he has included in the statement in support of his application for leave under rule 3 a claim for damages arising from any matter to which the application relates, and
(b) the Court is satisfied that, if the claim had been made in an action begun by the applicant at the time of making his application, he could have been awarded damages.

(2) Order 18, rule 12, shall apply to a statement relating to a claim for damages as it applies to a pleading.]

NOTES

Substituted as noted to Order 53, r 1.

(R 8 outside the scope of this work.)

[Order 53, r 9 Hearing of application for judicial review

(1) On the hearing of any motion or summons under rule 5, any person who desires to be heard in opposition to the motion or summons, and appears to the Court to be a proper person to be heard, shall be heard, notwithstanding that he has not been served with notice of the motion or the summons.

(2) Where the relief sought is or includes an order of certiorari to remove any proceedings for the purpose of quashing them, the applicant may not question the validity of any order, warrant, commitment, conviction, inquisition or record unless before the hearing of the motion or summons he has lodged in the Crown Office a copy thereof verified by affidavit or accounts for his failure to do so to the satisfaction of the Court hearing the motion or summons.

(3) Where an order of certiorari is made in any such case as is referred to in paragraph (2), the order shall, subject to paragraph (4), direct that the proceedings shall be quashed forthwith on their removal into the Queen's Bench Division.

(4) Where the relief sought is an order of certiorari and the Court is satisfied that there are grounds for quashing the decision to which the application relates, the Court may, in addition to quashing it, remit the matter to the court, tribunal or authority concerned with a direction to reconsider it and reach a decision in accordance with the findings of the Court.

(5) Where the relief sought is a declaration, an injunction or damages and the Court considers that it should not be granted on an application for judicial review but might have been granted if it had been sought in an action begun by writ by the applicant at the time of making his application, the Court may, instead of refusing the application, order the proceedings to continue as if they had been begun by writ; and Order 28, rule 8, shall apply as if, in the case of an application made by motion, it had been made by summons.]

NOTES

Substituted as noted to Order 53, r 1.

(Rr 10–14 outside the scope of this work.)

BRITISH NATIONALITY ACT 1981

(c 61)

An Act to make fresh provision about citizenship and nationality, and to amend the Immigration Act 1971 as regards the right of abode in the United Kingdom

[30 October 1981]

PART I
BRITISH CITIZENSHIP

Acquisition after commencement

1 Acquisition by birth or adoption

(1) A person born in the United Kingdom after commencement shall be a British citizen if at the time of the birth his father or mother is—

(a) a British citizen; or

(b) settled in the United Kingdom.

(2) A new-born infant who, after commencement, is found abandoned in the United Kingdom shall, unless the contrary is shown, be deemed for the purposes of subsection (1)—

(a) to have been born in the United Kingdom after commencement; and

(b) to have been born to a parent who at the time of the birth was a British citizen or settled in the United Kingdom.

(3) A person born in the United Kingdom after commencement who is not a British citizen by virtue of subsection (1) or (2) shall be entitled to be registered as a British citizen if, while he is a minor—

(a) his father or mother becomes a British citizen or becomes settled in the United Kingdom; and

(b) an application is made for his registration as a British citizen.

(4) A person born in the United Kingdom after commencement who is not a British citizen by virtue of subsection (1) or (2) shall be entitled, on an application for his registration as a British citizen made at any time after he has attained the age of ten years, to be registered as such a citizen if, as regards each of the first ten years of that person's life, the number of days on which he was absent from the United Kingdom in that year does not exceed 90.

(5) Where after commencement an order authorising the adoption of a minor who is not a British citizen is made by any court in the United Kingdom, he shall be a British citizen as from the date on which the order is made if the adopter or, in the case of a joint adoption, one of the adopters is a British citizen on that date.

(6) Where an order in consequence of which any person became a British citizen by virtue of subsection (5) ceases to have effect, whether on annulment or otherwise, the cesser shall not affect the status of that person as a British citizen.

(7) If in the special circumstances of any particular case the Secretary of State thinks fit, he may for the purposes of subsection (4) treat the person to whom the application relates as fulfilling the requirement specified in that subsection although, as regards any one or more of the first ten years of that person's life, the number of days on which he was absent from the United Kingdom in that year or each of the years in question exceeds 90.

(8) In this section and elsewhere in this Act "settled" has the meaning given by section 50.

2 Acquisition by descent

(1) A person born outside the United Kingdom after commencement shall be a British citizen if at the time of the birth his father or mother—

- (a) is a British citizen otherwise than by descent; or
- (b) is a British citizen and is serving outside the United Kingdom in service to which this paragraph applies, his or her recruitment for that service having taken place in the United Kingdom; or
- (c) is a British citizen and is serving outside the United Kingdom in service under a Community institution, his or her recruitment for that service having taken place in a country which at the time of the recruitment was a member of the Communities.

(2) Paragraph (b) of subsection (1) applies to—

- (a) Crown service under the government of the United Kingdom; and
- (b) service of any description for the time being designated under subsection (3).

(3) For the purposes of this section the Secretary of State may by order made by statutory instrument designate any description of service which he considers to be closely associated with the activities outside the United Kingdom of Her Majesty's government in the United Kingdom.

(4) Any order made under subsection (3) shall be subject to annulment in pursuance of a resolution of either House of Parliament.

3 Acquisition by registration: minors

(1) If while a person is a minor an application is made for his registration as a British citizen, the Secretary of State may, if he thinks fit, cause him to be registered as such a citizen.

(2) A person born outside the United Kingdom shall be entitled, on an application for his registration as a British citizen made within the period of twelve months from the date of the birth, to be registered as such a citizen if the requirements specified in subsection (3) or, in the case of a person born stateless, the requirements specified in paragraphs (a) and (b) of that subsection, are fulfilled in the case of either that person's father or his mother ("the parent in question").

(3) The requirements referred to in subsection (2) are—

- (a) that the parent in question was a British citizen by descent at the time of the birth; and
- (b) that the father or mother of the parent in question—
  - (i) was a British citizen otherwise than by descent at the time of the birth of the parent in question; or
  - (ii) became a British citizen otherwise than by descent at commencement, or would have become such a citizen otherwise than by descent at commencement but for his or her death; and
- (c) that, as regards some period of three years ending with a date not later than the date of the birth—
  - (i) the parent in question was in the United Kingdom at the beginning of that period; and
  - (ii) the number of days on which the parent in question was absent from the United Kingdom in that period does not exceed 270.

(4) If in the special circumstances of any particular case the Secretary of State thinks fit, he may treat subsection (2) as if the reference to twelve months were a reference to six years.

(5) A person born outside the United Kingdom shall be entitled, on an application for his registration as a British citizen made while he is a minor, to be registered as such a citizen if the following requirements are satisfied, namely—

- (a) that at the time of that person's birth his father or mother was a British citizen by descent; and
- (b) subject to subsection (6), that that person and his father and mother were in the United Kingdom at the beginning of the period of three years ending with the date of the application and that, in the case of each of them, the number of days on which the person in question was absent from the United Kingdom in that period does not exceed 270; and
- (c) subject to subsection (6), that the consent of his father and mother to the registration has been signified in the prescribed manner.

(6) In the case of an application under subsection (5) of the registration of a person as a British citizen—

- (a) if his father or mother died, or their marriage was terminated, on or before the date of the application, or his father and mother were legally separated on that date, the references to his father and mother in paragraph (b) of that subsection shall be read either as references to his father or as references to his mother;
- (b) if his father or mother died on or before that date, the reference to his father and mother in paragraph (c) of that subsection shall be read as a reference to either of them; and
- (c) if he was born illegitimate, all those references shall be read as references to his mother.

4 Acquisition by registration: British Dependent Territories citizens etc

(1) This section applies to any person who is a British Dependent Territories citizen, [a British National (Overseas),] a British Overseas citizen, a British subject under this Act or a British protected person.

(2) A person to whom this section applies shall be entitled, on an application for his registration as a British citizen, to be registered as such a citizen if the following requirements are satisfied in the case of that person, namely—

- (a) subject to subsection (3), that he was in the United Kingdom at the beginning of the period of five years ending with the date of the application and that the number of days on which he was absent from the United Kingdom in that period does not exceed 450; and
- (b) that the number of days on which he was absent from the United Kingdom in the period of twelve months so ending does not exceed 90; and
- (c) that he was not at any time in the period of twelve months so ending subject under the immigration laws to any restriction on the period for which he might remain in the United Kingdom; and
- (d) that he was not at any time in the period of five years so ending in the United Kingdom in breach of the immigration laws.

(3) So much of subsection (2)(a) as requires the person in question to have been in the United Kingdom at the beginning of the period there mentioned shall not apply in relation to a person who was settled in the United Kingdom immediately before commencement.

(4) If in the special circumstances of any particular case the Secretary of State thinks fit, he may for the purposes of subsection (2) do all or any of the following things, namely—

- (a) treat the person to whom the application relates as fulfilling the requirement specified in subsection (2)(a) or subsection (2)(b), or both, although the number of days on which he was absent from the United Kingdom in the period there mentioned exceeds the number there mentioned;
- (b) disregard any such restriction as is mentioned in subsection (2)(c), not being a restriction to which that person was subject on the date of the application;
- (c) treat that person as fulfilling the requirement specified in subsection (2)(d) although he was in the United Kingdom in breach of the immigration laws in the period there mentioned.

(5) If, on an application for registration as a British citizen made by a person to whom this section applies, the Secretary of State is satisfied that the applicant has at any time served in service to which this subsection applies, he may, if he thinks fit in the special circumstances of the applicant's case, cause him to be registered as such a citizen.

(6) Subsection (5) applies to—

- (a) Crown service under the government of a dependent territory; and
- (b) paid or unpaid service (not falling within paragraph (a)) as a member of any body established by law in a dependent territory members of which are appointed by or on behalf of the Crown.

NOTES

Sub-s (1): words in square brackets inserted by the Hong Kong (British Nationality) Order 1986, SI 1986/948, art 7(2).

5 Acquisition by registration: nationals for purposes of the Community treaties

A British Dependent Territories citizen who falls to be treated as a national of the United Kingdom for the purposes of the Community Treaties shall be entitled to be registered as a British citizen if an application is made for his registration as such a citizen.

6 Acquisition by naturalisation

(1) If, on an application for naturalisation as a British citizen made by a person of full age and capacity, the Secretary of State is satisfied that the applicant fulfils the requirements of Schedule 1 for naturalisation as such a citizen under this subsection, he may, if he thinks fit, grant to him a certificate of naturalisation as such a citizen.

(2) If, on an application for naturalisation as a British citizen made by a person of full age and capacity who on the date of the application is married to a British citizen, the Secretary of State is satisfied that the applicant fulfils the requirements of Schedule 1 for naturalisation as such a citizen under this subsection, he may, if he thinks fit, grant to him a certificate of naturalisation as such a citizen.

Acquisition at commencement

11 Citizens of UK and Colonies who are to become British citizens at commencement

(1) Subject to subsection (2), a person who immediately before commencement—
- (a) was a citizen of the United Kingdom and Colonies; and
- (b) had the right of abode in the United Kingdom under the Immigration Act 1971 as then in force,

shall at commencement become a British citizen.

(2) A person who was registered as a citizen of the United Kingdom and Colonies under section 1 of the British Nationality (No 2) Act 1964 (stateless persons) on the ground mentioned in subsection (1)(a) of that section (namely that his mother was a citizen of the United Kingdom and Colonies at the time when he was born) shall not become a British citizen under subsection (1) unless—
- (a) his mother becomes a British citizen under subsection (1) or would have done so but for her death; or
- (b) immediately before commencement he had the right of abode in the United Kingdom by virtue of section 2(1)(c) of the Immigration Act 1971 as then in force (settlement in United Kingdom, combined with five or more years' ordinary residence there as a citizen of the United Kingdom and Colonies).

(3) . . .

NOTES

Sub-s (3): outside the scope of this work.

Renunciation and resumption

12 Renunciation

(1) If any British citizen of full age and capacity makes in the prescribed manner a declaration of renunciation of British citizenship, then, subject to subsections (3) and (4), the Secretary of State shall cause the declaration to be registered.

(2) On the registration of a declaration made in pursuance of this section the person who made it shall cease to be a British citizen.

(3) A declaration made by a person in pursuance of this section shall not be registered unless the Secretary of State is satisfied that the person who made it will after the registration have or acquire some citizenship or nationality other than British citizenship; and if that person does not have any such citizenship or nationality on the date of registration and does not acquire some such citizenship or nationality within six months from that date, he shall be, and be deemed to have remained, a British citizen notwithstanding the registration.

(4) The Secretary of State may withhold registration of any declaration made in pursuance of this section if it is made during any war in which Her Majesty may be engaged in right of Her Majesty's government in the United Kingdom.

(5) For the purposes of this section any person who has been married shall be deemed to be of full age.

PART II
BRITISH DEPENDENT TERRITORIES CITIZENSHIP

Acquisition after commencement

15 Acquisition by birth or adoption

(1) A person born in a dependent territory after commencement shall be a British Dependent Territories citizen if at the time of the birth his father or mother is—

(a) a British Dependent Territories citizen; or
(b) settled in a dependent territory.

(2) A new-born infant who, after commencement, is found abandoned in a dependent territory shall, unless the contrary is shown, be deemed for the purposes of subsection (1)—

(a) to have been born in that territory after commencement; and
(b) to have been born to a parent who at the time of the birth was a British Dependent Territories citizen or settled in a dependent territory.

(3) A person born in a dependent territory after commencement who is not a British Dependent Territories citizen by virtue of subsection (1) or (2) shall be entitled to be registered as such a citizen if, while he is a minor—

(a) his father or mother becomes such a citizen or becomes settled in a dependent territory; and
(b) an application is made for his registration as such a citizen.

(4) A person born in a dependent territory after commencement who is not a British Dependent Territories citizen by virtue of subsection (1) or (2) shall be entitled, on an application for registration as a British Dependent Territories citizen made at any time after he has attained the age of ten years, to be registered as such a

citizen if, as regards each of the first ten years of that person's life, the number of days on which he was absent from that territory in that year does not exceed 90.

(5), (6) . . .

(7) If in the special circumstances of any particular case the Secretary of State thinks fit, he may for the purposes of subsection (4) treat the person to whom the application relates as fulfilling the requirements specified in that subsection although, as regards any one or more of the first ten years of that person's life, the number of days on which he was absent from the dependent territory there mentioned in that year or each of the years in question exceeds 90.

NOTES

Sub-ss (5), (6): outside the scope of this work.

16 Acquisition by descent

(1) A person born outside the dependent territories after commencement shall be a British Dependent Territories citizen if at the time of the birth his father or mother—

- (a) is such a citizen otherwise than by descent; or
- (b) is such a citizen and is serving outside the dependent territories in service to which this paragraph applies, his or her recruitment for that service having taken place in a dependent territory.

(2) Paragraph (b) of subsection (1) applies to—

- (a) Crown service under the government of a dependent territory; and
- (b) service of any description for the time being designated under subsection (3).

(3) For the purposes of this section the Secretary of State may by order made by statutory instrument designate any description of service which he considers to be closely associated with the activities outside the dependent territories of the government of any dependent territory.

(4) Any order made under subsection (3) shall be subject to annulment in pursuance of a resolution of either House of Parliament.

18 Acquisition by naturalisation

(1) If, on an application for naturalisation as a British Dependent Territories citizen made by a person of full age and capacity, the Secretary of State is satisfied that the applicant fulfils the requirements of Schedule 1 for naturalisation as such a citizen under this subsection, he may, if he thinks fit, grant to him a certificate of naturalisation as such a citizen.

(2) If, on an application for naturalisation as a British Dependent Territories citizen made by a person of full age and capacity who on the date of the application is married to such a citizen, the Secretary of State is satisfied that the applicant fulfils the requirements of Schedule 1 for naturalisation as such a citizen under this subsection, he may, if he thinks fit, grant to him a certificate of naturalisation as such a citizen.

(3) Every application under this section shall specify the dependent territory which is to be treated as the relevant territory for the purposes of that application; and, in relation to any such application, references in Schedule 1 to the relevant territory shall be construed accordingly.

PART III
BRITISH OVERSEAS CITIZENSHIP

26 Citizens of UK and Colonies who are to become British Overseas citizens at commencement

Any person who was a citizen of the United Kingdom and Colonies immediately before commencement and who does not at commencement become either a British citizen or a British Dependent Territories citizen shall at commencement become a British Overseas citizen.

PART V
MISCELLANEOUS AND SUPPLEMENTARY

37 Commonwealth citizenship

(1) Every person who—

(a) under [the British Nationality Acts 1981 and 1983] is a British citizen, a British Dependent Territories citizen, [a British National (Overseas),] a British Overseas citizen or a British subject; or

(b) under any enactment for the time being in force in any country mentioned in Schedule 3 is a citizen of that country,

shall have the status of a Commonwealth citizen.

(2) Her Majesty may by Order in Council amend Schedule 3 by the alteration of any entry, the removal of any entry, or the insertion of any additional entry.

(3) Any Order in Council made under this section shall be subject to annulment in pursuance of a resolution of either House of Parliament.

(4) After commencement no person shall have the status of a Commonwealth citizen or the status of a British subject otherwise than under this Act.

NOTES

Sub-s (1): in para (a), words in first pair of square brackets substituted by the British Nationality (Falkland Islands) Act 1983, s 4(3), words in second pair of square brackets inserted by the Hong Kong (British Nationality) Order 1986, SI 1986/948, art 7(3).

40 Deprivation of citizenship

(1) Subject to the provisions of this section, the Secretary of State may by order deprive any British citizen to whom this subsection applies of his British citizenship if the Secretary of State is satisfied that the registration or certificate of naturalisation by virtue of which he is such a citizen was obtained by means of fraud, false representation or the concealment of any material fact.

(2) Subsection (1) applies to any British citizen who—

(a) became a British citizen after commencement by virtue of—

(i) his registration as a British citizen under any provision of [the British Nationality Acts 1981 and 1983]; or

(ii) a certificate of naturalisation granted to him under section 6; or

(b) being immediately before commencement a citizen of the United Kingdom and Colonies by virtue of registration as such a citizen under any provision of the British Nationality Acts 1948 to 1964, became at commencement a British citizen; or

(c) at any time before commencement became a British subject (within the meaning of that expression at that time), or a citizen of Eire or of the Republic of Ireland, by virtue of a certificate of naturalisation granted to him or in which his name was included.

(3) Subject to the provisions of this section, the Secretary of State may by order deprive any British citizen to whom this subsection applies of his British citizenship if the Secretary of State is satisfied that that citizen—

(a) has shown himself by act or speech to be disloyal or disaffected towards Her Majesty; or

(b) has, during any war in which Her Majesty was engaged, unlawfully traded or communicated with an enemy or been engaged in or associated with any business that was to his knowledge carried on in such a manner as to assist an enemy in that war; or

(c) has, within the period of five years from the relevant date, been sentenced in any country to imprisonment for a term of not less than twelve months.

(4) Subsection (3) applies to any British citizen who falls within paragraph (a) or (c) of subsection (2); and in subsection (3) "the relevant date", in relation to a British citizen to whom subsection (3) applies, means the date of the registration by virtue of which he is such a citizen or, as the case may be, the date of the grant of the certificate of naturalisation by virtue of which he is such a citizen.

(5) The Secretary of State—

(a) shall not deprive a person of British citizenship under this section unless he is satisfied that it is not conducive to the public good that that person should continue to be a British citizen; and

(b) shall not deprive a person of British citizenship under subsection (3) on the ground mentioned in paragraph (c) of that subsection if it appears to him that that person would thereupon become stateless.

(6) Before making an order under this section the Secretary of State shall give the person against whom the order is proposed to be made notice in writing informing him of the ground or grounds on which it is proposed to be made and of his right to an inquiry under this section.

(7) If the person against whom the order is proposed to be made applies in the prescribed manner for an inquiry, the Secretary of State shall, and in any other case the Secretary of State may, refer the case to a committee of inquiry consisting of a chairman, being a person possessing judicial experience, appointed by the Secretary of State and of such other members appointed by the Secretary of State as he thinks proper.

(8)–(10) . . .

NOTES

Sub-s (2): words in square brackets in para (a) substituted by the British Nationality (Falkland Islands) Act 1983, s 4(3).

Sub-ss (8)–(10): outside the scope of this work.

42 Registration and naturalisation: general provisions

(1) Subject to subsection (2)—

(a) a person shall not be registered under any provision of this Act as a citizen of any description or as a British subject; and

(b) a certificate of naturalisation shall not be granted to a person under any provision of this Act,

unless—

(i) any fee payable by virtue of this Act in connection with the registration or, as the case may be, the grant of the certificate has been paid; and

(ii) the person concerned has within the prescribed time taken an oath of allegiance in the form indicated in Schedule 5.

(2) So much of subsection (1) as required the taking of an oath of allegiance shall not apply to a person who—

(a) is not of full age; or

(b) is already a British citizen, a British Dependent Territories citizen, [a British National (Overseas),] a British Overseas citizen, a British subject, or a citizen of any country of which Her Majesty is Queen.

(3) Any provision of this Act which provides for a person to be entitled to registration as a citizen of any description or as a British subject shall have effect subject to the preceding provisions of this section.

(4) A person registered under any provision of this Act as a British citizen, or as a British Dependent Territories citizen[, or as a British National (Overseas),] or as a British Overseas citizen, or as a British subject, shall be a citizen of that description or, as the case may be, [a British National (Overseas) or] a British subject as from the date on which he is so registered.

(5) A person to whom a certificate of naturalisation as a British citizen or as a British Dependent Territories citizen is granted under any provision of this Act shall be a citizen of that description as from the date on which the certificate is granted.

[(6) A person who applies for registration or naturalisation as a British Dependent Territories citizen under any provision of this Act by virtue (wholly or partly) of his having a connection with Hong Kong, may not be naturalised or registered, as the case may be, unless he makes his application on or before 31st March 1996.]

NOTES

Sub-ss (2), (4): words in square brackets inserted by the Hong Kong (British Nationality) Order 1986, SI 1986/948, art 7(5).

Sub-s (6): inserted by the Hong Kong (British Nationality) (Amendment) Order 1993, SI 1993/1795, art 3.

44 Decisions involving exercise of discretion

(1) Any discretion vested by or under this Act in the Secretary of State, a Governor or a Lieutenant-Governor shall be exercised without regard to the race, colour or religion of any person who may be affected by its exercise.

(2) The Secretary of State, a Governor or a Lieutenant-Governor, as the case may be, shall not be required to assign any reason for the grant or refusal of any application under this Act the decision on which is at his discretion; and the decision of the Secretary of State or a Governor or Lieutenant-Governor on any such application shall not be subject to appeal to, or review in, any court.

(3) Nothing in this section affects the jurisdiction of any court to entertain proceedings of any description concerning the rights of any person under any provision of this Act.

47 Legitimated children

(1) A person born out of wedlock and legitimated by the subsequent marriage of his parents shall, as from the date of the marriage, be treated for the purposes of this Act as if he had been born legitimate.

(2) A person shall be deemed for the purposes of this section to have been legitimated by the subsequent marriage of his parents if by the law of the place in which his father was domiciled at the time of the marriage the marriage operated immediately or subsequently to legitimate him, and not otherwise.

NOTES

Modification: references to the British Nationality Act 1981 modified to include the Hong Kong (British Nationality) Order 1986, by the Hong Kong (British Nationality) Order 1986, SI 1986/948, art 7(7).

50 Interpretation

(1) In this Act, unless the context otherwise requires—

"the 1948 Act" means the British Nationality Act 1948;

"alien" means a person who is neither a Commonwealth citizen nor a British protected person nor a citizen of the Republic of Ireland;

. . . . .

["British National (Overseas)" means a person who is a British National (Overseas) under the Hong Kong (British Nationality) Order 1986, and "status of a British National (Overseas)" shall be construed accordingly;

"British Overseas citizen" includes a person who is a British Overseas citizen under the Hong Kong (British Nationality) Order 1986;]

"British protected person" means a person who is a member of any class of person declared to be British protected persons by an Order in Council for the time being in force under section 38 or is a British protected person by virtue of the Solomon Islands Act 1978;

. . . . .

"Commonwealth citizen" means a person who has the status of a Commonwealth citizen under this Act;

. . . . .

"Crown service" means the service of the Crown, whether within Her Majesty's dominions or elsewhere;

"Crown service under the government of the United Kingdom" means Crown service under Her Majesty's government in the United Kingdom or under Her Majesty's government in Northern Ireland;

. . . . .

"foreign country" means a country other than the United Kingdom, a dependent territory, a country mentioned in Schedule 3 and the Republic of Ireland;

. . . . .

"immigration laws"—

(a) in relation to the United Kingdom, means the Immigration Act 1971 and any law for purposes similar to that Act which is for the time being or has at any time been in force in any part of the United Kingdom;

(b) in relation to a dependent territory, means any law for purposes similar to the Immigration Act 1971 which is for the time being or has at any time been in force in that territory;

. . . . . .

"the United Kingdom" means Great Britain, Northern Ireland and the Islands, taken together;

. . . . . .

(2) Subject to subsection (3), references in this Act to a person being settled in the United Kingdom or in a dependent territory are references to his being ordinarily resident in the United Kingdom or, as the case may be, in that territory without being subject under the immigration laws to any restriction on the period for which he may remain.

(3), (4) . . .

(5) It is hereby declared that a person is not to be treated for the purpose of any provision of this Act as ordinarily resident in the United Kingdom or in a dependent territory at a time when he is in the United Kingdom or, as the case may be, in that territory in breach of the immigration laws.

(6)–(8) . . .

(9) For the purposes of this Act—

(a) the relationship of mother and child shall be taken to exist between a woman and any child (legitimate or illegitimate) born to her; but

(b) subject to section 47, the relationship of father and child shall be taken to exist only between a man and any legitimate child born to him;

and the expressions "mother", "father", "parent", "child" and "descended" shall be construed accordingly.

(10)–(13) . . .

NOTES

Sub-s (1): definitions "British National (Overseas)" and "British Overseas citizen" inserted by the Hong Kong (British Nationality) Order 1986, SI 1986/948, art 7(8); definitions omitted outside the scope of this work.

Sub-ss (3), (4), (6)–(8), (10)–(13): outside the scope of this work.

53 Citation, commencement and extent

(1) This Act may be cited as the British Nationality Act 1981.

(2) This Act, . . . shall come into force on such day as the Secretary of State may by order made by statutory instrument appoint; and references to the commencement of this Act shall be construed as references to the beginning of that day.

(3) . . .

(4) This Act extends to Northern Ireland.

(5)–(7) . . .

NOTES

Words omitted from sub-s (2) and sub-ss (3), (5)–(7) outside the scope of this work.

SCHEDULE 1

Sections 6, 18

REQUIREMENTS FOR NATURALISATION

Naturalisation as a British citizen under section 6(1)

1.—(1) Subject to paragraph 2, the requirements for naturalisation as a British citizen under section 6(1) are, in the case of any person who applies for it—

- (a) the requirements specified in sub-paragraph (2) of this paragraph, or the alternative requirement specified in sub-paragraph (3) of this paragraph; and
- (b) that he is of good character; and
- (c) that he has a sufficient knowledge of the English, Welsh or Scottish Gaelic language; and
- (d) that either—
  - (i) his intentions are such that, in the event of a certificate of naturalisation as a British citizen being granted to him, his home or (if he has more than one) his principal home will be in the United Kingdom; or
  - (ii) he intends, in the event of such a certificate being granted to him, to enter into, or continue in, Crown service under the government of the United Kingdom, or service under an international organisation of which the United Kingdom or Her Majesty's government therein is a member, or service in the employment of a company or association established in the United Kingdom.

(2) The requirements referred to in sub-paragraph (1)(a) of this paragraph are—

- (a) that the applicant was in the United Kingdom at the beginning of the period of five years ending with the date of the application, and that the number of days on which he was absent from the United Kingdom in that period does not exceed 450; and
- (b) that the number of days on which he was absent from the United Kingdom in the period of twelve months so ending does not exceed 90; and
- (c) that he was not at any time in the period of twelve months so ending subject under the immigration laws to any restriction on the period for which he might remain in the United Kingdom; and
- (d) that he was not at any time in the period of five years so ending in the United Kingdom in breach of the immigration laws.

(3) The alternative requirement referred to in sub-paragraph (1)(a) of this paragraph is that on the date of the application he is serving outside the United Kingdom in Crown service under the government of the United Kingdom.

2. . . .

Naturalisation as a British citizen under section 6(2)

3. Subject to paragraph 4, the requirements for naturalisation as a British citizen under section 6(2) are, in the case of any person who applies for it—

- (a) that he was in the United Kingdom at the beginning of the period of three years ending with the date of the application, and that the number of days on which he was absent from the United Kingdom in that period does not exceed 270; and
- (b) that the number of days on which he was absent from the United Kingdom in the period of twelve months so ending does not exceed 90; and
- (c) that on the date of the application he was not subject under the immigration laws to any restriction on the period for which he might remain in the United Kingdom; and
- (d) that he was not at any time in the period of three years ending with the date of the application in the United Kingdom in breach of the immigration laws; and
- (e) the requirement specified in paragraph 1(1)(b).

4–10. . . .

NOTES

Paras 2, 4–10: outside the scope of this work.

REPRESENTATION OF THE PEOPLE ACT 1983

(C 2)

An Act to consolidate the Representation of the People Acts of 1949, 1969, 1977, 1978 and 1980, the Electoral Registers Acts of 1949 and 1953, the Elections (Welsh Forms) Act 1964, Part III of the Local Government Act 1972, sections 6 to 10 of the Local Government (Scotland) Act 1973, the Representation of the People (Armed Forces) Act 1976, the Returning Officers (Scotland) Act 1977, section 3 of the Representation of the People Act 1981, section 62 of and Schedule 2 to the Mental Health (Amendment) Act 1982, and connected provisions; and to repeal as obsolete the Representation of the People Act 1979 and other enactments related to the Representation of the People Acts

[8 February 1983]

PART I
PARLIAMENTARY AND LOCAL GOVERNMENT FRANCHISE AND ITS EXERCISE

Parliamentary and local government franchise

1 Parliamentary electors

(1) A person entitled to vote as an elector at a parliamentary election in any constituency is one who—

(a) is resident there on the qualifying date (subject to subsection (2) below in relation to Northern Ireland); and

(b) on that date and on the date of the poll—

(i) is not subject to any legal incapacity to vote (age apart); and

(ii) is either a Commonwealth citizen or a citizen of the Republic of Ireland;

and

(c) is of voting age (that is, 18 years or over) on the date of the poll.

(2) A person is not entitled to vote as an elector at a parliamentary election in any constituency in Northern Ireland unless he was resident in Northern Ireland during the whole of the period of three months ending on the qualifying date for that election.

(3) A person is not entitled to vote as an elector in any constituency unless registered there in the register of parliamentary electors to be used at the election.

(4) A person is not entitled to vote as an elector—

(a) more than once in the same constituency at any parliamentary election;

(b) in more than one constituency at a general election.

PART II
THE ELECTION CAMPAIGN

Election expenses

75 Prohibition of expenses not authorised by election agent

(1) No expenses shall, with a view to promoting or procuring the election of a candidate at an election, be incurred by any person other than the candidate, his election agent and persons authorised in writing by the election agent on account—

(a) of holding public meetings or organising any public display; or
(b) of issuing advertisements, circulars or publications; or
(c) of otherwise presenting to the electors the candidate or his views or the extent or nature of his backing or disparaging another candidate,

but paragraph (c) of this subsection shall not—
(i) restrict the publication of any matter relating to the election in a newspaper or other periodical or in a broadcast made by the British Broadcasting Corporation [or by Sianel Pedwar Cymru or in a programme included in any service licensed under Part I or III of the Broadcasting Act 1990 [or Part I or II of the Broadcasting Act 1996]]; or
(ii) apply to any expenses not exceeding in the aggregate the sum of [£5] which may be incurred by an individual and are not incurred in pursuance of a plan suggested by or concerted with others, or to expenses incurred by any person in travelling or in living away from home or similar personal expenses.

(2)–(6) . . .

NOTES

Sub-s (1): words in first (outer) pair of square brackets in para (i) substituted, subject to a transitional modification, by the Broadcasting Act 1990, s 203(1), (4), Sch 20, para 35(1), (2), Sch 22, para 5(1), (2); words in second (inner) pair of square brackets in para (i) inserted by the Broadcasting Act 1996, s 148(1), Sch 10, Pt III, para 28; reference to "£5" in para (ii) substituted by the Representation of the People Act 1985, s 14(3).

Sub-ss (2)–(6): outside the scope of this work.

Publicity at parliamentary elections

92 Broadcasting from outside United Kingdom

[(1) No person shall, with intent to influence persons to give or refrain from giving their votes at a parliamentary or local government election, include, or aid, abet, counsel or procure the inclusion of, any matter relating to the election in any programme service (within the meaning of the Broadcasting Act 1990) provided from a place outside the United Kingdom otherwise than in pursuance of arrangements made with—
(a) the British Broadcasting Corporation;
(b) Sianel Pedwar Cymru; or
(c) the holder of any licence granted by the Independent Television Commission or the Radio Authority,

for the reception and re-transmission of that matter by that body or the holder of that licence.]

(2) An offence under this section shall be an illegal practice, but the court before whom a person is convicted of an offence under this section may, if they think it just in the special circumstances of the case, mitigate or entirely remit any incapacity imposed by virtue of section 173 below.

(3) Where any act or omission of an association or body of persons, corporate or unincorporate, is an illegal practice under this section, any person who at the time of the act or omission was a director, general manager, secretary or other similar officer of the association or body, or was purporting to act in any such capacity, shall be deemed to be guilty of the illegal practice, unless he proves—
(a) that the act or omission took place without his consent or connivance; and

(b) that he exercised all such diligence to prevent the commission of the illegal practice as he ought to have exercised having regard to the nature of his functions in that capacity and to all the circumstances.

NOTES

Sub-s (1): substituted, subject to a transitional modification, by the Broadcasting Act 1990, s 203(1), (4), Sch 20, para 35(1), (3), Sch 22, para 6.

93 Broadcasting during elections

(1) In relation to a parliamentary or local government election—

(a) pending such an election it shall not be lawful for any item about the constituency or electoral area to be—

[(i) broadcast by the British Broadcasting Corporation or Sianel Pedwar Cymru, or

(ii) included in any service licensed under Part I or III of the Broadcasting Act 1990 or Part I or II of the Broadcasting Act 1996]

if any of the persons who are for the time being candidates at the election takes part in the item and the broadcast is not made with his consent; and

(b) where an item about a constituency or electoral area is so broadcast pending such an election there, then if the broadcast either is made before the latest time for delivery of nomination papers, or is made after that time but without the consent of any candidate remaining validly nominated, any person taking part in the item for the purpose of promoting or procuring his election shall be guilty of an illegal practice, unless the broadcast is so made without his consent.

(2), (3) . . .

NOTES

Sub-s (1): para (a)(i), (ii) substituted by the Broadcasting Act 1996, s 148(1), Sch 10, Pt III, para 29.

Sub-s (2): outside the scope of this work.

Sub-s (3): added by the Cable and Broadcasting Act 1984, s 57(1), Sch 5, para 44(2), and repealed by the Broadcasting Act 1990, s 203(1), (3), Sch 20, para 35(1), (4)(b), Sch 21.

Election meetings

95 Schools and rooms for parliamentary election meetings

(1) Subject to the provisions of this section, a candidate at a parliamentary election is entitled for the purpose of holding public meetings in furtherance of his candidature to the use [free of charge] at reasonable times between the receipt of the writ and [the day preceding] the date of the poll of—

(a) a suitable room in the premises of a school to which this section applies;

(b) any meeting room to which this section applies.

(2)–(8) . . .

NOTES

Similar provision in respect of schools and rooms for local election meetings is made by s 96 of this Act.

Sub-s (1): words in square brackets inserted by the Representation of the People Act 1985, s 24, Sch 4, para 37(a).

Sub-ss (2)–(8): outside the scope of this work.

97 Disturbances at election meetings

(1) A person who at a lawful public meeting to which this section applies acts, or incites others to act, in a disorderly manner for the purpose of preventing the transaction of the business for which the meeting was called together shall be guilty of an illegal practice.

(2) This section applies to—

(a) a political meeting held in any constituency between the date of the issue of a writ for the return of a member of Parliament for the constituency and the date at which a return to the writ is made;

(b) a meeting held with reference to a local government election in the electoral area for that election [in the period beginning with the last date on which notice of the election may be published in accordance with rules made under section 36 or, in Scotland, section 42 above and ending with] the day of election.

(3) If a constable reasonably suspects any person of committing an offence under subsection (1) above, he may if requested so to do by the chairman of the meeting require that person to declare to him immediately his name and address and, if that person refuses or fails so to declare his name and address or gives a false name and address, he shall be liable on summary conviction to a fine not exceeding level 1 on the standard scale, . . .

This subsection does not apply in Northern Ireland.

NOTES

Sub-s (2): words in square brackets in para (b) substituted by the Representation of the People Act 1985, s 24, Sch 4, para 39.

Sub-s (3): words omitted repealed by the Police and Criminal Evidence Act 1984, ss 26(1), 119(2), Sch 7, Pt I.

Agency by election officials and canvassing by police officers

100 Illegal canvassing by police officers

(1) No member of a police force shall by word, message, writing or in any other manner, endeavour to persuade any person to give, or dissuade any person from giving, his vote, whether as an elector or as proxy—

(a) at any parliamentary election for a constituency, or

(b) at any local government election for any electoral area,

wholly or partly within the police area.

(2) A person acting in contravention of subsection (1) above shall be liable [on summary conviction to a fine not exceeding level 3 on the standard scale, but] nothing in that subsection shall subject a member of a police force to any penalty for anything done in the discharge of his duty as a member of the force.

(3) In this section references to a member of a police force and to a police area are to be taken in relation to Northern Ireland as references to a member of the Royal Ulster Constabulary and to Northern Ireland.

NOTES

Sub-s (2): words in square brackets substituted by the Representation of the People Act 1985, s 23, Sch 3, para 5.

PART V
GENERAL AND SUPPLEMENTAL

Operation

207 Citation and commencement

(1) This Act may be cited as the Representation of the People Act 1983, and is included among the Acts which may be cited as the Representation of the People Acts.

(2) This Act shall come into force on such day as the Secretary of State may by order made by statutory instrument appoint.

NATIONAL AUDIT ACT 1983

(C 44)

An Act to strengthen Parliamentary control and supervision of expenditure of public money by making new provision for the appointment and status of the Comptroller and Auditor General, establishing a Public Accounts Commission and a National Audit Office and making new provision for promoting economy, efficiency and effectiveness in the use of such money by government departments and other authorities and bodies; to amend or repeal certain provisions of the Exchequer and Audit Departments Acts 1866 and 1921; and for connected purposes

[13 May 1983]

1 Appointment and status of Comptroller and Auditor General

(1) The power of Her Majesty under section 6 of the Exchequer and Audit Departments Act 1866 (appointment of Comptroller and Auditor General) shall be exercisable on an address presented by the House of Commons, and no motion shall be made for such an address except by the Prime Minister acting with the agreement of the Chairman of the Committee of Public Accounts.

(2) The Comptroller and Auditor General shall by virtue of his office be an officer of the House of Commons.

(3) Subject to any duty imposed on him by statute, the Comptroller and Auditor General shall have complete discretion in the discharge of his functions and, in particular, in determining whether to carry out any examination under Part II of this Act and as to the manner in which any such examination is carried out; but in determining whether to carry out any such examination he shall take into account any proposals made by the Committee of Public Accounts.

(4) Subsection (2) above shall not be construed as applying any provision of section 4 of the House of Commons (Administration) Act 1978 (House departments and persons employed in or for the purposes of the House) to the Comptroller and Auditor General, to the National Audit Office or to any member of its staff.

2 The Public Accounts Commission

(1) There shall be a body of Commissioners named the Public Accounts Commission (in this Act referred to as "the Commission") which shall perform the functions conferred on it by this Act.

(2) The Commission shall consist of—
(a) the Member of the House of Commons who is for the time being the Chairman of the Committee of Public Accounts;
(b) the Leader of the House of Commons; and
(c) seven other Members of the House of Commons appointed by the House, none of whom shall be a Minister of the Crown.

(3) The Commission shall from time to time present to the House of Commons a report on the exercise of its functions.

(4) Schedule 1 to this Act shall have effect as respects the Commission.

3 The National Audit Office

(1) There shall be a National Audit Office consisting of—
(a) the Comptroller and Auditor General, who shall be the head of that Office; and
(b) the staff appointed by him under this section.

(2) The Comptroller and Auditor General shall appoint such staff for the National Audit Office as he considers necessary for assisting him in the discharge of his functions.

(3) The staff shall be appointed at such remuneration and on such other terms and conditions as the Comptroller and Auditor General may determine.

(4) Employment as a member of the staff of the National Audit Office shall be included among the kinds of employment to which a superannuation scheme under section 1 of the Superannuation Act 1972 can apply; and in exercising his powers under subsection (3) above the Comptroller and Auditor General shall have regard to the desirability of keeping the remuneration and other terms and conditions of employment of the staff of that Office broadly in line with those applying to persons employed in the civil service of the State.

(5) . . . neither the Comptroller and Auditor General nor any member of the staff of the National Audit Office shall be regarded as holding office under Her Majesty or as discharging any functions on behalf of the Crown.

(6) In section 2(2) of the Exchequer and Audit Departments Act 1957 the reference to the department of the Comptroller and Auditor General shall be construed as a reference to the National Audit Office.

(7) Schedule 2 to this Act shall have effect for supplementing the provisions of this section.

NOTES

Sub-s (5): words omitted repealed by the Official Secrets Act 1989, s 16(4), Sch 2.

PART II
ECONOMY, EFFICIENCY AND EFFECTIVENESS EXAMINATIONS

6 Public departments etc

(1) The Comptroller and Auditor General may carry out examinations into the economy, efficiency and effectiveness with which any department, authority or other body to which this section applies has used its resources in discharging its functions.

(2) Subsection (1) above shall not be construed as entitling the Comptroller and Auditor General to question the merits of the policy objectives of any department, authority or body in respect of which an examination is carried out.

(3) Subject to subsections (4) and (5) below, this section applies to—

(a) any department in respect of which appropriation accounts are required to be prepared under the Exchequer and Audit Departments Act 1866;

(b) any body required to keep accounts under section 98 of the National Health Service Act 1977 or section 86 of the National Health Service (Scotland) Act 1978;

(c) any other authority or body whose accounts are required to be examined and certified by, or are open to the inspection of, the Comptroller and Auditor General by virtue of any enactment, including an enactment passed after this Act; and

(d) any authority or body which does not fall within section 7 below and whose accounts are required to be examined and certified by, or are open to the inspection of, the Comptroller and Auditor General by virtue of any agreement made, whether before or after the passing of this Act, between that authority or body and a Minister of the Crown.

(4)–(6) . . .

(7) In this section—

"authority" includes any person holding a public office;

"Minister" or "Minister of the Crown" includes any department falling within subsection (3)(a) above;

"policy", in relation to any such department, includes any policy of the government so far as relating to the functions of that department;

and references to an agreement made by a Minister include references to conditions imposed by him in pursuance of any statutory power in that behalf, whether in connection with the provision of financial assistance or otherwise.

NOTES

Sub-ss (4)–(6): outside the scope of this work.

7 Other bodies mainly supported by public funds

(1) If the Comptroller and Auditor General has reasonable cause to believe that any authority or body to which this section applies has in any of its financial years received more than half its income from public funds he may carry out an examination into the economy, efficiency and effectiveness with which it has in that year used its resources in discharging its functions.

(2) Subsection (1) above shall not be construed as entitling the Comptroller and Auditor General to question the merits of the policy objectives of any authority or body in respect of which an examination is carried out.

(3) In determining for the purposes of subsection (1) above whether the income of an authority or body is such as to bring it within that subsection the Comptroller and Auditor General shall consult that authority or body and the Treasury.

(4) This section applies to any authority or body appointed, or whose members are required to be appointed, by or on behalf of the Crown except a body specified in Schedule 4 to this Act.

(5), (6) . . .

NOTES

Sub-ss (5), (6): outside the scope of this work.

8 Right to obtain documents and information

(1) Subject to subsection (2) below, the Comptroller and Auditor General shall have a right of access at all reasonable times to all such documents as he may reasonably require for carrying out any examination under section 6 or 7 above and shall be entitled to require from any person holding or accountable for any such document such information and explanation as are reasonably necessary for that purpose.

(2) Subsection (1) above applies only to documents in the custody or under the control of the department, authority or body to which the examination relates.

9 Reports to House of Commons

The Comptroller and Auditor General may report to the House of Commons the results of any examination carried out by him under section 6 or 7 above.

PART III
MISCELLANEOUS AND SUPPLEMENTARY

15 Short title and commencement

(1) This Act may be cited as the National Audit Act 1983.

(2) Subject to subsection (3) below, this Act shall come into force on 1st January 1984.

(3) . . .

NOTES

Sub-s (3): outside the scope of this work.

POLICE AND CRIMINAL EVIDENCE ACT 1984

(C 60)

An Act to make further provision in relation to the powers and duties of the police, persons in police detention, criminal evidence, police discipline and complaints against the police; to provide for arrangements for obtaining the views of the community on policing and for a rank of deputy chief constable; to amend the law relating to the Police Federations and Police Forces and Police Cadets in Scotland; and for connected purposes

[31 October 1984]

PART I
POWERS TO STOP AND SEARCH

1 Power of constable to stop and search persons, vehicles etc

(1) A constable may exercise any power conferred by this section—

(a) in any place to which at the time when he proposes to exercise the power the public or any section of the public has access, on payment or otherwise, as of right or by virtue of express or implied permission; or

(b) in any other place to which people have ready access at the time when he proposes to exercise the power but which is not a dwelling.

(2) Subject to subsection (3) to (5) below, a constable—

(a) may search—

(i) any person or vehicle;

(ii) anything which is in or on a vehicle,

for stolen or prohibited articles [or any article to which subsection (8A) below applies]; and

(b) may detain a person or vehicle for the purpose of such a search.

(3) This section does not give a constable power to search a person or vehicle or anything in or on a vehicle unless he has reasonable grounds for suspecting that he will find stolen or prohibited articles [or any article to which subsection (8A) below applies].

(4) If a person is in a garden or yard occupied with and used for the purposes of a dwelling or on other land so occupied and used, a constable may not search him in the exercise of the power conferred by this section unless the constable has reasonable grounds for believing—

(a) that he does not reside in the dwelling; and

(b) that he is not in the place in question with the express or implied permission of a person who resides in the dwelling.

(5) If a vehicle is in a garden or yard occupied with and used for the purposes of a dwelling or on other land so occupied and used, a constable may not search the vehicle or anything in or on it in the exercise of the power conferred by this section unless he has reasonable grounds for believing—

(a) that the person in charge of the vehicle does not reside in the dwelling; and

(b) that the vehicle is not in the place in question with the express or implied permission of a person who resides in the dwelling.

(6) If in the course of such a search a constable discovers an article which he has reasonable grounds for suspecting to be a stolen or prohibited article [or an article to which subsection (8A) below applies], he may seize it.

(7) An article is prohibited for the purposes of this Part of this Act if it is—

(a) an offensive weapon; or

(b) an article—

(i) made or adapted for use in the course of or in connection with an offence to which this sub-paragraph applies; or

(ii) intended by the person having it with him for such use by him or by some other person.

(8) The offences to which subsection (7)(b)(i) above applies are—

(a) burglary;

(b) theft;

(c) offences under section 12 of the Theft Act 1968 (taking motor vehicle or other conveyance without authority); and

(d) offences under section 15 of that Act (obtaining property by deception).

[(8A) This subsection applies to any article in relation to which a person has committed, or is committing or is going to commit an offence under section 139 of the Criminal Justice Act 1988.]

(9) In this Part of this Act "offensive weapon" means any article—

(a) made or adapted for use for causing injury to persons; or

(b) intended by the person having it with him for such use by him or by some other person.

NOTES

Sub-s (2): words in square brackets in para (a) inserted by the Criminal Justice Act 1988, s 140(1)(a)(i).
Sub-s (3): words in square brackets inserted by the Criminal Justice Act 1988, s 140(1)(a)(ii).
Sub-s (6): words in square brackets inserted by the Criminal Justice Act 1988, s 140(1)(b).
Sub-s (8A): inserted by the Criminal Justice Act 1988, s 140(1)(c).

2 Provisions relating to search under section 1 and other powers

(1) A constable who detains a person or vehicle in the exercise—
- (a) of the power conferred by section 1 above; or
- (b) of any other power—
  - (i) to search a person without first arresting him; or
  - (ii) to search a vehicle without making an arrest,

need not conduct a search if it appears to him subsequently—
- (i) that no search is required; or
- (ii) that a search is impracticable.

(2) If a constable contemplates a search, other than a search of an unattended vehicle, in the exercise—
- (a) of the power conferred by section 1 above; or
- (b) of any other power, except the power conferred by section 6 below and the power conferred by section 27(2) of the Aviation Security Act 1982—
  - (i) to search a person without first arresting him; or
  - (ii) to search a vehicle without making an arrest,

it shall be his duty, subject to subsection (4) below, to take reasonable steps before he commences the search to bring to the attention of the appropriate person—
- (i) if the constable is not in uniform, documentary evidence that he is a constable; and
- (ii) whether he is in uniform or not, the matters specified in subsection (3) below;

and the constable shall not commence the search until he has performed that duty.

(3) The matters referred to in subsection (2)(ii) above are—
- (a) the constable's name and the name of the police station to which he is attached;
- (b) the object of the proposed search;
- (c) the constable's grounds for proposing to make it; and
- (d) the effect of section 3(7) or (8) below, as may be appropriate.

(4) A constable need not bring the effect of section 3(7) or (8) below to the attention of the appropriate person if it appears to the constable that it will not be practicable to make the record in section 3(1) below.

(5) In this section "the appropriate person" means—
- (a) if the constable proposes to search a person, that person; and
- (b) if he proposes to search a vehicle, or anything in or on a vehicle, the person in charge of the vehicle.

(6) On completing a search of an unattended vehicle or anything in or on such a vehicle in the exercise of any such power as is mentioned in subsection (2) above a constable shall leave a notice—

(a) stating that he has searched it;
(b) giving the name of the police station to which he is attached;
(c) stating that an application for compensation for any damage caused by the search may be made to that police station; and
(d) stating the effect of section 3(8) below.

(7) . . .

(8) The time for which a person or vehicle may be detained for the purposes of such a search is such time as is reasonably required to permit a search to be carried out either at the place where the person or vehicle was first detained or nearby.

(9) Neither the power conferred by section 1 above nor any other power to detain and search a person without first arresting him or to detain and search a vehicle without making an arrest is to be construed—
(a) as authorising a constable to require a person to remove any of his clothing in public other than an outer coat, jacket or gloves; or
(b) as authorising a constable not in uniform to stop a vehicle.

(10) . . .

NOTES

Sub-ss (7), (10): outside the scope of this work.

3 Duty to make records concerning searches

(1) Where a constable has carried out a search in the exercise of any such power as is mentioned in section 2(1) above, other than a search—
(a) under section 6 below; or
(b) under section 27(2) of the Aviation Security Act 1982,

he shall make a record of it in writing unless it is not practicable to do so.

(2) If—
(a) a constable is required by subsection (1) above to make a record of a search; but
(b) it is not practicable to make the record on the spot,

he shall make it as soon as practicable after the completion of the search.

(3) The record of a search of a person shall include a note of his name, if the constable knows it, but a constable may not detain a person to find out his name.

(4) If a constable does not know the name of the person whom he has searched, the record of the search shall include a note otherwise describing that person.

(5) The record of a search of a vehicle shall include a note describing the vehicle.

(6) The record of a search of a person or a vehicle—
(a) shall state—
(i) the object of the search;
(ii) the grounds for making it;
(iii) the date and time when it was made;
(iv) the place where it was made;
(v) whether anything, and if so what, was found;
(vi) whether any, and if so what, injury to a person or damage to property appears to the constable to have resulted from the search; and
(b) shall identify the constable making it.

(7) If a constable who conducted a search of a person made a record of it, the person who was searched shall be entitled to a copy of the record if he asks for one before the end of the period specified in subsection (9) below.

(8) If—

(a) the owner of a vehicle which has been searched or the person who was in charge of the vehicle at the time when it was searched asks for a copy of the record of the search before the end of the period specified in subsection (9) below; and

(b) the constable who conducted the search made a record of it,

the person who made the request shall be entitled to a copy.

(9) The period mentioned in subsections (7) and (8) above is the period of 12 months beginning with the date on which the search was made.

(10) . . .

NOTES

Sub-s (10): outside the scope of this work.

4 Road checks

(1) This section shall have effect in relation to the conduct of road checks by police officers for the purpose of ascertaining whether a vehicle is carrying—

(a) a person who has committed an offence other than a road traffic offence or a [vehicle] excise offence;

(b) a person who is a witness to such an offence;

(c) a person intending to commit such an offence; or

(d) a person who is unlawfully at large.

(2) For the purposes of this section a road check consists of the exercise in a locality of the power conferred by [section 163 of the Road Traffic Act 1988] in such a way as to stop during the period for which its exercise in that way in that locality continues all vehicles or vehicles selected by any criterion.

(3) Subject to subsection (5) below, there may only be such a road check if a police officer of the rank of superintendent or above authorises it in writing.

(4) An officer may only authorise a road check under subsection (3) above—

(a) for the purpose specified in subsection (1)(a) above, if he has reasonable grounds—

(i) for believing that the offence is a serious arrestable offence; and

(ii) for suspecting that the person is, or is about to be, in the locality in which vehicles would be stopped if the road check were authorised;

(b) for the purpose specified in subsection (1)(b) above, if he has reasonable grounds for believing that the offence is a serious arrestable offence;

(c) for the purpose specified in subsection (1)(c) above, if he has reasonable grounds—

(i) for believing that the offence would be a serious arrestable offence; and

(ii) for suspecting that the person is, or is about to be, in the locality in which vehicles would be stopped if the road check were authorised;

(d) for the purpose specified in subsection (1)(d) above, if he has reasonable grounds for suspecting that the person is, or is about to be, in that locality.

(5) An officer below the rank of superintendent may authorise such a road check if it appears to him that it is required as a matter of urgency for one of the purposes specified in subsection (1) above.

(6) If an authorisation is given under subsection (5) above, it shall be the duty of the officer who gives it—
  (a) to make a written record of the time at which he gives it; and
  (b) to cause an officer of the rank of superintendent or above to be informed that it has been given.

(7)–(12) . . .

(13) Every written authorisation shall specify—
  (a) the name of the officer giving it;
  (b) the purpose of the road check; and
  (c) the locality in which vehicles are to be stopped.

(14) . . .

(15) Where a vehicle is stopped in a road check, the person in charge of the vehicle at the time when it is stopped shall be entitled to obtain a written statement of the purpose of the road check if he applies for such a statement not later than the end of the period of twelve months from the day on which the vehicle was stopped.

(16) Nothing in this section affects the exercise by police officers of any power to stop vehicles for purposes other than those specified in subsection (1) above.

NOTES

Sub-s (1): word in square brackets in para (a) substituted by the Vehicle Excise and Registration Act 1994, s 63, Sch 3, para 19.

Sub-s (2): words in square brackets substituted by the Road Traffic (Consequential Provisions) Act 1988, s 4, Sch 3, para 27(1).

Sub-ss (7)–(12), (14): outside the scope of this work.

PART II
POWERS OF ENTRY, SEARCH AND SEIZURE

Search warrants

8 Power of justice of the peace to authorise entry and search of premises

(1) If on an application made by a constable a justice of the peace is satisfied that there are reasonable grounds for believing—
  (a) that a serious arrestable offence has been committed; and
  (b) that there is material on premises specified in the application which is likely to be of substantial value (whether by itself or together with other material) to the investigation of the offence; and
  (c) that the material is likely to be relevant evidence; and
  (d) that it does not consist of or include items subject to legal privilege, excluded material or special procedure material; and
  (e) that any of the conditions specified in subsection (3) below applies,

he may issue a warrant authorising a constable to enter and search the premises.

(2) A constable may seize and retain anything for which a search has been authorised under subsection (1) above.

(3) The conditions mentioned in subsection (1)(e) above are—

(a) that it is not practicable to communicate with any person entitled to grant entry to the premises;

(b) that it is practicable to communicate with a person entitled to grant entry to the premises but it is not practicable to communicate with any person entitled to grant access to the evidence;

(c) that entry to the premises will not be granted unless a warrant is produced;

(d) that the purpose of a search may be frustrated or seriously prejudiced unless a constable arriving at the premises can secure immediate entry to them.

(4) In this Act "relevant evidence", in relation to an offence, means anything that would be admissible in evidence at a trial for the offence.

(5) The power to issue a warrant conferred by this section is in addition to any such power otherwise conferred.

9 Special provisions as to access

(1) A constable may obtain access to excluded material or special procedure material for the purposes of a criminal investigation by making an application under Schedule 1 below and in accordance with that Schedule.

(2) Any Act (including a local Act) passed before this Act under which a search of premises for the purposes of a criminal investigation could be authorised by the issue of a warrant to a constable shall cease to have effect so far as it relates to the authorisation of searches—

(a) for items subject to legal privilege; or

(b) for excluded material; or

(c) for special procedure material consisting of documents or records other than documents.

10 Meaning of "items subject to legal privilege"

(1) Subject to subsection (2) below, in this Act "items subject to legal privilege" means—

(a) communications between a professional legal adviser and his client or any person representing his client made in connection with the giving of legal advice to the client;

(b) communications between a professional legal adviser and his client or any person representing his client or between such an adviser or his client or any such representative and any other person made in connection with or in contemplation of legal proceedings and for the purposes of such proceedings; and

(c) items enclosed with or referred to in such communications and made—

(i) in connection with the giving of legal advice; or

(ii) in connection with or in contemplation of legal proceedings and for the purposes of such proceedings,

when they are in the possession of a person who is entitled to possession of them.

(2) Items held with the intention of furthering a criminal purpose are not items subject to legal privilege.

11 Meaning of "excluded material"

(1) Subject to the following provisions of this section, in this Act "excluded material" means—

(a) personal records which a person has acquired or created in the course of any trade, business, profession or other occupation or for the purposes of any paid or unpaid office and which he holds in confidence;

(b) human tissue or tissue fluid which has been taken for the purposes of diagnosis or medical treatment and which a person holds in confidence;

(c) journalistic material which a person holds in confidence and which consists—

(i) of documents; or

(ii) of records other than documents.

(2) A person holds material other than journalistic material in confidence for the purposes of this section if he holds it subject—

(a) to an express or implied undertaking to hold it in confidence; or

(b) to a restriction on disclosure or an obligation of secrecy contained in any enactment, including an enactment contained in an Act passed after this Act.

(3) A person holds journalistic material in confidence for the purposes of this section if—

(a) he holds it subject to such an undertaking, restriction or obligation; and

(b) it has been continuously held (by one or more persons) subject to such an undertaking, restriction or obligation since it was first acquired or created for the purposes of journalism.

12 Meaning of "personal records"

In this Part of this Act "personal records" means documentary and other records concerning an individual (whether living or dead) who can be identified from them and relating—

(a) to his physical or mental health;

(b) to spiritual counselling or assistance given or to be given to him; or

(c) to counselling or assistance given or to be given to him, for the purposes of his personal welfare, by any voluntary organisation or by any individual who—

(i) by reason of his office or occupation has responsibilities for his personal welfare; or

(ii) by reason of an order of a court has responsibilities for his supervision.

13 Meaning of "journalistic material"

(1) Subject to subsection (2) below, in this Act "journalistic material" means material acquired or created for the purposes of journalism.

(2) Material is only journalistic material for the purposes of this Act if it is in the possession of a person who acquired or created it for the purposes of journalism.

(3) A person who receives material from someone who intends that the recipient shall use it for the purposes of journalism is to be taken to have acquired it for those purposes.

14 Meaning of "special procedure material"

(1) In this Act "special procedure material" means—
- (a) material to which subsection (2) below applies; and
- (b) journalistic material, other than excluded material.

(2) Subject to the following provisions of this section, this subsection applies to material, other than items subject to legal privilege and excluded material, in the possession of a person who—
- (a) acquired or created it in the course of any trade, business, profession or other occupation or for the purpose of any paid or unpaid office; and
- (b) holds it subject—
  - (i) to an express or implied undertaking to hold it in confidence; or
  - (ii) to a restriction or obligation such as is mentioned in section 11(2)(b) above.

(3) Where material is acquired—
- (a) by an employee from his employer and in the course of his employment; or
- (b) by a company from an associated company,

it is only special procedure material if it was special procedure material immediately before the acquisition.

(4)–(6) . . .

NOTES

Sub-ss (4)–(6): outside the scope of this work.

15 Search warrants—safeguards

(1) This section and section 16 below have effect in relation to the issue to constables under any enactment, including an enactment contained in an Act passed after this Act, of warrants to enter and search premises; and an entry on or search of premises under a warrant is unlawful unless it complies with this section and section 16 below.

(2) Where a constable applies for any such warrant, it shall be his duty—
- (a) to state—
  - (i) the ground on which he makes the application; and
  - (ii) the enactment under which the warrant would be issued;
- (b) to specify the premises which it is desired to enter and search; and
- (c) to identify, so far as is practicable, the articles or persons to be sought.

(3) An application for such a warrant shall be made ex parte and supported by an information in writing.

(4) The constable shall answer on oath any question that the justice of the peace or judge hearing the application asks him.

(5) A warrant shall authorise an entry on one occasion only.

(6) A warrant—
- (a) shall specify—
  - (i) the name of the person who applies for it;
  - (ii) the date on which it is issued;
  - (iii) the enactment under which it is issued; and

(iv) the premises to be searched; and

(b) shall identify, so far as is practicable, the articles or persons to be sought.

(7), (8) . . .

NOTES

Sub-ss (7), (8): outside the scope of this work.

16 Execution of warrants

(1) A warrant to enter and search premises may be executed by any constable.

(2) Such a warrant may authorise persons to accompany any constable who is executing it.

(3) Entry and search under a warrant must be within one month from the date of its issue.

(4) Entry and search under a warrant must be at a reasonable hour unless it appears to the constable executing it that the purpose of a search may be frustrated on an entry at a reasonable hour.

(5) Where the occupier of premises which are to be entered and searched is present at the time when a constable seeks to execute a warrant to enter and search them, the constable—

(a) shall identify himself to the occupier and, if not in uniform, shall produce to him documentary evidence that he is a constable;

(b) shall produce the warrant to him; and

(c) shall supply him with a copy of it.

(6) Where—

(a) the occupier of such premises is not present at the time when a constable seeks to execute such a warrant; but

(b) some other person who appears to the constable to be in charge of the premises is present,

subsection (5) above shall have effect as if any reference to the occupier were a reference to that other person.

(7) If there is no person present who appears to the constable to be in charge of the premises, he shall leave a copy of the warrant in a prominent place on the premises.

(8) A search under a warrant may only be a search to the extent required for the purpose for which the warrant was issued.

(9) A constable executing a warrant shall make an endorsement on it stating—

(a) whether the articles or persons sought were found; and

(b) whether any articles were seized, other than articles which were sought.

(10) A warrant which—

(a) has been executed; or

(b) has not been executed within the time authorised for its execution,

shall be returned—

(i) if it was issued by a justice of the peace, to the clerk to the justices for the petty sessions area for which he acts; and

(ii) if it was issued by a judge, to the appropriate officer of the court from which he issued it.

(11) A warrant which is returned under subsection (10) above shall be retained for 12 months from its return—

(a) by the clerk to the justices, if it was returned under paragraph (i) of that subsection; and

(b) by the appropriate officer, if it was returned under paragraph (ii).

(12) If during the period for which a warrant is to be retained the occupier of the premises to which it relates asks to inspect it, he shall be allowed to do so.

Entry and search without search warrant

17 Entry for purpose of arrest etc

(1) Subject to the following provisions of this section, and without prejudice to any other enactment, a constable may enter and search any premises for the purpose—

(a) of executing—

(i) a warrant of arrest issued in connection with or arising out of criminal proceedings; or

(ii) a warrant of commitment issued under section 76 of the Magistrates' Courts Act 1980;

(b) of arresting a person for an arrestable offence;

(c) of arresting a person for an offence under—

(i) section 1 (prohibition of uniforms in connection with political objects) . . . of the Public Order Act 1936;

(ii) any enactment contained in sections 6 to 8 or 10 of the Criminal Law Act 1977 (offences relating to entering and remaining on property);

(iii) section 4 of the Public Order Act 1986 (fear or provocation of violence);]

(iv) section 76 of the Criminal Justice and Public Order Act 1994 (failure to comply with interim possession order);]

[(ca) of arresting, in pursuance of section 32(1A) of the Children and Young Persons Act 1969, any child or young person who has been remanded or committed to local authority accommodation under section 23(1) of that Act;

(cb) of recapturing any person who is, or is deemed for any purpose to be, unlawfully at large while liable to be detained—

(i) in a prison, remand centre, young offender institution or secure training centre, or

(ii) in pursuance of section 53 of the Children and Young Persons Act 1933 (dealing with children and young persons guilty of grave crimes), in any other place;]

(d) of recapturing [any person whatever] who is unlawfully at large and whom he is pursuing; or

(e) of saving life or limb or preventing serious damage to property.

(2) Except for the purpose specified in paragraph (e) of subsection (1) above, the powers of entry and search conferred by this section—

(a) are only exercisable if the constable has reasonable grounds for believing that the person whom he is seeking is on the premises; and

(b) are limited, in relation to premises consisting of two or more separate dwellings, to powers to enter and search—

(i) any parts of the premises which the occupiers of any dwelling comprised in the premises use in common with the occupiers of any other such dwelling; and

(ii) any such dwelling in which the constable has reasonable grounds for believing that the person whom he is seeking may be.

(3) The powers of entry and search conferred by this section are only exercisable for the purposes specified in subsection (1)(c)(ii) [or (iv)] above by a constable in uniform.

(4) The power of search conferred by this section is only a power to search to the extent that is reasonably required for the purpose for which the power of entry is exercised.

(5) Subject to subsection (6) below, all the rules of common law under which a constable has power to enter premises without a warrant are hereby abolished.

(6) Nothing in subsection (5) above affects any power of entry to deal with or prevent a breach of the peace.

NOTES

Sub-s (1): words omitted from para (c)(i) repealed, and para (c)(iii) added, by the Public Order Act 1986, s 40(2), (3), Sch 2, para 7, Sch 3; para (c)(iv) added by the Criminal Justice and Public Order Act 1994, s 168(2), Sch 10, para 53(a); paras (ca), (cb) inserted, and words in square brackets in para (d) substituted, by the Prisoners (Return to Custody) Act 1995, s 2(1).

Sub-s (3): words in square brackets inserted by the Criminal Justice and Public Order Act 1994, s 168(2), Sch 10, para 53(b).

18 Entry and search after arrest

(1) Subject to the following provisions of this section, a constable may enter and search any premises occupied or controlled by a person who is under arrest for an arrestable offence, if he has reasonable grounds for suspecting that there is on the premises evidence, other than items subject to legal privilege, that relates—

(a) to that offence; or

(b) to some other arrestable offence which is connected with or similar to that offence.

(2) A constable may seize and retain anything for which he may search under subsection (1) above.

(3) The power to search conferred by subsection (1) above is only a power to search to the extent that is reasonably required for the purpose of discovering such evidence.

(4) Subject to subsection (5) below, the powers conferred by this section may not be exercised unless an officer of the rank of inspector or above has authorised them in writing.

(5) A constable may conduct a search under subsection (1) above—

(a) before taking the person to a police station; and

(b) without obtaining an authorisation under subsection (4) above,

if the presence of that person at a place other than a police station is necessary for the effective investigation of the offence.

(6) If a constable conducts a search by virtue of subsection (5) above, he shall inform an officer of the rank of inspector or above that he has made the search as soon as practicable after he has made it.

(7) An officer who—

(a) authorises a search; or

(b) is informed of a search under subsection (6) above, shall make a record in writing—

(i) of the grounds for the search; and
(ii) of the nature of the evidence that was sought.

(8) If the person who was in occupation or control of the premises at the time of the search is in police detention at the time the record is to be made, the officer shall make the record as part of his custody record.

Seizure etc

19 General power of seizure etc

(1) The powers conferred by subsections (2), (3) and (4) below are exercisable by a constable who is lawfully on any premises.

(2) The constable may seize anything which is on the premises if he has reasonable grounds for believing—

(a) that it has been obtained in consequence of the commission of an offence; and
(b) that it is necessary to seize it in order to prevent it being concealed, lost, damaged, altered or destroyed.

(3) The constable may seize anything which is on the premises if he has reasonable grounds for believing—

(a) that it is evidence in relation to an offence which he is investigating or any other offence; and
(b) that it is necessary to seize it in order to prevent the evidence being concealed, lost, altered or destroyed.

(4) The constable may require any information which is contained in a computer and is accessible from the premises to be produced in a form in which it can be taken away and in which it is visible and legible if he has reasonable grounds for believing—

(a) that—
(i) it is evidence in relation to an offence which he is investigating or any other offence; or
(ii) it has been obtained in consequence of the commission of an offence; and
(b) that it is necessary to do so in order to prevent it being concealed, lost, tampered with or destroyed.

(5) The powers conferred by this section are in addition to any power otherwise conferred.

(6) No power of seizure conferred on a constable under any enactment (including an enactment contained in an Act passed after this Act) is to be taken to authorise the seizure of an item which the constable exercising the power has reasonable grounds for believing to be subject to legal privilege.

20 Extension of powers of seizure to computerised information

(1) Every power of seizure which is conferred by an enactment to which this section applies on a constable who has entered premises in the exercise of a power conferred by an enactment shall be construed as including a power to require any information contained in a computer and accessible from the premises to be produced in a form in which it can be taken away and in which it is visible and legible.

(2) This section applies—
(a) to any enactment contained in an Act passed before this Act;
(b) to sections 8 and 18 above;
(c) to paragraph 13 of Schedule 1 to this Act; and
(d) to any enactment contained in an Act passed after this Act.

21 Access and copying

(1) A constable who seizes anything in the exercise of a power conferred by any enactment, including an enactment contained in an Act passed after this Act, shall, if so requested by a person showing himself—
(a) to be the occupier of premises on which it was seized; or
(b) to have had custody or control of it immediately before the seizure,

provide that person with a record of what he seized.

(2) The officer shall provide the record within a reasonable time from the making of the request for it.

(3) Subject to subsection (8) below, if a request for permission to be granted access to anything which—
(a) has been seized by a constable; and
(b) is retained by the police for the purpose of investigating an offence,

is made to the officer in charge of the investigation by a person who had custody or control of the thing immediately before it was so seized or by someone acting on behalf of such a person, the officer shall allow the person who made the request access to it under the supervision of a constable.

(4) Subject to subsection (8) below, if a request for a photograph or copy of any such thing is made to the officer in charge of the investigation by a person who had custody or control of the thing immediately before it was so seized, or by someone acting on behalf of such a person, the officer shall—
(a) allow the person who made the request access to it under the supervision of a constable for the purpose of photographing or copying it; or
(b) photograph or copy it, or cause it to be photographed or copied.

(5) A constable may also photograph or copy, or have photographed or copied, anything which he has power to seize, without a request being made under subsection (4) above.

(6) Where anything is photographed or copied under subsection (4)(b) above, the photograph or copy shall be supplied to the person who made the request.

(7) The photograph or copy shall be so supplied within a reasonable time from the making of the request.

(8) There is no duty under this section to grant access to, or to supply a photograph or copy of, anything if the officer in charge of the investigation for the purposes of which it was seized has reasonable grounds for believing that to do so would prejudice—
(a) that investigation;
(b) the investigation of an offence other than the offence for the purposes of investigating which the thing was seized; or
(c) any criminal proceedings which may be brought as a result of—
(i) the investigation of which he is in charge; or
(ii) any such investigation as is mentioned in paragraph (b) above.

22 Retention

(1) Subject to subsection (4) below, anything which has been seized by a constable or taken away by a constable following a requirement made by virtue of section 19 or 20 above may be retained so long as is necessary in all the circumstances.

(2) Without prejudice to the generality of subsection (1) above—

(a) anything seized for the purposes of a criminal investigation may be retained, except as provided by subsection (4) below—

(i) for use as evidence at a trial for an offence; or

(ii) for forensic examination or for investigation in connection with an offence; and

(b) anything may be retained in order to establish its lawful owner, where there are reasonable grounds for believing that it has been obtained in consequence of the commission of an offence.

(3) Nothing seized on the ground that it may be used—

(a) to cause physical injury to any person;

(b) to damage property;

(c) to interfere with evidence; or

(d) to assist in escape from police detention or lawful custody,

may be retained when the person from whom it was seized is no longer in police detention or the custody of a court or is in the custody of a court but has been released on bail.

(4) Nothing may be retained for either of the purposes mentioned in subsection (2)(a) above if a photograph or copy would be sufficient for that purpose.

(5) Nothing in this section affects any power of a court to make an order under section 1 of the Police (Property) Act 1897.

PART III
ARREST

24 Arrest without warrant for arrestable offences

(1) The powers of summary arrest conferred by the following subsections shall apply—

(a) to offences for which the sentence is fixed by law;

(b) to offences for which a person of 21 years of age or over (not previously convicted) may be sentenced to imprisonment for a term of five years (or might be so sentenced but for the restrictions imposed by section 33 of the Magistrates' Courts Act 1980); and

(c) to the offences to which subsection (2) below applies,

and in this Act "arrestable offence" means any such offence.

(2) The offences to which this subsection applies are—

(a) offences for which a person may be arrested under the customs and excise Acts, as defined in section 1(1) of the Customs and Excise Management Act 1979;

(b) offences under [the Official Secrets Acts 1920] that are not arrestable offences by virtue of the term of imprisonment for which a person may be sentenced in respect of them;

[(bb) offences under any provision of the Official Secrets Act 1989 except section 8(1), (4) or (5);]

(c) offences under section . . . 22 (causing prostitution of women) or 23 (procuration of girl under 21) of the Sexual Offences Act 1956;

(d) offences under section 12(1) (taking motor vehicle or other conveyance without authority etc) or 25(1) (going equipped for stealing, etc) of the Theft Act 1968; and

[(e) any offence under the Football (Offences) Act 1991.]

[(f) an offence under section 2 of the Obscene Publications Act 1959 (publication of obscene matter);

(g) an offence under section 1 of the Protection of Children Act 1978 (indecent photographs and pseudo-photographs of children);]

[(h) an offence under section 166 of the Criminal Justice and Public Order Act 1994 (sale of tickets by unauthorised persons);]

[(i) an offence under section 19 of the Public Order Act 1986 (publishing, etc material intended or likely to stir up racial hatred);]

[(j) an offence under section 167 of the Criminal Justice and Public Order Act 1994 (touting for hire car services);]

[(k) an offence under section 1(1) of the Prevention of Crime Act 1953 (prohibition of the carrying of offensive weapons without lawful authority or reasonable excuse);

(l) an offence under section 139(1) of the Criminal Justice Act 1988 (offence of having article with blade or point in public place);

(m) an offence under section 139A(1) or (2) of the Criminal Justice Act 1988 (offence of having article with blade or point (or offensive weapon) on school premises)].

[(n) an offence under section 2 of the Protection from Harassment Act 1997 (harassment).]

[(o) an offence under section 60(8)(b) of the Criminal Justice and Public Order Act 1994 (failing to comply with requirement to remove mask etc.);]

[(q) an offence under section 16(4) of the Football Spectators Act 1989 (failure to comply with reporting duty imposed by restriction order).]

(3) Without prejudice to section 2 of the Criminal Attempts Act 1981, the powers of summary arrest conferred by the following subsections shall also apply to the offences of—

(a) conspiring to commit any of the offences mentioned in subsection (2) above;

(b) attempting to commit any such offence [other than an offence under section 12(1) of the Theft Act 1968];

(c) inciting, aiding, abetting, counselling or procuring the commission of any such offence;

and such offences are also arrestable offences for the purposes of this Act.

(4) Any person may arrest without a warrant—

(a) anyone who is in the act of committing an arrestable offence;

(b) anyone whom he has reasonable grounds for suspecting to be committing such an offence.

(5) Where an arrestable offence has been committed, any person may arrest without a warrant—

(a) anyone who is guilty of the offence;

(b) anyone whom he has reasonable grounds for suspecting to be guilty of it.

(6) Where a constable has reasonable grounds for suspecting that an arrestable offence has been committed, he may arrest without a warrant anyone whom he has reasonable grounds for suspecting to be guilty of the offence.

(7) A constable may arrest without a warrant—

(a) anyone who is about to commit an arrestable offence;

(b) anyone whom he has reasonable grounds for suspecting to be about to commit an arrestable offence.

NOTES

Sub-s (2): words in square brackets in para (b) substituted, and para (bb) inserted, by the Official Secrets Act 1989, s 11(1); words omitted from para (c) repealed by the Sexual Offences Act 1985, s 5(3), Schedule; para (e) added by the Football (Offences) Act 1991, s 5(1) (original para (e) repealed by the Criminal Justice Act 1988, s 170(12), Sch 16); paras (f)–(j) added by the Criminal Justice and Public Order Act 1994, ss 85(1), (2), 155, 166(4), 167(7); paras (k)–(m) added by the Offensive Weapons Act 1996, s 1(1); para (n) added by the Protection from Harassment Act 1997, s 2(3); para (o) added by the Crime and Disorder Act 1998, s 27(1), as from a day to be appointed; para (q) added by the Crime and Disorder Act 1998, ss 84(2), 120(1), Sch 9, para 9, partly as from a day to be appointed, and does not apply to offences committed before 7 August 1998.

Sub-s (3): words in square brackets in para (b) added by the Criminal Justice Act 1988, s 170(11), Sch 15, paras 97, 98.

25. General arrest conditions

(1) Where a constable has reasonable grounds for suspecting that any offence which is not an arrestable offence has been committed or attempted, or is being committed or attempted, he may arrest the relevant person if it appears to him that service of a summons is impracticable or inappropriate because any of the general arrest conditions is satisfied.

(2) In this section "the relevant person" means any person whom the constable has reasonable grounds to suspect of having committed or having attempted to commit the offence or of being in the course of committing or attempting to commit it.

(3) The general arrest conditions are—

(a) that the name of the relevant person is unknown to, and cannot be readily ascertained by, the constable;

(b) that the constable has reasonable grounds for doubting whether a name furnished by the relevant person as his name is his real name;

(c) that—

(i) the relevant person has failed to furnish a satisfactory address for service; or

(ii) the constable has reasonable grounds for doubting whether an address furnished by the relevant person is a satisfactory address for service;

(d) that the constable has reasonable grounds for believing that arrest is necessary to prevent the relevant person—

(i) causing physical injury to himself or any other person;

(ii) suffering physical injury;

(iii) causing loss of or damage to property;

(iv) committing an offence against public decency; or

(v) causing an unlawful obstruction of the highway;

(e) that the constable has reasonable grounds for believing that arrest is necessary to protect a child or other vulnerable person from the relevant person.

(4) For the purposes of subsection (3) above an address is a satisfactory address for service if it appears to the constable—

- (a) that the relevant person will be at it for a sufficiently long period for it to be possible to serve him with a summons; or
- (b) that some other person specified by the relevant person will accept service of a summons for the relevant person at it.

(5) Nothing in subsection (3)(d) above authorises the arrest of a person under sub-paragraph (iv) of that paragraph except where members of the public going about their normal business cannot reasonably be expected to avoid the person to be arrested.

(6) This section shall not prejudice any power of arrest conferred apart from this section.

26 Repeal of statutory powers of arrest without warrant or order

(1) Subject to subsection (2) below, so much of any Act (including a local Act) passed before this Act as enables a constable—

- (a) to arrest a person for an offence without a warrant; or
- (b) to arrest a person otherwise than for an offence without a warrant or an order of a court,

shall cease to have effect.

(2) Nothing in subsection (1) above affects the enactments specified in Schedule 2 to this Act.

28 Information to be given on arrest

(1) Subject to subsection (5) below, where a person is arrested, otherwise than by being informed that he is under arrest, the arrest is not lawful unless the person arrested is informed that he is under arrest as soon as is practicable after his arrest.

(2) Where a person is arrested by a constable, subsection (1) above applies regardless of whether the fact of the arrest is obvious.

(3) Subject to subsection (5) below, no arrest is lawful unless the person arrested is informed of the ground for the arrest at the time of, or as soon as is practicable after, the arrest.

(4) Where a person is arrested by a constable, subsection (3) above applies regardless of whether the ground for the arrest is obvious.

(5) Nothing in this section is to be taken to require a person to be informed—

- (a) that he is under arrest; or
- (b) of the ground for the arrest,

if it was not reasonably practicable for him to be so informed by reason of his having escaped from arrest before the information could be given.

29 Voluntary attendance at police station etc

Where for the purpose of assisting with an investigation a person attends voluntarily at a police station or at any other place where a constable is present or accompanies a constable to a police station or any such other place without having been arrested—

- (a) he shall be entitled to leave at will unless he is placed under arrest;
- (b) he shall be informed at once that he is under arrest if a decision is taken by a constable to prevent him from leaving at will.

30 Arrest elsewhere than at police station

(1) Subject to the following provisions of this section, where a person—
- (a) is arrested by a constable for an offence; or
- (b) is taken into custody by a constable after being arrested for an offence by a person other than a constable,

at any place other than a police station, he shall be taken to a police station by a constable as soon as practicable after the arrest.

(2) Subject to subsections (3) and (5) below, the police station to which an arrested person is taken under subsection (1) above shall be a designated police station.

(3) A constable to whom this subsection applies may take an arrested person to any police station unless it appears to the constable that it may be necessary to keep the arrested person in police detention for more than six hours.

(4) Subsection (3) above applies—
- (a) to a constable who is working in a locality covered by a police station which is not a designated police station; and
- (b) to a constable belonging to a body of constables maintained by an authority other than a police authority.

(5) Any constable may take an arrested person to any police station if—
- (a) either of the following conditions is satisfied—
  - (i) the constable has arrested him without the assistance of any other constable and no other constable is available to assist him;
  - (ii) the constable has taken him into custody from a person other than a constable without the assistance of any other constable and no other constable is available to assist him; and
- (b) it appears to the constable that he will be unable to take the arrested person to a designated police station without the arrested person injuring himself, the constable or some other person.

(6) If the first police station to which an arrested person is taken after his arrest is not a designated police station, he shall be taken to a designated police station not more than six hours after his arrival at the first police station unless he is released previously.

(7) A person arrested by a constable at a place other than a police station shall be released if a constable is satisfied, before the person arrested reaches a police station, that there are no grounds for keeping him under arrest.

(8) A constable who releases a person under subsection (7) above shall record the fact that he has done so.

(9) The constable shall make the record as soon as is practicable after the release.

(10) Nothing in subsection (1) above shall prevent a constable delaying taking a person who has been arrested to a police station if the presence of that person elsewhere is necessary in order to carry out such investigations as it is reasonable to carry out immediately.

(11) Where there is delay in taking a person who has been arrested to a police station after his arrest, the reasons for the delay shall be recorded when he first arrives at a police station.

(12), (13) . . .

NOTES

Sub-ss (12), (13): outside the scope of this work.

31 Arrest for further offence

Where—

(a) a person—

(i) has been arrested for an offence; and

(ii) is at a police station in consequence of that arrest; and

(b) it appears to a constable that, if he were released from that arrest, he would be liable to arrest for some other offence,

he shall be arrested for that other offence.

32 Search upon arrest

(1) A constable may search an arrested person, in any case where the person to be searched has been arrested at a place other than a police station, if the constable has reasonable grounds for believing that the arrested person may present a danger to himself or others.

(2) Subject to subsections (3) to (5) below, a constable shall also have power in any such case—

(a) to search the arrested person for anything—

(i) which he might use to assist him to escape from lawful custody; or

(ii) which might be evidence relating to an offence; and

(b) to enter and search any premises in which he was when arrested or immediately before he was arrested for evidence relating to the offence for which he has been arrested.

(3) The power to search conferred by subsection (2) above is only a power to search to the extent that is reasonably required for the purpose of discovering any such thing or any such evidence.

(4) The powers conferred by this section to search a person are not to be construed as authorising a constable to require a person to remove any of his clothing in public other than an outer coat, jacket or gloves [but they do authorise a search of a person's mouth].

(5) A constable may not search a person in the exercise of the power conferred by subsection (2)(a) above unless he has reasonable grounds for believing that the person to be searched may have concealed on him anything for which a search is permitted under that paragraph.

(6) A constable may not search premises in the exercise of the power conferred by subsection (2)(b) above unless he has reasonable grounds for believing that there is evidence for which a search is permitted under that paragraph on the premises.

(7) In so far as the power of search conferred by subsection (2)(b) above relates to premises consisting of two or more separate dwellings, it is limited to a power to search—

(a) any dwelling in which the arrest took place or in which the person arrested was immediately before his arrest; and

(b) any parts of the premises which the occupier of any such dwelling uses in common with the occupiers of any other dwellings comprised in the premises.

(8) A constable searching a person in the exercise of the power conferred by subsection (1) above may seize and retain anything he finds, if he has reasonable grounds for believing that the person searched might use it to cause physical injury to himself or to any other person.

(9) A constable searching a person in the exercise of the power conferred by subsection (2)(a) above may seize and retain anything he finds, other than an item subject to legal privilege, if he has reasonable grounds for believing—

(a) that he might use it to assist him to escape from lawful custody; or

(b) that it is evidence of an offence or has been obtained in consequence of the commission of an offence.

(10) Nothing in this section shall be taken to affect the power conferred by [section 15(3), (4) and (5) of the Prevention of Terrorism (Temporary Provisions) Act 1989].

NOTES

Sub-s (4): words in square brackets added by the Criminal Justice and Public Order Act 1994, s 59(2).

Sub-s (10): words in square brackets substituted by the Prevention of Terrorism (Temporary Provisions) Act 1989, s 25(1), Sch 8, para 6(1), (3).

PART IV
DETENTION

Detention—conditions and duration

34 Limitations on police detention

(1) A person arrested for an offence shall not be kept in police detention except in accordance with the provisions of this Part of this Act.

(2) Subject to subsection (3) below, if at any time a custody officer—

(a) becomes aware, in relation to any person in police detention, that the grounds for the detention of that person have ceased to apply; and

(b) is not aware of any other grounds on which the continued detention of that person could be justified under the provisions of this Part of this Act,

it shall be the duty of the custody officer, subject to subsection (4) below, to order his immediate release from custody.

(3) No person in police detention shall be released except on the authority of a custody officer at the police station where his detention was authorised or, if it was authorised at more than one station, a custody officer at the station where it was last authorised.

(4) A person who appears to the custody officer to have been unlawfully at large when he was arrested is not to be released under subsection (2) above.

(5) A person whose release is ordered under subsection (2) above shall be released without bail unless it appears to the custody officer—

(a) that there is need for further investigation of any matter in connection with which he was detained at any time during the period of his detention; or

(b) that proceedings may be taken against him in respect of any such matter,

and, if it so appears, he shall be released on bail.

(6) . . .

[(7) For the purposes of this Part of this Act a person who returns to a police station to answer to bail or is arrested under section 46A below shall be treated as arrested for an offence and the offence in connection with which he was granted bail shall be deemed to be that offence.]

NOTES

Sub-s (6): outside the scope of this work.

Sub-s (7): added by the Criminal Justice and Public Order Act 1994, s 29(1), (3), and applies whether person released on bail was granted bail before or after 10 April 1995.

35 Designated police stations

(1) The chief officer of police for each police area shall designate the police stations in his area which, subject to section 30(3) and (5) above, are to be the stations in that area to be used for the purpose of detaining arrested persons.

(2) A chief officer's duty under subsection (1) above is to designate police stations appearing to him to provide enough accommodation for that purpose.

(3), (4) . . .

NOTES

Sub-ss (3), (4): outside the scope of this work.

36 Custody officers at police stations

(1) One or more custody officers shall be appointed for each designated police station.

(2) A custody officer for a designated police station shall be appointed—

- (a) by the chief officer of police for the area in which the designated police station is situated; or
- (b) by such other police officer as the chief officer of police for that area may direct.

(3) No officer may be appointed a custody officer unless he is of at least the rank of sergeant.

(4) An officer of any rank may perform the functions of a custody officer at a designated police station if a custody officer is not readily available to perform them.

(5) Subject to the following provisions of this section and to section 39(2) below, none of the functions of a custody officer in relation to a person shall be performed by an officer who at the time when the function falls to be performed is involved in the investigation of an offence for which that person is in police detention at that time.

(6) . . .

(7) Where an arrested person is taken to a police station which is not a designated police station, the functions in relation to him which at a designated police station would be the functions of a custody officer shall be performed—

- (a) by an officer who is not involved in the investigation of an offence for which he is in police detention, if such an officer is readily available; and
- (b) if no such officer is readily available, by the officer who took him to the station or any other officer.

(8)–(10) . . .

NOTES

Sub-ss (6), (8)–(10): outside the scope of this work.

37 Duties of custody officer before charge

(1) Where—

(a) a person is arrested for an offence—

(i) without a warrant; or

(ii) under a warrant not endorsed for bail, . . .

(b) . . . ,

the custody officer at each police station where he is detained after his arrest shall determine whether he has before him sufficient evidence to charge that person with the offence for which he was arrested and may detain him at the police station for such period as is necessary to enable him to do so.

(2) If the custody officer determines that he does not have such evidence before him, the person arrested shall be released either on bail or without bail, unless the custody officer has reasonable grounds for believing that his detention without being charged is necessary to secure or preserve evidence relating to an offence for which he is under arrest or to obtain such evidence by questioning him.

(3) If the custody officer has reasonable grounds for so believing, he may authorise the person arrested to be kept in police detention.

(4) Where a custody officer authorises a person who has not been charged to be kept in police detention, he shall, as soon as is practicable, make a written record of the grounds for the detention.

(5) Subject to subsection (6) below, the written record shall be made in the presence of the person arrested who shall at that time be informed by the custody officer of the grounds for his detention.

(6) Subsection (5) above shall not apply where the person arrested is, at the time when the written record is made—

(a) incapable of understanding what is said to him;

(b) violent or likely to become violent; or

(c) in urgent need of medical attention.

(7) Subject to section 41(7) below, if the custody officer determines that he has before him sufficient evidence to charge the person arrested with the offence for which he was arrested, the person arrested—

(a) shall be charged; or

(b) shall be released without charge, either on bail or without bail.

(8) . . .

(9) If the person arrested is not in a fit state to be dealt with under subsection (7) above, he may be kept in police detention until he is.

(10) The duty imposed on the custody officer under subsection (1) above shall be carried out by him as soon as practicable after the person arrested arrives at the police station or, in the case of a person arrested at the police station, as soon as practicable after the arrest.

(11)–(15) . . .

NOTES

Sub-s (1): para (b) and word "or" immediately preceding it repealed by the Criminal Justice and Public Order Act 1994, ss 29(1), (4)(a), (5), 168(3), Sch 11.

Sub-ss (8), (15): outside the scope of this work.

Sub-ss (11)–(14): repealed by the Criminal Justice Act 1991, ss 72, 101(2), Sch 13.

38 Duties of custody officer after charge

(1) Where a person arrested for an offence otherwise than under a warrant endorsed for bail is charged with an offence, the custody officer shall[, subject to section 25 of the Criminal Justice and Public Order Act 1994,] order his release from police detention, either on bail or without bail, unless—

(a) if the person arrested is not an arrested juvenile—

(i) his name or address cannot be ascertained or the custody officer has reasonable grounds for doubting whether a name or address furnished by him as his name or address is his real name or address;

[(ii) the custody officer has reasonable grounds for believing that the person arrested will fail to appear in court to answer to bail;

(iii) in the case of a person arrested for an imprisonable offence, the custody officer has reasonable grounds for believing that the detention of the person arrested is necessary to prevent him from committing an offence;

(iv) in the case of a person arrested for an offence which is not an imprisonable offence, the custody officer has reasonable grounds for believing that the detention of the person arrested is necessary to prevent him from causing physical injury to any other person or from causing loss of or damage to property;

(v) the custody officer has reasonable grounds for believing that the detention of the person arrested is necessary to prevent him from interfering with the administration of justice or with the investigation of offences or of a particular offence; or

(vi) the custody officer has reasonable grounds for believing that the detention of the person arrested is necessary for his own protection];

(b) if he is an arrested juvenile—

(i) any of the requirements of paragraph (a) above is satisfied; or

(ii) the custody officer has reasonable grounds for believing that he ought to be detained in his own interests.

(2) If the release of a person arrested is not required by subsection (1) above, the custody officer may authorise him to be kept in police detention.

[(2A) . . .

(3) Where a custody officer authorises a person who has been charged to be kept in police detention, he shall, as soon as practicable, make a written record of the grounds for the detention.

(4) Subject to subsection (5) below, the written record shall be made in the presence of the person charged who shall at that time be informed by the custody officer of the grounds for his detention.

(5) Subsection (4) above shall not apply where the person charged is, at the time when the written record is made—

(a) incapable of understanding what is said to him;

(b) violent or likely to become violent; or

(c) in urgent need of medical attention.

[[(6) Where a custody officer authorises an arrested juvenile to be kept in police detention under subsection (1) above, the custody officer shall, unless he certifies—

(a) that, by reason of such circumstances as are specified in the certificate, it is impracticable for him to do so; or

(b) in the case of an arrested juvenile who has attained the [age of 12 years] that no secure accommodation is available and that keeping him in other local authority accommodation would not be adequate to protect the public from serious harm from him,

secure that the arrested juvenile is moved to local authority accommodation.]

(6A), (6B), (7), (7A), (8) . . .

NOTES

Sub-s (1): words in first pair of square brackets inserted, and paras (a)(ii)–(vi) substituted for original sub-s (1)(a)(ii), (iii), by the Criminal Justice and Public Order Act 1994, ss 28(1), (2), 168(2), Sch 10, para 54.

Sub-s (2A): outside the scope of this work.

Sub-s (6): substituted (together with sub-s (6A)) for existing sub-ss (6), (6A), by the Criminal Justice Act 1991, s 59; words in square brackets in para (b) substituted by the Criminal Justice and Public Order Act 1994, s 24.

Sub-ss (6A), (6B), (7), (7A), (8): outside the scope of this work.

39 Responsibilities in relation to persons detained

(1) Subject to subsections (2) and (4) below, it shall be the duty of the custody officer at a police station to ensure—

(a) that all persons in police detention at that station are treated in accordance with this Act and any code of practice issued under it and relating to the treatment of persons in police detention; and

(b) that all matters relating to such persons which are required by this Act or by such codes of practice to be recorded are recorded in the custody records relating to such persons.

(2) If the custody officer, in accordance with any code of practice issued under this Act, transfers or permits the transfer of a person in police detention—

(a) to the custody of a police officer investigating an offence for which that person is in police detention; or

(b) to the custody of an officer who has charge of that person outside the police station,

the custody officer shall cease in relation to that person to be subject to the duty imposed on him by subsection (1)(a) above; and it shall be the duty of the officer to whom the transfer is made to ensure that he is treated in accordance with the provisions of this Act and of any such codes of practice as are mentioned in subsection (1) above.

(3)–(5) . . .

(6) Where—

(a) an officer of higher rank than the custody officer gives directions relating to a person in police detention; and

(b) the directions are at variance—

(i) with any decision made or action taken by the custody officer in the performance of a duty imposed on him under this Part of this Act; or

(ii) with any decision or action which would but for the directions have been made or taken by him in the performance of such a duty, the custody officer shall refer the matter at once to an officer of the rank of superintendent or above who is responsible for the police station for which the custody officer is acting as custody officer.

NOTES

Sub-ss (3), (4): outside the scope of this work.

Sub-s (5): repealed by the Children Act 1989, s 108(7), Sch 16.

40 Review of police detention

(1) Reviews of the detention of each person in police detention in connection with the investigation of an offence shall be carried out periodically in accordance with the following provisions of this section—

- (a) in the case of a person who has been arrested and charged, by the custody officer; and
- (b) in the case of a person who has been arrested but not charged, by an officer of at least the rank of inspector who has not been directly involved in the investigation.

(2) The officer to whom it falls to carry out a review is referred to in this section as a "review officer".

(3) Subject to subsection (4) below—

- (a) the first review shall be not later than six hours after the detention was first authorised;
- (b) the second review shall be not later than nine hours after the first;
- (c) subsequent reviews shall be at intervals of not more than nine hours.

(4) A review may be postponed—

- (a) if, having regard to all the circumstances prevailing at the latest time for it specified in subsection (3) above, it is not practicable to carry out the review at that time;
- (b) without prejudice to the generality of paragraph (a) above—
  - (i) if at that time the person in detention is being questioned by a police officer and the review officer is satisfied that an interruption of the questioning for the purpose of carrying out the review would prejudice the investigation in connection with which he is being questioned; or
  - (ii) if at that time no review officer is readily available.

(5) If a review is postponed under subsection (4) above it shall be carried out as soon as practicable after the latest time specified for it in subsection (3) above.

(6) If a review is carried out after postponement under subsection (4) above, the fact that it was so carried out shall not affect any requirement of this section as to the time at which any subsequent review is to be carried out.

(7) The review officer shall record the reasons for any postponement of a review in the custody record.

(8) Subject to subsection (9) below, where the person whose detention is under review has not been charged before the time of the review, section 37(1) to (6) above shall have effect in relation to him, but with the substitution—

- (a) of references to the person whose detention is under review for references to the person arrested; and
- (b) of references to the review officer for references to the custody officer.

(9) Where a person has been kept in police detention by virtue of section 37(9) above, section 37(1) to (6) shall not have effect in relation to him but it shall be the duty of the review officer to determine whether he is yet in a fit state.

(10) Where the person whose detention is under review has been charged before the time of the review, section 38(1) to (6) above shall have effect in relation to him, with the substitution of references to the person whose detention is under review for references to the person arrested.

(11) Where—

(a) an officer of higher rank than the review officer gives directions relating to a person in police detention; and

(b) the directions are at variance—

(i) with any decision made or action taken by the review officer in the performance of a duty imposed on him under this Part of this Act; or

(ii) with any decision or action which would but for the directions have been made or taken by him in the performance of such a duty,

the review officer shall refer the matter at once to an officer of the rank of superintendent or above who is responsible for the police station for which the review officer is acting as review officer in connection with the detention.

(12) Before determining whether to authorise a person's continued detention the review officer shall give—

(a) that person (unless he is asleep); or

(b) any solicitor representing him who is available at the time of the review,

an opportunity to make representations to him about the detention.

(13), (14) . . .

NOTES

Sub-ss (13), (14): outside the scope of this work.

41 Limits on period of detention without charge

(1) Subject to the following provisions of this section and to sections 42 and 43 below, a person shall not be kept in police detention for more than 24 hours without being charged.

(2) The time from which the period of detention of a person is to be calculated (in this Act referred to as "the relevant time")—

(a) in the case of a person to whom this paragraph applies, shall be—

(i) the time at which that person arrives at the relevant police station; or

(ii) the time 24 hours after the time of that person's arrest,

whichever is the earlier;

(b) in the case of a person arrested outside England and Wales, shall be—

(i) the time at which that person arrives at the first police station to which he is taken in the police area in England or Wales in which the offence for which he was arrested is being investigated; or

(ii) the time 24 hours after the time of that person's entry into England and Wales,

whichever is the earlier;

(c) in the case of a person who—

(i) attends voluntarily at a police station; or

(ii) accompanies a constable to a police station without having been arrested,

and is arrested at the police station, the time of his arrest;

(d) in any other case, except where subsection (5) below applies, shall be the time at which the person arrested arrives at the first police station to which he is taken after his arrest.

(3)–(6) . . .

(7) Subject to subsection (8) below, a person who at the expiry of 24 hours after the relevant time is in police detention and has not been charged shall be released at that time either on bail or without bail.

(8) Subsection (7) above does not apply to a person whose detention for more than 24 hours after the relevant time has been authorised or is otherwise permitted in accordance with section 42 or 43 below.

(9) A person released under subsection (7) above shall not be re-arrested without a warrant for the offence for which he was previously arrested unless new evidence justifying a further arrest has come to light since his release[; but this subsection does not prevent an arrest under section 46A below.]

NOTES

Sub-ss (3)–(6): outside the scope of this work.

Sub-s (9): words in square brackets added by the Criminal Justice and Public Order Act 1994, s 29(1), (4)(b), and apply whether person released on bail was granted bail before or after 10 April 1995.

42 Authorisation of continued detention

(1) Where a police officer of the rank of superintendent or above who is responsible for the police station at which a person is detained has reasonable grounds for believing that—

(a) the detention of that person without charge is necessary to secure or preserve evidence relating to an offence for which he is under arrest or to obtain such evidence by questioning him;

(b) an offence for which he is under arrest is a serious arrestable offence; and

(c) the investigation is being conducted diligently and expeditiously,

he may authorise the keeping of that person in police detention for a period expiring at or before 36 hours after the relevant time.

(2) Where an officer such as is mentioned in subsection (1) above has authorised the keeping of a person in police detention for a period expiring less than 36 hours after the relevant time, such an officer may authorise the keeping of that person in police detention for a further period expiring not more than 36 hours after that time if the conditions specified in subsection (1) above are still satisfied when he gives the authorisation.

(3) . . .

(4) No authorisation under subsection (1) above shall be given in respect of any person—

(a) more than 24 hours after the relevant time; or

(b) before the second review of his detention under section 40 above has been carried out.

(5) Where an officer authorises the keeping of a person in police detention under subsection (1) above, it shall be his duty—

(a) to inform that person of the grounds for his continued detention; and
(b) to record the grounds in that person's custody record.

(6) Before determining whether to authorise the keeping of a person in detention under subsection (1) or (2) above, an officer shall give—
(a) that person; or
(b) any solicitor representing him who is available at the time when it falls to the officer to determine whether to give the authorisation,

an opportunity to make representations to him about the detention.

(7), (8) . . .

(9) Where—
(a) an officer authorises the keeping of a person in detention under subsection (1) above; and
(b) at the time of the authorisation he has not yet exercised a right conferred on him by section 56 or 58 below,

the officer—
(i) shall inform him of that right;
(ii) shall decide whether he should be permitted to exercise it;
(iii) shall record the decision in his custody record; and
(iv) if the decision is to refuse to permit the exercise of the right, shall also record the grounds for the decision in that record.

(10) Where an officer has authorised the keeping of a person who has not been charged in detention under subsection (1) or (2) above, he shall be released from detention, either on bail or without bail, not later than 36 hours after the relevant time, unless—
(a) he has been charged with an offence; or
(b) his continued detention is authorised or otherwise permitted in accordance with section 43 below.

(11) A person released under subsection (10) above shall not be re-arrested without a warrant for the offence for which he was previously arrested unless new evidence justifying a further arrest has come to light since his release[; but this subsection does not prevent an arrest under section 46A below].

NOTES

Sub-ss (3), (7), (8): outside the scope of this work.

Sub-s (11): words in square brackets added by the Criminal Justice and Public Order Act 1994, s 29(1), (4)(b), (5), and apply whether person released on bail was granted bail before or after 10 April 1995.

43 Warrants of further detention

(1) Where, on an application on oath made by a constable and supported by an information, a magistrates' court is satisfied that there are reasonable grounds for believing that the further detention of the person to whom the application relates is justified, it may issue a warrant of further detention authorising the keeping of that person in police detention.

(2) A court may not hear an application for a warrant of further detention unless the person to whom the application relates—
(a) has been furnished with a copy of the information; and
(b) has been brought before the court for the hearing.

(3) The person to whom the application relates shall be entitled to be legally represented at the hearing and, if he is not so represented but wishes to be so represented—

- (a) the court shall adjourn the hearing to enable him to obtain representation; and
- (b) he may be kept in police detention during the adjournment.

(4) A person's further detention is only justified for the purposes of this section or section 44 below if—

- (a) his detention without charge is necessary to secure or preserve evidence relating to an offence for which he is under arrest or to obtain such evidence by questioning him;
- (b) an offence for which he is under arrest is a serious arrestable offence; and
- (c) the investigation is being conducted diligently and expeditiously.

(5) Subject to subsection (7) below, an application for a warrant of further detention may be made—

- (a) at any time before the expiry of 36 hours after the relevant time; or
- (b) in a case where—
  - (i) it is not practicable for the magistrates' court to which the application will be made to sit at the expiry of 36 hours after the relevant time; but
  - (ii) the court will sit during the 6 hours following the end of that period,

  at any time before the expiry of the said 6 hours.

(6) In a case to which subsection (5)(b) above applies—

- (a) the person to whom the application relates may be kept in police detention until the application is heard; and
- (b) the custody officer shall make a note in that person's custody record—
  - (i) of the fact that he was kept in police detention for more than 36 hours after the relevant time; and
  - (ii) of the reason why he was so kept.

(7) If—

- (a) an application for a warrant of further detention is made after the expiry of 36 hours after the relevant time; and
- (b) it appears to the magistrates' court that it would have been reasonable for the police to make it before the expiry of that period,

the court shall dismiss the application.

(8) Where on an application such as is mentioned in subsection (1) above a magistrates' court is not satisfied that there are reasonable grounds for believing that the further detention of the person to whom the application relates is justified, it shall be its duty—

- (a) to refuse the application; or
- (b) to adjourn the hearing of it until a time not later than 36 hours after the relevant time.

(9) The person to whom the application relates may be kept in police detention during the adjournment.

(10) A warrant of further detention shall—

- (a) state the time at which it is issued;
- (b) authorise the keeping in police detention of the person to whom it relates for the period stated in it.

(11) Subject to subsection (12) below, the period stated in a warrant of further detention shall be such period as the magistrates' court thinks fit, having regard to the evidence before it.

(12) The period shall not be longer than 36 hours.

(13) . . .

(14) Any information submitted in support of an application under this section shall state—

- (a) the nature of the offence for which the person to whom the application relates has been arrested;
- (b) the general nature of the evidence on which that person was arrested;
- (c) what inquiries relating to the offence have been made by the police and what further inquiries are proposed by them;
- (d) the reasons for believing the continued detention of that person to be necessary for the purposes of such further inquiries.

(15) Where an application under this section is refused, the person to whom the application relates shall forthwith be charged or, subject to subsection (16) below, released, either on bail or without bail.

(16) A person need not be released under subsection (15) above—

- (a) before the expiry of 24 hours after the relevant time; or
- (b) before the expiry of any longer period for which his continued detention is or has been authorised under section 42 above.

(17) Where an application under this section is refused, no further application shall be made under this section in respect of the person to whom the refusal relates, unless supported by evidence which has come to light since the refusal.

(18) Where a warrant of further detention is issued, the person to whom it relates shall be released from police detention, either on bail or without bail, upon or before the expiry of the warrant unless he is charged.

(19) A person released under subsection (18) above shall not be re-arrested without a warrant for the offence for which he was previously arrested unless new evidence justifying a further arrest has come to light since his release[; but this subsection does not prevent an arrest under section 46A below.]

NOTES

Sub-s (13): outside the scope of this work.

Sub-s (19): words in square brackets added by the Criminal Justice and Public Order Act 1994, s 29(1), (4)(b), (5), and apply whether person released on bail was granted bail before or after 10 April 1995.

44 Extension of warrants of further detention

(1) On an application on oath made by a constable and supported by an information a magistrates' court may extend a warrant of further detention issued under section 43 above if it is satisfied that there are reasonable grounds for believing that the further detention of the person to whom the application relates is justified.

(2) Subject to subsection (3) below, the period for which a warrant of further detention may be extended shall be such period as the court thinks fit, having regard to the evidence before it.

(3) The period shall not—

(a) be longer than 36 hours; or
(b) end later than 96 hours after the relevant time.

(4) Where a warrant of further detention has been extended under subsection (1) above, or further extended under this subsection, for a period ending before 96 hours after the relevant time, on an application such as is mentioned in that subsection a magistrates' court may further extend the warrant if it is satisfied as there mentioned; and subsections (2) and (3) above apply to such further extensions as they apply to extensions under subsection (1) above.

(5) A warrant of further detention shall, if extended or further extended under this section, be endorsed with a note of the period of the extension.

(6) Subsections (2), (3), and (14) of section 43 above shall apply to an application made under this section as they apply to an application made under that section.

(7) Where an application under this section is refused, the person to whom the application relates shall forthwith be charged or, subject to subsection (8) below, released, either on bail or without bail.

(8) A person need not be released under subsection (7) above before the expiry of any period for which a warrant of further detention issued in relation to him has been extended or further extended on an earlier application made under this section.

Detention—miscellaneous

46 Detention after charge

(1) Where a person—
  (a) is charged with an offence; and
  (b) after being charged—
    (i) is kept in police detention; or
    (ii) is detained by a local authority in pursuance of arrangements made under section 38(6) above,

he shall be brought before a magistrates' court in accordance with the provisions of this section.

(2) If he is to be brought before a magistrates' court for the petty sessions area in which the police station at which he was charged is situated, he shall be brought before such a court as soon as is practicable and in any event not later than the first sitting after he is charged with the offence.

(3) If no magistrates' court for that area is due to sit either on the day on which he is charged or on the next day, the custody officer for the police station at which he was charged shall inform the clerk to the justices for the area that there is a person in the area to whom subsection (2) above applies.

(4) If the person charged is to be brought before a magistrates' court for a petty sessions area other than that in which the police station at which he was charged is situated, he shall be removed to that area as soon as is practicable and brought before such a court as soon as is practicable after his arrival in the area and in any event not later than the first sitting of a magistrates' court for that area after his arrival in the area.

(5) If no magistrates' court for that area is due to sit either on the day on which he arrives in the area or on the next day—

(a) he shall be taken to a police station in the area; and
(b) the custody officer at that station shall inform the clerk to the justices for the area that there is a person in the area to whom subsection (4) applies.

(6) Subject to subsection (8) below, where a clerk to the justices for a petty sessions area has been informed—
(a) under subsection (3) above that there is a person in the area to whom subsection (2) above applies; or
(b) under subsection (5) above that there is a person in the area to whom subsection (4) above applies,

the clerk shall arrange for a magistrates' court to sit not later than the day next following the relevant day.

(7) In this section " the relevant day"—
(a) in relation to a person who is to be brought before a magistrates' court for the petty sessions area in which the police station at which he was charged is situated, means the day on which he was charged; and
(b) in relation to a person who is to be brought before a magistrates' court for any other petty sessions area, means the day on which he arrives in the area.

(8) Where the day next following the relevant day is Christmas Day, Good Friday or a Sunday, the duty of the clerk under subsection (6) above is a duty to arrange for a magistrates' court to sit not later than the first day after the relevant day which is not one of those days.

(9) Nothing in this section requires a person who is in hospital to be brought before a court if he is not well enough.

[46A Power of arrest for failure to answer to police bail

(1) A constable may arrest without a warrant any person who, having been released on bail under this Part of this Act subject to a duty to attend at a police station, fails to attend at that police station at the time appointed for him to do so.

(2) A person who is arrested under this section shall be taken to the police station appointed as the place at which he is to surrender to custody as soon as practicable after the arrest.

(3) For the purposes of—
(a) section 30 above (subject to the obligation in subsection (2) above), and
(b) section 31 above,

an arrest under this section shall be treated as an arrest for an offence.]

NOTES

Inserted by the Criminal Justice and Public Order Act 1994, s 29(1), (2), (5), and applies whether person released on bail was granted bail before or after 10 April 1995.

47 Bail after arrest

(1) Subject to subsection (2) below, a release on bail of a person under this Part of this Act shall be a release on bail granted in accordance with [sections 3, 3A, 5 and 5A of the Bail Act 1976 as they apply to bail granted by a constable].

[(1A) The normal powers to impose conditions of bail shall be available to him where a custody officer releases a person on bail under section 38(1) above (including that subsection as applied by section 40(10) above) but not in any other cases.

In this subsection "the normal powers to impose conditions of bail" has the meaning given in section 3(6) of the Bail Act 1976.]

(2) Nothing in the Bail Act 1976 shall prevent the re-arrest without warrant of a person released on bail subject to a duty to attend at a police station if new evidence justifying a further arrest has come to light since his release.

(3)–(6) . . .

(7) Where a person who was released on bail subject to a duty to attend at a police station is re-arrested, the provisions of this Part of this Act shall apply to him as they apply to a person arrested for the first time[; but this subsection does not apply to a person who is arrested under section 46A above or has attended a police station in accordance with the grant of bail (and who accordingly is deemed by section 34(7) above to have been arrested for the offence)].

(8) . . .

NOTES

Sub-s (1): words in square brackets substituted by the Criminal Justice and Public Order Act 1994, s 27(1)(a).

Sub-s (1A): inserted by the Criminal Justice and Public Order Act 1994, ss 27(1)(b).

Sub-ss (3), (4), (6): outside the scope of this work.

Sub-s (5): repealed by the Criminal Justice and Public Order Act 1994, s 29(1), (4)(c), (5), 168(3), Sch 11.

Sub-s (7): words in square brackets added by the Criminal Justice and Public Order Act 1994, s 29(1), (4)(e), (5).

Sub-s (8): substitutes the Magistrates' Courts Act 1980, ss 43, 117(3).

PART V
QUESTIONING AND TREATMENT OF PERSONS BY POLICE

53 Abolition of certain powers of constables to search persons

(1) Subject to subsection (2) below, there shall cease to have effect any Act (including a local Act) passed before this Act in so far as it authorises—

(a) any search by a constable of a person in police detention at a police station; or

(b) an intimate search of a person by a constable;

and any rule of common law which authorises a search such as is mentioned in paragraph (a) or (b) above is abolished.

(2) . . .

NOTES

Sub-s (2): repealed by the Prevention of Terrorism (Temporary Provisions) Act 1989, s 25(2), Sch 9, Pt I.

54 Searches of detained persons

(1) The custody officer at a police station shall ascertain and record or cause to be recorded everything which a person has with him when he is—

(a) brought to the station after being arrested elsewhere or after being committed to custody by an order or sentence of a court; or

[(b) arrested at the station or detained there[, as a person falling within section 34(7), under section 37 above]].

(2) In the case of an arrested person the record shall be made as part of his custody record.

(3) Subject to subsection (4) below, a custody officer may seize and retain any such thing or cause any such thing to be seized and retained.

(4) Clothes and personal effects may only be seized if the custody officer—
- (a) believes that the person from whom they are seized may use them—
  - (i) to cause physical injury to himself or any other person;
  - (ii) to damage property;
  - (iii) to interfere with evidence; or
  - (iv) to assist him to escape; or
- (b) has reasonable grounds for believing that they may be evidence relating to an offence.

(5) Where anything is seized, the person from whom it is seized shall be told the reason for the seizure unless he is —
- (a) violent or likely to become violent; or
- (b) incapable of understanding what is said to him.

(6) Subject to subsection (7) below, a person may be searched if the custody officer considers it necessary to enable him to carry out his duty under subsection (1) above and to the extent that the custody officer considers necessary for that purpose.

[(6A) A person who is in custody at a police station or is in police detention otherwise than at a police station may at any time be searched in order to ascertain whether he has with him anything which he could use for the purposes specified in subsection (4)(a) above.

(6B) Subject to subsection (6C) below, a constable may seize and retain, or cause to be seized and retained, anything found on such a search.

(6C) A constable may only seize clothes and personal effects in the circumstances specified in subsection (4) above.]

(7) An intimate search may not be conducted under this section.

(8) A search under this section shall be carried out by a constable.

(9) The constable carrying out a search shall be of the same sex as the person searched.

NOTES

Sub-s (1): para (b) substituted by the Criminal Justice Act 1988, s 147(a); words in square brackets in para (b) substituted by the Criminal Justice and Public Order Act 1994, s 168(2), Sch 10, para 55.

Sub-ss (6A)–(6C): inserted by the Criminal Justice Act 1988, s 147(b).

55 Intimate searches

(1) Subject to the following provisions of this section, if an officer of at least the rank of superintendent has reasonable grounds for believing—
- (a) that a person who has been arrested and is in police detention may have concealed on him anything which—
  - (i) he could use to cause physical injury to himself or others; and
  - (ii) he might so use while he is in police detention or in the custody of a court; or
- (b) that such a person—

(i) may have a Class A drug concealed on him; and
(ii) was in possession of it with the appropriate criminal intent before his arrest,

he may authorise [an intimate search] of that person.

(2) An officer may not authorise an intimate search of a person for anything unless he has reasonable grounds for believing that it cannot be found without his being intimately searched.

(3) . . .

(4) An intimate search which is only a drug offence search shall be by way of examination by a suitably qualified person.

(5) Except as provided by subsection (4) above, an intimate search shall be by way of examination by a suitably qualified person unless an officer of at least the rank of superintendent considers that this is not practicable.

(6) An intimate search which is not carried out as mentioned in subsection (5) above shall be carried out by a constable.

(7) A constable may not carry out an intimate search of a person of the opposite sex.

(8) No intimate search may be carried out except—
(a) at a police station;
(b) at a hospital;
(c) at a registered medical practitioner's surgery; or
(d) at some other place used for medical purposes.

(9) An intimate search which is only a drug offence search may not be carried out at a police station.

(10) If an intimate search of a person is carried out, the custody record relating to him shall state—
(a) which parts of his body were searched; and
(b) why they were searched.

(11) . . .

(12) The custody officer at a police station may seize and retain anything which is found on an intimate search of a person, or cause any such thing to be seized and retained—
(a) if he believes that the person from whom it is seized may use it—
(i) to cause physical injury to himself or any other person;
(ii) to damage property;
(iii) to interfere with evidence; or
(iv) to assist him to escape; or
(b) if he has reasonable grounds for believing that it may be evidence relating to an offence.

(13) Where anything is seized under this section, the person from whom it is seized shall be told the reason for the seizure unless he is—
(a) violent or likely to become violent; or
(b) incapable of understanding what is said to him.

(14), (14A), (15), (16) . . .

(17) In this section—

"the appropriate criminal intent" means an intent to commit an offence under—

(a) section 5(3) of the Misuse of Drugs Act 1971 (possession of controlled drug with intent to supply to another); or

(b) section 68(2) of the Customs and Excise Management Act 1979 (exportation etc with intent to evade a prohibition or restriction);

"Class A drug" has the meaning assigned to it by section 2(1)(b) of the Misuse of Drugs Act 1971;

"drug offence search" means an intimate search for a Class A drug which an officer has authorised by virtue of subsection (1)(b) above; and

"suitably qualified person" means—

(a) a registered medical practitioner; or

(b) a registered nurse.

NOTES

Sub-s (1): words in square brackets substituted by the Criminal Justice Act 1988, s 170(1), Sch 15, paras 97, 99.

Sub-ss (3), (11), (14), (14A), (15), (16): outside the scope of this work.

56 Right to have someone informed when arrested

(1) Where a person has been arrested and is being held in custody in a police station or other premises, he shall be entitled, if he so requests, to have one friend or relative or other person who is known to him or who is likely to take an interest in his welfare told, as soon as is practicable except to the extent that delay is permitted by this section, that he has been arrested and is being detained there.

(2) Delay is only permitted—

(a) in the case of a person who is in police detention for a serious arrestable offence; and

(b) if an officer of at least the rank of superintendent authorises it.

(3) In any case the person in custody must be permitted to exercise the right conferred by subsection (1) above within 36 hours from the relevant time, as defined in section 41(2) above.

(4) . . .

(5) [Subject to subsection (5A) below] an officer may only authorise delay where he has reasonable grounds for believing that telling the named person of the arrest—

(a) will lead to interference with or harm to evidence connected with a serious arrestable offence or interference with or physical injury to other persons; or

(b) will lead to the alerting of other persons suspected of having committed such an offence but not yet arrested for it; or

(c) will hinder the recovery of any property obtained as a result of such an offence.

[(5A) An officer may also authorise delay where the serious arrestable offence is a drug trafficking offence [or an offence to which Part VI of the Criminal Justice Act 1988 applies (offences in respect of which confiscation orders under that Part may be made)] and the officer has reasonable grounds for believing—

[(a) where the offence is a drug trafficking offence, that the detained person has benefited from drug trafficking and that the recovery of the value of that person's proceeds of drug trafficking will be hindered by telling the named person of the arrest; and

(b) where the offence is one to which Part VI of the Criminal Justice Act 1988 applies, that the detained person has benefited from the offence and that the recovery of the value of the property obtained by that person from or in connection with the offence or of the pecuniary advantage derived by him from or in connection with it will be hindered by telling the named person of the arrest].]

(6) If a delay is authorised—

(a) the detained person shall be told the reason for it; and
(b) the reason shall be noted on his custody record.

(7) The duties imposed by subsection (6) above shall be performed as soon as is practicable.

(8) The rights conferred by this section on a person detained at a police station or other premises are exercisable whenever he is transferred from one place to another; and this section applies to each subsequent occasion on which they are exercisable as it applies to the first such occasion.

(9) There may be no further delay in permitting the exercise of the right conferred by subsection (1) above once the reason for authorising delay ceases to subsist.

(10) In the foregoing provisions of this section references to a person who has been arrested include references to a person who has been detained under the terrorism provisions and "arrest" includes detention under those provisions.

(11) In its application to a person who has been arrested or detained under the terrorism provisions—

(a) subsection (2)(a) above shall have effect as if for the words "for a serious arrestable offence" there were substituted the words "under the terrorism provisions";
(b) subsection (3) above shall have effect as if for the words from "within" onwards there were substituted the words "before the end of the period beyond which he may no longer be detained without the authority of the Secretary of State"; and
(c) subsection (5) above shall have effect as if at the end there were added "or
  (d) will lead to interference with the gathering of information about the commission, preparation or instigation of acts of terrorism; or
  (e) by alerting any person, will make it more difficult—
    (i) to prevent an act of terrorism; or
    (ii) to secure the apprehension, prosecution or conviction of any person in connection with the commission, preparation or instigation of an act of terrorism.".

NOTES

Sub-s (4): outside the scope of this work.

Sub-s (5): words in square brackets inserted by the Drug Trafficking Offences Act 1986, s 32(1).

Sub-s (5A): inserted by the Drug Trafficking Offences Act 1986, s 32(1); words in square brackets inserted or substituted by the Criminal Justice Act 1988, s 99(1), (2).

58 Access to legal advice

(1) A person arrested and held in custody in a police station or other premises shall be entitled, if he so requests, to consult a solicitor privately at any time.

(2) Subject to subsection (3) below, a request under subsection (1) above and the time at which it was made shall be recorded in the custody record.

(3) Such a request need not be recorded in the custody record of a person who makes it at a time while he is at a court after being charged with an offence.

(4) If a person makes such a request, he must be permitted to consult a solicitor as soon as is practicable except to the extent that delay is permitted by this section.

(5) In any case he must be permitted to consult a solicitor within 36 hours from the relevant time, as defined in section 41(2) above.

(6) Delay in compliance with a request is only permitted—

(a) in the case of a person who is in police detention for a serious arrestable offence; and

(b) if an officer of at least the rank of superintendent authorises it.

(7) An officer may give an authorisation under subsection (6) above orally or in writing but, if he gives it orally, he shall confirm it in writing as soon as is practicable.

(8) [Subject to subsection (8A) below] an officer may only authorise delay where he has reasonable grounds for believing that the exercise of the right conferred by subsection (1) above at the time when the person detained desires to exercise it—

(a) will lead to interference with or harm to evidence connected with a serious arrestable offence or interference with or physical injury to other persons; or

(b) will lead to the alerting of other persons suspected of having committed such an offence but not yet arrested for it; or

(c) will hinder the recovery of any property obtained as a result of such an offence.

[(8A) An officer may also authorise delay where the serious arrestable offence is a drug trafficking offence [or an offence to which Part VI of the Criminal Justice Act 1988 applies] and the officer has reasonable grounds for believing—

[(a) where the offence is a drug trafficking offence, that the detained person has benefited from drug trafficking and that the recovery of the value of that person's proceeds of drug trafficking will be hindered by the exercise of the right conferred by subsection (1) above; and

(b) where the offence is one to which Part VI of the Criminal Justice Act 1988 applies, that the detained person has benefited from the offence and that the recovery of the value of the property obtained by that person from or in connection with the offence or of the pecuniary advantage derived by him from or in connection with it will be hindered by the exercise of the right conferred by subsection (1) above].]

(9) If delay is authorised—

(a) the detained person shall be told the reason for it; and

(b) the reason shall be noted on his custody record.

(10) The duties imposed by subsection (9) above shall be performed as soon as is practicable.

(11) There may be no further delay in permitting the exercise of the right conferred by subsection (1) above once the reason for authorising delay ceases to subsist.

(12) The reference in subsection (1) above to a person arrested includes a reference to a person who has been detained under the terrorism provisions.

(13) In the application of this section to a person who has been arrested or detained under the terrorism provisions—

(a) subsection (5) above shall have effect as if for the words from "within" onwards there were substituted the words "before the end of the period beyond which he may no longer be detained without the authority of the Secretary of State";

(b) subsection (6)(a) above shall have effect as if for the words "for a serious arrestable offence" there were substituted the words "under the terrorism provisions"; and

(c) subsection (8) above shall have effect as if at the end there were added "or

(d) will lead to interference with the gathering of information about the commission, preparation or instigation of acts of terrorism; or

(e) by alerting any person, will make it more difficult—

(i) to prevent an act of terrorism; or

(ii) to secure the apprehension, prosecution or conviction of any person in connection with the commission, preparation or instigation of an act of terrorism.".

(14) If an officer of appropriate rank has reasonable grounds for believing that, unless he gives a direction under subsection (15) below, the exercise by a person arrested or detained under the terrorism provisions of the right conferred by subsection (1) above will have any of the consequences specified in subsection (8) above (as it has effect by virtue of subsection (13) above), he may give a direction under that subsection.

(15) A direction under this subsection is a direction that a person desiring to exercise the right conferred by subsection (1) above may only consult a solicitor in the sight and hearing of a qualified officer of the uniformed branch of the force of which the officer giving the direction is a member.

(16) An officer is qualified for the purpose of subsection (15) above if—

(a) he is of at least the rank of inspector; and

(b) in the opinion of the officer giving the direction he has no connection with the case.

(17) An officer is of appropriate rank to give a direction under subsection (15) above if he is of at least the rank of Commander or Assistant Chief Constable.

(18) A direction under subsection (15) above shall cease to have effect once the reason for giving it ceases to subsist.

NOTES

Sub-s (8): words in square brackets inserted by the Drug Trafficking Offences Act 1986, s 32(2).

Sub-s (8A) inserted by the Drug Trafficking Offences Act 1986, s 32(2); words in square brackets inserted or substituted by the Criminal Justice Act 1988, s 99(1), (3).

---

60 Tape-recording of interviews

(1) It shall be the duty of the Secretary of State—

(a) to issue a code of practice in connection with the tape-recording of interviews of persons suspected of the commission of criminal offences which are held by police officers at police stations; and

(b) to make an order requiring the tape-recording of interviews of persons suspected of the commission of criminal offences, or of such descriptions of criminal offences as may be specified in the order, which are so held, in accordance with the code as it has effect for the time being.

(2) An order under subsection (1) above shall be made by statutory instrument and shall be subject to annulment in pursuance of a resolution of either House of Parliament.

61 Fingerprinting

(1) Except as provided by this section no person's fingerprints may be taken without the appropriate consent.

(2) Consent to the taking of a person's fingerprints must be in writing if it is given at a time when he is at a police station.

(3) The fingerprints of a person detained at a police station may be taken without the appropriate consent—
- (a) if an officer of at least the rank of superintendent authorises them to be taken; or
- (b) if—
  - (i) he has been charged with a recordable offence or informed that he will be reported for such an offence; and
  - (ii) he has not had his fingerprints taken in the course of the investigation of the offence by the police.

(4) An officer may only give an authorisation under subsection (3)(a) above if he has reasonable grounds—
- (a) for suspecting the involvement of the person whose fingerprints are to be taken in a criminal offence; and
- (b) for believing that his fingerprints will tend to confirm or disprove his involvement.

(5) . . .

(6) Any person's fingerprints may be taken without the appropriate consent if he has been convicted of a recordable offence.

(7), (7A) . . .

(8) If he is detained at a police station when the fingerprints are taken, the reason for taking them [and, in the case falling within subsection (7A) above, the fact referred to in paragraph (b) of that subsection] shall be recorded on his custody record.

(9) Nothing in this section—
- (a) affects any power conferred by paragraph 18(2) of Schedule 2 to the Immigration Act 1971; or
- (b) [except as provided in section 15(10) of, and paragraph 7(6) of Schedule 5 to, the Prevention of Terrorism (Temporary Provisions) Act 1989,] applies to a person arrested or detained under the terrorism provisions.

NOTES

Sub-ss (5), (7), (7A): outside the scope of this work.

Sub-s (8): words in square brackets inserted by the Criminal Justice and Public Order Act 1994, s 168(2), Sch 10, para 56(b).

Sub-s (9): words in square brackets in para (b) inserted by the Prevention of Terrorism (Temporary Provisions) Act 1989, s 25(1), Sch 8, para 6(1), (5).

62 Intimate samples

(1) An intimate sample may be taken from a person in police detention only—
- (a) if a police officer of at least the rank of superintendent authorises it to be taken; and

(b) if the appropriate consent is given.

[(1A) An intimate sample may be taken from a person who is not in police detention but from whom, in the course of the investigation of the offence, two or more non-intimate samples suitable for the same means of analysis have been taken which have proved insufficient—

(a) if a police officer of at least the rank of superintendent authorises it to be taken; and

(b) if the appropriate consent is given.]

(2) An officer may only give an authorisation [under subsection (1) or (1A) above] if he has reasonable grounds—

(a) for suspecting the involvement of the person from whom the sample is to be taken in a [recordable offence]; and

(b) for believing that the sample will tend to confirm or disprove his involvement.

(3) . . .

(4) The appropriate consent must be given in writing.

(5) Where—

(a) an authorisation has been given; and

(b) it is proposed that an intimate sample shall be taken in pursuance of the authorisation,

an officer shall inform the person from whom the sample is to be taken—

(i) of the giving of the authorisation; and

(ii) of the grounds for giving it.

(6) The duty imposed by subsection (5)(ii) above includes a duty to state the nature of the offence in which it is suspected that the person from whom the sample is to be taken has been involved.

(7) If an intimate sample is taken from a person—

(a) the authorisation by virtue of which it was taken;

(b) the grounds for giving the authorisation; and

(c) the fact that the appropriate consent was given,

shall be recorded as soon as is practicable after the sample is taken.

(7A), (8) . . .

(9) An intimate sample, other than a sample of urine [or a dental impression], may only be taken from a person by a registered medical practitioner [and a dental impression may only be taken by a registered dentist].

(10) Where the appropriate consent to the taking of an intimate sample from a person was refused without good cause, in any proceedings against that person for an offence—

(a) the court, in determining—

(i) whether to commit that person for trial; or

(ii) whether there is a case to answer; and

[(aa) a judge, in deciding whether to grant an application made by the accused under—

(i) section 6 of the Criminal Justice Act 1987 (application for dismissal of charge of serious fraud in respect of which notice of transfer has been given under section 4 of that Act); or

(ii) paragraph 5 of Schedule 6 to the Criminal Justice Act 1991 (application for dismissal of charge of violent or sexual offence involving child in respect of which notice of transfer has been given under section 53 of that Act; and]

(b) the court or jury, in determining whether that person is guilty of the offence charged,

may draw such inferences from the refusal as appear proper; . . .

(11) Nothing in this section affects [sections 4 to 11 of the Road Traffic Act 1988].

(12) . . .

NOTES

Sub-ss (1A): inserted by the Criminal Justice and Public Order Act 1994, s 54(1), (2).

Sub-s (2): words in first pair of square brackets inserted, and words in second pair of square brackets substituted, by the Criminal Justice and Public Order Act 1994, s 54(1), (3).

Sub-ss (3), (7A), (8), (12): outside the scope of this work.

Sub-s (9): words in first pair of square brackets in substituted, and words in second pair of square brackets added, by the Criminal Justice and Public Order Act 1994, s 54(1), (5).

Sub-s (10): para (aa) inserted, and words omitted repealed, by the Criminal Justice and Public Order Act 1994, s 168(1), Sch 9, para 24, Sch 11.

Sub-s (11): words in square brackets substituted by the Road Traffic (Consequential Provisions) Act 1988, s 4, Sch 3, para 27(4).

63 Other samples

(1) Except as provided by this section, a non-intimate sample may not be taken from a person without the appropriate consent.

(2) Consent to the taking of a non-intimate sample must be given in writing.

(3) A non-intimate sample may be taken from a person without the appropriate consent if—

(a) he is in police detention or is being held in custody by the police on the authority of a court; and

(b) an officer of at least the rank of superintendent authorises it to be taken without the appropriate consent.

[(3A) A non-intimate sample may be taken from a person (whether or not he falls within subsection (3)(a) above) without the appropriate consent if—

(a) he has been charged with a recordable offence or informed that he will be reported for such an offence; and

(b) either he has not had a non-intimate sample taken from him in the course of the investigation of the offence by the police or he has had a non-intimate sample taken from him but either it was not suitable for the same means of analysis or, though so suitable, the sample proved insufficient.

(3B) A non-intimate sample may be taken from a person without the appropriate consent if he has been convicted of a recordable offence.]

[(3C) A non-intimate sample may also be taken from a person without the appropriate consent if he is a person to whom section 2 of the Criminal Evidence (Amendment) Act 1997 applies (persons detained following acquittal on grounds of insanity or finding of unfitness to plead).]

(4) An officer may only give an authorisation under subsection (3) above if he has reasonable grounds—

(a) for suspecting the involvement of the person from whom the sample is to be taken in a [recordable offence]; and
(b) for believing that the sample will tend to confirm or disprove his involvement.

(5) An officer may give an authorisation under subsection (3) above orally or in writing but, if he gives it orally, he shall confirm it in writing as soon as is practicable.

(6) Where—
(a) an authorisation has been given; and
(b) it is proposed that a non-intimate sample shall be taken in pursuance of the authorisation,

an officer shall inform the person from whom the sample is to be taken—
(i) of the giving of the authorisation; and
(ii) of the grounds for giving it.

(7) The duty imposed by subsection (6)(ii) above includes a duty to state the nature of the offence in which it is suspected that the person from whom the sample is to be taken has been involved.

(8) If a non-intimate sample is taken from a person by virtue of subsection (3) above—
(a) the authorisation by virtue of which it was taken; and
(b) the grounds for giving the authorisation,

shall be recorded as soon as is practicable after the sample is taken.

(8A), (8B), (9), (9A), (10) . . .

NOTES

Sub-ss (3A), (3B): inserted by the Criminal Justice and Public Order Act 1994, s 55(2).

Sub-s (3C): inserted by the Criminal Evidence (Amendment) Act 1997, s 2(2).

Sub-s (4): words in square brackets substituted by the Criminal Justice and Public Order Act 1994, s 55(3).

Sub-ss (8A), (8B), (9), (9A), (10): outside the scope of this work.

Modification: modified, in relation to the investigation of offences conducted by a service policeman under the Army Act 1955, the Air Force Act 1955 or the Naval Discipline Act 1957, by the Police and Criminal Evidence Act 1984 (Application to the Armed Forces) Order 1997, SI 1997/15, art 2, Schedule.

64 Destruction of fingerprints and samples

(1) If—
(a) fingerprints or samples are taken from a person in connection with the investigation of an offence; and
(b) he is cleared of that offence,

they must[, except as provided in subsection (3A) below,] be destroyed as soon as is practicable after the conclusion of the proceedings.

(2) If—
(a) fingerprints or samples are taken from a person in connection with such an investigation; and
(b) it is decided that he shall not be prosecuted for the offence and he has not admitted it and been dealt with by way of being cautioned by a constable,

they must[, except as provided in subsection (3A) below,] be destroyed as soon as is practicable after that decision is taken.

(3) If—

(a) fingerprints or samples are taken from a person in connection with the investigation of an offence; and

(b) that person is not suspected of having committed the offence,

they must[, except as provided in subsection (3A) below,] be destroyed as soon as they have fulfilled the purpose for which they were taken.

[(3A) Samples which are required to be destroyed under subsection (1), (2) or (3) above need not be destroyed if they were taken for the purpose of the same investigation of an offence of which a person from whom one was taken has been convicted, but the information derived from the sample of any person entitled (apart from this subsection) to its destruction under subsection (1), (2) or (3) above shall not be used—

(a) in evidence against the person so entitled; or

(b) for the purposes of any investigation of an offence.

(3B) Where samples are required to be destroyed under subsections (1), (2) or (3) above, and subsection (3A) above does not apply, information derived from the sample of any person entitled to its destruction under subsection (1), (2) or (3) above shall not be used—

(a) in evidence against the person so entitled; or

(b) for the purposes of any investigation of an offence.]

(4)–(6), (6A), (6B), (7) . . .

NOTES

Sub-s (1): words in square brackets inserted by the Criminal Justice and Public Order Act 1994, s 57(1), (2).
Sub-s (2): words in square brackets inserted by the Criminal Justice and Public Order Act 1994, s 57(1), (2).
Sub-s (3): words in square brackets inserted by the Criminal Justice and Public Order Act 1994, s 57(1), (2).
Sub-s (3A): inserted by the Criminal Justice and Public Order Act 1994, s 57(1), (3)
Sub-s (3B): inserted by the Criminal Justice and Public Order Act 1994, s 57(1), (3).
Sub-ss (4)–(6), (6A), (6B), (7): outside the scope of this work.

65 Part V—supplementary

In this Part of this Act—

"appropriate consent" means—

(a) in relation to a person who has attained the age of 17 years, the consent of that person;

(b) in relation to a person who has not attained that age but has attained the age of 14 years, the consent of that person and his parent or guardian; and

(c) in relation to a person who has not attained the age of 14 years, the consent of his parent or guardian;

["drug trafficking" and "drug trafficking offence" have the same meaning as in the [Drug Trafficking Act 1994]]

"fingerprints" includes palm prints;

["intimate sample" means—

(a) a sample of blood, semen or any other tissue fluid, urine or pubic hair;

(b) a dental impression;

(c) a swab taken from a person's body orifice other than the mouth;]

["intimate search" means a search which consists of the physical examination of a person's body orifices other than the mouth;]

["non-intimate sample" means—

(a) a sample of hair other than pubic hair;

(b) a sample taken from a nail or from under a nail;
(c) a swab taken from any part of a person's body including the mouth but not any other body orifice;
(d) saliva;
(e) a footprint or a similar impression of any part of a person's body other than a part of his hand;]

. . . . .

["the terrorism provisions" means section 14(1) of the Prevention of Terrorism (Temporary Provisions) Act 1989 and any provision of Schedule 2 or 5 to that Act conferring a power of arrest or detention; and

"terrorism" has the meaning assigned to it by section 20(1) of that Act]

[. . . references in this Part to any person's proceeds of drug trafficking are to be construed in accordance with the [Drug Trafficking Act 1994]].

NOTES

Definition "drug trafficking" and "drug trafficking offence" inserted, and words in first (outer) pair of square brackets at end of section added, by the Drug Trafficking Offences Act 1986, s 32(3).

Words in square brackets in definition of "drug trafficking" and "drug trafficking offence" and words in second (inner) pair of square brackets at end of section substituted by the Drug Trafficking Act 1994, s 65(1), Sch 1, para 8.

Definitions "intimate sample" and "non-intimate sample" substituted, and definition "intimate search" inserted, by the Criminal Justice and Public Order Act 1994, ss 58(1)–(3), 59(1).

Definitions omitted outside the scope of this work.

Definitions "the terrorism provisions" and "terrorism" substituted by the Prevention of Terrorism (Temporary Provisions) Act 1989, s 25(1), Sch 8, para 6(1), (6).

Words omitted at end of section repealed by the Criminal Justice Act 1988, s 170, Sch 16.

PART VI
CODES OF PRACTICE—GENERAL

66 Codes of practice

The Secretary of State shall issue codes of practice in connection with—

(a) the exercise by police officers of statutory powers—
  (i) to search a person without first arresting him; or
  (ii) to search a vehicle without making an arrest;
(b) the detention, treatment, questioning and identification of persons by police officers;
(c) searches of premises by police officers; and
(d) the seizure of property found by police officers on persons or premises.

67 Codes of practice—supplementary

(1) When the Secretary of State proposes to issue a code of practice to which this section applies, he shall prepare and publish a draft of that code, shall consider any representations made to him about the draft and may modify the draft accordingly.

(2) This section applies to a code of practice under section 60 or 66 above.

(3) The Secretary of State shall lay before both Houses of Parliament a draft of any code of practice prepared by him under this section.

(4) When the Secretary of State has laid the draft of a code before Parliament, he may bring the code into operation by order made by statutory instrument.

(5) No order under subsection (4) above shall have effect until approved by a resolution of each House of Parliament.

(6) An order bringing a code of practice into operation may contain such transitional provisions or savings as appear to the Secretary of State to be necessary or expedient in connection with the code of practice thereby brought into operation.

(7) The Secretary of State may from time to time revise the whole or any part of a code of practice to which this section applies and issue that revised code; and the foregoing provisions of this section shall apply (with appropriate modifications) to such a revised code as they apply to the first issue of a code.

(8) . . .

(9) Persons other than police officers who are charged with the duty of investigating offences or charging offenders shall in the discharge of that duty have regard to any relevant provision of such a code.

(10) A failure on the part—

(a) of a police officer to comply with any provision of such a code; or

(b) of any person other than a police officer who is charged with the duty of investigating offences or charging offenders to have regard to any relevant provision of such a code in the discharge of that duty,

shall not of itself render him liable to any criminal or civil proceedings.

(11) In all criminal and civil proceedings any such code shall be admissible in evidence; and if any provision of such a code appears to the court or tribunal conducting the proceedings to be relevant to any question arising in the proceedings it shall be taken into account in determining that question.

(12) . . .

NOTES

Sub-s (8): repealed by the Police and Magistrates' Courts Act 1994, ss 37(a), 93, Sch 9, Pt I and by the Police Act 1996, s 103(3), Sch 9, Pt II.

Sub-s (12): outside the scope of this work.

See Appendix for extracts of relevant code of practice.

PART VIII
EVIDENCE IN CRIMINAL PROCEEDINGS—GENERAL

Confessions

76 Confessions

(1) In any proceedings a confession made by an accused person may be given in evidence against him in so far as it is relevant to any matter in issue in the proceedings and is not excluded by the court in pursuance of this section.

(2) If, in any proceedings where the prosecution proposes to give in evidence a confession made by an accused person, it is represented to the court that the confession was or may have been obtained—

(a) by oppression of the person who made it; or

(b) in consequence of anything said or done which was likely, in the circumstances existing at the time, to render unreliable any confession which might be made by him in consequence thereof, the court shall not allow the confession to be given in evidence against him except in so far as the prosecution proves to the court beyond reasonable doubt that the confession (notwithstanding that it may be true) was not obtained as aforesaid.

(3) In any proceedings where the prosecution proposes to give in evidence a confession made by an accused person, the court may of its own motion require the prosecution, as a condition of allowing it to do so, to prove that the confession was not obtained as mentioned in subsection (2) above.

(4) The fact that a confession is wholly or partly excluded in pursuance of this section shall not affect the admissibility in evidence—

- (a) of any facts discovered as a result of the confession; or
- (b) where the confession is relevant as showing that the accused speaks, writes or expresses himself in a particular way, of so much of the confession as is necessary to show that he does so.

(5) Evidence that a fact to which this subsection applies was discovered as a result of a statement made by an accused person shall not be admissible unless evidence of how it was discovered is given by him or on his behalf.

(6) Subsection (5) above applies—

- (a) to any fact discovered as a result of a confession which is wholly excluded in pursuance of this section; and
- (b) to any fact discovered as a result of a confession which is partly so excluded, if the fact is discovered as a result of the excluded part of the confession.

(7) Nothing in Part VII of this Act shall prejudice the admissibility of a confession made by an accused person.

(8) In this section "oppression" includes torture, inhuman or degrading treatment, and the use or threat of violence (whether or not amounting to torture).

(9) . . .

NOTES

Sub-s (9): outside the scope of this work.

77 Confessions by mentally handicapped persons

(1) Without prejudice to the general duty of the court at a trial on indictment to direct the jury on any matter on which it appears to the court appropriate to do so, where at such a trial—

- (a) the case against the accused depends wholly or substantially on a confession by him; and
- (b) the court is satisfied—
  - (i) that he is mentally handicapped; and
  - (ii) that the confession was not made in the presence of an independent person,

the court shall warn the jury that there is special need for caution before convicting the accused in reliance on the confession, and shall explain that the need arises because of the circumstances mentioned in paragraphs (a) and (b) above.

(2) In any case where at the summary trial of a person for an offence it appears to the court that a warning under subsection (1) above would be required if the trial were on indictment, the court shall treat the case as one in which there is a special need for caution before convicting the accused on his confession.

(3) In this section—

"independent person" does not include a police officer or a person employed for, or engaged on, police purposes;

"mentally handicapped", in relation to a person, means that he is in a state of arrested or incomplete development of mind which includes significant impairment of intelligence and social functioning; and

"police purposes" has the meaning assigned to it by [section 101(2) of the Police Act 1996].

NOTES

Sub-s (3): words in square brackets in definition of "police purposes" substituted by the Police Act 1996, s 103(1), Sch 7, Pt II, para 38.

Miscellaneous

78 Exclusion of unfair evidence

(1) In any proceedings the court may refuse to allow evidence on which the prosecution proposes to rely to be given if it appears to the court that, having regard to all the circumstances, including the circumstances in which the evidence was obtained, the admission of the evidence would have such an adverse effect on the fairness of the proceedings that the court ought not to admit it.

(2) Nothing in this section shall prejudice any rule of law requiring a court to exclude evidence.

(3) . . .

NOTES

Sub-s (3): outside the scope of this work.

Part VIII—supplementary

82 Part VIII—interpretation

(1) In this Part of this Act—

"confession" includes any statement wholly or partly adverse to the person who made it, whether made to a person in authority or not and whether made in words or otherwise;

. . . . .

"proceedings" means criminal proceedings . . .

(2) . . .

(3) Nothing in this Part of this Act shall prejudice any power of a court to exclude evidence (whether by preventing questions from being put or otherwise) at its discretion.

NOTES

Sub-s (1): definitions "court-martial" and "service court" and words omitted from definition "proceedings" outside the scope of this work.

Sub-s (2): outside the scope of this work.

PART XI
MISCELLANEOUS AND SUPPLEMENTARY

116 Meaning of "serious arrestable offence"

(1) This section has effect for determining whether an offence is a serious arrestable offence for the purposes of this Act.

(2) The following arrestable offences are always serious—

(a) an offence (whether at common law or under any enactment) specified in Part I of Schedule 5 to this Act;

[(aa) . . .]

(b) an offence under an enactment specified in Part II of that Schedule, [and

(c) any of the offences mentioned in paragraphs (a) to (f) of section 1(3) of the Drug Trafficking Act 1994.]

(3) Subject to subsections (4) and (5) below, any other arrestable offence is serious only if its commission—

(a) has led to any of the consequences specified in subsection (6) below; or

(b) is intended or is likely to lead to any of those consequences.

(4) An arrestable offence which consists of making a threat is serious if carrying out the threat would be likely to lead to any of the consequences specified in subsection (6) below.

(5) An offence under [section 2, 8, 9, 10 or 11 of the Prevention of Terrorism (Temporary Provisions) Act 1989] is always a serious arrestable offence for the purposes of section 56 or 58 above, and an attempt or conspiracy to commit any such offence is also always a serious arrestable offence for those purposes.

(6) The consequences mentioned in subsections (3) and (4) above are

(a) serious harm to the security of the State or to public order;

(b) serious interference with the administration of justice or with the investigation of offences or of a particular offence;

(c) the death of any person;

(d) serious injury to any person;

(e) substantial financial gain to any person; and

(f) serious financial loss to any person.

(7) Loss is serious for the purposes of this section if, having regard to all the circumstances, it is serious for the person who suffers it.

(8) In this section "injury" includes any disease and any impairment of a person's physical or mental condition.

NOTES

Sub-s (2): para (aa) repealed, and para (c) and word in square brackets immediately preceding it added, by the Drug Trafficking Act 1994, ss 65(1), 67(1), Sch 1, para 9, Sch 3.

Sub-s (5): words in square brackets substituted by the Prevention of Terrorism (Temporary Provisions) Act 1989, s 25(1), Sch 8, para 6(1), (7).

117 Power of constable to use reasonable force

Where any provision of this Act—

(a) confers a power on a constable; and

(b) does not provide that the power may only be exercised with the consent of some person, other than a police officer,

the officer may use reasonable force, if necessary, in the exercise of the power.

122 Short title

This Act may be cited as the Police and Criminal Evidence Act 1984.

SCHEDULES

SCHEDULE 1

Section 9

SPECIAL PROCEDURE

Making of orders by circuit judge

1. If on an application made by a constable a circuit judge is satisfied that one or other of the sets of access conditions is fulfilled, he may make an order under paragraph 4 below.

2. The first set of access conditions is fulfilled if—
   (a) there are reasonable grounds for believing—
      (i) that a serious arrestable offence has been committed;
      (ii) that there is material which consists of special procedure material or includes special procedure material and does not also include excluded material on premises specified in the application;
      (iii) that the material is likely to be of substantial value (whether by itself or together with other material) to the investigation in connection with which the application is made; and
      (iv) that the material is likely to be relevant evidence;
   (b) other methods of obtaining the material—
      (i) have been tried without success; or
      (ii) have not been tried because it appeared that they were bound to fail; and
   (c) it is in the public interest, having regard—
      (i) to the benefit likely to accrue to the investigation if the material is obtained; and
      (ii) to the circumstances under which the person in possession of the material holds it,

   that the material should be produced or that access to it should be given.

3. The second set of access conditions is fulfilled if—
   (a) there are reasonable grounds for believing that there is material which consists of or includes excluded material or special procedure material on premises specified in the application;
   (b) but for section 9(2) above a search of the premises for that material could have been authorised by the issue of a warrant to a constable under an enactment other than this Schedule; and
   (c) the issue of such a warrant would have been appropriate.

4. An order under this paragraph is an order that the person who appears to the circuit judge to be in possession of the material to which the application relates shall—
   (a) produce it to a constable for him to take away; or
   (b) give a constable access to it,

not later than the end of the period of seven days from the date of the order or the end of such longer period as the order may specify.

5. Where the material consists of information contained in a computer—
   (a) an order under paragraph 4(a) above shall have effect as an order to produce the material in a form in which it can be taken away and in which it is visible and legible; and

(b) an order under paragraph 4(b) above shall have effect as an order to give a constable access to the material in a form in which it is visible and legible.

6. For the purposes of sections 21 and 22 above material produced in pursuance of an order under paragraph 4(a) above shall be treated as if it were material seized by a constable.

Notices of applications for orders

7. An application for an order under paragraph 4 above shall be made inter partes.

8. Notice of an application for such an order may be served on a person either by delivering it to him or by leaving it at his proper address or by sending it by post to him in a registered letter or by the recorded delivery service.

9, 10. . . .

11. Where notice of an application for an order under paragraph 4 above has been served on a person, he shall not conceal, destroy, alter or dispose of the material to which the application relates except—

(a) with the leave of a judge; or
(b) with the written permission of a constable,

until—

(i) the application is dismissed or abandoned; or
(ii) he has complied with an order under paragraph 4 above made on the application.

Issue of warrants by circuit judge

12. If on an application made by a constable a circuit judge—

(a) is satisfied—
 (i) that either set of access conditions is fulfilled; and
 (ii) that any of the further conditions set out in paragraph 14 below is also fulfilled; or
(b) is satisfied—
 (i) that the second set of access conditions is fulfilled; and
 (ii) that an order under paragraph 4 above relating to the material has not been complied with,

he may issue a warrant authorising a constable to enter and search the premises.

13. A constable may seize and retain anything for which a search has been authorised under paragraph 12 above.

14. The further conditions mentioned in paragraph 12(a)(ii) above are—

(a) that it is not practicable to communicate with any person entitled to grant entry to the premises to which the application relates;
(b) that it is practicable to communicate with a person entitled to grant entry to the premises but it is not practicable to communicate with any person entitled to grant access to the material;
(c) that the material contains information which—
 (i) is subject to a restriction or obligation such as is mentioned in section 11(2)(b) above; and
 (ii) is likely to be disclosed in breach of it if a warrant is not issued;
(d) that service of notice of an application for an order under paragraph 4 above may seriously prejudice the investigation.

15.—(1) If a person fails to comply with an order under paragraph 4 above, a circuit judge may deal with him as if he had committed a contempt of the Crown Court.

(2) Any enactment relating to contempt of the Crown Court shall have effect in relation to such a failure as if it were such a contempt.

16. . . .

NOTES

Paras 9, 10, 16: outside the scope of this work.

Section 116

SCHEDULE 5

SERIOUS ARRESTABLE OFFENCES

PART I
OFFENCES MENTIONED IN SECTION 116(2)(A)

1. Treason.

2. Murder.

3. Manslaughter.

4. Rape.

5. Kidnapping.

6. Incest with a girl under the age of 13.

[7. Buggery with a person under the age of 16.]

8. Indecent assault which constitutes an act of gross indecency.

NOTES

Item 7: substituted by the Criminal Justice and Public Order Act 1994, s 168(2), Sch 10, para 59.

PART II
OFFENCES MENTIONED IN SECTION 116(2)(B)

Explosive Substances Act 1883 (c 3)

1. Section 2 (causing explosion likely to endanger life or property).

Sexual Offences Act 1956 (c 69)

2. Section 5 (intercourse with a girl under the age of 13).

Firearms Act 1968 (c 27)

3. Section 16 (possession of firearms with intent to injure).

4. Section 17(1) (use of firearms and imitation firearms to resist arrest).

5. Section 18 (carrying firearms with criminal intent).

. . . . .

Taking of Hostages Act 1982 (c 28)

7. Section 1 (hostage-taking).

Aviation Security Act 1982 (c 36)

8. Section 1 (hi-jacking).

[*Road Traffic Act 1988 (c 52)*

Section 1 (causing death by [dangerous] driving).]

[Section 3A (causing death by careless driving when under the influence of drink or drugs).]

[*Criminal Justice Act 1988 (c 33)*

Section 134 (Torture).]

[*Aviation and Maritime Security Act 1990 (c 31)*

11. Section 1 (endangering safety at aerodromes).

12. Section 9 (hijacking of ships).

13. Section 10 (seizing or exercising control of fixed platforms).]

[Channel Tunnel (Security) Order 1994 No [570]

14. Article 4 (hijacking of Channel Tunnel trains).

15. Article 5 (seizing or exercising control of the tunnel system).]

[Protection of Children Act 1978 (c 37)

14. Section 1 (indecent photographs and pseudo-photographs of children).

Obscene Publications Act 1959 (c 66)

15. Section 2 (publication of obscene matter).]

NOTES

Entry omitted repealed, and entry relating to the Road Traffic Act 1988, s 1 added, by the Road Traffic (Consequential Provisions) Act 1988, ss 3, 4, Schs 1, 3, para 27(5); word in square brackets in that entry substituted, and entry relating to s 3A of the 1988 Act added, by the Road Traffic Act 1991, s 48, Sch 4, para 39.

Entry relating to the Criminal Justice Act 1988 added by the Criminal Justice Act 1988, s 170(1), Sch 15, paras 97, 102.

Entries relating to the Aviation and Maritime Security Act 1990 added by the Aviation and Maritime Security Act 1990, s 53(1), Sch 3, para 8.

Entries relating to the Channel Tunnel (Security) Order 1994 added by the Channel Tunnel (Security) Order 1994, SI 1994/570, art 38, Sch 3, para 4; reference to "570" in square brackets in cross-heading omitted from Queen's Printer's copy.

Entries relating to offences under the Protection of Children Act 1978 and the Obscene Publications Act 1959 added by the Criminal Justice and Public Order Act 1994, s 85(1), (3).

A CODE OF PRACTICE FOR THE EXERCISE BY POLICE OFFICERS OF STATUTORY POWERS OF STOP AND SEARCH

Commencement—Transitional Arrangements

This code applies to any search by a police officer which commences after midnight on 14 May 1997.

1 General

1.1 This code of practice must be readily available at all police stations for consultation by police officers, detained persons and members of the public.

1.2 The notes for guidance included are not provisions of this code, but are guidance to police officers and others about its application and interpretation. Provisions in the annexes to the code are provisions of this code.

1.3, 1.4 . . .

1.5 This code applies to stops and searches under powers:

(a) requiring reasonable grounds for suspicion that articles unlawfully obtained or possessed are being carried;

(b) authorised under section 60 of the Criminal Justice and Public Order Act 1994 based upon a reasonable belief that incidents involving serious violence may take place within a locality;

(c) authorised under section 13A of the Prevention of Terrorism (Temporary Provisions) Act 1989 as amended by section 81 of the Criminal Justice and Public Order Act 1994;

(d) exercised under paragraph 4(2) of Schedule 5 to the Prevention of Terrorism (Temporary Provisions) Act 1989.

[See *Note 1A*]

(a) Powers requiring reasonable suspicion

1.6 Whether a reasonable ground for suspicion exists will depend on the circumstances in each case, but there must be some objective basis for it. An officer will need to consider the nature of the article suspected of being carried in the context of other factors such as the time and the place, and the behaviour of the person concerned or those with him. Reasonable suspicion may exist, for example, where information has been received such as a description of an article being carried or of a suspected offender; a person is seen acting covertly or warily or attempting to hide something; or a person is carrying a certain type of article at an unusual time or in a place where a number of burglaries or thefts are known to have taken place recently. But the decision to stop and search must be based on all the facts which bear on the likelihood that an article of a certain kind will be found.

1.6A For example, reasonable suspicion may be based upon reliable information or intelligence which indicates that members of a particular group or gang, or their associates, habitually carry knives unlawfully or weapons or controlled drugs.

1.7 Subject to the provision in paragraph 1.7AA below, reasonable suspicion can never be supported on the basis of personal factors alone without supporting intelligence or information. For example, a person's colour, age, hairstyle or manner of dress, or the fact that he is known to have a previous conviction for possession of an unlawful article, cannot be used alone or in combination with each other as the sole basis on which to search that person. Nor may it be founded on the basis of stereotyped images of certain persons or groups as more likely to be committing offences.

1.7AA However, where there is reliable information or intelligence that members of a group or gang who habitually carry knives unlawfully or weapons or controlled drugs, and wear a distinctive item of clothing or other means of identification to indicate membership of it, the members may be identified by means of that distinctive item of clothing or other means of identification. [See *Note 1H*]

1.7A Where a police officer has reasonable grounds to suspect that a person is in innocent possession of a stolen or prohibited article or other item for which he is empowered to search, the power of stop and search exists notwithstanding that there would be no power of arrest. However every effort should be made to secure the person's co-operation in the production of the article before resorting to the use of force.

(b) Authorisation under section 60 of the Criminal Justice and Public Order Act 1994

1.8 Authority to exercise the powers of stop and search under section 60 of the Criminal Justice and Public Order Act 1994 may be given where it is reasonably believed that incidents involving serious violence may take place in a locality, and it is expedient to use these powers to prevent their occurrence. Authorisation should normally be given by an officer of the rank of superintendent or above, in writing, specifying the locality in which the powers may be exercised and the period of time for which they are in force. Authorisation may be given by an inspector or chief inspector if he reasonably believes that violence is imminent and no superintendent is available. In either case the period authorised shall be no longer than appears reasonably necessary to prevent, or try to prevent incidents of serious violence, and it may not exceed 24 hours. A superintendent or the authorising officer may direct that the period shall be extended for a further six hours if violence has occurred or is suspected to have occurred and the continued use of the powers is considered necessary to prevent further violence. That direction must also be given in writing at the time or as soon as practicable afterwards. [See *Notes 1F* and *1G*]

(c) Authorisation under section 13A of the Prevention of Terrorism (Temporary Provisions) Act 1989, as amended by section 81 of the Criminal Justice and Public Order Act 1994

1.8A Authority to exercise the powers of stop and search under section 13A of the Prevention of Terrorism (Temporary Provisions) Act 1989 may be given where it appears expedient to do so to prevent acts of terrorism. Authorisation must be given by an officer of the rank of assistant chief constable (or equivalent) or above, in writing, specifying where the powers may be exercised and the period of time for which they are to remain in force. The period authorised may not exceed 28 days. Further periods of up to 28 days may be authorised. [See *Notes 1F* and *1G*]

Notes for Guidance

1A–1C . . .

1D Nothing in this code affects

a *the routine searching of persons entering sports grounds or other premises with their consent, or as a condition of entry; or*

b *the ability of an officer to search a person in the street with his consent where no search power exists. In these circumstances an officer should always make it clear that he is seeking the consent of the person concerned to the search being carried out by telling the person that he need not consent and that without his consent he will not be searched.*

1E If an officer acts in an improper manner this will invalidate a voluntary search. Juveniles, people suffering from a mental handicap or mental disorder and others who appear not to be capable of giving an informed consent should not be subject to a voluntary search.

1F–1H . . .

NOTES

Paras 1.3, 1.4: outside the scope of this work.

Notes for Guidance paras 1A–1C, 1F–1H: outside the scope of this work.

2 Action before a search is carried out

(a) Searches requiring reasonable suspicion

2.1 Where an officer has the reasonable grounds for suspicion necessary to exercise a power of stop and search he may detain the person concerned for the purposes of and with a view to searching him. There is no power to stop or detain a person against his will in order to find grounds for a search.

2.2 Before carrying out a search the officer may question the person about his behaviour or his presence in circumstances which gave rise to the suspicion, since he may have a satisfactory explanation which will make a search unnecessary. If, as a result of any questioning preparatory to a search, or other circumstances which come to the attention of the officer, there cease to be reasonable grounds for suspecting that an article is being carried of a kind for which there is a power of stop and search, no search may take place. [See *Note 2A*]

2.3 . . .

(b) All searches

2.4, 2.5. . .

2.6 Unless it appears to the officer that it will not be practicable to make a record of the search, he must also inform the person to be searched (or the owner or person in charge of a vehicle that is to be searched, as the case may be) that he is entitled to a copy of the record of the search if he asks for it within a year. If the person wishes to have a copy and is not given one on the spot, he shall be advised to which police station he should apply.

2.7 . . .

Note for Guidance

2A . . .

NOTES

Paras 2.3–2.5, 2.7: outside the scope of this work.

Notes for Guidance para 2A: outside the scope of this work.

3 Conduct of the search

3.1 Every reasonable effort must be made to reduce to the minimum the embarrassment that a person being searched may experience.

3.2 The co-operation of the person to be searched shall be sought in every case, even if he initially objects to the search. A forcible search may be made only if it has been established that the person is unwilling to co-operate (eg by opening a bag) or resists. Although force may only be used as a last resort, reasonable force may be used if necessary to conduct a search or to detain a person or vehicle for the purposes of a search.

3.3, 3.4 . . .

3.5 Searches in public must be restricted to superficial examination of outer clothing. There is no power to require a person to remove any clothing in public other than an outer coat, jacket or gloves. Where on reasonable grounds it is considered necessary to conduct a more thorough search (eg by requiring a person to take off a T-shirt or headgear), this shall be done out of public view for example, in a police van or police station if there is one nearby. Any search involving the removal of more than an outer coat, jacket, gloves, headgear or footwear may only be made by an officer of the same sex as the person searched and may not be made in the presence of anyone of the opposite sex unless the person being searched specifically requests it. [See *Note 3A*]

3.5A . . .

Notes for Guidance

3A, 3B . . .

NOTES

Paras 3.3, 3.4, 3.5A: outside the scope of this work.

Notes for Guidance paras 3A, 3B: outside the scope of this work.

(*Para 4 and Annex A outside the scope of this work.*)

B CODE OF PRACTICE FOR THE SEARCHING OF PREMISES BY POLICE OFFICERS AND THE SEIZURE OF PROPERTY FOUND BY POLICE OFFICERS ON PERSONS OR PREMISES

Commencement—Transitional Arrangements

This code applies to applications for warrants made after 9 April 1995 and to searches and seizures which take place after midnight on 9 April 1995.

1 General

1.1, 1.2 . . .

1.3 This code applies to searches of premises:

(a) undertaken for the purposes of an investigation into an alleged offence, with the occupier's consent, other than searches made in the following circumstances:
- — routine scenes of crime searches
- — calls to a fire or a burglary made by or on behalf of an occupier or searches following the activation of fire or burglar alarms
- — searches to which paragraph 4.4 applies
- — bomb threat calls;

(b) under powers conferred by sections 17, 18 and 32 of the Police and Criminal Evidence Act 1984;

(c) undertaken in pursuance of a search warrant issued in accordance with section 15 of, or Schedule 1 to the Police and Criminal Evidence Act 1984, or section 15 of, or Schedule 7 to the Prevention of Terrorism (Temporary Provisions) Act 1989.

'Premises' for the purpose of this code is defined in section 23 of the Police and Criminal Evidence Act 1984. It includes any place and, in particular, any vehicle, vessel, aircraft, hovercraft, tent or movable structure. It also includes any offshore installation as defined in section 1 of the Mineral Workings (Offshore Installations) Act 1971.

1.3A Any search of a person who has not been arrested which is carried out during a search of premises shall be carried out in accordance with Code A.

1.3B This code does not apply to the exercise of a statutory power to enter premises or to inspect goods, equipment or procedures if the exercise of that power is not dependent on the existence of grounds for suspecting that an offence may have been committed and the person exercising the power has no reasonable grounds for such suspicion.

NOTES

Paras 1.1, 1.2: outside the scope of this work.

---

2 Search warrants and production orders

(a) Action to be taken before an application is made

2.1 Where information is received which appears to justify an application, the officer concerned must take reasonable steps to check that the information is accurate, recent and has not been provided maliciously or irresponsibly. An application may not be made on the basis of information from an anonymous source where corroboration has not been sought. [See *Note 2A*]

2.2 The officer shall ascertain as specifically as is possible in the circumstances the nature of the articles concerned and their location.

2.3 . . .

2.4 No application for a search warrant may be made without the authority of an officer of at least the rank of inspector (or, in the case of urgency where no officer of this rank is readily available, the senior officer on duty). No application for a production order or warrant under Schedule 7 to the Prevention of Terrorism (Temporary Provisions) Act 1989, may be made without the authority of an officer of at least the rank of superintendent.

2.5 Except in a case of urgency, if there is reason to believe that a search might have an adverse effect on relations between the police and the community then the local police/community liaison officer shall be consulted before it takes place. In urgent cases, the local police/community liaison officer shall be informed of the search as soon as practicable after it has been made. [See *Note 2B*]

(b) Making an application

2.6 . . .

2.7 An application for a search warrant under paragraph 12(a) of Schedule 1 to the Police and Criminal Evidence Act 1984, or under Schedule 7 to the Prevention of Terrorism (Temporary Provisions) Act 1989, shall also, where appropriate, indicate why it is believed that service of notice of an application for a production order may seriously prejudice the investigation.

2.8 If an application is refused, no further application may be made for a warrant to search those premises unless supported by additional grounds.

Notes for Guidance

2A, 2B . . .

NOTES

Paras 2.3, 2.6: outside the scope of this work.

Notes for Guidance paras 2A, 2B: outside the scope of this work.

(*Para 3 outside the scope of this work.*)

4 Search with consent

4.1 Subject to paragraph 4.4 below, if it is proposed to search premises with the consent of a person entitled to grant entry to the premises the consent must, if practicable, be given in writing on the Notice of Powers and Rights before the search takes place. The officer must make enquiries to satisfy himself that the person is in a position to give such consent. [See *Notes 4A* and *4B* and paragraph 5.7(i)]

4.2 Before seeking consent the officer in charge of the search shall state the purpose of the proposed search and inform the person concerned that he is not obliged to consent and that anything seized may be produced in evidence. If at the time the person is not suspected of an offence, the officer shall tell him so when stating the purpose of the search.

4.3 An officer cannot enter and search premises or continue to search premises under 4.1 above if the consent has been given under duress or is withdrawn before the search is completed.

4.4 It is unnecessary to seek consent under paragraphs 4.1 and 4.2 above where in the circumstances this would cause disproportionate inconvenience to the person concerned. [See *Note 4C*]

Notes for Guidance

4A–4C . . .

NOTES

Notes for Guidance paras 4A–4C: outside the scope of this work.

5 Searching of premises: general considerations

5.1–5.6 . . .

(c) Notice of Powers and Rights

5.7 If an officer conducts a search to which this code applies he shall, unless it is impracticable to do so, provide the occupier with a copy of a notice in a standard format:

(i) specifying whether the search is made under warrant, or with consent, or in the exercise of the powers described in 3.1 to 3.3 above (the format of the notice shall provide for authority or consent to be indicated where appropriate—see 3.3 and 4.1 above);

(ii) summarising the extent of the powers of search and seizure conferred in the Act;

(iii) explaining the rights of the occupier, and of the owner of property seized in accordance with the provisions of 6.1 to 6.5 below, set out in the Act and in this code;

(iv) explaining that compensation may be payable in appropriate cases for damages caused in entering and searching premises, and giving the address to which an application for compensation should be directed;

(v) stating that a copy of this code is available to be consulted at any police station.

5.8 If the occupier is present, copies of the notice mentioned above, and of the warrant (if the search is made under warrant) shall if practicable be given to the occupier before the search begins, unless the officer in charge of the search reasonably believes that to do so would frustrate the object of the search or endanger the officers concerned or other people. If the occupier is not present, copies of the notice, and of the warrant where appropriate, shall be left in a prominent place on the premises or appropriate part of the premises and endorsed with the name of the officer in charge of the search (except in the case of enquiries linked to the investigation of terrorism, in which case the officer's warrant or other identification number shall be given), the name of the police station to which he is attached and the date and time of the search. The warrant itself shall be endorsed to show that this has been done.

(d) Conduct of searches

5.9 . . .

5.10 Searches must be conducted with due consideration for the property and privacy of the occupier of the premises searched, and with no more disturbance than necessary. Reasonable force may be used only where this is necessary because the co-operation of the occupier cannot be obtained or is insufficient for the purpose.

5.11–5.14 . . .

Notes for Guidance

5A–5C . . .

NOTES

Paras 5.1–5.6, 5.9, 5.11–5.14: outside the scope of this work.

Notes for Guidance paras 5A–5C: outside the scope of this work.

(*Para 6 outside the scope of this work.*)

7 Action to be taken after searches

7.1 Where premises have been searched in circumstances to which this code applies, other than in the circumstances covered by the exceptions to paragraph 1.3(a), the officer in charge of the search shall, on arrival at a police station, make or have made a record of the search. The record shall include:

(i) the address of the premises searched;

(ii) the date, time and duration of the search;

(iii) the authority under which the search was made. Where the search was made in the exercise of a statutory power to search premises without warrant, the record shall include the power under which the search was made; and where the search was made under warrant, or with written consent, a copy of the warrant or consent shall be appended to the record or kept in a place identified in the record;

(iv) the names of all the officers who conducted the search (except in the case of enquiries linked to the investigation of terrorism, in which case the record shall state the warrant or other identification number and duty station of each officer concerned);

(v) the names of any people on the premises if they are known;

(vi) either a list of any articles seized or a note of where such a list is kept and, if not covered by a warrant, the reason for their seizure;

(vii) whether force was used, and, if so, the reason why it was used;

(viii) details of any damage caused during the search, and the circumstances in which it was caused.

7.2 Where premises have been searched under warrant, the warrant shall be endorsed to show:

(i) whether any articles specified in the warrant were found;

(ii) whether any other articles were seized;

(iii) the date and time at which it was executed;

(iv) the names of the officers who executed it (except in the case of enquiries linked to the investigation of terrorism, in which case the warrant or other identification number and duty station of each officer concerned shall be shown);

(v) whether a copy, together with a copy of the Notice of Powers and Rights was handed to the occupier; or whether it was endorsed as required by paragraph 5.8, and left on the premises together with the copy notice and, if so, where.

7.3 . . .

NOTES

Para 7.3: outside the scope of this work.

(Para 8 outside the scope of this work.)

C CODE OF PRACTICE FOR THE DETENTION, TREATMENT AND QUESTIONING OF PERSONS BY POLICE OFFICERS

Commencement—Transitional Arrangements

This code applies to people in police detention after midnight on 9 April 1995, notwithstanding that their period of detention may have commenced before that time.

1 General

1.1 . . .

1.1A A custody officer is required to perform the functions specified in this code as soon as is practicable. A custody officer shall not be in breach of this code in the event of delay provided that the delay is justifiable and that every reasonable step is taken to prevent unnecessary delay. The custody record shall indicate where a delay has occurred and the reason why. [See *Note 1H*]

1.2, 1.3 . . .

1.4 If an officer has any suspicion, or is told in good faith, that a person of any age may be mentally disordered or mentally handicapped, or mentally incapable of understanding the significance of questions put to him or his replies, then that person shall be treated as a mentally disordered or mentally handicapped person for the purposes of this code. [See *Note 1G*]

1.5 If anyone appears to be under the age of 17 then he shall be treated as a juvenile for the purposes of this code in the absence of clear evidence to show that he is older.

1.6 If a person appears to be blind or seriously visually handicapped, deaf, unable to read, unable to speak or has difficulty orally because of a speech impediment, he shall be treated as such for the purposes of this code in the absence of clear evidence to the contrary.

1.7 In this code 'the appropriate adult' means:

(a) in the case of a juvenile:

(i) his parent or guardian (or, if he is in care, the care authority or voluntary organisation. The term 'in care' is used in this code to cover all cases in which a juvenile is 'looked after' by a local authority under the terms of the Children Act 1989);

(ii) a social worker;

(iii) failing either of the above, another responsible adult aged 18 or over who is not a police officer or employed by the police.

(b) in the case of a person who is mentally disordered or mentally handicapped:

(i) a relative, guardian or other person responsible for his care or custody;
(ii) someone who has experience of dealing with mentally disordered or mentally handicapped people but who is not a police officer or employed by the police (such as an approved social worker as defined by the Mental Health Act 1983 or a specialist social worker); or
(iii) failing either of the above, some other responsible adult aged 18 or over who is not a police officer or employed by the police.
[See *Note 1E*]

1.8 Whenever this code requires a person to be given certain information he does not have to be given it if he is incapable at the time of understanding what is said to him or is violent or likely to become violent or is in urgent need of medical attention, but he must be given it as soon as practicable.

1.9 Any reference to a custody officer in this code includes an officer who is performing the functions of a custody officer.

1.10 Subject to paragraph 1.12, this code applies to people who are in custody at police stations in England and Wales whether or not they have been arrested for an offence and to those who have been removed to a police station as a place of safety under sections 135 and 136 of the Mental Health Act 1983. Section 15 (reviews and extensions of detention) however applies solely to people in police detention, for example those who have been brought to a police station under arrest for an offence or have been arrested at a police station for an offence after attending there voluntarily.

1.11 People in police custody include anyone taken to a police station after being arrested under section 14 of the Prevention of Terrorism (Temporary Provisions) Act 1989 or under paragraph 6 of Schedule 5 to that Act by an examining officer who is a constable.

1.12 This code does not apply to the following groups of people in custody:
(i) people who have been arrested by officers from a police force in Scotland exercising their powers of detention under section 137(2) of the Criminal Justice and Public Order Act 1994 (Cross Border powers of arrest etc);
(ii) people arrested under section 3(5) of the Asylum and Immigration Appeals Act 1993 for the purpose of having their fingerprints taken;
(iii) people who have been served a notice advising them of their detention under powers contained in the Immigration Act 1971;
(iv) convicted or remanded prisoners held in police cells on behalf of the Prison Service under the Imprisonment (Temporary Provisions) Act 1980);

but the provisions on conditions of detention and treatment in sections 8 and 9 of this code must be considered as the minimum standards of treatment for such detainees.

Notes for Guidance

1A Although certain sections of this code (eg section 9—treatment of detained persons) apply specifically to people in custody at police stations, those there voluntarily to assist with an investigation should be treated with no less consideration (eg offered refreshments at appropriate times) and enjoy an absolute right to obtain legal advice or communicate with anyone outside the police station.

1B . . .

1C A person, including a parent or guardian, should not be an appropriate adult if he is suspected of involvement in the offence in question, is the victim, is a witness, is involved in the investigation or has received admissions prior to attending to act as the appropriate adult. If the parent of a juvenile is estranged from the juvenile, he should not be asked to act as the appropriate adult if the juvenile expressly and specifically objects to his presence.

1D–1EE . . .

1F A solicitor or lay visitor who is present at the police station in that capacity may not act as the appropriate adult.

1G, 1H . . .

1I It is important that the custody officer reminds the appropriate adult and the detained person of the right to legal advice and records any reasons for waiving it in accordance with section 6 of this code.

NOTES

Paras 1.1, 1.2, 1.3: outside the scope of this work.

Notes for Guidance paras 1B, 1D–1EE, 1G, 1H: outside the scope of this work.

---

2 Custody records

2.1 A separate custody record must be opened as soon as practicable for each person who is brought to a police station under arrest or is arrested at the police station having attended there voluntarily. All information which has to be recorded under this code must be recorded as soon as practicable in the custody record unless otherwise specified. Any audio or video recording made in the custody area is not part of the custody record.

2.2, 2.3 . . .

2.4 A solicitor or appropriate adult must be permitted to consult the custody record of a person detained as soon as practicable after their arrival at the police station. When a person leaves police detention or is taken before a court, he or his legal representative or his appropriate adult shall be supplied on request with a copy of the custody record as soon as practicable. This entitlement lasts for 12 months after his release.

2.5 The person who has been detained, the appropriate adult, or the legal representative shall be permitted to inspect the original custody record after the person has left police detention provided they give reasonable notice of their request. A note of any such inspection shall be made in the custody record.

2.6, 2.7 . . .

NOTES

Paras 2.2, 2.3, 2.6, 2.7: outside the scope of this work.

---

3 Initial action

(a) Detained persons: normal procedure

3.1 When a person is brought to a police station under arrest or is arrested at the police station having attended there voluntarily, the custody officer must tell him clearly of the following rights and of the fact that they are continuing rights which may be exercised at any stage during the period in custody:

(i) the right to have someone informed of his arrest in accordance with section 5 below;
(ii) the right to consult privately with a solicitor and the fact that independent legal advice is available free of charge; and
(iii) the right to consult these codes of practice.
[See *Note 3E*]

3.2 In addition the custody officer must give the person a written notice setting out the above three rights, the right to a copy of the custody record in accordance with paragraph 2.4 above and the caution in the terms prescribed in section 10 below. The notice must also explain the arrangements for obtaining legal advice. The custody officer must also give the person an additional written notice briefly setting out his entitlements while in custody. [See *Notes 3A and 3B*] The custody officer shall ask the person to sign the custody record to acknowledge receipt of these notices and any refusal to sign must be recorded on the custody record.

3.3 A citizen of an independent Commonwealth country or a national of a foreign country (including the Republic of Ireland) must be informed as soon as practicable of his rights of communication with his High Commission, Embassy or Consulate. [See *Section* 7]

3.4 The custody officer shall note on the custody record any comment the person may make in relation to the arresting officer's account but shall not invite comment. If the custody officer authorises a person's detention he must inform him of the grounds as soon as practicable and in any case before that person is then questioned about any offence. The custody officer shall note any comment the person may make in respect of the decision to detain him but, again, shall not invite comment. The custody officer shall not put specific questions to the person regarding his involvement in any offence, nor in respect of any comments he may make in response to the arresting officer's account or the decision to place him in detention. Such an exchange is likely to constitute an interview as defined by paragraph 11.1A and would require the associated safeguards included in section 11. [See also paragraph 11.13 in respect of unsolicited comments.]

3.5 The custody officer shall ask the detained person whether at this time he would like legal advice (see paragraph 6.5). The person shall be asked to sign the custody record to confirm his decision. The custody officer is responsible for ensuring that in confirming any decision the person signs in the correct place.

3.5A If video cameras are installed in the custody area, notices which indicate that cameras are in use shall be prominently displayed. Any request by a detained person or other person to have video cameras switched off shall be refused.

(b) Detained persons: special groups

3.6 If the person appears to be deaf or there is doubt about his hearing or speaking ability or ability to understand English, and the custody officer cannot establish effective communication, the custody officer must as soon as practicable call an interpreter and ask him to provide the information required above. [See *Section 13*]

3.7 If the person is a juvenile, the custody officer must, if it is practicable, ascertain the identity of a person responsible for his welfare. That person may be his parent or guardian (or, if he is in care, the care authority or voluntary organisation) or any other person who has, for the time being, assumed responsibility for his welfare. That person must be informed as soon as practicable that the juvenile has been arrested, why he has been arrested and where he is detained. This right is in addition to the juvenile's right in section 5 of the code not to be held incommunicado. [See *Note 3C*]

3.8 In the case of a juvenile who is known to be subject to a supervision order, reasonable steps must also be taken to notify the person supervising him.

3.9 If the person is a juvenile, is mentally handicapped or appears to be suffering from a mental disorder, then the custody officer must, as soon as practicable, inform the appropriate adult (who in the case of a juvenile may or may not be a person responsible for his welfare, in accordance with paragraph 3.7 above) of the grounds for his detention and his whereabouts and ask the adult to come to the police station to see the person.

3.10 It is imperative that a mentally disordered or mentally handicapped person who has been detained under section 136 of the Mental Health Act 1983 shall be assessed as soon as possible. If that assessment is to take place at the police station, an approved social worker and a registered medical practitioner shall be called to the police station as soon as possible in order to interview and examine the person. Once the person has been interviewed and examined and suitable arrangements have been made for his treatment or care, he can no longer be detained under section 136. The person should not be released until he has been seen by both the approved social worker and the registered medical practitioner.

3.11 If the appropriate adult is already at the police station, then the provisions of paragraphs 3.1 to 3.5 above must be complied with in his presence. If the appropriate adult is not at the police station when the provisions of paragraphs 3.1 to 3.5 above are complied with, then these provisions must be complied with again in the presence of the appropriate adult once that person arrives.

3.12 The person shall be advised by the custody officer that the appropriate adult (where applicable) is there to assist and advise him and that he can consult privately with the appropriate adult at any time.

3.13 If, having been informed of the right to legal advice under paragraph 3.11 above, either the appropriate adult or the person detained wishes legal advice to be taken, then the provisions of section 6 of this code apply. [See *Note 3G*]

3.14 If the person is blind or seriously visually handicapped or is unable to read, the custody officer shall ensure that his solicitor, relative, the appropriate adult or some other person likely to take an interest in him (and not involved in the investigation) is available to help in checking any documentation. Where this code requires written consent or signification then the person who is assisting may be asked to sign instead if the detained person so wishes. [See *Note 3F*]

(c) Persons attending a police station voluntarily

3.15 Any person attending a police station voluntarily for the purpose of assisting with an investigation may leave at will unless placed under arrest. If it is decided that he should not be allowed to leave then he must be informed at once that he is under arrest and brought before the custody officer, who is responsible for ensuring that he is notified of his rights in the same way as other detained persons. If he is not placed under arrest but is cautioned in accordance with section 10 below, the officer who gives the caution must at the same time inform him that he is not under arrest, that he is not obliged to remain at the police station but if he remains at the police station he may obtain free and independent legal advice if he wishes. The officer shall point out that the right to legal advice includes the right to speak with a solicitor on the telephone and ask him if he wishes to do so.

3.16 If a person who is attending the police station voluntarily (in accordance with paragraph 3.15) asks about his entitlement to legal advice, he shall be given a copy of the notice explaining the arrangements for obtaining legal advice. [See paragraph 3.2]

(d) Documentation

3.17 The grounds for a person's detention shall be recorded, in his presence if practicable.

3.18 Action taken under paragraphs 3.6 to 3.14 shall be recorded.

Notes for Guidance

3A–3F . . .

3G The purpose of paragraph 3.13 is to protect the rights of a juvenile, mentally disordered or mentally handicapped person who may not understand the significance of what is being said to him. If such a person wishes to exercise the right to legal advice the appropriate action should be taken straightaway and not delayed until the appropriate adult arrives.

NOTES

Notes for Guidance paras 3A–3F: outside the scope of this work.

(*Para 4 outside the scope of this work.*)

5 Right not to be held incommunicado

(a) Action

5.1–5.3 . . .

5.4 The person may receive visits at the custody officer's discretion. [See *Note 5B*]

5.5 Where an enquiry as to the whereabouts of the person is made by a friend, relative or person with an interest in his welfare, this information shall be given, if he agrees and if Annex B does not apply. [See *Note 5D*]

5.6 . . .

5.7 Before any letter or message is sent, or telephone call made, the person shall be informed that what he says in any letter, call or message (other than in the case of a communication to a solicitor) may be read or listened to as appropriate and may be given in evidence. A telephone call may be terminated if it is being abused. The costs can be at public expense at the discretion of the custody officer.

(b) Documentation

5.8 . . .

Notes for Guidance

5A . . .

5B In the exercise of his discretion the custody officer should allow visits where possible in the light of the availability of sufficient manpower to supervise a visit and a possible hindrance to the investigation.

5C–5E . . .

NOTES

Paras 5.1–5.3, 5.6, 5.8: outside the scope of this work.

Notes for Guidance paras 5A, 5C–5E: outside the scope of this work.

6 Right to legal advice

(a) Action

6.1 Subject to the provisos in Annex B all people in police detention must be informed that they may at any time consult and communicate privately, whether in person, in writing or by telephone with a solicitor, and that independent legal advice is available free of charge from the duty solicitor. [See paragraph 3.1 and *Note 6B* and *Note 6J*]

6.2 . . .

6.3 A poster advertising the right to have legal advice must be prominently displayed in the charging area of every police station. [See *Note 6H*]

6.4 No police officer shall at any time do or say anything with the intention of dissuading a person in detention from obtaining legal advice.

6.5 The exercise of the right of access to legal advice may be delayed only in accordance with Annex B to this code. Whenever legal advice is requested (and unless Annex B applies) the custody officer must act without delay to secure the provision of such advice to the person concerned. If, on being informed or reminded of the right to legal advice, the person declines to speak to a solicitor in person, the officer shall point out that the right to legal advice includes the right to speak with a solicitor on the telephone and ask him if he wishes to do so. If the person continues to waive his right to legal advice the officer shall ask him the reasons for doing so, and any reasons shall be recorded on the custody record or the interview record as appropriate. Reminders of the right to legal advice must be given in accordance with paragraphs 3.5, 11.2, 15.3, 16.4 and 16.5 of this code and paragraphs 2.15(ii) and 5.2 of Code D. Once it is clear that a person neither wishes to speak to a solicitor in person nor by telephone he should cease to be asked his reasons. [See *Note 6K*]

6.6 A person who wants legal advice may not be interviewed or continue to be interviewed until he has received it unless:

(a) Annex B applies; or

(b) an officer of the rank of superintendent or above has reasonable grounds for believing that:

  (i) delay will involve an immediate risk of harm to persons or serious loss of, or damage to, property; or

  (ii) where a solicitor, including a duty solicitor, has been contacted and has agreed to attend, awaiting his arrival would cause unreasonable delay to the process of investigation; or

(c) the solicitor nominated by the person, or selected by him from a list:

  (i) cannot be contacted; or

  (ii) has previously indicated that he does not wish to be contacted; or

  (iii) having been contacted, has declined to attend;

and the person has been advised of the Duty Solicitor Scheme but has declined to ask for the duty solicitor, or the duty solicitor is unavailable. (In these circumstances the interview may be started or continued without further delay provided that an officer of the rank of Inspector or above has given agreement for the interview to proceed in those circumstances—see *Note 6B*).

(d) the person who wanted legal advice changes his mind.

In these circumstances the interview may be started or continued without further delay provided that the person has given his agreement in writing or on tape to being interviewed without receiving legal advice and that an officer of the rank of Inspector or above, having inquired into the person's reasons for his change of mind, has given authority for the interview to proceed. Confirmation of the person's agreement, his change of mind, his reasons where given and the name of the authorising officer shall be recorded in the taped or written interview record at the beginning or re-commencement of interview. [See *Note 6I*]

6.7 Where 6.6(b)(i) applies, once sufficient information to avert the risk has been obtained, questioning must cease until the person has received legal advice unless 6.6(a), (b)(ii), (c) or (d) apply.

6.8 Where a person has been permitted to consult a solicitor and the solicitor is available (ie present at the station or on his way to the station or easily contactable by telephone) at the time the interview begins or is in progress, the solicitor must be allowed to be present while he is interviewed.

6.9 The solicitor may only be required to leave the interview if his conduct is such that the investigating officer is unable properly to put questions to the suspect. [See *Notes 6D* and *6E*]

6.10, 6.11 . . .

6.12 In Codes of Practice issued under the Police and Criminal Evidence Act 1984, 'solicitor' means a solicitor who holds a current practising certificate, a trainee solicitor, a duty solicitor representative or an accredited representative included on the register of representatives maintained by the Legal Aid Board. If a solicitor wishes to send a non-accredited or probationary representative to provide advice on his behalf, then that person shall be admitted to the police station for this purpose unless an officer of the rank of inspector or above considers that such a visit will hinder the investigation of crime and directs otherwise. (Hindering the investigation of a crime does not include giving proper legal advice to a detained person in accordance with *Note 6D*.) Once admitted to the police station, the provisions of paragraphs 6.6 to 6.10 apply.

6.13, 6.14 . . .

6.15 If a solicitor arrives at the station to see a particular person, that person must (unless Annex B applies) be informed of the solicitor's arrival whether or not he is being interviewed and asked whether he would like to see him. This applies even if the person concerned has already declined legal advice or having requested it, subsequently agreed to be interviewed without having received advice. The solicitor's attendance and the detained person's decision must be noted in the custody record.

(b) Documentation

6.16 Any request for legal advice and the action taken on it shall be recorded.

6.17 If a person has asked for legal advice and an interview is begun in the absence of a solicitor or his representative (or the solicitor or his representative has been required to leave an interview), a record shall be made in the interview record.

Notes for Guidance

6A . . .

6B A person who asks for legal advice should be given an opportunity to consult a specific solicitor or another solicitor from that solicitor's firm or the duty solicitor. If advice is not available by these means, or he does not wish to consult the duty solicitor, the person should be given an opportunity to choose a solicitor from a list of those willing to provide legal advice. If this solicitor is unavailable, he may choose up two alternatives. If these attempts to secure legal advice are unsuccessful, the custody officer has discretion to allow further attempts until a solicitor has been contacted and agrees to provide legal advice. Apart from carrying out his duties under Note 6B, a police officer must not advise the suspect about any particular firm of solicitors.

6C [Not Used]

6D A detained person has a right to free legal advice and to be represented by a solicitor. The solicitor's only role in the police station is to protect and advance the legal rights of his client. On occasions this may require the solicitor to give advice which has the effect of his client avoiding giving evidence which strengthens a prosecution case. The solicitor may intervene in order to seek clarification or to challenge an improper question to his client or the manner in which it is put, or to advise his client not to reply to particular questions, or if he wishes to give his client further legal advice. Paragraph 6.9 will only apply if the solicitor's approach or conduct prevents or unreasonably obstructs proper questions being put to the suspect or his response being recorded. Examples of unacceptable conduct include answering questions on a suspect's behalf or providing written replies for him to quote.

6E–6K . . .

NOTES

Paras 6.2, 6.10, 6.11, 6.13, 6.14: outside the scope of this work.

Notes for Guidance paras 6A, 6E–6K: outside the scope of this work.

(Para 7 outside the scope of this work.)

8 Conditions of Detention

(a) Action

8.1 So far as is practicable, not more than one person shall be detained in each cell.

8.2 Cells in use must be adequately heated, cleaned and ventilated. They must be adequately lit, subject to such dimming as is compatible with safety and security to allow people detained overnight to sleep. No additional restraints shall be used within a locked cell unless absolutely necessary, and then only suitable handcuffs. In the case of a mentally handicapped or mentally disordered person, particular care must be taken when deciding whether to use handcuffs. [See Annex E paragraph 13]

8.3, 8.4 . . .

8.5 If it is necessary to remove a person's clothes for the purposes of investigation, for hygiene or health reasons or for cleaning, replacement clothing of a reasonable standard of comfort and cleanliness shall be provided. A person may not be interviewed unless adequate clothing has been offered to him.

8.6 At least two light meals and one main meal shall be offered in any period of 24 hours. [See *Note 8C*] . . .

8.7, 8.8 . . .

8.9 Reasonable force may be used if necessary for the following purposes:

(i) to secure compliance with reasonable instructions, including instructions given in pursuance of the provisions of a code of practice; or
(ii) to prevent escape, injury, damage to property or the destruction of evidence.

8.10 . . .

(b) Documentation

8.11, 8.12 . . .

Notes for Guidance

8A–8C . . .

NOTES

Paras 8.3, 8.4, 8.7, 8.8, 8.10–8.12: outside the scope of this work.
Para 8.6: words omitted outside the scope of this work.
Notes for Guidance paras 8A–8C: outside the scope of this work.

---

9 Treatment of Detained Persons

(a) General

9.1 If a complaint is made by or on behalf of a detained person about his treatment since his arrest, or it comes to the notice of any officer that he may have been treated improperly, a report must be made as soon as practicable to an officer of the rank of inspector or above who is not connected with the investigation. If the matter concerns a possible assault or the possibility of the unnecessary or unreasonable use of force then the police surgeon must also be called as soon as practicable.

(b) Medical Treatment

9.2 The custody officer must immediately call the police surgeon (or, in urgent cases,—for example, where a person does not show signs of sensibility or awareness,—must send the person to hospital or call the nearest available medical practitioner) if a person brought to a police station or already detained there:
(a) appears to be suffering from physical illness or a mental disorder; or
(b) is injured; or
(c) [Not Used]
(d) fails to respond normally to questions or conversation (other than through drunkenness alone); or
(e) otherwise appears to need medical attention.

. . . . .

9.3–9.9 . . .

Notes for Guidance

9A–9C . . .

NOTES

Para 9.2: words omitted outside the scope of this work.
Paras 9.3–9.9: outside the scope of this work.
Notes for Guidance paras 9A–9C: outside the scope of this work.

---

10 Cautions

(a) When a caution must be given

10.1 A person whom there are grounds to suspect of an offence must be cautioned before any questions about it (or further questions if it is his answers to previous questions which provide the grounds for suspicion) are put to him regarding his involvement or suspected involvement in that offence if his answers or his silence (ie failure or refusal to answer a question or to answer satisfactorily) may be given in evidence to a court in a prosecution. He therefore need not be cautioned if questions are put for other purposes, for example, solely to establish his identity or his ownership of any vehicle or to obtain information in accordance with any relevant statutory requirement (see paragraph 10.5C) or in furtherance of the proper and effective conduct of a search, (for example to determine the need to search in the exercise of powers of stop and search or to seek co-operation while carrying out a search) or to seek verification of a written record in accordance with paragraph 11.13.

10.2 Whenever a person who is not under arrest is initially cautioned or is reminded that he is under caution (see paragraph 10.5) he must at the same time be told that he is not under arrest and is not obliged to remain with the officer (see paragraph 3.15).

10.3 A person must be cautioned upon arrest for an offence unless:
- (a) it is impracticable to do so by reason of his condition or behaviour at the time; or
- (b) he has already been cautioned immediately prior to arrest in accordance with paragraph 10.1 above.

(b) Action: general

10.4 The caution shall be in the following terms:

> 'You do not have to say anything. But it may harm your defence if you do not mention when questioned something which you later rely on in court. Anything you do say may be given in evidence.'

Minor deviations do not constitute a breach of this requirement provided that the sense of the caution is preserved. [See *Note 10C*]

10.5 When there is a break in questioning under caution the interviewing officer must ensure that the person being questioned is aware that he remains under caution. If there is any doubt the caution shall be given again in full when the interview resumes. [See *Note 10A*]

Special warnings under sections 36 and 37 of the Criminal Justice and Public Order Act 1994

10.5A When a suspect who is interviewed after arrest fails or refuses to answer certain questions, or to answer them satisfactorily, after due warning, a court or jury may draw such inferences as appear proper under sections 36 and 37 of the Criminal Justice and Public Order Act 1994. This applies when:
- (a) a suspect is arrested by a constable and there is found on his person, or in or on his clothing or footwear, or otherwise in his possession, or in the place where he was arrested, any objects, marks or substances, or marks on such objects, and the person fails or refuses to account for the objects, marks or substances found; or

(b) an arrested person was found by a constable at a place at or about the time the offence for which he was arrested, is alleged to have been committed, and the person fails or refuses to account for his presence at that place.

10.5B For an inference to be drawn from a suspect's failure or refusal to answer a question about one of these matters or to answer it satisfactorily, the interviewing officer must first tell him in ordinary language:

(a) what offence he is investigating;
(b) what fact he is asking the suspect to account for;
(c) that he believes this fact may be due to the suspect's taking part in the commission of the offence in question;
(d) that a court may draw a proper inference if he fails or refuses to account for the fact about which he is being questioned;
(e) that a record is being made of the interview and that it may be given in evidence if he is brought to trial.

10.5C Where, despite the fact that a person has been cautioned, failure to co-operate may have an effect on his immediate treatment, he should be informed of any relevant consequences and that they are not affected by the caution. Examples are when his refusal to provide his name and address when charged may render him liable to detention, or when his refusal to provide particulars and information in accordance with a statutory requirement, for example, under the Road Traffic Act 1988, may amount to an offence or may make him liable to arrest.

(c) Juveniles, the mentally disordered and the mentally handicapped

10.6 If a juvenile or a person who is mentally disordered or mentally handicapped is cautioned in the absence of the appropriate adult, the caution must be repeated in the adult's presence.

(d) Documentation

10.7 A record shall be made when a caution is given under this section, either in the officer's pocket book or in the interview record as appropriate.

Notes for Guidance

10A, 10B . . .

10C If it appears that a person does not understand what the caution means, the officer who has given it should go on to explain it in his own words.

10D . . .

NOTES

Notes for Guidance paras 10A, 10B, 10D: outside the scope of this work.

---

11 Interviews: general

(a) Action

11.1A An interview is the questioning of a person regarding his involvement or suspected involvement in a criminal offence or offences which, by virtue of paragraph 10.1 of Code C, is required to be carried out under caution. Procedures undertaken under section 7 of the Road Traffic Act 1988 do not constitute interviewing for the purpose of this code.

11.1 Following a decision to arrest a suspect he must not be interviewed about the relevant offence except at a police station or other authorised place of detention unless the consequent delay would be likely:

(a) to lead to interference with or harm to evidence connected with an offence or interference with or physical harm to other people; or
(b) to lead to the alerting of other people suspected of having committed an offence but not yet arrested for it; or
(c) to hinder the recovery of property obtained in consequence of the commission of an offence.

Interviewing in any of these circumstances shall cease once the relevant risk has been averted or the necessary questions have been put in order to attempt to avert that risk.

11.2 Immediately prior to the commencement or re-commencement of any interview at a police station or other authorised place of detention, the interviewing officer shall remind the suspect of his entitlement to free legal advice and that the interview can be delayed for him to obtain legal advice (unless the exceptions in paragraph 6.6 or Annex C apply). It is the responsibility of the interviewing officer to ensure that all such reminders are noted in the record of interview.

11.2A At the beginning of an interview carried out in a police station, the interviewing officer, after cautioning the suspect, shall put to him any significant statement or silence which occurred before his arrival at the police station, and shall ask him whether he confirms or denies that earlier statement or silence and whether he wishes to add anything. A 'significant' statement or silence is one which appears capable of being used in evidence against the suspect, in particular a direct admission of guilt, or failure or refusal to answer a question or to answer it satisfactorily, which might give rise to an inference under Part III of the Criminal Justice and Public Order Act 1994.

11.3 No police officer may try to obtain answers to questions or to elicit a statement by the use of oppression. Except as provided for in paragraph 10.5C, no police officer shall indicate, except in answer to a direct question, what action will be taken on the part of the police if the person being interviewed answers questions, makes a statement or refuses to do either. If the person asks the officer directly what action will be taken in the event of his answering questions, making a statement or refusing to do either, then the officer may inform the person what action the police propose to take in that event provided that action is itself proper and warranted.

11.4 As soon as a police officer who is making enquiries of any person about an offence believes that a prosecution should be brought against him and that there is sufficient evidence for it to succeed, he shall ask the person if he has anything further to say. If the person indicates that he has nothing more to say the officer shall without delay cease to question him about that offence. This should not, however, be taken to prevent officers in revenue cases or acting under the confiscation provisions of the Criminal Justice Act 1988 or the Drug Trafficking Offences Act 1986 from inviting suspects to complete a formal question and answer record after the interview is concluded.

(b) Interview records

11.5 (a) An accurate record must be made of each interview with a person suspected of an offence, whether or not the interview takes place at a police station.

(b) The record must state the place of the interview, the time it begins and ends, the time the record is made (if different), any breaks in the interview and the names of all those present; and must be made on the forms provided for this purpose or in the officer's pocket book or in accordance with the code of practice for the tape-recording of police interviews with suspects (Code E).

(c) The record must be made during the course of the interview, unless in the investigating officer's view this would not be practicable or would interfere with conduct of the interview, and must constitute either a verbatim record of what has been said or, failing this, an account of the interview which adequately and accurately summarises it.

11.6 The requirement to record the names of all those present at any interview does not apply to police officers interviewing people detained under the Prevention of Terrorism (Temporary Provisions) Act 1989. Instead the record shall state the warrant or other identification number and duty station of such officers.

11.7 If an interview record is not made during the course of the interview it must be made as soon as practicable after its completion.

11.8 Written interview records must be timed and signed by the maker.

11.9 If an interview record is not completed in the course of the interview the reason must be recorded in the officer's pocket book.

11.10 Unless it is impracticable the person interviewed shall be given the opportunity to read the interview record and to sign it as correct or to indicate the respects in which he considers it inaccurate. If the interview is tape-recorded the arrangements set out in Code E apply. If the person concerned cannot read or refuses to read the record or to sign it, the senior police officer present shall read it to him and ask him whether he would like to sign it as correct (or make his mark) or to indicate the respects in which he considers it inaccurate. The police officer shall then certify on the interview record itself what has occurred. [See *Note 11D*]

11.11 If the appropriate adult or the person's solicitor is present during the interview, he shall also be given an opportunity to read and sign the interview record (or any written statement taken down by a police officer).

11.12 Any refusal by a person to sign an interview record when asked to do so in accordance with the provisions of the code must itself be recorded.

11.13 A written record shall also be made of any comments made by a suspected person, including unsolicited comments, which are outside the context of an interview but which might be relevant to the offence. Any such record must be timed and signed by the maker. Where practicable the person shall be given the opportunity to read that record and to sign it as correct or to indicate the respects in which he considers it inaccurate. Any refusal to sign shall be recorded. [See *Note 11D*]

(c) Juveniles, mentally disordered people and mentally handicapped people

11.14 A juvenile or a person who is mentally disordered or mentally handicapped, whether suspected or not, must not be interviewed or asked to provide or sign a written statement in the absence of the appropriate adult unless paragraph 11.1 or Annex C applies.

11.15, 11.16 . . .

Notes for Guidance

11A–11D . . .

NOTES

Paras 11.15, 11.16: outside the scope of this work.

Notes for Guidance paras 11A–11D: outside the scope of this work.

12 Interviews in police stations

(a) Action

12.1 If a police officer wishes to interview, or conduct enquiries which require the presence of a detained person, the custody officer is responsible for deciding whether to deliver him into his custody.

12.2 In any period of 24 hours a detained person must be allowed a continuous period of at least 8 hours for rest, free from questioning, travel or any interruption by police officers in connection with the investigation concerned. This period should normally be at night. The period of rest may not be interrupted or delayed, except at the request of the person, his appropriate adult or his legal representative, unless there are reasonable grounds for believing that it would:

(i) involve a risk of harm to people or serious loss of, or damage to, property; or

(ii) delay unnecessarily the person's release from custody; or

(iii) otherwise prejudice the outcome of the investigation.

If a person is arrested at a police station after going there voluntarily, the period of 24 hours runs from the time of his arrest and not the time of arrival at the police station. Any action which is required to be taken in accordance with section 8 of this code, or in accordance with medical advice or at the request of the detained person, his appropriate adult or his legal representative, does not constitute an interruption to the rest period such that a fresh period must be allowed.

12.3 A detained person may not be supplied with intoxicating liquor except on medical directions. No person, who is unfit through drink or drugs to the extent that he is unable to appreciate the significance of questions put to him and his answers, may be questioned about an alleged offence in that condition except in accordance with Annex C. [See *Note 12B*]

12.4–12.7 . . .

12.8 If in the course of the interview a complaint is made by the person being questioned or on his behalf concerning the provisions of this code then the interviewing officer shall:

(i) record it in the interview record; and

(ii) inform the custody officer, who is then responsible for dealing with it in accordance with section 9 of this code.

(b) Documentation

12.9–12.13 . . .

Notes for Guidance

12A . . .

12B The police surgeon can give advice about whether or not a person is fit to be interviewed in accordance with paragraph 12.3 above.

12C . . .

NOTES

Paras 12.4–12.7, 12.9–12.13: outside the scope of this work.

Notes for Guidance paras 12A, 12C: outside the scope of this work.

(*Para 13 outside the scope of this work.*)

14 Questioning: special restrictions

14.1 If a person has been arrested by one police force on behalf of another and the lawful period of detention in respect of that offence has not yet commenced in accordance with section 41 of the Police and Criminal Evidence Act 1984 no questions may be put to him about the offence while he is in transit between the forces except in order to clarify any voluntary statement made by him.

14.2 If a person is in police detention at a hospital he may not be questioned without the agreement of a responsible doctor. [See *Note 14A*]

Note for Guidance

14A If questioning takes place at a hospital under paragraph 14.2 (or on the way to or from a hospital) the period concerned counts towards the total period of detention permitted.

15 Reviews and extensions of detention

(a) Action

15.1, 15.2 . . .

15.2A After hearing any representations, the review officer or officer determining whether further detention should be authorised shall note any comment the person may make if the decision is to keep him in detention. The officer shall not put specific questions to the suspect regarding his involvement in any offence, nor in respect of any comments he may make in response to the decision to keep him in detention. Such an exchange is likely to constitute an interview as defined by paragraph 11.1A and would require the associated safeguards included in section 11. [See also paragraph 11.13]

(b) Documentation

15.3–15.6 . . .

Notes for Guidance

15A–15C. . .

NOTES

Note that in Para 15.2A, the representations referred to are those made by the detainee or his representatives.

Paras 15.1, 15.2, 15.3–15.6: outside the scope of this work.

Notes for Guidance paras 15A–15C: outside the scope of this work.

16 Charging of detained persons

(a) Action

16.1 When an officer considers that there is sufficient evidence to prosecute a detained person, and that there is sufficient evidence for a prosecution to succeed, and that the person has said all that he wishes to say about the offence, he shall without delay (and subject to the following qualification) bring him before the custody officer who shall then be responsible for considering whether or not he should be charged. When a person is detained in respect of more than one offence it is permissible to delay bringing him before the custody officer until the above conditions are satisfied in respect of all the offences (but see paragraph 11.4). Any resulting action shall be taken in the presence of the appropriate adult if the person is a juvenile or mentally disordered or mentally handicapped.

16.2 When a detained person is charged with or informed that he may be prosecuted for an offence he shall be cautioned in the following terms:

> 'You do not have to say anything. But it may harm your defence if you do not mention now something which you later rely on in court. Anything you do say may be given in evidence.'

16.3 At the time a person is charged he shall be given a written notice showing particulars of the offence with which he is charged and including the name of the officer in the case (in terrorist cases, the officer's warrant or other identification number instead), his police station and the reference number for the case. So far as possible the particulars of the charge shall be stated in simple terms, but they shall also show the precise offence in law with which he is charged. The notice shall begin with the following words:

> 'You are charged with the offence(s) shown below. You do not have to say anything. But it may harm your defence if you do not mention now something which you later rely on in court. Anything you do say may be given in evidence.'

If the person is a juvenile or is mentally disordered or mentally handicapped the notice shall be given to the appropriate adult.

16.4 . . .

16.5 Questions relating to an offence may not be put to a person after he has been charged with that offence, or informed that he may be prosecuted for it, unless they are necessary for the purpose of preventing or minimising harm or loss to some other person or to the public or for clearing up an ambiguity in a previous answer or statement, or where it is in the interests of justice that the person should have put to him and have an opportunity to comment on information concerning the offence which has come to light since he was charged or informed that he might be prosecuted. Before any such questions are put to him, he shall be warned that he does not have to say anything but that anything he does say may be given in evidence and reminded of his right to legal advice in accordance with paragraph 6.5 above. [See *Note 16A*]

16.6 Where a juvenile is charged with an offence and the custody officer authorises his continued detention he must try to make arrangements for the juvenile to be taken into care of a local authority to be detained pending appearance in court unless he certifies that it is impracticable to do so, or, in the case of a juvenile of at least 12 years of age, no secure accommodation is available and there is a risk to the public of serious harm from that juvenile, in accordance with section 38(6) of the Police and Criminal Evidence Act 1984, as amended by section 59 of the Criminal Justice Act 1991 and section 24 of the Criminal Justice and Public Order Act 1994. [See *Note 16B*]

(b) Documentation

16.7 A record shall be made of anything a detained person says when charged.

16.8 Any questions put after charge and answers given relating to the offence shall be contemporaneously recorded in full on the forms provided and the record signed by that person or, if he refuses, by the interviewing officer and any third parties present. If the questions are tape-recorded the arrangements set out in Code E apply.

16.9 If it is not practicable to make arrangements for the transfer of a juvenile into local authority care in accordance with paragraph 16.6 above the custody officer must record the reasons and make out a certificate to be produced before the court together with the juvenile.

Notes for Guidance

16A, 16B . . .

NOTES

Para 16.4: outside the scope of this work.

Notes for Guidance paras 16A, 16B: outside the scope of this work.

ANNEX A
INTIMATE AND STRIP SEARCHES

[See paragraph 4.1]

(Part A outside the scope of this work.)

B. STRIP SEARCH

9 A strip search is a search involving the removal of more than outer clothing.

(a) Action

10 A strip search may take place only if it is considered necessary to remove an article which a person would not be allowed to keep, and the officer reasonably considers that the person might have concealed such an article. Strip searches shall not be routinely carried out where there is no reason to consider that articles have been concealed.

The conduct of strip searches

11 The following procedures shall be observed when strip searches are conducted:

(a) a police officer carrying out a strip search must be of the same sex as the person searched;

(b) the search shall take place in an area where the person being searched cannot be seen by anyone who does not need to be present, nor by a member of the opposite sex (except an appropriate adult who has been specifically requested by the person being searched);

(c) except in cases of urgency, where there is a risk of serious harm to the person detained or to others, whenever a strip search involves exposure of intimate parts of the body, there must be at least two people present other than the person searched, and if the search is of a juvenile or a mentally disordered or mentally handicapped person, one of the people must be the appropriate adult. Except in urgent cases as above, a search of a juvenile may take place in the absence of the appropriate adult only if the juvenile signifies in the presence of the appropriate adult that he prefers the search to be done in his absence and the appropriate adult agrees. A record shall be made of the juvenile's decision and signed by the appropriate adult. The presence of more than two people, other than an appropriate adult, shall be permitted only in the most exceptional circumstances.

(d) the search shall be conducted with proper regard to the sensitivity and vulnerability of the person in these circumstances and every reasonable effort shall be made to secure the person's co-operation and minimise embarrassment. People who are searched should not normally be required to have all their clothes removed at the same time, for example, a man shall be allowed to put on his shirt before removing his trousers, and a woman shall be allowed to put on her blouse and upper garments before further clothing is removed;

(e) where necessary to assist the search, the person may be required to hold his or her arms in the air or to stand with his or her legs apart and to bend forward so that a visual examination may be made of the genital and anal areas provided that no physical contact is made with any body orifice;

(f) if, during a search, articles are found, the person shall be asked to hand them over. If articles are found within any body orifice other than the mouth, and the person refuses to hand them over, their removal would constitute an intimate search, which must be carried out in accordance with the provisions of Part A of this Annex;

(g) a strip search shall be conducted as quickly as possible, and the person searched allowed to dress as soon as the procedure is complete.

(b) Documentation

12 A record shall be made on the custody record of a strip search including the reason it was considered necessary to undertake it, those present and any result.

ANNEX B
DELAY IN NOTIFYING ARREST OR ALLOWING ACCESS TO LEGAL ADVICE

(This Annex reproduces the statutory grounds for delay set out in the Police and Criminal Evidence Act 1984, ss 56, 58.)

ANNEX C
VULNERABLE SUSPECTS: URGENT INTERVIEWS AT POLICE STATIONS

1 When an interview is to take place in a police station or other authorised place of detention if, and only if, an officer of the rank of superintendent or above considers that delay will lead to the consequences set out in paragraph 11.1(a) to (c) of this Code:

(a) a person heavily under the influence of drink or drugs may be interviewed in that state; or

(b) a juvenile or a person who is mentally disordered or mentally handicapped may be interviewed in the absence of the appropriate adult; or

(c) a person who has difficulty in understanding English or who has a hearing disability may be interviewed in the absence of an interpreter.

2 Questioning in these circumstances may not continue once sufficient information to avert the immediate risk has been obtained.

3 A record shall be made of the grounds for any decision to interview a person under paragraph 1 above.

Note for Guidance

C1 The special groups referred to in this Annex are all particularly vulnerable. The provisions of the Annex, which override safeguards designed to protect them and to minimise the risk of interviews producing unreliable evidence, should be applied only in exceptional cases of need.

(Annexes D, E, F outside the scope of this work.)

PROSECUTION OF OFFENCES ACT 1985

(C 23)

An Act to provide for the establishment of a Crown Prosecution Service for England and Wales; to make provision as to costs in criminal cases; to provide for the imposition of time limits in relation to preliminary stages of criminal proceedings; to amend section 42 of the Supreme Court Act 1981 and section 3 of the Children and Young Persons Act 1969; to make provision with respect to consents to prosecutions; to repeal section 9 of the Perjury Act 1911; and for connected purposes

[23 May 1985]

PART I
THE CROWN PROSECUTION SERVICE

Constitution and functions of Service

1 The Crown Prosecution Service

(1) There shall be a prosecuting service for England and Wales (to be known as the "Crown Prosecution Service"), consisting of—

- (a) the Director of Public Prosecutions, who shall be head of the Service;
- (b) the Chief Crown Prosecutors, designated under subsection (4) below, each of whom shall be the member of the Service responsible to the Director for supervising the operation of the Service in his area; and
- (c) the other staff appointed by the Director under this section.

(2) The Director shall appoint such staff for the Service as, with the approval of the Treasury as to numbers, remuneration and other terms and conditions of service, he considers necessary for the discharge of his functions.

(3) The Director may designate any member of the Service [who has a general qualification (within the meaning of section 71 of the Courts and Legal Services Act 1990)] for the purposes of this subsection, and any person so designated shall be known as a Crown Prosecutor.

(4) The Director shall divide England and Wales into areas and, for each of those areas, designate a Crown Prosecutor for the purposes of this subsection and any person so designated shall be known as a Chief Crown Prosecutor.

(5) The Director may, from time to time, vary the division of England and Wales made for the purposes of subsection (4) above.

(6) Without prejudice to any functions which may have been assigned to him in his capacity as a member of the Service, every Crown Prosecutor shall have all the powers of the Director as to the institution and conduct of proceedings but shall exercise those powers under the direction of the Director.

(7) Where any enactment (whenever passed)—

- (a) prevents any step from being taken without the consent of the Director or without his consent or the consent of another; or
- (b) requires any step to be taken by or in relation to the Director;

any consent given by or, as the case may be, step taken by or in relation to, a Crown Prosecutor shall be treated, for the purposes of that enactment, as given by or, as the case may be, taken by or in relation to the Director.

NOTES

Sub-s (3): words in square brackets substituted by the Courts and Legal Services Act 1990, s 71(2), Sch 10, para 61(1).

2 The Director of Public Prosecutions

(1) The Director of Public Prosecutions shall be appointed by the Attorney General.

(2) The Director must be a [person who has a ten year general qualification, within the meaning of section 71 of the Courts and Legal Services Act 1990.]

(3) . . .

NOTES

Sub-s (2): words in square brackets substituted by the Courts and Legal Services Act 1990, s 71(2), Sch 10, para 60.

Sub-s (3): outside the scope of this work.

3 Functions of the Director

(1) The Director shall discharge his functions under this or any other enactment under the superintendence of the Attorney General.

(2) It shall be the duty of the Director[, subject to any provisions contained in the Criminal Justice Act 1987]—

- (a) to take over the conduct of all criminal proceedings, other than specified proceedings, instituted on behalf of a police force (whether by a member of that force or by any other person);
- (b) to institute and have the conduct of criminal proceedings in any case where it appears to him that—
  - (i) the importance or difficulty of the case makes it appropriate that proceedings should be instituted by him; or
  - (ii) it is otherwise appropriate for proceedings to be instituted by him;
- (c) to take over the conduct of all binding over proceedings instituted on behalf of a police force (whether by a member of that force or by any other person);
- (d) to take over the conduct of all proceedings begun by summons issued under section 3 of the Obscene Publications Act 1959 (forfeiture of obscene articles);
- (e) to give, to such extent as he considers appropriate, advice to police forces on all matters relating to criminal offences;
- (f) to appear for the prosecution, when directed by the court to do so, on any appeal under—
  - (i) section 1 of the Administration of Justice Act 1960 (appeal from the High Court in criminal cases);
  - (ii) Part I or Part II of the Criminal Appeal Act 1968 (appeals from the Crown Court to the criminal division of the Court of Appeal and thence to the House of Lords); or
  - (iii) section 108 of the Magistrates' Courts Act 1980 (right of appeal to Crown Court) as it applies, by virtue of subsection (5) of section 12 of the Contempt of Court Act 1981, to orders made under section 12 (contempt of magistrates' courts); and

(g) to discharge such other functions as may from time to time be assigned to him by the Attorney General in pursuance of this paragraph.

(3) In this section—

"the court" means—

(a) in the case of an appeal to or from the criminal division of the Court of Appeal, that division;

(b) in the case of an appeal from a Divisional Court of the Queen's Bench Division, the Divisional Court; and

(c) in the case of an appeal against an order of a magistrates' court, the Crown Court;

In section 3 of the Prosecution of Offences Act 1985 (functions of Director), in subsection (3), in the definition of "police force", after "1996" there shall be inserted ", the National Crime Squad".

"police force" means any police force maintained by a police authority under [the Police Act 1996][, the National Crime Squad] and any other body of constables for the time being specified by order made by the Secretary of State for the purposes of this section; and

"specified proceedings" means proceedings which fall within any category for the time being specified by order made by the Attorney General for the purposes of this section.

(4) The power to make orders under subsection (3) above shall be exercisable by statutory instrument subject to annulment in pursuance of a resolution of either House of Parliament.

NOTES

Sub-s (2): words in square brackets inserted by the Criminal Justice Act 1987, s 15, Sch 2, para 13.

Sub-s (3): in definition of "police force", words in first pair of square brackets substituted by the Police Act 1996, s 103(1), Sch 7, Pt II, para 39, words in second pair of square brackets inserted by the Police Act 1997, s 134(1), Sch 9, para 48.

6 Prosecutions instituted and conducted otherwise than by the service

(1) Subject to subsection (2) below, nothing in this Part shall preclude any person from instituting any criminal proceedings or conducting any criminal proceedings to which the Director's duty to take over the conduct of proceedings does not apply.

(2) Where criminal proceedings are instituted in circumstances in which the Director is not under a duty to take over their conduct, he may nevertheless do so at any stage.

Guidelines

10 Guidelines for Crown Prosecutors

(1) The Director shall issue a Code for Crown Prosecutors giving guidance on general principles to be applied by them—

(a) in determining, in any case—

(i) whether proceedings for an offence should be instituted or, where proceedings have been instituted, whether they should be discontinued; or

(ii) what charges should be preferred; and

(b) in considering, in any case, representations to be made by them to any magistrates' court about the mode of trial suitable for that case.

(2) The Director may from time to time make alterations in the Code.

(3) The provisions of the Code shall be set out in the Director's report under section 9 of this Act for the year in which the Code is issued; and any alteration in the Code shall be set out in his report under that section for the year in which the alteration is made.

PART IV
SUPPLEMENTAL

31 Short title, commencement and extent etc

(1) This Act may be cited as the Prosecution of Offences Act 1985.

(2)–(6) . . .

(7) This Act does not extend to Scotland or Northern Ireland.

NOTES

Sub-ss (2)–(6): outside the scope of this work.

REPRESENTATION OF THE PEOPLE ACT 1985

(C 50)

An Act to amend the law relating to parliamentary elections in the United Kingdom and local government elections in Great Britain, to provide for combining polls taken on the same date at such elections and elections to the European Parliament of the European Communities, to extend the franchise at elections to that European Parliament, to amend the law relating to the effect of the demise of the Crown on the summoning and duration of a new Parliament and to repeal section 21(3) of the Representation of the People Act 1918

[16 July 1985]

Extension of franchise to British citizens overseas

1 Extension of parliamentary franchise

(1) Subject to section 1(3) of the principal Act, a person is entitled (notwithstanding anything in section 1(2) of that Act) to vote as an elector at a parliamentary election in any constituency if—

(a) he qualifies as an overseas elector in respect of that constituency on the qualifying date, and

(b) on that date and on the date of the poll he is not subject to any legal incapacity to vote and is a British citizen.

(2) For the purposes of this and the principal Act, a person qualifies as an overseas elector in respect of a constituency on the qualifying date if—

(a) on that date he is not resident in the United Kingdom, and

(b) he satisfies [one of the following sets of] conditions.

(3) [The first set of conditions is] that—

(a) he was included in a register of parliamentary electors in respect of an address at a place that is situated within the constituency concerned,

(b) on the date by reference to which the register was prepared, he was resident or treated for the purposes of registration as resident at that address.

(c) that date fell within the period of [twenty years] ending immediately before the qualifying date, and

(d) if he was included in any register of parliamentary electors prepared by reference to a date later than the date referred to in paragraph (b) above, he was not resident or treated for the purposes of registration as resident at an address in the United Kingdom on that later date.

[(3A) The second set of conditions is that—

(a) he was last resident in the United Kingdom within the period of twenty years ending immediately before the qualifying date,

(b) he was by reason only of his age incapable of being included in any register of parliamentary electors prepared by reference to the last date within that period by reference to which such registers were prepared on which he was so resident, and

(c) the address at which he was resident on the date referred to in paragraph (b) above was at a place that is situated within the constituency concerned and a parent or guardian of his was included, in respect of that address, in a register of parliamentary electors or a register of local government electors prepared by reference to that date.]

(4) The reference in subsection (1) above to a person being subject to a legal incapacity to vote on the qualifying date does not include a reference to his being below the age of 18 on that date [and the reference in subsection (3A) above to a register of local government electors includes a reference to a register of electors prepared for the purposes of local elections (within the meaning of the Electoral Law Act (Northern Ireland) 1962)].

NOTES

Sub-s (2): words in square brackets in para (b) substituted by the Representation of the People Act 1989, s 3(1)(a).

Sub-s (3): words in square brackets substituted by the Representation of the People Act 1989, ss 1, 3(1)(b).

Sub-s (3A): inserted by the Representation of the People Act 1989, s 2(1).

Sub-s (4): words in square brackets added by the Representation of the People Act 1989, s 3(1)(c).

Miscellaneous and supplemental

29 Citation, commencement and extent

(1) This Act may be cited as the Representation of the People Act 1985 and shall be included among the Acts that may be cited as the Representation of the People Acts.

(2) This Act . . . shall come into force on such day as the Secretary of State may by order made by statutory instrument appoint, and different days may be appointed for different provisions and for different purposes.

(3) . . .

(4) This Act, except the provisions mentioned in subsection (5) below, extends to Northern Ireland; and section 10 of and Schedule 1 to this Act extend to Northern Ireland only.

(5) Those provisions are sections 15 to 18, 21 to 22 of this Act and any amendment or repeal by this Act of an enactment not extending to Northern Ireland.

NOTES

Words omitted from sub-s (2), and the whole of sub-s (3), outside the scope of this work.

INTERCEPTION OF COMMUNICATIONS ACT 1985

(C 56)

An Act to make new provision for and in connection with the interception of communications sent by post or by means of public telecommunication systems and to amend section 45 of the Telecommunications Act 1984

[25 July 1985]

1 Prohibition on interception

(1) Subject to the following provisions of this section, a person who intentionally intercepts a communication in the course of its transmission by post or by means of a public telecommunication system shall be guilty of an offence and liable—

(a) on summary conviction, to a fine not exceeding the statutory maximum;

(b) on conviction on indictment, to imprisonment for a term not exceeding two years or to a fine or to both.

(2) A person shall not be guilty of an offence under this section if—

(a) the communication is intercepted in obedience to a warrant issued by the Secretary of State under section 2 below; or

(b) that person has reasonable grounds for believing that the person to whom, or the person by whom, the communication is sent has consented to the interception.

(3) A person shall not be guilty of an offence under this section if—

(a) the communication is intercepted for purposes connected with the provision of postal or public telecommunication services or with the enforcement of any enactment relating to the use of those services; or

(b) the communication is being transmitted by wireless telegraphy and is intercepted, with the authority of the Secretary of State, for purposes connected with the issue of licences under the Wireless Telegraphy Act 1949 or the prevention or detection of interference with wireless telegraphy.

(4) No proceedings in respect of an offence under this section shall be instituted—

(a) in England and Wales, except by or with the consent of the Director of Public Prosecutions;

(b) in Northern Ireland, except by or with the consent of the Director of Public Prosecutions for Northern Ireland.

2 Warrants for interception

(1) Subject to the provisions of this section and section 3 below, the Secretary of State may issue a warrant requiring the person to whom it is addressed to intercept, in the course of their transmission by post or by means of a public telecommunication

system, such communications as are described in the warrant; and such a warrant may also require the person to whom it is addressed to disclose the intercepted material to such persons and in such manner as are described in the warrant.

(2) The Secretary of State shall not issue a warrant under this section unless he considers that the warrant is necessary—

(a) in the interests of national security;

(b) for the purpose of preventing or detecting serious crime; or

(c) for the purpose of safeguarding the economic well-being of the United Kingdom.

(3) The matters to be taken into account in considering whether a warrant is necessary as mentioned in subsection (2) above shall include whether the information which it is considered necessary to acquire could reasonably be acquired by other means.

(4) A warrant shall not be considered necessary as mentioned in subsection (2)(c) above unless the information which it is considered necessary to acquire is information relating to the acts or intentions of persons outside the British Islands.

(5) References in the following provisions of this Act to a warrant are references to a warrant under this section.

3 Scope of warrants

(1) Subject to subsection (2) below, the interception required by a warrant shall be the interception of—

(a) such communications as are sent to or from one or more addresses specified in the warrant, being an address or addresses likely to be used for the transmission of communications to or from—

(i) one particular person specified or described in the warrant; or

(ii) one particular set of premises so specified or described; and

(b) such other communications (if any) as it is necessary to intercept in order to intercept communications falling within paragraph (a) above.

(2) Subsection (1) above shall not apply to a warrant if—

(a) the interception required by the warrant is the interception, in the course of their transmission by means of a public telecommunication system, of—

(i) such external communications as are described in the warrant; and

(ii) such other communications (if any) as it is necessary to intercept in order to intercept such external communications as are so described; and

(b) at the time when the warrant is issued, the Secretary of State issues a certificate certifying the descriptions of intercepted material the examination of which he considers necessary as mentioned in section 2(2) above.

(3) A certificate such as is mentioned in subsection (2) above shall not specify an address in the British Islands for the purpose of including communications sent to or from that address in the certified material unless—

(a) the Secretary of State considers that the examination of communications sent to or from that address is necessary for the purpose of preventing or detecting acts of terrorism; and

(b) communications sent to or from that address are included in the certified material only in so far as they are sent within such a period, not exceeding three months, as is specified in the certificate.

(4) A certificate such as is mentioned in subsection (2) above shall not be issued except under the hand of the Secretary of State.

(5) References in the following provisions of this Act to a certificate are references to a certificate such as is mentioned in subsection (2) above.

4 Issue and duration of warrants

(1) A warrant shall not be issued except—

(a) under the hand of the Secretary of State; or

(b) in an urgent case where the Secretary of State has expressly authorised its issue and a statement of that fact is endorsed thereon, under the hand of an official of his department of or above the rank of Assistant Under Secretary of State.

(2) A warrant shall, unless renewed under subsection (3) below, cease to have effect at the end of the relevant period.

(3) The Secretary of State may, at any time before the end of the relevant period, renew a warrant if he considers that the warrant continues to be necessary as mentioned in section 2(2) above.

(4) If, at any time before the end of the relevant period, the Secretary of State considers that a warrant is no longer necessary as mentioned in section 2(2) above, he shall cancel the warrant.

(5), (6) . . .

NOTES

Sub-ss (5), (6): outside the scope of this work.

6 Safeguards

(1) Where the Secretary of State issues a warrant he shall, unless such arrangements have already been made, make such arrangements as he considers necessary for the purpose of securing—

(a) that the requirements of subsections (2) and (3) below are satisfied in relation to the intercepted material; and

(b) where a certificate is issued in relation to the warrant, that so much of the intercepted material as is not certified by the certificate is not read, looked at or listened to by any person.

(2) The requirements of this subsection are satisfied in relation to any intercepted material if each of the following, namely—

(a) the extent to which the material is disclosed;

(b) the number of persons to whom any of the material is disclosed;

(c) the extent to which the material is copied; and

(d) the number of copies made of any of the material,

is limited to the minimum that is necessary as mentioned in section 2(2) above.

(3) The requirements of this subsection are satisfied in relation to any intercepted material if each copy made of any of that material is destroyed as soon as its retention is no longer necessary as mentioned in section 2(2) above.

7 The Tribunal

(1) There shall be a tribunal (in this Act referred to as "the Tribunal") in relation to which the provisions of Schedule 1 to this Act shall apply.

(2) Any person who believes that communications sent to or by him have been intercepted in the course of their transmission by post or by means of a public telecommunication system may apply to the Tribunal for an investigation under this section.

(3) On such an application (other than one appearing to the Tribunal to be frivolous or vexatious), the Tribunal shall investigate—

- (a) whether there is or has been a relevant warrant or a relevant certificate; and
- (b) where there is or has been such a warrant or certificate, whether there has been any contravention of sections 2 to 5 above in relation to that warrant or certificate.

(4) If, on an investigation, the Tribunal, applying the principles applicable by a court on an application for judicial review, conclude that there has been a contravention of sections 2 to 5 above in relation to a relevant warrant or a relevant certificate, they shall—

- (a) give notice to the applicant stating that conclusion;
- (b) make a report of their findings to the Prime Minister; and
- (c) if they think fit, make an order under subsection (5) below.

(5) An order under this subsection may do one or more of the following, namely—

- (a) quash the relevant warrant or the relevant certificate;
- (b) direct the destruction of copies of the intercepted material or, as the case may be, so much of it as is certified by the relevant certificate;
- (c) direct the Secretary of State to pay to the applicant such sum by way of compensation as may be specified in the order.

(6), (7) . . .

(8) The decisions of the Tribunal (including any decisions as to their jurisdiction) shall not be subject to appeal or liable to be questioned in any court.

(9) . . .

NOTES

Sub-ss (6), (7), (9): outside the scope of this work.

8 The Commissioner

(1) The Prime Minister shall appoint a person who holds or has held a high judicial office (in this section referred to as "the Commissioner") to carry out the following functions, namely—

- (a) to keep under review the carrying out by the Secretary of State of the functions conferred on him by sections 2 to 5 above and the adequacy of any arrangements made for the purposes of section 6 above; and
- (b) to give to the Tribunal all such assistance as the Tribunal may require for the purpose of enabling them to carry out their functions under this Act.

(2) The Commissioner shall hold office in accordance with the terms of his appointment and there shall be paid to him out of money provided by Parliament such allowances as the Treasury may determine.

(3) It shall be the duty of every person holding office under the Crown or engaged in the business of the Post Office or in the running of a public telecommunication system to disclose or give to the Commissioner such documents or information as he may require for the purpose of enabling him to carry out his functions under this section.

(4) It shall be the duty of the Tribunal to send to the Commissioner a copy of every report made by them under section 7(4) above.

(5) If at any time it appears to the Commissioner—

(a) that there has been a contravention of sections 2 to 5 above which has not been the subject of a report made by the Tribunal under section 7(4) above; or

(b) that any arrangements made for the purposes of section 6 above have proved inadequate,

he shall make a report to the Prime Minister with respect to that contravention or those arrangements.

(6) As soon as practicable after the end of each calendar year, the Commissioner shall make a report to the Prime Minister with respect to the carrying out of his functions under this section.

(7) The Prime Minister shall lay before each House of Parliament a copy of every annual report made by the Commissioner under subsection (6) above together with a statement as to whether any matter has been excluded from that copy in pursuance of subsection (8) below.

(8) If it appears to the Prime Minister, after consultation with the Commissioner, that the publication of any matter in an annual report would be prejudicial to national security, to the prevention or detection of serious crime or to the economic well-being of the United Kingdom, the Prime Minister may exclude that matter from the copy of the report as laid before each House of Parliament.

9 Exclusion of evidence

(1) In any proceedings before any court or tribunal no evidence shall be adduced and no question in cross-examination shall be asked which (in either case) tends to suggest—

(a) that an offence under section 1 above has been or is to be committed by any of the persons mentioned in subsection (2) below; or

(b) that a warrant has been or is to be issued to any of those persons.

(2) The persons referred to in subsection (1) above are—

(a) any person holding office under the Crown;

(b) the Post Office and any person engaged in the business of the Post Office; and

(c) any public telecommunications operator and any person engaged in the running of a public telecommunication system.

(3) Subsection (1) above does not apply—

(a) in relation to proceedings for a relevant offence or proceedings before the Tribunal; or

(b) where the evidence is adduced or the question in cross-examination is asked for the purpose of establishing the fairness or unfairness of a dismissal on grounds of an offence under section 1 above or of conduct from which such an offence might be inferred;

and paragraph (a) of that subsection does not apply where a person has been convicted of the offence under that section.

(4) . . .

NOTES

Sub-s (4): outside the scope of this work.

12 Short title, commencement and extent

(1) This Act may be cited as the Interception of Communications Act 1985.

(2) This Act shall come into force on such day as the Secretary of State may by order made by statutory instrument appoint.

(3) This Act extends to Northern Ireland.

(4) . . .

NOTES

Sub-s (4): outside the scope of this work.

LOCAL GOVERNMENT ACT 1986

(C 10)

An Act to require rating authorities to set a rate on or before 1st April; to prohibit political publicity and otherwise restrain local authority publicity; to require the mortgagor's consent and make other provision in connection with the disposal of local authority mortgages; to amend the law as to to the effect of retirement and re-election of, and the allowances payable to, members of certain authorities; and for connected purposes [26 March 1986]

PART II
LOCAL AUTHORITY PUBLICITY

2 Prohibition of political publicity

(1) A local authority shall not publish any material which, in whole or in part, appears to be designed to affect public support for a political party.

[(2) In determining whether material falls within the prohibition regard shall be had to the content and style of the material, the time and other circumstances of publication and the likely effect on those to whom it is directed and, in particular, to the following matters—

(a) whether the material refers to a political party or to persons identified with a political party or promotes or opposes a point of view on a question of political controversy which is identifiable as the view of one political party and not of another;

(b) where the material is part of a campaign, the effect which the campaign appears to be designed to achieve.]

(3) A local authority shall not give financial or other assistance to a person for the publication of material which the authority are prohibited by this section from publishing themselves.

NOTES

Sub-s (2): substituted by the Local Government Act 1988, s 27(1).

[2A Prohibition on promoting homosexuality by teaching or by publishing material

(1) A local authority shall not—

(a) intentionally promote homosexuality or publish material with the intention of promoting homosexuality;

(b) promote the teaching in any maintained school of the acceptability of homosexuality as a pretended family relationship.

(2) Nothing in subsection (1) above shall be taken to prohibit the doing of anything for the purpose of treating or preventing the spread of disease.

(3) In any proceedings in connection with the application of this section a court shall draw such inferences as to the intention of the local authority as may reasonably be drawn from the evidence before it.

(4) In subsection (1)(b) above "maintained school" means,—

(a) in England and Wales, a *county school, voluntary school, nursery school or special school, within the meaning of [the Education Act 1996]*; and

(b) . . .

NOTES

Inserted by the Local Government Act 1988, s 28.

Sub-s (4): in para (a), words in square brackets substituted by the Education Act 1996, s 582(1), Sch 37, Pt I, para 63, and for words in italics there are substituted words "a maintained school or maintained nursery school, within the meaning of the School Standards and Framework Act 1998", by the School Standards and Framework Act 1998, s 140(1), Sch 30, para 13, as from a day to be appointed; para (b) outside the scope of this work.

PART IV
MISCELLANEOUS AND GENERAL

General

12 Short title, commencement and extent

(1) This Act may be cited as the Local Government Act 1986.

(2) . . .

(3) Part II and this section extend to England and Wales and Scotland; the other provisions of this Act extend to England and Wales only.

NOTES

Sub-s (2): outside the scope of this work.

PARLIAMENTARY CONSTITUENCIES ACT 1986

(C 56)

An Act to consolidate the House of Commons (Redistribution of Seats) Acts 1949 to 1979 and certain related enactments [7 November 1986]

1 Parliamentary constituencies

(1) There shall for the purpose of parliamentary elections be the county and borough constituencies (or in Scotland the county and burgh constituencies), each

returning a single member, which are described in Orders in Council made under this Act.

(2) In this Act and, except where the context otherwise requires, in any Act passed after the Representation of the People Act 1948, "constituency" means an area having separate representation in the House of Commons.

2 The Boundary Commissions

(1) For the purpose of the continuous review of the distribution of seats at parliamentary elections, there shall continue to be four permanent Boundary Commissions, namely a Boundary Commission for England, a Boundary Commission for Scotland, a Boundary Commission for Wales and a Boundary Commission for Northern Ireland.

(2) Schedule 1 to this Act shall have effect with respect to the constitution of, and other matters relating to, the Boundary Commissions.

3 Reports of the Commissions

(1) Each Boundary Commission shall keep under review the representation in the House of Commons of the part of the United Kingdom with which they are concerned and shall, in accordance with subsection (2) below, submit to the Secretary of State reports with respect to the whole of that part of the United Kingdom, either—

- (a) showing the constituencies into which they recommend that it should be divided in order to give effect to the rules set out in paragraphs 1 to 6 of Schedule 2 to this Act (read with paragraph 7 of that Schedule), or
- (b) stating that, in the opinion of the Commission, no alteration is required to be made in respect of that part of the United Kingdom in order to give effect to the said rules (read with paragraph 7).

(2) Reports under subsection (1) above shall be submitted by a Boundary Commission [not less than eight or more than twelve years] from the date of the submission of their last report under that subsection.

[(2A) A failure by a Boundary Commission to submit a report within the time limit which is appropriate to that report shall not be regarded as invalidating the report for the purposes of any enactment.]

(3) Any Boundary Commission may also from time to time submit to the Secretary of State reports with respect to the area comprised in any particular constituency or constituencies in the part of the United Kingdom with which they are concerned, showing the constituencies into which they recommend that that area should be divided in order to give effect to the rules set out in paragraphs 1 to 6 of Schedule 2 to this Act (read with paragraph 7 of that Schedule).

(4) A report of a Boundary Commission under this Act showing the constituencies into which they recommend that any area should be divided shall state, as respects each constituency, the name by which they recommend that it should be known, and whether they recommend that it should be a county constituency or a borough constituency (or in Scotland a county constituency or a burgh constituency).

(5) As soon as may be after a Boundary Commission have submitted a report to the Secretary of State under this Act, he shall lay the report before Parliament together, except in a case where the report states that no alteration is required to be made in

respect of the part of the United Kingdom with which the Commission are concerned, with the draft of an Order in Council for giving effect, whether with or without modifications, to the recommendations contained in the report.

(6) Schedule 2 to this Act which contains the rules referred to above and related provisions shall have effect.

(7), (8) . . .

NOTES

Sub-s (2): words in square brackets substituted by the Boundary Commissions Act 1992, ss 2(1), (3), subject to the exception in s 2(3) of that Act.

Sub-s (2A): inserted by the Boundary Commissions Act 1992, ss 2(1), (4).

Sub-ss (7), (8): outside the scope of this work.

4 Orders in Council

(1) The draft of any Order in Council laid before Parliament by the Secretary of State under this Act for giving effect, whether with or without modifications, to the recommendations contained in the report of a Boundary Commission may make provision for any matters which appear to him to be incidental to, or consequential on, the recommendations.

(2) Where any such draft gives effect to any such recommendations with modifications, the Secretary of State shall lay before Parliament together with the draft a statement of the reasons for the modifications.

(3) If any such draft is approved by resolution of each House of Parliament, the Secretary of State shall submit it to Her Majesty in Council.

(4) If a motion for the approval of any such draft is rejected by either House of Parliament or withdrawn by leave of the House, the Secretary of State may amend the draft and lay the amended draft before Parliament, and if the draft as so amended is approved by resolution of each House of Parliament, the Secretary of State shall submit it to Her Majesty in Council.

(5) . . .

(6) The coming into force of any such Order shall not affect any parliamentary election until a proclamation is issued by Her Majesty summoning a new Parliament, or affect the constitution of the House of Commons until the dissolution of the Parliament then in being.

(7) The validity of any Order in Council purporting to be made under this Act and reciting that a draft of the Order has been approved by resolution of each House of Parliament shall not be called in question in any legal proceedings whatsoever.

NOTES

Sub-s (5): outside the scope of this work.

5 Notices

(1) Where a Boundary Commission intend to consider making a report under this Act they shall, by notice in writing, inform the Secretary of State accordingly, and a copy of the notice shall be published—

(a) in a case where it was given by the Boundary Commission for England or the Boundary Commission for Wales, in the London Gazette,

(b) . . . , and

(c) in a case where it was given by the Boundary Commission for Northern Ireland, in the Belfast Gazette.

(2) Where a Boundary Commission have provisionally determined to make recommendations affecting any constituency, they shall publish in at least one newspaper circulating in the constituency a notice stating—

(a) the effect of the proposed recommendations and (except in a case where they propose to recommend that no alteration be made in respect of the constituency) that a copy of the recommendations is open to inspection at a specified place within the constituency, and

(b) that representations with respect to the proposed recommendations may be made to the Commission within one month after the publication of the notice;

and the Commission shall take into consideration any representations duly made in accordance with any such notice.

(3) Where a Boundary Commission revise any proposed recommendations after publishing a notice of them under subsection (2) above, the Commission shall comply again with that subsection in relation to the revised recommendations, as if no earlier notice had been published.

NOTES

Sub-s (1): para (b) outside the scope of this work.

6 Local inquiries

(1) A Boundary Commission may, if they think fit, cause a local inquiry to be held in respect of any constituency or constituencies.

(2) Where, on the publication of the notice under section 5(2) above of a recommendation of a Boundary Commission for the alteration of any constituencies, the Commission receive any representation objecting to the proposed recommendation from an interested authority or from a body of electors numbering one hundred or more, the Commission shall not make the recommendation unless, since the publication of the notice, a local inquiry has been held in respect of the constituencies.

(3) Where a local inquiry was held in respect of the constituencies before the publication of the notice mentioned in subsection (2) above, that subsection shall not apply if the Commission, after considering the matters discussed at the local inquiry, the nature of the representations received on the publication of the notice and any other relevant circumstances, are of opinion that a further local inquiry would not be justified.

(4)–(7) . . .

NOTES

Sub-ss (4)–(7): outside the scope of this work.

9 Citation, commencement and extent

(1) This Act may be cited as the Parliamentary Constituencies Act 1986, and shall be included among the Acts which may be cited as the Representation of the People Acts.

(2) This Act shall come into force at the end of the period of three months beginning with the day on which it is passed.

(3) This Act extends to Northern Ireland.

SCHEDULES

SCHEDULE 1

Section 2

THE BOUNDARY COMMISSIONS

Constitution

1. The Speaker of the House of Commons shall be the chairman of each of the four Commissions.

2. Each of the four Commissions shall consist of the chairman, a deputy chairman and two other members appointed by the Secretary of State.

3. The deputy chairman—
   (a) in the case of the Commission for England shall be a judge of the High Court appointed by the Lord Chancellor,
   (b) . . .
   (c) in the case of the Commission for Wales shall be a judge of the High Court appointed by the Lord Chancellor,
   (d) in the case of the Commission for Northern Ireland shall be a judge of the High Court in Northern Ireland appointed by the Lord Chief Justice of Northern Ireland.

4. A member of any Commission (other than the chairman) shall hold his appointment for such term and on such conditions as may be determined before his appointment by the person appointing him.

4A–12. . . .

NOTES

Para 3: para (b) outside the scope of this work.

Paras 4A–12: outside the scope of this work.

SCHEDULE 2

Section 3

RULES FOR REDISTRIBUTION OF SEATS

The rules

1.—(1) The number of constituencies in Great Britain shall not be substantially greater or less than 613.

(2) . . .

(3) The number of constituencies in Wales shall not be less than 35.

(4) The number of constituencies in Northern Ireland shall not be greater than 18 or less than 16, and shall be 17 unless it appears to the Boundary Commission for Northern Ireland that Northern Ireland should for the time being be divided into 16 or (as the case may be) into 18 constituencies.

2. Every constituency shall return a single member.

3. There shall continue to be a constituency which shall include the whole of the City of London and the name of which shall refer to the City of London.

4.—(1) So far as is practicable having regard to rules 1 to 3—
   (a) in England and Wales,—
      (i) no county or any part of a county shall be included in a constituency which includes the whole or part of any other county or the whole or part of a London borough,

(ii) no London borough or any part of a London borough shall be included in a constituency which includes the whole or part of any other London borough,

(b) . . .

(c) in Northern Ireland, no ward shall be included partly in one constituency and partly in another.

[(1A) In sub-paragraph (1)(a) above "county" means, in relation to Wales, a preserved county (as defined by section 64 of the Local Government (Wales) Act 1994).]

(2) . . .

5. The electorate of any constituency shall be as near the electoral quota as is practicable having regard to rules 1 to 4; and a Boundary Commission may depart from the strict application of rule 4 if it appears to them that a departure is desirable to avoid an excessive disparity between the electorate of any constituency and the electoral quota, or between the electorate of any constituency and that of neighbouring constituencies in the part of the United Kingdom with which they are concerned.

6. A Boundary Commission may depart from the strict application of rules 4 and 5 if special geographical considerations, including in particular the size, shape and accessibility of a constituency, appear to them to render a departure desirable.

General and supplementary

7. It shall not be the duty of a Boundary Commission to aim at giving full effect in all circumstances to the above rules, but they shall take account, so far as they reasonably can—

(a) of the inconveniences attendant on alterations of constituencies, other than alterations made for the purposes of rule 4, and

(b) of any local ties which would be broken by such alterations.

8, 9. . . .

NOTES

Para 1: sub-para (2) outside the scope of this work.

Para 4: sub-paras (1)(b), (2) outside the scope of this work; sub-para (1A) inserted by the Local Government (Wales) Act 1994, s 1(3), Sch 2, para 13.

Paras 8, 9: outside the scope of this work.

PUBLIC ORDER ACT 1986

(C 64)

An Act to abolish the common law offences of riot, rout, unlawful assembly and affray and certain statutory offences relating to public order; to create new offences relating to public order; to control public processions and assemblies; to control the stirring up of racial hatred; to provide for the exclusion of certain offenders from sporting events; to create a new offence relating to the contamination of or interference with goods; to confer power to direct certain trespassers to leave land; to amend section 7 of the Conspiracy and Protection of Property Act 1875, section 1 of the Prevention of Crime Act 1953, Part V of the Criminal Justice (Scotland) Act 1980 and the Sporting Events (Control of Alcohol etc) Act 1985; to repeal certain obsolete or unnecessary enactments; and for connected purposes

[7 November 1986]

PART I
NEW OFFENCES

1 Riot

(1) Where 12 or more persons who are present together use or threaten unlawful violence for a common purpose and the conduct of them (taken together) is such as

would cause a person of reasonable firmness present at the scene to fear for his personal safety, each of the persons using unlawful violence for the common purpose is guilty of riot.

(2) It is immaterial whether or not the 12 or more use or threaten unlawful violence simultaneously.

(3) The common purpose may be inferred from conduct.

(4) No person of reasonable firmness need actually be, or be likely to be, present at the scene.

(5) Riot may be committed in private as well as in public places.

(6) A person guilty of riot is liable on conviction on indictment to imprisonment for a term not exceeding ten years or a fine or both.

2 Violent disorder

(1) Where 3 or more persons who are present together use or threaten unlawful violence and the conduct of them (taken together) is such as would cause a person of reasonable firmness present at the scene to fear for his personal safety, each of the persons using or threatening unlawful violence is guilty of violent disorder.

(2) It is immaterial whether or not the 3 or more use or threaten unlawful violence simultaneously.

(3) No person of reasonable firmness need actually be, or be likely to be, present at the scene.

(4) Violent disorder may be committed in private as well as in public places.

(5) A person guilty of violent disorder is liable on conviction on indictment to imprisonment for a term not exceeding 5 years or a fine or both, or on summary conviction to imprisonment for a term not exceeding 6 months or a fine not exceeding the statutory maximum or both.

3 Affray

(1) A person is guilty of affray if he uses or threatens unlawful violence towards another and his conduct is such as would cause a person of reasonable firmness present at the scene to fear for his personal safety.

(2) Where 2 or more persons use or threaten the unlawful violence, it is the conduct of them taken together that must be considered for the purposes of subsection (1).

(3) For the purposes of this section a threat cannot be made by the use of words alone.

(4) No person of reasonable firmness need actually be, or be likely to be, present at the scene.

(5) Affray may be committed in private as well as in public places.

(6) A constable may arrest without warrant anyone he reasonably suspects is committing affray.

(7) A person guilty of affray is liable on conviction on indictment to imprisonment for a term not exceeding 3 years or a fine or both, or on summary conviction to imprisonment for a term not exceeding 6 months or a fine not exceeding the statutory maximum or both.

4 Fear or provocation of violence

(1) A person is guilty of an offence if he—

(a) uses towards another person threatening, abusive or insulting words or behaviour, or

(b) distributes or displays to another person any writing, sign or other visible representation which is threatening, abusive or insulting,

with intent to cause that person to believe that immediate unlawful violence will be used against him or another by any person, or to provoke the immediate use of unlawful violence by that person or another, or whereby that person is likely to believe that such violence will be used or it is likely that such violence will be provoked.

(2) An offence under this section may be committed in a public or a private place, except that no offence is committed where the words or behaviour are used, or the writing, sign or other visible representation is distributed or displayed, by a person inside a dwelling and the other person is also inside that or another dwelling.

(3) A constable may arrest without warrant anyone he reasonably suspects is committing an offence under this section.

(4) A person guilty of an offence under this section is liable on summary conviction to imprisonment for a term not exceeding 6 months or a fine not exceeding level 5 on the standard scale or both.

[4A Intentional harassment, alarm or distress

(1) A person is guilty of an offence if, with intent to cause a person harassment, alarm or distress, he—

(a) uses threatening, abusive or insulting words or behaviour, or disorderly behaviour, or

(b) displays any writing, sign or other visible representation which is threatening, abusive or insulting,

thereby causing that or another person harassment, alarm or distress.

(2) An offence under this section may be committed in a public place or a private place, except that no offence is committed where the words or behaviour are used, or the writing, sign or other visible representation is displayed, by a person inside a dwelling and the person who is harassed, alarmed or distressed is also inside that or another dwelling.

(3) It is a defence for the accused to prove—

(a) that he was inside a dwelling and had no reason to believe that the words or behaviour used, or the writing, sign or other visible representation displayed, would be heard or seen by a person outside that or any other dwelling, or

(b) that his conduct was reasonable.

(4) A constable may arrest without warrant anyone he reasonably suspects is committing an offence under this section.

(5) A person guilty of an offence under this section is liable on summary conviction to imprisonment for a term not exceeding 6 months or a fine not exceeding level 5 of the standard scale or both.]

NOTES

Inserted by the Criminal Justice and Public Order Act 1994, s 154.

5 Harassment, alarm or distress

(1) A person is guilty of an offence if he—

(a) uses threatening, abusive or insulting words or behaviour, or disorderly behaviour, or

(b) displays any writing, sign or other visible representation which is threatening, abusive or insulting,

within the hearing or sight of a person likely to be caused harassment, alarm or distress thereby.

(2) An offence under this section may be committed in a public or a private place, except that no offence is committed where the words or behaviour are used, or the writing, sign or other visible representation is displayed, by a person inside a dwelling and the other person is also inside that or another dwelling.

(3) It is a defence for the accused to prove—

(a) that he had no reason to believe that there was any person within hearing or sight who was likely to be caused harassment, alarm or distress, or

(b) that he was inside a dwelling and had no reason to believe that the words or behaviour used, or the writing, sign or other visible representation displayed, would be heard or seen by a person outside that or any other dwelling, or

(c) that his conduct was reasonable.

(4) A constable may arrest a person without warrant if—

(a) he engages in offensive conduct which [a] constable warns him to stop, and

(b) he engages in further offensive conduct immediately or shortly after the warning.

(5) In subsection (4) "offensive conduct" means conduct the constable reasonably suspects to constitute an offence under this section, and the conduct mentioned in paragraph (a) and the further conduct need not be of the same nature.

(6) A person guilty of an offence under this section is liable on summary conviction to a fine not exceeding level 3 on the standard scale.

NOTES

Sub-s (4): word in square brackets substituted by the Public Order (Amendment) Act 1996, s 1.

6 Mental element: miscellaneous

(1) A person is guilty of riot only if he intends to use violence or is aware that his conduct may be violent.

(2) A person is guilty of violent disorder or affray only if he intends to use or threaten violence or is aware that his conduct may be violent or threaten violence.

(3) A person is guilty of an offence under section 4 only if he intends his words or behaviour, or the writing, sign or other visible representation, to be threatening, abusive or insulting, or is aware that it may be threatening, abusive or insulting.

(4) A person is guilty of an offence under section 5 only if he intends his words or behaviour, or the writing, sign or other visible representation, to be threatening, abusive or insulting, or is aware that it may be threatening, abusive or insulting or (as the case may be) he intends his behaviour to be or is aware that it may be disorderly.

(5) For the purposes of this section a person whose awareness is impaired by intoxication shall be taken to be aware of that of which he would be aware if not

intoxicated, unless he shows either that his intoxication was not self-induced or that it was caused solely by the taking or administration of a substance in the course of medical treatment.

(6) In subsection (5) "intoxication" means any intoxication, whether caused by drink, drugs or other means, or by a combination of means.

(7) Subsections (1) and (2) do not affect the determination for the purposes of riot or violent disorder of the number of persons who use or threaten violence.

7 Procedure: miscellaneous

(1) No prosecution for an offence of riot or incitement to riot may be instituted except by or with the consent of the Director of Public Prosecutions.

(2)–(4) . . .

NOTES

Sub-ss (2)–(4): outside the scope of this work.

8 Interpretation

In this Part—

"dwelling" means any structure or part of a structure occupied as a person's home or as other living accommodation (whether the occupation is separate or shared with others) but does not include any part not so occupied, and for this purpose "structure" includes a tent, caravan, vehicle, vessel or other temporary or movable structure;

"violence" means any violent conduct, so that—

(a) except in the context of affray, it includes violent conduct towards property as well as violent conduct towards persons, and

(b) it is not restricted to conduct causing or intended to cause injury or damage but includes any other violent conduct (for example, throwing at or towards a person a missile of a kind capable of causing injury which does not hit or falls short).

9 Offences abolished

(1) The common law offences of riot, rout, unlawful assembly and affray are abolished.

(2) . . .

NOTES

Sub-s (2): outside the scope of this work.

PART II
PROCESSIONS AND ASSEMBLIES

11 Advance notice of public processions

(1) Written notice shall be given in accordance with this section of any proposal to hold a public procession intended—

(a) to demonstrate support for or opposition to the views or actions of any person or body of persons,

(b) to publicise a cause or campaign, or
(c) to mark or commemorate an event,

unless it is not reasonably practicable to give any advance notice of the procession.

(2) Subsection (1) does not apply where the procession is one commonly or customarily held in the police area (or areas) in which it is proposed to be held or is a funeral procession organised by a funeral director acting in the normal course of his business.

(3) The notice must specify the date when it is intended to hold the procession, the time when it is intended to start it, its proposed route, and the name and address of the person (or of one of the persons) proposing to organise it.

(4) Notice must be delivered to a police station—
(a) in the police area in which it is proposed the procession will start, or
(b) where it is proposed the procession will start in Scotland and cross into England, in the first police area in England on the proposed route.

(5) If delivered not less than 6 clear days before the date when the procession is intended to be held, the notice may be delivered by post by the recorded delivery service; but section 7 of the Interpretation Act 1978 (under which a document sent by post is deemed to have been served when posted and to have been delivered in the ordinary course of post) does not apply.

(6) If not delivered in accordance with subsection (5), the notice must be delivered by hand not less than 6 clear days before the date when the procession is intended to be held or, if that is not reasonably practicable, as soon as delivery is reasonably practicable.

(7) Where a public procession is held, each of the persons organising it is guilty of an offence if—
(a) the requirements of this section as to notice have not been satisfied, or
(b) the date when it is held, the time when it starts, or its route, differs from the date, time or route specified in the notice.

(8) It is a defence for the accused to prove that he did not know of, and neither suspected nor had reason to suspect, the failure to satisfy the requirements or (as the case may be) the difference of date, time or route.

(9) To the extent that an alleged offence turns on a difference of date, time or route, it is a defence for the accused to prove that the difference arose from circumstances beyond his control or from something done with the agreement of a police officer or by his direction.

(10) A person guilty of an offence under subsection (7) is liable on summary conviction to a fine not exceeding level 3 on the standard scale.

12 Imposing conditions on public processions

(1) If the senior police officer, having regard to the time or place at which and the circumstances in which any public procession is being held or is intended to be held and to its route or proposed route, reasonably believes that—
(a) it may result in serious public disorder, serious damage to property or serious disruption to the life of the community, or
(b) the purpose of the persons organising it is the intimidation of others with a view to compelling them not to do an act they have a right to do, or to do an act they have a right not to do,

he may give directions imposing on the persons organising or taking part in the procession such conditions as appear to him necessary to prevent such disorder, damage, disruption or intimidation, including conditions as to the route of the procession or prohibiting it from entering any public place specified in the directions.

(2) In subsection (1) "the senior police officer" means—

(a) in relation to a procession being held, or to a procession intended to be held in a case where persons are assembling with a view to taking part in it, the most senior in rank of the police officers present at the scene, and

(b) in relation to a procession intended to be held in a case where paragraph (a) does not apply, the chief officer of police.

(3) A direction given by a chief officer of police by virtue of subsection (2)(b) shall be given in writing.

(4) A person who organises a public procession and knowingly fails to comply with a condition imposed under this section is guilty of an offence, but it is a defence for him to prove that the failure arose from circumstances beyond his control.

(5) A person who takes part in a public procession and knowingly fails to comply with a condition imposed under this section is guilty of an offence, but it is a defence for him to prove that the failure arose from circumstances beyond his control.

(6) A person who incites another to commit an offence under subsection (5) is guilty of an offence.

(7) A constable in uniform may arrest without warrant anyone he reasonably suspects is committing an offence under subsection (4), (5) or (6).

(8) A person guilty of an offence under subsection (4) is liable on summary conviction to imprisonment for a term not exceeding 3 months or a fine not exceeding level 4 on the standard scale or both.

(9) A person guilty of an offence under subsection (5) is liable on summary conviction to a fine not exceeding level 3 on the standard scale.

(10) A person guilty of an offence under subsection (6) is liable on summary conviction to imprisonment for a term not exceeding 3 months or a fine not exceeding level 4 on the standard scale or both, notwithstanding section 45(3) of the Magistrates' Courts Act 1980 (inciter liable to same penalty as incited).

(11) . . .

NOTES

Sub-s (11): outside the scope of this work.

13 Prohibiting public processions

(1) If at any time the chief officer of police reasonably believes that, because of particular circumstances existing in any district or part of a district, the powers under section 12 will not be sufficient to prevent the holding of public processions in that district or part from resulting in serious public disorder, he shall apply to the council of the district for an order prohibiting for such period not exceeding 3 months as may be specified in the application the holding of all public processions (or of any class of public procession so specified) in the district or part concerned.

(2) On receiving such an application, a council may with the consent of the Secretary of State make an order either in the terms of the application or with such modifications as may be approved by the Secretary of State.

(3) Subsection (1) does not apply in the City of London or the metropolitan police district.

(4) If at any time the Commissioner of Police for the City of London or the Commissioner of Police of the Metropolis reasonably believes that, because of particular circumstances existing in his police area or part of it, the powers under section 12 will not be sufficient to prevent the holding of public processions in that area or part from resulting in serious public disorder, he may with the consent of the Secretary of State make an order prohibiting for such period not exceeding 3 months as may be specified in the order the holding of all public processions (or of any class of public procession so specified) in the area or part concerned.

(5) An order made under this section may be revoked or varied by a subsequent order made in the same way, that is, in accordance with subsections (1) and (2) or subsection (4), as the case may be.

(6) Any order under this section shall, if not made in writing, be recorded in writing as soon as practicable after being made.

(7) A person who organises a public procession the holding of which he knows is prohibited by virtue of an order under this section is guilty of an offence.

(8) A person who takes part in a public procession the holding of which he knows is prohibited by virtue of an order under this section is guilty of an offence.

(9) A person who incites another to commit an offence under subsection (8) is guilty of an offence.

(10) A constable in uniform may arrest without warrant anyone he reasonably suspects is committing an offence under subsection (7), (8) or (9).

(11) A person guilty of an offence under subsection (7) is liable on summary conviction to imprisonment for a term not exceeding 3 months or a fine not exceeding level 4 on the standard scale or both.

(12) A person guilty of an offence under subsection (8) is liable on summary conviction to a fine not exceeding level 3 on the standard scale.

(13) A person guilty of an offence under subsection (9) is liable on summary conviction to imprisonment for a term not exceeding 3 months or a fine not exceeding level 4 on the standard scale or both, notwithstanding section 45(3) of the Magistrates' Courts Act 1980.

14 Imposing conditions on public assemblies

(1) If the senior police officer, having regard to the time or place at which and the circumstances in which any public assembly is being held or is intended to be held, reasonably believes that—

- (a) it may result in serious public disorder, serious damage to property or serious disruption to the life of the community, or
- (b) the purpose of the persons organising it is the intimidation of others with a view to compelling them not to do an act they have a right to do, or to do an act they have a right not to do,

he may give directions imposing on the persons organising or taking part in the assembly such conditions as to the place at which the assembly may be (or continue to be) held, its maximum duration, or the maximum number of persons who may constitute it, as appear to him necessary to prevent such disorder, damage, disruption or intimidation.

(2) In subsection (1) "the senior police officer" means—
- (a) in relation to an assembly being held, the most senior in rank of the police officers present at the scene, and
- (b) in relation to an assembly intended to be held, the chief officer of police.

(3) A direction given by a chief officer of police by virtue of subsection (2)(b) shall be given in writing.

(4) A person who organises a public assembly and knowingly fails to comply with a condition imposed under this section is guilty of an offence, but it is a defence for him to prove that the failure arose from circumstances beyond his control.

(5) A person who takes part in a public assembly and knowingly fails to comply with a condition imposed under this section is guilty of an offence, but it is a defence for him to prove that the failure arose from circumstances beyond his control.

(6) A person who incites another to commit an offence under subsection (5) is guilty of an offence.

(7) A constable in uniform may arrest without warrant anyone he reasonably suspects is committing an offence under subsection (4), (5) or (6).

(8) A person guilty of an offence under subsection (4) is liable on summary conviction to imprisonment for a term not exceeding 3 months or a fine not exceeding level 4 on the standard scale or both.

(9) A person guilty of an offence under subsection (5) is liable on summary conviction to a fine not exceeding level 3 on the standard scale.

(10) A person guilty of an offence under subsection (6) is liable on summary conviction to imprisonment for a term not exceeding 3 months or a fine not exceeding level 4 on the standard scale or both, notwithstanding section 45(3) of the Magistrates' Courts Act 1980.

[14A Prohibiting trespassory assemblies

(1) If at any time the chief officer of police reasonably believes that an assembly is intended to be held in any district at a place on land to which the public has no right of access or only a limited right of access and that the assembly—
- (a) is likely to be held without the permission of the occupier of the land or to conduct itself in such a way as to exceed the limits of any permission of his or the limits of the public's right of access, and
- (b) may result—
  - (i) in serious disruption to the life of the community, or
  - (ii) where the land, or a building or monument on it, is of historical, architectural, archaeological or scientific importance, in significant damage to the land, building or monument,

he may apply to the council of the district for an order prohibiting for a specified period the holding of all trespassory assemblies in the district or a part of it, as specified.

(2) On receiving such an application, a council may—
- (a) in England and Wales, with the consent of the Secretary of State make an order either in the terms of the application or with such modifications as may be approved by the Secretary of State; or
- (b) . . .

(3) Subsection (1) does not apply in the City of London or the metropolitan police district.

(4) If at any time the Commissioner of Police for the City of London or the Commissioner of Police of the Metropolis reasonably believes that an assembly is intended to be held at a place on land to which the public has no right of access or only a limited right of access in his police area and that the assembly—

- (a) is likely to be held without the permission of the occupier of the land or to conduct itself in such a way as to exceed the limits of any permission of his or the limits of the public's right of access, and
- (b) may result—
  - (i) in serious disruption to the life of the community, or
  - (ii) where the land, or a building or monument on it, is of historical, architectural, archaeological or scientific importance, in significant damage to the land, building or monument,

he may with the consent of the Secretary of State make an order prohibiting for a specified period the holding of all trespassory assemblies in the area or a part of it, as specified.

(5) An order prohibiting the holding of trespassory assemblies operates to prohibit any assembly which—

- (a) is held on land to which the public has no right of access or only a limited right of access, and
- (b) takes place in the prohibited circumstances, that is to say, without the permission of the occupier of the land or so as to exceed the limits of any permission of his or the limits of the public's right of access.

(6) No order under this section shall prohibit the holding of assemblies for a period exceeding 4 days or in an area exceeding an area represented by a circle with a radius of 5 miles from a specified centre.

(7) An order made under this section may be revoked or varied by a subsequent order made in the same way, that is, in accordance with subsection (1) and (2) or subsection (4), as the case may be.

(8) Any order under this section shall, if not made in writing, be recorded in writing as soon as practicable after being made.

(9) In this section and sections 14B and 14C—

"assembly" means an assembly of 20 or more persons;

"land" means land in the open air;

"limited", in relation to a right of access by the public to land, means that their use of it is restricted to use for a particular purpose (as in the case of a highway or road) or is subject to other restrictions;

"occupier" means—

- (a) in England and Wales, the person entitled to possession of the land by virtue of an estate or interest held by him; or
- (b) . . .

and in subsections (1) and (4) includes the person reasonably believed by the authority applying for or making the order to be the occupier;

"public" includes a section of the public; and

"specified" means specified in an order under this section.

(10), (11) . . .

NOTES

Inserted by the Criminal Justice and Public Order Act 1994, s 70.

Sub-ss (2)(b), (9)(b), (10), (11): outside the scope of this work.

[14B Offences in connection with trespassory assemblies and arrest therefor

(1) A person who organises an assembly the holding of which he knows is prohibited by an order under section 14A is guilty of an offence.

(2) A person who takes part in an assembly which he knows is prohibited by an order under section 14A is guilty of an offence.

(3) In England and Wales, a person who incites another to commit an offence under subsection (2) is guilty of an offence.

(4) A constable in uniform may arrest without a warrant anyone he reasonably suspects to be committing an offence under this section.

(5)–(8) . . .

NOTES

Inserted by the Criminal Justice and Public Order Act 1994, s 70.

Sub-ss (5)–(8): outside the scope of this work.

[14C Stopping persons from proceeding to trespassory assemblies

(1) If a constable in uniform reasonably believes from proceeding that a person is on his way to an assembly within the area to which an order under section 14A applies which the constable reasonably believes is likely to be an assembly which is prohibited by that order, he may, subject to subsection (2) below—

(a) stop that person, and
(b) direct him not to proceed in the direction of the assembly.

(2) The power conferred by subsection (1) may only be exercised within the area to which the order applies.

(3) A person who fails to comply with a direction under subsection (1) which he knows has been given to him is guilty of an offence.

(4) A constable in uniform may arrest without a warrant anyone he reasonably suspects to be committing an offence under this section.

(5) A person guilty of an offence under subsection (3) is liable on summary conviction to a fine not exceeding level 3 on the standard scale.]

NOTES

Inserted by the Criminal Justice and Public Order Act 1994, s 71.

15 Delegation

(1) The chief officer of police may delegate, to such extent and subject to such conditions as he may specify, any of his functions under sections 12 to [14A] to [an] assistant chief constable; and references in those sections to the person delegating shall be construed accordingly.

(2) Subsection (1) shall have effect in the City of London and the metropolitan police district as if "[an] assistant chief constable" read "an assistant commissioner of police".

NOTES

Sub-s (1): figure in first pair of square brackets substituted by the Criminal Justice and Public Order Act 1994, s 168(2), Sch 10, para 60; word in second pair of square brackets substituted by the Police and Magistrates' Courts Act 1994, s 44, Sch 5, Pt II, para 37.

Sub-s (2): word in square brackets substituted by the Police and Magistrates' Courts Act 1994, s 44, Sch 5, Pt II, para 37.

16 Interpretation

In this Part—

"the City of London" means the City as defined for the purposes of the Acts relating to the City of London police;

"the metropolitan police district" means that district as defined in section 76 of the London Government Act 1963;

"public assembly" means an assembly of 20 or more persons in a public place which is wholly or partly open to the air;

"public place" means—

(a) . . .

(b) any place to which at the material time the public or any section of the public has access, on payment or otherwise, as of right or by virtue of express or implied permission;

"public procession" means a procession in a public place.

NOTES

In definition of "public place", para (a) outside the scope of this work.

PART III
RACIAL HATRED

Meaning of "racial hatred"

17 Meaning of "racial hatred"

In this Part "racial hatred" means hatred against a group of persons in Great Britain defined by reference to colour, race, nationality (including citizenship) or ethnic or national origins.

Acts intended or likely to stir up racial hatred

18 Use of words or behaviour or display of written material

(1) A person who uses threatening, abusive or insulting words or behaviour, or displays any written material which is threatening, abusive or insulting, is guilty of an offence if—

(a) he intends thereby to stir up racial hatred, or

(b) having regard to all the circumstances racial hatred is likely to be stirred up thereby.

(2) An offence under this section may be committed in a public or a private place, except that no offence is committed where the words or behaviour are used, or the written material is displayed, by a person inside a dwelling and are not heard or seen except by other persons in that or another dwelling.

(3) A constable may arrest without warrant anyone he reasonably suspects is committing an offence under this section.

(4) In proceedings for an offence under this section it is a defence for the accused to prove that he was inside a dwelling and had no reason to believe that the words or behaviour used, or the written material displayed, would be heard or seen by a person outside that or any other dwelling.

(5) A person who is not shown to have intended to stir up racial hatred is not guilty of an offence under this section if he did not intend his words or behaviour, or the written material, to be, and was not aware that it might be, threatening, abusive or insulting.

(6) This section does not apply to words or behaviour used, or written material displayed, solely for the purpose of being included in a programme [included in a programme service].

NOTES

Sub-s (6): words in square brackets substituted by the Broadcasting Act 1990, s 164(1), (2)(a).

19 Publishing or distributing written material

(1) A person who publishes or distributes written material which is threatening, abusive or insulting is guilty of an offence if—

(a) he intends thereby to stir up racial hatred, or

(b) having regard to all the circumstances racial hatred is likely to be stirred up thereby.

(2) In proceedings for an offence under this section it is a defence for an accused who is not shown to have intended to stir up racial hatred to prove that he was not aware of the content of the material and did not suspect, and had no reason to suspect, that it was threatening, abusive or insulting.

(3) References in this Part to the publication or distribution of written material are to its publication or distribution to the public or a section of the public.

20 Public performance of play

(1) If a public performance of a play is given which involves the use of threatening, abusive or insulting words or behaviour, any person who presents or directs the performance is guilty of an offence if—

(a) he intends thereby to stir up racial hatred, or

(b) having regard to all the circumstances (and, in particular, taking the performance as a whole) racial hatred is likely to be stirred up thereby.

(2) If a person presenting or directing the performance is not shown to have intended to stir up racial hatred, it is a defence for him to prove—

(a) that he did not know and had no reason to suspect that the performance would involve the use of the offending words or behaviour, or

(b) that he did not know and had no reason to suspect that the offending words or behaviour were threatening, abusive or insulting, or

(c) that he did not know and had no reason to suspect that the circumstances in which the performance would be given would be such that racial hatred would be likely to be stirred up.

(3)–(6) . . .

NOTES

Sub-ss (3)–(6): outside the scope of this work.

21 Distributing, showing or playing a recording

(1) A person who distributes, or shows or plays, a recording of visual images or sounds which are threatening, abusive or insulting is guilty of an offence if—

(a) he intends thereby to stir up racial hatred, or

(b) having regard to all the circumstances racial hatred is likely to be stirred up thereby.

(2) In this Part "recording" means any record from which visual images or sounds may, by any means, be reproduced; and references to the distribution, showing or playing of a recording are to its distribution, showing or playing to the public or a section of the public.

(3) In proceedings for an offence under this section it is a defence for an accused who is not shown to have intended to stir up racial hatred to prove that he was not aware of the content of the recording and did not suspect, and had no reason to suspect, that it was threatening, abusive or insulting.

(4) This section does not apply to the showing or playing of a recording solely for the purpose of enabling the recording to be [included in a programme service].

NOTES

Sub-s (4): words in square brackets substituted by the Broadcasting Act 1990, s 164(1), (2)(c).

22 Broadcasting or including programme in cable programme service

(1) If a programme involving threatening, abusive or insulting visual images or sounds is [included in a programme service], each of the persons mentioned in subsection (2) is guilty of an offence if—

(a) he intends thereby to stir up racial hatred, or

(b) having regard to all the circumstances racial hatred is likely to be stirred up thereby.

(2) The persons are—

(a) the person providing the . . . programme service,

(b) any person by whom the programme is produced or directed, and

(c) any person by whom offending words or behaviour are used.

(3) If the person providing the service, or a person by whom the programme was produced or directed, is not shown to have intended to stir up racial hatred, it is a defence for him to prove that—

(a) he did not know and had no reason to suspect that the programme would involve the offending material, and

(b) having regard to the circumstances in which the programme was [included in a programme service], it was not reasonably practicable for him to secure the removal of the material.

(4), (5) . . .

(6) A person who is not shown to have intended to stir up racial hatred is not guilty of an offence under this section if he did not know, and had no reason to suspect, that the offending material was threatening, abusive or insulting.

(7), (8) . . .

NOTES

Sub-s (1): words in square brackets substituted by the Broadcasting Act 1990, s 164(1), (3)(a).

Sub-s (2): words omitted from para (a) repealed by the Broadcasting Act 1990, ss 164(1), (3)(b)(i), 203(3), Sch 21.

Sub-s (3): words in square brackets in para (b) substituted by the Broadcasting Act 1990, s 164(1), (3)(a).

Sub-ss (4), (5): outside the scope of this work.

Sub-s (7): repealed by the Broadcasting Act 1990, ss 164(1), (3)(b)(iii), 203(3), Sch 21.

Sub-s (8): repealed by the Broadcasting Act 1990, ss 164(1), (3)(b)(iv), 203(3), Sch 21.

Racially inflammatory material

23 Possession of racially inflammatory material

(1) A person who has in his possession written material which is threatening, abusive or insulting, or a recording of visual images or sounds which are threatening, abusive or insulting, with a view to—

(a) in the case of written material, its being displayed, published, distributed, [or included in a programme service], whether by himself or another, or

(b) in the case of a recording, its being distributed, shown, played, [or included in a programme service], whether by himself or another,

is guilty of an offence if he intends racial hatred to be stirred up thereby or, having regard to all the circumstances, racial hatred is likely to be stirred up thereby.

(2) For this purpose regard shall be had to such display, publication, distribution, showing, playing, [or inclusion in a programme service] as he has, or it may reasonably be inferred that he has, in view.

(3) In proceedings for an offence under this section it is a defence for an accused who is not shown to have intended to stir up racial hatred to prove that he was not aware of the content of the written material or recording and did not suspect, and had no reason to suspect, that it was threatening, abusive or insulting.

(4) . . .

NOTES

Sub-s (1): words in square brackets substituted by the Broadcasting Act 1990, s 164(1), (4)(a),

Sub-s (2): words in square brackets substituted by the Broadcasting Act 1990, s 164(1), (4)(b).

Sub-s (4): repealed by the Broadcasting Act 1990, ss 164(1), (4)(c), 203(3), Sch 21.

24 Powers of entry and search

(1) If in England and Wales a justice of the peace is satisfied by information on oath laid by a constable that there are reasonable grounds for suspecting that a person has possession of written material or a recording in contravention of section 23, the justice may issue a warrant under his hand authorising any constable to enter and search the premises where it is suspected the material or recording is situated.

(2) . . .

(3) A constable entering or searching premises in pursuance of a warrant issued under this section may use reasonable force if necessary.

(4) . . .

NOTES

Sub-ss (2), (4): outside the scope of this work.

Supplementary provisions

26 Savings for reports of parliamentary or judicial proceedings

(1) Nothing in this Part applies to a fair and accurate report of proceedings in Parliament.

(2) Nothing in this Part applies to a fair and accurate report of proceedings publicly heard before a court or tribunal exercising judicial authority where the report is published contemporaneously with the proceedings or, if it is not reasonably practicable or would be unlawful to publish a report of them contemporaneously, as soon as publication is reasonably practicable and lawful.

27 Procedure and punishment

(1) No proceedings for an offence under this Part may be instituted in England and Wales except by or with the consent of the Attorney General.

(2) For the purposes of the rules in England and Wales against charging more than one offence in the same count or information, each of sections 18 to 23 creates one offence.

(3) A person guilty of an offence under this Part is liable—

(a) on conviction on indictment to imprisonment for a term not exceeding two years or a fine or both;

(b) on summary conviction to imprisonment for a term not exceeding six months or a fine not exceeding the statutory maximum or both.

PART V
MISCELLANEOUS AND GENERAL

40 Amendments, repeals and savings

(1) Schedule 1, which amends the Sporting Events (Control of Alcohol etc) Act 1985 and Part V of the Criminal Justice (Scotland) Act 1980, shall have effect.

(2)–(5) . . .

NOTES

Sub-ss (2)–(5): outside the scope of this work.

41 Commencement

(1) This Act shall come into force on such day as the Secretary of State may appoint by order made by statutory instrument, and different days may be appointed for different provisions or different purposes.

(2) Nothing in a provision of this Act applies in relation to an offence committed or act done before the provision comes into force.

(3) Where a provision of this Act comes into force for certain purposes only, the references in subsection (2) to the provision are references to it so far as it relates to those purposes.

42 Extent

(1) The provisions of this Act extend to England and Wales except so far as they—
(a) amend or repeal an enactment which does not so extend, or
(b) relate to the extent of provisions to Scotland or Northern Ireland.

(2) . . .

(3) The following provisions of this Act extend to Northern Ireland—
sections 38, 41, this subsection, [and section 43].

NOTES

Sub-s (2): outside the scope of this work.

Sub-s (3): words in square brackets substituted by the Public Order (Northern Ireland) Order 1987, SI 1987/463, art 28(1), Sch 1, para 6.

43 Short title

This Act may be cited as the Public Order Act 1986.

EDUCATION (NO 2) ACT 1986

(C 61)

An Act to amend the law relating to education [7 November 1986]

PART IV
MISCELLANEOUS

43 Freedom of speech in universities, polytechnics and colleges

(1) Every individual and body of persons concerned in the government of any establishment to which this section applies shall take such steps as are reasonably practicable to ensure that freedom of speech within the law is secured for members, students and employees of the establishment and for visiting speakers.

(2) The duty imposed by subsection (1) above includes (in particular) the duty to ensure, so far as is reasonably practicable, that the use of any premises of the establishment is not denied to any individual or body of persons on any ground connected with—
(a) the beliefs or views of that individual or of any member of that body; or
(b) the policy or objectives of that body.

(3) The governing body of every such establishment shall, with a view to facilitating the discharge of the duty imposed by subsection (1) above in relation to that establishment, issue and keep up to date a code of practice setting out—
(a) the procedures to be followed by members, students and employees of the establishment in connection with the organisation—
(i) of meetings which are to be held on premises of the establishment and which fall within any class of meeting specified in the code; and

(ii) of other activities which are to take place on those premises and which fall within any class of activity so specified; and

(b) the conduct required of such persons in connection with any such meeting or activity;

and dealing with such other matters as the governing body consider appropriate.

(4) Every individual and body of persons concerned in the government of any such establishment shall take such steps as are reasonably practicable (including where appropriate the initiation of disciplinary measures) to secure that the requirements of the code of practice for that establishment, issued under subsection (3) above, are complied with.

(5) The establishments to which this section applies are—

(a) any university;

[(aa) any institution other than a university within the higher education sector;]

[(b) any establishment of higher or further education which is maintained by a local education authority;] and

[(ba) any institution within the further education sector]

(c) . . .

(6) . . .

(7) Where any establishment—

(a) falls within subsection (5)(b) above; or

(b) . . . ;

the local education authority . . . shall, for the purposes of this section, be taken to be concerned in its government.

(8) Where a students' union occupies premises which are not premises of the establishment in connection with which the union is constituted, any reference in this section to the premises of the establishment shall be taken to include a reference to the premises occupied by the students' union.

NOTES

Sub-s (5): para (aa) substituted, para (ba) inserted, and para (c) omitted, by the Further and Higher Education Act 1992, s 93, Sch 8, Pt I, para 22(a); para (b) substituted by the Education Reform Act 1988, s 237(1), Sch 12, Pt III, para 100(1), (3).

Sub-s (6): outside the scope of this work.

Sub-s (7): para (b) and other words omitted repealed by the Further and Higher Education Act 1992, s 93, Sch 8, Pt I, para 22(b).

PART V
SUPPLEMENTAL

67 Short title etc

(1) This Act may be cited as the Education (No 2) Act 1986.

(2) . . .

(3) This Act shall be construed as one with [the Education Act 1996].

(4)–(6) . . .

(7) [In this Act section 48 and this section extend to Scotland,] but otherwise this Act extends only to England and Wales.

NOTES

Sub-ss (2), (5), (6): repealed by the Education Act 1996, s 582(1), (2), Sch 37, Pt I, para 66(1), (2), Sch 38, Pt I.

Sub-s (3): words in square brackets substituted by the Education Act 1996, s 582(1), Sch 37, Pt I, para 66(1), (3), Sch 38, Pt I.

Sub-s (4): outside the scope of this work.

Sub-s (7): words in square brackets substituted by the Education Act 1996, s 582(1), Sch 37, Pt I, para 66(1), (4), Sch 38, Pt I.

IMMIGRATION (CARRIERS' LIABLITY) ACT 1987

(C 24)

An Act to require carriers to make payments to the Secretary of State in respect of passengers brought by them to the United Kingdom without proper documents

[15 May 1987]

1 Liability of carriers for passengers without proper documents

(1) Where a person requiring leave to enter the United Kingdom arrives in the United Kingdom by ship or aircraft and, on being required to do so by an immigration officer, fails to produce—

(a) either a valid passport with photograph or some other document satisfactorily establishing his identity and nationality or citizenship; and

(b) if he is a person who under the immigration rules requires a visa for entry into the United Kingdom [or by virtue of section 1A below requires a visa for passing through the United Kingdom, a visa valid for the purpose of entering or (as the case may be) passing through the United Kingdom,]

the owners or agents of the ship or aircraft shall, in respect of that person, be liable to pay the Secretary of State on demand the sum of [£2,000] or such other sum as may be prescribed.

(2) No liability shall be incurred under subsection (1) above in respect of any person who is shown by the owners or agents to have produced to them or an employee of theirs the document or documents specified in that subsection when embarking on the ship or aircraft for the voyage or flight to the United Kingdom.

(3) In subsection (1) above "prescribed" means prescribed by an order made by the Secretary of State by statutory instrument subject to annulment in pursuance of a resolution of either House of Parliament.

(4), (5) . . .

NOTES

Sub-s (1): words in square brackets in para (b) substituted by the Asylum and Immigration Appeals Act 1993, s 12(1), (2); sum in square brackets substituted by virtue of the Immigration (Carriers' Liability Prescribed Sum) Order 1991, SI 1991/1497, art 2.

Sub-ss (4), (5): outside the scope of this work.

[1A Visas for transit passengers]

[(1) The Secretary of State may by order require persons of any description specified in the order who on arrival in the United Kingdom pass through to another country or territory without entering the United Kingdom to hold a visa for that purpose.

(2) An order under this section—
- (a) may specify a description of persons by reference to nationality, citizenship, origin or other connection with any particular country or territory, but not by reference to race, colour or religion;
- (b) shall not provide for the requirement imposed by the order to apply to any person who under the Immigration Act 1971 has the right of abode in the United Kingdom and may provide for any category of persons of a description specified in the order to be exempted from the requirement imposed by the order; and
- (c) may make provision about the method of application for visas required by the order.

(3) An order under this section shall be made by statutory instrument which shall be subject to annulment in pursuance of a resolution of either House of Parliament.]

NOTES

Inserted by the Asylum and Immigration Appeals Act 1993, s 12(1), (3).

2 Short title, interpretation, extent and commencement

(1) This Act may be cited as the Immigration (Carriers' Liability) Act 1987.

(2) In this Act any expression which is also used in the Immigration Act 1971 has the same meaning as in that Act.

(3) This Act extends to Northern Ireland; . . .

(4) This Act has effect in relation to persons arriving in the United Kingdom at any time after 4th March 1987 except persons arriving by a voyage or flight for which they embarked on the ship or aircraft in question on or before that date.

NOTES

Sub-s (3): words omitted outside the scope of this work.

IMMIGRATION ACT 1988

(C 14)

An Act to make further provision for the regulation of immigration into the United Kingdom; and for connected purposes

[10 May 1988]

2 Restriction on exercise of right of abode in cases of polygamy

(1) This section applies to any woman who—
- (a) has the right of abode in the United Kingdom under section 2(1)(b) of the principal Act as, or as having been, the wife of a man ("the husband")—
  - (i) to whom she is or was polygamously married; and

(ii) who is or was such a citizen of the United Kingdom and Colonies, Commonwealth citizen or British subject as is mentioned in section 2(2)(a) or (b) of that Act as in force immediately before the commencement of the British Nationality Act 1981; and

(b) has not before the coming into force of this section and since her marriage to the husband been in the United Kingdom.

(2) A woman to whom this section applies shall not be entitled to enter the United Kingdom in the exercise of the right of abode mentioned in subsection (1)(a) above or to be granted a certificate of entitlement in respect of that right if there is another woman living (whether or not one to whom this section applies) who is the wife or widow of the husband and who—

(a) is, or at any time since her marriage to the husband has been, in the United Kingdom; or

(b) has been granted a certificate of entitlement in respect of the right of abode mentioned in subsection (1)(a) above or an entry clearance to enter the United Kingdom as the wife of the husband.

(3)–(10) . . .

NOTES

Commencement: 1 August 1988, subject to exception set out in the Immigration Act 1988 (Commencement No 1) Order 1988, SI 1988/1133, art 3(1).

Sub-ss (3)–(10): outside the scope of this work.

7 Persons exercising Community rights and nationals of member States

(1) A person shall not under the principal Act require leave to enter or remain in the United Kingdom in any case in which he is entitled to do so by virtue of an enforceable Community right or of any provision made under section 2(2) of the European Communities Act 1972.

(2) The Secretary of State may by order made by statutory instrument give leave to enter the United Kingdom for a limited period to any class of persons who are nationals of member States but who are not entitled to enter the United Kingdom as mentioned in subsection (1) above; and any such order may give leave subject to such conditions as may be imposed by the order.

(3) References in the principal Act to limited leave shall include references to leave given by an order under subsection (2) above and a person having leave by virtue of such an order shall be treated as having been given that leave by a notice given to him by an immigration officer within the period specified in paragraph 6(1) of Schedule 2 to that Act.

NOTES

Commencement: 10 July 1988 (sub-ss (2), (3)); 20 July 1994 (sub-s (1)).

12 Short title, interpretation, commencement and extent

(1) This Act may be cited as the Immigration Act 1988.

(2) In this Act "the principal Act" means the Immigration Act 1971 and any expression which is also used in that Act has the same meaning as in that Act.

(3) Except as provided in subsection (4) below this Act shall come into force at the end of the period of two months beginning with the day on which it is passed.

(4) . . .

(5) This Act extends to Northern Ireland . . .

NOTES

Commencement: 10 July 1988.

Sub-s (4), and words omitted from sub-s (5): outside the scope of this work.

CRIMINAL JUSTICE ACT 1988

(C 33)

An Act to make fresh provision for extradition; to amend the rules of evidence in criminal proceedings; to provide for the reference by the Attorney General of certain questions relating to sentencing to the Court of Appeal; to amend the law with regard to the jurisdiction and powers of criminal courts, the collection, enforcement and remission of fines imposed by coroners, juries, supervision orders, the detention of children and young persons, probation and the probation service, criminal appeals, anonymity in cases of rape and similar cases, orders under sections 4 and 11 of the Contempt of Court Act 1981 relating to trials on indictment, orders restricting the access of the public to the whole or any part of a trial on indictment or to any proceedings ancillary to such a trial and orders restricting the publication of any report of the whole or any part of a trial on indictment or any such ancillary proceedings, the alteration of names of petty sessions areas, officers of inner London magistrates' courts and the costs and expenses of prosecution witnesses and certain other persons; to make fresh provision for the payment of compensation by the Criminal Injuries Compensation Board; to make provision for the payment of compensation for a miscarriage of justice which has resulted in a wrongful conviction; to create an offence of torture and an offence of having an article with a blade or point in a public place; to create further offences relating to weapons; to create a summary offence of possession of an indecent photograph of a child; to amend the Police and Criminal Evidence Act 1984 in relation to searches, computer data about fingerprints and bail for persons in customs detention; to make provision in relation to the taking of body samples by the police in Northern Ireland; to amend the Bail Act 1976; to give a justice of the peace power to authorise entry and search of premises for offensive weapons; to provide for the enforcement of the Video Recordings Act 1984 by officers of a weights and measures authority and in Northern Ireland by officers of the Department of Economic Development; to extend to the purchase of easements and other rights over land the power to purchase land conferred on the Secretary of State by section 36 of the Prison Act 1952; and for connected purposes

[29 July 1988]

PART XI
MISCELLANEOUS

Miscarriages of justice

133 Compensation for miscarriages of justice

(1) Subject to subsection (2) below, when a person has been convicted of a criminal offence and when subsequently his conviction has been reversed or he has been pardoned on the ground that a new or newly discovered fact shows beyond reasonable doubt that there has been a miscarriage of justice, the Secretary of State shall pay compensation for the miscarriage of justice to the person who has suffered punishment as a result of such conviction or, if he is dead, to his personal

representatives, unless the non-disclosure of the unknown fact was wholly or partly attributable to the person convicted.

(2) No payment of compensation under this section shall be made unless an application for such compensation has been made to the Secretary of State.

(3) The question whether there is a right to compensation under this section shall be determined by the Secretary of State.

(4) If the Secretary of State determines that there is a right to such compensation, the amount of the compensation shall be assessed by an assessor appointed by the Secretary of State.

[(4A) In assessing so much of any compensation payable under this section to or in respect of a person as is attributable to suffering, harm to reputation or similar damage, the assessor shall have regard in particular to—

(a) the seriousness of the offence of which the person was convicted and the severity of the punishment resulting from the conviction;

(b) the conduct of the investigation and prosecution of the offence; and

(c) any other convictions of the person and any punishment resulting from them.]

(5)–(7) . . .

NOTES

Sub-s (4A): inserted by the Criminal Appeal Act 1995, s 28.

Sub-ss (5)–(7): outside the scope of this work.

Torture

134 Torture

(1) A public official or person acting in an official capacity, whatever his nationality, commits the offence of torture if in the United Kingdom or elsewhere he intentionally inflicts severe pain or suffering on another in the performance or purported performance of his official duties.

(2) A person not falling within subsection (1) above commits the offence of torture, whatever his nationality, if—

(a) in the United Kingdom or elsewhere he intentionally inflicts severe pain or suffering on another at the instigation or with the consent or acquiescence—

(i) of a public official; or

(ii) of a person acting in an official capacity; and

(b) the official or other person is performing or purporting to perform his official duties when he instigates the commission of the offence or consents to or acquiesces in it.

(3) It is immaterial whether the pain or suffering is physical or mental and whether it is caused by an act or an omission.

(4) It shall be a defence for a person charged with an offence under this section in respect of any conduct of his to prove that he had lawful authority, justification or excuse for that conduct.

(5) . . .

(6) A person who commits the offence of torture shall be liable on conviction on indictment to imprisonment for life.

NOTES

Sub-s (5): outside the scope of this work.

135 Requirement of Attorney General's consent for prosecutions

Proceedings for an offence under section 134 above shall not be begun—

(a) in England and Wales, except by, or with the consent of, the Attorney General; or

(b) in Northern Ireland, except by, or with the consent of, the Attorney General for Northern Ireland.

Articles with blades or points and offensive weapons

142 Power of justice of the peace to authorise entry and search of premises for offensive weapons

(1) If on an application made by a constable a justice of the peace (including, in Scotland, the sheriff) is satisfied that there are reasonable grounds for believing—

(a) that there are on premises specified in the application—

(i) knives such as are mentioned in section 1(1) of the Restriction of Offensive Weapons Act 1959; or

(ii) weapons to which section 141 above applies; and

(b) that an offence under section 1 of the Restriction of Offensive Weapons Act 1959 or section 141 above has been or is being committed in relation to them; and

(c) that any of the conditions specified in subsection (3) below applies,

he may issue a warrant authorising a constable to enter and search the premises.

(2) A constable may seize and retain anything for which a search has been authorised under subsection (1) above.

(3) The conditions mentioned in subsection (1)(b) above are—

(a) that it is not practicable to communicate with any person entitled to grant entry to the premises;

(b) that it is practicable to communicate with a person entitled to grant entry to the premises but it is not practicable to communicate with any person entitled to grant access to the knives or weapons to which the application relates;

(c) that entry to the premises will not be granted unless a warrant is produced;

(d) that the purpose of a search may be frustrated or seriously prejudiced unless a constable arriving at the premises can secure immediate entry to them.

(4) Subsection (1)(a)(i) shall be omitted in the application of this section to Northern Ireland.

Reports of criminal proceedings

159 Crown Court proceedings—orders restricting or preventing reports or restricting public access

(1) A person aggrieved may appeal to the Court of Appeal, if that court grants leave, against—

(a) an order under section 4 or 11 of the Contempt of Court Act 1981 made in relation to a trial on indictment;

[(aa) an order made by the Crown Court under section 58(7) or (8) of the Criminal Procedure and Investigations Act 1996 in a case where the Court has convicted a person on a trial on indictment;]

(b) any order restricting the access of the public to the whole or any part of a trial on indictment or to any proceedings ancillary to such a trial; and

(c) any order restricting the publication of any report of the whole or any part of a trial on indictment or any such ancillary proceedings;

and the decision of the Court of Appeal shall be final.

(2) Subject to Rules of Court, the jurisdiction of the Court of Appeal under this section shall be exercised by the criminal division of the Court, and references to the Court of Appeal in this section shall be construed as references to that division.

(3)–(7) . . .

NOTES

Sub-s (1): para (aa) inserted by the Criminal Procedure and Investigations Act 1996, s 61(6), in relation to offences committed on or after 1 April 1997.

Sub-ss (3)–(7): outside the scope of this work.

Possession of indecent photograph of child

160 Summary offence of possession of indecent photograph of child

(1) It is an offence for a person to have any indecent photograph [or pseudo-photograph] of a child . . . in his possession.

(2) Where a person is charged with an offence under subsection (1) above, it shall be a defence for him to prove—

(a) that he had a legitimate reason for having the photograph [or pseudo-photograph] in his possession; or

(b) that he had not himself seen the photograph [or pseudo-photograph] and did not know, nor had any cause to suspect, it to be indecent; or

(c) that the photograph [or pseudo-photograph] was sent to him without any prior request made by him or on his behalf and that he did not keep it for an unreasonable time.

(3) A person shall be liable on summary conviction of an offence under this section to [imprisonment for a term not exceeding six months or] a fine not exceeding level 5 on the standard scale[, or both].

(4) Sections 1(3), 2(3), 3 and 7 of the Protection of Children Act 1978 shall have effect as if any reference in them to that Act included a reference to this section.

(5) . . .

NOTES

Sub-s (1): words in square brackets inserted, and words omitted repealed, by the Criminal Justice and Public Order Act 1994, ss 84(4)(a), 168(3), Sch 11.

Sub-s (2): words in square brackets in paras (a), (b), (c) inserted by the Criminal Justice and Public Order Act 1994, s 84(4)(b).

Sub-s (3): words in both pairs of square brackets inserted the Criminal Justice and Public Order Act 1994, s 86(1).

Sub-s (5): repealed by the Criminal Justice and Public Order Act 1994, s 168(3), Sch 11.

PART XII
GENERAL AND SUPPLEMENTARY

171 Commencement

(1) Subject to the following provisions of this section, this Act shall come into force on such day as the Secretary of State may by order made by statutory instrument appoint and different days may be appointed in pursuance of this subsection for different provisions or different purposes of the same provision.

(2), (3), (4) . . .

(5) The following provisions shall come into force on the day this Act is passed—

. . .
section 142;
. . .
sections 172 and 173.

(6) The following provisions—

. . .
section 134;
section 135;
. . .
sections 160 and 161;
. . .

shall come into force at the end of the period of two months beginning with the day this Act is passed.

(7) . . .

NOTES

Sub-ss (2), (7): outside the scope of this work.
Sub-ss (3), (4): repealed by the Criminal Injuries Compensation Act 1995, s 12(7), Schedule.
Sub-ss (5), (6): words omitted outside the scope of this work.

172 Extent

(1) Subject to the following provisions of this section, and to sections 19, 20 and 21 above, this Act extends to England and Wales only.

(2) . . .

(3) The following provisions extend also to Northern Ireland—

. . .
section 134;
section 135;
. . .
section 141;
section 142;
. . .
section 152;
section 159;
. . .
section 171;

this section; and
section 173.

(4)–(12) . . .

NOTES
Sub-ss (2), (4)–(12): outside the scope of this work.
Sub-s (3): words omitted outside the scope of this work.

173 Citation

This Act may be cited as the Criminal Justice Act 1988.

COPYRIGHT, DESIGNS AND PATENTS ACT 1988

(C 48)

An Act to restate the law of copyright, with amendments; to make fresh provision as to the rights of performers and others in performances; to confer a design right in original designs; to amend the Registered Designs Act 1949; to make provision with respect to patent agents and trade mark agents; to confer patents and designs jurisdiction on certain county courts; to amend the law of patents; to make provision with respect to devices designed to circumvent copy-protection of works in electronic form; to make fresh provision penalising the fraudulent reception of transmissions; to make the fraudulent application or use of a trade mark an offence; to make provision for the benefit of the Hospital for Sick Children, Great Ormond Street, London; to enable financial assistance to be given to certain international bodies; and for connected purposes

[15 November 1988]

PART I
COPYRIGHT

CHAPTER III
ACTS PERMITTED IN RELATION TO COPYRIGHT WORKS

Public administration

45 Parliamentary and judicial proceedings

(1) Copyright is not infringed by anything done for the purposes of parliamentary or judicial proceedings.

(2) Copyright is not infringed by anything done for the purposes of reporting such proceedings; but this shall not be construed as authorising the copying of a work which is itself a published report of the proceedings.

49 Public records

Material which is comprised in public records within the meaning of the Public Records Act 1958, the Public Records (Scotland) Act 1937 or the Public Records Act (Northern Ireland) 1923 which are open to public inspection in pursuance of that Act, may be copied, and a copy may be supplied to any person, by or with the authority of any officer appointed under that Act, without infringement of copyright.

CHAPTER IX
QUALIFICATION FOR AND EXTENT OF COPYRIGHT PROTECTION

Extent and application of this Part

157 Countries to which this Part extends

(1) This Part extends to England and Wales, Scotland and Northern Ireland.

(2)–(5) . . .

NOTES
Sub-ss (2)–(5): outside the scope of this work.

CHAPTER X
MISCELLANEOUS AND GENERAL

Crown and Parliamentary copyright

166 Copyright in Parliamentary Bills

(1) Copyright in every Bill introduced into Parliament belongs, in accordance with the following provisions, to one or both of the Houses of Parliament.

(2) Copyright in a public Bill belongs in the first instance to the House into which the Bill is introduced, and after the Bill has been carried to the second House to both Houses jointly, and subsists from the time when the text of the Bill is handed in to the House in which it is introduced.

(3) Copyright in a private Bill belongs to both Houses jointly and subsists from the time when a copy of the Bill is first deposited in either House.

(4) Copyright in a personal Bill belongs in the first instance to the House of Lords, and after the Bill has been carried to the House of Commons to both Houses jointly, and subsists from the time when it is given a First Reading in the House of Lords.

(5) Copyright under this section ceases—
- (a) on Royal Assent, or
- (b) if the Bill does not receive Royal Assent, on the withdrawal or rejection of the Bill or the end of the Session:

Provided that, copyright in a Bill continues to subsist notwithstanding its rejection in any Session by the House of Lords if, by virtue of the Parliament Acts 1911 and 1949, it remains possible for it to be presented for Royal Assent in that Session.

(6), (7) . . .

NOTES
Sub-ss (6), (7): outside the scope of this work.

PART VII
MISCELLANEOUS AND GENERAL

General

306 Short title

This Act may be cited as the Copyright, Designs and Patents Act 1988.

ROAD TRAFFIC ACT 1988

(C 52)

An Act to consolidate certain enactments relating to road traffic with amendments to give effect to recommendations of the Law Commission and the Scottish Law Commission

[15 November 1988]

PART VII
MISCELLANEOUS AND GENERAL

Powers of constables and other authorised persons

163 Power of police to stop vehicles

(1) A person driving a [mechanically propelled vehicle] on a road must stop the vehicle on being required to do so by a constable in uniform.

(2) A person riding a cycle on a road must stop the cycle on being required to do so by a constable in uniform.

(3) If a person fails to comply with this section he is guilty of an offence.

NOTES

Sub-s (1): words in square brackets substituted by the Road Traffic Act 1991, s 48, Sch 4, para 67.

164 Power of constables to require production of driving licence and in certain cases statement of date of birth

(1) Any of the following persons—

(a) a person driving a motor vehicle on a road,

(b) a person whom a constable [or vehicle examiner] has reasonable cause to believe to have been the driver of a motor vehicle at a time when an accident occurred owing to its presence on a road,

(c) a person whom a constable [or vehicle examiner] has reasonable cause to believe to have committed an offence in relation to the use of a motor vehicle on a road, or

(d) a person—

(i) who supervises the holder of a provisional licence while the holder is driving a motor vehicle on a road, or

(ii) whom a constable [or vehicle examiner] has reasonable cause to believe was supervising the holder of a provisional licence while driving, at a time when an accident occurred owing to the presence of the vehicle on a road or at a time when an offence is suspected of having been committed by the holder of the provisional licence in relation to the use of the vehicle on a road,

must, on being so required by a constable [or vehicle examiner], produce his licence [and its counterpart] for examination, so as to enable the constable [or vehicle examiner] to ascertain the name and address of the holder of the licence, the date of issue, and the authority by which [they were] issued.

(2) [A person required by a constable under subsection (1) above to produce his licence] must in prescribed circumstances, on being so required by the constable, state his date of birth.

(3)–(11) . . .

NOTES

Sub-s (1): words "or vehicle examiner" wherever it occurs inserted by the Road Traffic Act 1991, s 48, Sch 4, para 68(1), (2); words "and its counterpart" inserted, and words "they were", substituted, by the Driving Licences (Community Driving Licence) Regulations 1990, SI 1990/144, regs 2(1), 3, Sch 1, para 9(a), in relation to licences which came into force after 31 May 1990.

Sub-s (2): words in square brackets substituted by the Road Traffic Act 1991, s 48, Sch 4, para 68(1), (3).

Sub-ss (3)–(11): outside the scope of this work.

165 Power of constables to obtain names and addresses of drivers and others, and to require production of evidence of insurance or security and test certificates

(1) Any of the following persons—

(a) a person driving a motor vehicle (other than an invalid carriage) on a road, or

(b) a person whom a constable [or vehicle examiner] has reasonable cause to believe to have been the driver of a motor vehicle (other than an invalid carriage) at a time when an accident occurred owing to its presence on a road, or

(c) a person whom a constable [or vehicle examiner] has reasonable cause to believe to have committed an offence in relation to the use on a road of a motor vehicle (other than an invalid carriage),

must, on being so required by a constable [or vehicle examiner], give his name and address and the name and address of the owner of the vehicle and produce the following documents for examination.

(2) Those documents are—

(a) the relevant certificate of insurance or certificate of security (within the meaning of Part VI of this Act), or such other evidence that the vehicle is not or was not being driven in contravention of section 143 of this Act as may be prescribed by regulations made by the Secretary of State,

(b) in relation to a vehicle to which section 47 of this Act applies, a test certificate issued in respect of the vehicle as mentioned in subsection (1) of that section, and

(c) in relation to a goods vehicle the use of which on a road without a plating certificate or goods vehicle test certificate is an offence under section 53(1) or (2) of this Act, any such certificate issued in respect of that vehicle or any trailer drawn by it.

(3) Subject to subsection (4) below, a person who fails to comply with a requirement under subsection (1) above is guilty of an offence.

(4) A person shall not be convicted of an offence under [subsection (3)] above by reason only of failure to produce any certificate or other evidence . . . if in proceedings against him for the offence he shows that—

(a) within seven days after the date on which the production of the certificate or other evidence was required it was produced at a police station that was specified by him at the time when its production was required, or

(b) it was produced there as soon as was reasonably practicable, or

(c) it was not reasonably practicable for it to be produced there before the day on which the proceedings were commenced,

and for the purposes of this subsection the laying of the information or, in Scotland, the service of the complaint on the accused shall be treated as the commencement of the proceedings.

(5)–(7) . . .

NOTES

Sub-s (1): words in square brackets inserted by the Road Traffic Act 1991, s 48, Sch 4, para 69(1), (2).

Sub-s (4): words in square brackets substituted by the Road Traffic (Driver Licensing and Information Systems) Act 1989, s 7, Sch 3, para 19.

Sub-ss (5)–(7): outside the scope of this work.

Duty to give name and address

168 Failure to give, or giving false, name and address in case of reckless or careless or inconsiderate driving or cycling

Any of the following persons—

(a) the driver of a [mechanically propelled vehicle] who is alleged to have committed an offence under section 2 or 3 of this Act, or

(b) the rider of a cycle who is alleged to have committed an offence under section 28 or 29 of this Act,

who refuses, on being so required by any person having reasonable ground for so requiring, to give his name or address, or gives a false name or address, is guilty of an offence.

NOTES

Words in square brackets in para (a) substituted by the Road Traffic Act 1991, s 48, Sch 4, para 71.

Supplementary

197 Short title, commencement and extent

(1) This Act may be cited as the Road Traffic Act 1988.

(2) This Act shall come into force, subject to the transitory provisions in Schedule 5 to the Road Traffic (Consequential Provisions) Act 1988, at the end of the period of six months beginning with the day on which it is passed.

(3) This Act, except section 80 and except as provided by section 184, does not extend to Northern Ireland.

ELECTED AUTHORITIES (NORTHERN IRELAND) ACT 1989

(C 3)

An Act to amend the law relating to the franchise at elections to district councils in Northern Ireland, to make provision in relation to a declaration against terrorism to be made by candidates at such elections and at elections to the Northern Ireland Assembly and by persons co-opted as members of district councils, to amend sections 3 and 4 of the Local Government Act (Northern Ireland) 1972, and for connected purposes

[15 March 1989]

Disqualification for breach of declaration against terrorism or in consequence of imprisonment or detention

3 Declaration against terrorism: local elections

(1) A person is not validly nominated as a candidate at a local election unless his consent to nomination includes a declaration in the form set out in Part I of Schedule 2 to this Act.

(2) . . .

NOTES

Sub-s (2): outside the scope of this work.

4 Declaration against terrorism: councillors co-opted to fill casual vacancies

(1) A person is not eligible to be chosen by a district council to fill a casual vacancy in the council unless he has made, and served on the clerk of the council, a declaration in the form set out in Part II of Schedule 2 to this Act.

(2) . . .

NOTES

Sub-s (2): amends the Electoral Law Act (Northern Ireland) 1962, s 11(4B).

5 Declaration against terrorism: Assembly elections

A person is not validly nominated as a candidate at an election to the Northern Ireland Assembly unless his consent to nomination includes a declaration in the form set out in Part I of Schedule 2 to this Act.

6 Breach of terms of declaration

(1) A person who has made a declaration required for the purposes of section 3, 4 or 5 of this Act in connection with a local election, an election to the Northern Ireland Assembly or the filling of a casual vacancy in a district council acts in breach of the terms of the declaration if at any time after he is declared to be elected at that election or is chosen to fill that vacancy and while he remains a member of the district council or of the Assembly—

(a) he expresses support for or approval of—

(i) a proscribed organisation, or

(ii) acts of terrorism (that is to say, violence for political ends) connected with the affairs of Northern Ireland, and

(b) he does so—

(i) at a public meeting, or

(ii) knowing, or in such circumstances that he can reasonably be expected to know, that the fact that he has made that expression of support or approval is likely to become known to the public.

(2) For the purposes of subsection (1) above a person shall be taken to express support for, or approval of, any matter if his words or actions could reasonably be understood a expressing support for, or approval of, it.

(3) It is immaterial for the purposes of subsection (1) above—

(a) whether the expression of support or approval is made by spoken or written words, by the display of written matter or by other behaviour, and

(b) whether it is made in the United Kingdom or elsewhere.

(4) This section has effect notwithstanding section 26(1) of the Northern Ireland Constitution Act 1973 (privileges of the Northern Ireland Assembly).

(5) In this section—
"proscribed organisation" has the same meaning as in [section 30 of the Northern Ireland (Emergency Provisions) Act 1996],

. . . . .

NOTES

Sub-s (5): words in square brackets in definition "proscribed organisation" substituted by the Northern Ireland (Emergency Provisions) Act 1996 s 63(6), Sch 6, paras 1, 2; definitions omitted outside the scope of this work.

General

13 Short title, commencement, transitional provision and extent

(1) This Act may be cited as the Elected Authorities (Northern Ireland) Act 1989.

(2)–(6) . . .

(7) This Act, except section 11(8), extends to Northern Ireland only.

NOTES

Sub-ss (2)–(6): outside the scope of this work.

SCHEDULE 2

Sections 3, 4, 5

DECLARATION AGAINST TERRORISM

PART I
FORM FOR INCLUSION IN CONSENT TO NOMINATION

I declare that, if elected, I will not by word or deed express support for or approval of—

(a) any organisation that is for the time being a proscribed organisation specified in Schedule 2 to the Northern Ireland (Emergency Provisions) Act 1978; or

(b) acts of terrorism (that is to say, violence for political ends) connected with the affairs of Northern Ireland.

PART II
FORM FOR USE IN CASE OF DISTRICT COUNCILLOR CHOSEN TO FILL CASUAL VACANCY

I, (name in full), of (home address in full) declare that, if I am chosen to be a councillor for the District of (name of district), I will not by word or deed express support for or approval of—

(a) any organisation that is for the time being a proscribed organisation specified in [Schedule 2 to the Northern Ireland (Emergency Provisions) Act 1996]; or

(b) acts of terrorism (that is to say, violence for political ends) connected with the affairs of Northern Ireland.

Signed .. ..

Date .. ..

NOTES

Words in square brackets substituted by the Northern Ireland (Emergency Provisions) Act 1996, s 63(6), Sch 6, paras 1, 3.

PREVENTION OF TERRORISM (TEMPORARY PROVISIONS) ACT 1989

(C 4)

An Act to make provision in place of the Prevention of Terrorism (Temporary Provisions) Act 1984; to make further provision in relation to powers of search under, and persons convicted of scheduled offences within the meaning of, the Northern Ireland (Emergency Provisions) Act 1978; and to enable the Secretary of State to prevent the establishment of new explosives factories, magazines and stores in Northern Ireland

[15 March 1989]

PART I
PROSCRIBED ORGANISATIONS

1 Proscribed organisations

(1) Any organisation for the time being specified in Schedule 1 to this Act is a proscribed organisation for the purposes of this Act; and any organisation which passes under a name mentioned in that Schedule shall be treated as proscribed whatever relationship (if any) it has to any other organisation of the same name.

(2) The Secretary of State may by order made by statutory instrument—
- (a) add to Schedule 1 to this Act any organisation that appears to him to be concerned in, or in promoting or encouraging, terrorism occurring in the United Kingdom and connected with the affairs of Northern Ireland;
- (b) remove an organisation from that Schedule.

(3) No order shall be made under this section unless—
- (a) a draft of the order has been laid before and approved by a resolution of each House of Parliament; or
- (b) it is declared in the order that it appears to the Secretary of State that by reason of urgency it is necessary to make the order without a draft having been so approved.

(4) An order under this section of which a draft has not been approved under subsection (3) above—
- (a) shall be laid before Parliament; and
- (b) shall cease to have effect at the end of the period of forty days beginning with the day on which it was made unless, before the end of that period, the order has been approved by a resolution of each House of Parliament, but without prejudice to anything previously done or to the making of a new order.

(5) In reckoning for the purposes of subsection (4) above any period of forty days, no account shall be taken of any period during which Parliament is dissolved or prorogued or during which both Houses are adjourned for more than four days.

(6) In this section "organisation" includes any association or combination of persons.

2 Membership, support and meetings

(1) Subject to subsection (3) below, a person is guilty of an offence if he—
- (a) belongs or professes to belong to a proscribed organisation;

(b) solicits or invites support for a proscribed organisation other than support with money or other property; or

(c) arranges or assists in the arrangement or management of, or addresses, any meeting of three or more persons (whether or not it is a meeting to which the public are admitted) knowing that the meeting is—

(i) to support a proscribed organisation;

(ii) to further the activities of such an organisation; or

(iii) to be addressed by a person belonging or professing to belong to such an organisation.

(2) A person guilty of an offence under subsection (1) above is liable—

(a) on conviction on indictment, to imprisonment for a term not exceeding ten years or a fine or both;

(b) on summary conviction, to imprisonment for a term not exceeding six months or a fine not exceeding the statutory maximum or both.

(3) A person belonging to a proscribed organisation is not guilty of an offence under this section by reason of belonging to the organisation if he shows—

(a) that he became a member when it was not a proscribed organisation under the current legislation; and

(b) that he has not since he became a member taken part in any of its activities at any time while it was a proscribed organisation under that legislation.

(4), (5) . . .

NOTES

Sub-ss (4), (5): outside the scope of this work.

[2A Evidence and inferences

(1) This section applies where a person is charged with an offence under section 2(1)(a) above; and references here to a specified organisation must be construed in accordance with section 2B below.

(2) Subsection (3) below applies if a police officer of or above the rank of superintendent states in oral evidence that in his opinion the accused—

(a) belongs to an organisation which is specified, or

(b) belonged at a particular time to an organisation which was then specified.

(3) If this subsection applies—

(a) the statement shall be admissible as evidence of the matter stated, but

(b) the accused shall not be committed for trial in England and Wales, or be found to have a case to answer or be convicted, solely on the basis of the statement.

(4) Subsection (6) below applies if evidence is given that—

(a) at any time before being charged with the offence the accused, on being questioned under caution by a constable, failed to mention a fact which is material to the offence and which he could reasonably be expected to mention, and

(b) before being questioned he was permitted to consult a solicitor.

(5) Subsection (6) below also applies if evidence is given that—

(a) on being charged with the offence or informed by a constable that he might be prosecuted for it the accused failed to mention a fact which is material to the offence and which he could reasonably be expected to mention, and

(b) before being charged or informed he was permitted to consult a solicitor.

(6) If this subsection applies—
  (a) the court or jury, in considering any question whether the accused belongs or belonged at a particular time to a specified organisation, may draw from the failure inferences relating to that question, but
  (b) the accused shall not be committed for trial in England and Wales, or be found to have a case to answer or be convicted, solely on the basis of the inferences.

(7) Subject to any directions by the court, evidence tending to establish the failure may be given before or after evidence tending to establish the fact which the accused is alleged to have failed to mention.

(8) This section does not—
  (a) prejudice the admissibility of evidence admissible apart from this section;
  (b) preclude the drawing of inferences which could be drawn apart from this section;
  (c) prejudice an enactment providing (in whatever words) that an answer or evidence given by a person in specified circumstances is not admissible in evidence against him or some other person in any proceedings or class of proceedings (however described, and whether civil or criminal).

(9) In subsection (8)(c) above the reference to giving evidence is a reference to giving it in any manner (whether by giving information, making discovery or disclosure, producing documents or otherwise).

(10) . . .

(11) In this section "police officer" means a member of—
  (a) a police force within the meaning of the Police Act 1996 or the Police (Scotland) Act 1967, or
  (b) the Royal Ulster Constabulary.

(12) This section does not apply to a statement made or failure occurring before the day on which the Criminal Justice (Terrorism and Conspiracy) Act 1998 was passed.]

NOTES

Commencement: 4 September 1998.
Inserted by the Criminal Justice (Terrorism and Conspiracy) Act 1998, s 1(1).
Sub-s (10): outside the scope of this work.

[2B Specified organisations

(1) For the purposes of section 2A above an organisation is specified at a particular time if at that time—
  (a) it is specified under section 3(8) of the Northern Ireland (Sentences) Act 1998 or under subsection (2) below, and
  (b) it is, or forms part of, an organisation which is proscribed for the purposes of this Act.

(2) If the condition in subsection (3) below is satisfied the Secretary of State may by order specify an organisation which is not specified under section 3(8) of the Northern Ireland (Sentences) Act 1998.

(3) The condition is that the Secretary of State believes that the organisation—
  (a) is concerned in terrorism connected with the affairs of Northern Ireland, or in promoting or encouraging it, and

(b) has not established or is not maintaining a complete and unequivocal ceasefire.

(4) An order under this section shall be made by statutory instrument; and no order shall be made unless a draft has been laid before, and approved by resolution of, each House of Parliament.]

NOTES

Commencement: 4 September 1998.
Inserted by the Criminal Justice (Terrorism and Conspiracy) Act 1998, s 1(1).

3 Display of support in public

(1) Any person who in a public place—

(a) wears any item of dress; or
(b) wears, carries or displays any article,

in such a way or in such circumstances as to arouse reasonable apprehension that he is a member or supporter of a proscribed organisation, is guilty of an offence and liable on summary conviction to imprisonment for a term not exceeding six months or a fine not exceeding level 5 on the standard scale or both.

(2) . . .

(3) In this section "public place" includes any highway or, in Scotland, any road within the meaning of the Roads (Scotland) Act 1984 and any premises to which at the material time the public have, or are permitted to have, access, whether on payment or otherwise.

NOTES

Sub-ss (2), (3): outside the scope of this work.

PART II
EXCLUSION ORDERS

4 Exclusion orders: general

(1) The Secretary of State may exercise the powers conferred on him by this Part of this Act in such a way as appears to him expedient to prevent acts of terrorism to which this Part of this Act applies.

(2) The acts of terrorism to which this Part of this Act applies are acts of terrorism connected with the affairs of Northern Ireland.

(3) An order under section 5, 6 or 7 below is referred to in this Act as an "exclusion order".

(4) Schedule 2 to this Act shall have effect with respect to the duration of exclusion orders, the giving of notices, the right to make representations, powers of removal and detention and other supplementary matters for this Part of this Act.

(5) The exercise of the detention powers conferred by that Schedule shall be subject to supervision in accordance with Schedule 3 to this Act.

5 Orders excluding persons from Great Britain

(1) If the Secretary of State is satisfied that any person—

(a) is or has been concerned in the commission, preparation or instigation of acts of terrorism to which this Part of this Act applies; or

(b) is attempting or may attempt to enter Great Britain with a view to being concerned in the commission, preparation or instigation of such acts of terrorism,

the Secretary of State may make an exclusion order against him.

(2) An exclusion order under this section is an order prohibiting a person from being in, or entering, Great Britain.

(3) In deciding whether to make an exclusion order under this section against a person who is ordinarily resident in Great Britain, the Secretary of State shall have regard to the question whether that person's connection with any country or territory outside Great Britain is such as to make it appropriate that such an order should be made.

(4) An exclusion order shall not be made under this section against a person who is a British citizen and who—

(a) is at the time ordinarily resident in Great Britain and has then been ordinarily resident in Great Britain throughout the last three years; or

(b) is at the time subject to an order under section 6 below.

6 Orders excluding persons from Northern Ireland

(1) If the Secretary of State is satisfied that any person—

(a) is or has been concerned in the commission, preparation or instigation of acts of terrorism to which this Part of this Act applies; or

(b) is attempting or may attempt to enter Northern Ireland with a view to being concerned in the commission, preparation or instigation of such acts of terrorism,

the Secretary of State may make an exclusion order against him.

(2) An exclusion order under this section is an order prohibiting a person from being in, or entering, Northern Ireland.

(3) In deciding whether to make an exclusion order under this section against a person who is ordinarily resident in Northern Ireland, the Secretary of State shall have regard to the question whether that person's connection with any country or territory outside Northern Ireland is such as to make it appropriate that such an order should be made.

(4) An exclusion order shall not be made under this section against a person who is a British citizen and who—

(a) is at the time ordinarily resident in Northern Ireland and has then been ordinarily resident in Northern Ireland throughout the last three years; or

(b) is at the time subject to an order under section 5 above.

7 Orders excluding persons from the United Kingdom

(1) If the Secretary of State is satisfied that any person—

(a) is or has been concerned in the commission, preparation or instigation of acts of terrorism to which this Part of this Act applies; or

(b) is attempting or may attempt to enter Great Britain or Northern Ireland with a view to being concerned in the commission, preparation or instigation of such acts of terrorism,

the Secretary of State may make an exclusion order against him.

(2) An exclusion order under this section is an order prohibiting a person from being in, or entering, the United Kingdom.

(3) In deciding whether to make an exclusion order under this section against a person who is ordinarily resident in the United Kingdom, the Secretary of State shall have regard to the question whether that person's connection with any country or territory outside the United Kingdom is such as to make it appropriate that such an order should be made.

(4) An exclusion order shall not be made under this section against a person who is a British citizen.

8 Offences in respect of exclusion orders

(1) A person who is subject to an exclusion order is guilty of an offence if he fails to comply with the order at a time after he has been, or has become liable to be, removed under Schedule 2 to this Act.

(2) A person is guilty of an offence—

(a) if he is knowingly concerned in arrangements for securing or facilitating the entry into Great Britain, Northern Ireland or the United Kingdom of a person whom he knows, or has reasonable grounds for believing, to be an excluded person; or

(b) if he knowingly harbours such a person in Great Britain, Northern Ireland or the United Kingdom.

(3) . . .

(4) A person guilty of an offence under this section is liable—

(a) on conviction on indictment, to imprisonment for a term not exceeding five years or a fine or both;

(b) on summary conviction, to imprisonment for a term not exceeding six months or a fine not exceeding the statutory maximum or both.

NOTES

Sub-s (3): outside the scope of this work.

PART III
FINANCIAL ASSISTANCE FOR TERRORISM

9 Contributions towards acts of terrorism

(1) A person is guilty of an offence if he—

(a) solicits or invites any other person to give, lend or otherwise make available, whether for consideration or not, any money or other property; . . .

(b) receives or accepts from any other person, whether for consideration or not, any money or other property;[or

(c) uses or has possession of, whether for consideration or not, any money or other property,] intending that it shall be applied or used for the commission of, or in furtherance of or in connection with, acts of terrorism to which this section applies or having reasonable cause to suspect that it may be so used or applied.

(2) A person is guilty of an offence if he—

(a) gives, lends or otherwise makes available to any other person, whether for consideration or not, any money or other property; or

(b) enters into or is otherwise concerned in an arrangement whereby money or other property is or is to be made available to another person,

knowing or having reasonable cause to suspect that it will or may be applied or used as mentioned in subsection (1) above.

(3) The acts of terrorism to which this section applies are—

(a) acts of terrorism connected with the affairs of Northern Ireland; and

(b) subject to subsection (4) below, acts of terrorism of any other description except acts connected solely with the affairs of the United Kingdom or any part of the United Kingdom other than Northern Ireland.

(4) Subsection (3)(b) above does not apply to an act done or to be done outside the United Kingdom unless it constitutes or would constitute an offence triable in the United Kingdom.

(5) In proceedings against a person for an offence under this section in relation to an act within subsection (3)(b) above done or to be done outside the United Kingdom—

(a) the prosecution need not prove that that person knew or had reasonable cause to suspect that the act constituted or would constitute such an offence as is mentioned in subsection (4) above; but

(b) it shall be a defence to prove that he did not know and had no reasonable cause to suspect that the facts were such that the act constituted or would constitute such an offence.

NOTES

Sub-s (1): word omitted repealed, and words in square brackets inserted, by the Criminal Justice Act 1993, ss 49(1), 79(14), Sch 6, Pt I.

10 Contributions to resources of proscribed organisations

(1) A person is guilty of an offence if he—

(a) solicits or invites any other person to give, lend or otherwise make available, whether for consideration or not, any money or other property for the benefit of a proscribed organisation;

(b) gives, lends or otherwise makes available or receives or accepts [or uses or has possession of], whether for consideration or not, any money or other property for the benefit of such an organisation; or

(c) enters into or is otherwise concerned in an arrangement whereby money or other property is or is to be made available for the benefit of such an organisation.

(2) In proceedings against a person for an offence under subsection (1)(b) above it is a defence to prove that he did not know and had no reasonable cause to suspect that the money or property was for the benefit of a proscribed organisation; and in proceedings against a person for an offence under subsection (1)(c) above it is a defence to prove that he did not know and had no reasonable cause to suspect that the arrangement related to a proscribed organisation.

(3) In this section and sections 11 and 13 below "proscribed organisation" includes a proscribed organisation for the purposes of [section 30 of the Northern Ireland (Emergency Provisions) Act 1996].

NOTES

Sub-s (1): words in square brackets in para (b) inserted by the Criminal Justice Act 1993, s 49(2).

Sub-s (3): words in square brackets substituted by the Northern Ireland (Emergency Provisions) Act 1996, s 63(6), Sch 6, paras 4, 5.

11 Assisting in retention or control of terrorist funds

(1) A person is guilty of an offence if he enters into or is otherwise concerned in an arrangement whereby the retention or control by or on behalf of another person of terrorist funds is facilitated, whether by concealment, removal from the jurisdiction, transfer to nominees or otherwise.

(2) In proceedings against a person for an offence under this section it is a defence to prove that he did not know and had no reasonable cause to suspect that the arrangement related to terrorist funds.

(3) In this section and section 12 below "terrorist funds" means—

(a) funds which may be applied or used for the commission of, or in furtherance of or in connection with, acts of terrorism to which section 9 above applies;

(b) the proceeds of the commission of such acts of terrorism or of activities engaged in furtherance of or in connection with such acts; and

(c) the resources of a proscribed organisation.

(4) Paragraph (b) of subsection (3) includes any property which in whole or in part directly or indirectly represents such proceeds as are mentioned in that paragraph; and paragraph (c) of that subsection includes any money or other property which is or is to be applied or made available for the benefit of a proscribed organisation.

13 Penalties and forfeiture

(1) A person guilty of an offence under section 9, 10 or 11 above is liable—

(a) on conviction on indictment, to imprisonment for a term not exceeding fourteen years or a fine or both;

(b) on summary conviction, to imprisonment for a term not exceeding six months or a fine not exceeding the statutory maximum or both.

(2) Subject to the provisions of this section, the court by or before which a person is convicted of an offence under section 9(1) or (2)(a) above may order the forfeiture of any money or other property—

(a) which, at the time of the offence, he had in his possession or under his control; and

(b) which, at that time—

(i) in the case of an offence under subsection (1) of section 9, he intended should be applied or used, or had reasonable cause to suspect might be applied or used, as mentioned in that subsection;

(ii) in the case of an offence under subsection (2)(a) of that section, he knew or had reasonable cause to suspect would or might be applied or used as mentioned in subsection (1) of that section.

(3) Subject to the provisions of this section, the court by or before which a person is convicted of an offence under section 9(2)(b), 10(1)(c) or 11 above may order the

forfeiture of the money or other property to which the arrangement in question related and which, in the case of an offence under section 9(2)(b), he knew or had reasonable cause to suspect would or might be applied or used as mentioned in section 9(1) above.

(4) Subject to the provisions of this section, the court by or before which a person is convicted of an offence under section 10(1)(a) or (b) above may order the forfeiture of any money or other property which, at the time of the offence, he had in his possession or under his control for the use or benefit of a proscribed organisation.

(5) The court shall not under this section make an order forfeiting any money or other property unless the court considers that the money or property may, unless forfeited, be applied or used as mentioned in section 9(1) above but the court may, in the absence of evidence to the contrary, assume that any money or property may be applied or used as there mentioned.

(6) Where a person other than the convicted person claims to be the owner of or otherwise interested in anything which can be forfeited by an order under this section, the court shall, before making such an order in respect of it, gave him an opportunity to be heard.

(7), (8) . . .

NOTES

Sub-ss (7), (8): outside the scope of this work.

PART IV
[POWERS OF ARREST, STOP AND SEARCH, DETENTION AND CONTROL OF ENTRY]

NOTES

Part heading substituted by the Criminal Justice and Public Order Act 1994, s 81(2).

[13A Powers to stop and search vehicles etc and persons

(1) Where it appears to—

(a) any officer of police of or above the rank of commander of the metropolitan police, as respects the metropolitan police [district];

(b) any officer of police of or above the rank of commander of the City of London police, as respects the City of London; or

(c) any officer of police of or above the rank of assistant chief constable for any other police area,

that it is expedient to do so in order to prevent acts of terrorism to which this section applies he may give an authorisation that the powers to stop and search vehicles and persons conferred by this section shall be exercisable at any place within his area or a specified locality in his area for a specified period not exceeding twenty eight days.

(2) The acts of terrorism to which this section applies are—

(a) acts of terrorism connected with the affairs of Northern Ireland; and

(b) acts of terrorism of any other description except acts connected solely with the affairs of the United Kingdom or any part of the United Kingdom other than Northern Ireland.

(3) This section confers on any constable in uniform power—

(a) to stop any vehicle;

(b) to search any vehicle, its driver or any passenger for articles of a kind which could be used for a purpose connected with the commission, preparation or instigation of acts of terrorism to which this section applies;

(c) . . .

[(4) A constable may exercise his powers under this section whether or not he has any grounds for suspecting the presence of articles of that kind.

(4A) Nothing in this section authorises a constable to require a person to remove any of his clothing in public other than any headgear, footwear, outer coat, jacket or gloves.]

(5) This section applies (with the necessary modifications) to ships and aircraft as it applies to vehicles.

(6) A person is guilty of an offence if he—

(a) fails to stop . . . the vehicle when required to do so by a constable in the exercise of his powers under this section; or

(b) wilfully obstructs a constable in the exercise of those powers.

(7)–(10A) . . .

(11) Nothing in this section affects the exercise by constables of any power to stop vehicles for purposes other than those specified in subsection (1) above.]

NOTES

Inserted by the Criminal Justice and Public Order Act 1994, s 81(1).

Sub-s (1): word in square brackets in para (a) substituted by the Prevention of Terrorism (Additional Powers) Act 1996, s 1(2), (7).

Sub-s (3): para (c) repealed by the Prevention of Terrorism (Additional Powers) Act 1996, s 1(2), (3).

Sub-ss (4), (4A): substituted for original sub-s (4) by the Prevention of Terrorism (Additional Powers) Act 1996, s 1(2), (4).

Sub-s (6): words omitted from para (a) repealed by the Prevention of Terrorism (Additional Powers) Act 1996, s 1(2), (3)(a).

Sub-ss (7)–(10A): outside the scope of this work.

[13B Power to stop and search pedestrians

(1) Where it appears to a police officer of the rank mentioned in subsection (1)(a), (b) or (as the case may be) (c) of section 13A above that it is expedient to do so in order to prevent acts of terrorism to which that section applies, he may give an authorisation that the powers to stop and search persons conferred by this section shall be exercisable at any place within his area or a locality in his area which is specified in the authorisation.

(2) This section confers on any constable in uniform power to stop any pedestrian and search him, or anything carried by him, for articles of a kind which could be used for a purpose connected with the commission, preparation or instigation of such acts of terrorism.

(3) A constable may exercise his powers under this section whether or not he has any grounds for suspecting the presence of articles of that kind.

(4) Nothing in this section authorises a constable to require a person to remove any of his clothing in public other than any headgear, footwear, outer coat, jacket or gloves.

(5) A person is guilty of an offence if he—

(a) fails to stop when required to do so by a constable in the exercise of his powers under this section; or

(b) wilfully obstructs a constable in the exercise of those powers.

(6), (7) . . .

(8) A person giving an authorisation under this section must cause the Secretary of State to be informed, as soon as is reasonably practicable, that it was given.

(9) An authorisation under this section—

(a) may be cancelled by the Secretary of State with effect from such time as he may direct;

(b) ceases to have effect if it is not confirmed by the Secretary of State before the end of the period of 48 hours beginning with the time when it was given; but

(c) if confirmed, continues in force—

(i) for such period, not exceeding 28 days beginning with the day on which it was given, as may be specified in the authorisation; or

(ii) for such shorter period as the Secretary of State may direct.

(10) . . .

NOTES

Inserted by the Prevention of Terrorism (Additional Powers) Act 1996, s 1(1).

Sub-ss (6), (7), (10): outside the scope of this work.

14 Arrest and detention of suspected persons

(1) Subject to subsection (2) below, a constable may arrest without warrant a person whom he has reasonable grounds for suspecting to be—

(a) a person guilty of an offence under section 2, 8, 9, 10 or 11 above [or under section 30 of the Northern Ireland (Emergency Provisions) Act 1996];

(b) a person who is or has been concerned in the commission, preparation or instigation of acts of terrorism to which this section applies; or

(c) a person subject to an exclusion order.

(2) The acts of terrorism to which this section applies are—

(a) acts of terrorism connected with the affairs of Northern Ireland; and

(b) acts of terrorism of any other description except acts connected solely with the affairs of the United Kingdom or any part of the United Kingdom other than Northern Ireland.

(3) The power of arrest conferred by subsection (1)(c) above is exercisable only—

(a) in Great Britain if the exclusion order was made under section 5 above; and

(b) in Northern Ireland if it was made under section 6 above.

(4) Subject to subsection (5) below, a person arrested under this section shall not be detained in right of the arrest for more than forty-eight hours after his arrest.

(5) The Secretary of State may, in any particular case, extend the period of forty-eight hours mentioned in subsection (4) above by a period or periods specified by him, but any such further period or periods shall not exceed five days in all and if an application for such an extension is made the person detained shall as soon as practicable be given written notice of that fact and of the time when the application was made.

(6) The exercise of the detention powers conferred by this section shall be subject to supervision in accordance with Schedule 3 to this Act.

(7) The provisions of this section are without prejudice to any power of arrest exercisable apart from this section.

NOTES

Sub-s (1): words in square brackets inserted by the Criminal Justice (Terrorism and Conspiracy) Act 1998, s 3, in relation to offences suspected to have been committed before or after 4 September 1998.

15 Provisions supplementary to s 14

(1) If a justice of the peace is satisfied that there are reasonable grounds for suspecting that a person whom a constable believes to be liable to arrest under section 14(1)(b) above is to be found on any premises he may grant a search warrant authorising any constable to enter those premises for the purpose of searching for and arresting that person.

(2) . . .

(3) In any circumstances in which a constable has power under section 14 above to arrest a person, he may also, for the purpose of ascertaining whether he has in his possession any document or other article which may constitute evidence that he is a person liable to arrest, stop that person and search him.

(4) Where a constable has arrested a person under that section for any reason other than the commission of a criminal offence, he, or any other constable, may search him for the purpose of ascertaining whether he has in his possession any document or other article which may constitute evidence that he is a person liable to arrest.

(5) A search of a person under subsection (3) or (4) above may only be carried out by a person of the same sex.

(6)–(14) . . .

NOTES

Sub-ss (2), (6)–(14): outside the scope of this work.

PART V
INFORMATION, PROCEEDINGS AND INTERPRETATION

17 Investigation of terrorist activities

(1) Schedule 7 to this Act shall have effect for conferring powers to obtain information for the purposes of terrorist investigations, . . .

[(2) A person is guilty of an offence if, knowing or having reasonable cause to suspect that a constable is acting, or is proposing to act, in connection with a terrorist investigation which is being, or is about to be, conducted, he—

(a) discloses to any other person information or any other matter which is likely to prejudice the investigation or proposed investigation, or

(b) falsifies, conceals or destroys or otherwise disposes of, or causes or permits the falsification, concealment, destruction or disposal of, material which is or is likely to be relevant to the investigation, or proposed investigation.

(2A) A person is guilty of an offence if, knowing or having reasonable cause to suspect that a disclosure ("the disclosure") has been made to a constable under section 12, 18 or 18A of this Act or . . . , he—

(a) discloses to any other person information or any other matter which is likely to prejudice any investigation which might be conducted following the disclosure; or

(b) falsifies, conceals or destroys or otherwise disposes of, or causes or permits the falsification, concealment, destruction or disposal of, material which is or is likely to be relevant to any such investigation.

(2B) A person is guilty of an offence if, knowing or having reasonable cause to suspect that a disclosure ("the disclosure") of a kind mentioned in section 12(4) or 18A(5) of this Act . . . has been made, he—

(a) discloses to any person information or any other matter which is likely to prejudice any investigation which might be conducted following the disclosure; or

(b) falsifies, conceals or destroys or otherwise disposes of, or causes or permits the falsification, concealment, destruction or disposal of, material which is or is likely to be relevant to any such investigation.

(2C) Nothing in subsections (2) to (2B) above makes it an offence for a professional legal adviser to disclose any information or other matter—

(a) to, or to a representative of, a client of his in connection with the giving by the adviser of legal advice to the client; or

(b) to any person–

(i) in contemplation of, or in connection with, legal proceedings; and

(ii) for the purpose of those proceedings.

(2D) Subsection (2C) above does not apply in relation to any information or other matter which is disclosed with a view to furthering any criminal purpose.

(2E) No constable or other person shall be guilty of an offence under this section in respect of anything done by him in the course of acting in connection with the enforcement, or intended enforcement, of any provision of this Act or of any other enactment relating to terrorism or the proceeds or resources of terrorism.]

(3) In proceedings against a person for an offence under subsection (2)(a) above it is a defence to prove—

(a) that he did not know and had no reasonable cause to suspect that the disclosure was likely to prejudice the investigation [or proposed investigation]; or

(b) that he had lawful authority or reasonable excuse for making the disclosure.

[(3A) In proceedings against a person for an offence under subsection (2A)(a) or (2B)(a) above it is a defence to prove—

(a) that he did not know and had no reasonable cause to suspect that his disclosure was likely to prejudice the investigation in question; or

(b) that he had lawful authority or reasonable excuse for making his disclosure.]

(4) In proceedings against a person for an offence under subsection (2)(b) above it is a defence to prove that he had no intention of concealing any information contained in the material in question from [any person conducting, or likely to be conducting, the investigation or proposed investigation].

[(4A) In proceedings against a person for an offence under subsection (2A)(b) or (2B)(b) above, it is a defence to prove that he had no intention of concealing any information contained in the material in question from any person who might carry out the investigation in question.]

(5) A person guilty of an offence under subsection (2) [(2A) or (2B)] above is liable—

(a) on conviction on indictment, to imprisonment for a term not exceeding five years or a fine or both;

(b) on summary conviction, to imprisonment for a term not exceeding six months or a fine not exceeding the statutory maximum or both.

[(6) For the purposes of subsection (1) above, as it applies in relation to any offence under section 18 or 18A below . . . "act" includes omission.]

NOTES

Sub-s (1): words omitted outside the scope of this work.

Sub-ss (2)–(2E): substituted for original sub-s (2) by the Criminal Justice Act 1993, s 50(1), (3).

Sub-s (2A): words omitted repealed by the Northern Ireland (Emergency Provisions) Act 1996, s 63(6), (7), Sch 6, paras 4, 6(1), (5), Sch 7, Pt I.

Sub-s (2B): words omitted repealed by the Northern Ireland (Emergency Provisions) Act 1996, s 63(6), (7), Sch 6, paras 4, 6(1), (6), Sch 7, Pt I.

Sub-s (3): words in square brackets inserted by the Criminal Justice Act 1993, s 50(1), (4).

Sub-s (3A): inserted by the Criminal Justice Act 1993, s 50(1), (5).

Sub-s (4): words in square brackets substituted by the Criminal Justice Act 1993, s 50(1), (6).

Sub-s (4A): inserted by the Criminal Justice Act 1993, s 50(1), (7).

Sub-s (5): words in square brackets inserted by the Criminal Justice Act 1993, s 50(1), (8).

Sub-s (6): added by the Criminal Justice Act 1993, s 50(1), (9); words omitted repealed by the Northern Ireland (Emergency Provisions) Act 1996, s 63(6), (7), Sch 6, paras 4, 6(1), (7), Sch 7, Pt I.

[18A Failure to disclose knowledge or suspicion of offences under sections 9 to 11

(1) A person is guilty of an offence if—

(a) he knows, or suspects, that another person is providing financial assistance for terrorism;

(b) the information, or other matter, on which that knowledge or suspicion is based came to his attention in the course of his trade, profession, business or employment; and

(c) he does not disclose the information or other matter to a constable as soon as is reasonably practicable after it comes to his attention.

(2) Subsection (1) above does not make it an offence for a professional legal adviser to fail to disclose any information or other matter which has come to him in privileged circumstances.

(3) It is a defence to a charge of committing an offence under this section that the person charged had a reasonable excuse for not disclosing the information or other matter in question.

(4) Where a person discloses to a constable—

(a) his suspicion or belief that another person is providing financial assistance for terrorism; or

(b) any information or other matter on which that suspicion or belief is based;

the disclosure shall not be treated as a breach of any restriction imposed by statute or otherwise.

(5) Without prejudice to subsection (3) or (4) above, in the case of a person who was in employment at the relevant time, it is a defence to a charge of committing an

offence under this section that he disclosed the information or other matter in question to the appropriate person in accordance with the procedure established by his employer for the making of such disclosures.

(6)–(9) . . .

(10) No information or other matter shall be treated as coming to a professional legal adviser in privileged circumstances if it is communicated or given with a view to furthering any criminal purpose.

(11) . . .

NOTES

Sub-ss (6)–(9), (11): outside the scope of this work.

Inserted by the Criminal Justice Act 1993, s 51.

PART VII
SUPPLEMENTARY

27 Commencement and duration

(1), (2) . . .

(3) Schedule 3 and paragraphs 8 to 10, 18 to 20, 28 to 30 and 34 of Schedule 4 shall come into force on such day as the Secretary of State may appoint by an order made by statutory instrument; and different days may be appointed for different provisions and for England and Wales, for Scotland and for Northern Ireland.

(4) . . .

(5) The provisions of Parts I to V of this Act and of subsection (6)(c) below shall remain in force until 22nd March 1990 and shall then expire unless continued in force by an order under subsection (6) below.

(6) The Secretary of State may by order made by statutory instrument provide—

(a) that all or any of those provisions which are for the time being in force (including any in force by virtue of an order under this paragraph or paragraph (c) below) shall continue in force for a period not exceeding twelve months from the coming into operation of the order;

(b) that all or any of those provisions which are for the time being in force shall cease to be in force; or

(c) that all or any of those provisions which are not for the time being in force shall come into force again and remain in force for a period not exceeding twelve months from the coming into operation of the order.

(7) No order shall be made under subsection (6) above unless—

(a) a draft of the order has been laid before and approved by a resolution of each House of Parliament; or

(b) it is declared in the order that it appears to the Secretary of State that by reason of urgency it is necessary to make the order without a draft having been so approved.

(8) An order under that subsection of which a draft has not been approved under section (7) above—

(a) shall be laid before Parliament; and

(b) shall cease to have effect at the end of the period of forty days beginning with the day on which it was made unless, before the end of that period, the order has been approved by a resolution of each House of Parliament, but without prejudice to anything previously done or to the making of a new order.

(9) . . .

(10) In subsection (5) above the reference to Parts I to V of this Act does not include a reference to the provisions of Parts III and V so far as they have effect in Northern Ireland and relate to proscribed organisations for the purposes of [section 30 of the Northern Ireland (Emergency Provisions) Act 1996] or offences or orders under that section.

[(11) The provisions excluded by subsection (10) above from subsection (5) shall remain in force until [15th June 1999] and then expire but shall be—

(a) included in the provisions to which subsection (3) of section 62 of the said Act of 1996 applies (provisions that can be continued in force, repealed or revived by order); and

(b) treated as part of that Act for the purposes of subsection (10) of that section [(repeal at end of 24th August 2000)].]

(12) . . .

NOTES

Sub-ss (1), (4), (9): outside the scope of this work.

Sub-ss (2), (12): repealed by the Northern Ireland (Emergency Provisions) Act 1991, s 70(4), Sch 8, Pt I.

Sub-s (10): words in square brackets substituted by the Northern Ireland (Emergency Provisions) Act 1996, s 63(6), Sch 6, paras 4, 7(1), (2).

Sub-s (11): substituted by the Northern Ireland (Emergency Provisions) Act 1996, s 63(6), Sch 6, paras 4, 7(1), (3); words in square brackets substituted by the Northern Ireland (Emergency Provisions) Act 1998, s 7(1), Sch 1, para 1.

28 Short title and extent

(1) This Act may be cited as the Prevention of Terrorism (Temporary Provisions) Act 1989.

(2) This Act extends to the whole of the United Kingdom except that—

(a) Part I, sections 13A [13B] and 15(1) . . . do not extend to Northern Ireland . . .

(b), (c) . . .

(d) Part I of Schedule 7 [except paragraph 2A] extends only to England, Wales and Northern Ireland; and

(e) . . .

(3) . . .

NOTES

This section is printed as amended by the Criminal Justice and Public Order Act 1994 and the Prevention of Terrorism (Additional Powers) Act 1996 (in so far as relevant); words omitted outside the scope of this work.

SCHEDULES

SCHEDULE 1

Section 1

PROSCRIBED ORGANISATIONS

Irish Republican Army

Irish National Liberation Army

SCHEDULE 2

Section 4(4)

EXCLUSION ORDERS

Duration

1.—(1) An exclusion order may be revoked at any time by a further order made by the Secretary of State.

(2) An exclusion order shall, unless revoked earlier, expire at the end of the period of three years beginning with the day on which it is made.

(3), (4) . . .

[*Notice that exclusion order is being considered*

2.—(1) Where the Secretary of State is considering whether to make an exclusion order against a person—
- (a) if the person is in the United Kingdom, notice in writing shall be served on him that the Secretary of State is considering that question; and
- (b) if the person is not in the United Kingdom, notice in writing may be served on him that the Secretary of State is considering that question.

(2) A notice under sub-paragraph (1) above shall—
- (a) specify whether the order under consideration is an order under section 5, 6 or 7 of this Act; and
- (b) set out the rights afforded by paragraph 4 below and specify the manner in which those rights are to be exercised.

(3) . . .

Advice

3. Where notice is served on a person under paragraph 2(1) above, the matter shall be referred for the advice of one or more persons nominated by the Secretary of State.

Representations and interview

4.—(1) Where a person on whom notice is served under paragraph 2(1) above objects to the making against him of the exclusion order under consideration, he may—
- (a) make representations in writing to the Secretary of State setting out the grounds of his objections; and
- (b) include in those representations a request for a personal interview with the person or persons nominated by the Secretary of State under paragraph 3 above.

(2) The person on whom the notice is served may exercise the rights conferred by sub-paragraph (1) above—
- (a) if he is outside the relevant territory when the notice is served, within fourteen days of the service of the notice;
- (b) if he is inside the relevant territory when the notice is served but departs with the Secretary of State's approval within seven days of the service of the notice, within fourteen days of his departure; and
- (c) in any other case, within seven days of the service of the notice.

(3) In sub-paragraph (2) above "the relevant territory" means—

(a) Great Britain if the notice relates to the making of an order under section 5 of this Act;

(b) Northern Ireland if it relates to the making of an order under section 6 of this Act; and

(c) the United Kingdom if it relates to the making of an order under section 7 of this Act.

(4) A person who requests a personal interview under sub-paragraph (1)(b) above shall be granted one unless—

(a) sub-paragraph (2)(a) or (b) above applies to him; and

(b) it appears to the Secretary of State that it is not reasonably practicable to grant him such an interview in an appropriate country or territory within a reasonable period from the date on which he made his representations.

(5) Where, in the case of a person to whom sub-paragraph (2)(a) or (b) above applies, it appears to the Secretary of State that it is reasonably practicable to grant him a personal interview in more than one appropriate country or territory, the Secretary of State may grant him the personal interview in whichever of them he thinks fit.

(6) In sub-paragraphs (4) and (5) above "appropriate country or territory" means—

(a) Northern Ireland or the Republic of Ireland if the notice served on the person under paragraph 2(1) above relates to the making of an order under section 5 of this Act;

(b) Great Britain or the Republic of Ireland if it relates to the making of an order under section 6 of this Act; and

(c) the Republic of Ireland if it relates to the making of an order under section 7 of this Act.

(7) . . .

Making of exclusion order

5.—(1) In deciding whether to make an exclusion order against any person, the Secretary of State shall take into account everything which appears to him to be relevant; and where a notice has been served on the person concerned under paragraph 2(1) above the Secretary of State shall in particular take account of—

(a) the advice of the person or persons to whom the matter was referred under paragraph 3 above;

(b) any representations made by the person under paragraph 4 above; and

(c) the report of any personal interview granted under that paragraph.

(2) The question whether to make an exclusion order against a person on whom notice has been served under paragraph 2(1) above shall be decided as soon as is reasonably practicable after—

(a) the Secretary of State has received the advice of the person or persons to whom the matter was referred under paragraph 3 above; and

(b) sub-paragraph (3) below is satisfied.

(3) This sub-paragraph is satisfied if—

(a) the Secretary of State has received representations made by the person under paragraph 4 above and the report of any personal interview granted under that paragraph;

(b) the Secretary of State has received from the person a statement in writing that he does not intend to make representations under that paragraph; or

(c) the period during which the person may make representations under that paragraph has expired.

(4) If the Secretary of State—

(a) makes an exclusion order against a person; or

(b) decides not to make an exclusion order against a person on whom notice has been served under paragraph 2(1) above,

notice in writing of the making of the order or the decision not to make an order shall be served on him if it is reasonably practicable to do so.

Detention pending decision whether to make exclusion order

5A.—(1) A person on whom notice has been served under paragraph 2(1) above may be detained under the authority of the Secretary of State until the Secretary of State has either made an exclusion order against him or decided not to make an exclusion order against him.

(2) A person liable to be detained under sub-paragraph (1) above may be arrested without warrant by an examining officer.

(3) The power of detention and the power of arrest conferred by sub-paragraphs (1) and (2) above are exercisable only—

(a) in Great Britain if the notice relates to the making of an order under section 5 of this Act; and

(b) in Northern Ireland if it relates to the making of an order under section 6 of this Act.

(4) . . .]

6–9. . . .

NOTES

Para 1: sub-paras (3), (4) outside the scope of this work.

Paras 2–5A: substituted for original paras 2–5 by the Prevention of Terrorism (Exclusion Orders) Regulations 1996, SI 1996/892, reg 2.

Para 2: sub-para (3) outside the scope of this work.

Para 4: sub-para (7) outside the scope of this work.

Para 5A: sub-para (4) outside the scope of this work.

Paras 6–9: outside the scope of this work.

SCHEDULE 7

Section 17

TERRORIST INVESTIGATIONS

PART I
ENGLAND, WALES AND NORTHERN IRELAND

Interpretation

1. In this Part of this Schedule a "terrorist investigation" means any investigation to which section 17(1) of this Act applies and "items subject to legal privilege", "excluded material" and "special procedure material" have the meanings given in sections 10 to 14 of the Police and Criminal Evidence Act 1984.

Search for material other than excluded or special procedure material

2.—(1) A justice of the peace may, on an application made by a constable, issue a warrant under this paragraph if satisfied that a terrorist investigation is being carried out and that there are reasonable grounds for believing—

(a) that there is material on premises specified in the application which is likely to be of substantial value (whether by itself or together with other material) to the investigation;

(b) that the material does not consist of or include items subject to legal privilege, excluded material or special procedure material; and

(c) that any of the conditions in sub-paragraph (2) below are fulfilled.

(2) The conditions referred to in sub-paragraph (1)(c) above are—

(a) that it is not practicable to communicate with any person entitled to grant entry to the premises;

(b) that it is practicable to communicate with a person entitled to grant entry to the premises but it is not practicable to communicate with any person entitled to grant access to the material;

(c) that entry to the premises will not be granted unless a warrant is produced;

(d) that the purpose of a search may be frustrated or seriously prejudiced unless a constable arriving at the premises can secure immediate entry to them.

(3) A warrant under this paragraph shall authorise a constable to enter the premises specified in the warrant and to search the premises and any person found there and to seize and retain anything found there or on any such person, other than items subject to legal privilege, if he has reasonable grounds for believing—

(a) that it is likely to be of substantial value (whether by itself or together with other material) to the investigation; and

(b) that it is necessary to seize it in order to prevent it being concealed, lost, damaged, altered or destroyed.

(4) . . .

[*Search of non-residential premises*

2A.—(1) A justice of the peace may, on an application made by a police officer of at least the rank of superintendent, issue a warrant under this paragraph if satisfied that a terrorist investigation is being carried out and that there are reasonable grounds for believing—

(a) that there is material which is likely to be of substantial value (whether by itself or together with other material) to the investigation to be found on one or more of the premises specified in the application; and

(b) that the material does not consist of or include items subject to legal privilege, excluded material or special procedure material.

(2) The officer making an application under this paragraph may not include in the premises specified in the application any which he has reasonable cause to believe are used wholly or mainly as a dwelling.

(3) A warrant under this paragraph shall authorise a constable to enter any of the premises specified in the warrant and to search the premises and any person found there and to seize and retain anything found there or on any such person, other than an item subject to legal privilege, if he has reasonable grounds for believing—

(a) that it is likely to be of substantial value (whether by itself or together with other material) to the investigation; and

(b) that it is necessary to seize it in order to prevent it from being concealed, lost, damaged, altered or destroyed.

(4) Entry and search under a warrant issued under this paragraph must be within 24 hours from the time when the warrant is issued.]

3, 4. . . .

Search for excluded or special procedure material

5.—(1) A constable may apply to a Circuit judge for a warrant under this paragraph in relation to specified premises.

(2) On such an application the judge may issue a warrant under this paragraph if satisfied—

(a) that an order made under paragraph 3 above in relation to material on the premises has not been complied with; or

(b) that there are reasonable grounds for believing that there is on the premises material consisting of or including excluded material or special procedure material, that it does not include items subject to legal privilege and that the conditions in sub-paragraph (5) of that paragraph and the condition in sub-paragraph (3) below are fulfilled in respect of that material.

(3) The condition referred to in sub-paragraph (2)(b) above is that it would not be appropriate to make an order under paragraph 3 above in relation to the material because—

(a) it is not practicable to communicate with any person entitled to produce the material; or

(b) it is not practicable to communicate with any person entitled to grant access to the material or entitled to grant entry to the premises on which the material is situated; or

(c) the investigation for the purposes of which the application is made might be seriously prejudiced unless a constable could secure immediate access to the material.

(4) A warrant under this paragraph shall authorise a constable to enter the premises specified in the warrant and to search the premises and any person found there and to seize and retain anything found there or on any such person, other than items subject to legal privilege, if he has reasonable grounds for believing that it is likely to be of substantial value (whether by itself or together with other material) to the investigation for the purposes of which the application was made.

(5) . . .

6. . . .

Urgent cases

7.—(1) If a police officer of at least the rank of superintendent has reasonable grounds for believing that the case is one of great emergency and that in the interests of the State immediate action is necessary, he may by a written order signed by him give to any constable the authority which may be given by a search warrant under paragraph 2[, 2A] or 5 above.

(2) Where an authority is given under this paragraph particulars of the case shall be notified as soon as may be to the Secretary of State.

(3) An order under this paragraph may not authorise a search for items subject to legal privilege.

(4) If such a police officer as is mentioned in sub-paragraph (1) above has reasonable grounds for believing that the case is such as is there mentioned he may by a notice in writing signed by him require any person specified in the notice to provide an explanation of any material seized in pursuance of an order under this paragraph.

(5) Any person who without reasonable excuse fails to comply with a notice under sub-paragraph (4) above is guilty of an offence and liable on summary conviction to imprisonment for a term not exceeding six months or a fine not exceeding level 5 on the standard scale or both.

(6) Sub-paragraphs (2) to (5) of paragraph 6 above shall apply to a requirement imposed under sub-paragraph (4) above as they apply to a requirement under that paragraph.

8–17. . . .

NOTES

Para 2: sub-para (4) outside the scope of this work.

Para 2A: inserted by the Prevention of Terrorism (Additional Powers) Act 1996, s 2(1), (2).

Para 5: sub-para (5) outside the scope of this work.

Para 7: words in square brackets in sub-para (1) inserted by the Prevention of Terrorism (Additional Powers) Act 1996, s 2(1), (4).

Paras 3, 4, 6, 8–17: outside the scope of this work.

SECURITY SERVICE ACT 1989

(C 5)

An Act to place the Security Service on a statutory basis; to enable certain actions to be taken on the authority of warrants issued by the Secretary of State, with provision for the issue of such warrants to be kept under review by a Commissioner; to establish a procedure for the investigation by a Tribunal or, in some cases, by the Commissioner of complaints about the Service; and for connected purposes

[27 April 1989]

1 The Security Service

(1) There shall continue to be a Security Service (in this Act referred to as "the Service") under the authority of the Secretary of State.

(2) The function of the Service shall be the protection of national security and, in particular, its protection against threats from espionage, terrorism and sabotage, from the activities of agents of foreign powers and from actions intended to overthrow or undermine parliamentary democracy by political, industrial or violent means.

(3) It shall also be the function of the Service to safeguard the economic well-being of the United Kingdom against threats posed by the actions or intentions of persons outside the British Islands.

[(4) It shall also be the function of the Service to act in support of the activities of police forces[, the National Criminal Intelligence Service, the National Crime Squad] and other law enforcement agencies in the prevention and detection of serious crime.]

NOTES

Sub-s (4): added by the Security Service Act 1996, s 1(1); words in square brackets inserted by the Police Act 1997, s 134(1), Sch 9, para 60.

2 The Director-General

(1) The operations of the Service shall continue to be under the control of a Director-General appointed by the Secretary of State.

(2) The Director-General shall be responsible for the efficiency of the Service and it shall be his duty to ensure—

- (a) that there are arrangements for securing that no information is obtained by the Service except so far as necessary for the proper discharge of its functions or disclosed by it except so far as necessary for that purpose or for the purpose of preventing or detecting serious crime [or for the purpose of any criminal proceedings]; and
- (b) that the Service does not take any action to further the interests of any political party[; and
- (c) that there are arrangements, agreed with [the Director General of the National Criminal Intelligence Service], for co-ordinating the activities of the Service in pursuance of section 1(4) of this Act with the activities of police forces[, the National Criminal Intelligence Service, the National Crime Squad] and other law enforcement agencies].

(3) The arrangements mentioned in subsection (2)(a) above shall be such as to ensure that information in the possession of the Service is not disclosed for use in determining whether a person should be employed, or continue to be employed, by any person, or in any office or capacity, except in accordance with provisions in that behalf approved by the Secretary of State.

(3A), (3B) . . .

(4) The Director-General shall make an annual report on the work of the Service to the Prime Minister and the Secretary of State and may at any time report to either of them on any matter relating to its work.

NOTES

Sub-s (2): words in square brackets in para (a) inserted by the Intelligence Services Act 1994, s 11(2), Sch 4, para 1(1); para (c) and word immediately preceding it inserted by the Security Service Act 1996, s 1(2); in para (c), words in first pair of square brackets substituted, and words in second pair of square brackets inserted, by the Police Act 1997, ss 12, 134(1), Sch 9, para 61.

Sub-s (3A): outside the scope of this work.

Sub-s (3B): repealed by the Police Act 1997, s 134(2), Sch 10.

---

4 The Security Service Commissioner

(1) The Prime Minister shall appoint as a Commissioner for the purposes of this Act a person who holds or has held high judicial office within the meaning of the Appellate Jurisdiction Act 1876.

(2) The Commissioner shall hold office in accordance with the terms of his appointment and there shall be paid to him by the Secretary of State such allowances as the Treasury may determine.

(3) In addition to his functions under the subsequent provisions of this Act the Commissioner shall keep under review the exercise by the Secretary of State of his [powers, so far as they relate to applications made by the Service, under sections 5 and 6 of the Intelligence Act 1994.]

(4) It shall be the duty of every member of the Service and of every official of the department of the Secretary of State to disclose or give to the Commissioner such documents or information as he may require for the purpose of enabling him to discharge his functions.

(5) The Commissioner shall make an annual report on the discharge of his functions to the Prime Minister and may at any time report to him on any matter relating to his discharge of those functions.

(6) The Prime Minister shall lay before each House of Parliament a copy of each annual report made by the Commissioner under subsection (5) above together with a statement as to whether any matter has been excluded from that copy in pursuance of subsection (7) below.

(7) If it appears to the Prime Minister, after consultation with the Commissioner, that the publication of any matter in a report would be prejudicial to the continued discharge of the functions of the Service, the Prime Minister may exclude that matter from the copy of the report as laid before each House of Parliament.

(8) The Secretary of State may, after consultation with the Commissioner and with the approval of the Treasury as to numbers, provide the Commissioner with such staff as the Secretary of State thinks necessary for the discharge of his functions.

NOTES

Sub-s (3): words in square brackets substituted by the Intelligence Services Act 1994, s 11(2), Sch 4, para 2.

5 Investigation of complaints

(1) There shall be a Tribunal for the purpose of investigating complaints about the Service in the manner specified in Schedule 1 to this Act.

(2) . . .

(3) The Commissioner shall have the functions conferred on him by Schedule 1 to this Act and give the Tribunal all such assistance in discharging their functions under that Schedule as they may require.

(4) The decisions of the Tribunal and the Commissioner under that Schedule (including decisions as to their jurisdictions) shall not be subject to appeal or liable to be questioned in any court.

NOTES

Sub-s (2): outside the scope of this work.

7 Short title, commencement and extent

(1) This Act may be cited as the Security Service Act 1989.

(2) This Act shall come into force on such day as the Secretary of State may by an order made by statutory instrument appoint, and different days may be appointed for different provisions or different purposes.

(3) This Act extends to Northern Ireland.

(4) . . .

NOTES

Sub-s (4): outside the scope of this work.

SCHEDULE 1

Section 5(1)

INVESTIGATION OF COMPLAINTS

Preliminary

1. Any person may complain to the Tribunal if he is aggrieved by anything which he believes the Service has done in relation to him or to any property of his; and, unless the Tribunal consider that the complaint is frivolous or vexatious, they shall investigate it in accordance with this Schedule.

Investigations and determinations

2.—(1) The Tribunal shall investigate whether the complainant has been the subject of inquiries by the Service.

(2) If the Tribunal find that the Service has made inquiries about the complainant but that those inquiries had ceased at the time when the complaint was made, they shall determine whether, at the time when the inquiries were instituted, the Service had reasonable grounds for deciding to institute inquiries about the complainant in the discharge of its functions.

(3) If the Tribunal find that inquiries by the Service about the complainant were continuing at the time when the complaint was made, they shall determine whether, at that time, the Service had reasonable grounds for deciding to continue inquiries about the complainant in the discharge of its functions.

(4) Where it appears to the Tribunal that the inquiries had been or were being made about the complainant on the ground of his membership of a category of persons regarded by the Service as requiring investigation in the discharge of its functions, the Tribunal shall regard the Service as having reasonable grounds for deciding to institute or continue inquiries about the complainant if the Tribunal consider that the Service had reasonable grounds for believing him to be a member of that category.

3. If and so far as the complainant alleges that the Service has disclosed information for use in determining whether he should be employed, or continue to be employed, by any person or in any office or capacity specified by him, the Tribunal shall investigate whether the Service has disclosed information for that purpose and, if the Tribunal find that it has done so, they shall determine whether the Service had reasonable grounds for believing the information to be true.

4.—(1) If and so far as the complainant alleges that anything has been done by the Service in relation to any property of his, the Tribunal shall refer the complaint to the Commissioner who shall investigate whether a warrant has been issued under section 3 of this Act [or section 5 of the Intelligence Services Act 1994] in respect of that property and if he finds that such a warrant has been issued he shall, applying the principles applied by a court on an application for judicial review, determine whether the Secretary of State was acting properly in issuing or renewing the warrant.

(2) The Commissioner shall inform the Tribunal of his conclusion on any complaint so far as referred to him under this paragraph.

Report of conclusions

5.—(1) Where the Tribunal determine under paragraph 2 or 3 above that the Service did not have reasonable grounds for the decision or belief in question, they shall—

(a) give notice to the complainant that they have made a determination in his favour under that paragraph; and

(b) make a report of their findings to the Secretary of State and to the Commissioner.

(2) The Tribunal shall also give notice to the complainant of any determination in his favour by the Commissioner under paragraph 4 above.

(3) Where in the case of any complaint no such determination as is mentioned in sub-paragraph (1) or (2) above is made by the Tribunal or the Commissioner the Tribunal shall give notice to the complainant that no determination in his favour has been made on his complaint.

6, 7. . . .

Supplementary

8.—(1) The persons who may complain to the Tribunal under this Schedule include any organisation and any association or combination of persons.

(2) References in this Schedule to a complainant's property include references to any place where the complainant resides or works.

9. . . .

NOTES

Para 4: words in square brackets in sub-para (1) inserted by the Intelligence Services Act 1994, s 11(2), Sch 4, para 3.

Paras 6, 7, 9: outside the scope of this work.

OFFICIAL SECRETS ACT 1989

(C 6)

An Act to replace section 2 of the Official Secrets Act 1911 by provisions protecting more limited classes of official information

[11 May 1989]

1 Security and intelligence

(1) A person who is or has been—

(a) a member of the security and intelligence services; or

(b) a person notified that he is subject to the provisions of this subsection,

is guilty of an offence if without lawful authority he discloses any information, document or other article relating to security or intelligence which is or has been in his possession by virtue of his position as a member of any of those services or in the course of his work while the notification is or was in force.

(2) The reference in subsection (1) above to disclosing information relating to security or intelligence includes a reference to making any statement which purports to be a disclosure of such information or is intended to be taken by those to whom it is addressed as being such a disclosure.

(3) A person who is or has been a Crown servant or government contractor is guilty of an offence if without lawful authority he makes a damaging disclosure of any information, document or other article relating to security or intelligence which is or has been in his possession by virtue of his position as such but otherwise than as mentioned in subsection (1) above.

(4) For the purposes of subsection (3) above a disclosure is damaging if—

(a) it causes damage to the work of, or of any part of, the security and intelligence services; or

(b) it is of information or a document or other article which is such that its unauthorised disclosure would be likely to cause such damage or which falls within a class or description of information, documents or articles the unauthorised disclosure of which would be likely to have that effect.

(5) It is a defence for a person charged with an offence under this section to prove that at the time of the alleged offence he did not know, and had no reasonable cause to believe, that the information, document or article in question related to security or intelligence or, in the case of an offence under subsection (3), that the disclosure would be damaging within the meaning of that subsection.

(6) Notification that a person is subject to subsection (1) above shall be effected by a notice in writing served on him by a Minister of the Crown; and such a notice may be served if, in the Minister's opinion, the work undertaken by the person in question is or includes work connected with the security and intelligence services and its nature is such that the interests of national security require that he should be subject to the provisions of that subsection.

(7) Subject to subsection (8) below, a notification for the purposes of subsection (1) above shall be in force for the period of five years beginning with the day on which it is served but may be renewed by further notices under subsection (6) above for periods of five years at a time.

(8) A notification for the purposes of subsection (1) above may at any time be revoked by a further notice in writing served by the Minister on the person concerned; and the Minister shall serve such a further notice as soon as, in his opinion, the work undertaken by that person ceases to be such as is mentioned in subsection (6) above.

(9) In this section "security or intelligence" means the work of, or in support of, the security and intelligence services or any part of them, and references to information relating to security or intelligence include references to information held or transmitted by those services or by persons in support of, or of any part of, them.

2 Defence

(1) A person who is or has been a Crown servant or government contractor is guilty of an offence if without lawful authority he makes a damaging disclosure of any information, document or other article relating to defence which is or has been in his possession by virtue of his position as such.

(2) For the purposes of subsection (1) above a disclosure is damaging if—

(a) it damages the capability of, or of any part of, the armed forces of the Crown to carry out their tasks or leads to loss of life or injury to members of those forces or serious damage to the equipment or installations of those forces; or

(b) otherwise than as mentioned in paragraph (a) above, it endangers the interests of the United Kingdom abroad, seriously obstructs the promotion or protection by the United Kingdom of those interests or endangers the safety of British citizens abroad; or

(c) it is of information or of a document or article which is such that its unauthorised disclosure would be likely to have any of those effects.

(3) It is a defence for a person charged with an offence under this section to prove that at the time of the alleged offence he did not know, and had no reasonable cause to believe, that the information, document or article in question related to defence or that its disclosure would be damaging within the meaning of subsection (1) above.

(4) In this section "defence" means—

(a) the size, shape, organisation, logistics, order of battle, deployment, operations, state of readiness and training of the armed forces of the Crown;

(b) the weapons, stores or other equipment of those forces and the invention, development, production and operation of such equipment and research relating to it;

(c) defence policy and strategy and military planning and intelligence;

(d) plans and measures for the maintenance of essential supplies and services that are or would be needed in time of war.

3 International relations

(1) A person who is or has been a Crown servant or government contractor is guilty of an offence if without lawful authority he makes a damaging disclosure of—

(a) any information, document or other article relating to international relations; or

(b) any confidential information, document or other article which was obtained from a State other than the United Kingdom or an international organisation, being information or a document or article which is or has been in his possession by virtue of his position as a Crown servant or government contractor.

(2) For the purposes of subsection (1) above a disclosure is damaging if—

(a) it endangers the interests of the United Kingdom abroad, seriously obstructs the promotion or protection by the United Kingdom of those interests or endangers the safety of British citizens abroad; or

(b) it is of information or of a document or article which is such that its unauthorised disclosure would be likely to have any of those effects.

(3) In the case of information or a document or article within subsection (1)(b) above—

(a) the fact that it is confidential, or

(b) its nature or contents,

may be sufficient to establish for the purposes of subsection (2)(b) above that the information, document or article is such that its unauthorised disclosure would be likely to have any of the effects there mentioned.

(4) It is a defence for a person charged with an offence under this section to prove that at the time of the alleged offence he did not know, and had no reasonable cause to believe, that the information, document or article in question was such as is mentioned in subsection (1) above or that its disclosure would be damaging within the meaning of that subsection.

(5) In this section "international relations" means the relations between States, between international organisations or between one or more States and one or more such organisations and includes any matter relating to a State other than the United Kingdom or to an international organisation which is capable of affecting the relations of the United Kingdom with another State or with an international organisation.

(6) For the purposes of this section any information, document or article obtained from a State or organisation is confidential at any time while the terms on which it was obtained require it to be held in confidence or while the circumstances in which it was obtained make it reasonable for the State or organisation to expect that it would be so held.

4 Crime and special investigation powers

(1) A person who is or has been a Crown servant or government contractor is guilty of an offence if without lawful authority he discloses any information, document or other article to which this section applies and which is or has been in his possession by virtue of his position as such.

(2) This section applies to any information, document or other article—

(a) the disclosure of which—

(i) results in the commission of an offence; or

(ii) facilitates an escape from legal custody or the doing of any other act prejudicial to the safekeeping of persons in legal custody; or

(iii) impedes the prevention or detection of offences or the apprehension or prosecution of suspected offenders; or

(b) which is such that its unauthorised disclosure would be likely to have any of those effects.

(3) This section also applies to—

(a) any information obtained by reason of the interception of any communication in obedience to a warrant issued under section 2 of the Interception of Communications Act 1985, any information relating to the obtaining of information by reason of any such interception and any document or other article which is or has been used or held for use in, or has been obtained by reason of, any such interception; and

(b) any information obtained by reason of action authorised by a warrant issued under section 3 of the Security Service Act 1989 [or under section 5 of the Intelligence Services Act 1994 or by an authorisation given under section 7 of that Act], any information relating to the obtaining of information by reason of any such action and any document or other article which is or has been used or held for use in, or has been obtained by reason of, any such action.

(4) It is a defence for a person charged with an offence under this section in respect of a disclosure falling within subsection (2)(a) above to prove that at the time of the alleged offence he did not know, and had no reasonable cause to believe, that the disclosure would have any of the effects there mentioned.

(5) It is a defence for a person charged with an offence under this section in respect of any other disclosure to prove that at the time of the alleged offence he did not know, and had no reasonable cause to believe, that the information, document or article in question was information or a document or article to which this section applies.

(6) In this section "legal custody" includes detention in pursuance of any enactment or any instrument made under an enactment.

NOTES

Sub-s (3): words in square brackets in para (b) inserted by the Intelligence Services Act 1994, s 11(2), Sch 4, para 4.

5 Information resulting from unauthorised disclosures or entrusted in confidence

(1) Subsection (2) below applies where—

(a) any information, document or other article protected against disclosure by the foregoing provisions of this Act has come into a person's possession as a result of having been—

(i) disclosed (whether to him or another) by a Crown servant or government contractor without lawful authority; or

(ii) entrusted to him by a Crown servant or government contractor on terms requiring it to be held in confidence or in circumstances in which the Crown servant or government contractor could reasonably expect that it would be so held; or

(iii) disclosed (whether to him or another) without lawful authority by a person to whom it was entrusted as mentioned in sub-paragraph (ii) above; and

(b) the disclosure without lawful authority of the information, document or article by the person into whose possession it has come is not an offence under any of those provisions.

(2) Subject to subsections (3) and (4) below, the person into whose possession the information, document or article has come is guilty of an offence if he discloses it

without lawful authority knowing, or having reasonable cause to believe, that it is protected against disclosure by the foregoing provisions of this Act and that it has come into his possession as mentioned in subsection (1) above.

(3) In the case of information or a document or article protected against disclosure by sections 1 to 3 above, a person does not commit an offence under subsection (2) above unless—

(a) the disclosure by him is damaging; and

(b) he makes it knowing, or having reasonable cause to believe, that it would be damaging;

and the question whether a disclosure is damaging shall be determined for the purposes of this subsection as it would be in relation to a disclosure of that information, document or article by a Crown servant in contravention of section 1(3), 2(1) or 3(1) above.

(4) A person does not commit an offence under subsection (2) above in respect of information or a document or other article which has come into his possession as a result of having been disclosed—

(a) as mentioned in subsection (1)(a)(i) above by a government contractor; or

(b) as mentioned in subsection (1)(a)(iii) above,

unless that disclosure was by a British citizen or took place in the United Kingdom, in any of the Channel Islands or in the Isle of Man or a colony.

(5) For the purposes of this section information or a document or article is protected against disclosure by the foregoing provisions of this Act if—

(a) it relates to security or intelligence, defence or international relations within the meaning of section 1, 2 or 3 above or is such as is mentioned in section 3(1)(b) above; or

(b) it is information or a document or article to which section 4 above applies;

and information or a document or article is protected against disclosure by sections 1 to 3 above if it falls within paragraph (a) above.

(6) A person is guilty of an offence if without lawful authority he discloses any information, document or other article which he knows, or has reasonable cause to believe, to have come into his possession as a result of a contravention of section 1 of the Official Secrets Act 1911.

6 Information entrusted in confidence to other States or international organisations

(1) This section applies where—

(a) any information, document or other article which—

  (i) relates to security or intelligence, defence or international relations; and

  (ii) has been communicated in confidence by or on behalf of the United Kingdom to another State or to an international organisation,

has come into a person's possession as a result of having been disclosed (whether to him or another) without the authority of that State or organisation or, in the case of an organisation, of a member of it; and

(b) the disclosure without lawful authority of the information, document or article by the person into whose possession it has come is not an offence under any of the foregoing provisions of this Act.

(2) Subject to subsection (3) below, the person into whose possession the information, document or article has come is guilty of an offence if he makes a damaging disclosure of it knowing, or having reasonable cause to believe, that it is such as is mentioned in subsection (1) above, that it has come into his possession as there mentioned and that its disclosure would be damaging.

(3) A person does not commit an offence under subsection (2) above if the information, document or article is disclosed by him with lawful authority or has previously been made available to the public with the authority of the State or organisation concerned or, in the case of an organisation, of a member of it.

(4) For the purposes of this section "security or intelligence", "defence" and "international relations" have the same meaning as in sections 1, 2 and 3 above and the question whether a disclosure is damaging shall be determined as it would be in relation to a disclosure of the information, document or article in question by a Crown servant in contravention of section 1(3), 2(1) and 3(1) above.

(5) For the purposes of this section information or a document or article is communicated in confidence if it is communicated on terms requiring it to be held in confidence or in circumstances in which the person communicating it could reasonably expect that it would be so held.

7 Authorised disclosures

(1) For the purposes of this Act a disclosure by—

(a) a Crown servant; or

(b) a person, not being a Crown servant or government contractor, in whose case a notification for the purposes of section 1(1) above is in force,

is made with lawful authority if, and only if, it is made in accordance with his official duty.

(2) For the purposes of this Act a disclosure by a government contractor is made with lawful authority if, and only if, it is made—

(a) in accordance with an official authorisation; or

(b) for the purposes of the functions by virtue of which he is a government contractor and without contravening an official restriction.

(3) For the purposes of this Act a disclosure made by any other person is made with lawful authority if, and only if, it is made—

(a) to a Crown servant for the purposes of his functions as such; or

(b) in accordance with an official authorisation.

(4) It is a defence for a person charged with an offence under any of the foregoing provisions of this Act to prove that at the time of the alleged offence he believed that he had lawful authority to make the disclosure in question and had no reasonable cause to believe otherwise.

(5) In this section "official authorisation" and "official restriction" mean, subject to subsection (6) below, an authorisation or restriction duly given or imposed by a Crown servant or government contractor or by or on behalf of a prescribed body or a body of a prescribed class.

(6) In relation to section 6 above "official authorisation" includes an authorisation duly given by or on behalf of the State or organisation concerned or, in the case of an organisation, a member of it.

8 Safeguarding of information

(1) Where a Crown servant or government contractor, by virtue of his position as such, has in his possession or under his control any document or other article which it would be an offence under any of the foregoing provisions of this Act for him to disclose without lawful authority he is guilty of an offence if—

(a) being a Crown servant, he retains the document or article contrary to his official duty; or

(b) being a government contractor, he fails to comply with an official direction for the return or disposal of the document or article,

or if he fails to take such care to prevent the unauthorised disclosure of the document or article as a person in his position may reasonably be expected to take.

(2) It is a defence for a Crown servant charged with an offence under subsection (1)(a) above to prove that at the time of the alleged offence he believed that he was acting in accordance with his official duty and had no reasonable cause to believe otherwise.

(3) In subsections (1) and (2) above references to a Crown servant include any person, not being a Crown servant or government contractor, in whose case a notification for the purposes of section 1(1) above is in force.

(4) Where a person has in his possession or under his control any document or other article which it would be an offence under section 5 above for him to disclose without lawful authority, he is guilty of an offence if—

(a) he fails to comply with an official direction for its return or disposal; or

(b) where he obtained it from a Crown servant or government contractor on terms requiring it to be held in confidence or in circumstances in which that servant or contractor could reasonably expect that it would be so held, he fails to take such care to prevent its unauthorised disclosure as a person in his position may reasonably be expected to take.

(5) Where a person has in his possession or under his control any document or other article which it would be an offence under section 6 above for him to disclose without lawful authority, he is guilty of an offence if he fails to comply with an official direction for its return or disposal.

(6) A person is guilty of an offence if he discloses any official information, document or other article which can be used for the purpose of obtaining access to any information, document of other article protected against disclosure by the foregoing provisions of this Act and the circumstances in which it is disclosed are such that it would be reasonable to expect that it might be used for that purpose without authority.

(7) For the purposes of subsection (6) above a person discloses information or a document or article which is official if—

(a) he has or has had it in his possession by virtue of his position as a Crown servant or government contractor; or

(b) he knows or has reasonable cause to believe that a Crown servant or government contractor has or has had it in his possession by virtue of his position as such.

(8) Subsection (5) of section 5 above applies for the purposes of subsection (6) above as it applies for the purposes of that section.

(9) In this section "official direction" means a direction duly given by a Crown servant or government contractor or by or on behalf of a prescribed body or a body of a prescribed class.

9 Prosecutions

(1) Subject to subsection (2) below, no prosecution for an offence under this Act shall be instituted in England and Wales or in Northern Ireland except by or with the consent of the Attorney General or, as the case may be, the Attorney General for Northern Ireland.

(2) Subsection (1) above does not apply to an offence in respect of any such information, document or article as is mentioned in section 4(2) above but no prosecution for such an offence shall be instituted in England and Wales or in Northern Ireland except by or with the consent of the Director of Public Prosecutions or, as the case may be, the Director of Public Prosecutions for Northern Ireland.

10 Penalties

(1) A person guilty of an offence under any provision of this Act other than section 8(1), (4) or (5) shall be liable—

(a) on conviction on indictment, to imprisonment for a term not exceeding two years or a fine or both;

(b) on summary conviction, to imprisonment for a term not exceeding six months or a fine not exceeding the statutory maximum or both.

(2) A person guilty of an offence under section 8(1), (4) or (5) above shall be liable on summary conviction to imprisonment for a term not exceeding three months or a fine not exceeding level 5 on the standard scale or both.

11 Arrest, search and trial

(1), (2) . . .

(3) Section 9(1) of the Official Secrets Act 1911 (search warrants) shall have effect as if references to offences under that Act included references to offences under any provision of this Act other than section 8(1), (4) or (5); and the following provisions of the Police and Criminal Evidence Act 1984, that is to say—

(a) section 9(2) (which excludes items subject to legal privilege and certain other material from powers of search conferred by previous enactments); and

(b) paragraph 3(b) of Schedule 1 (which prescribes access conditions for the special procedure laid down in that Schedule),

shall apply to section 9(1) of the said Act of 1911 as extended by this subsection as they apply to that section as originally enacted.

[(3A) In the application of subsection (3) above to Northern Ireland—

(a) the reference to the Police and Criminal Evidence Act 1984 shall be construed as a reference to the Police and Criminal Evidence (Northern Ireland) Order 1989;

(b) the reference to section 9(2) of that Act shall be construed as a reference to Article 11(2) of that Order; and

(c) the reference to paragraph 3(b) of Schedule 1 to that Act shall be construed as a reference to paragraph 3(b) of Schedule 1 to that Order.]

(4) Section 8(4) of the Official Secrets Act 1920 (exclusion of public from hearing on grounds of national safety) shall have effect as if references to offences under that Act included references to offences under any provision of this Act other than section 8(1), (4) or (5).

(5) Proceedings for an offence under this Act may be taken in any place in the United Kingdom.

NOTES

Sub-s (1): amends the Police and Criminal Evidence Act 1984, s 24(2).

Sub-s (2): repealed by the Police and Criminal Evidence (Northern Ireland) Order 1989, SI 1989/1341, art 90(1), (2), Sch 6, para 19(a), Sch 7, Pt I.

Sub-s (3A) inserted by the Police and Criminal Evidence (Northern Ireland) Order 1989, SI 1989/1341, art 90(1), Sch 6, para 19(b).

12 "Crown servant" and "government contractor"

(1) In this Act "Crown servant" means—

(a) a Minister of the Crown;

(b) a person appointed under section 8 of the Northern Ireland Constitution Act 1973 (the Northern Ireland Executive etc);

(c) any person employed in the civil service of the Crown, including Her Majesty's Diplomatic Service, Her Majesty's Overseas Civil Service, the civil service of Northern Ireland and the Northern Ireland Court Service;

(d) any member of the naval, military or air forces of the Crown, including any person employed by an association established for the purposes of [Part XI of the Reserve Forces Act 1996];

(e) any constable and any other person employed or appointed in or for the purposes of any police force (including a police force within the meaning of the *Police Act (Northern Ireland) 1970*) [or of the National Criminal Intelligence Service or the National Crime Squad];

(f) any person who is a member or employee of a prescribed body or a body of a prescribed class and either is prescribed for the purposes of this paragraph or belongs to a prescribed class of members or employees of any such body;

(g) any person who is the holder of a prescribed office or who is an employee of such a holder and either is prescribed for the purposes of this paragraph or belongs to a prescribed class of such employees.

(2) In this Act "government contractor" means, subject to subsection (3) below, any person who is not a Crown servant but who provides, or is employed in the provision of, goods or services—

(a) for the purposes of any Minister or person mentioned in paragraph (a) or (b) of subsection (1) above, of any of the services, forces or bodies mentioned in that subsection or of the holder of any office prescribed under that subsection; or

(b) under an agreement or arrangement certified by the Secretary of State as being one to which the government of a State other than the United Kingdom or an international organisation is a party or which is subordinate to, or made for the purposes of implementing, any such agreement or arrangement.

(3) Where an employee or class of employees of any body, or of any holder of an office, is prescribed by an order made for the purposes of subsection (1) above—

(a) any employee of that body, or of the holder of that office, who is not prescribed or is not within the prescribed class; and

(b) any person who does not provide, or is not employed in the provision of, goods or services for the purposes of the performance of those functions of the body or the holder of the office in connection with which the employee or prescribed class of employees is engaged,

shall not be a government contractor for the purposes of this Act.

NOTES

Sub-s (1): words in square brackets in para (d) substituted by the Reserve Forces Act 1996, s 131(1), Sch 10, para 22; in para (e), for words in italics there are substituted words "Police (Northern Ireland) Act 1998", by the Police (Northern Ireland) Act 1998, s 74(1), Sch 4, para 17, as from a day to be appointed, and words in second pair of square brackets inserted by the Police Act 1997, s 134(1), Sch 9, para 62.

13 Other interpretation provisions

(1) In this Act—

"disclose" and "disclosure", in relation to a document or other article, include parting with possession of it;

"international organisation" means, subject to subsections (2) and (3) below, an organisation of which only States are members and includes a reference to any organ of such an organisation;

"prescribed" means prescribed by an order made by the Secretary of State;

"State" includes the government of a State and any organ of its government and references to a State other than the United Kingdom include references to any territory outside the United Kingdom.

(2) In section 12(2)(b) above the reference to an international organisation includes a reference to any such organisation whether or not one of which only States are members and includes a commercial organisation.

(3) In determining for the purposes of subsection (1) above whether only States are members of an organisation, any member which is itself an organisation of which only States are members, or which is an organ of such an organisation, shall be treated as a State.

15 Acts done abroad and extent

(1) Any act—

(a) done by a British citizen or Crown servant; or

(b) done by any person in any of the Channel Islands or the Isle of Man or any colony,

shall, if it would be an offence by that person under any provision of this Act other than section 8(1), (4) or (5) when done by him in the United Kingdom, be an offence under that provision.

(2) This Act extends to Northern Ireland.

(3) Her Majesty may by Order in Council provide that any provision of this Act shall extend, with such exceptions, adaptations and modifications as may be specified in the Order, to any of the Channel Islands or the Isle of Man or any colony.

16 Short title, citation, consequential amendments, repeals, revocation and commencement

(1) This Act may be cited as the Official Secrets Act 1989.

(2) This Act and the Official Secrets Acts 1911 to 1939 may be cited together as the Official Secrets Acts 1911 to 1989.

(3), (4) . . .

(5) Subject to any Order under subsection (3) of section 15 above the repeals in the Official Secrets Act 1911 and the Official Secrets Act 1920 do not extend to any of the territories mentioned in that subsection.

(6) This Act shall come into force on such day as the Secretary of State may by order appoint.

NOTES

Sub-ss (3), (4): outside the scope of this work.

EXTRADITION ACT 1989

(C 33)

An Act to consolidate enactments relating to extradition under the Criminal Justice Act 1988, the Fugitive Offenders Act 1967 and the Extradition Acts 1870 to 1935, with amendments to give effect to recommendations of the Law Commission and the Scottish Law Commission

[27 July 1989]

PART I
INTRODUCTORY

General

1 Liability to extradition

(1) Where extradition procedures under Part III of this Act are available as between the United Kingdom and a foreign state, a person in the United Kingdom who—

(a) is accused in that state of the commission of an extradition crime; or

(b) is alleged to be unlawfully at large after conviction of an extradition crime by a court in that state,

may be arrested and returned to that state in accordance with those procedures.

(2) Subject to the provisions of this Act, a person in the United Kingdom who is accused of an extradition crime—

(a) in a Commonwealth country designated for the purposes of this subsection under section 5(1) below; or

(b) in a colony,

or who is alleged to be unlawfully at large after conviction of such an offence in any such country or in a colony, may be arrested and returned to that country or colony in accordance with extradition procedures under Part III of this Act.

(2A), (3) . . .

NOTES

Sub-ss (2A), (3): outside the scope of this work.

Extradition crimes

2 Meaning of "extradition crime"

(1) In this Act, except in Schedule 1, "extradition crime" means—

(a) conduct in the territory of a foreign state, a designated Commonwealth country[, a colony or the Hong Kong Special Administrative Region] which, if it occurred in the United Kingdom, would constitute an offence punishable with imprisonment for a term of 12 months, or any greater punishment, and which, however described in the law of the foreign state, Commonwealth country or colony [or of the Hong Kong Special Administrative Region], is so punishable under that law;

(b) an extra-territorial offence against the law of a foreign state, designated Commonwealth country or colony[, or of the Hong Kong Special Administrative Region,] which is punishable under that law with imprisonment for a term of 12 months, or any greater punishment, and which satisfies—

(i) the condition specified in subsection (2) below; or

(ii) all the conditions specified in subsection (3) below.

(2) The condition mentioned in subsection (1)(b)(i) above is that in corresponding circumstances equivalent conduct would constitute an extra-territorial offence against the law of the United Kingdom punishable with imprisonment for a term of 12 months, or any greater punishment.

(3) The conditions mentioned in subsection (1)(b)(ii) above are—

(a) that the foreign state, Commonwealth country or colony [or the Hong Kong Special Administrative Region] bases its jurisdiction on the nationality of the offender;

(b) that the conduct constituting the offence occurred outside the United Kingdom; and

(c) that, if it occurred in the United Kingdom, it would constitute an offence under the law of the United Kingdom punishable with imprisonment for a term of 12 months, or any greater punishment.

(4) For the purposes of [this Act, except Schedule 1]—

(a) the law of a foreign state, designated Commonwealth country or colony includes the law of any part of it and the law of the United Kingdom includes the law of any part of the United Kingdom;

(b) conduct in a colony or dependency of a foreign state or of a designated Commonwealth country, or a vessel, aircraft or hovercraft of a foreign state or of such a country, shall be treated as if it were conduct in the territory of that state or country; . . .

(c) conduct in a vessel, aircraft or hovercraft of a colony of the United Kingdom shall be treated as if it were conduct in that colony[; and

(d) conduct in a vessel, aircraft or hovercraft of the Hong Kong Special Administrative Region shall be treated as if it were conduct in that Region.][; but—

[(d) reference shall be made to the law of the colony or dependency of a foreign state or of a designated Commonwealth country, and not (where different) to the law of the foreign state or Commonwealth country, to determine the level of punishment applicable to conduct in that colony or dependency.]

NOTES

Sub-s (1): in para (a), words in first pair of square brackets substituted, and words in second pair of square brackets inserted, by the Hong Kong (Extradition) Order 1997, SI 1997/1178, art 2, Schedule, para 2(1), (2)(a); words in square brackets in para (b) inserted by the Hong Kong (Extradition) Order 1997, SI 1997/1178, art 2, Schedule, para 2(1), (2)(b).

Sub-s (3): words in square brackets in para (a) inserted by the Hong Kong (Extradition) Order 1997, SI 1997/1178, art 2, Schedule, para 2(1), (3).

Sub-s (4): words in first pair of square brackets substituted, and second para (d) and word immediately preceding it inserted, by the Criminal Justice and Public Order Act 1994, s 168(1), Sch 9, para 37(1), (2); word omitted from para (b) repealed, and first para (d) and word immediately preceding it inserted, by the Hong Kong (Extradition) Order 1997, SI 1997/1178, art 2, Schedule, para 2(1), (4).

PART II
RESTRICTIONS ON RETURN

6 General restrictions on return

(1) A person shall not be returned under Part III of this Act, or committed or kept in custody for the purposes of return, if it appears to an appropriate authority—

(a) that the offence of which that person is accused or was convicted is an offence of a political character;

(b) that it is an offence under military law which is not also an offence under the general criminal law;

(c) that the request for his return (though purporting to be made on account of an extradition crime) is in fact made for the purpose of prosecuting or punishing him on account of his race, religion, nationality or political opinions; or

(d) that he might, if returned, be prejudiced at his trial or punished, detained or restricted in his personal liberty by reason of his race, religion, nationality or political opinions.

(2) A person who is alleged to be unlawfully at large after conviction of an extradition crime shall not be returned to a foreign state [or to the Hong Kong Special Administrative Region], or committed or kept in custody for the purposes of return to a foreign state[or to that Region], if it appears to an appropriate authority—

(a) that the conviction was obtained in his absence; and

(b) that it would not be in the interests of justice to return him on the ground of that conviction.

(3) A person accused of an offence shall not be returned, or committed or kept in custody for the purposes of return, if it appears to an appropriate authority that if charged with that offence in the United Kingdom he would be entitled to be discharged under any rule of law relating to previous acquittal or conviction.

(4) A person shall not be returned, or committed or kept in custody for the purposes of such return, unless provision is made by the relevant law, or by an arrangement made with the relevant foreign state, Commonwealth country or colony [or with the Hong Kong Special Administrative Region], for securing that he will not, unless he has first had an opportunity to leave it, be dealt with there for or in respect of any offence committed before his return to it other than—

(a) the offence in respect of which his return is ordered;

(b) an offence, other than an offence excluded by subsection (5) below, which is disclosed by the facts in respect of which his return was ordered; or

(c) subject to subsection (6) below, any other offence being an extradition crime in respect of which the Secretary of State may consent to his being dealt with.

(5) The offences excluded from paragraph (b) of subsection (4) above are offences in relation to which an order for the return of the person concerned could not lawfully be made.

(6) The Secretary of State may not give consent under paragraph (c) of that subsection in respect of an offence in relation to which it appears to him that an order for the return of the person concerned could not lawfully be made, or would not in fact be made.

(7) Any such arrangement as is mentioned in subsection (4) above which is made with a designated Commonwealth country or a colony may be an arrangement made for the particular case or an arrangement of a more general nature; and for the purposes of that subsection a certificate issued by or under the authority of the Secretary of State confirming the existence of an arrangement with a Commonwealth country or a colony and stating its terms shall be conclusive evidence of the matters contained in the certificate.

(8) In relation to a Commonwealth country or a colony the reference in subsection (1) above to an offence of a political character does not include an offence against the life or person of the Head of the Commonwealth or attempting or conspiring to commit, or assisting, counselling or procuring the commission of or being accessory before or after the fact to such an offence, or of impeding the apprehension or prosecution of persons guilty of such an offence.

(9) In this Act "appropriate authority" means—

(a) the Secretary of State;

(b) the court of committal;

(c) the High Court or High Court of Justiciary on an application for habeas corpus or for review of the order of committal.

(10) In this section, in relation to Commonwealth countries and colonies, "race" includes tribe.

NOTES

Sub-s (2): words in square brackets inserted by the Hong Kong (Extradition) Order 1997, SI 1997/1178, art 2, Schedule, para 4(a), subject to transitional provisions.

Sub-s (4): words in square brackets inserted by the Hong Kong (Extradition) Order 1997, SI 1997/1178, art 2, Schedule, para 4(b), subject to transitional provisions.

PART III
PROCEDURE

Custody

17 Custody

(1) Any person remanded or committed to custody under this Part of this Act shall be committed to the like institution as a person charged with an offence before the court of committal.

(2) If any person who is in custody by virtue of a warrant under this Act escapes out of custody, he may be retaken in any part of the United Kingdom in like manner as a person escaping from custody under a warrant for his arrest issued in that part in respect of an offence committed in that part.

(3) Where a person, being in custody in any part of the United Kingdom whether under this Part of this Act or otherwise, is required to be removed in custody under this Act to another part of the United Kingdom and is so removed by sea or by air, he shall be deemed to continue in legal custody until he reaches the place to which he is required to be removed.

(4) A warrant for the return of any person shall be sufficient authority for all persons to whom it is directed and all constables to receive that person, keep him in custody and convey him into the jurisdiction to which he is to be returned.

PART VI
MISCELLANEOUS AND SUPPLEMENTARY

Supplementary

38 Short title, commencement and extent

(1) This Act may be cited as the Extradition Act 1989.

(2) The provisions of this Act other than any provision to which subsection (3) below applies shall come into force at the end of the period of two months beginning with the day on which it is passed.

(3), (4) . . .

(5) This Act extends to Northern Ireland.

NOTES

Sub-ss (3), (4): outside the scope of this work.

COURTS AND LEGAL SERVICES ACT 1990

(C 41)

An Act to make provision with respect to the procedure in, and allocation of business between, the High Court and other courts; to make provision with respect to legal services; to establish a body to be known as the Lord Chancellor's Advisory Committee on Legal Education and Conduct and a body to be known as the Authorised Conveyancing Practitioners Board; to provide for the appointment of a Legal Services Ombudsman; to make provision for the establishment of a Conveyancing Ombudsman Scheme; to provide for the establishment of Conveyancing Appeal Tribunals; to amend the law relating to judicial and related pensions and judicial and other appointments; to make provision with respect to certain officers of the Supreme Court; to amend the Solicitors Act 1974; to amend the Arbitration Act 1950; to make provision with respect to certain loans in respect of residential property; to make provision with respect to the jurisdiction of the Parliamentary Commissioner for Administration in connection with the functions of court staff; to amend the Children Act 1989 and make further provision in connection with that Act; and for connected purposes

[1 November 1990]

PART II
LEGAL SERVICES

Introductory

17 The statutory objective and the general principle

(1) The general objective of this Part is the development of legal services in England and Wales (and in particular the development of advocacy, litigation, conveyancing and probate services) by making provision for new or better ways of

providing such services and a wider choice of persons providing them, while maintaining the proper and efficient administration of justice.

(2) In this Act that objective is referred to as "the statutory objective".

(3) As a general principle the question whether a person should be granted a right of audience, or be granted a right to conduct litigation in relation to any court or proceedings, should be determined only by reference to—

(a) whether he is qualified in accordance with the educational and training requirements appropriate to the court or proceedings;

(b) whether he is a member of a professional or other body which—

(i) has rules of conduct (however described) governing the conduct of its members;

(ii) has an effective mechanism for enforcing the rules of conduct; and

(iii) is likely to enforce them;

(c) whether, in the case of a body whose members are or will be providing advocacy services, the rules of conduct make satisfactory provision in relation to the court or proceedings in question requiring any such member not to withhold those services—

(i) on the ground that the nature of the case is objectionable to him or any section of the public;

(ii) on the ground that the conduct, opinions or beliefs of the prospective client are unacceptable to him or to any section of the public;

(iii) on any ground relating to the source of any financial support which may properly be given to the prospective client for the proceedings in question (for example, on the ground that such support will be available under the Legal Aid Act 1988); and

(d) whether the rules of conduct are, in relation to the court or proceedings, appropriate in the interests of the proper and efficient administration of justice.

(4) In this Act that principle is referred to as "the general principle".

(5) Rules of conduct which allow a member of the body in question to withhold his services if there are reasonable grounds for him to consider that, having regard to—

(a) the circumstances of the case;

(b) the nature of his practice; or

(c) his experience and standing,

he is not being offered a proper fee, are not on that account to be taken as being incompatible with the general principle.

18 The statutory duty

(1) Where any person is called upon to exercise any functions which are conferred by this Part with respect to—

(a) the granting of rights of audience;

(b) the granting of rights to conduct litigation;

(c) the approval of qualification regulations or rules of conduct; or

(d) the giving of advice with respect to any matter mentioned in paragraphs (*a*) to (*c*),

it shall be the duty of that person to exercise those functions as soon as is reasonably practicable and consistent with the provisions of this Part.

(2) A person exercising any such functions shall act in accordance with the general principle and, subject to that, shall—

(a) so far as it is possible to do so in the circumstances of the case, act to further the statutory objective; and

(b) not act in any way which would be incompatible with the statutory objective.

The Advisory Committee

19 The Lord Chancellor's Advisory Committee on Legal Education and Conduct

(1) There shall be a body corporate to be known as the Lord Chancellor's Advisory Committee on Legal Education and Conduct (in this Act referred to as "the Advisory Committee").

(2) The Advisory Committee shall consist of a Chairman, and 16 other members, appointed by the Lord Chancellor.

(3) The Chairman shall be a Lord of Appeal in Ordinary or a judge of the Supreme Court of England and Wales.

(4) Of the 16 other members of the Advisory Committee—

(a) one shall be a judge who is or has been a Circuit judge;

(b) 2 shall be practising barristers appointed after consultation with the General Council of the Bar;

(c) 2 shall be practising solicitors appointed after consultation with the Law Society;

(d) 2 shall be persons with experience in the teaching of law, appointed after consultation with such institutions concerned with the teaching of law and such persons representing teachers of law as the Lord Chancellor considers appropriate; and

(e) 9 shall be persons other than—

(i) salaried judges of any court;

(ii) practising barristers;

(iii) practising solicitors; or

(iv) teachers of law,

appointed after consultation with such organisations as the Lord Chancellor considers appropriate.

(5) In appointing any member who falls within subsection (4)(*e*), the Lord Chancellor shall have regard to the desirability of appointing persons who have experience in, or knowledge of—

(a) the provision of legal services;

(b) civil or criminal proceedings and the working of the courts;

(c) the maintenance of professional standards among barristers or solicitors;

(d) social conditions;

(e) consumer affairs;

(f) commercial affairs; or

(g) the maintenance of professional standards in professions other than the legal profession.

(6) The Advisory Committee shall not be regarded as the servant or agent of the Crown, or as enjoying any status, immunity or privilege of the Crown.

(7)–(9) . . .

NOTES

Sub-ss (7)–(9): outside the scope of this work.

20 Duties of the Advisory Committee

(1) The Advisory Committee shall have the general duty of assisting in the maintenance and development of standards in the education, training and conduct of those offering legal services.

(2), (3) . . .

NOTES

Sub-ss (2), (3): outside the scope of this work.

The Legal Services Ombudsman

21 The Legal Services Ombudsman

(1) The Lord Chancellor shall appoint a person for the purpose of conducting investigations under this Act.

(2) The person appointed shall be known as "the Legal Services Ombudsman".

(3) The Legal Services Ombudsman—

(a) shall be appointed for a period of not more than three years; and

(b) shall hold and vacate office in accordance with the terms of his appointment.

(4) At the end of his term of appointment the Legal Services Ombudsman shall be eligible for re-appointment.

(5) The Legal Services Ombudsman shall not be an authorised advocate, authorised litigator, licensed conveyancer, authorised practitioner or notary.

(6) . . .

NOTES

Sub-s (6): outside the scope of this work.

22 Ombudsman's functions

(1) Subject to the provisions of this Act, the Legal Services Ombudsman may investigate any allegation which is properly made to him and which relates to the manner in which a complaint made to a professional body with respect to—

(a) a person who is or was an authorised advocate, authorised litigator, licensed conveyancer, registered foreign lawyer, recognised body or duly certificated notary public and a member of that professional body; or

(b) any employee of such a person,

has been dealt with by that professional body.

(2)–(6) . . .

(7) The Ombudsman shall not investigate—

(a) any issue which is being or has been determined by—

(i) a court;
(ii) the Solicitors Disciplinary Tribunal;
(iii) the Disciplinary Tribunal of the Council of the Inns of Court; or
(iv) any tribunal specified in an order made by the Lord Chancellor for the purposes of this subsection; or

(b) any allegation relating to a complaint against any person which concerns an aspect of his conduct in relation to which he has immunity from any action in negligence or contract.

(8)–(11) . . .

NOTES

Sub-ss (2)–(6), (8)–(11): outside the scope of this work.

24 Advisory functions

(1) The Legal Services Ombudsman may make recommendations to any professional body about the arrangements which that body has in force for the investigation of complaints made with respect to persons who are subject to that body's control.

(2) It shall be the duty of any professional body to whom a recommendation is made under this section to have regard to it.

(3) The Ombudsman may refer to the Advisory Committee any matters which come to his notice in the exercise of his functions and which appear to him to be relevant to the Committee's functions.

Miscellaneous

62 Immunity of advocates from actions in negligence and for breach of contract

(1) A person—
(a) who is not a barrister; but
(b) who lawfully provides any legal services in relation to any proceedings,

shall have the same immunity from liability for negligence in respect of his acts or omissions as he would have if he were a barrister lawfully providing those services.

(2) No act or omission on the part of any barrister or other person which is accorded immunity from liability for negligence shall give rise to an action for breach of any contract relating to the provision by him of the legal services in question.

63 Legal professional privilege

(1) This section applies to any communication made to or by a person who is not a barrister or solicitor at any time when that person is—
(a) providing advocacy or litigation services as an authorised advocate or authorised litigator;
(b) providing conveyancing services as an authorised practitioner; or
(c) providing probate services as a probate practitioner.

(2) Any such communication shall in any legal proceedings be privileged from disclosure in like manner as if the person in question had at all material times been acting as his client's solicitor.

(3) In subsection (1), "probate practitioner" means a person to whom section 23(1) of the Solicitors Act 1974 (unqualified person not to prepare probate papers etc.) does not apply.

PART VI
MISCELLANEOUS AND SUPPLEMENTAL

Supplemental

125 Short title, minor and consequential amendments, transitionals and repeals

(1) This Act may be cited as the Courts and Legal Services Act 1990.

(2)–(7) . . .

NOTES

Sub-ss (2)–(7): outside the scope of this work.

BROADCASTING ACT 1990

(C 42)

An Act to make new provision with respect to the provision and regulation of independent television and sound programme services and of other services provided on television or radio frequencies; to make provision with respect to the provision and regulation of local delivery services; to amend in other respects the law relating to broadcasting and the provision of television and sound programme services and to make provision with respect to the supply and use of information about programmes; to make provision with respect to the transfer of the property, rights and liabilities of the Independent Broadcasting Authority and the Cable Authority and the dissolution of those bodies; to make new provision relating to the Broadcasting Complaints Commission; to provide for the establishment and functions of a Broadcasting Standards Council; to amend the Wireless Telegraphy Acts 1949 to 1967 and the Marine, &c, Broadcasting (Offences) Act 1967; to revoke a class licence granted under the Telecommunications Act 1984 to run broadcast relay systems; and for connected purposes

[1 November 1990]

PART I
INDEPENDENT TELEVISION SERVICES

CHAPTER I
REGULATION BY COMMISSION OF TELEVISION SERVICES GENERALLY

Establishment of Independent Television Commission

1 The Independent Television Commission

(1) There shall be a commission to be called the Independent Television Commission (in this Part referred to as "the Commission").

(2) The Commission shall consist of—

(a) a chairman and a deputy chairman appointed by the Secretary of State; and

(b) such number of other members appointed by the Secretary of State, not being less than eight nor more than ten, as he may from time to time determine.

(3) . . .

NOTES

Sub-s (3): outside the scope of this work.

Function of Commission

2 Regulation by Commission of provision of television services

(1) It shall be the function of the Commission to regulate, in accordance with this Part, the provision of the following services, namely—

(a) television programme services which are provided from places in the United Kingdom by persons other than the BBC and the Welsh Authority, and

(b) additional services which are provided from places in the United Kingdom,

and to regulate, in accordance with Part II, the provision of local delivery services (within the meaning of that Part) which are so provided.

(2) It shall be the duty of the Commission—

(a) to discharge their functions under this Part and Part II as respects the licensing of the services referred to in subsection (1) in the manner which they consider is best calculated—

(i) to ensure that a wide range of such services is available throughout the United Kingdom, and

(ii) to ensure fair and effective competition in the provision of such services and services connected with them; and

(b) to discharge their functions under this Part as respects the licensing of television programme services in the manner which they consider is best calculated to ensure the provision of such services which (taken as a whole) are of high quality and offer a wide range of programmes calculated to appeal to a variety of tastes and interests.

(3)–(6) . . .

NOTES

Sub-ss (3)–(6): outside the scope of this work.

General provisions about licensed services

6 General requirements as to licensed services

(1) The Commission shall do all that they can to secure that every licensed service complies with the following requirements, namely—

(a) that nothing is included in its programmes which offends against good taste or decency or is likely to encourage or incite to crime or to lead to disorder or to be offensive to public feeling;

(b) that any news given (in whatever form) in its programmes is presented with due accuracy and impartiality;

(c) that due impartiality is preserved on the part of the person providing the service as respects matters of political or industrial controversy or relating to current public policy;

(d) that due responsibility is exercised with respect to the content of any of its programmes which are religious programmes, and that in particular any such programmes do not involve—
  (i) any improper exploitation of any susceptibilities of those watching the programmes, or
  (ii) any abusive treatment of the religious views and beliefs of those belonging to a particular religion or religious denomination; and

(e) that its programmes do not include any technical device which, by using images of very brief duration or by any other means, exploits the possibility of conveying a message to, or otherwise influencing the minds of, persons watching the programmes without their being aware, or fully aware, of what has occurred.

(2) In applying subsection (1)(c) a series of programmes may be considered as a whole.

(3)–(8) . . .

NOTES

Sub-ss (3)–(8): outside the scope of this work.

7 General code for programmes

(1) The Commission shall draw up, and from time to time review, a code giving guidance—

(a) as to the rules to be observed with respect to the showing of violence, or the inclusion of sounds suggestive of violence, in programmes included in licensed services, particularly when large numbers of children and young persons may be expected to be watching the programmes;

(b) as to the rules to be observed with respect to the inclusion in such programmes of appeals for donations; and

(c) as to such other matters concerning standards and practice for such programmes as the Commission may consider suitable for inclusion in the code;

and the Commission shall do all that they can to secure that the provisions of the code are observed in the provision of licensed services.

(2) In considering what other matters ought to be included in the code in pursuance of subsection (1)(c), the Commission shall have special regard to programmes included in licensed services in circumstances such that large numbers of children and young persons may be expected to be watching the programmes.

(3) The Commission shall, in drawing up or revising the code under this section, take account of such of the international obligations of the United Kingdom as the Secretary of State may notify to them for the purposes of this subsection.

(4) The Commission shall publish the code drawn up under this section, and every revision of it, in such manner as they consider appropriate.

8 General provisions as to advertisements

(1) The Commission shall do all that they can to secure that the rules specified in subsection (2) are complied with in relation to licensed services.

(2) Those rules are as follows—

(a) a licensed service must not include—
  (i) any advertisement which is inserted by or on behalf of any body whose objects are wholly or mainly of a political nature,
  (ii) any advertisement which is directed towards any political end, or
  (iii) any advertisement which has any relation to any industrial dispute (other than an advertisement of a public service nature inserted by, or on behalf of, a government department);

(b) in the acceptance of advertisements for inclusion in a licensed service there must be no unreasonable discrimination either against or in favour of any particular advertiser; and

(c) a licensed service must not, without the previous approval of the Commission, include a programme which is sponsored by any person whose business consists, wholly or mainly, in the manufacture or supply of a product, or in the provision of a service, which the licence holder is prohibited from advertising by virtue of any provision of section 9.

(3) Nothing in subsection (2) shall be construed as prohibiting the inclusion in a licensed service of any party political broadcast which complies with the rules (so far as applicable) made by the Commission for the purposes of section 36.

(4) After consultation with the Commission the Secretary of State may make regulations amending, repealing, or adding to the rules specified in subsection (2); but no such regulations shall be made unless a draft of the regulations has been laid before and approved by a resolution of each House of Parliament.

(5) The Commission shall not act as an advertising agent.

9 Control of advertisements

(1) It shall be the duty of the Commission—

(a) after the appropriate consultation, to draw up, and from time to time review, a code—
  (i) governing standards and practice in advertising and in the sponsoring of programmes, and
  (ii) prescribing the advertisements and methods of advertising or sponsorship to be prohibited, or to be prohibited in particular circumstances; and

(b) to do all that they can to secure that the provisions of the code are observed in the provision of licensed services;

and the Commission may make different provision in the code for different kinds of licensed services.

(2)–(6) . . .

(7) The Commission may give directions to persons holding any class of licences with respect to the times when advertisements are to be allowed.

(8) Directions under this section may be, to any degree, either general or specific and qualified or unqualified; and directions under subsection (7) may, in particular, relate to—

(a) the maximum amount of time to be given to advertisements in any hour or other period,

(b) the minimum interval which must elapse between any two periods given over to advertisements and the number of such periods to be allowed in any programme or in any hour or day,

(c) the exclusion of advertisements from a specified part of a licensed service,

and may make different provision for different parts of the day, different days of the week, different types of programmes or for other differing circumstances.

(9) The Commission shall—

(a) in drawing up or revising the code, or

(b) in giving any directions under subsection (7),

take account of such of the international obligations of the United Kingdom as the Secretary of State may notify to them for the purposes of this subsection.

NOTES

Sub-ss (2)–(6): outside the scope of this work.

10 Government control over licensed services

(1) If it appears to him to be necessary or expedient to do so in connection with his functions as such, the Secretary of State or any other Minister of the Crown may at any time by notice require the Commission to direct the holders of any licences specified in the notice to publish in their licensed services, at such times as may be specified in the notice, such announcement as is so specified, with or without visual images of any picture, scene or object mentioned in the announcement; and it shall be the duty of the Commission to comply with the notice.

(2) Where the holder of a licence publishes any announcement in pursuance of a direction under subsection (1), he may announce that he is doing so in pursuance of such a direction.

(3) The Secretary of State may at any time by notice require the Commission to direct the holders of any licences specified in the notice to refrain from including in the programmes included in their licensed services any matter or classes of matter specified in the notice; and it shall be the duty of the Commission to comply with the notice.

(4) Where the Commission—

(a) have given the holder of any licence a direction in accordance with a notice under subsection (3), or

(b) in consequence of the revocation by the Secretary of State of such a notice, have revoked such a direction,

or where such a notice has expired, the holder of the licence in question may publish in the licensed service an announcement of the giving or revocation of the direction or of the expiration of the notice, as the case may be.

(5), (6) . . .

NOTES

Sub-ss (5), (6): outside the scope of this work.

Prohibition on providing unlicensed television services

13 Prohibition on providing television services without a licence

(1) Subject to subsection (2), any person who provides any service falling within section 2(1)(a)[, (aa)][, (b), (c) or (d)] without being authorised to do so by or under a licence under this Part [or Part I of the Broadcasting Act 1996] shall be guilty of an offence.

(2) The Secretary of State may, after consultation with the Commission, by order provide that subsection (1) shall not apply to such services or descriptions of services as are specified in the order.

(3) A person guilty of an offence under this section shall be liable—
- (a) on summary conviction, to a fine not exceeding the statutory maximum;
- (b) on conviction on indictment, to a fine.

(4) No proceedings in respect of an offence under this section shall be instituted—
- (a) in England and Wales, except by or with the consent of the Director of Public Prosecutions;
- (b) in Northern Ireland, except by or with the consent of the Director of Public Prosecutions for Northern Ireland.

(5) Without prejudice to subsection (3), compliance with this section shall be enforceable by civil proceedings by the Crown for an injunction or interdict or for any other appropriate relief.

(6) Any order under this section shall be subject to annulment in pursuance of a resolution of either House of Parliament.

NOTES

Sub-s (1): words in first pair of square brackets inserted by the Satellite Television Service Regulations 1997, SI 1997/1682, reg 2, Schedule, para 2; words in second pair of square brackets substituted, and words in third pair of square brackets inserted, by the Broadcasting Act 1996, s 148(1), Sch 10, Pt I, para 2.

CHAPTER II
TELEVISION BROADCASTING ON CHANNELS 3, 4 AND 5

Miscellaneous provisions relating to Channels 3, 4 and 5

36 Party political broadcasts

(1) Subject to subsection (2), any regional Channel 3 licence or licence to provide Channel 4 or 5 shall include—
- (a) conditions requiring the licence holder to include party political broadcasts in the licensed service; and
- (b) conditions requiring the licence holder to observe such rules with respect to party political broadcasts as the Commission may determine.

(2) Where any determination under section 28(3) is in force, a licence to provide Channel 5 may (but need not) include any such conditions as are mentioned in subsection (1)(a) and (b).

(3) Without prejudice to the generality of paragraph (b) of subsection (1), the Commission may determine for the purposes of that subsection—
- (a) the political parties on whose behalf party political broadcasts may be made; and
- (b) in relation to any political party on whose behalf such broadcasts may be made, the length and frequency of such broadcasts.

(4) Any rules made by the Commission for the purposes of this section may make different provision for different cases or circumstances.

PART X
MISCELLANEOUS AND GENERAL

General

204 Short title, commencement and extent

(1) This Act may be cited as the Broadcasting Act 1990.

(2) This Act shall come into force on such day as the Secretary of State may by order appoint; and different days may be so appointed for different provisions or for different purposes.

(3) Subject to subsections (4) and (5), this Act extends to the whole of the United Kingdom.

(4) . . .

(5) The amendments and repeals in Schedules 20 and 21 have the same extent as the enactments to which they refer.

(6) . . .

NOTES

Sub-ss (4), (6): outside the scope of this work.

WAR CRIMES ACT 1991

(C 13)

An Act to confer jurisdiction on United Kingdom courts in respect of certain grave violations of the laws and customs of war committed in German-held territory during the Second World War; and for connected purposes

[9 May 1991]

1 Jurisdiction over certain war crimes

(1) Subject to the provisions of this section, proceedings for murder, manslaughter or culpable homicide may be brought against a person in the United Kingdom irrespective of his nationality at the time of the alleged offence if that offence—

(a) was committed during the period beginning with 1st September 1939 and ending with 5th June 1945 in a place which at the time was part of Germany or under German occupation; and

(b) constituted a violation of the laws and customs of war.

(2) No proceedings shall by virtue of this section be brought against any person unless he was on 8th March 1990, or has subsequently become, a British citizen or resident in the United Kingdom, the Isle of Man or any of the Channel Islands.

(3) No proceedings shall by virtue of this section be brought in England and Wales or in Northern Ireland except by or with the consent of the Attorney General or, as the case may be, the Attorney General for Northern Ireland.

(4) . . .

NOTES

Sub-s (4): repealed by the Criminal Procedure and Investigations Act 1996, ss 46(1)(a), 79(4), 80, Sch 4, paras 1–3, 19, Sch 5(2).

3 Short title, consequential amendments, commencement and extent

(1) This Act may be cited as the War Crimes Act 1991.

(2)–(4) . . .

(5) This Act extends to Northern Ireland.

(6) . . .

NOTES

Sub-s (2): repealed by the Criminal Procedure and Investigations Act 1996, s 80, Sch 5(2).

Sub-s (3) : repealed by the Criminal Procedure and Investigations Act 1996, s 79(4), Sch 4, paras 1–3, 36.

Sub-ss (4), (6): outside the scope of this work.

LOCAL GOVERNMENT ACT 1992

(C 19)

An Act to make new provision, by giving effect to proposals in Cm 1599 (The Citizen's Charter) relating to publicity and competition, for securing economy, efficiency and effectiveness in the manner in which local authorities carry on certain activities; and to make new provision in relation to local government in England for effecting structural, boundary and electoral changes

[6 March 1992]

PART II
LOCAL GOVERNMENT CHANGES FOR ENGLAND

The Local Government Commission

12 The Local Government Commission for England

(1) There shall be a body corporate to be known as the Local Government Commission for England (in this Part referred to as "the Local Government Commission") for the purpose of carrying out the functions assigned to it by section 13 below.

(2) . . .

NOTES

Sub-s (2): outside the scope of this work.

Functions of the Local Government Commission

13 Duty to conduct reviews and make recommendations

(1) If the Secretary of State so directs, the Local Government Commission shall, in accordance with this Part and any directions given under it—

(a) conduct a review of such areas in England as are specified in the direction or are of a description so specified; and

(b) recommend to the Secretary of State as respects each of those areas either—

(i) that he should make such structural, boundary or electoral changes as are specified in the recommendations; or

(ii) that he should make no such changes.

[(1A) If the Secretary of State so directs, the Local Government Commission shall, in accordance with this Part and any directions given under it—

(a) conduct a review of such areas in England as are specified in the direction or are of a description so specified; and

(b) recommend to the Secretary of State as respects each of those areas either—

(i) that he should make such parish boundary changes or parish electoral changes as are specified in the recommendations; or

(ii) that he should make no such changes.]

(1B), (1C) . . .

(2) It shall also be the duty of the Local Government Commission—

(a) independently of any reviews under subsection (1) above, to conduct periodic reviews of every principal area in England for the purpose of determining whether recommendations should be made for electoral changes in that area; and

(b) as respects any area reviewed, to recommend to the Secretary of State either—

(i) that he should make such electoral changes as are specified in the recommendations; or

(ii) that he should make no such changes.

(3), (4) . . .

(5) Any structural, boundary or electoral changes recommended to the Secretary of State under this section shall be such as appear to the Local Government Commission desirable having regard to the need—

(a) to reflect the identities and interests of local communities; and

(b) to secure effective and convenient local government.

(6) The Secretary of State may give directions as to the exercise by the Local Government Commission of any functions under this section; and such directions may require that Commission to have regard to any guidance given by the Secretary of State as respects matters to be taken into account.

NOTES

Sub-s (1A): added by the Local Government and Rating Act 1997, s 19(1).

Sub-ss (1B), (1C), (3), (4): outside the scope of this work.

14 Changes that may be recommended

(1) For the purposes of this Part—

(a) a structural change is the replacement, in any non-metropolitan area, of the two principal tiers of local government with a single tier;

(b) a boundary change is any of the changes specified in subsection (3) below, whether made for the purpose of facilitating a structural change or independently of any such change; and

(c) an electoral change is a change of electoral arrangements for any local government area, whether made in consequence of any structural or boundary change or independently of any such change;

and recommendations by the Local Government Commission for any structural or boundary changes shall include such recommendations as to the matters mentioned in subsection (5) below as the Commission thinks appropriate in connection with the recommended changes.

(2)–(7) . . .

NOTES

Sub-ss (2)–(7): outside the scope of this work.

15 Procedure on a review

(1) As soon as reasonably practicable after being directed to conduct a review, the Local Government Commission shall take such steps as it considers sufficient to secure that persons who may be interested in the review are informed of—

- (a) the direction requiring that review to be conducted;
- (b) any other directions under this Part which are relevant to the review; and
- (c) the period within which representations with respect to the subject-matter of the review may be made.

(2) As soon as reasonably practicable after deciding to conduct a periodic review of any area under section 13(2) above, the Local Government Commission shall take such steps as it considers sufficient to secure that persons who may be interested in the review are informed of—

- (a) the fact that the Commission is to conduct a periodic review of that area;
- (b) any directions under this Part which are relevant to the review; and
- (c) the period within which representations with respect to the subject-matter of the review may be made.

(3) In conducting a review, the Local Government Commission shall—

- (a) take into consideration any representations made to it within the period mentioned in subsection (1)(c) or (2)(c) above;
- (b) prepare draft recommendations and take such steps as it considers sufficient to secure that persons who may be interested in the recommendations are informed of them and of the period within which representations with respect to them may be made;
- (c) deposit copies of the draft recommendations at the principal office of any principal council [or police authority] appearing to that Commission to be likely to be affected by them; and
- (d) take into consideration any representations made to that Commission within that period.

(4) As soon as the Local Government Commission is in a position to submit to the Secretary of State a report on a review, it shall—

- (a) submit such a report to him together with its recommendations;
- (b) take such steps as it considers sufficient to secure that persons who may be interested in the recommendations are informed of them and of the period within which they may be inspected; and
- (c) deposit copies of the recommendations at the principal office of any principal council [or police authority] appearing to that Commission to be likely to be affected by them.

(5)–(8) . . .

NOTES

Sub-s (3): words in square brackets in para (c) inserted by the Police and Magistrates' Courts Act 1994, s 39(1), (3).

Sub-s (4): words in square brackets in para (c) inserted by the Police and Magistrates' Courts Act 1994, s 39(1), (3).

Sub-ss (5)–(8): outside the scope of this work.

Implementation of recommendations

17 Implementation of recommendations by order

(1) Where the Local Government Commission submit to the Secretary of State a report on a review together with its recommendations, he may, if he thinks fit, by order give effect to all or any of the recommendations, with or without modifications.

(2)–(6) . . .

NOTES

Sub-ss (2)–(6): outside the scope of this work.

PART III
GENERAL

30 Short title, commencement and extent

(1) This Act may be cited as the Local Government Act 1992.

(2)–(4) . . .

(5) Except for the purposes of—

(a) . . .

(b) so much of Part II of Schedule 4 as makes a repeal in the House of Commons Disqualification Act 1975,

this Act does not extend to Northern Ireland.

NOTES

Sub-s (2): repealed by the Audit Commission Act 1998, s 54(3), Sch 5.

Sub-ss (3), (4): outside the scope of this work.

Sub-s (5): para (a) outside the scope of this work.

TRADE UNION AND LABOUR RELATIONS (CONSOLIDATION) ACT 1992

(C 52)

An Act to consolidate the enactments relating to collective labour relations, that is to say, to trade unions, employers' associations, industrial relations and industrial action

[16 July 1992]

PART V
INDUSTRIAL ACTION

Criminal offences

241 Intimidation or annoyance by violence or otherwise

(1) A person commits an offence who, with a view to compelling another person to abstain from doing or to do any act which that person has a legal right to do or abstain from doing, wrongfully and without legal authority—

(a) uses violence to or intimidates that person or his wife or children, or injures his property,
(b) persistently follows that person about from place to place,
(c) hides any tools, clothes or other property owned or used by that person, or deprives him of or hinders him in the use thereof,
(d) watches or besets the house or other place where that person resides, works, carries on business or happens to be, or the approach to any such house or place, or
(e) follows that person with two or more other persons in a disorderly manner in or through any street or road.

(2) A person guilty of an offence under this section is liable on summary conviction to imprisonment for a term not exceeding six months or a fine not exceeding level 5 on the standard scale, or both.

(3) A constable may arrest without warrant anyone he reasonably suspects is committing an offence under this section.

PART VII
MISCELLANEOUS AND GENERAL

Final provisions

301 Extent

(1) This Act extends to England and Wales and [(apart from section 212A(6)) to] Scotland.

(2), (3) . . .

NOTES

Sub-s (1): words in square brackets inserted by the Employment Rights (Dispute Resolution) Act 1998, s 15, Sch 1, para 10.

Sub-ss (2), (3): outside the scope of this work.

302 Commencement

This Act comes into force at the end of the period of three months beginning with the day on which it is passed.

303 Short title

This Act may be cited as the Trade Union and Labour Relations (Consolidation) Act 1992.

TRIBUNALS AND INQUIRIES ACT 1992

(C 53)

An Act to consolidate the Tribunals and Inquiries Act 1971 and certain other enactments relating to tribunals and inquiries [16 July 1992]

The Council on Tribunals and their functions

1 The Council on Tribunals

(1) There shall continue to be a council entitled the Council on Tribunals (in this Act referred to as "the Council")—

(a) to keep under review the constitution and working of the tribunals specified in Schedule 1 (being the tribunals constituted under or for the purposes of the statutory provisions specified in that Schedule) and, from time to time, to report on their constitution and working;

(b) to consider and report on such particular matters as may be referred to the Council under this Act with respect to tribunals other than the ordinary courts of law, whether or not specified in Schedule 1, or any such tribunal; and

(c) to consider and report on such matters as may be referred to the Council under this Act, or as the Council may determine to be of special importance, with respect to administrative procedures involving, or which may involve, the holding by or on behalf of a Minister of a statutory inquiry, or any such procedure.

(2) Nothing in this section authorises or requires the Council to deal with any matter with respect to which the Parliament of Northern Ireland had power to make laws.

2 Composition of the Council and the Scottish Committee

(1) Subject to subsection (3), the Council shall consist of not more than fifteen nor less than ten members appointed by the Lord Chancellor and the Lord Advocate, and one of the members shall be so appointed to be chairman of the Council.

(2) . . .

(3) In addition to the persons appointed or designated under subsection (1) or (2), the Parliamentary Commissioner for Administration shall, by virtue of his office, be a member of the Council and of the Scottish Committee.

(4) In appointing members of the Council regard shall be had to the need for representation of the interests of persons in Wales.

NOTES

Sub-s (2): outside the scope of this work.

Composition and procedure of tribunals and inquiries

5 Recommendations of Council as to appointment of members of tribunals

(1) Subject to section 6 but without prejudice to the generality of section 1(1)(a), the Council may make to the appropriate Minister general recommendations as to the making of appointments to membership of any tribunals mentioned in Schedule 1 or of panels constituted for the purposes of any such tribunals; and (without prejudice to any statutory provisions having effect with respect to such appointments) the appropriate Minister shall have regard to recommendations under this section.

(2) In this section "the appropriate Minister", in relation to appointments of any description, means the Minister making the appointments or, if they are not made by a Minister, the Minister in charge of the government department concerned with the tribunals in question.

(3) . . .

NOTES

Sub-s (3): outside the scope of this work.

6 Appointment of chairmen of certain tribunals

(1) The chairman, or any person appointed to act as chairman, of any of the tribunals to which this subsection applies shall (without prejudice to any statutory provisions as to qualifications) be selected by the appropriate authority from a panel of persons appointed by the Lord Chancellor.

(2) Members of panels constituted under this section shall hold and vacate office under the terms of the instruments under which they are appointed, but may resign office by notice in writing to the Lord Chancellor; and any such member who ceases to hold office shall be eligible for re-appointment.

(3)–(9) . . .

NOTES

Sub-ss (3)–(9): outside the scope of this work.

7 Concurrence required for removal of members of certain tribunals

(1) Subject to subsection (2), the power of a Minister, other than the Lord Chancellor, to terminate a person's membership of any tribunal specified in Schedule 1, or of a panel constituted for the purposes of any such tribunal, shall be exercisable only with the consent of—

(a) the Lord Chancellor, the Lord President of the Court of Session and the Lord Chief Justice of Northern Ireland, if the tribunal sits in all parts of the United Kingdom;

(b) the Lord Chancellor and the Lord President of the Court of Session, if the tribunal sits in all parts of Great Britain;

(c) the Lord Chancellor and the Lord Chief Justice of Northern Ireland, if the tribunal sits both in England and Wales and in Northern Ireland;

(d) the Lord Chancellor, if the tribunal does not sit outside England and Wales;

(e) . . .

(f) the Lord Chief Justice of Northern Ireland, if the tribunal sits only in Northern Ireland.

(2), (3) . . .

NOTES

Sub-s (1): para (e) outside the scope of this work.

Sub-ss (2), (3): outside the scope of this work.

8 Procedural rules for tribunals

(1) The power of a Minister, the Lord President of the Court of Session, the Commissioners of Inland Revenue or the Foreign Compensation Commission to make, approve, confirm or concur in procedural rules for any tribunal specified in Schedule 1 shall be exercisable only after consultation with the Council.

(2)–(4) . . .

NOTES

Sub-ss (2)–(4): outside the scope of this work.

9 Procedure in connection with statutory inquiries

(1) The Lord Chancellor, after consultation with the Council, may make rules regulating the procedure to be followed in connection with statutory inquiries held by or on behalf of Ministers; and different provision may be made by any such rules in relation to different classes of such inquiries.

(2) Any rules made by the Lord Chancellor under this section shall have effect, in relation to any statutory inquiry, subject to the provisions of the enactment under which the inquiry is held, and of any rules or regulations made under that enactment.

(3), (4) . . .

NOTES

Sub-ss (3), (4): outside the scope of this work.

Judicial control of tribunals etc

10 Reasons to be given for decisions of tribunals and Ministers

(1) Subject to the provisions of this section and of section 14, where—

(a) any tribunal specified in Schedule 1 gives any decision, or

(b) any Minister notifies any decision taken by him—

(i) after a statutory inquiry has been held by him or on his behalf, or

(ii) in a case in which a person concerned could (whether by objecting or otherwise) have required a statutory inquiry to be so held,

it shall be the duty of the tribunal or Minister to furnish a statement, either written or oral, of the reasons for the decision if requested, on or before the giving or notification of the decision, to state the reasons.

(2) The statement referred to in subsection (1) may be refused, or the specification of the reasons restricted, on grounds of national security.

(3) A tribunal or Minister may refuse to furnish a statement under subsection (1) to a person not primarily concerned with the decision if of the opinion that to furnish it would be contrary to the interests of any person primarily concerned.

(4) . . .

(5) Subsection (1) does not apply—

(a) to decisions in respect of which any statutory provision has effect, apart from this section, as to the giving of reasons,

(b) to decisions of a Minister in connection with the preparation, making, approval, confirmation, or concurrence in regulations, rules or byelaws, or orders or schemes of a legislative and not executive character, or

[(ba) to decisions of the Pensions Compensation Board referred to in paragraph 35(h) of Schedule 1]

(c) . . .

(6) Any statement of the reasons for a decision referred to in paragraph (a) or (b) of subsection (1), whether given in pursuance of that subsection or of any other statutory provision, shall be taken to form part of the decision and accordingly to be incorporated in the record.

(7), (8) . . .

NOTES

Sub-ss (4), (7), (8): outside the scope of this work.

Sub-s (5): para (ba) inserted, and para (c) repealed, by the Pensions Act 1995, ss 122, 151, 177, Sch 3, para 21(b), Sch 5, para 16(1), (3), Sch 7, Pt III.

11 Appeals from certain tribunals

(1) Subject to subsection (2), if any party to proceedings before any tribunal specified in paragraph 8, [15(a), (d) or (e)], 16, 18, 24, 26, 31, 33(b), 37[, 40A], 44 or 45 of Schedule 1 is dissatisfied in point of law with a decision of the tribunal he may, according as rules of court may provide, either appeal from the tribunal to the High Court or require the tribunal to state and sign a case for the opinion of the High Court.

(2)–(4) . . .

(5) An appeal to the Court of Appeal shall not be brought by virtue of this section except with the leave of the High Court or the Court of Appeal.

(6)–(10) . . .

NOTES

Sub-s (1): words in first pair of square brackets substituted by the Education Act 1993, s 181(2), and continues to have effect by virtue of the Education Act 1996, s 582(1), Sch 37, Pt I, para 118(1), (2); number in second pair of square brackets inserted by the Sea Fish (Conservation) Act 1992, s 9(1), (2).

Sub-s (2): words in first pair of square brackets substituted b the Employment Rights Act 1996, s 240, Sch 1, para 57; words in second pair of square brackets substituted by the Employment Rights (Dispute Resolution) Act 1998, s 1(2)(b); words in third (outer) pair of square brackets substituted by the Employment Tribunals Act 1996, s 43, Sch 1, para 9(1), (2); words in fourth (inner) pair of square brackets substituted by the Employment Rights (Dispute Resolution) Act 1998, s 1(2)(c).

Sub-ss (2)–(4), (6)–(10): outside the scope of this work.

12 Supervisory functions of superior courts not excluded by Acts passed before 1st August 1958

(1) As respects England and Wales—

(a) any provision in an Act passed before 1st August 1958 that any order or determination shall not be called into question in any court, or

(b) any provision in such an Act which by similar words excludes any of the powers of the High Court,

shall not have effect so as to prevent the removal of the proceedings into the High Court by order of certiorari or to prejudice the powers of the High Court to make orders of mandamus.

(2) . . .

(3) Nothing in this section shall apply—

(a) to any order or determination of a court of law, or

(b) where an Act makes special provision for application to the High Court or the Court of Session within a time limited by the Act.

NOTES

Sub-s (2): outside the scope of this work.

Supplementary provisions

19 Short title, commencement and extent

(1) This Act may be cited as the Tribunals and Inquiries Act 1992.

(2) This Act shall come into force on 1st October 1992.

(3) This Act extends to Northern Ireland.

JUDICIAL PENSIONS AND RETIREMENT ACT 1993

(C 8)

An Act to make further provision with respect to the pensions and other benefits payable in respect of service in certain judicial, and related, offices and in certain senior public investigative offices; to amend the law relating to the date on which the holders of certain judicial, and related, offices are required to vacate those offices; and for purposes connected therewith

[29 March 1993]

PART II MISCELLANEOUS, GENERAL AND SUPPLEMENTARY PROVISIONS

Retirement date for certain judicial officers etc

26 Retirement date for holders of certain judicial offices etc

(1) Subject to the following provisions of this section, a person holding any of the offices for the time being specified in Schedule 5 to this Act (a "relevant office") shall vacate that office on the day on which he attains the age of 70 or such lower age as may for the time being be specified for the purpose in the enactments and instruments relating to that office, whenever passed or made.

(2)–(12) . . .

NOTES

Commencement: 31 March 1995.

Sub-ss (2)–(12): outside the scope of this work.

Miscellaneous and supplementary provisions

31 Short title, supplementary provisions and extent

(1) This Act may be cited as the Judicial Pensions and Retirement Act 1993.

(2) The provisions of this Act shall come into force on such day as the appropriate Minister may by order made by statutory instrument appoint; and different days may be appointed for different provisions or for different purposes of the same provision.

(3)–(7) . . .

NOTES

Commencement: 31 March 1995.

Sub-ss (3)–(7): outside the scope of this work.

SCHEDULE 5

Section 26

RETIREMENT PROVISIONS: THE RELEVANT OFFICES

Lord of Appeal in Ordinary

Judge of the Supreme Court of England and Wales, other than the Lord Chancellor

Deputy judge of the High Court

Lord President of the Court of Session

Lord Justice Clerk

Judge of the Court of Session

Temporary Judge of the Court of Session

Lord Chief Justice of Northern Ireland

Lord Justice of Appeal in Northern Ireland

Judge of the High Court of Justice in Northern Ireland

Circuit judge

. . . . .

NOTES

Commencement: 31 March 1995.

Entries omitted outside the scope of this work.

ASYLUM AND IMMIGRATION APPEALS ACT 1993

(C 23)

An Act to make provision about persons who claim asylum in the United Kingdom and their dependants; to amend the law with respect to certain rights of appeal under the Immigration Act 1971; and to extend the provisions of the Immigration (Carriers' Liability) Act 1987 to transit passengers

[1 July 1993]

Introductory

1 Interpretation

In this Act—

"the 1971 Act" means the Immigration Act 1971;

"claim for asylum" means a claim made by a person (whether before or after the coming into force of this section) that it would be contrary to the United Kingdom's obligations under the Convention for him to be removed from, or required to leave, the United Kingdom; and

"the Convention" means the Convention relating to the Status of Refugees done at Geneva on 28th July 1951 and the Protocol to that Convention.

2 Primacy of Convention

Nothing in the immigration rules (within the meaning of the 1971 Act) shall lay down any practice which would be contrary to the Convention.

Treatment of persons who claim asylum

3 Fingerprinting

(1) Where a person ("the claimant") has made a claim for asylum, an immigration officer, constable, prison officer or officer of the Secretary of State authorised for the purposes of this section may—

- (a) take such steps as may be reasonably necessary for taking the claimant's fingerprints; or
- (b) by notice in writing require the claimant to attend at a place specified in the notice in order that such steps may be taken.

(2) The powers conferred by subsection (1) above may be exercised not only in relation to the claimant but also in relation to any dependant of his; but in the exercise of the power conferred by paragraph (a) of that subsection, fingerprints shall not be taken from a person under the age of sixteen ("the child") except in the presence of a person of full age who is—

- (a) the child's parent or guardian; or
- (b) a person who for the time being takes responsibility for the child and is not an immigration officer, constable, prison officer or officer of the Secretary of State.

(3) Where the claimant's claim for asylum has been finally determined or abandoned—

- (a) the powers conferred by subsection (1) above shall not be exercisable in relation to him or any dependant of his; and
- (b) any requirement imposed on him or any dependant of his by a notice under subsection (1)(b) above shall no longer have effect.

(4) A notice given to any person under paragraph (b) of subsection (1) above—

- (a) shall give him a period of at least seven days within which he is to attend as mentioned in that paragraph; and
- (b) may require him so to attend at a specified time of day or between specified times of day.

(5) Any immigration officer or constable may arrest without warrant a person who has failed to comply with a requirement imposed on him by a notice under subsection (1)(b) above (unless the requirement no longer has effect) and, where a person is arrested under this subsection,—

- (a) he may be removed to a place where his fingerprints may conveniently be taken, and
- (b) (whether or not he is so removed) there may be taken such steps as may be reasonably necessary for taking his fingerprints,

before he is released.

(6) Fingerprints of a person which are taken by virtue of this section must be destroyed not later than the earlier of—

- (a) the end of the period of one month beginning with any day on which he is given indefinite leave under the 1971 Act to enter or remain in the United Kingdom; and

(b) the end of the period of ten years beginning with the day on which the fingerprints are taken.

(7) Where fingerprints taken by virtue of this section are destroyed—
(a) any copies of the fingerprints shall also be destroyed; and
(b) if there are any computer data relating to the fingerprints, the Secretary of State shall, as soon as it is practicable to do so, make it impossible for access to be gained to the data.

(8) If—
(a) subsection (7)(b) above falls to be complied with, and
(b) the person to whose fingerprints the data relate asks for a certificate that it has been complied with,

such a certificate shall be issued to him by the Secretary of State not later than the end of the period of three months beginning with the day on which he asks for it.

(9) In this section—
(a) "immigration officer" means an immigration officer appointed for the purposes of the 1971 Act; and
(b) "dependant", in relation to the claimant, means a person—
(i) who is his spouse or a child of his under the age of eighteen; and
(ii) who has neither a right of abode in the United Kingdom nor indefinite leave under the 1971 Act to enter or remain in the United Kingdom.

(10) . . .

NOTES
Sub-s (10): outside the scope of this work.

6 Protection of claimants from deportation etc

During the period beginning when a person makes a claim for asylum and ending when the Secretary of State gives him notice of the decision on the claim, he may not be removed from, or required to leave, the United Kingdom.

7 Curtailment of leave to enter or remain

(1) Where—
(a) a person who has limited leave under the 1971 Act to enter or remain in the United Kingdom claims that it would be contrary to the United Kingdom's obligations under the Convention for him to be required to leave the United Kingdom after the time limited by the leave, and
(b) the Secretary of State has considered the claim and given to the person notice in writing of his rejection of it,

the Secretary of State may by notice in writing, given to the person concurrently with the notice under paragraph (b) above, curtail the duration of the leave.

[(1A) Where the Secretary of State by notice under subsection (1) above curtails the duration of any person's leave to enter or remain in the United Kingdom, he may also by notice in writing given to any dependant of that person curtail to the same extent the duration of that dependant's leave so to enter or remain.]

(2) No appeal may be brought under section 14 of the 1971 Act or section 8(2) below against the curtailment of leave under [subsection (1) or (1A) above].

(3) . . .

(4) Where—

(a) the duration of a person's leave under the 1971 Act to enter or remain in the United Kingdom has been curtailed under [subsection (1) or (1A) above], and

(b) the Secretary of State has decided to make a deportation order against him by virtue of section 3(5) of that Act,

he may be detained under the authority of the Secretary of State pending the making of the deportation order; and the references to sub-paragraph (2) of paragraph 2 of Schedule 3 to that Act in sub-paragraphs (3), (4) and (6) of that paragraph (provisions about detention under sub-paragraph (2)) shall include references to this subsection.

NOTES

Sub-s (1A): inserted by the Asylum and Immigration Act 1996, s 12(2), Sch 3, para 1(1).

Sub-ss (2), (4): words in square brackets substituted by the Asylum and Immigration Act 1996, s 12(2), Sch 3, para 1(2).

Sub-s (3): outside the scope of this work.

Rights of appeal

8 Appeals to special adjudicator

(1) A person who is refused leave to enter the United Kingdom under the 1971 Act may appeal against the refusal to a special adjudicator on the ground that his removal in consequence of the refusal would be contrary to the United Kingdom's obligations under the Convention.

(2) A person who has limited leave under the 1971 Act to enter or remain in the United Kingdom may appeal to a special adjudicator against any variation of, or refusal to vary, the leave on the ground that it would be contrary to the United Kingdom's obligations under the Convention for him to be required to leave the United Kingdom after the time limited by the leave.

(3) Where the Secretary of State—

(a) has decided to make a deportation order against a person by virtue of section 3(5) of the 1971 Act, or

(b) has refused to revoke a deportation order made against a person by virtue of section 3(5) or (6) of that Act,

the person may appeal to a special adjudicator against the decision or refusal on the ground that his removal in pursuance of the order would be contrary to the United Kingdom's obligations under the Convention; . . .

[(3A) A person may not appeal under paragraph (b) of subsection (3) above if he has had the right to appeal under paragraph (a) of that subsection, whether or not he has exercised it.]

(4) . . .

(5) The Lord Chancellor shall designate such number of the adjudicators appointed for the purposes of Part II of the 1971 Act as he thinks necessary to act as special adjudicators for the purposes of this section and may from time to time vary that number and the persons who are so designated.

(6) . . .

NOTES

Sub-s (3): words omitted repealed by the Asylum and Immigration Act 1996, s 12(2), (3), Sch 3, para 2(1), Sch 4.

Sub-s (3A): inserted by the Asylum and Immigration Act 1996, s 12(2), Sch 3, para 2(2).

Sub-ss (4), (6): outside the scope of this work.

9 Appeals from Immigration Appeal Tribunal

(1) Where the Immigration Appeal Tribunal has made a final determination of an appeal brought under Part II of the 1971 Act (including that Part as it applies by virtue of Schedule 2 to this Act) any party to the appeal may bring a further appeal to the appropriate appeal court on any question of law material to that determination.

(2) An appeal under this section may be brought only with the leave of the Immigration Appeal Tribunal or, if such leave is refused, with the leave of the appropriate appeal court.

(3) In this section "the appropriate appeal court" means—

(a) if the appeal is from the determination of an adjudicator or special adjudicator and that determination was made in Scotland, the Court of Session; and

(b) in any other case, the Court of Appeal.

(4), (5) . . .

NOTES

Sub-s (4): outside the scope of this work.

Sub-s (5): amends the Immigration Act 1971, s 33(4).

Supplementary

14 Commencement

(1) Sections 4 to 11 above (and section 1 above so far as it relates to those sections) shall not come into force until such day as the Secretary of State may by order appoint, and different days may be appointed for different provisions or for different purposes.

(2) An order under subsection (1) above—

(a) shall be made by statutory instrument; and

(b) may contain such transitional and supplemental provisions as the Secretary of State thinks necessary or expedient.

(3) Without prejudice to the generality of subsections (1) and (2) above, with respect to any provision of section 4 above an order under subsection (1) above may appoint different days in relation to different descriptions of asylum-seekers and dependants of asylum-seekers; and any such descriptions may be framed by reference to nationality, citizenship, origin or other connection with any particular country or territory, but not by reference to race, colour or religion.

15 Extent

(1) Her Majesty may by Order in Council direct that any of the provisions of this Act shall extend, with such modifications as appear to Her Majesty to be appropriate, to any of the Channel Islands or the Isle of Man.

(2) This Act extends to Northern Ireland.

16 Short title

This Act may be cited as the Asylum and Immigration Appeals Act 1993.

EUROPEAN COMMUNITIES (AMENDMENT) ACT 1993

(C 32)

An Act to make provision consequential on the Treaty on European Union signed at Maastricht on 7th February 1992

[20 July 1993]

1 Treaty on European Union

(1) . . .

(2) For the purpose of section 6 of the European Parliamentary Elections Act 1978 (approval of treaties increasing the Parliament's powers) the Treaty on European Union signed at Maastricht on 7th February 1992 is approved.

NOTES

Sub-s (1): amends the European Communities Act 1972, s 1(2).

2 Economic and monetary union

No notification shall be given to the Council of the European Communities that the United Kingdom intends to move to the third stage of economic and monetary union (in accordance with the Protocol on certain provisions relating to the United Kingdom adopted at Maastricht on 7th February 1992) unless a draft of the notification has first been approved by Act of Parliament and unless Her Majesty's Government has reported to Parliament on its proposals for the co-ordination of economic policies, its role in the European Council of Finance Ministers (ECOFIN) in pursuit of the objectives of Article 2 of the Treaty establishing the European Community as provided for in Articles 103 and 102a, and the work of the European Monetary Institute in preparation for economic and monetary union.

3 Annual report by Bank of England

In implementing Article 108 of the Treaty establishing the European Community, and ensuring compatibility of the statutes of the national central bank, Her Majesty's Government shall, by order, make provision for the Governor of the Bank of England to make an annual report to Parliament, which shall be subject to approval by a Resolution of each House of Parliament.

6 Committee of the Regions

A person may be proposed as a member or alternate member for the United Kingdom of the Committee of the Regions constituted under Article 198a of the Treaty establishing the European Community only if, at the time of the proposal, he is an elected member of a local authority.

7 Commencement (Protocol on Social Policy)

This Act shall come into force only when each House of Parliament has come to a Resolution on a motion tabled by a Minister of the Crown considering the question of adopting the Protocol on Social Policy.

8 Short title

This Act may be cited as the European Communities (Amendment) Act 1993.

WELSH LANGUAGE ACT 1993

(C 38)

An Act to establish a Board having the function of promoting and facilitating the use of the Welsh language, to provide for the preparation by public bodies of schemes giving effect to the principle that in the conduct of public business and the administration of justice in Wales the English and Welsh languages should be treated on a basis of equality, to make further provision relating to the Welsh language, to repeal certain spent enactments relating to Wales, and for connected purposes [21 October 1993]

PART I
THE BOARD

1 Establishment of the Board

There shall be a body corporate to be known as Bwrdd yr Iaith Gymraeg or the Welsh Language Board.

NOTES

Commencement: 21 December 1993.

2 Membership of the Board

(1) The Board established under section 1 above (referred to in this Act as "the Board") shall consist of not more than fifteen members appointed by the Secretary of State.

(2) In exercising his power of appointment under subsection (1) above the Secretary of State shall have regard to the desirability of securing that, within the Board's membership, there are reflected both the varying extent to which the Welsh language is used by those living in Wales, and the range of interests of the persons to whom the Board will offer advice.

NOTES

Commencement: 21 December 1993.

3 Functions of the Board

(1) The Board shall have the function of promoting and facilitating the use of the Welsh language.

(2) Without prejudice to the generality of subsection (1) above, the Board shall in carrying out the function mentioned there—

(a) advise the Secretary of State on matters concerning the Welsh language;
(b) advise persons exercising functions of a public nature on the ways in which effect may be given to the principle that, in the conduct of public business and the administration of justice in Wales, the English and Welsh languages should be treated on a basis of equality;
(c) advise those and other persons providing services to the public on the use of the Welsh language in their dealings with the public in Wales.

(3) Subject to the following provisions, the Board may do anything which is incidental or conducive to the performance of its functions, and may in particular—
(a) make grants and loans and give guarantees;
(b) make charges for the provision of advice or other services;
(c) accept gifts of money or other property.

(4) The Board shall not—
(a) make a grant or loan,
(b) give a guarantee, or
(c) acquire or dispose of any interest in land,

except with the approval of the Secretary of State given with the consent of the Treasury.

NOTES
Commencement: 21 December 1993.

PART III
MISCELLANEOUS

Supplementary

37 Short title

This Act may be cited as the Welsh Language Act 1993.

NOTES
Commencement: 21 December 1993.

EUROPEAN PARLIAMENTARY ELECTIONS ACT 1993

(C 41)

An Act to give effect to a Decision of the Council of the European Communities, 93/81/Euratom, ECSC, EEC, of 1st February 1993 having the effect of increasing the number of United Kingdom representatives to be elected to the European Parliament; and for connected purposes

[5 November 1993]

2 Initial drawing up of the new constituencies

(1) The provisions of this section have effect for the purpose of determining the European Parliamentary constituencies into which England and Wales shall initially

be divided in order to give effect to paragraph 1(2)(a) and (c) of Schedule 1 to the principal Act, as amended by section 1 above.

(2) For each of England and Wales there shall be a European Parliamentary Constituencies Committee (in this Act referred to as a "Committee") appointed (whether before or after the passing of this Act) by the Secretary of State; and the provisions of Part I of the Schedule to this Act shall have effect with respect to each Committee.

(3) Part II of the Schedule to this Act (which is derived, with modifications, from provisions of Part I of Schedule 2 to the principal Act) shall have effect with respect to reports of the Committees and Orders in Council consequent thereon.

(4) Parts II and III of Schedule 2 to the principal Act (criteria for dividing Great Britain into European Parliamentary constituencies) shall have effect in relation to reports of the Committees and Orders in Council consequent thereon as they have effect in relation to reports of Boundary Commissions and Orders in Council under that Schedule, except that for the definition of "enumeration date" in Part III there shall be substituted—

"enumeration date" means 16th February 1993.

(5) For the purposes of the principal Act, an Order in Council which has been made under Part II of the Schedule to this Act shall have effect as if it had been made under Schedule 2 to the principal Act.

(6) Any appointment made or other thing done by or in relation to a Committee at a time before the passing of this Act shall be regarded as valid if it would have been valid at that time, had this Act then been in force.

NOTES

Commencement: 5 November 1993.

Sub-s (1): "the principal Act" is the European Parliamentary Elections Act 1978.

3 Short title, consequential amendment and commencement

(1) This Act may be cited as the European Parliamentary Elections Act 1993.

(2) . . .

(3) Section 1 of this Act shall come into force on such day as the Secretary of State may by order made by statutory instrument appoint; and different days may be so appointed for different purposes.

NOTES

Commencement: 5 November 1993.

Sub-s (2): amends the European Communities Act 1972, s 1(2).

SCHEDULE

Section 2

PART I
THE EUROPEAN PARLIAMENTARY CONSTITUENCIES COMMITTEES

1. Each Committee shall consist of a Chairman and two other members appointed by the Secretary of State.

2. Each member of a Committee (including the Chairman) shall hold his appointment for such term and on such conditions as may be (or have been) determined before his appointment by the Secretary of State.

3, 4. . . .

PART II
REPORTS OF COMMITTEES AND ORDERS IN COUNCIL

5. As soon as practicable after the passing of this Act, each of the Committees shall submit to the Secretary of State a report showing the European Parliamentary constituencies into which they recommend that England or, as the case may be, Wales should be divided.

6. A report of a Committee under this Part of this Schedule showing the European Parliamentary constituencies into which they recommend that England or Wales should be divided shall state, as respects each European Parliamentary constituency, the name by which they recommend that it should be known.

7. As soon as may be after a Committee have submitted a report to the Secretary of State under this Part of this Schedule, he shall lay the report before Parliament together with the draft of an Order in Council for giving effect, whether with or without modifications, to the recommendations contained in the report.

8.—(1) The draft of any Order in Council laid before Parliament by the Secretary of State under this Part of this Schedule for giving effect, whether with or without modifications, to the recommendations contained in a report of a Committee may make provision for any matters which appear to him to be incidental to, or consequential on, the recommendations.

(2) Where any such draft gives effect to any such recommendations with modifications, the Secretary of State shall lay before Parliament together with the draft a statement of the reasons for the modifications.

(3) If any such draft is approved by a resolution of each House of Parliament, the Secretary of State shall submit it to Her Majesty in Council.

(4) If a motion for the approval of any such draft is rejected by either House of Parliament or withdrawn by leave of the House, the Secretary of State may amend the draft and lay the amended draft before Parliament, and if the draft as so amended is approved by a resolution of each House of Parliament, the Secretary of State shall submit it to Her Majesty in Council.

(5) Where the draft of an Order in Council is submitted to Her Majesty in Council under this Part of this Schedule, Her Majesty in Council may make an Order in terms of the draft which, subject to paragraph 8 of Schedule 2 to the principal Act, shall come into force on such date as may be specified in or determined under the Order and shall have effect notwithstanding anything in any enactment.

(6) The validity of any Order in Council purporting to be made under this Part of this Schedule and reciting that a draft of the Order has been approved by a resolution of each House of Parliament shall not be called in question in any legal proceedings whatsoever.

9. Nothing in paragraphs 7 and 8 above shall be taken as enabling the Secretary of State to modify any recommendation or draft Order in Council in a manner conflicting with the provisions of Part II of Schedule 2 to the principal Act.

NOTES

Commencement: 5 November 1993.

Paras 3, 4: outside the scope of this work.

HEALTH SERVICE COMMISSIONERS ACT 1993

(C 46)

An Act to consolidate the enactments relating to the Health Service Commissioners for England, for Wales and for Scotland with amendments to give effect to recommendations of the Law Commission and the Scottish Law Commission

[5 November 1993]

Health Service Commissioners

1 The Commissioners

(1) For the purpose of conducting investigations in accordance with this Act, there shall continue to be—

(a) a Health Service Commissioner for England,
(b) a Health Service Commissioner for Wales, and
(c) . . .

(2), (3) . . .

NOTES

Commencement: 5 February 1994.
Sub-s (1): para (c) outside the scope of this work.
Sub-ss (2), (3): outside the scope of this work.

Health service bodies subject to investigation

2 The bodies subject to investigation

(1) The bodies subject to investigation by the Health Service Commissioner for England are—

[(a) Health Authorities whose areas are in England,]
(c) Special Health Authorities to which this section applies exercising functions only or mainly in England,
(d) National Health Service trusts managing a hospital, or other establishment or facility, in England,
(e) . . .
(f) the Dental Practice Board, and
(g) the Public Health Laboratory Service Board.

(2)–(6) . . .

NOTES

Commencement: 5 February 1994.
Sub-s (1): para (a) substituted for original paras (a), (b), and para (e) repealed, by the Health Authorities Act 1995, ss 2(1), 5(1), Sch 1, Pt III, para 126(1), (2)(a), Sch 3.
Sub-ss (2)–(6): outside the scope of this work.

[*Persons subject to investigation*

2A Health service providers subject to investigation

(1) Persons are subject to investigation by the Health Service Commissioner for England if they are persons (whether individuals or bodies) undertaking to provide in

England general medical services, general dental services, general ophthalmic services or pharmaceutical services under the National Health Service Act 1977.

(2) Persons are subject to investigation by the Health Service Commissioner for Wales if they are persons (whether individuals or bodies) undertaking to provide in Wales general medical services, general dental services, general ophthalmic services or pharmaceutical services under the National Health Service Act 1977.

(3) . . .

(4) In this Act—

(a) references to a family health service provider are to any person mentioned in subsection (1), (2) or (3);

(b) references to family health services are to any of the services so mentioned.]

NOTES

Inserted by the Health Service Commissioners (Amendment) Act 1996, s 1.

Sub-s (3): outside the scope of this work.

[2B Independent providers subject to investigation

(1) Persons are subject to investigation by the Health Service Commissioner for England if—

(a) they are persons (whether individuals or bodies) providing services in England under arrangements with health service bodies or family health service providers, and

(b) they are not themselves health service bodies or family health service providers.

(2) Persons are subject to investigation by the Health Service Commissioner for Wales if—

(a) they are persons (whether individuals or bodies) providing services in Wales under arrangements with health service bodies or family health service providers, and

(b) they are not themselves health service bodies or family health service providers.

(3) . . .

(4) The services provided under arrangements mentioned in subsection (1)(a), (2)(a) or (3)(a) may be services of any kind.

(5) In this Act references to an independent provider are to any person providing services as mentioned in subsection (1), (2) or (3).]

NOTES

Inserted by the Health Service Commissioners (Amendment) Act 1996, s 1.

Sub-s (3): outside the scope of this work.

Matters subject to investigation

3 General remit of Commissioners

(1) On a complaint duly made to a Commissioner by or on behalf of a person that he has sustained injustice or hardship in consequence of—

(a) a failure in a service provided by a health service body,
(b) a failure of such a body to provide a service which it was a function of the body to provide, or
(c) maladministration connected with any other action taken by or on behalf of such a body,

the Commissioner may, subject to the provisions of this Act, investigate the alleged failure or other action.

[(1ZA) Any failure or maladministration mentioned in subsection (1) may arise from action of—
(a) the health service body,
(b) a person employed by that body,
(c) a person acting on behalf of that body, or
(d) a person to whom that body has delegated any functions.]

[(1A) Where a family health service provider has undertaken to provide any family health services and a complaint is duly made to a Commissioner by or on behalf of a person that he has sustained injustice or hardship in consequence of—
(a) action taken by the family health service provider in connection with the services,
(b) action taken in connection with the services by a person employed by the family health service provider in respect of the services,
(c) action taken in connection with the services by a person acting on behalf of the family health service provider in respect of the services, or
(d) action taken in connection with the services by a person to whom the family health service provider has delegated any functions in respect of the services,

the Commissioner may, subject to the provisions of this Act, investigate the alleged action.

(1B) Where the family health service provider mentioned in subsection (1A) is a member of a recognised fund-holding practice, references there to action taken by any person in connection with family health services include references to action taken by the person concerned in connection with any allotted sum paid to the members of the practice.

(1C) Where an independent provider has made an arrangement with a health service body or a family health service provider to provide a service (of whatever kind) and a complaint is duly made to a Commissioner by or on behalf of a person that he has sustained injustice or hardship in consequence of—
(a) a failure in the service provided by the independent provider,
(b) a failure of the independent provider to provide the service, or
(c) maladministration connected with any other action taken in relation to the service,

the Commissioner may, subject to the provisions of this Act, investigate the alleged failure or other action.

(1D) Any failure or maladministration mentioned in subsection (1C) may arise from action of—
(a) the independent provider,
(b) a person employed by the provider,
(c) a person acting on behalf of the provider, or
(d) a person to whom the provider has delegated any functions.]

(2) In determining whether to initiate, continue or discontinue an investigation under this Act, a Commissioner shall act in accordance with his own discretion.

(3) Any question whether a complaint is duly made to a Commissioner shall be determined by him.

(4) Nothing in this Act authorises or requires a Commissioner to question the merits of a decision taken without maladministration by a health service body in the exercise of a discretion vested in that body.

[(5) Nothing in this Act authorises or requires a Commissioner to question the merits of a decision taken without maladministration by—

- (a) a family health service provider,
- (b) a person employed by a family health service provider,
- (c) a person acting on behalf of a family health service provider, or
- (d) a person to whom a family health service provider has delegated any functions.

(6) Nothing in this Act authorises or requires a Commissioner to question the merits of a decision taken without maladministration by—

- (a) an independent provider,
- (b) a person employed by an independent provider,
- (c) a person acting on behalf of an independent provider, or
- (d) a person to whom an independent provider has delegated any functions.]

[(7) Subsections (4) to (6) do not apply to the merits of a decision to the extent that it was taken in consequence of the exercise of clinical judgment.]

NOTES

Commencement: 5 February 1994.

Sub-s (1ZA): inserted by the National Health Service (Primary Care) Act 1997, s 41(10), Sch 2, Pt I, para 68(1), (5).

Sub-ss (1A)–(1D): inserted by the Health Service Commissioners (Amendment) Act 1996, s 2(1), (2).

Sub-ss (5), (6): inserted by the Health Service Commissioners (Amendment) Act 1996, s 2(1), (3).

Sub-s (7): added by the Health Service Commissioners (Amendment) Act 1996, s 6(2).

Matters excluded from investigation

4 Availability of other remedy

(1) A Commissioner shall not conduct an investigation in respect of action in relation to which the person aggrieved has or had—

- (a) a right of appeal, reference or review to or before a tribunal constituted by or under any enactment or by virtue of Her Majesty's prerogative, or
- (b) a remedy by way of proceedings in any court of law,

unless the Commissioner is satisfied that in the particular circumstances it is not reasonable to expect that person to resort or have resorted to it.

(2)–(6) . . .

NOTES

Commencement: 5 February 1994.

Sub-ss (2)–(6): outside the scope of this work.

7 Personnel, contracts etc

(1) A Commissioner shall not conduct an investigation in respect of action taken in respect of appointments or removals, pay, discipline, superannuation or other personnel matters in relation to service under the National Health Service Act 1977 or the National Health Service (Scotland) Act 1978 [or the National Health Service and Community Care Act 1990].

(2) A Commissioner shall not conduct an investigation in respect of action taken in matters relating to contractual or other commercial transactions, except for—

- (a) matters relating to NHS contracts (as defined by section 4 of the National Health Service and Community Care Act 1990 and, in relation to Scotland, by section 17A of the National Health Service (Scotland) Act 1978), . . .
- (b) matters arising from arrangements between a health service body and [an independent provider for the provision of services by the provider] [and
- (c) matters arising from arrangements between a family health service provider and an independent provider for the provision of services by the independent provider.]

(3) In determining what matters arise from arrangements mentioned in subsection (2)(b) the Health Service Commissioners for England and for Wales shall disregard any arrangements for the provision of services at an establishment maintained by a Minister of the Crown mainly for patients who are members of the armed forces of the Crown.

[(3A) A Commissioner shall not conduct an investigation in pursuance of a complaint if—

- (a) the complaint is in respect of action taken in any matter relating to arrangements made by a health service body and a family health service provider for the provision of family health services,
- (b) the action is taken by or on behalf of the body or by the provider, and
- (c) the complaint is made by the provider or the body.]

[(3B) Nothing in the preceding provisions of this section prevents a Commissioner conducting an investigation in respect of action taken by a health service body in operating a procedure established to examine complaints.]

(4) Her Majesty may by Order in Council amend this section so as to permit the investigation by a Commissioner of any of the matters mentioned in subsection (1) or (2).

(5) A statutory instrument containing an Order in Council made by virtue of subsection (4) shall be subject to annulment in pursuance of a resolution of either House of Parliament.

NOTES

Commencement: 5 February 1994.

Sub-s (1): words in square brackets inserted by the Health Service Commissioners (Amendment) Act 1996, s 8(1), (2).

Sub-s (2): word omitted at end of para (a) repealed, words in square brackets in para (b) substituted, and para (c) and word immediately preceding it added, by the Health Service Commissioners (Amendment) Act 1996, ss 3, 13, Sch 1, paras 1, 2(1)–(4), Sch 2.

Sub-ss (3A), (3B): inserted by the Health Service Commissioners (Amendment) Act 1996, ss 3, 8(1), (3), Sch 1, paras 1, 2(1), (5).

Complaints

8 Individuals and bodies entitled to complain

(1) A complaint under this Act may be made by an individual or a body of persons, whether incorporated or not, other than a public authority.

(2) . . .

NOTES

Commencement: 5 February 1994.
Sub-s (2): outside the scope of this work.

9 Requirements to be complied with

(1) The following requirements apply in relation to a complaint made to a Commissioner.

(2)–(6) . . .

NOTES

Commencement: 5 February 1994.
Sub-ss (2)–(4): outside the scope of this work.
Sub-ss (5), (6): repealed by the Health Service Commissioners (Amendment) Act 1996, ss 9, 13, Sch 2.

Investigations

12 Evidence

(1) For the purposes of an investigation [pursuant to a complaint under section 3(1)] a Commissioner may require any officer or member of the health service body concerned or any other person who in his opinion is able to supply information or produce documents relevant to the investigation to supply any such information or produce any such document.

[(1A) For the purposes of an investigation pursuant to a complaint under section 3(1A) or (1C) a Commissioner may require any person who in his opinion is able to supply information or produce documents relevant to the investigation to supply any such information or produce any such document.]

(2) For the purposes of an investigation a Commissioner shall have the same powers as the Court in respect of—

(a) the attendance and examination of witnesses (including the administration of oaths and affirmations and the examination of witnesses abroad), and
(b) the production of documents.

(3) No obligation to maintain secrecy or other restriction on the disclosure of information obtained by or supplied to persons in Her Majesty's service, whether imposed by any enactment or by any rule of law, shall apply to the disclosure of information for the purposes of an investigation.

(4) The Crown shall not be entitled in relation to an investigation to any such privilege in respect of the production of documents or the giving of evidence as is allowed by law in legal proceedings.

(5) No person shall be required or authorised by this Act—

(a) to supply any information or answer any question relating to proceedings of the Cabinet or of any Committee of the Cabinet, or

(b) to produce so much of any document as relates to such proceedings;

and for the purposes of this subsection a certificate issued by the Secretary of the Cabinet with the approval of the Prime Minister and certifying that any information, question, document or part of a document relates to such proceedings shall be conclusive.

(6) Subject to subsections (3) and (4), no person shall be compelled for the purposes of an investigation to give any evidence or produce any document which he could not be compelled to give or produce in civil proceedings before the Court.

NOTES

Commencement: 5 February 1994.

Sub-s (1): words in square brackets inserted by the Health Service Commissioners (Amendment) Act 1996, s 3, Sch 1, paras 1, 4(1), (2).

Sub-s (1A): inserted by the Health Service Commissioners (Amendment) Act 1996, s 3, Sch 1, paras 1, 4(1), (3).

Reports

14 Reports by Commissioners

(1) [In any case where a Commissioner conducts an investigation pursuant to a complaint under section 3(1) he shall send a report of the results of an investigation]—

(a) to the person who made the complaint,

(b) to any member of the House of Commons who to the Commissioner's knowledge assisted in the making of the complaint (or if he is no longer a member to such other member as the Commissioner thinks appropriate),

[(c) to the health service body who at the time the report is made provides the service, or has the function, in relation to which the complaint was made,]

(d) to any person who is alleged in the complaint to have taken or authorised the action complained of, [and]

[(e) to the Secretary of State.]

(2) In any case where a Commissioner decides not to conduct an investigation [pursuant to a complaint under section 3(1)] he shall send a statement of his reasons—

(a) to the person who made the complaint, [and]

(b) to any such member of the House of Commons as is mentioned in subsection (1)(b), . . .

(c) . . .

[(2A) In any case where a Commissioner conducts an investigation pursuant to a complaint under section 3(1A) he shall send a report of the results of the investigation—

(a) to the person who made the complaint,

(b) to any member of the House of Commons who to the Commissioner's knowledge assisted in the making of the complaint (or if he is no longer a member to such other member as the Commissioner thinks appropriate),

(c) to any person by reference to whose action the complaint is made,

(d) to the family health service provider (if he does not fall within paragraph (c)),

(e) to any health service body with whom the family health service provider is subject to an undertaking to provide family health services, and

(f) to the Secretary of State.

(2B) In any case where a Commissioner decides not to conduct an investigation pursuant to a complaint under section 3(1A) he shall send a statement of his reasons—
- (a) to the person who made the complaint, and
- (b) to any such member of the House of Commons as is mentioned in subsection (2A)(b).

(2C) In any case where a Commissioner conducts an investigation pursuant to a complaint under section 3(1C) he shall send a report of the results of the investigation—
- (a) to the person who made the complaint,
- (b) to any member of the House of Commons who to the Commissioner's knowledge assisted in the making of the complaint (or if he is no longer a member to such other member as the Commissioner thinks appropriate),
- (c) to any person who is alleged in the complaint to have taken or authorised the action complained of,
- (d) to the independent provider,
- (e) to the health service body or family health service provider with whom the independent provider made the arrangement to provide the service concerned, and
- (f) to the Secretary of State.

(2D) In any case where a Commissioner decides not to conduct an investigation pursuant to a complaint under section 3(1C) he shall send a statement of his reasons—
- (a) to the person who made the complaint, and
- (b) to any such member of the House of Commons as is mentioned in subsection (2C)(b).]

(3) If after conducting an investigation it appears to a Commissioner that—
- (a) the person aggrieved has sustained such injustice or hardship as is mentioned in section 3(1)[, (1A) or (1C)], and
- (b) the injustice or hardship has not been and will not be remedied,

he may if he thinks fit [lay before each House of Parliament a special report on the case.]

[(4) Each of the Commissioners—
- (a) shall annually lay before each House of Parliament a general report on the performance of his functions under this Act, and
- (b) may from time to time lay before each House of Parliament such other reports with respect to those functions as he thinks fit.]

(5) For the purposes of the law of defamation, the publication of any matter by a Commissioner in sending or making a report or statement in pursuance of this section shall be absolutely privileged.

NOTES

Commencement: 5 February 1994.

Sub-s (1): words in square brackets and para (c) substituted by the Health Service Commissioners (Amendment) Act 1996, ss 3, 10(1), (2), Sch 1, paras 1, 5(1), (2); word in square brackets in para (d) inserted, and para (e) substituted for original paras (e), (f), by the Health Authorities Act 1995, s 2(1), Sch 1, Pt III, para 126(1), (4).

Sub-s (2): words in square brackets and word at end of para (a) inserted, and para (c) and word immediately preceding it repealed, by the Health Service Commissioners (Amendment) Act 1996, ss 3, 10(1), (3), 13, Sch 1, paras 1, 5(1), (3), Sch 2.

Sub-ss (2A)–(2D): inserted by the Health Service Commissioners (Amendment) Act 1996, s 3, Sch 1, paras 1, 5(1), (4).

Sub-s (3): words in square brackets in para (a) inserted, and words in other pair of square brackets substituted, by the Health Service Commissioners (Amendment) Act 1996, s 3, 10(1), (4), Sch 1, paras 1, 5(1), (5).

Sub-s (4): substituted by the Health Service Commissioners (Amendment) Act 1996, s 10(1), (5).

Information and consultation

16 Information prejudicial to the safety of the State

(1) A Minister of the Crown may give notice in writing to a Commissioner with respect to any document or information specified in the notice that in the Minister's opinion the disclosure of the document or information would be prejudicial to the safety of the State or otherwise contrary to the public interest.

(2) Where such a notice is given to a Commissioner, nothing in this Act shall be construed as authorising or requiring him or any of his officers to communicate to any person or for any purpose any document or information specified in the notice.

(3) References above to a document or information include references to a class of document or a class of information.

NOTES

Commencement: 5 February 1994.

Supplementary

22 Short title, extent and commencement

(1) This Act may be cited as the Health Service Commissioners Act 1993.

(2) The following provisions of this Act extend to Northern Ireland—

(a) sections . . . , 12, 13, 14(5), 15, 16 and this section;

(b)–(d) . . .

(3) . . .

(4) This Act shall come into force at the end of the period of three months beginning with the day on which it is passed.

NOTES

Commencement: 5 February 1994.

Sub-s (2): words omitted from para (a) and paras (b)–(d) outside the scope of this work.

Sub-s (3): outside the scope of this work.

EUROPEAN ECONOMIC AREA ACT 1993

(C 51)

An Act to make provision in relation to the European Economic Area established under the Agreement signed at Oporto on 2nd May 1992 as adjusted by the Protocol signed at Brussels on 17th March 1993 [5 November 1993]

2 Consistent application of law to whole of EEA

(1) Where—

(a) the operation of any relevant enactment is limited (expressly or by implication) by reference to the Communities or by reference to some connection with the Communities, and

(b) the enactment relates to a matter to which the Agreement (as it has effect on the date on which it comes into force) relates, then, unless the context otherwise requires, the enactment shall have effect on and after that date in relation to that matter with the substitution of a corresponding limitation relating to the European Economic Area (or, where appropriate, to both the Communities and the European Economic Area).

(2) Subsection (1) above shall have effect—

(a) . . .

(b) subject to such exceptions and modifications as may be prescribed by regulations made by a Minister of the Crown.

(3) Subsection (1) above shall not be regarded—

(a) as having an effect which is inconsistent with the operation, by virtue of the Agreement, of section 2(1) of the 1972 Act, or

(b) as prejudicing any power to make provision for the purpose of implementing any obligation of the United Kingdom created or arising by or under the Agreement, or for any other purpose mentioned in section 2(2)(a) or (b) of the 1972 Act relating to the Agreement;

and any instrument made for such a purpose under section 2(2) of the 1972 Act or under any other enactment may exclude the operation of subsection (1) above.

(4) In relation to matters to which the Agreement (as it has effect on the date on which it comes into force or subsequently) relates, the powers conferred by section 2(2) of the 1972 Act shall include power to make provision for the elimination or reduction of any difference between—

(a) the application of any relevant enactment in cases having a connection with member States, and

(b) its application in cases having a connection with other States within the European Economic Area;

and paragraph 1(1)(a), (c) and (d) of Schedule 2 to the 1972 Act shall not apply to the powers conferred by section 2(2) of that Act so far as they are exercisable by virtue of this subsection.

(5) In relation to matters to which the Agreement (as it has effect on the date on which it comes into force or subsequently) relates, the powers conferred by section 2(2) of the 1972 Act shall include power to make provision for the avoidance, elimination or reduction of any difference between—

(a) the application of an instrument made under that section on or after the date on which the Agreement comes into force in cases having a connection with member States, and

(b) its application in cases having a connection with other States within the European Economic Area.

(6) . . .

(7) In this section (and in the Schedule to this Act) "relevant enactment" means a provision of an Act passed, or of any subordinate legislation made, before the date on which the Agreement comes into force.

NOTES

Commencement: 5 November 1993.

Sub-s (2): para (a) outside the scope of this work.

Sub-s (6): outside the scope of this work.

3 General implementation of Agreement

(1) Subject to section 2 above, where by virtue of the Agreement (as it has effect on the date on which it comes into force) it is necessary for a purpose mentioned in section 2(2)(a) or (b) of the 1972 Act that any relevant provision should have effect with modifications which can be ascertained from the Agreement, then on and after that date the provision shall have effect with those modifications.

(2) A Minister of the Crown may by regulations modify or exclude the operation of subsection (1) above in relation to a relevant provision where it appears to him appropriate to do so because of the suspension of any part of the Agreement in accordance with the terms of the Agreement.

(3) Subsection (1) above shall not be regarded—

- (a) as providing for modifications the effect of which is achieved through the operation, by virtue of the Agreement, of section 2(1) of the 1972 Act, or
- (b) as prejudicing any power to make provision for the purpose of implementing any obligation of the United Kingdom created or arising by or under the Agreement, or for any other purpose mentioned in section 2(2)(a) or (b) of the 1972 Act relating to the Agreement;

and any instrument made for such a purpose under section 2(2) of the 1972 Act or under any other enactment may exclude the operation of subsection (1) above.

(4) Subsection (1) above shall not apply so as to require a modification if that modification, or a corresponding modification limited so as to relate only to the Communities,—

- (a) could have been made, by Act passed before the date on which the Agreement comes into force, for a purpose mentioned in section 2(2)(a) or (b) of the 1972 Act, but
- (b) was not made (by that or other means).

(5) In this section "relevant provision" means—

- (a) a provision of an Act passed, or of any subordinate legislation made, before the date on which the Agreement comes into force;
- (b) a provision of any other instrument made before that date by a person as against whom the effect of a directive issued by a Community institution (if such a directive were relevant) might be relied upon in proceedings to which he was a party.

NOTES

Commencement: 5 November 1993.

5 Regulations

The power to make regulations under section 2(2) or section 3(2) above shall be exercisable by statutory instrument; and any statutory instrument containing such regulations, if made without a draft having been approved by resolution of each House of Parliament, shall be subject to annulment in pursuance of a resolution of either House.

NOTES

Commencement: 5 November 1993.

6 Interpretation

(1) In this Act, except where the context otherwise requires,—

"the 1972 Act" means the European Communities Act 1972;

"Act" includes an Act of the Parliament of Northern Ireland and a Measure of the Northern Ireland Assembly;

"the Agreement" means the Agreement on the European Economic Area signed at Oporto on 2nd May 1992 as adjusted by the Protocol signed at Brussels on 17th March 1993;

"Minister of the Crown" includes the Treasury;

"subordinate legislation" means Orders in Council, orders, rules, regulations, schemes, warrants, byelaws and other instruments made under any Act.

(2) References in this Act to the date on which the Agreement comes into force are references to the date on which (in accordance with the Protocol signed at Brussels on 17th March 1993) it comes into force otherwise than as regards Liechtenstein.

NOTES

Commencement: 5 November 1993.

7 Short title

This Act may be cited as the European Economic Area Act 1993.

NOTES

Commencement: 5 November 1993.

INTELLIGENCE SERVICES ACT 1994

(C 13)

An Act to make provision about the Secret Intelligence Service and the Government Communications Headquarters, including provision for the issue of warrants and authorisations enabling certain actions to be taken and for the issue of such warrants and authorisations to be kept under review; to make further provision about warrants issued on applications by the Security Service; to establish a procedure for the investigation of complaints about the Secret Intelligence Service and the Government Communications Headquarters; to make provision for the establishment of an Intelligence and Security Committee to scrutinise all three of those bodies; and for connected purposes.

[26 May 1994]

The Secret Intelligence Service

1 The Secret Intelligence Service

(1) There shall continue to be a Secret Intelligence Service (in this Act referred to as "the Intelligence Service") under the authority of the Secretary of State; and, subject to subsection (2) below, its functions shall be—

(a) to obtain and provide information relating to the actions or intentions of persons outside the British Islands; and

(b) to perform other tasks relating to the actions or intentions of such persons.

(2) The functions of the Intelligence Service shall be exercisable only—
- (a) in the interests of national security, with particular reference to the defence and foreign policies of Her Majesty's Government in the United Kingdom; or
- (b) in the interests of the economic well-being of the United Kingdom; or
- (c) in support of the prevention or detection of serious crime.

NOTES
Commencement: 15 December 1994.

2 The Chief of the Intelligence Service

(1) The operations of the Intelligence Service shall continue to be under the control of a Chief of that Service appointed by the Secretary of State.

(2) The Chief of the Intelligence Service shall be responsible for the efficiency of that Service and it shall be his duty to ensure—
- (a) that there are arrangements for securing that no information is obtained by the Intelligence Service except so far as necessary for the proper discharge of its functions and that no information is disclosed by it except so far as necessary—
  - (i) for that purpose;
  - (ii) in the interests of national security;
  - (iii) for the purpose of the prevention or detection of serious crime; or
  - (iv) for the purpose of any criminal proceedings; and
- (b) that the Intelligence Service does not take any action to further the interests of any United Kingdom political party.

(3) Without prejudice to the generality of subsection (2)(a) above, the disclosure of information shall be regarded as necessary for the proper discharge of the functions of the Intelligence Service if it consists of—
- (a) the disclosure of records subject to and in accordance with the Public Records Act 1958; or
- (b) the disclosure, subject to and in accordance with arrangements approved by the Secretary of State, of information to the Comptroller and Auditor General for the purposes of his functions.

(4) The Chief of the Intelligence Service shall make an annual report on the work of the Intelligence Service to the Prime Minister and the Secretary of State and may at any time report to either of them on any matter relating to its work.

NOTES
Commencement: 15 December 1994.

GCHQ

3 The Government Communications Headquarters

(1) There shall continue to be a Government Communications Headquarters under the authority of the Secretary of State; and, subject to subsection (2) below, its functions shall be—
- (a) to monitor or interfere with electromagnetic, acoustic and other emissions and any equipment producing such emissions and to obtain and provide information derived from or related to such emissions or equipment and from encrypted material; and

(b) to provide advice and assistance about—
  (i) languages, including terminology used for technical matters, and
  (ii) cryptography and other matters relating to the protection of information and other material,

to the armed forces of the Crown, to Her Majesty's Government in the United Kingdom or to a Northern Ireland Department or to any other organisation which is determined for the purposes of this section in such manner as may be specified by the Prime Minister.

(2) The functions referred to in subsection (1)(a) above shall be exercisable only—

(a) in the interests of national security, with particular reference to the defence and foreign policies of Her Majesty's Government in the United Kingdom; or

(b) in the interests of the economic well-being of the United Kingdom in relation to the actions or intentions of persons outside the British Islands; or

(c) in support of the prevention or detection of serious crime.

(3) In this Act the expression "GCHQ" refers to the Government Communications Headquarters and to any unit or part of a unit of the armed forces of the Crown which is for the time being required by the Secretary of State to assist the Government Communications Headquarters in carrying out its functions.

NOTES

Commencement: 15 December 1994.

4 The Director of GCHQ

(1) The operations of GCHQ shall continue to be under the control of a Director appointed by the Secretary of State.

(2) The Director shall be responsible for the efficiency of GCHQ and it shall be his duty to ensure—

(a) that there are arrangements for securing that no information is obtained by GCHQ except so far as necessary for the proper discharge of its functions and that no information is disclosed by it except so far as necessary for that purpose or for the purpose of any criminal proceedings; and

(b) that GCHQ does not take any action to further the interests of any United Kingdom political party.

(3) Without prejudice to the generality of subsection (2)(a) above, the disclosure of information shall be regarded as necessary for the proper discharge of the functions of GCHQ if it consists of—

(a) the disclosure of records subject to and in accordance with the Public Records Act 1958; or

(b) the disclosure, subject to and in accordance with arrangements approved by the Secretary of State, of information to the Comptroller and Auditor General for the purposes of his functions.

(4) The Director shall make an annual report on the work of GCHQ to the Prime Minister and the Secretary of State and may at any time report to either of them on any matter relating to its work.

NOTES

Commencement: 15 December 1994.

Authorisation of certain actions

5 Warrants: general

(1) No entry on or interference with property or with wireless telegraphy shall be unlawful if it is authorised by a warrant issued by the Secretary of State under this section.

(2) The Secretary of State may, on an application made by the Security Service, the Intelligence Service or GCHQ, issue a warrant under this section authorising the taking, subject to subsection (3) below, of such action as is specified in the warrant in respect of any property so specified or in respect of wireless telegraphy so specified if the Secretary of State—

- (a) thinks it necessary for the action to be taken on the ground that it is likely to be of substantial value in assisting, as the case may be,—
  - (i) the Security Service in carrying out any of its functions under the 1989 Act; or
  - (ii) the Intelligence Service in carrying out any of its functions under section 1 above; or
  - (iii) GCHQ in carrying out any function which falls within section 3(1)(a) above; and
- (b) is satisfied that what the action seeks to achieve cannot reasonably be achieved by other means; and
- (c) is satisfied that satisfactory arrangements are in force under section 2(2)(a) of the 1989 Act (duties of the Director-General of the Security Service), section 2(2)(a) above or section 4(2)(a) above with respect to the disclosure of information obtained by virtue of this section and that any information obtained under the warrant will be subject to those arrangements.

[(3) A warrant issued on the application of the Intelligence Service or GCHQ for the purposes of the exercise of their functions by virtue of section 1(2)(c) or 3(2)(c) above may not relate to property in the British Islands.

(3A) A warrant issued on the application of the Security Service for the purposes of the exercise of their function under section 1(4) of the Security Service Act 1989 may not relate to property in the British Islands unless it authorises the taking of action in relation to conduct within subsection (3B) below.

(3B) Conduct is within this subsection if it constitutes (or, if it took place in the United Kingdom, would constitute) one or more offences, and either—

- (a) it involves the use of violence, results in substantial financial gain or is conduct by a large number of persons in pursuit of a common purpose; or
- (b) the offence or one of the offences is an offence for which a person who has attained the age of twenty-one and has no previous convictions could reasonably be expected to be sentenced to imprisonment for a term of three years or more.]

(4) Subject to subsection (5) below, the Security Service may make an application under subsection (2) above for a warrant to be issued authorising that Service (or a person acting on its behalf) to take such action as is specified in the warrant on behalf of the Intelligence Service or GCHQ and, where such a warrant is issued, the functions of the Security Service shall include the carrying out of the action so specified, whether or not it would otherwise be within its functions.

(5) The Security Service may not make an application for a warrant by virtue of subsection (4) above except where the action proposed to be authorised by the warrant—

(a) is action in respect of which the Intelligence Service or, as the case may be, GCHQ could make such an application; and

(b) is to be taken otherwise than in support of the prevention or detection of serious crime.

NOTES

Commencement: 15 December 1994.

Sub-ss (3), (3A), (3B): substituted for original sub-s (3) by the Security Service Act 1996, s 2.

6 Warrants: procedure and duration, etc

(1) A warrant shall not be issued except—

(a) under the hand of the Secretary of State; or

(b) in an urgent case where the Secretary of State has expressly authorised its issue and a statement of that fact is endorsed on it, under the hand of a senior official of his department.

(2) A warrant shall, unless renewed under subsection (3) below, cease to have effect—

(a) if the warrant was under the hand of the Secretary of State, at the end of the period of six months beginning with the day on which it was issued; and

(b) in any other case, at the end of the period ending with the second working day following that day.

(3) If at any time before the day on which a warrant would cease to have effect the Secretary of State considers it necessary for the warrant to continue to have effect for the purpose for which it was issued, he may by an instrument under his hand renew it for a period of six months beginning with that day.

(4) The Secretary of State shall cancel a warrant if he is satisfied that the action authorised by it is no longer necessary.

(5) In the preceding provisions of this section "warrant" means a warrant under section 5 above.

(6) As regards the Security Service, this section and section 5 above have effect in place of section 3 (property warrants) of the 1989 Act, and accordingly—

(a) a warrant issued under that section of the 1989 Act and current when this section and section 5 above come into force shall be treated as a warrant under section 5 above, but without any change in the date on which the warrant was in fact issued or last renewed; and

(b) section 3 of the 1989 Act shall cease to have effect.

NOTES

Commencement: 15 December 1994.

7 Authorisation of acts outside the British Islands

(1) If, apart from this section, a person would be liable in the United Kingdom for any act done outside the British Islands, he shall not be so liable if the act is one which is authorised to be done by virtue of an authorisation given by the Secretary of State under this section.

(2) In subsection (1) above "liable in the United Kingdom" means liable under the criminal or civil law of any part of the United Kingdom.

(3) The Secretary of State shall not give an authorisation under this section unless he is satisfied—

(a) that any acts which may be done in reliance on the authorisation or, as the case may be, the operation in the course of which the acts may be done will be necessary for the proper discharge of a function of the Intelligence Service; and

(b) that there are satisfactory arrangements in force to secure—

(i) that nothing will be done in reliance on the authorisation beyond what is necessary for the proper discharge of a function of the Intelligence Service; and

(ii) that, in so far as any acts may be done in reliance on the authorisation, their nature and likely consequences will be reasonable, having regard to the purposes for which they are carried out; and

(c) that there are satisfactory arrangements in force under section 2(2)(a) above with respect to the disclosure of information obtained by virtue of this section and that any information obtained by virtue of anything done in reliance on the authorisation will be subject to those arrangements.

(4) Without prejudice to the generality of the power of the Secretary of State to give an authorisation under this section, such an authorisation—

(a) may relate to a particular act or acts, to acts of a description specified in the authorisation or to acts undertaken in the course of an operation so specified;

(b) may be limited to a particular person or persons of a description so specified; and

(c) may be subject to conditions so specified.

(5) An authorisation shall not be given under this section except—

(a) under the hand of the Secretary of State; or

(b) in an urgent case where the Secretary of State has expressly authorised it to be given and a statement of that fact is endorsed on it, under the hand of a senior official of his department.

(6) An authorisation shall, unless renewed under subsection (7) below, cease to have effect—

(a) if the authorisation was given under the hand of the Secretary of State, at the end of the period of six months beginning with the day on which it was given;

(b) in any other case, at the end of the period ending with the second working day following the day on which it was given.

(7) If at any time before the day on which an authorisation would cease to have effect the Secretary of State considers it necessary for the authorisation to continue to have effect for the purpose for which it was given, he may by an instrument under his hand renew it for a period of six months beginning with that day.

(8) The Secretary of State shall cancel an authorisation if he is satisfied that any act authorised by it is no longer necessary.

NOTES

Commencement: 15 December 1994.

The Commissioner, the Tribunal and the investigation of complaints

8 The Commissioner

(1) The Prime Minister shall appoint as a Commissioner for the purposes of this Act a person who holds or has held high judicial office within the meaning of the Appellate Jurisdiction Act 1876.

(2) The Commissioner shall hold office in accordance with the terms of his appointment and there shall be paid to him by the Secretary of State such allowances as the Treasury may determine.

(3) In addition to his functions under the subsequent provisions of this Act, the Commissioner shall keep under review the exercise by the Secretary of State of his powers under sections 5 to 7 above, except in so far as the powers under sections 5 and 6 above relate to the Security Service.

(4) It shall be the duty of—

(a) every member of the Intelligence Service,

(b) every member of GCHQ, and

(c) every official of the department of the Secretary of State,

to disclose or give to the Commissioner such documents or information as he may require for the purpose of enabling him to discharge his functions.

(5) The Commissioner shall make an annual report on the discharge of his functions to the Prime Minister and may at any time report to him on any matter relating to his discharge of those functions.

(6) The Prime Minister shall lay before each House of Parliament a copy of each annual report made by the Commissioner under subsection (5) above together with a statement as to whether any matter has been excluded from that copy in pursuance of subsection (7) below.

(7) If it appears to the Prime Minister, after consultation with the Commissioner, that the publication of any matter in a report would be prejudicial to the continued discharge of the functions of the Intelligence Service or, as the case may be, GCHQ, the Prime Minister may exclude that matter from the copy of the report as laid before each House of Parliament.

(8) The Secretary of State may, after consultation with the Commissioner and with the approval of the Treasury as to numbers, provide the Commissioner with such staff as the Secretary of State thinks necessary for the discharge of his functions.

NOTES

Commencement: 15 December 1994.

---

9 Investigation of complaints

(1) There shall be a Tribunal for the purpose of investigating complaints about the Intelligence Service or GCHQ in the manner specified in Schedule 1 to this Act.

(2) The Commissioner shall have the functions conferred on him by Schedule 1 to this Act and give the Tribunal all such assistance in discharging their functions under that Schedule as they may require.

(3) Schedule 2 to this Act shall have effect with respect to the constitution, procedure and other matters relating to the Tribunal.

(4) The decisions of the Tribunal and the Commissioner under Schedule 1 to this Act (including decisions as to their jurisdictions) shall not be subject to appeal or liable to be questioned in any court.

NOTES

Commencement: 15 December 1994.

The Intelligence and Security Committee

10 The Intelligence and Security Committee

(1) There shall be a Committee, to be known as the Intelligence and Security Committee and in this section referred to as "the Committee", to examine the expenditure, administration and policy of—

- (a) the Security Service;
- (b) the Intelligence Service; and
- (c) GCHQ.

(2) The Committee shall consist of nine members—

- (a) who shall be drawn both from the members of the House of Commons and from the members of the House of Lords; and
- (b) none of whom shall be a Minister of the Crown.

(3) The members of the Committee shall be appointed by the Prime Minister after consultation with the Leader of the Opposition, within the meaning of the Ministerial and other Salaries Act 1975; and one of those members shall be so appointed as Chairman of the Committee.

(4) Schedule 3 to this Act shall have effect with respect to the tenure of office of members of, the procedure of and other matters relating to, the Committee; and in that Schedule "the Committee" has the same meaning as in this section.

(5) The Committee shall make an annual report on the discharge of their functions to the Prime Minister and may at any time report to him on any matter relating to the discharge of those functions.

(6) The Prime Minister shall lay before each House of Parliament a copy of each annual report made by the Committee under subsection (5) above together with a statement as to whether any matter has been excluded from that copy in pursuance of subsection (7) below.

(7) If it appears to the Prime Minister, after consultation with the Committee, that the publication of any matter in a report would be prejudicial to the continued discharge of the functions of either of the Services or, as the case may be, GCHQ, the Prime Minister may exclude that matter from the copy of the report as laid before each House of Parliament.

NOTES

Commencement: 15 December 1994.

Supplementary

12 Short title, commencement and extent

(1) This Act may be cited as the Intelligence Services Act 1994.

(2) This Act shall come into force on such day as the Secretary of State may by an order made by statutory instrument appoint, and different days may be so appointed for different provisions or different purposes.

(3) This Act extends to Northern Ireland.

(4) . . .

NOTES
Commencement: 15 December 1994.
Sub-s (4): outside the scope of this work.

POLICE AND MAGISTRATES' COURTS ACT 1994

NOTES
See Notes to the Justices of the Peace Act 1979.

CRIMINAL JUSTICE AND PUBLIC ORDER ACT 1994

(C 33)

An Act to make further provision in relation to criminal justice (including employment in the prison service); to amend or extend the criminal law and powers for preventing crime and enforcing that law; to amend the Video Recordings Act 1984; and for purposes connected with those purposes

[3 November 1994]

PART III
COURSE OF JUSTICE: EVIDENCE, PROCEDURE, ETC

Inferences from accused's silence

34 Effect of accused's failure to mention facts when questioned or charged

(1) Where, in any proceedings against a person for an offence, evidence is given that the accused—

(a) at any time before he was charged with the offence, on being questioned under caution by a constable trying to discover whether or by whom the offence had been committed, failed to mention any fact relied on in his defence in those proceedings; or

(b) on being charged with the offence or officially informed that he might be prosecuted for it, failed to mention any such fact,

being a fact which in the circumstances existing at the time the accused could reasonably have been expected to mention when so questioned, charged or informed, as the case may be, subsection (2) below applies.

(2) Where this subsection applies—

[(a) a magistrates' court inquiring into the offence as examining justices;]
(b) a judge, in deciding whether to grant an application made by the accused under—
(i) section 6 of the Criminal Justice Act 1987 (application for dismissal of charge of serious fraud in respect of which notice of transfer has been given under section 4 of that Act); or
(ii) paragraph 5 of Schedule 6 to the Criminal Justice Act 1991 (application for dismissal of charge of violent or sexual offence involving child in respect of which notice of transfer has been given under section 53 of that Act);
(c) the court, in determining whether there is a case to answer; and
(d) the court or jury, in determining whether the accused is guilty of the offence charged,

may draw such inferences from the failure as appear proper.

(3) Subject to any directions by the court, evidence tending to establish the failure may be given before or after evidence tending to establish the fact which the accused is alleged to have failed to mention.

(4) This section applies in relation to questioning by persons (other than constables) charged with the duty of investigating offences or charging offenders as it applies in relation to questioning by constables; and in subsection (1) above "officially informed" means informed by a constable or any such person.

(5) This section does not—
(a) prejudice the admissibility in evidence of the silence or other reaction of the accused in the face of anything said in his presence relating to the conduct in respect of which he is charged, in so far as evidence thereof would be admissible apart from this section; or
(b) preclude the drawing of any inference from any such silence or other reaction of the accused which could properly be drawn apart from this section.

(6), (7) . . .

NOTES

Commencement: 10 April 1995.

Sub-s (2): para (a) substituted by the Criminal Procedure and Investigations 1996, s 44(1), (3), (7), in relation to an inquiry into an offence by a magistrates' court as examining justices begun after 4 July 1996.

Sub-s (6): outside the scope of this work.

Sub-s (7): repealed by the Criminal Procedure and Investigations Act 1996, ss 44(1), (4), (7), 80, Sch 5, in relation to an inquiry into an offence by a magistrates' court as examining justices begun after 4 July 1996.

Modification: modified, in relation to the Armed Forces, by the Criminal Justice and Public Order Act 1994 (Application to the Armed Forces) Order 1997, SI 1997/16, art 2, Schedule.

35 Effect of accused's silence at trial

(1) At the trial of any person who has attained the age of fourteen years for an offence, subsections (2) and (3) below apply unless—
(a) the accused's guilt is not in issue; or
(b) it appears to the court that the physical or mental condition of the accused makes it undesirable for him to give evidence;

but subsection (2) below does not apply if, at the conclusion of the evidence for the prosecution, his legal representative informs the court that the accused will give evidence or, where he is unrepresented, the court ascertains from him that he will give evidence.

(2) Where this subsection applies, the court shall, at the conclusion of the evidence for the prosecution, satisfy itself (in the case of proceedings on indictment, in the presence of the jury) that the accused is aware that the stage has been reached at which evidence can be given for the defence and that he can, if he wishes, give evidence and that, if he chooses not to give evidence, or having been sworn, without good cause refuses to answer any question, it will be permissible for the court or jury to draw such inferences as appear proper from his failure to give evidence or his refusal, without good cause, to answer any question.

(3) Where this subsection applies, the court or jury, in determining whether the accused is guilty of the offence charged, may draw such inferences as appear proper from the failure of the accused to give evidence or his refusal, without good cause, to answer any question.

(4) This section does not render the accused compellable to give evidence on his own behalf, and he shall accordingly not be guilty of contempt of court by reason of a failure to do so.

(5) For the purposes of this section a person who, having been sworn, refuses to answer any question shall be taken to do so without good cause unless—

(a) he is entitled to refuse to answer the question by virtue of any enactment, whenever passed or made, or on the ground of privilege; or

(b) the court in the exercise of its general discretion excuses him from answering it.

(6), (7) . . .

NOTES

Commencement: 10 April 1995.

Sub-ss (6), (7): outside the scope of this work.

Modification: modified, in relation to the Armed Forces, by the Criminal Justice and Public Order Act 1994 (Application to the Armed Forces) Order 1997, SI 1997/16, art 2, Schedule.

36 Effect of accused's failure or refusal to account for objects, substances or marks

(1) Where—

(a) a person is arrested by a constable, and there is—

(i) on his person; or

(ii) in or on his clothing or footwear; or

(iii) otherwise in his possession; or

(iv) in any place in which he is at the time of his arrest,

any object, substance or mark, or there is any mark on any such object; and

(b) that or another constable investigating the case reasonably believes that the presence of the object, substance or mark may be attributable to the participation of the person arrested in the commission of an offence specified by the constable; and

(c) the constable informs the person arrested that he so believes, and requests him to account for the presence of the object, substance or mark; and

(d) the person fails or refuses to do so,

then if, in any proceedings against the person for the offence so specified, evidence of those matters is given, subsection (2) below applies.

(2) Where this subsection applies—

[(a) a magistrates' court inquiring into the offence as examining justices;]

(b) a judge, in deciding whether to grant an application made by the accused under—
  (i) section 6 of the Criminal Justice Act 1987 (application for dismissal of charge of serious fraud in respect of which notice of transfer has been given under section 4 of that Act); or
  (ii) paragraph 5 of Schedule 6 to the Criminal Justice Act 1991 (application for dismissal of charge of violent or sexual offence involving child in respect of which notice of transfer has been given under section 53 of that Act);
(c) the court, in determining whether there is a case to answer; and
(d) the court or jury, in determining whether the accused is guilty of the offence charged,

may draw such inferences from the failure or refusal as appear proper.

(3) Subsections (1) and (2) above apply to the condition of clothing or footwear as they apply to a substance or mark thereon.

(4) Subsections (1) and (2) above do not apply unless the accused was told in ordinary language by the constable when making the request mentioned in subsection (1)(c) above what the effect of this section would be if he failed or refused to comply with the request.

(5) This section applies in relation to officers of customs and excise as it applies in relation to constables.

(6) This section does not preclude the drawing of any inference from a failure or refusal of the accused to account for the presence of an object, substance or mark or from the condition of clothing or footwear which could properly be drawn apart from this section.

(7), (8) . . .

NOTES

Commencement: 10 April 1995.

Sub-s (2): para (a) substituted by the Criminal Procedure and Investigations 1996, s 44(1), (3), (7), in relation to an inquiry into an offence by a magistrates' court as examining justices begun after 4 July 1996.

Sub-s (7): outside the scope of this work.

Sub-s (8): repealed by the Criminal Procedure and Investigations Act 1996, ss 44(1), (4), (7), 80, Sch 5, in relation to an inquiry into an offence by a magistrates' court as examining justices begun after 4 July 1996.

Modification: modified, in relation to the Armed Forces, by the Criminal Justice and Public Order Act 1994 (Application to the Armed Forces) Order 1997, SI 1997/16, art 2, Schedule.

---

37 Effect of accused's failure or refusal to account for presence at a particular place

(1) Where—
(a) a person arrested by a constable was found by him at a place at or about the time the offence for which he was arrested is alleged to have been committed; and
(b) that or another constable investigating the offence reasonably believes that the presence of the person at that place and at that time may be attributable to his participation in the commission of the offence; and
(c) the constable informs the person that he so believes, and requests him to account for that presence; and
(d) the person fails or refuses to do so,

then if, in any proceedings against the person for the offence, evidence of those matters is given, subsection (2) below applies.

(2) Where this subsection applies—

[(a) a magistrates' court inquiring into the offence as examining justices;]

(b) a judge, in deciding whether to grant an application made by the accused under—

(i) section 6 of the Criminal Justice Act 1987 (application for dismissal of charge of serious fraud in respect of which notice of transfer has been given under section 4 of that Act); or

(ii) paragraph 5 of Schedule 6 to the Criminal Justice Act 1991 (application for dismissal of charge of violent or sexual offence involving child in respect of which notice of transfer has been given under section 53 of that Act);

(c) the court, in determining whether there is a case to answer; and

(d) the court or jury, in determining whether the accused is guilty of the offence charged,

may draw such inferences from the failure or refusal as appear proper.

(3) Subsections (1) and (2) do not apply unless the accused was told in ordinary language by the constable when making the request mentioned in subsection (1)(c) above what the effect of this section would be if he failed or refused to comply with the request.

(4) This section applies in relation to officers of customs and excise as it applies in relation to constables.

(5) This section does not preclude the drawing of any inference from a failure or refusal of the accused to account for his presence at a place which could properly be drawn apart from this section.

(6) This section does not apply in relation to a failure or refusal which occurred before the commencement of this section.

(7) . . .

NOTES

Commencement: 10 April 1995.

Sub-s (2): para (a) substituted by the Criminal Procedure and Investigations 1996, s 44(1), (3), (7), in relation to an inquiry into an offence by a magistrates' court as examining justices begun after 4 July 1996.

Sub-s (7): repealed by the Criminal Procedure and Investigations Act 1996, ss 44(1), (4), (7), 80, Sch 5, in relation to an inquiry into an offence by a magistrates' court as examining justices begun after 4 July 1996.

Modification: modified, in relation to the Armed Forces, by the Criminal Justice and Public Order Act 1994 (Application to the Armed Forces) Order 1997, SI 1997/16, art 2, Schedule.

38 Interpretation and savings for sections 34, 35, 36 and 37

(1) In sections 34, 35, 36 and 37 of this Act—

"legal representative" means an authorised advocate or authorised litigator, as defined by section 119(1) of the Courts and Legal Services Act 1990; and

"place" includes any building or part of a building, any vehicle, vessel, aircraft or hovercraft and any other place whatsoever.

(2) In sections 34(2), 35(3), 36(2) and 37(2), references to an offence charged include references to any other offence of which the accused could lawfully be convicted on that charge.

(3) A person shall not have the proceedings against him transferred to the Crown Court for trial, have a case to answer or be convicted of an offence solely on an inference drawn from such a failure or refusal as is mentioned in section 34(2), 35(3), 36(2) or 37(2).

(4) A judge shall not refuse to grant such an application as is mentioned in section 34(2)(b), 36(2)(b) and 37(2)(b) solely on an inference drawn from such a failure as is mentioned in section 34(2), 36(2) or 37(2).

(5) Nothing in sections 34, 35, 36 or 37 prejudices the operation of a provision of any enactment which provides (in whatever words) that any answer or evidence given by a person in specified circumstances shall not be admissible in evidence against him or some other person in any proceedings or class of proceedings (however described, and whether civil or criminal).

In this subsection, the reference to giving evidence is a reference to giving evidence in any manner, whether by furnishing information, making discovery, producing documents or otherwise.

(6) Nothing in sections 34, 35, 36 or 37 prejudices any power of a court, in any proceedings, to exclude evidence (whether by preventing questions being put or otherwise) at its discretion.

NOTES

Commencement; 10 April 1995.

Modification: modified, in relation to the Armed Forces, by the Criminal Justice and Public Order Act 1994 (Application to the Armed Forces) Order 1997, SI 1997/16, art 2, Schedule.

Sentencing: guilty pleas

48 Reduction in sentences for guilty pleas

(1) In determining what sentence to pass on an offender who has pleaded guilty to an offence in proceedings before that or another court a court shall take into account—

- (a) the stage in the proceedings for the offence at which the offender indicated his intention to plead guilty, and
- (b) the circumstances in which this indication was given.

(2) If, as a result of taking into account any matter referred to in subsection (1) above, the court imposes a punishment on the offender which is less severe than the punishment it would otherwise have imposed, it shall state in open court that it has done so.

[(3) In the case of an offence the sentence for which falls to be imposed under subsection (2) of section 3 or 4 of the Crime (Sentences) Act 1997, nothing in that subsection shall prevent the court, after taking into account any matter referred to in subsection (1) above, from imposing any sentence which is not less than 80 per cent of that specified in that subsection.]

NOTES

Commencement: 3 February 1995.

Sub-s (3): inserted by the Crime (Sentences) Act 1997, s 55, Sch 4, para 17, as from 1 October 1997, in so far as relating to offences the sentences for which fall to be imposed under the Crime (Sentences) Act 1997, s 57(2); to be appointed, otherwise.

PART IV
POLICE POWERS

Powers of police to stop and search

60 Powers to stop and search in anticipation of violence

(1) Where a police officer of or above the rank of superintendent reasonably believes that—
- *(a) incidents involving serious violence may take place in any locality in his area, and*
- *(b) it is expedient to do so to prevent their occurrence,*

he may give an authorisation that the powers to stop and search persons and vehicles conferred by this section shall be exercisable at any place within that locality for a period not exceeding twenty four hours.

(2) The power conferred by subsection (1) above may be exercised by a chief inspector or an inspector if he reasonably believes that incidents involving serious violence are imminent and no superintendent is available.

(3) If it appears to *the officer who gave the authorisation or to a* superintendent that it is expedient to do so, having regard to offences which have, or are reasonably suspected to have, been committed in connection with any *incident* falling within the authorisation, he may direct that the authorisation shall continue in being for a further *six* hours.

[(3A) If an inspector gives an authorisation under subsection (1) he must, as soon as it is practicable to do so, cause an officer of or above the rank of superintendent to be informed.]

(4) This section confers on any constable in uniform power—
- (a) to stop any pedestrian and search him or anything carried by him for offensive weapons or dangerous instruments;
- (b) to stop any vehicle and search the vehicle, its driver and any passenger for offensive weapons or dangerous instruments.

[(4A) This section also confers on any constable in uniform power—
- (a) to require any person to remove any item which the constable reasonably believes that person is wearing wholly or mainly for the purpose of concealing his identity;
- (b) to seize any item which the constable reasonably believes any person intends to wear wholly or mainly for that purpose.]

(5) A constable may, in the exercise of *those powers*, stop any person or vehicle and make any search he thinks fit whether or not he has any grounds for suspecting that the person or vehicle is carrying weapons or articles of that kind.

(6) If in the course of a search under this section a constable discovers a dangerous instrument or an article which he has reasonable grounds for suspecting to be an offensive weapon, he may seize it.

(7) This section applies (with the necessary modifications) to ships, aircraft and hovercraft as it applies to vehicles.

(8) A person who fails *to stop or (as the case may be) to stop the vehicle* when required to do so by a constable in the exercise of his powers under this section shall be liable on summary conviction to imprisonment for a term not exceeding one month or to a fine not exceeding level 3 on the standard scale or both.

(2) A direction under subsection (1) above, if not communicated to the persons referred to in subsection (1) by the police officer giving the direction, may be communicated to them by any constable at the scene.

(3) If a person knowing that a direction under subsection (1) above has been given which applies to him—

(a) fails to leave the land as soon as practicable, or

(b) having left again enters the land as a trespasser within the period of three months beginning with the day on which the direction was given,

he commits an offence and is liable on summary conviction to imprisonment for a term not exceeding three months or a fine not exceeding level 4 on the standard scale, or both.

(4) In proceedings for an offence under subsection (3) it is a defence for the accused to show—

(a) that he was not trespassing on the land, or

(b) that he had a reasonable excuse for failing to leave the land as soon as practicable or, as the case may be, for again entering the land as a trespasser.

(5) A constable in uniform who reasonably suspects that a person is committing an offence under this section may arrest him without a warrant.

(6) In this section "lawful activity" and "land" have the same meaning as in section 68.

NOTES

Commencement: 3 November 1994.

PART XII
MISCELLANEOUS AND GENERAL

Closed-circuit television by local authorities

163 Local authority powers to provide closed-circuit television

(1) Without prejudice to any power which they may exercise for those purposes under any other enactment, a local authority may take such of the following steps as they consider will, in relation to their area, promote the prevention of crime or the welfare of the victims of crime—

(a) providing apparatus for recording visual images of events occurring on any land in their area;

(b) providing within their area a telecommunications system which, under Part II of the Telecommunications Act 1984, may be run without a licence;

(c) arranging for the provision of any other description of telecommunications system within their area or between any land in their area and any building occupied by a public authority.

(2)–(5) . . .

NOTES

Commencement: 3 February 1995.

Sub-ss (2)–(5): outside the scope of this work.

General

172 Short title, commencement and extent

(1) This Act may be cited as the Criminal Justice and Public Order Act 1994.

(2)–(16) . . .

NOTES

Commencement: 3 November 1994.

Sub-ss (2)–(16): outside the scope of this work.

DRUG TRAFFICKING ACT 1994

(C 37)

An Act to consolidate the Drug Trafficking Offences Act 1986 and certain provisions of the Criminal Justice (International Co-operation) Act 1990 relating to drug trafficking

[3 November 1994]

PART IV
MISCELLANEOUS AND SUPPLEMENTAL

Investigations into drug trafficking

55 Order to make material available

(1) A constable may, for the purpose of an investigation into drug trafficking, apply to a Circuit judge for an order under subsection (2) below in relation to particular material or material of a particular description.

(2) If on such an application the judge is satisfied that the conditions in subsection (4) below are fulfilled, he may make an order that the person who appears to him to be in possession of the material to which the application relates shall—

(a) produce it to a constable for him to take away, or

(b) give a constable access to it,

within such period as the order may specify.

This subsection has effect subject to section 59(11) of this Act.

(3) The period to be specified in an order under subsection (2) above shall be seven days unless it appears to the judge that a longer or shorter period would be appropriate in the particular circumstances of the application.

(4) The conditions referred to in subsection (2) above are—

(a) that there are reasonable grounds for suspecting that a specified person has carried on or has benefited from drug trafficking;

(b) that there are reasonable grounds for suspecting that the material to which the application relates—

(i) is likely to be of substantial value (whether by itself or together with other material) to the investigation for the purpose of which the application is made; and

(ii) does not consist of or include items subject to legal privilege or excluded material; and

(c) that there are reasonable grounds for believing that it is in the public interest, having regard—

(i) to the benefit likely to accrue to the investigation if the material is obtained, and

(ii) to the circumstances under which the person in possession of the material holds it,

that the material should be produced or that access to it should be given.

(5) Where the judge makes an order under subsection (2)(b) above in relation to material on any premises he may, on the application of a constable, order any person who appears to him to be entitled to grant entry to the premises to allow a constable to enter the premises to obtain access to the material.

(6) An application under subsection (1) or (5) above may be made ex parte to a judge in chambers.

(7)–(9) . . .

(10) An order under subsection (2) above—

(a) shall not confer any right to production of, or access to, items subject to legal privilege or excluded material;

(b) shall have effect notwithstanding any obligation as to secrecy or other restriction upon the disclosure of information imposed by statute or otherwise; and

(c) may be made in relation to material in the possession of an authorised government department;

and in this subsection "authorised government department" means a government department which is an authorised department for the purposes of the Crown Proceedings Act 1947.

NOTES

Commencement: 3 February 1995.

Sub-ss (7)–(9): outside the scope of this work.

56 Authority for search

(1) A constable may, for the purpose of an investigation into drug trafficking, apply to a Circuit judge for a warrant under this section in relation to specified premises.

(2) On such application the judge may issue a warrant authorising a constable to enter and search the premises if the judge is satisfied—

(a) that an order made under section 55 of this Act in relation to material on the premises has not been complied with;

(b) that the conditions in subsection (3) below are fulfilled; or

(c) that the conditions in subsection (4) below are fulfilled.

(3) The conditions referred to in subsection (2)(b) above are—

(a) that there are reasonable grounds for suspecting that a specified person has carried on or has benefited from drug trafficking;

(b) that the conditions in subsection (4)(b) and (c) of section 55 of this Act are fulfilled in relation to any material on the premises; and

(c) that it would not be appropriate to make an order under that section in relation to the material because—

(i) it is not practicable to communicate with any person entitled to produce the material;

(ii) it is not practicable to communicate with any person entitled to grant access to the material or entitled to grant entry to the premises on which the material is situated; or

(iii) the investigation for the purpose of which the application is made might be seriously prejudiced unless a constable could secure immediate access to the material.

(4) The conditions referred to in subsection (2)(c) above are—

(a) that there are reasonable grounds for suspecting that a specified person has carried on or has benefited from drug trafficking;

(b) that there are reasonable grounds for suspecting that there is on the premises material relating to the specified person or to drug trafficking which is likely to be of substantial value (whether by itself or together with other material) to the investigation for the purpose of which the application is made, but that the material cannot at the time of the application be particularised; and

(c) that—

(i) it is not practicable to communicate with any person entitled to grant entry to the premises;

(ii) entry to the premises will not be granted unless a warrant is produced; or

(iii) the investigation for the purpose of which the application is made might be seriously prejudiced unless a constable arriving at the premises could secure immediate entry to them.

(5) Where a constable has entered premises in the execution of a warrant issued under this section, he may seize and retain any material, other than items subject to legal privilege and excluded material, which is likely to be of substantial value (whether by itself or together with other material) to the investigation for the purpose of which the warrant was issued.

NOTES

Commencement: 3 February 1995.

59 Disclosure of information held by government departments

(1) Subject to subsection (4) below, the High Court may on an application by the prosecutor order any material mentioned in subsection (3) below which is in the possession of an authorised government department to be produced to the court within such period as the court may specify.

(2) The power to make an order under subsection (1) above is exercisable if—

(a) the powers conferred on the court by sections 26(1) and 27(1) of this Act are exercisable by virtue of subsection (1) of section 25 of this Act; or

(b) those powers are exercisable by virtue of subsection (3) of that section and the court has made a restraint or charging order which has not been discharged;

but where the power to make an order under subsection (1) above is exercisable by virtue only of paragraph (b) above, subsection (4) of section 25 of this Act shall apply for the purposes of this section as it applies for the purposes of sections 26 and 27 of this Act.

(3) The material referred to in subsection (1) above is any material which—

(a) has been submitted to an officer of an authorised government department by the defendant or by a person who has at any time held property which was realisable property;

(b) has been made by an officer of an authorised government department in relation to the defendant or such a person; or

(c) is correspondence which passed between an officer of an authorised government department and the defendant or such a person;

and an order under that subsection may require the production of all such material or of a particular description of such material, being material in the possession of the department concerned.

(4) An order under subsection (1) above shall not require the production of any material unless it appears to the High Court that the material is likely to contain information that would facilitate the exercise of the powers conferred on the court by sections 26 to 29 of this Act or on a receiver appointed under section 26 or 29 of this Act or in pursuance of a charging order.

(5)–(13) . . .

NOTES

Commencement: 3 February 1995.

Sub-ss (5)–(13): outside the scope of this work.

Supplemental

68 Extent

(1) Subject to the following provisions of this section, this Act extends to England and Wales only.

(2)–(7) . . .

NOTES

Commencement: 3 February 1995.

Sub-ss (2)–(7): outside the scope of this work.

69 Short title and commencement

(1) This Act may be cited as the Drug Trafficking Act 1994.

(2) This Act comes into force at the end of the period of three months beginning with the day on which it is passed.

NOTES

Commencement: 3 February 1995.

DEREGULATION AND CONTRACTING OUT ACT 1994

(C 40)

An Act to amend, and make provision for the amendment of, statutory provisions and rules of law in order to remove or reduce certain burdens affecting persons in the carrying on of trades, businesses or professions or otherwise, and for other deregulatory purposes; to make further provision in connection with the licensing of operators of goods vehicles; to make provision for and in connection with the contracting out of certain functions vested in Ministers of the Crown, local authorities, certain governmental bodies and the holders of certain offices; and for purposes connected therewith

[3 November 1994]

PART I
DEREGULATION

CHAPTER I
GENERAL

Removal or reduction of burdens

1 Power to remove or reduce certain statutory burdens on businesses, individuals etc

(1) If, with respect to any provision made by an enactment, a Minister of the Crown is of the opinion—

(a) that the effect of the provision is such as to impose, or authorise or require the imposition of, a burden affecting any person in the carrying on of any trade, business or profession or otherwise, and

(b) that, by amending or repealing the enactment concerned and, where appropriate, by making such other provision as is referred to in subsection (4)(a) below, it would be possible, without removing any necessary protection, to remove or reduce the burden or, as the case may be, the authorisation or requirement by virtue of which the burden may be imposed,

he may, subject to the following provisions of this section and sections 2 to 4 below, by order amend or repeal that enactment.

(2) The reference in subsection (1)(b) above to reducing the authorisation or requirement by virtue of which a burden may be imposed includes a reference to shortening any period of time within which the burden may be so imposed.

(3) In this section and sections 2 to 4 below, in relation to an order under this section,—

(a) "the existing provision" means the provision by which the burden concerned is imposed or, as the case may be, is authorised or required to be imposed; and

(b) "the relevant enactment" means the enactment containing the existing provision.

(4) An order under this section shall be made by statutory instrument and may do all or any of the following—

(a) make provision (whether by amending any enactment or otherwise) creating a burden which relates to the subject matter of, but is less onerous than that imposed by, the existing provision;

(b) make such modifications of enactments as, in the opinion of the Minister concerned, are consequential upon, or incidental to, the amendment or repeal of the relevant enactment;

(c) contain such transitional provisions and savings as appear to the Minister to be appropriate;

(d) make different provision for different cases or different areas;

but no order shall be made under this section unless a draft of the order has been laid before and approved by a resolution of each House of Parliament.

(5) In this section and sections 2 to 4 below—

(a) "Minister of the Crown" has the same meaning as in the Ministers of the Crown Act 1975 and "Minister" shall be construed accordingly;

(b) "burden" includes a restriction, requirement or condition (including one requiring the payment of fees), together with—

(i) any sanction (whether criminal or otherwise) for failure to observe the restriction or to comply with the requirement or condition; and

(ii) any procedural provisions (including provisions for appeal) relevant to that sanction; and

(c) "enactment", subject to subsection (6) below, means an enactment contained in this Act or in any other Act passed before or in the same Session as this Act, or any provision of an order under this section.

(6) In paragraph (c) of subsection (5) above—

(a) "Act" does not include anything contained in Northern Ireland legislation, within the meaning of section 24 of the Interpretation Act 1978; and

(b) the reference to an enactment is a reference to an enactment as for the time being amended, extended or applied by or under any Act mentioned in that paragraph.

(7) Where a restriction, requirement or condition is subject to a criminal sanction (as mentioned in subsection (5)(b)(i) above), nothing in this section shall authorise the making of an amendment which would have the effect of leaving the restriction, requirement or condition in place but producing a different criminal sanction or altering any procedural provisions relevant to the criminal sanction.

NOTES

Commencement: 3 November 1994.

2 Limitations on the power under section 1

(1) If an order under section 1 above creates a new criminal offence, then, subject to subsections (2) and (3) below, that offence shall not be punishable—

(a) on indictment with imprisonment for a term of more than two years; or

(b) on summary conviction with imprisonment for a term exceeding six months or a fine exceeding level 5 on the standard scale or both.

(2) In the case of an offence which, if committed by an adult, is triable either on indictment or summarily and is not an offence triable on indictment only by virtue of—

(a) Part V of the Criminal Justice Act 1988, or

(b) . . .

the reference in subsection (1)(b) above to level 5 on the standard scale shall be construed as a reference to the statutory maximum.

(3) If an order under section 1 above abolishes an offence contained in the relevant enactment and the maximum penalties for that offence are greater than those

specified in subsection (1) above, the order may create a new criminal offence having maximum penalties not exceeding those applicable to the offence which is abolished.

(4) An order under section 1 above shall not contain any provision—
  (a) providing for any forcible entry, search or seizure, or
  (b) compelling the giving of evidence,

unless, and then only to the extent that, a provision to that effect is contained in the relevant enactment and is abolished by the order.

NOTES
Commencement: 3 November 1994.
Sub-s (2): para (b) outside the scope of this work.

3 Preliminary consultation

(1) Before a Minister makes an order under section 1 above, he shall—
  (a) consult such organisations as appear to him to be representative of interests substantially affected by his proposals; and
  (b) consult such other persons as he considers appropriate.

(2) If it appears to the Minister, as a result of the consultation required by subsection (1) above, that it is appropriate to vary the whole or any part of his proposals, he shall undertake such further consultation with respect to the variations as appears to him to be appropriate.

(3) If, after the conclusion of—
  (a) the consultation required by subsection (1) above, and
  (b) any further consultation undertaken as mentioned in subsection (2) above,

the Minister considers it appropriate to proceed with the making of an order under section 1 above, he shall lay before Parliament a document containing his proposals in the form of a draft of the order, together with details of the matters specified in subsection (4) below.

(4) The matters referred to in subsection (3) above are—
  (a) the burden, authorisation or requirement which it is proposed to remove or reduce;
  (b) whether the existing provision affords any necessary protection and, if so, how that protection is to be continued if the burden, authorisation or requirement is removed or reduced;
  (c) whether any savings in cost are estimated to result from the proposals and, if so, either the estimated amount or the reasons why savings should be expected;
  (d) any other benefits which are expected to flow from the removal or reduction of the burden, authorisation or requirement;
  (e) any consultation undertaken as required by subsection (1) or subsection (2) above;
  (f) any representations received as a result of that consultation; and
  (g) the changes (if any) which the Minister has made to his original proposals in the light of those representations.

(5) In giving details of the representations referred to in subsection (4)(f) above, the Minister shall not disclose any information relating to a particular person or business except—
  (a) with the consent of that person or of the person carrying on that business; or
  (b) in such a manner as not to identify that person or business.

(6) If, before the day on which this section comes into force, any consultation was undertaken which, had it been undertaken after that day, would to any extent have satisfied the requirements of subsection (1) above, those requirements shall to that extent be taken to have been satisfied.

NOTES
Commencement: 3 November 1994.

4 Parliamentary consideration of proposals

(1) Where a document has been laid before Parliament under section 3(3) above, no draft of an order under section 1 above to give effect (with or without variations) to proposals in that document shall be laid before Parliament until after the expiry of the period for Parliamentary consideration, as defined in subsection (2) below.

(2) In this section "the period for Parliamentary consideration", in relation to a document, means the period of sixty days beginning on the day on which it was laid before Parliament.

(3) In reckoning the period of sixty days referred to in subsection (2) above, no account shall be taken of any time during which Parliament is dissolved or prorogued or during which either House is adjourned for more than four days.

(4) In preparing a draft of an order under section 1 above to give effect, with or without variations, to proposals in a document laid before Parliament under section 3(3) above, the Minister concerned shall have regard to any representations made during the period for Parliamentary consideration and, in particular, to any resolution or report of, or of any committee of, either House of Parliament with regard to the document.

(5) Together with a draft of an order laid before Parliament under section 1(4) above, the Minister concerned shall lay a statement giving details of—

- (a) any representations, resolution or report falling within subsection (4) above; and
- (b) the changes (if any) which, in the light of any such representations, resolution or report, the Minister has made to his proposals as contained in the document previously laid before Parliament under section 3(3) above.

(6) Subsection (5) of section 3 above shall apply in relation to the representations referred to in subsection (5)(a) above as it applies in relation to the representations referred to in subsection (4)(f) of that section.

NOTES
Commencement: 3 November 1994.

Enforcement procedures and appeals

5 Powers to improve enforcement procedures

(1) If, with respect to any provision made by an enactment, a Minister of the Crown is of the opinion—

- (a) that the effect of the provision is such as to impose, or authorise or require the imposition of, a restriction, requirement or condition affecting any person in the carrying on of any trade, business or profession or otherwise, and

(b) that, by exercising any one or more of the powers conferred by Schedule 1 to this Act, it would be possible, without jeopardising any necessary protection, to improve (so far as fairness, transparency and consistency are concerned) the procedures for enforcing the restriction, requirement or condition,

he may, subject to the following provisions of this section, by order exercise the power or powers accordingly.

(2) No order shall be made under this section in any case where the sole or main effect which the restriction, requirement or condition may be expected to have on each person on whom it is imposed is an effect on him in his personal capacity, and not as a person carrying on a trade, business or profession.

(3) Where the relevant enactment—

(a) contains a power for the Minister to make regulations or orders; and

(b) provides for that power to be exercisable so as to give effect, with or without modifications, to proposals submitted by some other person,

the Minister shall consult with that person before he makes an order under this section.

(4) An order under this section shall be made by statutory instrument and may do all or any of the following—

(a) make provision as to the consequences of any failure to comply with a provision made by the order;

(b) contain provisions (including provisions modifying enactments relating to the periods within which proceedings must be brought) which are consequential upon, or supplemental or incidental to, the provisions made by the order;

(c) contain such transitional provisions and savings as appear to the Minister to be appropriate;

(d) make different provision for different cases or different areas;

and a statutory instrument containing an order under this section shall be subject to annulment in pursuance of a resolution of either House of Parliament.

(5) Nothing in any order made under this section shall—

(a) preclude an enforcement officer from taking immediate enforcement action against any person, or from requiring any person to take immediate remedial action, in any case where it appears to the officer to be necessary to take such action or impose such a requirement; or

(b) require such an officer to disclose any information the disclosure of which would be contrary to the public interest.

(6) In this section and Schedule 1 to this Act—

"enactment" means an enactment within the meaning of section 1 above, and any subordinate legislation made under such an enactment;

"enforcement action"—

(a) in relation to any restriction, requirement or condition, means any action taken with a view to or in connection with imposing any sanction (whether criminal or otherwise) for failure to observe or comply with it; and

(b) in relation to a restriction, requirement or condition relating to the grant or renewal of licences, includes any refusal to grant, renew or vary a licence, the imposition of any condition on the grant or renewal of a licence and any variation or revocation of a licence;

"enforcement officer" does not include—

(a) the Director of Public Prosecutions;

(b) the Lord Advocate or a procurator fiscal; or

(c) the Director of Public Prosecutions for Northern Ireland,

but, subject to that, means any person who is authorised, whether by or under the relevant enactment or otherwise, to take enforcement action;

"licence" includes any authorisation (by whatever name called) to do anything which would otherwise be unlawful;

"Minister of the Crown" and "Minister" have the same meanings as in section 1 above;

"the relevant enactment" means the enactment containing the provision by which the restriction, requirement or condition is imposed or, as the case may be, is authorised or required to be imposed;

"remedial action" means action taken by any person in order to avoid enforcement action being taken against him;

"subordinate legislation" has the same meaning as in the Interpretation Act 1978.

NOTES

Commencement: 3 November 1994.

PART III
SUPPLEMENTARY

82 Short title, commencement and extent

(1) This Act may be cited as the Deregulation and Contracting Out Act 1994.

(2)–(7) . . .

(8) Except in so far as any provision of this Act otherwise provides, this Act, other than Chapter I of Part I and this section, does not extend to Northern Ireland.

NOTES

Commencement: 3 November 1994.
Sub-ss (2)–(7): outside the scope of this work.

CRIMINAL APPEAL ACT 1995

(C 35)

An Act to amend provisions relating to appeals and references to the Court of Appeal in criminal cases; to establish a Criminal Cases Review Commission and confer functions on, and make other provision in relation to, the Commission; to amend section 142 of the Magistrates' Courts Act 1980 and introduce in Northern Ireland provisions similar to those of that section; to amend section 133 of the Criminal Justice Act 1988; and for connected purposes

[19 July 1995]

PART II
THE CRIMINAL CASES REVIEW COMMISSION

The Commission

8 The Commission

(1) There shall be a body corporate to be known as the Criminal Cases Review Commission.

(2) The Commission shall not be regarded as the servant or agent of the Crown or as enjoying any status, immunity or privilege of the Crown; and the Commission's property shall not be regarded as property of, or held on behalf of, the Crown.

(3) The Commission shall consist of not fewer than eleven members.

(4) The members of the Commission shall be appointed by Her Majesty on the recommendation of the Prime Minister.

(5) At least one third of the members of the Commission shall be persons who are legally qualified; and for this purpose a person is legally qualified if—
- (a) he has a ten year general qualification, within the meaning of section 71 of the Courts and Legal Services Act 1990, or
- (b) he is a member of the Bar of Northern Ireland, or solicitor of the Supreme Court of Northern Ireland, of at least ten years' standing.

(6) At least two thirds of the members of the Commission shall be persons who appear to the Prime Minister to have knowledge or experience of any aspect of the criminal justice system and of them at least one shall be a person who appears to him to have knowledge or experience of any aspect of the criminal justice system in Northern Ireland; and for the purposes of this subsection the criminal justice system includes, in particular, the investigation of offences and the treatment of offenders.

(7) . . .

NOTES

Commencement: 12 December 1996, for purpose of making recommendations and appointments; 1 January 1997, otherwise (sub-ss (1)–(6)).

Sub-s (7): outside the scope of this work.

References to court

9 Cases dealt with on indictment in England and Wales

(1) Where a person has been convicted of an offence on indictment in England and Wales, the Commission—
- (a) may at any time refer the conviction to the Court of Appeal, and
- (b) (whether or not they refer the conviction) may at any time refer to the Court of Appeal any sentence (not being a sentence fixed by law) imposed on, or in subsequent proceedings relating to, the conviction.

(2) A reference under subsection (1) of a person's conviction shall be treated for all purposes as an appeal by the person under section 1 of the 1968 Act against the conviction.

(3) A reference under subsection (1) of a sentence imposed on, or in subsequent proceedings relating to, a person's conviction on an indictment shall be treated for all purposes as an appeal by the person under section 9 of the 1968 Act against—
- (a) the sentence, and
- (b) any other sentence (not being a sentence fixed by law) imposed on, or in subsequent proceedings relating to, the conviction or any other conviction on the indictment.

(4) On a reference under subsection (1) of a person's conviction on an indictment the Commission may give notice to the Court of Appeal that any other conviction on the indictment which is specified in the notice is to be treated as referred to the Court of Appeal under subsection (1).

(5), (6) . . .

NOTES

Commencement: 31 March 1997, subject to transitional provisions.
Sub-ss (5), (6): outside the scope of this work.

11 Cases dealt with summarily in England and Wales

(1) Where a person has been convicted of an offence by a magistrates' court in England and Wales, the Commission—

(a) may at any time refer the conviction to the Crown Court, and
(b) (whether or not they refer the conviction) may at any time refer to the Crown Court any sentence imposed on, or in subsequent proceedings relating to, the conviction.

(2) A reference under subsection (1) of a person's conviction shall be treated for all purposes as an appeal by the person under section 108(1) of the Magistrates' Courts Act 1980 against the conviction (whether or not he pleaded guilty).

(3) A reference under subsection (1) of a sentence imposed on, or in subsequent proceedings relating to, a person's conviction shall be treated for all purposes as an appeal by the person under section 108(1) of the Magistrates' Courts Act 1980 against—

(a) the sentence, and
(b) any other sentence imposed on, or in subsequent proceedings relating to, the conviction or any related conviction.

(4) On a reference under subsection (1) of a person's conviction the Commission may give notice to the Crown Court that any related conviction which is specified in the notice is to be treated as referred to the Crown Court under subsection (1).

(5) For the purposes of this section convictions are related if they are convictions of the same person by the same court on the same day.

(6) On a reference under this section the Crown Court may not award any punishment more severe than that awarded by the court whose decision is referred.

(7) The Crown Court may grant bail to a person whose conviction or sentence has been referred under this section; and any time during which he is released on bail shall not count as part of any term of imprisonment or detention under his sentence.

NOTES

Commencement: 31 March 1997, subject to transitional provisions.

13 Conditions for making of references

(1) A reference of a conviction, verdict, finding or sentence shall not be made under any of sections 9 to 12 unless—

(a) the Commission consider that there is a real possibility that the conviction, verdict, finding or sentence would not be upheld were the reference to be made,
(b) the Commission so consider—
  (i) in the case of a conviction, verdict or finding, because of an argument, or evidence, not raised in the proceedings which led to it or on any appeal or application for leave to appeal against it, or
  (ii) in the case of a sentence, because of an argument on a point of law, or information, not so raised, and

(c) an appeal against the conviction, verdict, finding or sentence has been determined or leave to appeal against it has been refused.

(2) Nothing in subsection (1)(b)(i) or (c) shall prevent the making of a reference if it appears to the Commission that there are exceptional circumstances which justify making it.

NOTES
Commencement: 31 March 1997, subject to transitional provisions.

14 Further provisions about references

(1) A reference of a conviction, verdict, finding or sentence may be made under any of sections 9 to 12 either after an application has been made by or on behalf of the person to whom it relates or without an application having been so made.

(2) In considering whether to make a reference of a conviction, verdict, finding or sentence under any of sections 9 to 12 the Commission shall have regard to—

(a) any application or representations made to the Commission by or on behalf of the person to whom it relates,

(b) any other representations made to the Commission in relation to it, and

(c) any other matters which appear to the Commission to be relevant.

(3) In considering whether to make a reference under section 9 or 10 the Commission may at any time refer any point on which they desire the assistance of the Court of Appeal to that Court for the Court's opinion on it; and on a reference under this subsection the Court of Appeal shall consider the point referred and furnish the Commission with the Court's opinion on the point.

(4) Where the Commission make a reference under any of sections 9 to 12 the Commission shall—

(a) give to the court to which the reference is made a statement of the Commission's reasons for making the reference, and

(b) send a copy of the statement to every person who appears to the Commission to be likely to be a party to any proceedings on the appeal arising from the reference.

(5) Where a reference under any of sections 9 to 12 is treated as an appeal against any conviction, verdict, finding or sentence, the appeal may be on any ground relating to the conviction, verdict, finding or sentence (whether or not the ground is related to any reason given by the Commission for making the reference).

(6) In every case in which—

(a) an application has been made to the Commission by or on behalf of any person for the reference under any of sections 9 to 12 of any conviction, verdict, finding or sentence, but

(b) the Commission decide not to make a reference of the conviction, verdict, finding or sentence,

the Commission shall give a statement of the reasons for their decision to the person who made the application.

NOTES
Commencement: 31 March 1997, subject to transitional provisions.

Investigations and assistance

16 Assistance in connection with prerogative of mercy

(1) Where the Secretary of State refers to the Commission any matter which arises in the consideration of whether to recommend the exercise of Her Majesty's prerogative of mercy in relation to a conviction and on which he desires their assistance, the Commission shall—

(a) consider the matter referred, and

(b) give to the Secretary of State a statement of their conclusions on it;

and the Secretary of State shall, in considering whether so to recommend, treat the Commission's statement as conclusive of the matter referred.

(2) Where in any case the Commission are of the opinion that the Secretary of State should consider whether to recommend the exercise of Her Majesty's prerogative of mercy in relation to the case they shall give him the reasons for their opinion.

NOTES

Commencement: 31 March 1997, subject to transitional provisions.

Supplementary powers

17 Power to obtain documents etc

(1) This section applies where the Commission believe that a person serving in a public body has possession or control of a document or other material which may assist the Commission in the exercise of any of their functions.

(2) Where it is reasonable to do so, the Commission may require the person who is the appropriate person in relation to the public body—

(a) to produce the document or other material to the Commission or to give the Commission access to it, and

(b) to allow the Commission to take away the document or other material or to make and take away a copy of it in such form as they think appropriate,

and may direct that person that the document or other material must not be destroyed, damaged or altered before the direction is withdrawn by the Commission.

(3) The documents and other material covered by this section include, in particular, any document or other material obtained or created during any investigation or proceedings relating to—

(a) the case in relation to which the Commission's function is being or may be exercised, or

(b) any other case which may be in any way connected with that case (whether or not any function of the Commission could be exercised in relation to that other case).

(4) The duty to comply with a requirement under this section is not affected by any obligation of secrecy or other limitation on disclosure (including any such obligation or limitation imposed by or by virtue of an enactment) which would otherwise prevent the production of the document or other material to the Commission or the giving of access to it to the Commission.

NOTES

Commencement: 31 March 1997, subject to transitional provisions.

PART IV
SUPPLEMENTARY

32 Commencement

(1) This Act shall come into force on such day as the Secretary of State may by order made by statutory instrument appoint; and different days may be appointed for different provisions or for different purposes.

(2) An order under subsection (1) may include such transitional provisions and savings as appear to the Secretary of State to be necessary or desirable.

NOTES

Commencement: 1 January 1996, subject to transitional provisions.

33 Extent

(1) . . .

(2) Section 8 and Schedule 1 and sections 13 to 25 extend only to England and Wales and Northern Ireland.

(3) Sections 9 and 11 extend only to England and Wales.

(4) Sections 10 and 12 extend only to Northern Ireland.

NOTES

Commencement: 1 January 1996, subject to transitional provisions.
Sub-s (1): outside the scope of this work.

34 Short title

This Act may be cited as the Criminal Appeal Act 1995.

NOTES

Commencement: 1 January 1996, subject to transitional provisions.

DISABILITY DISCRIMINATION ACT 1995

(C 50)

An Act to make it unlawful to discriminate against disabled persons in connection with employment, the provision of goods, facilities and services or the disposal or management of premises; to make provision about the employment of disabled persons; and to establish a National Disability Council.

[8 November 1995]

PART I
DISABILITY

1 Meaning of "disability" and "disabled person"

(1) Subject to the provisions of Schedule 1, a person has a disability for the purposes of this Act if he has a physical or mental impairment which has a substantial and long-term adverse effect on his ability to carry out normal day-to-day activities.

(2) In this Act "disabled person" means a person who has a disability.

NOTES

Commencement: 17 May 1996 (England and Wales); 30 May 1996 (Northern Ireland).

2 Past disabilities

(1) The provisions of this Part and Parts II and III apply in relation to a person who has had a disability as they apply in relation to a person who has that disability.

(2) . . .

(3) Any regulations or order made under this Act may include provision with respect to persons who have had a disability.

(4) In any proceedings under Part II or Part III of this Act, the question whether a person had a disability at a particular time ("the relevant time") shall be determined, for the purposes of this section, as if the provisions of, or made under, this Act in force when the act complained of was done had been in force at the relevant time.

(5) The relevant time may be a time before the passing of this Act.

NOTES

Commencement: 17 May 1996 (England and Wales); 30 May 1996 (Northern Ireland).
Sub-s (2): outside the scope of this work.

3 Guidance

(1) The Secretary of State may issue guidance about the matters to be taken into account in determining—

(a) whether an impairment has a substantial adverse effect on a person's ability to carry out normal day-to-day activities; or

(b) whether such an impairment has a long-term effect.

(2) . . .

(3) A tribunal or court determining, for any purpose of this Act, whether an impairment has a substantial and long-term adverse effect on a person's ability to carry out normal day-to-day activities, shall take into account any guidance which appears to it to be relevant.

(4) . . .

(5) Where the Secretary of State proposes to issue any guidance, he shall publish a draft of it, consider any representations that are made to him about the draft and, if he thinks it appropriate, modify his proposals in the light of any of those representations.

(6) If the Secretary of State decides to proceed with any proposed guidance, he shall lay a draft of it before each House of Parliament.

(7) If, within the 40-day period, either House resolves not to approve the draft, the Secretary of State shall take no further steps in relation to the proposed guidance.

(8)–(10) . . .

(11) The Secretary of State may—

(a) from time to time revise the whole or part of any guidance and re-issue it;

(b) by order revoke any guidance.

(12) . . .

NOTES

Commencement: 17 May 1996 (England and Wales); 30 May 1996 (Northern Ireland).

Sub-ss (2), (4), (8)–(10), (12): outside the scope of this work.

PART II
EMPLOYMENT

Discrimination by employers

4 Discrimination against applicants and employees

(1) It is unlawful for an employer to discriminate against a disabled person—

(a) in the arrangements which he makes for the purpose of determining to whom he should offer employment;

(b) in the terms on which he offers that person employment; or

(c) by refusing to offer, or deliberately not offering, him employment.

(2) It is unlawful for an employer to discriminate against a disabled person whom he employs—

(a) in the terms of employment which he affords him;

(b) in the opportunities which he affords him for promotion, a transfer, training or receiving any other benefit;

(c) by refusing to afford him, or deliberately not affording him, any such opportunity; or

(d) by dismissing him, or subjecting him to any other detriment.

(3) Subsection (2) does not apply to benefits of any description if the employer is concerned with the provision (whether or not for payment) of benefits of that description to the public, or to a section of the public which includes the employee in question, unless—

(a) that provision differs in a material respect from the provision of the benefits by the employer to his employees; or

(b) the provision of the benefits to the employee in question is regulated by his contract of employment; or

(c) the benefits relate to training.

(4) In this Part "benefits" includes facilities and services.

(5) In the case of an act which constitutes discrimination by virtue of section 55, this section also applies to discrimination against a person who is not disabled.

(6) This section applies only in relation to employment at an establishment in Great Britain.

NOTES

Commencement: 2 December 1996.

5 Meaning of "discrimination"

(1) For the purposes of this Part, an employer discriminates against a disabled person if—

(a) for a reason which relates to the disabled person's disability, he treats him less favourably than he treats or would treat others to whom that reason does not or would not apply; and
(b) he cannot show that the treatment in question is justified.

(2) For the purposes of this Part, an employer also discriminates against a disabled person if—
(a) he fails to comply with a section 6 duty imposed on him in relation to the disabled person; and
(b) he cannot show that his failure to comply with that duty is justified.

(3) Subject to subsection (5), for the purposes of subsection (1) treatment is justified if, but only if, the reason for it is both material to the circumstances of the particular case and substantial.

(4) For the purposes of subsection (2), failure to comply with a section 6 duty is justified if, but only if, the reason for the failure is both material to the circumstances of the particular case and substantial.

(5) If, in a case falling within subsection (1), the employer is under a section 6 duty in relation to the disabled person but fails without justification to comply with that duty, his treatment of that person cannot be justified under subsection (3) unless it would have been justified even if he had complied with the section 6 duty.

(6) Regulations may make provision, for purposes of this section, as to circumstances in which—
(a) treatment is to be taken to be justified;
(b) failure to comply with a section 6 duty is to be taken to be justified;
(c) treatment is to be taken not to be justified;
(d) failure to comply with a section 6 duty is to be taken not to be justified.

(7) Regulations under subsection (6) may, in particular—
(a) make provision by reference to the cost of affording any benefit; and
(b) in relation to benefits under occupational pension schemes, make provision with a view to enabling uniform rates of contributions to be maintained.

NOTES

Commencement: 2 December 1996 (sub-ss (1)–(5), England and Wales, Northern Ireland); 6 June 1996 (sub-ss (6), (7), England and Wales); 11 July 1996 (sub-ss (6), (7), Northern Ireland).

6 Duty of employer to make adjustments

(1) Where—
(a) any arrangements made by or on behalf of an employer, or
(b) any physical feature of premises occupied by the employer,

place the disabled person concerned at a substantial disadvantage in comparison with persons who are not disabled, it is the duty of the employer to take such steps as it is reasonable, in all the circumstances of the case, for him to have to take in order to prevent the arrangements or feature having that effect.

(2) Subsection (1)(a) applies only in relation to—
(a) arrangements for determining to whom employment should be offered;
(b) any term, condition or arrangements on which employment, promotion, a transfer, training or any other benefit is offered or afforded.

(3) The following are examples of steps which an employer may have to take in relation to a disabled person in order to comply with subsection (1)—

- (a) making adjustments to premises;
- (b) allocating some of the disabled person's duties to another person;
- (c) transferring him to fill an existing vacancy;
- (d) altering his working hours;
- (e) assigning him to a different place of work;
- (f) allowing him to be absent during working hours for rehabilitation, assessment or treatment;
- (g) giving him, or arranging for him to be given, training;
- (h) acquiring or modifying equipment;
- (i) modifying instructions or reference manuals;
- (j) modifying procedures for testing or assessment;
- (k) providing a reader or interpreter;
- (l) providing supervision.

(4) In determining whether it is reasonable for an employer to have to take a particular step in order to comply with subsection (1), regard shall be had, in particular, to—

- (a) the extent to which taking the step would prevent the effect in question;
- (b) the extent to which it is practicable for the employer to take the step;
- (c) the financial and other costs which would be incurred by the employer in taking the step and the extent to which taking it would disrupt any of his activities;
- (d) the extent of the employer's financial and other resources;
- (e) the availability to the employer of financial or other assistance with respect to taking the step.

This subsection is subject to any provision of regulations made under subsection (8).

(5) . . .

(6) Nothing in this section imposes any duty on an employer in relation to a disabled person if the employer does not know, and could not reasonably be expected to know—

- (a) in the case of an applicant or potential applicant, that the disabled person concerned is, or may be, an applicant for the employment; or
- (b) in any case, that that person has a disability and is likely to be affected in the way mentioned in subsection (1).

(7) Subject to the provisions of this section, nothing in this Part is to be taken to require an employer to treat a disabled person more favourably than he treats or would treat others.

(8) Regulations may make provision, for the purposes of subsection (1)—

- (a) as to circumstances in which arrangements are, or a physical feature is, to be taken to have the effect mentioned in that subsection;
- (b) as to circumstances in which arrangements are not, or a physical feature is not, to be taken to have that effect;
- (c) as to circumstances in which it is reasonable for an employer to have to take steps of a prescribed description;
- (d) as to steps which it is always reasonable for an employer to have to take;
- (e) as to circumstances in which it is not reasonable for an employer to have to take steps of a prescribed description;
- (f) as to steps which it is never reasonable for an employer to have to take;

(g) as to things which are to be treated as physical features;
(h) as to things which are not to be treated as such features.

(9) Regulations made under subsection (8)(c), (d), (e) or (f) may, in particular, make provision by reference to the cost of taking the steps concerned.

(10) Regulations may make provision adding to the duty imposed on employers by this section, including provision of a kind which may be made under subsection (8).

(11) This section does not apply in relation to any benefit under an occupational pension scheme or any other benefit payable in money or money's worth under a scheme or arrangement for the benefit of employees in respect of—
(a) termination of service;
(b) retirement, old age or death;
(c) accident, injury, sickness or invalidity; or
(d) any other prescribed matter.

(12) This section imposes duties only for the purpose of determining whether an employer has discriminated against a disabled person; and accordingly a breach of any such duty is not actionable as such.

NOTES

Commencement: 2 December 1996 (sub-ss (1)–(4), (6), (7), (11), (12), England and Wales, Northern Ireland); 6 June 1996 (sub-ss (8)–(10), England and Wales); 11 July 1996 (sub-ss (8)–(10), Northern Ireland).

Sub-s (5): outside the scope of this work.

7 Exemption for small businesses

(1) Nothing in this Part applies in relation to an employer who has fewer than 20 employees.

(2) The Secretary of State may by order amend subsection (1) by substituting a different number (not greater than 20) for the number for the time being specified there.

(3)–(10) . . .

NOTES

Commencement: 2 December 1996.

Sub-ss (3)–(10): outside the scope of this work.

Enforcement etc

8 Enforcement, remedies and procedure

(1) A complaint by any person that another person—
(a) has discriminated against him in a way which is unlawful under this Part, or
(b) is, by virtue of section 57 or 58, to be treated as having discriminated against him in such a way,

may be presented to an [employment tribunal].

(2) Where an [employment tribunal] finds that a complaint presented to it under this section is well-founded, it shall take such of the following steps as it considers just and equitable—

(a) making a declaration as to the rights of the complainant and the respondent in relation to the matters to which the complaint relates;
(b) ordering the respondent to pay compensation to the complainant;
(c) recommending that the respondent take, within a specified period, action appearing to the tribunal to be reasonable, in all the circumstances of the case, for the purpose of obviating or reducing the adverse effect on the complainant of any matter to which the complaint relates.

(3)–(8) . . .

NOTES

Commencement: 2 December 1996 (sub-ss (1)–(5)).

Sub-ss (1), (2), (5): words in square brackets substituted by the Employment Rights (Dispute Resolution) Act 1998, s 1(2)(a).

Sub-ss (3)–(8): outside the scope of this work.

9 Validity of certain agreements

(1) Any term in a contract of employment or other agreement is void so far as it purports to—
(a) require a person to do anything which would contravene any provision of, or made under, this Part;
(b) exclude or limit the operation of any provision of this Part; or
(c) prevent any person from presenting a complaint to an [employment tribunal] under this Part.

(2) Paragraphs (b) and (c) of subsection (1) do not apply to an agreement not to institute proceedings under section 8(1), or to an agreement not to continue such proceedings, if—
(a) a conciliation officer has acted under [section 18 of the [Employment Tribunals Act 1996]] in relation to the matter; or
(b) the conditions set out in subsection (3) are satisfied.

(3) The conditions are that—
(a) the complainant must have received [advice from a relevant independent adviser] as to the terms and effect of the proposed agreement (and in particular its effect on his ability to pursue his complaint before an [employment tribunal]);
(b) when the adviser gave the advice there must have been in force a [contract of insurance, or an indemnity provided for members of a professional body] covering the risk of a claim by the complainant in respect of loss arising in consequence of the advice; and
(c) the agreement must be in writing, relate to the particular complaint, identify the adviser and state that the conditions are satisfied.

(4)–(6) . . .

NOTES

Commencement: 2 December 1996.

Sub-s (1): words in square brackets in para (c) substituted by the Employment Rights (Dispute Resolution) Act 1998, s 1(2)(a).

Sub-s (2): in para (a), words in first (outer) pair of square brackets substituted by the Employment Tribunals Act 1996, s 43, Sch 1, para 12(1), (3), as from 22 August 1996; words in second (inner) pair of square brackets substituted by the Employment Rights (Dispute Resolution) Act 1998, s 1(2)(c).

Sub-s (3): words in square brackets in paras (a), (b) substituted by the Employment Rights (Dispute Resolution) Act 1998, ss 1(2)(a), 9(1), (2)(d), 10(1), (2)(d).

Sub-ss (4)–(6): outside the scope of this work.

10 Charities and support for particular groups of persons

(1) Nothing in this Part—

(a) affects any charitable instrument which provides for conferring benefits on one or more categories of person determined by reference to any physical or mental capacity; or

(b) makes unlawful any act done by a charity or recognised body in pursuance of any of its charitable purposes, so far as those purposes are connected with persons so determined.

(2)–(5) . . .

NOTES

Commencement: 2 December 1996.

Sub-ss (2)–(5): outside the scope of this work.

Discrimination by other persons

12 Discrimination against contract workers

(1) It is unlawful for a principal, in relation to contract work, to discriminate against a disabled person—

(a) in the terms on which he allows him to do that work;

(b) by not allowing him to do it or continue to do it;

(c) in the way he affords him access to any benefits or by refusing or deliberately omitting to afford him access to them; or

(d) by subjecting him to any other detriment.

(2) Subsection (1) does not apply to benefits of any description if the principal is concerned with the provision (whether or not for payment) of benefits of that description to the public, or to a section of the public which includes the contract worker in question, unless that provision differs in a material respect from the provision of the benefits by the principal to contract workers.

(3) The provisions of this Part (other than subsections (1) to (3) of section 4) apply to any principal, in relation to contract work, as if he were, or would be, the employer of the contract worker and as if any contract worker supplied to do work for him were an employee of his.

(4) In the case of an act which constitutes discrimination by virtue of section 55, this section also applies to discrimination against a person who is not disabled.

(5) This section applies only in relation to contract work done at an establishment in Great Britain (the provisions of section 68 about the meaning of "employment at an establishment in Great Britain" applying for the purposes of this subsection with the appropriate modifications).

(6) . . .

NOTES

Commencement: 2 December 1996 (sub-ss (1), (2), (4), (5), England and Wales, Northern Ireland); 6 June 1996 (sub-s (3), England and Wales); 11 July 1996 (sub-s (3), Northern Ireland).

Sub-s (6): outside the scope of this work.

13 Discrimination by trade organisations

(1) It is unlawful for a trade organisation to discriminate against a disabled person—

(a) in the terms on which it is prepared to admit him to membership of the organisation; or

(b) by refusing to accept, or deliberately not accepting, his application for membership.

(2) It is unlawful for a trade organisation, in the case of a disabled person who is a member of the organisation, to discriminate against him—

(a) in the way it affords him access to any benefits or by refusing or deliberately omitting to afford him access to them;

(b) by depriving him of membership, or varying the terms on which he is a member; or

(c) by subjecting him to any other detriment.

(3) In the case of an act which constitutes discrimination by virtue of section 55, this section also applies to discrimination against a person who is not disabled.

(4) . . .

NOTES

Commencement: 2 December 1996.

Sub-s (4): outside the scope of this work.

14 Meaning of "discrimination" in relation to trade organisations

(1) For the purposes of this Part, a trade organisation discriminates against a disabled person if—

(a) for a reason which relates to the disabled person's disability, it treats him less favourably than it treats or would treat others to whom that reason does not or would not apply; and

(b) it cannot show that the treatment in question is justified.

(2) For the purposes of this Part, a trade organisation also discriminates against a disabled person if—

(a) it fails to comply with a section 15 duty imposed on it in relation to the disabled person; and

(b) it cannot show that its failure to comply with that duty is justified.

(3) Subject to subsection (5), for the purposes of subsection (1) treatment is justified if, but only if, the reason for it is both material to the circumstances of the particular case and substantial.

(4) For the purposes of subsection (2), failure to comply with a section 15 duty is justified if, but only if, the reason for the failure is both material to the circumstances of the particular case and substantial.

(5) If, in a case falling within subsection (1), the trade organisation is under a section 15 duty in relation to the disabled person concerned but fails without justification to comply with that duty, its treatment of that person cannot be justified under subsection (3) unless the treatment would have been justified even if the organisation had complied with the section 15 duty.

(6) . . .

NOTES

Commencement: 2 December 1996 (sub-ss (1), (3)); to be appointed (sub-ss (2), (4), (5)).

Sub-s (6): outside the scope of this work.

15 Duty of trade organisation to make adjustments

(1) Where—

(a) any arrangements made by or on behalf of a trade organisation, or

(b) any physical feature of premises occupied by the organisation,

place the disabled person concerned at a substantial disadvantage in comparison with persons who are not disabled, it is the duty of the organisation to take such steps as it is reasonable, in all the circumstances of the case, for it to have to take in order to prevent the arrangements or feature having that effect.

(2) Subsection (1)(a) applies only in relation to—

(a) arrangements for determining who should become or remain a member of the organisation;

(b) any term, condition or arrangements on which membership or any benefit is offered or afforded.

(3)–(10) . . .

NOTES

Commencement: to be appointed.

Sub-ss (3)–(10): outside the scope of this work.

PART VIII
MISCELLANEOUS

70 Short title, commencement, extent etc

(1) This Act may be cited as the Disability Discrimination Act 1995.

(2) This section (apart from subsections (4), (5) and (7)) comes into force on the passing of this Act.

(3) The other provisions of this Act come into force on such day as the Secretary of State may by order appoint and different days may be appointed for different purposes.

(4), (5) . . .

(6) This Act extends to Northern Ireland, but in their application to Northern Ireland the provisions of this Act mentioned in Schedule 8 shall have effect subject to the modifications set out in that Schedule.

(7) . . .

(8) Consultations which are required by any provision of this Act to be held by the Secretary of State may be held by him before the coming into force of that provision.

NOTES

Commencement: 8 November 1995 (sub-ss (1)).

Sub-ss (4), (5), (7): outside the scope of this work.

PREVENTION OF TERRORISM (ADDITIONAL POWERS) ACT 1996

(C 7)

(NOTE)

NOTES

Section 1(1) of this Act inserts the Prevention of Terrorism Act 1989, s 13B; s 1(2)–(7) of this Act amend s 13A of the 1989 Act; and s 2 of this Act makes a number of amendments to Sch 7 of the 1989 Act. All of these amendments are reproduced in this work.

POLICE ACT 1996

(C 16)

An Act to consolidate the Police Act 1964, Part IX of the Police and Criminal Evidence Act 1984, Chapter I of Part I of the Police and Magistrates' Courts Act 1994 and certain other enactments relating to the police

[22 May 1996]

PART I
ORGANISATION OF POLICE FORCES

Police areas

1 Police areas

(1) England and Wales shall be divided into police areas.

(2) The police areas referred to in subsection (1) shall be—

(a) those listed in Schedule 1 (subject to any amendment made to that Schedule by an order under section 32 below, section 58 of the Local Government Act 1972, or section 17 of the Local Government Act 1992),

(b) the metropolitan police district, and

(c) the City of London police area.

(3) References in Schedule 1 to any local government area are to that area as it is for the time being, but excluding any part of it within the metropolitan police district.

NOTES

Commencement: 22 August 1996.

Forces outside London

2 Maintenance of police forces

A police force shall be maintained for every police area for the time being listed in Schedule 1.

NOTES

Commencement: 22 August 1996.

3 Establishment of police authorities

(1) There shall be a police authority for every police area for the time being listed in Schedule 1.

(2) A police authority established under this section for any area shall be a body corporate to be known by the name of the area with the addition of the words "Police Authority".

NOTES

Commencement: 22 August 1996.

4 Membership of police authorities etc

(1) Subject to subsection (2), each police authority established under section 3 shall consist of seventeen members.

(2) The Secretary of State may by order provide in relation to a police authority specified in the order that the number of its members shall be a specified odd number greater than seventeen.

(3) A statutory instrument containing an order under subsection (2) shall be laid before Parliament after being made.

(4) Schedules 2 and 3 shall have effect in relation to police authorities established under section 3 and the appointment of their members.

NOTES

Commencement: 22 August 1996.

5 Reductions in size of police authorities

(1) This section applies to any order under section 4(2) which varies or revokes an earlier order so as to reduce the number of a police authority's members.

(2) Before making an order to which this section applies, the Secretary of State shall consult—

(a) the authority,

(b) the councils which are relevant councils in relation to the authority for the purposes of Schedule 2, and

(c) any selection panel, constituted under regulations made in accordance with [section 29(2) of the Justices of the Peace Act 1997], which is responsible, or is represented on a joint committee which is responsible, for the appointment of members of the authority.

(3) An order to which this section applies may include provision as to the termination of the appointment of the existing members of the authority and the making of new appointments or re-appointments.

NOTES

Commencement: 22 August 1996.

Sub-s (2): words in square brackets in para (c) substituted by the Justices of the Peace Act 1997, s 73(2), Sch 5, para 37(1), (2).

6 General functions of police authorities

(1) Every police authority established under section 3 shall secure the maintenance of an efficient and effective police force for its area.

(2) In discharging its functions, every police authority established under section 3 shall have regard to—

(a) any objectives determined by the Secretary of State under section 37,

(b) any objectives determined by the authority under section 7,

(c) any performance targets established by the authority, whether in compliance with a direction under section 38 or otherwise, and

(d) any local policing plan issued by the authority under section 8.

(3) In discharging any function to which a code of practice issued under section 39 relates, a police authority established under section 3 shall have regard to the code.

(4) A police authority shall comply with any direction given to it by the Secretary of State under section 38 or 40.

NOTES

Commencement: 22 August 1996.

7 Local policing objectives

(1) Every police authority established under Section 3 shall, before the beginning of each financial year, determine objectives for the policing of the authority's area during that year.

(2) Objectives determined under this section may relate to matters to which objectives determined under section 37 also relate, or to other matters, but in any event shall be so framed as to be consistent with the objectives determined under that section.

(3) Before determining objectives under this section, a police authority shall—

(a) consult the chief constable for the area, and

(b) consider any views obtained by the authority in accordance with arrangements made under section 96.

NOTES

Commencement: 22 August 1996.

8 Local policing plans

(1) Every police authority established under section 3 shall, before the beginning of each financial year, issue a plan setting but the proposed arrangements for the policing of the authority's area during the year ("the local policing plan").

(2) The local policing plan shall include a statement of the authority's priorities for the year, of the financial resources expected to be available and of the proposed allocation of those resources, and shall give particulars of—

(a) any objectives determined by the Secretary of State under section 37,

(b) any objectives determined by the authority under section 7, and

(c) any performance targets established by the authority, whether in compliance with a direction under section 38 or otherwise.

(3) A draft of the local policing plan shall be prepared by the chief constable for the area and submitted by him to the police authority for it to consider.

(4) Before issuing a local policing plan which differs from the draft submitted by the chief constable under subsection (3), a police authority shall consult the chief constable.

(5) A police authority shall arrange for every local policing plan issued by it under this section to be published in such manner as appears to it to be appropriate, and shall send a copy of the plan to the Secretary of State.

NOTES

Commencement: 22 August 1996.

9 Annual reports by police authorities

(1) As soon as possible after the end of each financial year every police authority established under section 3 shall issue a report relating to the policing of the authority's area for the year.

(2) A report issued by a police authority under this section for any year shall include an assessment of the extent to which the local policing plan for that year issued under section 8 has been carried out.

(3) A police authority shall arrange for every report issued by it under this Section to be published in such manner as appears to it to be appropriate, and shall send a copy of the report to the Secretary of State.

NOTES

Commencement: 22 August 1996.

10 General functions of chief constables

(1) A police force maintained under section 2 shall be under the direction and control of the chief constable appointed under section 11.

(2) In discharging his functions, every chief constable shall have regard to the local policing plan issued by the police authority for his area under section 8.

NOTES

Commencement: 22 August 1996.

Modification: by the Police Act 1997, s 23, this section does not apply to constables or other assistance provided by the Director General of the National Criminal Intelligence Service under the Police Act 1997, Pt I.

11 Appointment and removal of chief constables

(1) The chief constable of a police force maintained under section 2 shall be appointed by the police authority responsible for maintaining the force, but subject to the approval of the Secretary of State and to regulations under section 50.

(2) Without prejudice to any regulations under section 50 or under the Police Pensions Act 1976, the police authority, acting with the approval of the Secretary of State, may call upon the chief constable to retire in the interests of efficiency or effectiveness.

(3) Before seeking the approval of the Secretary of State under subsection (2), the police authority shall give the chief constable an opportunity to make representations and shall consider any representations that he makes.

(4) A chief constable who is called upon to retire under subsection (2) shall retire on such date as the police authority may specify or on such earlier date as may be agreed upon between him and the authority.

NOTES
Commencement: 22 August 1996.

13 Other members of police forces

(1), (2) . . .

(3) Appointments and promotions to any rank below that of assistant chief constable in any police force maintained under section 2 shall be made, in accordance with regulations under section 50, by the chief constable.

NOTES
Commencement: 22 August 1996.
Sub-ss (1), (2): outside the scope of this work.

14 Police fund

(1) Each police authority established under section 3 shall keep a fund to be known as the police fund.

(2) Subject to any regulations under the Police Pensions Act 1976, all receipts of the police authority shall be paid into the police fund and all expenditure of the authority shall be paid out of that fund.

(3) Accounts shall be kept by each police authority of payments made into or out of the police fund.

NOTES
Commencement: 22 August 1996.

20 Questions on police matters at council meetings

(1) Every relevant council shall make arrangements (whether by standing orders or otherwise) for enabling questions on the discharge of the functions of a police authority to be put by members of the council at a meeting of the council for answer by a person nominated by the authority for that purpose.

(2) On being given reasonable notice by a relevant council of a meeting of that council at which questions on the discharge of the police authority's functions are to be put, the police authority shall nominate one or more of its members to attend the meeting to answer those questions.

(3) In this section "relevant council" has the same meaning as in Schedule 2.

NOTES
Commencement: 22 August 1996.

General provisions

22 Reports by chief constables to police authorities

(1) Every chief constable shall, as soon as possible after the end of each financial year, submit to the police authority a general report on the policing during that year of the area for which his force is maintained.

(2) A chief constable shall arrange for a report submitted by him under subsection (1) to be published in such manner as appears to him to be appropriate.

(3) The chief constable of a police force shall, whenever so required by the police authority, submit to that authority a report on such matters as may be specified in the requirement, being matters connected with the policing of the area for which the force is maintained.

(4) A report submitted under subsection (3) shall be in such form as the police authority may specify.

(5) If it appears to the chief constable that a report in compliance with subsection (3) would contain information which in the public interest ought not to be disclosed, or is not needed for the discharge of the functions of the police authority, he may request that authority to refer the requirement to submit the report to the Secretary of State; and in any such case the requirement shall be of no effect unless it is confirmed by the Secretary of State.

(6) The police authority may arrange, or require the chief constable to arrange, for a report submitted under subsection (3) to be published in such manner as appears to the authority to be appropriate.

(7) This section shall apply in relation to the City of London police force as if for references to a chief constable there were substituted references to the Commissioner.

NOTES

Commencement: 22 August 1996.

23 Collaboration agreements

(1) If it appears to the chief officers of police of two or more police forces that any police functions can more efficiently or effectively be discharged by members of those forces acting jointly, they may, with the approval of the police authorities which maintain those forces, make an agreement for that purpose.

(2) If it appears to any two or more police authorities that any premises, equipment or other material or facilities can with advantage be provided jointly for the police forces maintained by those authorities, they may make an agreement for that purpose.

(3) Any expenditure incurred under an agreement made under this section shall be borne by the police authorities in such proportions as they may agree or as may, in the absence of agreement, be determined by the Secretary of State.

(4)–(8) . . .

NOTES

Commencement: 22 August 1996.
Sub-ss (4)–(8): outside the scope of this work.

24 Aid of one police force by another

(1) The chief officer of police of any police force may, on the application of the chief officer of police of any other police force, provide constables or other assistance for the purpose of enabling the other force to meet any special demand on its resources.

(2) If it appears to the Secretary of State to be expedient in the interests of public safety or order that any police force should be reinforced or should receive other assistance for the purpose of enabling it to meet any special demand on its resources, and that satisfactory arrangements under subsection (1) cannot be made, or cannot be

made in time, he may direct the chief officer of police of any police force to provide such constables or other assistance for that purpose as may be specified in the direction.

(3) While a constable is provided under this section for the assistance of another police force he shall, notwithstanding section 10(1), be under the direction and control of the chief officer of police of that other force.

(4) . . .

[(5) This section shall apply in relation to the Service Authority for the National Crime Squad, the National Crime Squad and the Director General of that Squad as it applies to a police authority, a police force and a chief officer of police respectively, and accordingly the reference in subsection (3) to section 10(1) shall be construed, in a case where constables are provided by the Director General of the National Crime Squad, as including a reference to section 56(1) of the Police Act 1997.]

NOTES

Commencement: 22 August 1996.
Sub-s (4): outside the scope of this work.
Sub-s (5): added by the Police Act 1997, s 134(1), Sch 9, paras 72, 74.

25 Provision of special services

(1) The chief officer of police of a police force may provide, at the request of any person, special police services at any premises or in any locality in the police area for which the force is maintained, subject to the payment to the police authority of charges on such scales as may be determined by that authority.

(2) In the application of this section to the metropolitan police force, for the reference in subsection (1) to the police authority there shall be substituted a reference to the Receiver for the Metropolitan Police District.

NOTES

Commencement: 22 August 1996.

29 Attestation of constables

Every member of a police force maintained for a police area and every special constable appointed for a police area shall, on appointment, be attested as a constable by making a declaration in the form set out in Schedule 4—

(a) in the case of a member of the metropolitan police force or a Special constable appointed for the metropolitan police district, before the Commissioner or an Assistant Commissioner of Police of the Metropolis, and

(b) in any other case, before a justice of the peace having jurisdiction within the police area.

NOTES

Commencement: 22 August 1996.

30 Jurisdiction of constables

(1) A member of a police force shall have all the powers and privileges of a constable throughout England and Wales and the adjacent United Kingdom waters.

(2) A special constable shall have all the powers and privileges of a constable in the police area for which he is appointed and, where the boundary of that area includes the coast, in the adjacent United Kingdom waters.

(3)–(6) . . .

NOTES

Commencement: 22 August 1996.
Sub-ss (3)–(6): outside the scope of this work.

Alteration of police areas

32 Power to alter police areas by order

(1) The Secretary of State may by order make alterations in police areas in England and Wales other than the City of London police area.

(2) The alterations that may be made by an order under this section include alterations that result in a reduction or an increase in the number of police areas, but not alterations that result in the abolition of the metropolitan police district.

(3) The Secretary of State shall not exercise his power under this section to make alterations unless either—

(a) he has received a request to make the alterations from the police authority for each of the areas (other than the metropolitan police district) affected by them, or

(b) it appears to him to be expedient to make the alterations in the interests of efficiency or effectiveness.

(4), (5) . . .

NOTES

Commencement: 22 August 1996.
Sub-ss (4), (5): outside the scope of this work.

PART II
CENTRAL SUPERVISION, DIRECTION AND FACILITIES

Functions of Secretary of State

36 General duty of Secretary of State

(1) The Secretary of State shall exercise his powers under the provisions of this Act referred to in subsection (2) in such manner and to such extent as appears to him to be best calculated to promote the efficiency and effectiveness of the police.

(2) The provisions of this Act mentioned in subsection (1) are—

(a) Part I;
(b) this Part;
(c) Part III (other than sections 61 and 62);
(d) in Chapter II of Part IV, section 85 and Schedule 6; and
(e) in Part V, Section 95.

NOTES

Commencement: 22 August 1996.

37 Setting of objectives for police authorities

(1) The Secretary of State may by order determine objectives for the policing of the areas of all police authorities established under section 3.

(2) Before making an order under this section the Secretary of State shall consult—

(a) persons whom he considers to represent the interests of police authorities established under section 3, and

(b) persons whom he considers to represent the interests of chief constables of forces maintained by those authorities.

(3) A statutory instrument containing an order under this section shall be laid before Parliament after being made.

NOTES

Commencement: 22 August 1996.

38 Setting of performance targets

(1) Where an objective has been determined under section 37, the Secretary of State may direct police authorities to establish levels of performance ("performance targets") to be aimed at in seeking to achieve the objective.

(2) A direction under this section may be given to all police authorities established under section 3 or to one or more particular authorities.

(3) A direction given under this section may impose conditions with which the performance targets must conform, and different conditions may be imposed for different authorities.

(4) The Secretary of State shall arrange for any direction given under this section to be published in such manner as appears to him to be appropriate.

NOTES

Commencement: 22 August 1996.

39 Codes of practice

(1) The Secretary of State may issue codes of practice relating to the discharge by police authorities established under section 3 of any of their functions.

(2) The Secretary of State may from time to time revise the whole or part of any code of practice issued under this section.

(3) The Secretary of State shall lay before Parliament a copy of any code of practice, and of any revision of a code of practice, issued by him under this section.

NOTES

Commencement: 22 August 1996.

40 Power to give directions to police authorities after adverse reports

(1) The Secretary of State may at any time require the inspectors of constabulary to carry out, for the purposes of this section, an inspection under Section 54 of any police force maintained under section 2.

(2) Where a report made to the Secretary of State under section 54 on an inspection carried out for the purposes of this section states—

(a) that, in the opinion of the person making the report, the force inspected is not efficient or not effective, or

(b) that in his opinion, unless remedial measures are taken, the force will cease to be efficient or will cease to be effective,

the Secretary of State may direct the police authority responsible for maintaining the force to take such measures as may be specified in the direction.

NOTES

Commencement: 22 August 1996.

42 Removal of chief constables, etc

(1) The Secretary of State may require a police authority to exercise its power under section 11 to call upon the chief constable to retire in the interests of efficiency or effectiveness.

(2) Before requiring the exercise of that power or approving the exercise of that or the similar power exercisable with respect to an assistant chief constable, the Secretary of State shall give the chief constable or assistant chief constable an opportunity to make representations to him and shall consider any representations so made.

(3) Where representations are made under this section the Secretary of State may, and in a case where he proposes to require the exercise of the power mentioned in subsection (1) shall, appoint one or more persons (one at least of whom shall be a person who is not an officer of police or of a Government department) to hold an inquiry and report to him and shall consider any report made under this subsection.

(4) The costs incurred by a chief constable or assistant chief constable in respect of an inquiry under this section, taxed in such manner as the Secretary of State may direct, shall be defrayed out of the police fund.

NOTES

Commencement: 22 August 1996.

43 Reports from police authorities

(1) A police authority shall, whenever so required by the Secretary of State, submit to the Secretary of State a report on such matters connected with the discharge of the authority's functions, or otherwise with the policing of its area, as may be specified in the requirement.

(2) A requirement under subsection (1) may specify the form in which a report is to be given.

(3) The Secretary of State may arrange, or require the police authority to arrange, for a report under this section to be published in such manner as appears to him to be appropriate.

NOTES

Commencement: 22 August 1996.

44 Reports from chief constables

(1) The Secretary of State may require a chief constable to submit to him a report on such matters as may be specified in the requirement, being matters connected with the policing of the chief constable's police area.

(2) A requirement under subsection (1) may specify the form in which a report is to be given.

(3) The Secretary of State may arrange, or require the chief constable to arrange, for a report under this section to be published in such manner as appears to the Secretary of State to be appropriate.

(4) Every chief constable shall, as soon as possible after the end of each financial year, submit to the Secretary of State the like report as is required by section 22(1) to be submitted to the police authority.

(5) This section shall apply in relation to the City of London police force as if for references to a chief constable there were substituted references to the Commissioner.

NOTES

Commencement: 22 August 1996.

46 Police grant

(1) Subject to the following provisions of this section, the Secretary of State shall for each financial year make grants for police purposes to—

(a) police authorities for areas other than the metropolitan police district, and

(b) the Receiver for the Metropolitan Police District;

and in those provisions references to police authorities shall be taken as including references to the Receiver.

(2) For each financial year the Secretary of State shall with the approval of the Treasury determine—

(a) the aggregate amount of grants to be made under this section, and

(b) the amount of the grant to be made to each authority;

and any determination may be varied by further determinations under this subsection.

(3) The Secretary of State shall prepare a report setting out any determination under subsection (2), and stating the considerations which he took into account in making the determination.

(4) In determining the allocation among police authorities of the whole or any part of the aggregate amount of grants, the Secretary of State may exercise his discretion by applying such formulae or other rules as he considers appropriate.

(5) The considerations which the Secretary of State takes into account making a determination under subsection (2), and the formulae and other rules referred to in subsection (4), may be different for different authorities or different classes of authority.

(6) A copy of every report prepared under subsection (3) shall be laid before the House of Commons, and no payment of grant shall be made unless the report setting out the determination of its amount has been approved by resolution of that House.

(7), (8) . . .

NOTES

Commencement: 22 August 1996.

Sub-ss (7), (8): outside the scope of this work.

50 Regulations for police forces

(1) Subject to the provisions of this section, the Secretary of State may make regulations as to the government, administration and conditions of service of police forces.

(2) Without prejudice to the generality of subsection (1), regulations under this section may make provision with respect to—

- (a) the ranks to be held by members of police forces;
- (b) the qualifications for appointment and promotion of members of police forces;
- (c) periods of service on probation;
- (d) voluntary retirement of members of police forces;
- (e) the conduct, efficiency and effectiveness of members of police forces and the maintenance of discipline;
- (f) the suspension of members of a police force from membership of that force and from their office as constable;
- (g) the maintenance of personal records of members of police forces;
- (h) the duties which are or are not to be performed by members of police forces;
- (i) the treatment as occasions of police duty of attendance at meetings of the Police Federations and of any body recognised by the Secretary of State for the purposes of section 64;
- (i) the hours of duty, leave, pay and allowances of members of police forces; and
- (k) the issue, use and return of police clothing, personal equipment and accoutrements

(3)–(8) . . .

NOTES

Commencement: 22 August 1996 (sub-s (1)).
Sub-ss (3)–(8): outside the scope of this work.

Inspectors of constabulary

54 Appointment and functions of inspectors of constabulary

(1) Her Majesty may appoint such number of inspectors (to be known as "Her Majesty's Inspectors of Constabulary") as the Secretary of State may with the consent of the Treasury determine, and of the persons so appointed one may be appointed as chief inspector of constabulary.

(2) The inspectors of constabulary shall inspect, and report to the Secretary of State on the efficiency and effectiveness of, every police force maintained for a police area [and the National Criminal Intelligence Service and the National Crime Squad].

(3) The inspectors of constabulary shall carry out such other duties for the purpose of furthering police efficiency and effectiveness as the Secretary of State may from time to time direct.

(4) The chief inspector of constabulary shall in each year submit to the Secretary of State a report in such form as the Secretary of State may direct, and the Secretary of State shall lay a copy of that report before Parliament.

(5) The inspectors of constabulary shall be paid such salary and allowances as the Secretary of State may with the consent of the Treasury determine.

NOTES

Commencement: 22 August 1996.

Sub-s (2): words in square brackets added by the Police Act 1997, s 134(1), Sch 9, paras 72, 76.

Modification: by the Police Act 1997, ss 30(1)(a), 75(1), inspectors appointed under this section may be required by the Secretary of State to carry out an inspection of the National Criminal Intelligence Service or the National Crime Squad established under the Police Act 1997, Pts I, II.

55 Publication of reports

(1) Subject to subsection (2), the Secretary of State shall arrange for any report received by him under section 54(2) to be published in such manner as appears to him to be appropriate.

(2) The Secretary of State may exclude from publication under subsection (1) any part of a report if, in his opinion, the publication of that part—

- (a) would be against the interests of national security, or
- (b) might jeopardise the safety of any person.

(3) The Secretary of State shall send a copy of the published report—

- (a) (except where he is himself the police authority) to the police authority maintaining the police force to which the report relates, and
- (b) to the chief officer of police of that police force.

(4) The police authority shall invite the chief officer of police to submit comments on the published report to the authority before such date as it may specify.

(5) The police authority shall prepare comments on the published report and shall arrange for—

- (a) its comments,
- (b) any comments submitted by the chief officer of police in accordance with subsection (4), and
- (c) any response which the authority has to the comments submitted by the chief officer of police,

to be published in such manner as appears to the authority to be appropriate.

(6) The police authority (except where it is the Secretary of State) shall send a copy of any document published under subsection (5) to the Secretary of State.

[(7) Subsections (3) to (6) above shall apply in relation to a report relating to the National Criminal Intelligence Service or the National Crime Squad as if—

- (a) the body to which the report relates were a police force,
- (b) the Service Authority which maintains that body were the police authority which maintains that force, and
- (c) the Director General of that body were the chief officer of police of that force.]

NOTES

Commencement: 22 August 1996.

Sub-s (7): added by the Police Act 1997, s 134(1), Sch 9, paras 72, 77.

PART III
POLICE REPRESENTATIVE INSTITUTIONS

59 Police Federations

(1) There shall continue to be a Police Federation for England and Wales and a Police Federation for Scotland for the purpose of representing members of the police forces in those countries respectively in all matters affecting their welfare and efficiency, except for—

(a) questions of promotion affecting individuals, and
(b) (subject to subsection (2)) questions of discipline affecting individuals.

(2) A Police Federation may represent a member of a police force at any proceedings brought under regulations made in accordance with section 50(3) above or section 26(2A) of the Police (Scotland) Act 1967 or on an appeal from any such proceedings.

(3) Except on an appeal to a police appeals tribunal or as provided by section 84, a member of a police force may only be represented under subsection (2) by another member of a police force.

(4) . . .

(5) The Police Federations and every branch of a Federation shall be entirely independent of, and subject to subsection (6) unassociated with, any body or person outside the police service, but may employ persons outside the police service in an administrative or advisory capacity.

(6)–(8) . . .

NOTES
Commencement: 22 August 1996.
Sub-ss (4), (6)–(8): outside the scope of this work.

60 Regulations for Police Federations

(1) The Secretary of State may by regulations—

(a) prescribe the constitution and proceedings of the Police Federations, or
(b) authorise the Federations to make rules concerning such matters relating to their constitution and proceedings as may be specified in the regulations.

(2)–(6) . . .

NOTES
Commencement: 22 August 1996.
Sub-ss (2)–(6): outside the scope of this work.

64 Membership of trade unions

(1) Subject to the following provisions of this section, a member of a police force shall not be a member of any trade union, or of any association having for its objects, or one of its objects, to control or influence the pay, pensions or conditions of service of any police force.

(2) Where a person was a member of a trade union before becoming a member of a police force, he may, with the consent of the chief officer of police, continue to be a member of that union during the time of his service in the police force.

(3)–(5) . . .

NOTES

Commencement: 22 August 1996.

Sub-ss (3)–(5): outside the scope of this work.

PART IV
COMPLAINTS, DISCIPLINARY PROCEEDINGS ETC

CHAPTER I
COMPLAINTS

Interpretation

65 Interpretation of Chapter I

In this Chapter—

"the appropriate authority" means—

(a) in relation to a member of the metropolitan police force, the Commissioner of Police of the Metropolis, and

(b) in relation to a member of any other police force—

(i) if he is a senior officer, the police authority for the force's area, and

(ii) if he is not a senior officer, the chief officer of police of the force;

"the Authority" means the Police Complaints Authority;

"complaint" means a complaint about the conduct of a member of a police force which is submitted—

(a) by a member of the public, or

(b) on behalf of a member of the public and with his written consent;

"disciplinary proceedings" means proceedings identified as such by regulations under section 50;

"investigating officer" means a member of a police force appointed under section 68(3) or, as the case may be, section 69(5) or (6) to investigate a complaint;

"senior officer" means a member of a police force holding a rank above that of superintendent;

"serious injury" means a fracture, damage to an internal organ, impairment of bodily function, a deep cut or a deep laceration.

NOTES

Commencement: to be appointed.

The Police Complaints Authority

66 The Police Complaints Authority

(1) The authority known as "the Police Complaints Authority" shall continue in existence as a body corporate.

(2) Schedule 5 shall have effect in relation to the Authority.

NOTES

Commencement: to be appointed.

Handling of Complaints etc

67 Preliminary

(1) Where a complaint is submitted to the chief officer of police for a police area, he shall take any steps that appear to him to be desirable for the purpose of obtaining or preserving evidence relating to the conduct complained of.

(2) After complying with subsection (1), the chief officer shall determine whether he is the appropriate authority in relation to the member of a police force whose conduct is the subject of the complaint.

(3) If the chief officer determines that he is not the appropriate authority, he shall—

(a) send the complaint or, if it was submitted orally, particulars of it, to the appropriate authority, and
(b) give notice that he has done so to the person by whom or on whose behalf the complaint was submitted.

(4) Nothing in this Chapter shall have effect in relation to a complaint in so far as it relates to the direction or control of a police force by the chief officer of police or the person performing the functions of the chief officer of police.

(5) If any conduct to which a complaint wholly or partly relates is or has been the subject of criminal or disciplinary proceedings, none of the provisions of this Chapter which relate to the recording and investigation of complaints shall have effect in relation to the complaint in so far as it relates to that conduct.

NOTES

Commencement: to be appointed.

68 Investigation of complaints: senior officers

(1) Where a complaint about the conduct of a senior officer—

(a) is submitted to the appropriate authority, or
(b) is sent to the appropriate authority under section 67(3),

the appropriate authority shall record and, subject to subsection (2), investigate it.

(2) If satisfied that the conduct complained of, even if proved, would not justify criminal or disciplinary proceedings, the appropriate authority may deal with the complaint according to the appropriate authority's discretion.

(3) In any other case, the appropriate authority shall appoint a member of the appropriate authority's force or of some other force to investigate the complaint.

(4) If the appropriate authority requests the chief officer of police of a police force to provide a member of his force for appointment under subsection (3), the chief officer shall comply with the request.

(5) No member of a police force of a rank lower than that of the member whose conduct is the subject of the complaint may be appointed under subsection (3).

(6) Unless an investigation under this section is supervised by the Authority under section 72, the investigating officer shall submit his report on it to the appropriate authority.

NOTES

Commencement: to be appointed.

69 Investigation of complaints: standard procedure

(1) If a chief officer of police determines that he is the appropriate authority in relation to a member of a police force—

(a) whose conduct is the subject of a complaint, and

(b) who is not a senior officer, he shall record the complaint.

(2) After recording a complaint under subsection (1), the chief officer of police shall consider whether the complaint is suitable for informal resolution and may appoint a member of his force to assist him.

(3) A complaint is not suitable for informal resolution unless—

(a) the member of the public concerned gives his consent, and

(b) the chief officer of police is satisfied that the conduct complained of, even if proved, would not justify criminal or disciplinary proceedings.

(4) If it appears to the chief officer of police that the complaint is suitable for informal resolution, he shall seek to resolve it informally and may appoint a member of his force to do so on his behalf.

(5) If it appears to the chief officer of police that the complaint is not suitable for informal resolution, he shall appoint a member of his own or some other force to investigate it formally.

(6) If, after attempts have been made to resolve a complaint informally, it appears to the chief officer of police—

(a) that informal resolution of the complaint is impossible, or

(b) that the complaint is for any other reason not suitable for informal resolution,

he shall appoint a member of his own or some other force to investigate it formally.

(7) A member of a police force may not be appointed to investigate a complaint formally if he has previously been appointed to act in relation to it under subsection (4).

(8) If a chief officer of police requests the chief officer of police of some other force to provide a member of that other force for appointment under subsection (5) or (6), that chief officer shall comply with the request.

(9) Unless the investigation is supervised by the Authority under section 72, the investigating officer shall submit his report on it to the chief officer of police who appointed him.

NOTES

Commencement: to be appointed.

70 References of complaints to Authority

(1) The appropriate authority—

(a) shall refer to the Authority—

(i) any complaint alleging that the conduct complained of resulted in the death of, or serious injury to, some other person, and

(ii) any complaint of a description specified for the purposes of this section in regulations made by the Secretary of State, and

(b) may refer to the Authority any complaint which is not required to be referred to them.

(2) The Authority may require the submission to them for consideration of any complaint not referred to them by the appropriate authority; and the appropriate authority shall comply with any such requirement not later than the end of the period specified for the purposes of this subsection in regulations made by the Secretary of State.

(3) Where a complaint falls to be referred to the Authority under subsection (1)(a), the appropriate authority shall refer it to them not later than the end of the period specified for the purposes of sub-paragraph (i) or, as the case may be, (ii) of that subsection in regulations made by the Secretary of State.

NOTES

Commencement: to be appointed.

71 References of other matters to Authority

(1) The appropriate authority may refer to the Authority any matter to which this section applies, if it appears to the appropriate authority that the matter ought to be referred by reason—

(a) of its gravity, or

(b) of exceptional circumstances.

(2) This section applies to any matter which—

(a) appears to the appropriate authority to indicate that a member of a police force may have committed a criminal offence or behaved in a manner which would justify disciplinary proceedings, and

(b) is not the subject of a complaint.

NOTES

Commencement: to be appointed.

72 Supervision of investigations by Authority

(1) The Authority shall supervise the investigation of—

(a) any complaint alleging that the conduct of a member of a police force resulted in the death of, or serious injury to, some other person,

(b) any other description of complaint specified for the purposes of this section in regulations made by the Secretary of State, and

(c) any complaint which is not within paragraph (a) or (b), and any matter referred to the Authority under section 71, if the Authority determine that it is desirable in the public interest that they should do so.

(2) Where the Authority have made a determination under subsection (1)(c), they shall notify it to the appropriate authority.

(3) Where an investigation is to be supervised by the Authority, they may require—

(a) that no appointment is made under section 68(3) or 69(5) unless they have given notice to the appropriate authority that they approve the person whom that authority propose to appoint, or

(b) if such an appointment has already been made and the Authority are not satisfied with the person appointed, that—

(i) the appropriate authority, as soon as is reasonably practicable, select another member of a police force and notify the Authority that it proposes to appoint him, and

(ii) the appointment is not made unless the Authority give notice to the appropriate authority that they approve that person.

(4) The Secretary of State shall by regulations authorise the Authority, subject to any restrictions or conditions specified in the regulations, to impose requirements as to a particular investigation additional to any requirements imposed by virtue of subsection (3).

(5) A member of a police force shall comply with any requirement imposed on him by virtue of regulations under subsection (4).

NOTES

Commencement: to be appointed.

73 Reports on investigations etc

(1) At the end of an investigation which the Authority have supervised, the investigating officer shall—

(a) submit a report on the investigation to the Authority, and

(b) send a copy of the report to the appropriate authority.

(2) After considering a report submitted to them under subsection (1), the Authority shall submit an appropriate statement to the appropriate authority.

(3) If it is practicable to do so, the Authority, when submitting the appropriate statement under subsection (2), shall send a copy of it to the member of a police force whose conduct has been investigated.

(4) If—

(a) the investigation related to a complaint, and

(b) it is practicable to do so,

the Authority shall also send a copy of the appropriate statement to the person by or on behalf of whom the complaint was submitted.

(5) The power to issue an appropriate statement includes power to issue separate statements in respect of the disciplinary and criminal aspects of an investigation.

(6) No disciplinary proceedings shall be brought before the appropriate statement is submitted to the appropriate authority.

(7) Subject to subsection (8), neither the appropriate authority nor the Director of Public Prosecutions shall bring criminal proceedings before the appropriate statement is submitted to the appropriate authority.

(8) The restriction imposed by subsection (7) does not apply if it appears to the Director that there are exceptional circumstances which make it undesirable to wait for the submission of the appropriate statement.

(9) In this section "appropriate statement" means a statement—

(a) as to whether the investigation was or was not conducted to the Authority's satisfaction,

(b) specifying any respect in which it was not so conducted, and

(c) dealing with any such other matters as the Secretary of State may by regulations provide.

NOTES

Commencement: to be appointed.

74 Steps to be taken after investigation: senior officers

On receiving—

(a) a report concerning the conduct of a senior officer which is submitted to it under section 68(6), or

(b) a copy of a report concerning the conduct of a senior officer which is sent to it under section 73(1),

the appropriate authority shall send a copy of the report to the Director of Public Prosecutions unless the report satisfies the appropriate authority that no criminal offence has been committed.

NOTES

Commencement: to be appointed.

75 Steps to be taken after investigation: standard procedure

(1) Nothing in this section or section 76 has effect in relation to senior officers.

(2) On receiving—

(a) a report concerning the conduct of a member of a police force who is not a senior officer which is submitted to him under section 69(9), or

(b) a copy of a report concerning the conduct of such a member which is sent to him under section 73(1),

a chief officer of police shall determine whether the report indicates that a criminal offence may have been committed by a member of the police force for his area.

(3) If the chief officer determines that the report indicates that a criminal offence may have been committed by a member of the police force for his area, he shall send a copy of the report to the Director of Public Prosecutions.

(4) After the Director has dealt with the question of criminal proceedings, the chief officer shall, in such cases as may be prescribed by regulations made by the Secretary of State, send the Authority a memorandum which—

(a) is signed by the chief officer,

(b) states whether he has brought (or proposes to bring) disciplinary proceedings in respect of the conduct which was the subject of the investigation, and

(c) if he has not brought (or does not propose to bring) such proceedings, gives his reasons.

(5) If the chief officer considers that the report does not indicate that a criminal offence may have been committed by a member of the police force for his area, he shall, in such cases as may be prescribed by regulations made by the Secretary of State, send the Authority a memorandum to that effect which—

(a) is signed by the chief officer,

(b) states whether he has brought (or proposes to bring) disciplinary proceedings in respect of the conduct which was the subject of the investigation, and

(c) if he has not brought (or does not propose to bring) such proceedings, gives his reasons.

(6) Where the investigation—

(a) related to conduct which was the subject of a complaint, and

(b) was not supervised by the Authority,

the chief officer shall, if he is required by virtue of regulations under subsection (4) or (5) to send the Authority a memorandum, at the same time send them a copy of the complaint, or of the record of the complaint, and a copy of the report of the investigation.

(7) Where a chief officer has sent the Authority a memorandum under subsection (4) or (5), he shall—

(a) if the memorandum states that he proposes to bring disciplinary proceedings, bring and proceed with them, and

(b) if the memorandum states that he has brought such proceedings, proceed with them.

NOTES

Commencement: to be appointed.

76 Powers of Authority as to disciplinary proceedings

(1) Where a memorandum under section 75 states that a chief officer of police has not brought disciplinary proceedings or does not propose to bring such proceedings, the Authority may recommend him to bring such proceedings.

(2) Where a chief officer has brought disciplinary proceedings in accordance with a recommendation under subsection (1), he shall proceed with them.

(3) If after the Authority have made a recommendation under this section and consulted the chief officer he is still unwilling to bring disciplinary proceedings, they may direct him to do so.

(4) Where the Authority give a chief officer a direction under this section, they shall supply him with a written statement of their reasons for doing so.

(5) Subject to subsection (6), it shall be the duty of a chief officer to comply with such a direction.

(6) The Authority may withdraw a direction given under this section.

(7) A chief officer shall—

(a) advise the Authority of what action he has taken in response to a recommendation or direction under this section, and

(b) supply the Authority with such other information as they may reasonably require for the purposes of discharging their functions under this section.

NOTES

Commencement: to be appointed.

79 Reports

(1) The Authority shall, at the request of the Secretary of State, report to him on such matters relating generally to their functions as the Secretary of State may specify, and the Authority may for that purpose carry out research into any such matters.

(2) The Authority may make a report to the Secretary of State on any matters coming to their notice under this Chapter to which they consider that his attention should be drawn by reason of their gravity or of other exceptional circumstances.

(3) The Authority shall send a copy of any report under subsection (2)—

(a) to the police authority and the chief officer of police of any police force which appears to the Authority to be concerned, or

(b) if the report concerns a body of constables such as is mentioned in section 78, to the authority maintaining it and the officer having the direction and the control of it.

(4) As soon as practicable after the end of each calendar year the Authority shall make to the Secretary of State a report on the discharge of their functions during that year.

(5) The Secretary of State shall lay before Parliament a copy of every report received by him under this section and shall cause every such report to be published.

(6) . . .

NOTES

Commencement: to be appointed.

Sub-s (6): outside the scope of this work.

80 Restriction on disclosure of information

(1) No information received by the Authority in connection with any of their functions under sections 67 to 79 or regulations made by virtue of section 81 shall be disclosed by any person who is or has been a member, officer or servant of the Authority except—

(a) to the Secretary of State or to a member, officer or servant of the Authority or, so far as may be necessary for the proper discharge of the functions of the Authority, to other persons,

(b) for the purposes of any criminal, civil or disciplinary proceedings, or

(c) in the form of a summary or other general statement made by the Authority which does not identify the person from whom the information was received or any person to whom it relates.

(2) Any person who discloses information in contravention of this section shall be guilty of an offence and liable on summary conviction to a fine of an amount not exceeding level 5 on the standard scale.

NOTES

Commencement: to be appointed.

81 Regulations

(1) The Secretary of State may make regulations as to the procedure to be followed under this Chapter.

(2) The Secretary of State shall by regulations provide—

(a) that, subject to such exceptions, and in accordance with such procedures, as may be specified in the regulations, the chief officer of police of a police force shall supply a copy of, or of the record of, any complaint concerning the conduct of a member of his force—

(i) to that member, and

(ii) to the person by or on behalf of whom the complaint was submitted;

(b) procedures for the informal resolution of complaints of such descriptions as may be specified in the regulations, and for giving the person by or on behalf of whom the complaint was submitted a record of the outcome of any such procedure if he applies for one within such period as the regulations may provide;

(c) procedures for giving a member of a police force, whose conduct is the subject of a complaint which falls to be resolved informally, an opportunity to comment orally or in writing on the complaint;

(d) for cases in which any provision of this Chapter is not to apply where—

(i) a complaint, other than a complaint which falls to be resolved informally, is withdrawn, or

(ii) the complainant indicates that he does not wish any further steps to be taken;

(e) for enabling the Authority to dispense with any requirement of this Chapter;

(f) for enabling the Authority to relinquish the supervision of the investigation of any complaint or other matter;

(g) procedures for the reference or submission of complaints or other matters to the Authority;

(h) for the time within which the Authority are to give a notification under section 72(2);

(i) that the Authority shall be supplied with such information or documents of such description as may be specified in the regulations at such time or in such circumstances as may be so specified;

(j) that any action or decision of the Authority which they take in consequence of their receipt of a memorandum under section 75 shall, if it is an action or decision of a description specified in the regulations, be notified to the person concerned and that, in connection with such a notification, the Authority shall have power to supply that person with any relevant information;

(k) that chief officers of police shall have power to delegate any functions conferred on them by or by virtue of this Chapter.

(3) In this section "document" means anything in which information of any description is recorded.

NOTES

Commencement: to be appointed.

82 Regulations—supplementary

(1) Regulations under this Chapter may make different provision for different circumstances and may authorise the Secretary of State to make provision for any purposes specified in the regulations.

(2) Subject to subsection (3), a statutory instrument containing regulations under this Chapter shall be subject to annulment in pursuance of a resolution of either House of Parliament.

(3) Regulations to which this subsection applies shall not be made unless a draft of them has been laid before and approved by resolution of each House of Parliament.

(4) Subsection (3) applies to regulations made by virtue of section 70(1)(a)(ii), 72(1)(b) or (4), 75(4) or (5) or 81(2)(b), (e) or (f).

NOTES

Commencement: to be appointed.

83 Guidance concerning complaints etc

(1) The Secretary of State may issue guidance to police authorities, chief officers of police and other members of police forces concerning the discharge of their functions under this Chapter and they shall have regard to any such guidance in the discharge of their functions.

(2) Guidance may not be issued under subsection (1) in relation to the handling of a particular case.

(3) A failure on the part of a person to whom guidance is issued under subsection (1) to have regard to such guidance shall be admissible in evidence on any appeal from a decision taken in proceedings under regulations made in accordance with section 50(3).

(4) In discharging their functions under section 76 the Authority shall have regard to any guidance given to them by the Secretary of State with respect to such matters as are for the time being the subject of guidance under subsection (1), and they shall have regard in particular, but without prejudice to the generality of this subsection, to any such guidance as to the principles to be applied in cases that involve any question of criminal proceedings.

(5) The report of the Authority under section 79(4) shall contain a statement of any guidance given to the Authority under subsection (4) above during the year to which the report relates.

NOTES

Commencement: to be appointed.

CHAPTER II
DISCIPLINARY AND OTHER PROCEEDINGS

86 Admissibility of statements in subsequent proceedings

(1) Subject to subsection (2), no statement made by a person for the purpose of the informal resolution of a complaint shall be admissible in any subsequent criminal, civil or disciplinary proceedings.

(2) A statement is not rendered inadmissible by subsection (1) if it consists of or includes an admission relating to a matter which does not fall to be resolved informally.

(3) In this section "complaint" and "disciplinary proceedings" have the meanings given in section 65.

NOTES

Commencement: to be appointed.

88 Liability for wrongful acts of constables

(1) The chief officer of police for a police area shall be liable in respect of torts committed by constables under his direction and control in the performance or purported performance of their functions in like manner as a master is liable in

respect of torts committed by his servants in the course of their employment, and accordingly shall in respect of any such tort be treated for all purposes as a joint tortfeasor.

(2) There shall be paid out of the police fund—

(a) any damages or costs awarded against the chief officer of police in any proceedings brought against him by virtue of this section and any costs incurred by him in any such proceedings so far as not recovered by him in the proceedings; and

(b) any sum required in connection with the settlement of any claim made against the chief officer of police by virtue of this section, if the settlement is approved by the police authority.

(3) Any proceedings in respect of a claim made by virtue of this section shall be brought against the chief officer of police for the time being or, in the case of a vacancy in that office, against the person for the time being performing the functions of the chief officer of police; and references in subsections (1) and (2) to the chief officer of police shall be construed accordingly.

(4) A police authority may, in such cases and to such extent as appear to it to be appropriate, pay out of the police fund—

(a) any damages or costs awarded against a person to whom this subsection applies in proceedings for a tort committed by that person,

(b) any costs incurred and not recovered by such a person in such proceedings, and

(c) any sum required in connection with the settlement of a claim that has or might have given rise to such proceedings.

(5) Subsection (4) applies to a person who is—

(a) a member of the police force maintained by the police authority,

(b) a constable for the time being required to serve with that force by virtue of section 24 or 98 [of this Act or section 23 of the Police Act 1997], or

(c) a special constable appointed for the authority's police area.

NOTES

Commencement: 22 August 1996.

Sub-s (5): words in square brackets in para (b) inserted by the Police Act 1997, s 134(1), Sch 9, paras 72, 85.

PART V
MISCELLANEOUS AND GENERAL

Offences

89 Assaults on constables

(1) Any person who assaults a constable in the execution of his duty, or a person assisting a constable in the execution of his duty, shall be guilty of an offence and liable on summary conviction to imprisonment for a term not exceeding six months or to a fine not exceeding level 5 on the standard scale, or to both.

(2) Any person who resists or wilfully obstructs a constable in the execution of his duty, or a person assisting a constable in the execution of his duty, shall be guilty of an offence and liable on summary conviction to imprisonment for a term not exceeding one month or to a fine not exceeding level 3 on the standard scale, or to both.

(3) This section also applies to a constable who is a member of a police force maintained in Scotland or Northern Ireland when he is executing a warrant, or otherwise acting in England or Wales, by virtue of any enactment conferring powers on him in England and Wales.

NOTES

Commencement: 22 August 1996.

91 Causing disaffection

(1) Any person who causes, or attempts to cause, or does any act calculated to cause, disaffection amongst the members of any police force, or induces or attempts to induce, or does any act calculated to induce, any member of a police force to withhold his services, shall be guilty of an offence and liable—

- (a) on summary conviction, to imprisonment for a term not exceeding six months or to a fine not exceeding the statutory maximum, or to both;
- (b) on conviction on indictment, to imprisonment for a term not exceeding two years or to a fine, or to both.

(2) This section applies to special constables appointed for a police area as it applies to members of a police force.

NOTES

Commencement: 22 August 1996.

Miscellaneous

96 Arrangements for obtaining the views of the community on policing

(1) Arrangements shall be made for each police area for obtaining—

- (a) the views of people in that area about matters concerning the policing of the area, and
- (b) their co-operation with the police in preventing crime in that area.

(2) Except as provided by subsections (3) to (6), arrangements for each police area shall be made by the police authority after consulting the chief constable as to the arrangements that would be appropriate.

(3) The Secretary of State shall issue guidance to the Commissioner of Police of the Metropolis concerning arrangements for the metropolitan police district; and the Commissioner shall make arrangements under this section after taking account of that guidance.

(4) The Commissioner shall make separate arrangements—

- (a) for each London borough;
- (b) for each district which falls wholly within the metropolitan police district; and
- (c) in the case of districts which fall partly within the metropolitan police district, for each part of such a district which falls within that police district.

(5) The Commissioner shall—

- (a) consult the council of each London borough as to the arrangements that would be appropriate for the borough,
- (b) consult the council of each district mentioned in subsection (4)(b) as to the arrangements that would be appropriate for the district, and

(c) consult the council of each district mentioned in subsection (4)(c) as to the arrangements that would be appropriate for the part of the district which falls within the metropolitan police district.

(6) The Common Council of the City of London shall issue guidance to the Commissioner of Police for the City of London concerning arrangements for the City of London police area; and the Commissioner shall make arrangements under this section after taking account of that guidance.

(7) A body or person whose duty it is to make arrangements under this section shall review the arrangements so made from time to time.

(8) If it appears to the Secretary of State that arrangements for a police area are not adequate for the purposes set out in subsection (1), he may require the body or person whose duty it is to make arrangements for that area to submit a report to him concerning the arrangements.

(9) After considering a report submitted under subsection (8), the Secretary of State may require the body or person who submitted it to review the arrangements and submit a further report to him concerning them.

(10) A body or person whose duty it is to make arrangements shall be under the same duties to consult when reviewing arrangements as when making them.

NOTES
Commencement: 22 August 1996.

Supplemental

104 Commencement

(1) Except as provided by subsection (2), this Act shall come into force at the end of the period of three months beginning with the day on which it is passed.

(2)–(5) . . .

NOTES
Commencement: 22 August 1996.
Sub-ss (2)–(5): outside the scope of this work.

105 Extent

(1) Except as provided by subsections (2) to (5), this Act extends to England and Wales only.

(2)–(5) . . .

NOTES
Commencement: 22 August 1996.
Sub-ss (2)–(5): outside the scope of this work.

106 Short title

This Act may be cited as the Police Act 1996.

NOTES
Commencement: 22 August 1996.

SCHEDULES

SCHEDULE 2

Section 4

POLICE AUTHORITIES ESTABLISHED UNDER SECTION 3

Membership of police authorities

1.—(1) Where, by virtue of section 4, a police authority is to consist of seventeen members—

(a) nine of those members shall be members of a relevant council appointed under paragraph 2,

(b) five shall be persons appointed under paragraph 5, and

(c) three shall be magistrates appointed under paragraph 8.

(2) Where, by virtue of an order under subsection (2) of that section, a police authority is to consist of more than seventeen members—

(a) a number which is greater by one than the number of members provided for in paragraphs (b) and (c) below shall be members of a relevant council appointed under paragraph 2,

(b) such number as may be prescribed by the order, not exceeding one third of the total membership, shall be persons appointed under paragraph 5, and

(c) the remainder shall be magistrates appointed under paragraph 8.

Appointment of members by relevant councils

2.—(1) In the case of a police authority in relation to which there is only one relevant council, the members of the police authority referred to in paragraph 1(1)(a) or (2)(a) shall be appointed by that council.

(2) In any other case, those members shall be appointed by a joint committee consisting of persons appointed by the relevant councils from among their own members.

3. The number of members of the joint committee, and the number of those members to be appointed by each relevant council, shall be such as the councils may agree or, in the absence of agreement, as may be determined by the Secretary of State.

4.—(1) A council or joint committee shall exercise its power to appoint members of a police authority under paragraph 2 so as to ensure that, so far as practicable, the members for whose appointment it is responsible reflect—

(a) in the case of appointments by a council, the balance of parties for the time being prevailing among the members of the council, and

(b) in the case of appointments by a joint committee, the balance of parties for the time being prevailing among the members of the relevant councils taken as a whole.

(2) The members referred to in sub-paragraph (1)(a) and (b) do not include any member of a relevant council who is disqualified for being appointed as or being a member of the police authority under paragraph 12.

Appointment of independent members

5. The members of a police authority referred to in paragraph 1(1)(b) or (2)(b) shall be appointed—

(a) by the members of the police authority appointed under paragraph 2 or 8,

(b) from among persons on a short-list prepared by the Secretary of State in accordance with Schedule 3.

6.—(1) Every police authority shall arrange for a notice stating—

(a) the name of each of its members appointed under paragraph 5, and

(b) such other information relating to him as the authority considers appropriate,

to be published in such manner as appears to it to be appropriate.

(2) A police authority shall send to the Secretary of State a copy of any notice which it has arranged to be published under sub-paragraph (1).

Appointment of magistrates

7. The members of a police authority referred to in paragraph 1(1)(c) or (2)(c)—
   (a) must be magistrates for an area all or part of which constitutes or forms part of the authority's area, and
   (b) shall be appointed in accordance with paragraph 8;

and in that paragraph references to a panel are references to a selection panel constituted under regulations made in accordance with [section 29(2) of the Justices of the Peace Act 1997].

8–27. . . .

NOTES

Commencement: 22 August 1996.

Para 7: words in square brackets substituted by the Justices of the Peace Act 1997, s 73(2), Sch 5, para 37(1), (3)(a).

Paras 8–27: outside the scope of this work.

SCHEDULE 4

Section 29

FORM OF DECLARATION

I, ... of .. .. do solemnly and sincerely declare and affirm that I will well and truly serve Our Sovereign Lady the Queen in the office of constable, without favour or affection, malice or ill will; and that I will to the best of my power cause the peace to be kept and preserved, and prevent all offences against the persons and properties of Her Majesty's subjects; and that while I continue to hold the said office I will to the best of my skill and knowledge discharge all the duties thereof faithfully according to law.

NOTES

Commencement: 22 August 1996.

SCHEDULE 5

Section 66

THE POLICE COMPLAINTS AUTHORITY

Constitution of Authority

1.—(1) The Police Complaints Authority shall consist of a chairman and not less than eight other members.

(2) The chairman shall be appointed by Her Majesty.

(3) The other members shall be appointed by the Secretary of State.

(4) The members of the Authority shall not include any person who is or has been a constable in any part of the United Kingdom.

(5) Persons may be appointed as whole-time or part-time members of the Authority.

(6) The Secretary of State may appoint not more than two of the members of the Authority to be deputy chairmen.

Status of Authority

2. The Authority shall not be regarded as the servant or agent of the Crown or as enjoying any status, privilege or immunity of the Crown; and the Authority's property shall not be regarded as property of or property held on behalf of the Crown.

Members

3.—(1) Subject to the following provisions of this Schedule, a person shall hold an office to which he is appointed under paragraph 1(2), (3) or (6) in accordance with the terms of his appointment.

(2) A person shall not be appointed to such an office for more than three years at a time.

(3) A person may at any time resign such an office.

(4) The Secretary of State may at any time remove a person from such an office if satisfied that—

(a) he has without reasonable excuse failed to carry out his duties for a continuous period of three months beginning not earlier than six months before that time;
(b) he has been convicted of a criminal offence;
(c) he has become bankrupt or made an arrangement with his creditors;
(d) he is incapacitated by physical or mental illness;
(e) he has acted improperly in relation to his duties; or
(f) he is otherwise unable or unfit to perform his duties.

4–9. . . .

Proceedings

10. . . .

11. The validity of any proceedings of the Authority shall not be affected by—

(a) any defect in the appointment of the chairman or any other member, or
(b) any vacancy in the office of chairman or among the other members.

12, 13. . . .

NOTES

Commencement: to be appointed.
Paras 4–10, 12, 13: outside the scope of this work.

EMPLOYMENT RIGHTS ACT 1996

(C 18)

An Act to consolidate enactments relating to employment rights

[22 May 1996]

PART XIII
MISCELLANEOUS

CHAPTER I
PARTICULAR TYPES OF EMPLOYMENT

Crown employment etc

191 Crown employment

(1) Subject to sections 192 and 193, the provisions of this Act to which this section applies have effect in relation to Crown employment and persons in Crown employment as they have effect in relation to other employment and other employees or workers.

(2) This section applies to—

(a) Parts I to III,
[(aa) Part IVA,]
(b) Part V, apart from section 45,
(c) Parts VI to VIII,
(d) in Part IX, sections 92 and 93,
(e) Part X, apart from section 101, and
(f) this Part and Parts XIV and XV.

(3) In this Act "Crown employment" means employment under or for the purposes of a government department or any officer or body exercising on behalf of the Crown functions conferred by a statutory provision.

(4) For the purposes of the application of provisions of this Act in relation to Crown employment in accordance with subsection (1)—
(a) references to an employee or a worker shall be construed as references to a person in Crown employment,
(b) references to a contract of employment, or a worker's contract, shall be construed as references to the terms of employment of a person in Crown employment,
(c) references to dismissal, or to the termination of a worker's contract, shall be construed as references to the termination of Crown employment,
(d) references to redundancy shall be construed as references to the existence of such circumstances as are treated, in accordance with any arrangements falling within section 177(3) for the time being in force, as equivalent to redundancy in relation to Crown employment, and
(e) references to an undertaking shall be construed—
(i) in relation to a Minister of the Crown, as references to his functions or (as the context may require) to the department of which he is in charge, and
(ii) in relation to a government department, officer or body, as references to the functions of the department, officer or body or (as the context may require) to the department, officer or body.

(5) Where the terms of employment of a person in Crown employment restrict his right to take part in—
(a) certain political activities, or
(b) activities which may conflict with his official functions,

nothing in section 50 requires him to be allowed time off work for public duties connected with any such activities.

(6) . . .

NOTES

Commencement: 22 August 1996.

Sub-s (2): para (aa) inserted by the Public Interest Disclosure Act 1998, ss 10, 18(2), partly as from a day to be appointed.

Sub-s (6): outside the scope of this work.

192 Armed forces

(1) Section 191—
(a) applies to service as a member of the naval, military or air forces of the Crown but subject to the following provisions of this section, and
(b) applies to employment by an association established for the purposes of Part XI of the Reserve Forces Act 1996.

(2) The provisions of this Act which have effect by virtue of section 191 in relation to service as a member of the naval, military or air forces of the Crown are—

(a) Part I,

[(aa) in Part V, section 45A, and sections 48 and 49 so far as relating to that section,]

(b) in Part VI, sections 55 to 57,

(c) Parts VII and VIII,

(d) in Part IX, sections 92 and 93,

(e) Part X, apart from sections 100 to 103 and 134, and

(f) this Part and Parts XIV and XV.

(3) Her Majesty may by Order in Council—

(a) amend subsection (2) by making additions to, or omissions from, the provisions for the time being specified in that subsection, and

(b) make any provision for the time being so specified apply to service as a member of the naval, military or air forces of the Crown subject to such exceptions and modifications as may be specified in the Order in Council,

but no provision contained in Part II may be added to the provisions for the time being specified in subsection (2).

(4)–(8) . . .

NOTES

Commencement: 22 August 1996.

Sub-s (2): para (aa) inserted by the Working Time Regulations 1998, SI 1998/1833, regs 2(1), 31(4).

Sub-ss (4)–(8): outside the scope of this work.

193 National security

(1) The provisions of this Act to which this section applies do not have effect in relation to any Crown employment in respect of which there is in force a certificate issued by or on behalf of a Minister of the Crown certifying that employment of a description specified in the certificate, or the employment of a particular person so specified, is (or, at a time specified in the certificate, was) required to be excepted from those provisions for the purpose of safeguarding national security.

(2) This section applies to—

(a) Part I, so far as it relates to itemised pay statements,

(b) Part III,

[(bb) Part IVA,

(bc) in Part V, section 47B,]

(c) in Part VI, sections 50 to 54,

(d) in Part VII, sections 64 and 65, and sections 69 and 70 so far as relating to those sections,

(e) in Part IX, sections 92 and 93, except where they apply by virtue of section 92(4),

(f) Part X, except so far as relating to a dismissal which is treated as unfair—

(i) by section 99(1) to (3), 100 or 103, or

(ii) by subsection (1) of section 105 by reason of the application of subsection (2), (3) or (6) of that section, and

(g) this Part and Parts XIV and XV (so far as relating to any of the provisions specified in paragraphs (a) to (f)).

(3) Any document purporting to be a certificate issued as mentioned in subsection (1)—

(a) shall be received in evidence, and

(b) unless the contrary is proved, shall be deemed to be such a certificate.

[(4) Part IVA and sections 47B and 103A do not have effect in relation to employment for the purposes of the Security Service, the Secret Intelligence Service or the Government Communications Headquarters.]

NOTES

Commencement: 22 August 1996.

Sub-s (2): paras (bb), (bc) inserted by the Public Interest Disclosure Act 1998, ss 11(1), (2), 18(2), partly as from a day to be appointed.

Sub-s (4): added by the Public Interest Disclosure Act 1998, ss 11(1), (3), 18(2), partly as from a day to be appointed.

PART XV
GENERAL AND SUPPLEMENTARY

Final provisions

243 Commencement

This Act shall come into force at the end of the period of three months beginning with the day on which it is passed.

NOTES

Commencement: 22 August 1996.

244 Extent

(1) Subject to the following provisions, this Act extends to England and Wales and Scotland but not to Northern Ireland.

(2) The provisions of this Act which refer to shop workers and betting workers extend to England and Wales only.

(3) Sections 201 and 238 (and sections 236 and 243, this section and section 245) extend to Northern Ireland (as well as to England and Wales and Scotland).

(4) . . .

NOTES

Commencement: 22 August 1996.

Sub-s (4): outside the scope of this work.

245 Short title

This Act may be cited as the Employment Rights Act 1996.

NOTES

Commencement: 22 August 1996.

DEFAMATION ACT 1996

(C 31)

An Act to amend the law of defamation and to amend the law of limitation with respect to actions for defamation or malicious falsehood [4 July 1996]

Evidence concerning proceedings in Parliament

13 Evidence concerning proceedings in Parliament

(1) Where the conduct of a person in or in relation to proceedings in Parliament is in issue in defamation proceedings, he may waive for the purposes of those

proceedings, so far as concerns him, the protection of any enactment or rule of law which prevents proceedings in Parliament being impeached or questioned in any court or place out of Parliament.

(2) Where a person waives that protection—
- (a) any such enactment or rule of law shall not apply to prevent evidence being given, questions being asked or statements, submissions, comments or findings being made about his conduct, and
- (b) none of those things shall be regarded as infringing the privilege of either House of Parliament.

(3) The waiver by one person of that protection does not affect its operation in relation to another person who has not waived it.

(4) Nothing in this section affects any enactment or rule of law so far as it protects a person (including a person who has waived the protection referred to above) from legal liability for words spoken or things done in the course of, or for the purposes of or incidental to, any proceedings in Parliament.

(5) Without prejudice to the generality of subsection (4), that subsection applies to—
- (a) the giving of evidence before either House or a committee;
- (b) the presentation or submission of a document to either House or a committee;
- (c) the preparation of a document for the purposes of or incidental to the transacting of any such business;
- (d) the formulation, making or publication of a document, including a report, by or pursuant to an order of either House or a committee; and
- (e) any communication with the Parliamentary Commissioner for Standards or any person having functions in connection with the registration of members' interests.

In this subsection "a committee" means a committee of either House or a joint committee of both Houses of Parliament.

NOTES
Commencement: 4 September 1996.

Statutory privilege

14 Reports of court proceedings absolutely privileged

(1) A fair and accurate report of proceedings in public before a court to which this section applies, if published contemporaneously with proceedings, is absolutely privileged.

(2) A report of proceedings which by an order of the court, or as a consequence of any statutory provision, is required to be postponed shall be treated as published contemporaneously if it is published as soon as practicable after publication is permitted.

(3) This section applies to—
- (a) any court in the United Kingdom,
- (b) the European Court of Justice or any court attached to that court,
- (c) the European Court of Human Rights, and

(d) any international criminal tribunal established by the Security Council of the United Nations or by an international agreement to which the United Kingdom is a party.

In paragraph (a) "court" includes any tribunal or body exercising the judicial power of the State.

(4) . . .

NOTES

Commencement: to be appointed.

Sub-s (4): outside the scope of this work.

15 Reports, &c protected by qualified privilege

(1) The publication of any report or other statement mentioned in Schedule 1 to this Act is privileged unless the publication is shown to be made with malice, subject as follows.

(2) In defamation proceedings in respect of the publication of a report or other statement mentioned in Part II of that Schedule, there is no defence under this section if the plaintiff shows that the defendant—

(a) was requested by him to publish in a suitable manner a reasonable letter or statement by way of explanation or contradiction, and

(b) refused or neglected to do so.

For this purpose "in a suitable manner" means in the same manner as the publication complained of or in a manner that is adequate and reasonable in the circumstances.

(3) This section does not apply to the publication to the public, or a section of the public, of matter which is not of public concern and the publication of which is not for the public benefit.

(4) Nothing in this section shall be construed—

(a) as protecting the publication of matter the publication of which is prohibited by law, or

(b) as limiting or abridging any privilege subsisting apart from this section.

NOTES

Commencement: to be appointed.

General provisions

18 Extent

(1) The following provisions of this Act extend to England and Wales—

. . .

section 13 (evidence concerning proceedings in Parliament),

sections 14 and 15 and Schedule 1 (statutory privilege),

. . .

this subsection,

. . .

section 20 (short title and saving).

(2) . . .

(3) The following provisions of this Act extend to Northern Ireland—

. . .

section 13 (evidence concerning proceedings in Parliament),
sections 14 and 15 and Schedule 1 (statutory privilege),

. . .

this subsection,

. . .

section 20 (short title and saving).

NOTES
Commencement: 4 July 1996.
Sub-ss (1), (3): words omitted outside the scope of this work.
Sub-s (2): outside the scope of this work.

20 Short title and saving

(1) This Act may be cited as the Defamation Act 1996.

(2) Nothing in this Act affects the law relating to criminal libel.

NOTES
Commencement: 4 July 1996.

SCHEDULE 1

Section 15

QUALIFIED PRIVILEGE

PART I
STATEMENTS HAVING QUALIFIED PRIVILEGE WITHOUT EXPLANATION OR CONTRADICTION

1. A fair and accurate report of proceedings in public of a legislature anywhere in the world.

2. A fair and accurate report of proceedings in public before a court anywhere in the world.

3. A fair and accurate report of proceedings in public of a person appointed to hold a public inquiry by a government or legislature anywhere in the world.

4. A fair and accurate report of proceedings in public anywhere in the world of an international organisation or an international conference.

5. A fair and accurate copy of or extract from any register or other document required by law to be open to public inspection.

6. A notice or advertisement published by or on the authority of a court, or of a judge or officer of a court, anywhere in the world.

7. A fair and accurate copy of or extract from matter published by or on the authority of a government or legislature anywhere in the world.

8. A fair and accurate copy of or extract from matter published anywhere in the world by an international organisation or an international conference.

PART II
STATEMENTS PRIVILEGED SUBJECT TO EXPLANATION OR CONTRADICTION

9.—(1) A fair and accurate copy of or extract from a notice or other matter issued for the information of the public by or on behalf of—

- (a) a legislature in any member State or the European Parliament;
- (b) the government of any member State, or any authority performing governmental functions in any member State or part of a member State, or the European Commission;
- (c) an international organisation or international conference.

(2) In this paragraph "governmental functions" includes police functions.

10. A fair and accurate copy of or extract from a document made available by a court in any member State or the European Court of Justice (or any court attached to that court), or by a judge or officer of any such court.

11.—(1) A fair and accurate report of proceedings at any public meeting or sitting in the United Kingdom of—

- (a) a local authority or local authority committee;
- (b) a justice or justices of the peace acting otherwise than as a court exercising judicial authority;
- (c) a commission, tribunal, committee or person appointed for the purposes of any inquiry by any statutory provision, by Her Majesty or by a Minister of the Crown or a Northern Ireland Department;
- (d) a person appointed by a local authority to hold a local inquiry in pursuance of any statutory provision;
- (e) any other tribunal, board, committee or body constituted by or under, and exercising functions under, any statutory provision.

(2) In sub-paragraph (1)(a)—

"local authority" means—

- (a) in relation to England and Wales, a principal council within the meaning of the Local Government Act 1972, any body falling within any paragraph of section 100J(1) of that Act or an authority or body to which the Public Bodies (Admission to Meetings) Act 1960 applies,
- (b) in relation to Scotland, a council constituted under section 2 of the Local Government etc (Scotland) Act 1994 or an authority or body to which the Public Bodies (Admission to Meetings) Act 1960 applies,
- (c) in relation to Northern Ireland, any authority or body to which sections 23 to 27 of the Local Government Act (Northern Ireland) 1972 apply; and

"local authority committee" means any committee of a local authority or of local authorities, and includes—

- (a) any committee or sub-committee in relation to which sections 100A to 100D of the Local Government Act 1972 apply by virtue of section 100E of that Act (whether or not also by virtue of section 100J of that Act), and
- (b) any committee or sub-committee in relation to which sections 50A to 50D of the Local Government (Scotland) Act 1973 apply by virtue of section 50E of that Act.

(3) A fair and accurate report of any corresponding proceedings in any of the Channel Islands or the Isle of Man or in another member State.

12–17. . . .

NOTES

Commencement: to be appointed.

Paras 12–17: outside the scope of this work.

SECURITY SERVICE ACT 1996

(C 35)

(NOTE)

NOTES

Section 1 of this Act amends the Security Service Act 1989, s 1; s 2 of this Act substitutes the Intelligence Services Act 1994, s 5(3), (3A), (3B) for the original sub-s (3) of that section. Both the 1989 Act and the 1994 Act are printed in this work. S 3 of this Act provides that this Act applies to Northern Ireland.

ASYLUM AND IMMIGRATION ACT 1996

(C 49)

An Act to amend and supplement the Immigration Act 1971 and the Asylum and Immigration Appeals Act 1993; to make further provision with respect to persons subject to immigration control and the employment of such persons; and for connected purposes [24 July 1996]

Asylum claims

2 Removal etc of asylum claimants to safe third countries

(1) Nothing in section 6 of the 1993 Act (protection of claimants from deportation etc) shall prevent a person who has made a claim for asylum being removed from the United Kingdom if—

(a) the Secretary of State has certified that, in his opinion, the conditions mentioned in subsection (2) below are fulfilled;

(b) the certificate has not been set aside on an appeal under section 3 below; and

(c) except in the case of a person who is to be sent to a country or territory to which subsection (3) below applies, the time for giving notice of such an appeal has expired and no such appeal is pending.

(2) The conditions are—

(a) that the person is not a national or citizen of the country or territory to which he is to be sent;

(b) that his life and liberty would not be threatened in that country or territory by reason of his race, religion, nationality, membership of a particular social group, or political opinion; and

(c) that the government of that country or territory would not send him to another country or territory otherwise than in accordance with the Convention.

(3) This subsection applies to any country or territory which is or forms part of a member State, or is designated for the purposes of this subsection in an order made by the Secretary of State by statutory instrument.

(4) The first order under this section shall not be made unless a draft of the order has been laid before and approved by a resolution of each House of Parliament.

(5) A statutory instrument containing a subsequent order under this section shall be subject to annulment in pursuance of a resolution of either House of Parliament.

(6) For the purposes of this section, an appeal under section 3 below is pending during the period beginning when notice of appeal is duly given and ending when the appeal is finally determined or withdrawn.

(7) In this section "claim for asylum" and "the Convention" have the same meanings as in the 1993 Act.

NOTES

Commencement: 1 September 1996.

3 Appeals against certificates under section 2

(1) Where a certificate has been issued under section 2(1) above in respect of any person—

- (a) that person may appeal against the certificate to a special adjudicator on the ground that any of the conditions mentioned in section 2(2) above was not fulfilled when the certificate was issued, or has since ceased to be fulfilled; but
- (b) unless and until the certificate is set aside on such an appeal, he shall not be entitled to bring or pursue any appeal under—
  - (i) Part II of the 1971 Act (appeals: general); or
  - (ii) section 8 of the 1993 Act (appeals to special adjudicator on Convention grounds),

  as respects matters arising before his removal from the United Kingdom.

(2) A person who has been, or is to be, sent to a country or territory to which section 2(3) above applies shall not be entitled to bring or pursue an appeal under this section so long as he is in the United Kingdom.

(3) The Lord Chancellor shall designate such number of the adjudicators appointed for the purposes of Part II of the 1971 Act as he thinks necessary to act as special adjudicators for the purposes of this section and may from time to time vary that number and the persons who are so designated.

(4) Subject to subsection (5) below, the following provisions of the 1971 Act, namely—

- (a) section 18 (notice of decisions appealable under that Part and statement of appeal rights etc);
- (b) section 19 (determination of appeals under that Part by adjudicators);
- (c) section 21 (references of cases by Secretary of State for further consideration);
- (d) section 22(1) to (4), (6) and (7) (rules of procedure for appeals);
- (e) section 23 (grants to voluntary organisations helping persons with rights of appeal); and
- (f) Schedule 5 (provisions about adjudicators and Immigration Appeal Tribunal),

shall have effect as if this section were contained in Part II of that Act.

(5) Rules of procedure under section 22 of the 1971 Act—

- (a) may make special provision in relation to appeals under this section; and
- (b) may make different provision in relation to appeals by persons who have been, or are to be, sent to countries or territories of different descriptions;

and so much of paragraph 5 of Schedule 5 to that Act as relates to the allocation of duties among the adjudicators shall have effect subject to subsection (3) above.

(6) Paragraph 29 of Schedule 2 to the 1971 Act (grant of bail pending appeal) shall have effect as if the references to appeals under sections 13(1), 15(1)(a) and 16 of that Act included references to appeals under this section.

NOTES

Commencement: 1 September 1996 (sub-ss (1), (2), (4), (6)); 26 July 1996 (sub-ss (3), (5)).

Immigration offences

7 Power of arrest and search warrants

(1) A constable or immigration officer may arrest without warrant anyone whom he has reasonable grounds for suspecting to have committed an offence to which this section applies.

(2) If—

- (a) a justice of the peace is by written information on oath satisfied that there is reasonable ground for suspecting that a person who is liable to be arrested under subsection (1) above is to be found on any premises; or
- (b) . . .

he may grant a warrant authorising any constable to enter, if need be by force, the premises named in the warrant for the purposes of searching for and arresting that person.

(3)–(5) . . .

NOTES

Commencement: 1 October 1996.

Sub-ss (3)–(5): outside the scope of this work.

Persons subject to immigration control

8 Restrictions on employment

(1) Subject to subsection (2) below, if any person ("the employer") employs a person subject to immigration control ("the employee") who has attained the age of 16, the employer shall be guilty of an offence if—

- (a) the employee has not been granted leave to enter or remain in the United Kingdom; or
- (b) the employee's leave is not valid and subsisting, or is subject to a condition precluding him from taking up the employment,

and (in either case) the employee does not satisfy such conditions as may be specified in an order made by the Secretary of State.

(2) Subject to subsection (3) below, in proceedings under this section, it shall be a defence to prove that—

- (a) before the employment began, there was produced to the employer a document which appeared to him to relate to the employee and to be of a description specified in an order made by the Secretary of State; and
- (b) either the document was retained by the employer, or a copy or other record of it was made by the employer in a manner specified in the order in relation to documents of that description.

(3) The defence afforded by subsection (2) above shall not be available in any case where the employer knew that his employment of the employee would constitute an offence under this section.

(4) A person guilty of an offence under this section shall be liable on summary conviction to a fine not exceeding level 5 on the standard scale.

(5)–(8) . . .

NOTES

Commencement: 1 December 1996, for purpose only of making orders; 27 January 1997, otherwise, subject to saving for employment beginning before 27 January 1997 (sub-ss (1), (2)); 27 January 1997, subject to saving for employment beginning before 27 January 1997 (sub-ss (3)–(8)).

Sub-ss (5)–(8): outside the scope of this work.

11 Saving for social security regulations

(1) Notwithstanding any enactment or rule of law, regulations may exclude any person who has made a claim for asylum from entitlement to any of the following benefits, namely—

- (a) income support, housing benefit and council tax benefit under the Social Security Contributions and Benefits Act 1992;
- (b) income support and housing benefit under the Social Security Contributions and Benefits (Northern Ireland) Act 1992; and
- (c) jobseeker's allowance under the Jobseekers Act 1995 or the Jobseekers (Northern Ireland) Order 1995.

(2) Regulations may provide that, where such a person who is so excluded is subsequently recorded by the Secretary of State as a refugee within the meaning of the Convention—

- (a) that person may, within a prescribed period, claim the whole or any prescribed proportion of any income support, housing benefit or council tax benefit to which he would have been entitled had he been recorded as a refugee immediately after he made the claim for asylum; and
- (b) where he makes such a claim as is mentioned in paragraph (a) above in respect of housing benefit or council tax benefit having resided in the areas of two or more local authorities in Great Britain, the claim shall be investigated and determined, and any benefit awarded shall be paid or allowed, by such one of those authorities as may be prescribed.

(3) Regulations making such provision as is mentioned in subsection (2)(b) above may require the other authorities there mentioned to supply the prescribed authority with such information as it may reasonably require in connection with the exercise of its functions under the regulations.

(4) Schedule 1 to this Act—

- (a) Part I of which modifies the Social Security (Persons from Abroad) Miscellaneous Amendments Regulations 1996; and
- (b) Part II of which modifies the Social Security (Persons from Abroad) (Miscellaneous Amendments) Regulations (Northern Ireland) 1996,

shall have effect.

(5), (6) . . .

NOTES

Commencement:: 24 July 1996.

Sub-ss (5), (6): outside the scope of this work.

Miscellaneous and supplemental

13 Short title, interpretation, commencement and extent

(1) This Act may be cited as the Asylum and Immigration Act 1996.

(2) In this Act—
"the 1971 Act" means the Immigration Act 1971;
"the 1993 Act" means the Asylum and Immigration Appeals Act 1993;
"person subject to immigration control" means a person who under the 1971 Act requires leave to enter or remain in the United Kingdom (whether or not such leave has been given).

(3) This Act, except section 11 and Schedule 1, shall come into force on such day as the Secretary of State may by order made by statutory instrument appoint, and different days may be appointed for different purposes.

(4) An order under subsection (3) above may make such transitional and supplemental provision as the Secretary of State thinks necessary or expedient.

(5) . . .

(6) This Act extends to Northern Ireland.

NOTES
Commencement: 26 July 1996.
Sub-s (5): outside the scope of this work.

BROADCASTING ACT 1996

(C 55)

An Act to make new provision about the broadcasting in digital form of television and sound programme services and the broadcasting in that form on television or radio frequencies of other services; to amend the Broadcasting Act 1990; to make provision about rights to televise sporting or other events of national interest; to amend in other respects the law relating to the provision of television and sound programme services; to provide for the establishment and functions of a Broadcasting Standards Commission and for the dissolution of the Broadcasting Complaints Commission and the Broadcasting Standards Council; to make provision for the transfer to other persons of property, rights and liabilities of the British Broadcasting Corporation relating to their transmission network; and for connected purposes

[24 July 1996]

PART I
DIGITAL TERRESTRIAL TELEVISION BROADCASTING

Introductory

1 Multiplex services and digital programme services

(1) In this Part "multiplex service" means a service provided by any person which consists in the broadcasting for general reception of two or more services specified in

subsection (3) by combining the relevant information in digital form, together with any broadcasting in digital form of digital additional services (as defined by section 24(1)).

(2) . . .

(3) The services referred to in subsections (1) and (2) are—
 (a) a digital programme service (as defined by subsection (4)), or
 (b) a qualifying service (as defined by section 2(2)).

(4) In this Part "digital programme service" means a service consisting in the provision by any person of television programmes (together with any ancillary services, as defined by section 24(2)) with a view to their being broadcast in digital form for general reception, whether by him or by some other person, but does not include—
 (a) a qualifying service,
 (b) a teletext service, or
 (c) any service in the case of which the visual images to be broadcast do not consist wholly or mainly of images capable of being seen as moving pictures,

except, in the case of a service falling within paragraph (b) or (c), to the extent that it is an ancillary service.

(5), (6) . . .

(7) In this section—
 "broadcast" means broadcast otherwise than—
 (a) by satellite, or
 (b) in the provision of a local delivery service (as defined by section 72(1) of the 1990 Act), and
 "for general reception" means for general reception in, or in any area in, the United Kingdom.

NOTES
Commencement: 1 October 1996.
Sub-ss (2), (5), (6): outside the scope of this work.

General provisions about licences

3 Licences under Part I

(1) Any licence granted by the Independent Television Commission (in this Part referred to as "the Commission") under this Part shall be in writing and (subject to the provisions of this Part) shall continue in force for such period as is provided, in relation to a licence of the kind in question, by the relevant provision of this Part.

(2) . . .

(3) The Commission—
 (a) shall not grant a licence to any person unless they are satisfied that he is a fit and proper person to hold it, and
 (b) shall do all that they can to secure that, if they cease to be so satisfied in the case of any person holding a licence, that person does not remain the holder of the licence;

and nothing in this Part shall be construed as affecting the operation of this subsection or of section 5(1) or (2)(b) or (c).

(4)–(8) . . .

NOTES

Commencement: 1 October 1996.

Sub-ss (2), (4)–(8): outside the scope of this work.

Digital programme services

18 Licensing of digital programme services

(1)–(3) . . .

(4) Where an application for a digital programme licence is made to the Commission in accordance with the provisions of this section, they shall grant the licence unless precluded from doing so by section 3(3)(a) or 5(1).

(5) Subject to subsection (6), sections 6 to 12 of the 1990 Act (general provisions relating to services licensed under Part I of that Act) shall apply in relation to a digital programme service licensed under this Part as they apply in relation to a service licensed under that Part of that Act.

(6) In its application in relation to a digital programme service—

(a) section 6 of the 1990 Act shall have effect with the omission of subsection (8), and

(b) section 12(1)(b) of that Act shall have effect as if the reference to the Commission's functions under Chapter II of Part I of that Act included a reference to their functions under this Part.

NOTES

Commencement: 1 October 1996.

Sub-ss (1)–(3): outside the scope of this work.

Miscellaneous and supplemental

34 Promotion of equal opportunities and fair treatment

(1) Any multiplex licence or digital programme licence shall include conditions requiring the licence holder—

(a) to make arrangements for promoting, in relation to employment by him, equality of opportunity between men and women and between persons of different racial groups,

(b) to make arrangements for promoting, in relation to employment by him, the fair treatment of disabled persons, and

(c) to review those arrangements from time to time.

(2) In subsection (1) "racial group" has the same meaning as in the Race Relations Act 1976 [or, in Northern Ireland, the Race Relations (Northern Ireland) Order 1997], and "disabled person" has the same meaning as in the Disability Discrimination Act 1995.

NOTES

Commencement: 1 October 1996.

Sub-s (2): words in square brackets inserted by the Race Relations (Northern Ireland) Order 1997, SI 1997/869 (NI 6), art 73, Sch 2, para 9.

PART II
DIGITAL TERRESTRIAL SOUND BROADCASTING

Introductory

40 Radio multiplex services

(1) In this Part "radio multiplex service" means a service provided by any person which consists in the broadcasting for general reception of two or more services specified in subsection (3) by combining the relevant information in digital form, together with any broadcasting in digital form of digital additional services (as defined by section 63(1)).

(2) A service in respect of which a licence under section 46 or 50 is in force is not prevented from being a radio multiplex service at a particular time merely because only one service specified in subsection (3) is being broadcast in digital form at that time.

(3) The services referred to in subsections (1) and (2) are—
- (a) a digital sound programme service (as defined by subsection (5)), or
- (b) a simulcast radio service (as defined by section 41(2)).

(4)–(7) . . .

(8) In this section—

"broadcast" means broadcast otherwise than—
- (a) by satellite, or
- (b) in the provision of a local delivery service (as defined by section 72(1) of the 1990 Act), and

. . .

NOTES

Commencement: 1 October 1996.

Sub-ss (4)–(7) and words omitted from sub-s (8) outside the scope of this work.

General provisions about licences

42 Licences under Part II

(1) Any licence granted by the Radio Authority (in this Part referred to as "the Authority") under this Part shall be in writing and (subject to the provisions of this Part) shall continue in force for such period as is provided, in relation to a licence of the kind in question, by the relevant provision of this Part.

(2) The Authority—
- (a) shall not grant a licence to any person unless they are satisfied that he is a fit and proper person to hold it, and

(b) shall do all that they can to secure that, if they cease to be so satisfied in the case of any person holding a licence, that person does not remain the holder of the licence;

and nothing in this Part shall be construed as affecting the operation of this subsection or of section 44(1) or (2)(b) or (c).

(3)–(7) . . .

NOTES

Commencement: 1 October 1996.

Sub-ss (3)–(7): outside the scope of this work.

PART V
THE BROADCASTING STANDARDS COMMISSION

Establishment of Broadcasting Standards Commission

106 The Broadcasting Standards Commission

(1) There shall be a commission, to be known as the Broadcasting Standards Commission (in this Part referred to as "the BSC").

(2) The BSC shall consist of—

(a) a chairman appointed by the Secretary of State,

(b) a deputy chairman or two deputy chairmen so appointed, and

(c) such number of other members appointed by the Secretary of State as he may from time to time determine,

but so that the total number of members does not exceed fifteen.

(3) Schedule 3 shall have effect with respect to the BSC.

NOTES

Commencement: 1 April 1997.

Unjust or unfair treatment or unwarranted infringement of privacy

107 Preparation by BSC of code relating to avoidance of unjust or unfair treatment or interference with privacy

(1) It shall be the duty of the BSC to draw up, and from time to time review, a code giving guidance as to principles to be observed, and practices to be followed, in connection with the avoidance of—

(a) unjust or unfair treatment in programmes to which this section applies, or

(b) unwarranted infringement of privacy in, or in connection with the obtaining of material included in, such programmes.

(2) It shall be the duty of each broadcasting or regulatory body, when drawing up or revising any code relating to principles and practice in connection with programmes, or in connection with the obtaining of material to be included in programmes, to reflect the general effect of so much of the code referred to in subsection (1) (as for the time being in force) as is relevant to the programmes in question.

(3) The BSC shall from time to time publish the code (as for the time being in force).

(4) Before drawing up or revising the code, the BSC shall consult—
- (a) each broadcasting or regulatory body, and
- (b) such other persons as appear to the BSC to be appropriate.

(5) This section applies to—
- (a) any programme broadcast by the BBC,
- (b) any programme broadcast by the Welsh Authority or included in the service referred to in section 57(1A)(a) of the 1990 Act, and
- (c) any programme included in a licensed service.

NOTES

Commencement: 1 April 1997.

Portrayal of violence or sexual conduct etc

108 Preparation by BSC of code relating to broadcasting standards generally

(1) It shall be the duty of the BSC to draw up, and from time to time review, a code giving guidance as to—
- (a) practices to be followed in connection with the portrayal of violence in programmes to which this section applies,
- (b) practices to be followed in connection with the portrayal of sexual conduct in such programmes, and
- (c) standards of taste and decency for such programmes generally.

(2) It shall be the duty of each broadcasting or regulatory body, when drawing up or revising any code relating to standards and practice for programmes, to reflect the general effect of so much of the code referred to in subsection (1) (as for the time being in force) as is relevant to the programmes in question.

(3) The BSC shall from time to time publish the code referred to in subsection (1) (as for the time being in force).

(4) Before drawing up or revising the code the BSC shall consult—
- (a) each broadcasting or regulatory body, and
- (b) such other persons as appear to the BSC to be appropriate.

(5) This section applies to—
- (a) any programme broadcast by the BBC,
- (b) any programme broadcast by the Welsh Authority or included in the service referred to in section 57(1A)(a) of the 1990 Act,
- (c) any programme included in a licensed service, and
- (d) any programme included in so much of a local delivery service licensed under Part II of the 1990 Act as is, by virtue of section 79(2) or (4) of that Act, treated for certain purposes as the provision of a service licensed under Part I of that Act.

(6) The code drawn up by the Broadcasting Standards Council under section 152 of the 1990 Act, as that code is in force immediately before the commencement of this section, shall be taken to have been drawn up by the BSC under this section.

NOTES

Commencement: 1 April 1997.

Complaints

110 General functions of BSC in relation to complaints

(1) Subject to the provisions of this Part, it shall be the duty of the BSC to consider and adjudicate on complaints which are made to them in accordance with sections 111 and 114 and relate—

(a) to unjust or unfair treatment in programmes to which section 107 applies, or

(b) to unwarranted infringement of privacy in, or in connection with the obtaining of material included in, such programmes.

(2) Subject to those provisions, it shall also be the duty of the BSC to consider, and make findings on, complaints which are made to them in accordance with sections 113 and 114 and relate—

(a) to the portrayal of violence or sexual conduct in programmes to which section 108 applies, or

(b) to alleged failures on the part of such programmes to attain standards of taste and decency.

(3) In exercising their functions under subsection (1), the BSC shall take into account any relevant provisions of the code maintained by them under section 107; and in exercising their functions under subsection (2) they shall take into account any relevant provisions of the code maintained by them under section 108.

(4) In this Part—

"a fairness complaint" means a complaint to the BSC in respect of any of the matters referred to in subsection (1)(a) and (b), and

"a standards complaint" means a complaint to the BSC in respect of any of the matters referred to in subsection (2)(a) and (b).

NOTES

Commencement: 1 April 1997.

111 Complaints of unfair treatment etc

(1) A fairness complaint may be made by an individual or by a body of persons, whether incorporated or not, but, subject to subsection (2), shall not be entertained by the BSC unless made by the person affected or by a person authorised by him to make the complaint for him.

(2) Where the person affected is an individual who has died, a fairness complaint may be made by his personal representative or by a member of the family of the person affected, or by some other person or body closely connected with him (whether as his employer, or as a body of which he was at his death a member, or in any other way).

(3) Where the person affected is an individual who is for any reason both unable to make a complaint himself and unable to authorise another person to do so for him, a fairness complaint may be made by a member of the family of the person affected, or by some other person or body closely connected with him (whether as his employer, or as a body of which he is a member, or in any other way).

(4) The BSC shall not entertain, or proceed with the consideration of, a fairness complaint if it appears to them that the complaint relates to the broadcasting of the relevant programme, or to its inclusion in a licensed service, on an occasion more than five years after the death of the person affected, unless it appears to them that in the particular circumstances it is appropriate to do so.

(5) The BSC may refuse to entertain a fairness complaint if it appears to them not to have been made within a reasonable time after the last occasion on which the relevant programme was broadcast or, as the case may be, included in a licensed service.

(6) Where, in the case of a fairness complaint, the relevant programme was broadcast or included in a licensed service after the death of the person affected, subsection (5) shall apply as if at the end there were added "within five years (or such longer period as may be allowed by the BSC in the particular case under subsection (4)) after the death of the person affected".

(7) The BSC may refuse to entertain—
  (a) a fairness complaint which is a complaint of unjust or unfair treatment if the person named as the person affected was not himself the subject of the treatment complained of and it appears to the BSC that he did not have a sufficiently direct interest in the subject-matter of that treatment to justify the making of a complaint with him as the person affected, or
  (b) a complaint made under subsection (2) or (3) by a person other than the person affected or a person authorised by him, if it appears to the BSC that the complainant's connection with the person affected is not sufficiently close to justify the making of the complaint by him.

NOTES
Commencement: 1 April 1997.

119 Publication of BSC's findings

(1) Where the BSC have—
  (a) considered and adjudicated upon a fairness complaint, or
  (b) considered and made their findings on a standards complaint,

they may give directions of the kind specified in subsection (2).

(2) Those directions are—
  (a) where the relevant programme was broadcast by a broadcasting body, directions requiring that body to publish the matters mentioned in subsection (3) in such manner, and within such period, as may be specified in the directions, and
  (b) where the relevant programme was included in a licensed service, directions requiring the appropriate regulatory body to direct the licence holder to publish those matters in such manner, and within such period, as may be so specified.

(3) Those matters are—
  (a) a summary of the complaint;
  (b) the BSC's findings on the complaint or a summary of them;
  (c) in the case of a standards complaint, any observations by the BSC on the complaint or a summary of any such observations.

(4) References in subsection (2) to the publication of any matter are references to the publication of that matter without its being accompanied by any observations made by a person other than the BSC and relating to the complaint.

(5) The form and content of any such summary as is mentioned in subsection (3)(a), (b) or (c) shall be such as may be approved by the BSC.

(6) A broadcasting or regulatory body shall comply with any directions given to them under this section.

(7) Any licence to provide a licensed service which is granted by a regulatory body under this Act shall include conditions requiring the licence holder to comply with such directions as may be given to him by that body for the purpose of enabling them to comply with any directions given to them under this section.

(8) The BSC shall publish, monthly or at such other intervals as they think fit and in such manner as they think fit, reports each containing, as regards every fairness complaint or standards complaint which falls within this subsection and has been dealt with by them in the period covered by the report—

- (a) a summary of the complaint and the action taken by them on it,
- (b) where they have adjudicated on it, a summary of—
  - (i) their findings,
  - (ii) any direction given under subsection (1), or other action taken by them, in relation to the complaint, and
- (c) where a direction has been given under subsection (1) in relation to the complaint, a summary of any action taken by a broadcasting body, a regulatory body or the holder of a licence to provide a licensed service in pursuance of the direction.

(9) A fairness complaint or standards complaint made to the BSC falls within subsection (8) unless it is one which under section 111(1), (4) or (5), 113(1) or 114(2) they have refused to entertain.

(10) The BSC may, if they think fit, omit from any summary which is included in a report under subsection (8) and relates to a fairness complaint any information which could lead to the disclosure of the identity of any person connected with the complaint in question other than—

- (a) a broadcasting or regulatory body, or
- (b) a person providing a licensed service.

(11), (12) . . .

NOTES

Commencement: 1 April 1997.

Sub-ss (11), (12): outside the scope of this work.

121 Certain statements etc protected by qualified privilege for purposes of defamation

(1) For the purposes of the law relating to defamation—

- (a) publication of any statement in the course of the consideration by the BSC of, and their adjudication on, a fairness complaint,
- (b) publication by the BSC of directions under section 119(1) relating to a fairness complaint, or
- (c) publication of a report of the BSC, so far as the report relates to fairness complaints,

is privileged unless the publication is shown to be made with malice.

(2) Nothing in subsection (1) shall be construed as limiting any privilege subsisting apart from that subsection.

NOTES

Commencement: 1 April 1997.

PART VIII
MISCELLANEOUS AND GENERAL

General

150 Short title and extent

(1) This Act may be cited as the Broadcasting Act 1996.

(2) This Act, . . . extends to Northern Ireland.

(3), (4) . . .

NOTES

Commencement: 24 July 1996.
Sub-s (2): words omitted outside the scope of this work.
Sub-ss (3), (4): outside the scope of this work.

EDUCATION ACT 1996

(C 56)

An Act to consolidate the Education Act 1944 and certain other enactments relating to education, with amendments to give effect to recommendations of the Law Commission

[24 July 1996]

PART V
THE CURRICULUM

CHAPTER IV
MISCELLANEOUS AND SUPPLEMENTARY PROVISIONS

Politics

406 Political indoctrination

(1) The local education authority, governing body and head teacher shall forbid—

(a) the pursuit of partisan political activities by any of those registered pupils at a maintained school who are junior pupils, and

(b) the promotion of partisan political views in the teaching of any subject in the school.

(2) In the case of activities which take place otherwise than on the school premises, subsection (1)(a) applies only where arrangements for junior pupils to take part in the activities are made by—

(a) any member of the school's staff (in his capacity as such), or

(b) anyone acting on behalf of the school or of a member of the school's staff (in his capacity as such).

(3) In this section "maintained school" includes *a maintained special school* established in a hospital.

NOTES

Commencement: 1 November 1996.

Sub-s (3): for words in italics there are substituted words "a community or foundation special school", by the School Standards and Framework Act 1998, s 140(1), Sch 30, paras 57, 104, partly as from a day to be appointed.

407 Duty to secure balanced treatment of political issues

(1) The local education authority, governing body and head teacher shall take such steps as are reasonably practicable to secure that where political issues are brought to the attention of pupils while they are—

(a) in attendance at a maintained school, or

(b) taking part in extra-curricular activities which are provided or organised for registered pupils at the school by or on behalf of the school,

they are offered a balanced presentation of opposing views.

(2) In this section "maintained school" includes *a maintained special school* established in a hospital.

NOTES

Commencement: 1 November 1996.

Sub-s (2): for words in italics there are substituted words "a community or foundation special school", by the School Standards and Framework Act 1998, s 140(1), Sch 30, paras 57, 104, partly as from a day to be appointed.

PART X
MISCELLANEOUS AND GENERAL

CHAPTER VI
GENERAL

Final provisions

583 Short title, commencement and extent

(1) This Act may be cited as the Education Act 1996.

(2) Subject to subsection (3), this Act shall come into force on 1st November 1996 (and references to the commencement of this Act are to its coming into force on that date).

(3) . . .

(4) The Secretary of State may by order make such incidental, supplemental, saving or transitional provision as he thinks fit in connection with the coming into force in accordance with subsection (2) of any provision of this Act reproducing the effect of a provision of the Education Act 1993 which has not previously been brought into force by an order under section 308(3) of that Act (commencement).

(5) . . .

(6) Subject to subsections (7) and (8), this Act extends to England and Wales only.

(7), (8) . . .

NOTES

Commencement: 1 November 1996.

Sub-ss (3), (5), (7), (8): outside the scope of this work.

NORTHERN IRELAND (EMERGENCY PROVISIONS) ACT 1996

(C 22)

An Act to re-enact, with omissions and amendments, the Northern Ireland (Emergency Provisions) Act 1991; and for connected purposes

[17 June 1996]

PART II
POWERS OF ARREST, SEARCH AND SEIZURE, ETC

17 Entry and search of premises for purpose of arresting terrorists

For the purpose of arresting a person under section 14(1)(b) of the of premises for Prevention of Terrorism (Temporary Provisions) Act 1989 (arrest of persons suspected of being concerned in acts of terrorism) a constable may enter and search any premises or other place where that person is or where the constable has reasonable grounds for suspecting him to be.

NOTES
Commencement: 25 August 1996.

18 Constables' general power of arrest and seizure

(1) Any constable may arrest without warrant any person who he has reasonable grounds to suspect is committing, has committed or is about to commit a scheduled offence or an offence under this Act which is not a scheduled offence.

(2) For the purpose of arresting a person under this section a constable may enter and search any premises or other place where that person is or where the constable has reasonable grounds for suspecting him to be.

(3) A constable may seize anything which he has reasonable grounds to suspect is being, has been or is intended to be used in the commission of a scheduled offence or an offence under this Act which is not a scheduled offence.

NOTES
Commencement: 25 August 1996.

19 Powers of arrest and seizure by members of Her Majesty's forces

(1) Any member of Her Majesty's forces on duty may arrest without warrant, and detain for not more than four hours, a person who he has reasonable grounds to suspect is committing, has committed or is about to commit any offence.

(2) A person effecting an arrest under this section complies with any rule of law requiring him to state the ground of arrest if he states that he is effecting the arrest as a member of Her Majesty's forces.

(3) For the purpose of arresting a person under this section a member of Her Majesty's forces may enter and search any premises or other place—
- (a) where that person is, or
- (b) if there are reasonable grounds for suspecting that that person is a terrorist

or has committed an offence involving the use or possession of an explosive substance or firearm, where there are reasonable grounds for suspecting him to be.

(4) Any member of Her Majesty's forces may seize, and detain for not more than four hours, anything which he has reasonable grounds to suspect is being, has been or is intended to be used in the commission of an offence under section 26 or 27.

NOTES

Commencement: 25 August 1996.

20 Power to search for munitions, radio transmitters and scanning receivers

(1) Any member of Her Majesty's forces on duty or any constable may enter any premises or other place other than a dwelling-house for the purpose of ascertaining—

(a) whether there are any munitions unlawfully at that place;

(b) whether there is a transmitter at that place;

and may search the place for any munitions or transmitter with a view to exercising the powers conferred by subsection (7).

(2) Any member of Her Majesty's forces on duty authorised by a commissioned officer of those forces or any constable authorised by an officer of the Royal Ulster Constabulary not below the rank of inspector may enter any dwelling-house in which there are reasonable grounds for suspecting that there are unlawfully any munitions or that there is a transmitter and may search it for any munitions or transmitter with a view to exercising the said powers.

(3)–(5) . . .

(6) Any member of Her Majesty's forces on duty or any constable may—

(a) stop any person in any public place and, with a view to exercising the powers conferred by subsection (7), search him for the purpose of ascertaining whether he has any munitions unlawfully with him or any transmitter with him; and

(b) with a view to exercising the said powers—

(i) search any person not in a public place who he has reasonable grounds to suspect has any munitions unlawfully with him or any transmitter with him; and

(ii) search any person entering or found in a dwelling-house entered under subsection (2).

(7) Where a member of Her Majesty's forces or a constable is empowered by virtue of any provision of this Act to search any premises or other place or any person—

(a) he may seize any munitions found in the course of the search (unless it appears to him that the munitions are being, have been and will be used only lawfully) and may retain and, if necessary, destroy them; and

(b) he may seize any transmitter found in the course of the search (unless it appears to him that the transmitter has been, is being and is likely to be used only lawfully) and may retain it.

(8) The preceding provisions of this section shall have effect in relation to scanning receivers as they have effect in relation to transmitters.

(9) In this section—

"munitions" means—

(a) explosives, explosive substances, firearms and ammunition; and

(b) anything used or capable of being used in the manufacture of any explosive, explosive substance, firearm or ammunition;

"scanning receiver" means—

(a) any apparatus for wireless telegraphy designed or adapted for the purpose of automatically monitoring selected frequencies, or automatically scanning a selected range of frequencies, so as to enable transmissions on any of those frequencies to be detected or intercepted; or

(b) part of any such apparatus;

"transmitter" means any apparatus for wireless telegraphy designed or adapted for emission, as opposed to reception, or part of any such apparatus;

"wireless telegraphy" has the same meaning as in section 19(1) of the wireless Telegraphy Act 1949.

NOTES

Commencement: 25 August 1996.

Sub-ss (3)–(5): outside the scope of this work.

21 Section 20: supplementary provisions

(1) Where a member of Her Majesty's forces or a constable carries out a search under section 20(1) or (2) he shall, unless it is not practicable to make a written record of the search which shall specify—

(a) the address of the premises, or a description of the place, which is searched;

(b) the date and time of the search;

(c) any damage caused in the course of the search; and

(d) anything seized in the course of the search.

(2) Such a record shall also include the name (if known) of any person appearing to the person making the record to be the occupier of the premises or other place searched; but—

(a) a person may not be detained to find out his name; and

(b) if the person making the record does not know the name of a person appearing to him to be the occupier of the premises or other place searched, he shall include in the record a note otherwise describing him.

(3) . . .

(4) Where a record of a search is made under this section a copy of the record shall be supplied at once or, where that is not practicable, as soon as is practicable to any person appearing to the person making the record to be the occupier of the premises or other place searched.

(5) A person who wilfully fails to comply with a requirement imposed under section 20(4) or wilfully obstructs, or seeks to frustrate the object of, a search in relation to which such a requirement has been or could be imposed is guilty of an offence and liable—

(a) on conviction on indictment, to imprisonment for a term not exceeding two years or a fine or both;

(b) on summary conviction, to imprisonment for a term not exceeding six months or a fine not exceeding the statutory maximum or both.

(6) A person who fails to stop when required to do so under subsection (6) of section 20 is guilty of an offence and liable on summary conviction to a fine not exceeding level 5 on the standard scale.

NOTES

Commencement: 25 August 1996.

Sub-s (3): outside the scope of this work.

23 Entry to search for persons unlawfully detained

(1) Where any person is believed to be unlawfully detained in such circumstances that his life is in danger, any member of Her Majesty's forces on duty or any constable may, subject to subsection (2), enter any premises or other place for the purpose of ascertaining whether that person is so detained there.

(2) A dwelling-house may be entered in pursuance of subsection (1)—

(a) by a member of Her Majesty's forces, only when authorised to do so by a commissioned officer of those forces; and

(b) by a constable, only when authorised to do so by an officer of the Royal Ulster Constabulary not below the rank of inspector.

NOTES

Commencement: 25 August 1996.

25 Power to stop and question

(1) Any member of Her Majesty's forces on duty or any constable may stop any person for so long as is necessary in order to question him for the purpose of ascertaining—

(a) that person's identity and movements;

(b) what he knows concerning any recent explosion or any other recent incident endangering life or concerning any person killed or injured in any such explosion or incident; or

(c) any one or more of the matters referred to in paragraphs (a) and (b).

(2) Any person who—

(a) fails to stop when required to do so under this section, or

(b) refuses to answer, or fails to answer to the best of his knowledge and ability, any question addressed to him under this section,

is guilty of an offence and liable on summary conviction to a fine not exceeding level 5 on the standard scale.

NOTES

Commencement: 25 August 1996.

26 General powers of entry and interference with rights of property and with highways

(1) Any member of Her Majesty's forces on duty or any constable may enter any premises or other place—

(a) if he considers it necessary to do so in the course of operations for the preservation of the peace or the maintenance of order; or

(b) if authorised to do so by or on behalf of the Secretary of State.

(2) Any member of Her Majesty's forces on duty, any constable or any person specifically authorised to do so by or on behalf of the Secretary of State may, if authorised to do so by or on behalf of the Secretary of State—

(a) take possession of any land or other property;
(b) take steps to place buildings or other structures in a state of defence;
(c) detain any property or cause it to be destroyed or moved;
(d) do any other act interfering with any public right or with any private rights of property, including carrying out any works on any land of which possession has been taken under this subsection.

(3) Any member of Her Majesty's forces on duty, any constable or any person specifically authorised to do so by or on behalf of the Secretary of State may, so far as he considers it immediately necessary for the preservation of the peace or the maintenance of order—

(a) wholly or partly close a highway or divert or otherwise interfere with a highway or the use of a highway; or
(b) prohibit or restrict the exercise of any right of way or the use of any waterway.

(4) Any person who, without lawful authority or reasonable excuse (the proof of which lies on him), interferes with works executed, or any apparatus, equipment or any other thing used, in or in connection with the exercise of powers conferred by this section is guilty of an offence and liable on summary conviction to imprisonment for a term not exceeding six months or a fine not exceeding level 5 on the standard scale or both.

(5) Any authorisation to exercise any powers under any provision of this section may authorise the exercise of all those powers, or powers of any class or a particular power specified, either by all persons by whom they are capable of being exercised or by persons of any class or a particular person specified.

NOTES
Commencement: 25 August 1996.

PART III
OFFENCES AGAINST PUBLIC SECURITY AND PUBLIC ORDER

30 Proscribed organisations

(1) Subject to subsection (6), any person who—

(a) belongs or professes to belong to a proscribed organisation; or
(b) solicits or invites support for a proscribed organisation other than support with money or other property; or
(c) solicits or invites any person to become a member of a proscribed organisation or to carry out on behalf of a proscribed organisation orders or directions given, or requests made, by a member of that organisation; or
(d) arranges or assists in the arrangement or management of, or addresses, any meeting of three or more persons (whether or not it is a meeting to which the public are admitted) knowing that the meeting—
  (i) is to support a proscribed organisation;
  (ii) is to further the activities of such an organisation; or
  (iii) is to be addressed by a person belonging or professing to belong to such an organisation,

is guilty of an offence and liable on conviction on indictment to imprisonment for a term not exceeding ten years or a fine or both and on summary conviction to imprisonment for a term not exceeding six months or a fine not exceeding the statutory maximum or both.

(2) The organisations specified in Schedule 2 to this Act are proscribed organisations for the purposes of this Act; and any organisation which passes under a name mentioned in that Schedule shall be treated as proscribed, whatever relationship (if any) it has to any other organisation of the same name.

(3) The Secretary of State may by order add to Schedule 2 to this Act any organisation that appears to him to be concerned in terrorism or in promoting or encouraging it.

(4) The Secretary of State may also by order remove an organisation from Schedule 2 to this Act.

(5) The possession by a person of a document—

(a) addressed to him as a member of a proscribed organisation; or

(b) relating or purporting to relate to the affairs of a proscribed organisation; or

(c) emanating or purporting to emanate from a proscribed organisation or officer of a proscribed organisation,

shall be evidence of that person belonging to the organisation at the time when he had the document in his possession.

(6) A person belonging to a proscribed organisation shall—

(a) if the organisation is a proscribed organisation by virtue of an order under subsection (3); or

(b) if this section has ceased to be in force but has been subsequently brought into force by an order under section 62(3),

not be guilty of an offence under this section by reason of belonging to the organisation if he has not after the coming into force of the order under subsection (3) or the coming into force again of this section, as the case may be, taken part in any activities of the organisation.

(7) Subsection (6) shall apply in relation to a person belonging to the Red Hand Commando, the Ulster Freedom Fighters, the Ulster Volunteer Force, the Irish National Liberation Army, the Irish People's Liberation Organisation or the Ulster Defence Association as if the organisation were proscribed by virtue of an order under subsection (3) with the substitution in subsection (6) for the reference to the coming into force of such an order of a reference—

(a) as respects a person belonging to the Red Hand Commando or the Ulster Freedom Fighters, to 12th November 1973;

(b) as respects a person belonging to the Ulster Volunteer Force, to 4th October 1975;

(c) as respects a person belonging to the Irish National Liberation Army, to 3rd July 1979;

(d) as respects a person belonging tb the Irish People's Liberation Organisation, to 29th March 1990;

(e) as respects a person belonging to the Ulster Defence Association, to 11th August 1992

[30A Evidence and inferences

(1) This section applies where a person is charged with an offence under section 30(1)(a); and references here to a specified organisation must be construed in accordance with section 30B.

(2)–(11) . . .

NOTES

Commencement: 4 September 1998.

Inserted by the Criminal Justice (Terrorism and Conspiracy) Act 1998, s 2.

Sub-ss (2)–(11): replicate the Prevention of Terrorism (Temporary Provisions) Act 1989, s 2A (with the omission of the words "in England and Wales" wherever occurring.

[30B Specified organisations

(1) For the purposes of section 30A an organisation is specified at a particular time if at that time—

(a) it is specified under section 3(8) of the Northern Ireland (Sentences) Act 1998 or under subsection (2) below, and

(b) it is, or forms part of, an organisation which is proscribed for the purposes of this Act.

(2) If the condition in subsection (3) is satisfied the Secretary of State may by order specify an organisation which is not specified under section 3(8) of the Northern Ireland (Sentences) Act 1998.

(3) The condition is that the Secretary of State believes that the organisation—

(a) is concerned in terrorism connected with the affairs of Northern Ireland, or in promoting or encouraging it, and

(b) has not established or is not maintaining a complete and unequivocal ceasefire.

(4) An order under this section shall be made by statutory instrument; and no order shall be made unless a draft has been laid before, and approved by resolution of, each House of Parliament.]

NOTES

Commencement: 4 September 1998.

Inserted by the Criminal Justice (Terrorism and Conspiracy) Act 1998, s 2.

31 Display of support in public for a proscribed organisation

Any person who in a public place—

(a) wears any item of dress; or

(b) wears, carries or displays any article,

in such a way or in such circumstances as to arouse reasonable apprehension that he is a member or supporter of a proscribed organisation is guilty of an offence and liable—

(i) on conviction on indictment, to imprisonment for a term not exceeding one year or a fine or both;

(ii) on summary conviction, to imprisonment for a term not exceeding six months or a fine not exceeding the statutory maximum or both.

NOTES

Commencement: 25 August 1996.

PART VI
PERSONS IN POLICE CUSTODY UNDER TERRORISM PROVISIONS

45 The terrorism provisions and police custody

(1) In this Part of this Act "the terrorism provisions" means section 14 of the Prevention of Terrorism (Temporary Provisions) Act 1989 and any provision of Schedule 2 or 5 to that Act conferring a power of arrest or detention.

(2) A person is held in police custody for the purposes of this Part of this Act if he is detained at a police station or is detained elsewhere in the charge of a constable except that a person who is at a court after being charged with an offence is not held in police custody for the purposes of section 46 below.

NOTES

Commencement: 25 August 1996.

46 Right to have someone informed of detention under terrorism provisions

(1) A person who is detained under the terrorism provisions is being held in police custody shall be entitled, if he so requests, to have one friend or relative or other person who is known to him or is likely to take an interest in his welfare told that he is being detained under those provisions and where he is being held in police custody.

(2) A person shall be informed of the right conferred on him by subsection (1) as soon as practicable after he has become a person to whom that subsection applies.

(3) A request made by a person under subsection (1), and the time at which it is made, shall be recorded in writing.

(4) If a person makes such a request, it must be complied with as soon as is practicable except to the extent that any delay is permitted by this section.

(5) Any delay in complying with such a request is only permitted if—

(a) it is authorised by an officer of at least the rank of superintendent; and

(b) it does not extend beyond the end of the period referred to in subsection (6).

(6) That period is—

(a) except where paragraph (b) applies, the period of forty-eight hours beginning with the time when the detained person was first detained under the terrorism provisions;

(b) where the detained person was, prior to the time when he was first so detained, being examined in accordance with paragraph 2 of Schedule 5 to the Prevention of Terrorism (Temporary Provisions) Act 1989, the period of forty-eight hours beginning with the time when he was first so examined.

(7) An officer may give an authorisation under subsection (5) orally or in writing but, if he gives it orally, he shall confirm it in writing as soon as is practicable.

(8) An officer may only authorise a delay in complying with a request under subsection (1) where he has reasonable grounds for believing that telling the person named in the request of the detention of the detained person—

(a) will lead to interference with or harm to evidence connected with a scheduled offence or interference with or physical injury to any person; or
(b) will lead to the alerting of any person suspected of having committed such an offence but not yet arrested for it; or
(c) will hinder the recovery of any property obtained as a result of such an offence; or
(d) will lead to interference with the gathering of information about the commission, preparation or instigation of acts of terrorism; or
(e) by alerting any person, will make it more difficult—
(i) to prevent an act of terrorism; or
(ii) to secure the apprehension, prosecution or conviction of any person in connection with the commission, preparation or instigation of an act of terrorism.

(9) If any delay is authorised, then, as soon as is practicable—

(a) the detained person shall be told the reason for authorising it; and
(b) the reason shall be recorded in writing.

(10) Any authorisation under subsection (5) shall cease to have effect once the reason for giving it ceases to subsist.

(11) The right conferred by subsection (1) may be exercised by a person to whom that subsection applies on each occasion when he is transferred from one place to another; and this section applies to each subsequent occasion on which that right is so exercised as it applies to the first such occasion.

(12) Subsection (11) shall not be construed as prejudicing the operation of a request by a person to whom subsection (1) applies which was made, but not complied with, before he was transferred.

NOTES
Commencement: 25 August 1996.

47 Right of access to legal advice

(1) A person who is detained under the terrorism provisions and is being held in police custody shall be entitled, if he so requests, to consult a solicitor privately.

(2) A person shall be informed of the right conferred on him by subsection (1) as soon as practicable after he has become a person to whom that subsection applies.

(3) A request made by a person under subsection (1), and the time at which it is made, shall be recorded in writing unless it is made by him while at a court after being charged with an offence.

(4) If a person makes such a request, he must be permitted to consult a solicitor as soon as is practicable except to the extent that any delay is permitted by this section.

(5) Any delay in complying with a request under subsection (1) is only permitted if—

(a) it is authorised by an officer of at least the rank of superintendent; and
(b) it does not extend beyond the relevant time.

(6) In subsection (5) "the relevant time" means—

(a) where the request is the first request made by the detained person under subsection (1), the end of the period referred to in section 46(6); or

(b) where the request follows an earlier request made by the detained person under that subsection in pursuance of which he has consulted a solicitor, the end of the period of forty-eight hours beginning with the time when that consultation began.

(7) An officer may give an authorisation under subsection (5) orally or in writing but, if he gives it orally, he shall confirm it in writing as soon as is practicable.

(8) An officer may only authorise a delay in complying with a request under subsection (1) where he has reasonable grounds for believing that the exercise of the right conferred by that subsection at the time when the detained person desires to exercise it—

(a) will lead to interference with or harm to evidence connected with a scheduled offence or interference with or physical injury to any person; or

(b) will lead to the alerting of any person suspected of having committed such an offence but not yet arrested for it; or

(c) will hinder the recovery of any property obtained as a result of such an offence; or

(d) will lead to interference with the gathering of information about the commission, preparation or instigation of acts of terrorism; or

(e) by alerting any person, will make it more difficult—

(i) to prevent an act of terrorism; or

(ii) to secure the apprehension, prosecution or conviction of any person in connection with the commission, preparation or instigation of an act of terrorism.

(9) If any delay is authorised, then, as soon as is practicable—

(a) the detained person shall be told the reason for authorising it; and

(b) the reason shall be recorded in writing.

(10) If an officer of at least the rank of Assistant Chief Constable has reasonable grounds for believing that, unless he gives a direction under subsection (11), the exercise by a person of the right conferred by subsection (1) will have any of the consequences specified in subsection (8), he may give a direction under subsection (11).

(11) A direction under this subsection is a direction that a person desiring to exercise the right conferred by subsection (1) may only consult a solicitor in the sight and hearing of a qualified officer of the uniformed branch of the Royal Ulster Constabulary.

(12) An officer is qualified for the purposes of subsection (11) if—

(a) he is of at least the rank of inspector; and

(b) in the opinion of the officer giving the direction, he has no connection with the case.

(13) Any authorisation under subsection (5) or direction under subsection (11) shall cease to have effect once the reason for giving it ceases to subsist.

NOTES

Commencement: 25 August 1996.

PART VIII
SUPPLEMENTARY

62 Commencement, duration, expiry and revival of provisions of this Act

(1) This Act shall come into force on 25th August 1996.

(2) The temporary provisions of this Act, that is to say, Parts I to VII except—
- (a) section 7, Part III of Schedule 1 and, so far as they relate to offences which are scheduled offences by virtue of that Part, sections 3, 10 and 11; and
- (b) sections 55 and 56,

shall (subject and without prejudice to subsection (3)) expire with [15th June 1999].

(3) The Secretary of State may by order provide—
- (a) that all or any of the temporary provisions of this Act which are for the time being in force (including any in force by virtue of an order under this section) shall continue in force for a period not exceeding twelve months from the coming into operation of the order;
- (b) that all or any of those provisions which are for the time being in force shall cease to be in force; or
- (c) that all or any of those provisions which are not for the time being in force shall come into force again and remain in force for a period not exceeding twelve months from the coming into operation of the order.

(4) An order under subsection (3) which relates to section 20, 23, 24, 25 or 26 may provide for the continuance, cessation or revival of that section—
- (a) generally,
- (b) only in so far as it concerns powers of members of Her Majesty's Forces, or
- (c) except in so far as it concerns powers of members of Her Majesty's Forces.

(5) . . .

(6)–(9) . . .

(10) This Act shall, by virtue of this subsection, be repealed as from the end of [24th August 2000].

NOTES

Commencement: 25 August 1996.

Sub-s (2): words in square brackets substituted by the Northern Ireland (Emergency Provisions) Act 1998, s 1(1), (2).

Sub-s (5): repealed by the Northern Ireland (Emergency Provisions) Act 1998, s 7, Sch 1, para 3(1), (4), Sch 2.

Sub-ss (6)–(9): outside the scope of this work.

Sub-s (10): words in square brackets substituted by the Northern Ireland (Emergency Provisions) Act 1998, s 1(1), (3).

64 Short title and extent

(1) This Act may be cited as the Northern Ireland (Emergency Provisions) Act 1996.

(2) This Act extends to Northern Ireland only . . .

NOTES

Commencement: 25 August 1996.

Sub-s (2): words omitted outside the scope of this work.

FIREARMS (AMENDMENT) ACT 1997

(C 5)

An Act to amend the Firearms Acts 1968 to 1992; to make provision in relation to the licensing and regulation of pistol clubs; to make further provision for regulating the possession of, and transactions relating to, firearms and ammunition; and for connected purposes

[27 February 1997]

PART III
REGULATION OF FIREARMS AND AMMUNITION

Miscellaneous

43 Power of search with warrant

(1) For section 46 of the 1968 Act (power of search with warrant), there shall be substituted the following section—

"46 Power of search with warrant

(1) If a justice of the peace or, in Scotland, the sheriff, is satisfied by information on oath that there is reasonable ground for suspecting—

(a) that an offence relevant for the purposes of this section has been, is being, or is about to be committed; or

(b) that, in connection with a firearm or ammunition, there is a danger to the public safety or to the peace,

he may grant a warrant for any of the purposes mentioned in subsection (2) below.

(2) A warrant under this section may authorise a constable or civilian officer—

(a) to enter at any time any premises or place named in the warrant, if necessary by force, and to search the premises or place and every person found there;

(b) to seize and detain anything which he may find on the premises or place, or on any such person, in respect of which or in connection with which he has reasonable ground for suspecting—

(i) that an offence relevant for the purposes of this section has been, is being or is about to be committed; or

(ii) that in connection with a firearm, imitation firearm or ammunition there is a danger to the public safety or to the peace.

(3) The power of a constable or civilian officer under subsection (2)(b) above to seize and detain anything found on any premises or place shall include power to require any information which is kept by means of a computer and is accessible from the premises or place to be produced in a form in which it is visible and legible and can be taken away.

(4) The offences relevant for the purposes of this section are all offences under this Act except an offence under section 22(3) or an offence relating specifically to air weapons.

(5) It is an offence for any person intentionally to obstruct a constable or civilian officer in the exercise of his powers under this section."

(2), (3) . . .

NOTES

Commencement: 1 July 1997.
"1968 Act" is the Firearms Act 1968.
Sub-s (2): amends the Firearms Act 1968, s 57(4).
Sub-s (3): amends the Firearms Act 1968, Sch 6, Pt I.

PART IV
FINAL PROVISIONS

53 Short title, commencement and extent

(1) This Act may be cited as the Firearms (Amendment) Act 1997.

(2) This Act and the Firearms Acts 1968 to 1992 may be cited together as the Firearms Acts 1968 to 1997.

(3) This Act shall come into force on such day as the Secretary of State may by order made by statutory instrument appoint; and different days may be appointed for different purposes and different areas.

(4) . . .

NOTES

Commencement: 27 February 1997.
Sub-s (4): outside the scope of this work.

CIVIL PROCEDURE ACT 1997

(C 12)

An Act to amend the law about civil procedure in England and Wales; and for connected purposes
[27 February 1997]

Rules and directions

1 Civil Procedure Rules

(1) There are to be rules of court (to be called "Civil Procedure Rules") governing the practice and procedure to be followed in—

(a) the civil division of the Court of Appeal,
(b) the High Court, and
(c) county courts.

(2) . . .

(3) The power to make Civil Procedure Rules is to be exercised with a view to securing that the civil justice system is accessible, fair and efficient.

NOTES

Commencement: 27 April 1997.
Sub-s (2): outside the scope of this work.

2 Rule Committee

(1) Civil Procedure Rules are to be made by a committee known as the Civil Procedure Rule Committee, which is to consist of—

(a) the Master of the Rolls,
(b) the Vice-Chancellor, and
(c) the persons currently appointed by the Lord Chancellor under subsection (2).

(2) The Lord Chancellor must appoint—

(a) one judge of the Supreme Court,
(b) one Circuit judge,
(c) one district judge,
(d) one person who is a Master referred to in Part II of Schedule 2 to the Supreme Court Act 1981,
(e) three persons who have a Supreme Court qualification (within the meaning of section 71 of the Courts and Legal Services Act 1990), including at least one with particular experience of practice in county courts,
(f) three persons who have been granted by an authorised body, under Part II of that Act, the right to conduct litigation in relation to all proceedings in the Supreme Court, including at least one with particular experience of practice in county courts,
(g) one person with experience in and knowledge of consumer affairs, and
(h) one person with experience in and knowledge of the lay advice sector.

(3)–(5) . . .

(6) The Civil Procedure Rule Committee must, before making or amending Civil Procedure Rules—

(a) consult such persons as they consider appropriate, and
(b) meet (unless it is inexpedient to do so).

(7) The Civil Procedure Rule Committee must, when making Civil Procedure Rules, try to make rules which are both simple and simply expressed.

(8) Rules made by the Civil Procedure Rule Committee must be signed by at least eight members of the Committee and be submitted to the Lord Chancellor, who may allow or disallow them.

NOTES

Commencement: 27 April 1997.
Sub-ss (3)–(5): outside the scope of this work.

3 Section 2: supplementary

(1) Rules made and allowed under section 2 are to—

(a) come into force on such day as the Lord Chancellor may direct, and
(b) be contained in a statutory instrument to which the Statutory Instruments Act 1946 is to apply as if it contained rules made by a Minister of the Crown.

(2) A statutory instrument containing Civil Procedure Rules shall be subject to annulment in pursuance of a resolution of either House of Parliament.

NOTES

Commencement: 27 April 1997.

4 Power to make consequential amendments

(1) The Lord Chancellor may by order amend, repeal or revoke any enactment to the extent he considers necessary or desirable in consequence of—

(a) section 1 or 2, or

(b) Civil Procedure Rules.

(2) The Lord Chancellor may by order amend, repeal or revoke any enactment passed or made before the commencement of this section to the extent he considers necessary or desirable in order to facilitate the making of Civil Procedure Rules.

(3) . . .

(4) A statutory instrument containing an order under subsection (1) shall be subject to annulment in pursuance of a resolution of either House of Parliament.

(5) No order may be made under subsection (2) unless a draft of it has been laid before and approved by resolution of each House of Parliament.

NOTES

Commencement: 27 April 1997.

Sub-s (3): outside the scope of this work.

5 Practice directions

(1) Practice directions may provide for any matter which, by virtue of paragraph 3 of Schedule 1, may be provided for by Civil Procedure Rules.

(2) . . .

NOTES

Commencement: 27 April 1997.

Sub-s (2): outside the scope of this work.

Civil Justice Council

6 Civil Justice Council

(1) The Lord Chancellor is to establish and maintain an advisory body, to be known as the Civil Justice Council.

(2) The Council must include—

(a) members of the judiciary,

(b) members of the legal professions,

(c) civil servants concerned with the administration of the courts,

(d) persons with experience in and knowledge of consumer affairs,

(e) persons with experience in and knowledge of the lay advice sector, and

(f) persons able to represent the interests of particular kinds of litigants (for example, businesses or employees).

(3) The functions of the Council are to include—

(a) keeping the civil justice system under review,

(b) considering how to make the civil justice system more accessible, fair and efficient,

(c) advising the Lord Chancellor and the judiciary on the development of the civil justice system,

(d) referring proposals for changes in the civil justice system to the Lord Chancellor and the Civil Procedure Rule Committee, and

(e) making proposals for research.

(4) . . .

NOTES

Commencement: 27 April 1997.

Sub-s (4): outside the scope of this work.

General

11 Short title, commencement and extent

(1) This Act may be cited as the Civil Procedure Act 1997.

(2) Sections 1 to 10 are to come into force on such day as the Lord Chancellor may by order made by statutory instrument appoint, and different days may be appointed for different purposes.

(3) This Act extends to England and Wales only.

NOTES

Commencement: 27 April 1997.

SCHEDULES

SCHEDULE 1

Section 1

CIVIL PROCEDURE RULE

Matters dealt with by the former rules

1. Among the matters which Civil Procedure Rules may be made about are any matters which were governed by the former Rules of the Supreme Court or the former county court rules (that is, the Rules of the Supreme Court (Revision) 1965 and the County Court Rules 1981).

Exercise of jurisdiction

2. Civil Procedure Rules may provide for the exercise of the jurisdiction of any court within the scope of the rules by officers or other staff of the court.

3. . . .

Evidence

4. Civil Procedure Rules may modify the rules of evidence as they apply to proceedings in any court within the scope of the rules.

Application of other rules

5.—(1) Civil Procedure Rules may apply any rules of court which relate to a court which is outside the scope of Civil Procedure Rules.

(2)–(4) . . .

6, 7. . . .

NOTES

Commencement: 27 April 1997.

Paras 3, 6, 7: outside the scope of this work.

Para 5: sub-paras (2)–(4) outside the scope of this work.

KNIVES ACT 1997

(C 21)

An Act to create new criminal offences in relation to the possession or marketing of, and publications relating to, knives; to confer powers on the police to stop and search people or vehicles for knives and other offensive weapons and to seize items found; and for connected purposes

[19 March 1997]

Supplementary powers

5 Supplementary powers of entry, seizure and retention

(1) If, on an application made by a constable, a justice of the peace or sheriff is satisfied that there are reasonable grounds for suspecting—

(a) that a person ("the suspect") has committed an offence under section 1 in relation to knives of a particular description, and

(b) that knives of that description and in the suspect's possession or under his control are to be found on particular premises,

the justice or sheriff may issue a warrant authorising a constable to enter those premises, search for the knives and seize and remove any that he finds.

(2) If, on an application made by a constable, a justice of the peace or sheriff is satisfied that there are reasonable grounds for suspecting—

(a) that a person ("the suspect") has committed an offence under section 2 in relation to particular material, and

(b) that publications consisting of or containing that material and in the suspect's possession or under his control are to be found on particular premises,

the justice or sheriff may issue a warrant authorising a constable to enter those premises, search for the publications and seize and remove any that he finds.

(3) A constable, in the exercise of his powers under a warrant issued under this section, may if necessary use reasonable force.

(4) Any knives or publications which have been seized and removed by a constable under a warrant issued under this section may be retained until the conclusion of proceedings against the suspect.

(5) . . .

(6) In this section "premises" includes any place and, in particular, any vehicle, vessel, aircraft or hovercraft and any tent or movable structure.

NOTES

Commencement: 1 September 1997.

Sub-s (5): outside the scope of this work.

Miscellaneous

11 Short title, commencement, extent etc

(1) This Act may be cited as the Knives Act 1997.

(2)–(6) . . .

(7) . . . , this Act extends to Northern Ireland.

NOTES

Commencement: 19 March 1997.

Sub-ss (2)–(6) and words omitted from sub-s (7) outside the scope of this work.

JUSTICES OF THE PEACE ACT 1997

(C 25)

An Act to consolidate the Justices of the Peace Act 1979 and provisions of Part IV of the Police and Magistrates' Courts Act 1994

[19 March 1997]

PART II
JUSTICES OF THE PEACE

Justices other than stipendiary magistrates

5 Appointment and removal of justices of the peace

(1) Subject to the following provisions of this Act, justices of the peace for any commission area shall be appointed by the Lord Chancellor by instrument on behalf and in the name of Her Majesty and a justice so appointed may be removed from office in like manner.

(2) Subsection (1) above—

(a) does not apply to stipendiary magistrates; and

(b) is without prejudice to the position of the Lord Mayor and aldermen as justices for the City of London by virtue of the charters of the City.

NOTES

Commencement: 19 June 1997.

Stipendiary magistrates

11 Appointment and removal of stipendiary magistrates

(1) Her Majesty may appoint a person who has a 7 year general qualification (within the meaning of section 71 of the Courts and Legal Services Act 1990) to be, during Her Majesty's pleasure, a whole-time stipendiary magistrate in any commission area or areas outside the inner London area and the City of London, and may appoint more than one such magistrate in the same area or areas.

(2) A person so appointed to be a stipendiary magistrate in any commission area shall by virtue of his office be a justice of the peace for that area.

(3) Any stipendiary magistrate appointed under this section—

(a) shall be a person recommended to Her Majesty by the Lord Chancellor; and

(b) shall not be removed from office except on the Lord Chancellor's recommendation.

(4) The number of stipendiary magistrates appointed under this section shall not at any time exceed 50 or such other number (which is not less than 40) as Her Majesty may from time to time by Order in Council specify.

(5) No Order in Council may be made under subsection (4) above unless a draft of the Order has been laid before Parliament and approved by resolution of each House.

NOTES

Commencement: 19 June 1997.

Metropolitan stipendiary magistrates

16 Appointment, removal and retirement of metropolitan stipendiary magistrates

(1) Metropolitan stipendiary magistrates shall be appointed by Her Majesty, and Her Majesty shall from time to time appoint such number of persons as is necessary; but the number of metropolitan stipendiary magistrates shall not at any time exceed 60 or such larger number as Her Majesty may from time to time by Order in Council specify.

(2) A person shall not be qualified to be appointed a metropolitan stipendiary magistrate unless he has a 7 year general qualification (within the meaning of section 71 of the Courts and Legal Services Act 1990).

(3) The Lord Chancellor shall designate one of the metropolitan stipendiary magistrates to be the chief metropolitan stipendiary magistrate.

(4) Each metropolitan stipendiary magistrate—

- (a) shall by virtue of his office be a justice of the peace for each of the London commission areas and for the retained counties of Essex, Hertfordshire, Kent and Surrey; and
- (b) may be removed from office by the Lord Chancellor for inability or misbehaviour.

(5) . . .

(6) No Order in Council shall be made under subsection (1) above unless a draft of the Order has been laid before Parliament and approved by resolution of each House.

NOTES

Commencement: 19 June 1997.

Sub-s (5): outside the scope of this work.

PART IV
JUSTICES' CHIEF EXECUTIVES, JUSTICES' CLERKS AND STAFF

48 Independence of justices' clerk and staff in relation to legal functions

(1) When exercising the functions specified in subsection (2) below or giving advice to justices of the peace in an individual case—

- (a) a justices' clerk shall not be subject to the direction of the magistrates' courts committee, the justices' chief executive or any other person; and
- (b) any member of the staff of a magistrates' courts committee shall not be subject to the direction of that committee or of the justices' chief executive (when acting as such).

(2) The functions referred to in subsection (1) above are functions conferred by rules made in accordance with section 144 of the Magistrates' Courts Act 1980 by virtue of section 45(1) or (2) above.

NOTES
Commencement: 19 June 1997.

PART V
PROTECTION AND INDEMNIFICATION OF JUSTICES AND JUSTICES' CLERKS

51 Immunity for acts within jurisdiction

No action shall lie against any justice of the peace or justices' clerk in respect of any act or omission of his—

(a) in the execution of his duty—
  (i) as such a justice; or
  (ii) as such a clerk exercising, by virtue of any statutory provision, any of the functions of a single justice; and
(b) with respect to any matter within his jurisdiction.

NOTES
Commencement: 19 June 1997.

52 Immunity for certain acts beyond jurisdiction

An action shall lie against any justice of the peace or justices' clerk in respect of any act or omission of his—

(a) in the purported execution of his duty—
  (i) as such a justice; or
  (ii) as such a clerk exercising, by virtue of any statutory provision, any of the functions of a single justice; but
(b) with respect to a matter which is not within his jurisdiction,

if, but only if, it is proved that he acted in bad faith.

NOTES
Commencement: 19 June 1997.

PART VIII
MISCELLANEOUS AND SUPPLEMENTARY PROVISIONS

75 Short title and extent

(1) This Act may be cited as the Justices of the Peace Act 1997.

(2)–(5) . . .

NOTES
Commencement: 19 June 1997.
Sub-ss (2)–(5): outside the scope of this work.

PROTECTION FROM HARASSMENT ACT 1997

(C 40)

An Act to make provision for protecting persons from harassment and similar conduct

[21 March 1997]

England and Wales

1 Prohibition of harassment

(1) A person must not pursue a course of conduct—

(a) which amounts to harassment of another, and

(b) which he knows or ought to know amounts to harassment of the other.

(2) For the purposes of this section, the person whose course of conduct is in question ought to know that it amounts to harassment of another if a reasonable person in possession of the same information would think the course of conduct amounted to harassment of the other.

(3) Subsection (1) does not apply to a course of conduct if the person who pursued it shows—

(a) that it was pursued for the purpose of preventing or detecting crime,

(b) that it was pursued under any enactment or rule of law or to comply with any condition or requirement imposed by any person under any enactment, or

(c) that in the particular circumstances the pursuit of the course of conduct was reasonable.

NOTES

Commencement: 16 June 1997.

2 Offence of harassment

(1) A person who pursues a course of conduct in breach of section 1 is guilty of an offence.

(2), (3) . . .

NOTES

Commencement: 16 June 1997.

Sub-s (2): outside the scope of this work

Sub-s (3): amends the Police and Criminal Evidence Act 1984, s 24(2).

3 Civil remedy

(1) An actual or apprehended breach of section 1 may be the subject of a claim in civil proceedings by the person who is or may be the victim of the course of conduct in question.

(2) On such a claim, damages may be awarded for (among other things) any anxiety caused by the harassment and any financial loss resulting from the harassment.

(3) Where—

(a) in such proceedings the High Court or a county court grants an injunction for the purpose of restraining the defendant from pursuing any conduct which amounts to harassment, and

(b) the plaintiff considers that the defendant has done anything which he is prohibited from doing by the injunction,

the plaintiff may apply for the issue of a warrant for the arrest of the defendant.

(4) . . .

(5) The judge or district judge to whom an application under subsection (3) is made may only issue a warrant if—

(a) the application is substantiated on oath, and

(b) the judge or district judge has reasonable grounds for believing that the defendant has done anything which he is prohibited from doing by the injunction.

(6) Where—

(a) the High Court or a county court grants an injunction for the purpose mentioned in subsection (3)(a), and

(b) without reasonable excuse the defendant does anything which he is prohibited from doing by the injunction,

he is guilty of an offence.

(7) Where a person is convicted of an offence under subsection (6) in respect of any conduct, that conduct is not punishable as a contempt of court.

(8) A person cannot be convicted of an offence under subsection (6) in respect of any conduct which has been punished as a contempt of court.

(9) . . .

NOTES

Commencement: 16 June 1997 (sub-ss (1), (2)); 1 September 1998 (sub-ss (3), (5)–(8)).
Sub-ss (4), (9): outside the scope of this work.

4 Putting people in fear of violence

(1) A person whose course of conduct causes another to fear, on at least two occasions, that violence will be used against him is guilty of an offence if he knows or ought to know that his course of conduct will cause the other so to fear on each of those occasions.

(2) For the purposes of this section, the person whose course of conduct is in question ought to know that it will cause another to fear that violence will be used against him on any occasion if a reasonable person in possession of the same information would think the course of conduct would cause the other so to fear on that occasion.

(3) It is a defence for a person charged with an offence under this section to show that—

(a) his course of conduct was pursued for the purpose of preventing or detecting crime,

(b) his course of conduct was pursued under any enactment or rule of law or to comply with any condition or requirement imposed by any person under any enactment, or

(c) the pursuit of his course of conduct was reasonable for the protection of himself or another or for the protection of his or another's property.

(4) . . .

(5) If on the trial on indictment of a person charged with an offence under this section the jury find him not guilty of the offence charged, they may find him guilty of an offence under section 2.

(6) . . .

NOTES

Commencement: 16 June 1997.

Sub-ss (4), (6): outside the scope of this work.

5 Restraining orders

(1) A court sentencing or otherwise dealing with a person ("the defendant") convicted of an offence under section 2 or 4 may (as well as sentencing him or dealing with him in any other way) make an order under this section.

(2) The order may, for the purpose of protecting the victim of the offence, or any other person mentioned in the order, from further conduct which—

(a) amounts to harassment, or

(b) will cause a fear of violence,

prohibit the defendant from doing anything described in the order.

(3) The order may have effect for a specified period or until further order.

(4) The prosecutor, the defendant or any other person mentioned in the order may apply to the court which made the order for it to be varied or discharged by a further order.

(5) If without reasonable excuse the defendant does anything which he is prohibited from doing by an order under this section, he is guilty of an offence.

(6) . . .

NOTES

Commencement: 16 June 1997.

Sub-s (6): outside the scope of this work.

General

14 Extent

(1) Sections 1 to 7 extend to England and Wales only.

(2) . . .

(3) This Act (except section 13) does not extend to Northern Ireland.

NOTES

Commencement: 21 March 1997.

Sub-s (2): outside the scope of this work.

15 Commencement

(1) Sections 1, 2, 4, 5 and 7 to 12 are to come into force on such day as the Secretary of State may by order made by statutory instrument appoint.

(2) Sections 3 and 6 are to come into force on such day as the Lord Chancellor may by order made by statutory instrument appoint.

(3) Different days may be appointed under this section for different purposes.

NOTES
Commencement: 21 March 1997.

16 Short title

This Act may be cited as the Protection from Harassment Act 1997.

NOTES
Commencement: 21 March 1997.

POLICE ACT 1997

(C 50)

An Act to make provision for the National Criminal Intelligence Service and the National Crime Squad; to make provision about entry on and interference with property and with wireless telegraphy in the course of the prevention or detection of serious crime; to make provision for the Police Information Technology Organisation; to provide for the issue of certificates about criminal records; to make provision about the administration and organisation of the police; to repeal certain enactments about rehabilitation of offenders; and for connected purposes.

[21 March 1997]

PART III
AUTHORISATION OF ACTION IN RESPECT OF PROPERTY

The Commissioners

91 The Commissioners

(1) The Prime Minister shall appoint for the purposes of this Part—

(a) a Chief Commissioner, and

(b) such number of other Commissioners as the Prime Minister thinks fit.

(2) The persons appointed under subsection (1) shall be persons who hold or have held high judicial office within the meaning of the Appellate Jurisdiction Act 1876.

(3) Subject to subsections (4) to (7), each Commissioner shall hold and vacate office in accordance with the terms of his appointment.

(4) Each Commissioner shall be appointed for a term of three years.

(5) A person who ceases to be a Commissioner (otherwise than under subsection (7)) may be reappointed under this section.

(6) Subject to subsection (7), a Commissioner shall not be removed from office before the end of the term for which he is appointed unless a resolution approving his removal has been passed by each House of Parliament.

(7) A Commissioner may be removed from office by the Prime Minister if after his appointment—

- (a) a bankruptcy order is made against him or his estate is sequestrated or he makes a composition or arrangement with, or grants a trust deed for, his creditors;
- (b) a disqualification order under the Company Directors Disqualification Act 1986 or Part II of the Companies (Northern Ireland) Order 1989, or an order under section 429(2)(b) of the Insolvency Act 1986 (failure to pay under county court administration order), is made against him; or
- (c) he is convicted in the United Kingdom, the Channel Islands or the Isle of Man of an offence and has passed on him a sentence of imprisonment (whether suspended or not).

(8), (9) . . .

(10) The decisions of the Chief Commissioner or, subject to sections 104 and 106, any other Commissioner (including decisions as to his jurisdiction) shall not be subject to appeal or liable to be questioned in any court.

NOTES

Commencement: 1 September 1997 (sub-ss (1)–(7)); to be appointed (sub-s (10)).
Sub-ss (8), (9): outside the scope of this work.

Authorisations

92 Effect of authorisation under Part III

No entry on or interference with property or with wireless telegraphy shall be unlawful if it is authorised by an authorisation having effect under this Part.

NOTES

Commencement: to be appointed.

93 Authorisations to interfere with property etc

(1) Where subsection (2) applies, an authorising officer may authorise—

- (a) the taking of such action, in respect of such property in the relevant area, as he may specify, or
- (b) the taking of such action in the relevant area as he may specify, in respect of wireless telegraphy.

(2) This subsection applies where the authorising officer believes—

- (a) that it is necessary for the action specified to be taken on the ground that it is likely to be of substantial value in the prevention or detection of serious crime, and
- (b) that what the action seeks to achieve cannot reasonably be achieved by other means.

(3) An authorising officer shall not give an authorisation under this section except on an application made—

- (a) if the authorising officer is within subsection (5)(a) to (e), by a member of his police force,

(b) if the authorising officer is within subsection (5)(f), by a member of the National Criminal Intelligence Service,
(c) if the authorising officer is within subsection (5)(g), by a member of the National Crime Squad, or
(d) if the authorising officer is within subsection (5)(h), by a customs officer.

(4) For the purposes of subsection (2), conduct which constitutes one or more offences shall be regarded as serious crime if, and only if,—
(a) it involves the use of violence, results in substantial financial gain or is conduct by a large number of persons in pursuit of a common purpose, or
(b) the offence or one of the offences is an offence for which a person who has attained the age of twenty-one and has no previous convictions could reasonably be expected to be sentenced to imprisonment for a term of three years or more,

and, where the authorising officer is within subsection (5)(h), it relates to an assigned matter within the meaning of section 1(1) of the Customs and Excise Management Act 1979.

(5) In this section "authorising officer" means—
(a) the chief constable of a police force maintained under section 2 of the Police Act 1996 (maintenance of police forces for areas in England and Wales except London);
(b) the Commissioner, or an Assistant Commissioner, of Police of the Metropolis;
(c) the Commissioner of Police for the City of London;
(d) . . .
(e) the Chief Constable or a Deputy Chief Constable of the Royal Ulster Constabulary;
(f) the Director General of the National Criminal Intelligence Service;
(g) the Director General of the National Crime Squad; or
(h) the customs officer designated by the Commissioners of Customs and Excise for the purposes of this paragraph.

(6) . . .

(7) The powers conferred by, or by virtue of, this section are additional to any other powers which a person has as a constable either at common law or under or by virtue of any other enactment and are not to be taken to affect any of those other powers.

NOTES
Commencement: to be appointed.
Sub-s (5): para (d) outside the scope of this work.
Sub-s (6): outside the scope of this work.

94 Authorisations given in absence of authorising officer

(1) Subsection (2) applies where it is not reasonably practicable for an authorising officer to consider an application for an authorisation under section 93 and—
(a) if the authorising officer is within paragraph (b) or (e) of section 93(5), it is also not reasonably practicable for the application to be considered by any of the other persons within the paragraph concerned; or
(b) if the authorising officer is within paragraph (a), (c), (d) [(f), (g) or (h)] of section 93(5), it is also not reasonably practicable for the application to be considered by his designated deputy.

(2) Where this subsection applies, the powers conferred on the authorising officer by section 93 may, in an urgent case, be exercised—

(a) where the authorising officer is within paragraph (a) or (d) of subsection (5) of that section, by a person holding the rank of assistant chief constable in his force;

(b) where the authorising officer is within paragraph (b) of that subsection, by a person holding the rank of commander in the metropolitan police force;

(c) where the authorising officer is within paragraph (c) of that subsection, by a person holding the rank of commander in the City of London police force;

(d) where the authorising officer is within paragraph (e) of that subsection, by a person holding the rank of assistant chief constable in the Royal Ulster Constabulary;

(e) where the authorising officer is within paragraph (f) or (g) of that subsection by a person designated for the purposes of this section by the Director General of the National Criminal Intelligence Service or, as the case may be, of the National Crime Squad;

(f) where the authorising officer is within paragraph (h) of that subsection, by a customs officer designated by the Commissioners of Customs and Excise for the purposes of this section.

(3), (4) . . .

NOTES

Commencement: to be appointed.

Sub-s (1): words in square brackets substituted by the Crime and Disorder Act 1998, s 113(1).

Sub-ss (3), (4): outside the scope of this work.

95 Authorisations: form and duration etc

(1) An authorisation shall be in writing, except that in an urgent case an authorisation (other than one given by virtue of section 94) may be given orally.

(2) An authorisation shall, unless renewed under subsection (3), cease to have effect—

(a) if given orally or by virtue of section 94, at the end of the period of 72 hours beginning with the time when it took effect;

(b) in any other case, at the end of the period of three months beginning with the day on which it took effect.

(3) If at any time before an authorisation would cease to have effect the authorising officer who gave the authorisation, or in whose absence it was given, considers it necessary for the authorisation to continue to have effect for the purpose for which it was issued, he may, in writing, renew it for a period of three months beginning with the day on which it would cease to have effect.

(4) A person shall cancel an authorisation given by him if satisfied that the action authorised by it is no longer necessary.

(5) An authorising officer shall cancel an authorisation given in his absence if satisfied that the action authorised by it is no longer necessary.

(6) If the authorising officer who gave the authorisation is within paragraph (b) or (e) of section 93(5), the power conferred on that person by subsections (3) and (4) above shall also be exercisable by each of the other persons within the paragraph concerned.

(7) Nothing in this section shall prevent a designated deputy from exercising the powers conferred on an authorising officer within paragraph (a), (c), (d), (f) or (g) of section 93(5) by subsections (3), (4) and (5) above.

NOTES

Commencement: to be appointed.

96 Notification of authorisations etc

(1) Where a person gives, renews or cancels an authorisation, he shall, as soon as is reasonably practicable and in accordance with arrangements made by the Chief Commissioner, give notice in writing that he has done so to a Commissioner appointed under section 91(1)(b).

(2) Subject to subsection (3), a notice under this section shall specify such matters as the Secretary of State may by order prescribe.

(3) A notice under this section of the giving or renewal of an authorisation shall specify—

- (a) whether section 97 applies to the authorisation or renewal, and
- (b) where that section does not apply by virtue of subsection (3) of that section, the grounds on which the case is believed to be one of urgency.

(4) Where a notice is given to a Commissioner under this section, he shall, as soon as is reasonably practicable, scrutinise the notice.

(5) An order under subsection (2) shall be made by statutory instrument.

(6) A statutory instrument which contains an order under subsection (2) shall not be made unless a draft has been laid before, and approved by a resolution of, each House of Parliament.

NOTES

Commencement: 1 September 1997, for purpose of making orders; to be appointed, otherwise.

Authorisations requiring approval

97 Authorisations requiring approval

(1) An authorisation to which this section applies shall not take effect until—

- (a) it has been approved in accordance with this section by a Commissioner appointed under section 91(1)(b), and
- (b) the person who gave the authorisation has been notified under subsection (4).

(2) Subject to subsection (3), this section applies to an authorisation if, at the time it is given, the person who gives it believes—

- (a) that any of the property specified in the authorisation—
  - (i) is used wholly or mainly as a dwelling or as a bedroom in a hotel, or
  - (ii) constitutes office premises, or
- (b) that the action authorised by it is likely to result in any person acquiring knowledge of—
  - (i) matters subject to legal privilege,
  - (ii) confidential personal information, or
  - (iii) confidential journalistic material.

(3) This section does not apply to an authorisation where the person who gives it believes that the case is one of urgency.

(4) Where a Commissioner receives a notice under section 96 which specifies that this section applies to the authorisation, he shall as soon as is reasonably practicable—
- (a) decide whether to approve the authorisation or refuse approval, and
- (b) give written notice of his decision to the person who gave the authorisation.

(5) A Commissioner shall approve an authorisation if, and only if, he is satisfied that there are reasonable grounds for believing the matters specified in section 93(2).

(6) Where a Commissioner refuses to approve an authorisation, he shall, as soon as is reasonably practicable, make a report of his findings to the authorising officer who gave it or in whose absence it was given (and paragraph 7 of Schedule 7 shall apply for the purposes of this subsection as it applies for the purposes of that Schedule).

(7) This section shall apply in relation to a renewal of an authorisation as it applies in relation to an authorisation (the references in subsection (2)(a) and (b) to the authorisation being construed as references to the authorisation renewed).

(8) . . .

NOTES

Commencement: to be appointed.

Sub-s (8): outside the scope of this work.

98 Matters subject to legal privilege

(1) Subject to subsection (5) below, in section 97 "matters subject to legal privilege" means matters to which subsection (2), (3) or (4) below applies.

(2) This subsection applies to communications between a professional legal adviser and—
- (a) his client, or
- (b) any person representing his client,

which are made in connection with the giving of legal advice to the client.

(3) This subsection applies to communications—
- (a) between a professional legal adviser and his client or any person representing his client, or
- (b) between a professional legal adviser or his client or any such representative and any other person,

which are made in connection with or in contemplation of legal proceedings and for the purposes of such proceedings.

(4) This subsection applies to items enclosed with or referred to in communications of the kind mentioned in subsection (2) or (3) and made—
- (a) in connection with the giving of legal advice, or
- (b) in connection with or in contemplation of legal proceedings and for the purposes of such proceedings.

(5) For the purposes of section 97—
- (a) communications and items are not matters subject to legal privilege when they are in the possession of a person who is not entitled to possession of them, and
- (b) communications and items held, or oral communications made, with the intention of furthering a criminal purpose are not matters subject to legal privilege.

NOTES

Commencement: to be appointed.

99 Confidential personal information

(1) In section 97 "confidential personal information" means—

(a) personal information which a person has acquired or created in the course of any trade, business, profession or other occupation or for the purposes of any paid or unpaid office, and which he holds in confidence, and

(b) communications as a result of which personal information—

(i) is acquired or created as mentioned in paragraph (a), and

(ii) is held in confidence.

(2) For the purposes of this section "personal information" means information concerning an individual (whether living or dead) who can be identified from it and relating—

(a) to his physical or mental health, or

(b) to spiritual counselling or assistance given or to be given to him.

(3) A person holds information in confidence for the purposes of this section if he holds it subject—

(a) to an express or implied undertaking to hold it in confidence, or

(b) to a restriction on disclosure or an obligation of secrecy contained in any enactment (including an enactment contained in an Act passed after this Act).

NOTES

Commencement: to be appointed.

100 Confidential journalistic material

(1) In section 97 "confidential journalistic material" means—

(a) material acquired or created for the purposes of journalism which—

(i) is in the possession of persons who acquired or created it for those purposes,

(ii) is held subject to an undertaking, restriction or obligation of the kind mentioned in section 99(3), and

(iii) has been continuously held (by one or more persons) subject to such an undertaking, restriction or obligation since it was first acquired or created for the purposes of journalism, and

(b) communications as a result of which information is acquired for the purposes of journalism and held as mentioned in paragraph (a)(ii).

(2) For the purposes of subsection (1), a person who receives material, or acquires information, from someone who intends that the recipient shall use it for the purposes of journalism is to be taken to have acquired it for those purposes.

NOTES

Commencement: to be appointed.

Code of Practice

101 Code of Practice

(1) The Secretary of State shall issue a code of practice in connection with the performance of functions under this Part by persons other than Commissioners appointed under section 91.

(2) Before issuing a code of practice under subsection (1), the Secretary of State shall prepare and publish a draft of that code, shall consider any representations made to him about the draft and may modify the draft accordingly.

(3) The Secretary of State shall lay before both Houses of Parliament a draft of the code of practice prepared by him under this section.

(4) The code of practice laid before Parliament in draft under subsection (3) shall not be brought into operation except in accordance with an order made by the Secretary of State by statutory instrument.

(5) A statutory instrument which contains an order under subsection (4) shall not be made unless a draft has been laid before, and approved by a resolution of, each House of Parliament.

(6) An order bringing the code into operation may contain such transitional provisions or savings as appear to the Secretary of State to be necessary or expedient in connection with the bringing into operation of that code.

(7) The Secretary of State may from time to time revise the whole or any part of a code to which this section applies and issue that revised code; and the foregoing provision of this section shall apply (with appropriate modifications) to such a revised code as they apply to the first issue of the code.

(8) Persons, other than Commissioners appointed under section 91, shall have regard to any code of practice issued under this section in the performance of their functions under this Part.

(9) A failure on the part of any person to comply with any provision of a code of practice issued under this section shall not of itself render him liable to any criminal or civil proceedings.

(10) A code issued under this section shall be admissible in evidence in criminal and civil proceedings; and if any provision of such a code appears to the court or tribunal conducting the proceedings to be relevant to any question arising in the proceedings it shall be taken into account in determining that question.

NOTES

Commencement: 5 August 1997.

Complaints etc

102 Complaints

(1) Where a complaint is made, in accordance with arrangements made by the Chief Commissioner, to a Commissioner appointed under section 91(1)(b), the Commissioner shall investigate the complaint if and so far as it alleges that anything has been done in relation to any property of the complainant in pursuance of an authorisation under section 93(1)(a) or (b).

(2) For the purposes of subsection (1), a place where the complainant works or resides shall be treated as property of the complainant.

(3) A Commissioner's duty under this section does not extend to a complaint if he considers that it is frivolous or vexatious.

(4) Schedule 7 makes further provision in relation to the investigation of complaints by a Commissioner.

NOTES

Commencement: to be appointed.

103 Quashing of authorisations etc

(1) Where, at any time, a Commissioner appointed under section 91(1)(b) is satisfied that, at the time an authorisation was given or renewed, there were no reasonable grounds for believing the matters specified in section 93(2), he may quash the authorisation or, as the case may be, renewal.

(2) Where, in the case of an authorisation or renewal to which section 97 does not apply, a Commissioner appointed under section 91(1)(b) is at any time satisfied that, at the time the authorisation was given or, as the case may be, renewed,—

(a) there were reasonable grounds for believing any of the matters specified in subsection (2) of section 97, and

(b) there were no reasonable grounds for believing the case to be one of urgency for the purposes of subsection (3) of that section,

he may quash the authorisation or, as the case may be, renewal.

(3) Where a Commissioner quashes an authorisation or renewal under subsection (1) or (2), he may order the destruction of any records relating to information obtained by virtue of the authorisation (or, in the case of a renewal, relating wholly or partly to information so obtained after the renewal) other than records required for pending criminal or civil proceedings.

(4) If a Commissioner appointed under section 91(1)(b) is satisfied that, at any time after an authorisation was given or, in the case of an authorisation renewed under section 95, after it was renewed, there were no reasonable grounds for believing the matters specified in section 93(2), he may cancel the authorisation.

(5) Where—

(a) an authorisation has ceased to have effect (otherwise than by virtue of subsection (1) or (2)), and

(b) a Commissioner appointed under section 91(1)(b) is satisfied that, at any time during the period of the authorisation, there were no reasonable grounds for believing the matters specified in section 93(2),

he may order the destruction of any records relating, wholly or partly, to information which was obtained by virtue of the authorisation after that time (other than records required for pending criminal or civil proceedings).

(6) Where a Commissioner exercises his powers under subsection (1), (2) or (4), he shall, if he is satisfied that there are reasonable grounds for doing so, order that the authorisation shall be effective, for such period as he shall specify, so far as it authorises the taking of action to retrieve anything left on property in accordance with the authorisation.

(7) Where a Commissioner exercises a power conferred by this section, he shall, as soon as is reasonably practicable, make a report of his findings—

(a) to the authorising officer who gave the authorisation or in whose absence it was given, and

(b) to the Chief Commissioner;

and paragraph 7 of Schedule 7 shall apply for the purposes of this subsection as it applies for the purposes of that Schedule.

(8) Where—

(a) a decision is made under subsection (1) or (2) and an order for the destruction of records is made under subsection (3), or

(b) a decision to order the destruction of records is made under subsection (5),

the order shall not become operative until the period for appealing against the decision has expired and, where an appeal is made, a decision dismissing it has been made by the Chief Commissioner.

(9) A Commissioner may exercise any of the powers conferred by this section notwithstanding any approval given under section 97.

NOTES

Commencement: to be appointed.

Appeals

104 Appeals by authorising officers

(1) An authorising officer who gives an authorisation, or in whose absence it is given, may, within the prescribed period, appeal to the Chief Commissioner against—

(a) any refusal to approve the authorisation or any renewal of it under section 97;

(b) any decision to quash the authorisation, or any renewal of it, under subsection (1) of section 103;

(c) any decision to quash the authorisation, or any renewal of it, under subsection (2) of that section;

(d) any decision to cancel the authorisation under subsection (4) of that section;

(e) any decision to order the destruction of records under subsection (5) of that section;

(f) any refusal to make an order under subsection (6) of that section;

(g) any determination in favour of a complainant under Schedule 7.

(2) In subsection (1), "the prescribed period" means the period of seven days beginning with the day on which the refusal, decision or, as the case may be, determination appealed against is reported to the authorising officer.

(3) In determining an appeal within subsection (1)(a), the Chief Commissioner shall, if he is satisfied that there are reasonable grounds for believing the matters specified in section 93(2), allow the appeal and direct the Commissioner to approve the authorisation or renewal under that section.

(4) In determining—

(a) an appeal within subsection (1)(b), or

(b) an appeal within subsection (1)(g), in a case where paragraph 2(2) of Schedule 7 applies, the Chief Commissioner shall allow the appeal unless he is satisfied that, at the time the authorisation was given or, as the case may be, renewed there were no reasonable grounds for believing the matters specified in section 93(2).

(5) In determining—

(a) an appeal within subsection (1)(c), or

(b) an appeal within subsection (1)(g), in a case where paragraph 2(3) of Schedule 7 applies,

the Chief Commissioner shall allow the appeal unless he is satisfied as mentioned in section 103(2).

(6) In determining—

(a) an appeal within subsection (1)(d) or (e), or

(b) an appeal within subsection (1)(g), in a case where paragraph 2(4) of Schedule 7 applies,

the Chief Commissioner shall allow the appeal unless he is satisfied that at the time to which the decision relates there were no reasonable grounds for believing the matters specified in section 93(2).

(7) In determining an appeal within subsection (1)(f), the Chief Commissioner shall allow the appeal and order that the authorisation shall be effective to the extent mentioned in section 103(6), for such period as he shall specify, if he is satisfied that there are reasonable grounds for making such an order.

(8) Where an appeal is allowed under this section, the Chief Commissioner shall—

(a) in the case of an appeal within subsection (1)(b) or (c), also quash any order made by the Commissioner to destroy records relating to information obtained by virtue of the authorisation concerned, and

(b) in the case of an appeal within subsection (1)(g), also quash any direction to pay compensation to the complainant.

NOTES

Commencement: to be appointed.

105 Appeals by authorising officers: supplementary

(1) . . .

(2) Subject to subsection (1)(b), the Chief Commissioner shall not give any reasons for a determination under section 104.

(3) . . .

NOTES

Commencement: to be appointed.

Sub-ss (1), (3): outside the scope of this work.

106 Appeals by complainants

(1) Where a complainant is notified under paragraph 3(2) of Schedule 7 that no determination in his favour has been made on a complaint, he may, within the period of seven days beginning with the day on which he receives the notice, appeal to the Chief Commissioner against the decision.

(2) Where a complainant appeals under this section, the Chief Commissioner shall have—

(a) all the powers and duties conferred by Schedule 7 on a Commissioner appointed under section 91(1)(b) who is required to investigate a complaint, and

(b) where the Chief Commissioner makes a determination in favour of the complainant by virtue of paragraph (a), all the powers and duties conferred by section 103.

(3) Where, by virtue of subsection (2), the Chief Commissioner makes an order to destroy records under section 103 or directs the payment of compensation under Schedule 7, subsection (8) of that section and paragraph 5(2) of that Schedule shall not apply.

(4) The Chief Commissioner shall make a report of his findings on an appeal under this section—

(a) to the Commissioner who made the decision appealed against, and

(b) where he allows the appeal, to the Prime Minister under section 107(2).

NOTES

Commencement: to be appointed.

General

107 Supplementary provisions relating to Commissioners

(1) . . .

(2) The Chief Commissioner shall make an annual report on the discharge of functions under this Part to the Prime Minister and may at any time report to him on any matter relating to those functions.

(3) The Prime Minister shall lay before each House of Parliament a copy of each annual report made by the Chief Commissioner under subsection (2) together with a statement as to whether any matter has been excluded from that copy in pursuance of subsection (4) below.

(4) The Prime Minister may exclude a matter from the copy of a report as laid before each House of Parliament, if it appears to him, after consultation with the Chief Commissioner, that the publication of that matter in the report would be prejudicial to the prevention or detection of serious crime or otherwise to the discharge of—

(a) the functions of any police authority,

(b) the functions of the Service Authority for the National Criminal Intelligence Service or the Service Authority for the National Crime Squad, or

(c) the duties of the Commissioners of Customs and Excise.

(5) Any person having functions under this Part, and any person taking action in relation to which an authorisation was given, shall comply with any request of a Commissioner for documents or information required by him for the purpose of enabling him to discharge his functions.

(6) In this section, "serious crime" shall be construed in accordance with section 93(4).

NOTES

Commencement: to be appointed.

Sub-s (1): outside the scope of this work.

PART IV
POLICE INFORMATION TECHNOLOGY ORGANISATION

109 Police Information Technology Organisation

(1) There shall be a body corporate to be known as the Police Information Technology Organisation ("the Organisation").

(2) . . .

(3) The Organisation may carry out activities (including the commissioning of research) relating to information technology equipment and systems for the use of—
- (a) police authorities and police forces, and
- (b) such other bodies as the Secretary of State may determine by order made by statutory instrument.

(4) The Organisation may also procure or assist in procuring other equipment, systems and services for any body falling within subsection (3)(a) or (b).

(5) Any statutory instrument made by virtue of subsection (3)(b) shall be subject to annulment in pursuance of a resolution of either House of Parliament.

(6) In this Part "information technology" includes any computer or other technology by means of which information or other matter may be recorded or communicated without being reduced to documentary form.

NOTES

Commencement: 1 September 1997 (sub-s (1)); 1 September 1997, for purpose of making orders; 1 April 1998, otherwise (sub-ss (3, (5)); 1 April 1998 (sub-ss (4), (6)).

Sub-s (2): outside the scope of this work.

PART VII
GENERAL

135 Commencement

(1) The preceding provisions of this Act shall come into force on such day as the Secretary of State may by order made by statutory instrument appoint.

(2) An order under this section may—
- (a) appoint different days for different purposes or different areas, and
- (b) make transitional provision and savings (including provision modifying this Act).

(3) . . .

(4) Any day appointed by an order under this section for the coming into force of section 93, 94 or 95 of this Act shall not be earlier than the day on which a code of practice issued under section 101 comes into operation.

(5) . . .

NOTES
Commencement: 21 March 1997.
Sub-ss (3), (5): outside the scope of this work.

137 Extent

(1) Subject to subsections (2) to (4), this Act extends throughout the United Kingdom.

(2) The following provisions of this Act extend to England and Wales only—
(a) Part II;
(b)–(e) . . .

(3) Sections 130 to 132 extend to Northern Ireland only.

(4) The amendments in Schedules 6 and 9, and the repeals in Schedule 10, have the same extent as the enactments to which they refer.

NOTES
Commencement: 21 March 1997.
Sub-s (2): paras (b)–(e) outside the scope of this work.
Sub-s (3): repealed by the Police (Northern Ireland) Act 1998, s 74(3), Sch 6, as from a day to be appointed.

138 Short title

This Act may be cited as the Police Act 1997.

NOTES
Commencement: 21 March 1997.

SCHEDULE 7

Section 102(4)

INVESTIGATION OF COMPLAINTS BY COMMISSIONERS ETC

Investigation

1. Where a Commissioner appointed under section 91(1)(b) is required by virtue of section 102 to investigate a complaint, he shall investigate whether an authorisation was given under section 93 in relation to the doing of the act or acts in question in relation to the property concerned ("a relevant authorisation").

2.—(1) In a case where the Commissioner determines that a relevant authorisation was given he shall, if sub-paragraph (2), (3) or (4) applies, make a determination in favour of the complainant.

(2) This sub-paragraph applies if the Commissioner is satisfied that there were, at the time the relevant authorisation was given or renewed, no reasonable grounds for believing the matters specified in section 93(2).

(3) This sub-paragraph applies where section 97 did not apply to the relevant authorisation or its renewal, but the Commissioner is satisfied as mentioned in section 103(2).

(4) This sub-paragraph applies if the Commissioner is satisfied that anything has been done in relation to any property of the complainant in pursuance of the relevant authorisation (other than by virtue of section 103(6) or section 104(7)) at a time when there were no reasonable grounds for believing the matters specified in section 93(2).

Report of conclusions

3.—(1) If the Commissioner makes a determination in favour of the complainant under paragraph 2, he shall—

(a) give notice to the complainant that he has done so, and
(b) make a report of his findings to the authorising officer who gave the authorisation, or in whose absence it was given, and to the Chief Commissioner.

(2) In any other case, the Commissioner shall give notice to the complainant that no determination in his favour has been made on the complaint.

(3) Subject to sub-paragraph (1)(b), the Commissioner shall not give any reasons for the making of, or any refusal to make, a determination in favour of the complainant.

4. Where—

(a) the Chief Commissioner receives a report of the Commissioner's findings under paragraph 3(1)(b), and
(b) no appeal is made against the determination in favour of the complainant,

the Chief Commissioner shall, under section 107(2), make a report of those findings to the Prime Minister.

Remedies

5.—(1) Where the Commissioner gives a complainant notice that a determination in his favour has been made on the complaint, he may (whether or not he has exercised, or intends to exercise, any of the powers under section 103) direct the authorising officer who gave the authorisation, or in whose absence it was given, to pay the complainant such sum by way of compensation as may be specified in the direction.

(2) Where a direction to pay compensation has been made under subparagraph (1), it shall not become operative until—

(a) the period for appealing against the determination in favour of the complainant has expired, and
(b) where such an appeal is made, a decision dismissing it has been made by the Chief Commissioner.

6, 7. . . .

NOTES

Commencement: to be appointed.
Paras 6, 7: outside the scope of this work.

LOCAL GOVERNMENT (CONTRACTS) ACT 1997

(C 65)

An Act to make provision about the powers of local authorities (including probation committees and the Receiver for the Metropolitan Police District) to enter into contracts; to enable expenditure of local authorities making administrative arrangements for magistrates' courts to be treated for some purposes as not being capital expenditure; and for connected purposes [27 November 1997]

Contracts for provision of assets or services

1 Functions to include power to enter into contracts

(1) Every statutory provision conferring or imposing a function on a local authority confers power on the local authority to enter into a contract with another

person for the provision or making available of assets or services, or both, (whether or not together with goods) for the purposes of, or in connection with, the discharge of the function by the local authority.

(2) Where—

(a) a local authority enters into a contract such as is mentioned in subsection (1) ("the provision contract") under any statutory provision, and

(b) in connection with the provision contract, a person ("the financier") makes a loan to, or provides any other form of finance for, a party to the provision contract other than the local authority,

the statutory provision also confers power on the local authority to enter into a contract with the financier, or any insurer of or trustee for the financier, in connection with the provision contract.

(3)–(5) . . .

NOTES

Commencement: 27 November 1997; and applies to any contract which a local authority enters into after 12 June 1997.

Sub-ss (3)–(5): outside the scope of this work.

Certified contracts

2 Certified contracts to be intra vires

(1) Where a local authority has entered into a contract, the contract shall, if it is a certified contract, have effect (and be deemed always to have had effect) as if the local authority had had power to enter into it (and had exercised that power properly in entering into it).

(2) For the purposes of this Act a contract entered into by a local authority is a certified contract if (and, subject to subsections (3) and (4), only if) the certification requirements have been satisfied by the local authority with respect to the contract and they were so satisfied before the end of the certification period.

(3) A contract entered into by a local authority shall be treated as a certified contract during the certification period if the contract provides that the certification requirements are intended to be satisfied by the local authority with respect to the contract before the end of that period.

(4) . . .

(5) In this Act "the certification period", in relation to a contract entered into by a local authority, means the period of six weeks beginning with the day on which the local authority entered into the contract.

(6) Subsection (1) is subject to section 5 (special provisions about judicial reviews and audit reviews).

(7) The application of subsection (1) in relation to a contract entered into by a local authority does not affect any claim for damages made by a person who is not (and has never been) a party to the contract in respect of a breach by the local authority of any duty to do, or not to do, something before entering into the contract (including, in particular, any such duty imposed by a statutory provision for giving effect to any

Community obligation relating to public procurement or by section 17(1) of the Local Government Act 1988).

NOTES

Commencement: 30 December 1997 and applies to any contract which a local authority enters into after 12 June 1997.

Sub-s (4): outside the scope of this work.

3 The certification requirements

(1) In this Act "the certification requirements", in relation to a contract entered into by a local authority, means the requirements specified in subsections (2) to (4).

(2) The requirement specified in this subsection is that the local authority must have issued a certificate (whether before or after the contract is entered into)—

- (a) including details of the period for which the contract operates or is to operate,
- (b) describing the purpose of the contract,
- (c) containing a statement that the contract is or is to be a contract falling within section 4(3) or (4),
- (d) stating that the local authority had or has power to enter into the contract and specifying the statutory provision, or each of the statutory provisions, conferring the power,
- (e) stating that a copy of the certificate has been or is to be given to each person to whom a copy is required to be given by regulations,
- (f) dealing in a manner prescribed by regulations with any matters required by regulations to be dealt with in certificates under this section, and
- (g) confirming that the local authority has complied with or is to comply with any requirement imposed by regulations with respect to the issue of certificates under this section.

(3) The requirement specified in this subsection is that the local authority must have secured that the certificate is signed by any person who is required by regulations to sign it.

(4) The requirement specified in this subsection is that the local authority must have obtained consent to the issue of a certificate under this section from each of the persons with whom the local authority has entered, or is to enter, into the contract.

NOTES

Commencement: 30 December 1997 (sub-ss (1), (2)(a)–(d), (g), (4)); 1 December 1997, so far as they confer power on Secretary of State to make regulations; 30 December, otherwise (sub-ss (2)(e), (f), (3)); and applies to any contract which a local authority enters into after 12 June 1997.

5 Special provision for judicial reviews and audit reviews

(1) Section 2(1) does not apply for the purposes of determining any question arising on—

- (a) an application for judicial review, or
- (b) an audit review,

as to whether a local authority had power to enter into a contract (or exercised any power properly in entering into a contract).

(2) Section 2(1) has effect subject to any determination or order made in relation to a certified contract on—

(a) an application for judicial review, or

(b) an audit review.

(3) Where, on an application for judicial review or an audit review relating to a certified contract entered into by a local authority, a court—

(a) is of the opinion that the local authority did not have power to enter into the contract (or exercised any power improperly in entering into it), but

(b) (having regard in particular to the likely consequences for the financial position of the local authority, and for the provision of services to the public, of a decision that the contract should not have effect) considers that the contract should have effect,

the court may determine that the contract has (and always has had) effect as if the local authority had had power to enter into it (and had exercised that power properly in entering into it).

(4) In this section and sections 6 and 7 references to an application for judicial review include any appeal (or further appeal) against a determination or order made on such an application.

NOTES

Commencement: 30 December 1997 and applies to any contract which a local authority enters into after 12 June 1997.

6 Relevant discharge terms

(1) No determination or order made in relation to a certified contract on—

(a) an application for judicial review, or

(b) an audit review,

shall affect the enforceability of any relevant discharge terms relating to the contract.

(2) In this section and section 7 "relevant discharge terms", in relation to a contract entered into by a local authority, means terms—

(a) which have been agreed by the local authority and any person with whom the local authority entered into the contract,

(b) which either form part of the contract or constitute or form part of another agreement entered into by them not later than the day on which the contract was entered into, and

(c) which provide for a consequence mentioned in subsection (3) to ensue in the event of the making of a determination or order in relation to the contract on an application for judicial review or an audit review.

(3) Those consequences are—

(a) the payment of compensatory damages (measured by reference to loss incurred or loss of profits or to any other circumstances) by one of the parties to the other,

(b) the adjustment between the parties of rights and liabilities relating to any assets or goods provided or made available under the contract, or

(c) both of those things.

(4) Where a local authority has agreed relevant discharge terms with any person with whom it has entered into a contract and the contract is a certified contract, the relevant discharge terms shall have effect (and be deemed always to have had effect) as if the local authority had had power to agree them (and had exercised that power properly in agreeing them).

NOTES

Commencement: 30 December 1997 and applies to any contract which a local authority enters into after 12 June 1997.

7 Absence of relevant discharge terms

(1) Subsection (2) applies where—

(a) the result of a determination or order made by a court on an application for judicial review or an audit review is that a certified contract does not have effect, and

(b) there are no relevant discharge terms having effect between the local authority and a person who is a party to the contract.

(2) That person shall be entitled to be paid by the local authority such sums (if any) as he would have been entitled to be paid by the local authority if the contract—

(a) had had effect until the time when the determination or order was made, but

(b) had been terminated at that time by acceptance by him of a repudiatory breach by the local authority.

(3) For the purposes of this section the circumstances in which there are no relevant discharge terms having effect between the local authority and a person who is a party to the contract include (as well as circumstances in which no such terms have been agreed) circumstances in which the result of a determination or order of a court, made (despite section 6(4)) on an application for judicial review or an audit review, is that such terms do not have effect.

NOTES

Commencement: 30 December 1997 and applies to any contract which a local authority enters into after 12 June 1997.

Supplementary

12 Short title, commencement and extent

(1) This Act may be cited as the Local Government (Contracts) Act 1997.

(2) Sections 2 to 9 shall not come into force until a day appointed by the Secretary of State by order made by statutory instrument; and different days may be appointed for different provisions or purposes.

(3) Sections 1 to 9 apply to any contract which a local authority enters into after 12th June 1997; but in relation to a contract entered into before the day on which section 2 comes into force "the certification period" means the period of six weeks beginning with that day.

(4) . . .

(5) This Act does not extend to Northern Ireland.

NOTES
Commencement: 27 November 1997.
Sub-s (4): outside the scope of this work.

SPECIAL IMMIGRATION APPEALS COMMISSION ACT 1997

(C 68)

An Act to establish the Special Immigration Appeals Commission; to make provision with respect to its jurisdiction; and for connected purposes

[17 December 1997]

1 Establishment of the Commission

(1) There shall be a commission, known as the Special Immigration Appeals Commission, for the purpose of exercising the jurisdiction conferred by this Act.

(2) . . .

NOTES
Commencement: 3 August 1998.
Sub-s (2): outside the scope of this work.

2 Jurisdiction: appeals

(1) A person may appeal to the Special Immigration Appeals Commission against—

(a) any matter in relation to which he would be entitled to appeal under subsection (1) of section 13 of the Immigration Act 1971 (appeal to an adjudicator against refusal of leave to enter), but for subsection (5) of that section (exclusion conducive to public good),

(b) any matter in relation to which he would be entitled to appeal under subsection (1) of section 14 of that Act (appeal to an adjudicator against variation of limited leave or any refusal to vary it), but for subsection (3) of that section (departure conducive to public good),

(c) any matter in relation to which he would be entitled to appeal under subsection (1)(a) of section 15 of that Act (appeal to an adjudicator or the Appeal Tribunal against a decision to make a deportation order), but for subsection (3) of that section (deportation conducive to public good),

(d) any matter in relation to which he would be entitled to appeal under Article 15(1) of the Immigration (European Economic Area) Order 1994 (appeal against refusal of admission), but for Article 20(2)(b) of that Order (exclusion conducive to public good),

(e) any matter in relation to which he would be entitled to appeal under Article 15(2) of that Order (appeal against decision to remove), but for Article 20(2)(d) of that Order (removal conducive to public good),

(f) any matter in relation to which he would be entitled to appeal under Article 18 of that Order (appeal against refusal or withdrawal of residence permit or residence document), but for Article 20(2)(c) of that Order (departure conducive to public good), and

(g) any matter in relation to which he would be entitled to appeal under section 8(1), (2) or (3) of the Asylum and Immigration Appeals Act 1993 (appeal to special adjudicator in cases involving claim to asylum), but for paragraph 6 of Schedule 2 to that Act (exclusion, departure or deportation in the interests of national security).

(2) A person may appeal to the Special Immigration Appeals Commission against the refusal of an entry clearance if he would be entitled to appeal against the refusal under subsection (2) of section 13 of the Immigration Act 1971, but for subsection (5) of that section (exclusion conducive to public good), and—

(a) he seeks to rely on an enforceable Community right or any provision made under section 2(2) of the European Communities Act 1972, or

(b) he seeks to enter the United Kingdom under immigration rules making provision about entry—

(i) to exercise rights of access to a child resident there,

(ii) as the spouse or fiancé of a person present and settled there, or

(iii) as the parent, grandparent or other dependent relative of a person present and settled there.

(3) . . .

(4) In this section, "immigration rules" has the same meaning as in the Immigration Act 1971.

NOTES

Commencement: 3 August 1998.

Sub-s (3): outside the scope of this work.

4 Determination of appeals

(1) The Special Immigration Appeals Commission on an appeal to it under this Act—

(a) shall allow the appeal if it considers—

(i) that the decision or action against which the appeal is brought was not in accordance with the law or with any immigration rules applicable to the case, or

(ii) where the decision or action involved the exercise of a discretion by the Secretary of State or an officer, that the discretion should have been exercised differently, and

(b) in any other case, shall dismiss the appeal.

(2) Where an appeal is allowed, the Commission shall give such directions for giving effect to the determination as it thinks requisite, and may also make recommendations with respect to any other action which it considers should be taken in the case under the Immigration Act 1971; and it shall be the duty of the Secretary of State and of any officer to whom directions are given under this subsection to comply with them.

(3) . . .

NOTES

Commencement: 3 August 1998.

Sub-s (3): outside the scope of this work.

5 Procedure in relation to jurisdiction under sections 2 and 3

(1) The Lord Chancellor may make rules—

(a) for regulating the exercise of the rights of appeal conferred by section 2 above,

(b) for prescribing the practice and procedure to be followed on or in connection with appeals under that section, including the mode and burden of proof and admissibility of evidence on such appeals, and

(c) for other matters preliminary or incidental to or arising out of such appeals, including proof of the decisions of the Special Immigration Appeals Commission.

(2) Rules under this section shall provide that an appellant has the right to be legally represented in any proceedings before the Commission on an appeal under section 2 above, subject to any power conferred on the Commission by such rules.

(3) Rules under this section may, in particular—

(a) make provision enabling proceedings before the Commission to take place without the appellant being given full particulars of the reasons for the decision which is the subject of the appeal,

(b) make provision enabling the Commission to hold proceedings in the absence of any person, including the appellant and any legal representative appointed by him,

(c) make provision about the functions in proceedings before the Commission of persons appointed under section 6 below, and

(d) make provision enabling the Commission to give the appellant a summary of any evidence taken in his absence.

(4), (5) . . .

(6) In making rules under this section, the Lord Chancellor shall have regard, in particular, to—

(a) the need to secure that decisions which are the subject of appeals are properly reviewed, and

(b) the need to secure that information is not disclosed contrary to the public interest.

(7) Section 9(1) of the Interception of Communications Act 1985 (exclusion of evidence) shall not apply to proceedings before the Commission.

(8) The power to make rules under this section shall be exercisable by statutory instrument.

(9) No rules shall be made under this section unless a draft of them has been laid before and approved by resolution of each House of Parliament.

NOTES

Commencement: 11 June 1998.

Sub-ss (4), (5): outside the scope of this work.

6 Appointment of person to represent the appellant's interests

(1) The relevant law officer may appoint a person to represent the interests of an appellant in any proceedings before the Special Immigration Appeals Commission from which the appellant and any legal representative of his are excluded.

(2) For the purposes of subsection (1) above, the relevant law officer is—

(a) in relation to proceedings before the Commission in England and Wales, the Attorney General,

(b) . . . , and

(c) in relation to proceedings before the Commission in Northern Ireland, the Attorney General for Northern Ireland.

(3) A person appointed under subsection (1) above—

(a) if appointed for the purposes of proceedings in England and Wales, shall have a general qualification for the purposes of section 71 of the Courts and Legal Services Act 1990,

(b) . . . , and

(c) if appointed for the purposes of proceedings in Northern Ireland, shall be a member of the Bar of Northern Ireland.

(4) . . .

NOTES

Commencement: 3 August 1998.

Sub-s (2): para (b) outside the scope of this work.

Sub-s (3); para (b): outside the scope of this work.

Sub-s (4): outside the scope of this work.

7 Appeals from the Commission

(1) Where the Special Immigration Appeals Commission has made a final determination of an appeal, any party to the appeal may bring a further appeal to the appropriate appeal court on any question of law material to that determination.

(2) An appeal under this section may be brought only with the leave of the Commission or, if such leave is refused, with the leave of the appropriate appeal court.

(3) In this section "the appropriate appeal court" means—

(a) in relation to a determination made by the Commission in England and Wales, the Court of Appeal,

(b) . . . , and

(c) in relation to a determination made by the Commission in Northern Ireland, the Court of Appeal in Northern Ireland.

(4) . . .

NOTES

Commencement: 3 August 1998.

Sub-s (3): para (b) outside the scope of this work.

Sub-s (4): outside the scope of this work.

9 Short title, commencement and extent

(1) This Act may be cited as the Special Immigration Appeals Commission Act 1997.

(2) This Act, except for this section, shall come into force on such day as the Secretary of State may by order made by statutory instrument appoint; and different days may be so appointed for different purposes.

(3) . . .

(4) This Act extends to Northern Ireland.

NOTES

Commencement: 17 December 1997.

Sub-s (3): outside the scope of this work.

PUBLIC PROCESSIONS (NORTHERN IRELAND) ACT 1998

(C 2)

An Act to amend the law relating to public processions in Northern Ireland; to provide for the establishment and functions of the Parades Commission for Northern Ireland; and for connected purposes

[16 February 1998]

The Commission

1 The Commission

(1) There shall be established a body to be known as the Parades Commission for Northern Ireland (in this Act referred to as "the Commission").

(2) . . .

NOTES

Commencement: 16 February 1998.

Sub-s (2): outside the scope of this work.

2 Functions of the Commission

(1) It shall be the duty of the Commission—

(a) to promote greater understanding by the general public of issues concerning public processions;

(b) to promote and facilitate mediation as a means of resolving disputes concerning public processions;

(c) to keep itself generally informed as to the conduct of public processions and protest meetings;

(d) to keep under review, and make such recommendations as it thinks fit to the Secretary of State concerning, the operation of this Act.

(2) The Commission may in accordance with the following provisions of this Act—

(a) facilitate mediation between parties to particular disputes concerning proposed public processions and take such other steps as appear to the Commission to be appropriate for resolving such disputes;

(b) issue determinations in respect of particular proposed public processions.

(3) . . .

NOTES

Commencement: 2 March 1998.

Sub-s (3): outside the scope of this work.

3 Code of Conduct

(1) The Commission shall issue a code (in this Act referred to as "the Code of Conduct")—

(a) providing guidance to persons organising a public procession or protest meeting; and

(b) regulating the conduct of persons organising or taking part in a public procession or protest meeting.

(2) The Commission—

(a) shall keep the Code of Conduct under review; and

(b) may from time to time revise the whole or any part of the Code of Conduct and issue the revised Code of Conduct.

(3) . . .

NOTES

Commencement: 16 February 1998.

Sub-s (3): outside the scope of this work.

4 Procedural rules

(1) The Commission shall issue a set of rules (in this Act referred to as "the procedural rules") for the purpose of regulating and prescribing the practice and procedure to be followed—

(a) by the Commission in exercising the functions mentioned in section 2(2); and

(b) by other persons or bodies in their dealings with the Commission in connection with the exercise of those functions.

(2) In particular (but without prejudice to the generality of subsection (1)) the procedural rules may—

(a) provide for the determination by the Commission of the particular cases in relation to which the functions mentioned in section 2(2) are to be exercised;

(b) prescribe the manner in which, and the time within which, specified actions may or must be taken (whether by the Commission or by other persons or bodies) for the purposes of the exercise by the Commission of those functions;

(c) require notice of specified determinations of the Commission made in the exercise of those functions to be published in such form and manner as may be specified.

(3) In subsection (2) "specified" means specified in the procedural rules.

(4) The Commission—

(a) shall keep the procedural rules under review; and

(b) may from time to time revise the whole or any part of the procedural rules and issue the revised procedural rules.

(5) . . .

NOTES

Commencement: 16 February 1998.

Sub-s (5): outside the scope of this work.

5 Guidelines

(1) The Commission shall issue a set of guidelines (in this Act referred to as "the guidelines") as to the exercise by the Commission of its functions under section 8.

(2) The Commission—
- (a) shall keep the guidelines under review; and
- (b) may from time to time revise the whole or any part of the guidelines and issue the revised guidelines.

(3) . . .

NOTES

Commencement: 16 February 1998.

Sub-s (3): outside the scope of this work.

Advance notice of public processions and related protest meetings

6 Advance notice of public processions

(1) A person proposing to organise a public procession shall give notice of that proposal in accordance with subsections (2) to (4) to a member of the Royal Ulster Constabulary not below the rank of sergeant by leaving the notice with him at the police station nearest to the proposed starting place of that procession.

(2) Notice under this section shall be given—
- (a) not less than 28 days before the date on which the procession is to be held; or
- (b) if that is not reasonably practicable, as soon as it is reasonably practicable to give such notice.

(3) Notice under this section shall—
- (a) be given in writing in such form as may be prescribed by regulations made by the Secretary of State; and
- (b) be signed by the person giving the notice.

(4) The form prescribed under subsection (3)(a) shall require a person giving notice under this section to specify—
- (a) the date and time when the procession is to be held;
- (b) its route;
- (c) the number of persons likely to take part in it;
- (d) the names of any bands which are to take part in it;
- (e) the arrangements for its control being made by the person proposing to organise it;
- (f) the name and address of that person;
- (g) where the notice is given as mentioned in paragraph (b) of subsection (2), the reason why it was not reasonably practicable to give notice in accordance with paragraph (a) of that subsection; and
- (h) such other matters as appear to the Secretary of State to be necessary for, or appropriate for facilitating, the exercise by the Commission, the Secretary of State or members of the Royal Ulster Constabulary of any function in relation to the procession.

(5) This section does not apply where the procession is—
- (a) a funeral procession; or
- (b) a procession of a class or description specified in an order made by the Secretary of State.

(6) The Chief Constable shall ensure that a copy of a notice given under this section is immediately sent to the Commission.

(7) A person who organises or takes part in a public procession—
- (a) in respect of which the requirements of this section as to notice have not been satisfied; or
- (b) which is held on a date, at a time or along a route which differs from the date, time or route specified in relation to it in the notice given under this section,

shall be guilty of an offence.

(8) In proceedings for an offence under subsection (7) it is a defence for the accused to prove that he did not know of, and neither suspected nor had reason to suspect, the failure to satisfy the requirements of this section or (as the case may be) the difference of date, time or route.

(9) To the extent that an alleged offence under subsection (7) turns on a difference of date, time or route it is a defence for the accused to prove that the difference arose from—
- (a) circumstances beyond his control;
- (b) something done in compliance with conditions imposed under section 8; or
- (c) something done with the agreement of a member of the Royal Ulster Constabulary not below the rank of inspector or by his direction.

(10) . . .

NOTES

Commencement: 2 March 1998.

Sub-s (10): outside the scope of this work.

7 Advance notice of protest meetings related to public processions

(1) Where notice has been given under section 6 in relation to a public procession, a person proposing to organise a related protest meeting shall give notice of that proposal in accordance with subsections (2) to (4) to a member of the Royal Ulster Constabulary not below the rank of sergeant by leaving the notice with him at the police station nearest to the place at which the meeting is to be held.

(2) Notice under this section shall be given—
- (a) not later than 14 days before the date on which the meeting is to be held; or
- (b) if that is not reasonably practicable, as soon as it is reasonably practicable to give such notice.

(3) Notice under this section shall—
- (a) be given in writing in such form as may be prescribed by regulations made by the Secretary of State; and
- (b) be signed by the person giving the notice.

(4) The form prescribed under subsection (3)(a) shall require a person giving notice under this section to specify—
- (a) the date and time when the meeting is to be held;
- (b) the place at which it is to be held;
- (c) the number of persons likely to take part in it;

(d) the arrangements for its control being made by the person proposing to organise it;
(e) the name and address of that person;
(f) where the notice is given as mentioned in paragraph (b) of subsection (2), the reason why it was not reasonably practicable to give notice in accordance with paragraph (a) of that subsection; and
(g) such other matters as appear to the Secretary of State to be necessary for, or appropriate for facilitating, the exercise by the Secretary of State or members of the Royal Ulster Constabulary of any function in relation to the meeting.

(5) The Chief Constable shall ensure that a copy of a notice given under this section is immediately sent to the Commission.

(6) A person who organises or takes part in a protest meeting—
(a) in respect of which the requirements of this section as to notice have not been satisfied; or
(b) which is held on a date or at a time or place which differs from the date, time or place specified in relation to it in the notice given under this section,

shall be guilty of an offence.

(7) In proceedings for an offence under subsection (6) it is a defence for the accused to prove that he did not know of, and neither suspected nor had reason to suspect, the failure to satisfy the requirements of this section or (as the case may be) the difference of date, time or place.

(8) To the extent that an alleged offence under subsection (6) turns on a difference of date, time or place it is a defence for the accused to prove that the difference arose from—
(a) circumstances beyond his control;
(b) something done in compliance with conditions imposed under Article 4(2) of the Public Order (Northern Ireland) Order 1987; or
(c) something done with the agreement of a member of the Royal Ulster Constabulary not below the rank of inspector or by his direction.

(9) . . .

NOTES
Commencement: 2 March 1998.
Sub-s (9): outside the scope of this work.

The Commission's powers to impose conditions on public processions

8 The Commission's powers to impose conditions on public processions

(1) The Commission may issue a determination in respect of a proposed public procession imposing on the persons organising or taking part in it such conditions as the Commission considers necessary.

(2) Without prejudice to the generality of subsection (1), the conditions imposed under that subsection may include conditions as to the route of the procession or prohibiting it from entering any place.

(3) Conditions imposed under subsection (1) may incorporate or be framed by reference to—

(a) the Code of Conduct; or

(b) any other document—

(i) prepared by the person or body organising the procession in question; and

(ii) approved by the Commission for the purposes of this section.

(4) The Commission may, in accordance with the procedural rules, amend or revoke any determination issued under this section.

(5) In considering in any particular case—

(a) whether to issue a determination under this section;

(b) whether to amend or revoke a determination issued under this section; or

(c) what conditions should be imposed by a determination (or amended determination) issued under this section,

the Commission shall have regard to the guidelines.

(6) The guidelines shall in particular (but without prejudice to the generality of section 5(1)) provide for the Commission to have regard to—

(a) any public disorder or damage to property which may result from the procession;

(b) any disruption to the life of the community which the procession may cause;

(c) any impact which the procession may have on relationships within the community;

(d) any failure of a person of a description specified in the guidelines to comply with the Code of Conduct (whether in relation to the procession in question or any related protest meeting or in relation to any previous procession or protest meeting); and

(e) the desirability of allowing a procession customarily held along a particular route to be held along that route.

(7) A person who knowingly fails to comply with a condition imposed under this section shall be guilty of an offence, but it is a defence for him to prove that the failure arose—

(a) from circumstances beyond his control; or

(b) from something done by direction of a member of the Royal Ulster Constabulary not below the rank of inspector.

(8) A person who incites another to commit an offence under subsection (7) shall be guilty of an offence.

(9) . . .

NOTES

Commencement: 2 March 1998 (sub-ss (1)–(5), (7), (8)); 16 February 1998 (sub-s (6)).

Sub-s (9): outside the scope of this work.

9 Review by Secretary of State of determination of Commission under section 8

(1) The Secretary of State shall, on an application made by the Chief Constable, review a determination issued by the Commission under section 8.

(2) On a review of a determination under this section the Secretary of State may—

(a) revoke the determination;

(b) amend the determination by amending or revoking any condition imposed by the determination or by adding any new condition; or

(c) confirm the determination.

(3) In considering in any particular case—

(a) whether to revoke, amend or confirm a determination; or

(b) what amendments should be made to a determination,

the Secretary of State shall have regard to the guidelines.

(4) Wherever practicable the Secretary of State shall before revoking, amending or confirming a determination under this section consult the Commission; but nothing in this subsection shall affect the validity of any revocation, amendment or confirmation under this section.

(5)–(7) . . .

NOTES

Commencement: 2 March 1998.

Sub-ss (5)–(7): outside the scope of this work.

10 Saving for powers of a constable

Nothing in section 8 or 9 or in any determination of the Commission affects the common law powers of a constable to take action to deal with or prevent a breach of the peace.

NOTES

Commencement: 2 March 1998.

Secretary of State's powers to prohibit public processions

11 Secretary of State's powers to prohibit public processions

(1) If, in the case of any proposed public procession, the Secretary of State is of the opinion that, having regard to—

(a) any serious public disorder or serious damage to property which may result from the procession;

(b) any serious disruption to the life of the community which the procession may cause;

(c) any serious impact which the procession may have on relationships within the community; and

(d) any undue demands which the procession may cause to be made on the police or military forces,

it is necessary in the public interest to do so, he may by order prohibit the holding of that procession.

(2) If, in relation to any area and any period of time not exceeding 28 days, the Secretary of State is of the opinion that, having regard to—

(a) any serious public disorder or serious damage to property which may result from public processions of a particular class or description in that area in that period;

(b) any serious disruption to the life of the community which such processions may cause;

(c) any serious impact which such processions may have on relationships within the community;

(d) any undue demands which such processions may cause to be made on the police or military forces; and

(e) the extent of the powers exercisable under subsection (1),

it is necessary in the public interest to do so, he may by order prohibit the holding of all public processions of that class or description in that area in that period.

(3) If, in relation to any area and any period of time not exceeding 28 days, the Secretary of State is of the opinion that, having regard to—

(a) any serious public disorder or serious damage to property which may result from public processions in that area in that period;

(b) any serious disruption to the life of the community which such processions may cause;

(c) any serious impact which such processions may have on relationships within the community;

(d) any undue demands which such processions may cause to be made on the police or military forces; and

(e) the extent of the powers exercisable under subsections (1) and (2),

it is necessary in the public interest to do so, he may by order prohibit the holding of all public processions in that area in that period.

(4) An order under subsection (2) or (3) may exempt any procession, or any procession of any class or description, specified in the order.

(5) Wherever practicable the Secretary of State shall before making an order under this section consult—

(a) the Commission; and

(b) the Chief Constable,

but nothing in this subsection shall affect the validity of any such order.

(6), (7) . . .

(8) A person who organises or takes part in a public procession the holding of which he knows is prohibited by an order under this section shall be guilty of an offence.

(9) . . .

NOTES

Commencement: 2 March 1998.

Sub-ss (6), (7), (9): outside the scope of this work.

General regulation of public processions

12 Registration of bands taking part in public processions

(1) The Secretary of State may by order provide for the registration of bands.

(2), (3) . . .

(4) A person who knowingly takes part in a public procession as a member of a band which—

(a) is one to which an order under subsection (1) applies, but is not registered under that order; or

(b) does not comply with any condition subject to which it is registered under such an order,

shall be guilty of an offence.

(5) . . .

NOTES
Commencement: 2 March 1998.
Sub-ss (2), (3), (5): outside the scope of this work.

14 Breaking up public procession

(1) A person who for the purpose of preventing or hindering any lawful public procession or of annoying persons taking part in or endeavouring to take part in any such procession—

(a) hinders, molests or obstructs those persons or any of them;
(b) acts in a disorderly way towards those persons or any of them; or
(c) behaves offensively and abusively towards those persons or any of them,

shall be guilty of an offence.

(2) . . .

NOTES
Commencement: 2 March 1998.
Sub-s (2): outside the scope of this work.

Supplementary

15 Powers of arrest

A constable in uniform may arrest without warrant anyone he reasonably suspects is committing an offence under this Act.

NOTES
Commencement: 2 March 1998.

19 Short title, commencement, transitional provision and extent

(1) This Act may be cited as the Public Processions (Northern Ireland) Act 1998.

(2)–(4) . . .

(5) Except for—

(a) paragraphs 1 and 2 of Schedule 3 and section 18(1) so far as relating thereto; and
(b) this section,

this Act extends to Northern Ireland only.

NOTES
Commencement: 16 February 1998.
Sub-ss (2)–(4): outside the scope of this work.

NORTHERN IRELAND (ELECTIONS) ACT 1998

(C 12)

An Act to make provision for the establishment of the New Northern Ireland Assembly and for the election of its members.

[7 May 1998]

The New Northern Ireland Assembly

1 The Assembly

(1) There shall be an Assembly called the New Northern Ireland Assembly, for the purpose of taking part in preparations to give effect to the agreement reached at the multi-party talks on Northern Ireland set out in Command Paper 3883.

(2) The Secretary of State may refer to the Assembly—
- (a) specific matters arising from that agreement, and
- (b) such other matters as he thinks fit.

(3) The Assembly shall consist of 108 members.

(4) The initial members shall be returned at an election for the constituencies in Northern Ireland which would return members to the Parliament of the United Kingdom if a general election were held on the date of the passing of this Act.

(5) Each constituency shall return six members.

(6) The Schedule to this Act (which makes supplementary provision about the Assembly) shall have effect.

NOTES

Commencement: 28 May 1998.

2 The election

(1) The poll for the election of the initial members of the Assembly shall be held on 25th June 1998.

(2) A person is entitled to vote at the election in a constituency if on the day of the poll—
- (a) he would be entitled to vote as an elector at a local election in a district electoral area wholly or partly comprised in the constituency, and
- (b) he is registered at an address in the constituency in a register of local electors.

(3) Each vote in the poll shall be a single transferable vote.

(4)–(6) . . .

NOTES

Commencement: 28 May 1998 (sub-ss (1)–(3)).
Sub-ss (4)–(6): outside the scope of this work.

3 Vacancies

(1) The Secretary of State may by order make provision for the filling of vacancies occurring in the Assembly's membership after the election under section 2.

(2) Such provision may be made by reference to by-elections or substitutes or such other method of filling vacancies as the Secretary of State thinks fit.

NOTES

Commencement: 7 May 1998.

4 Disqualification

(1) Subject to subsections (3) and (4) a person is disqualified for membership of the Assembly if he is disqualified for membership of the House of Commons, whether under the House of Commons Disqualification Act 1975 or otherwise.

(2) A person who is Her Majesty's Lord-Lieutenant or Lieutenant for a county or county borough in Northern Ireland is disqualified for membership of the Assembly for a constituency comprising the whole or part of the county or county borough.

(3) A person is not disqualified for membership of the Assembly by reason only—

(a) that he is a peer (other than a Lord of Appeal in Ordinary), or

(b) that he is a member of the Seanad Eireann (Senate of the Republic of Ireland).

(4)–(6) . . .

NOTES

Commencement: 28 May 1998.

Sub-ss (4)–(6): outside the scope of this work.

5 Disqualification: judicial proceedings

(1) Any person who claims that a person purporting to be a member of the Assembly—

(a) is disqualified, or

(b) was disqualified when, or at any time since, he was returned,

may apply to the High Court of Justice in Northern Ireland for a declaration to that effect.

(2)–(4) . . .

NOTES

Commencement: 28 May 1998.

Sub-ss (2)–(4): outside the scope of this work.

General

6 Orders

(1) Any power to make an order under this Act shall be exercised by statutory instrument.

(2) An order under section 2(5) or 3(1)—

(a) shall not be made unless a draft has been laid before, and approved by resolution of, each House of Parliament, and

(b) may apply (with or without modifications) any provision of, or made under, any enactment.

NOTES

Commencement: 7 May 1998.

8 Commencement

(1) Sections 2(5) and (6), 3 and 6 and this section shall come into force on the day on which this Act is passed.

(2) The remaining provisions of this Act shall come into force on such day as the Secretary of State may appoint by order.

(3) The Secretary of State shall appoint a day only if—

(a) a referendum is held about the agreement reached at the multi-party talks on Northern Ireland set out in Command Paper 3883, and

(b) a majority of those voting support the agreement.

NOTES

Commencement: 7 May 1998.

9 Short title

This Act may be cited as the Northern Ireland (Elections) Act 1998.

NOTES

Commencement: 28 May 1998.

SCHEDULE

Section 1

THE ASSEMBLY

Meetings

1. Meetings shall be held at such times and places as the Secretary of State directs.

Proceedings

2. Proceedings shall be conducted in accordance with standing orders.

Presiding officer

3.—(1) The Secretary of State shall appoint—

(a) the initial presiding officer, and

(b) the initial deputy presiding officer.

(2) Standing orders may make provision for the replacement of the presiding officer or the deputy presiding officer by the Secretary of State or by the Assembly.

4–6. . . .

Vacancies

7. If a seat becomes vacant by reason of resignation, death or disqualification the presiding officer shall as soon as reasonably practicable inform the Chief Electoral Officer for Northern Ireland.

Privilege

8. A written or oral statement made by a member in or for the purposes of the Assembly (or any committee it may establish) shall be privileged from action for defamation unless it is proved to have been made with malice.

9. . . .

Standing orders

10.—(1) References to standing orders are to orders determined by the Secretary of State from time to time and notified to the presiding officer.

(2) Section 6(1) does not apply to standing orders.

NOTES
Commencement: 28 May 1998.
Paras 4–6, 9: outside the scope of this work.

EUROPEAN COMMUNITIES (AMENDMENT) ACT 1998

(C 21)

An Act to make provision consequential on the Treaty signed at Amsterdam on 2nd October 1997 amending the Treaty on European Union, the Treaties establishing the European Communities and certain related Acts

[11 June 1998]

2 European Parliament

For the purpose of section 6 of the European Parliamentary Elections Act 1978 (approval of treaties increasing the Parliament's powers) the Treaty signed at Amsterdam on 2nd October 1997 amending the Treaty on European Union, the Treaties establishing the European Communities and certain related Acts is approved.

NOTES
Commencement: 11 June 1998.

3 Short title

This Act may be cited as the European Communities (Amendment) Act 1998.

NOTES
Commencement: 11 June 1998.

PUBLIC INTEREST DISCLOSURE ACT 1998

(C 23)

An Act to protect individuals who make certain disclosures of information in the public interest; to allow such individuals to bring action in respect of victimisation; and for connected purposes.

[2 July 1998]

1 Protected disclosures

After Part IV of the Employment Rights Act 1996 (in this Act referred to as "the 1996 Act") there is inserted—

"PART IVA
PROTECTED DISCLOSURES

43A Meaning of "protected disclosure"

In this Act a "protected disclosure" means a qualifying disclosure (as defined by section 43B) which is made by a worker in accordance with any of sections 43C to 43H.

43B Disclosures qualifying for protection

(1) In this Part a "qualifying disclosure" means any disclosure of information which, in the reasonable belief of the worker making the disclosure, tends to show one or more of the following—

(a) that a criminal offence has been committed, is being committed or is likely to be committed,

(b) that a person has failed, is failing or is likely to fail to comply with any legal obligation to which he is subject,

(c) that a miscarriage of justice has occurred, is occurring or is likely to occur,

(d) that the health or safety of any individual has been, is being or is likely to be endangered,

(e) that the environment has been, is being or is likely to be damaged, or

(f) that information tending to show any matter falling within any one of the preceding paragraphs has been, or is likely to be deliberately concealed.

(2) For the purposes of subsection (1), it is immaterial whether the relevant failure occurred, occurs or would occur in the United Kingdom or elsewhere, and whether the law applying to it is that of the United Kingdom or of any other country or territory.

(3) A disclosure of information is not a qualifying disclosure if the person making the disclosure commits an offence by making it.

(4) A disclosure of information in respect of which a claim to legal professional privilege (or, in Scotland, to confidentiality as between client and professional legal adviser) could be maintained in legal proceedings is not a qualifying disclosure if it is made by a person to whom the information had been disclosed in the course of obtaining legal advice.

(5) In this Part "the relevant failure", in relation to a qualifying disclosure, means the matter falling within paragraphs (a) to (f) of subsection (1).

43C Disclosure to employer or other responsible person

(1) A qualifying disclosure is made in accordance with this section if the worker makes the disclosure in good faith—

(a) to his employer, or

(b) where the worker reasonably believes that the relevant failure relates solely or mainly to—

(i) the conduct of a person other than his employer, or

(ii) any other matter for which a person other than his employer has legal responsibility,

to that other person.

(2) A worker who, in accordance with a procedure whose use by him is authorised by his employer, makes a qualifying disclosure to a person other than his employer, is to be treated for the purposes of this Part as making the qualifying disclosure to his employer.

43D Disclosure to legal adviser

A qualifying disclosure is made in accordance with this section if it is made in the course of obtaining legal advice.

43E Disclosure to Minister of the Crown

A qualifying disclosure is made in accordance with this section if—

(a) the worker's employer is—

(i) an individual appointed under any enactment by a Minister of the Crown, or

(ii) a body any of whose members are so appointed, and

(b) the disclosure is made in good faith to a Minister of the Crown.

43F Disclosure to prescribed person

(1) A qualifying disclosure is made in accordance with this section if the worker—

(a) makes the disclosure in good faith to a person prescribed by an order made by the Secretary of State for the purposes of this section, and

(b) reasonably believes—

(i) that the relevant failure falls within any description of matters in respect of which that person is so prescribed, and

(ii) that the information disclosed, and any allegation contained in it, are substantially true.

(2) An order prescribing persons for the purposes of this section may specify persons or descriptions of persons, and shall specify the descriptions of matters in respect of which each person, or persons of each description, is or are prescribed.

43G Disclosure in other cases

(1) A qualifying disclosure is made in accordance with this section if—

(a) the worker makes the disclosure in good faith,

(b) he reasonably believes that the information disclosed, and any allegation contained in it, are substantially true,

(c) he does not make the disclosure for purposes of personal gain,

(d) any of the conditions in subsection (2) is met, and

(e) in all the circumstances of the case, it is reasonable for him to make the disclosure.

(2) The conditions referred to in subsection (1)(d) are—

(a) that, at the time he makes the disclosure, the worker reasonably believes that he will be subjected to a detriment by his employer if he makes a disclosure to his employer or in accordance with section 43F,

(b) that, in a case where no person is prescribed for the purposes of section 43F in relation to the relevant failure, the worker reasonably believes that it is likely that evidence relating to the relevant failure will be concealed or destroyed if he makes a disclosure to his employer, or

(c) that the worker has previously made a disclosure of substantially the same information—

(i) to his employer, or

(ii) in accordance with section 43F.

(3) In determining for the purposes of subsection (1)(e) whether it is reasonable for the worker to make the disclosure, regard shall be had, in particular, to—

(a) the identity of the person to whom the disclosure is made,

(b) the seriousness of the relevant failure,

(c) whether the relevant failure is continuing or is likely to occur in the future,

(d) whether the disclosure is made in breach of a duty of confidentiality owed by the employer to any other person,

(e) in a case falling within subsection (2)(c)(i) or (ii), any action which the employer or the person to whom the previous disclosure in accordance with section 43F was made has taken or might reasonably be expected to have taken as a result of the previous disclosure, and

(f) in a case falling within subsection (2)(c)(i), whether in making the disclosure to the employer the worker complied with any procedure whose use by him was authorised by the employer.

(4) For the purposes of this section a subsequent disclosure may be regarded as a disclosure of substantially the same information as that disclosed by a previous disclosure as mentioned in subsection (2)(c) even though the subsequent disclosure extends to information about action taken or not taken by any person as a result of the previous disclosure.

43H Disclosure of exceptionally serious failure

(1) A qualifying disclosure is made in accordance with this section if—

(a) the worker makes the disclosure in good faith,

(b) he reasonably believes that the information disclosed, and any allegation contained in it, are substantially true,

(c) he does not make the disclosure for purposes of personal gain,

(d) the relevant failure is of an exceptionally serious nature, and

(e) in all the circumstances of the case, it is reasonable for him to make the disclosure.

(2) In determining for the purposes of subsection (1)(e) whether it is reasonable for the worker to make the disclosure, regard shall be had, in particular, to the identity of the person to whom the disclosure is made.

43J Contractual duties of confidentiality

(1) Any provision in an agreement to which this section applies is void in so far as it purports to preclude the worker from making a protected disclosure.

(2) This section applies to any agreement between a worker and his employer (whether a worker's contract or not), including an agreement to refrain from instituting or continuing any proceedings under this Act or any proceedings for breach of contract.

. . . . ."

NOTES

Commencement: 2 July 1998, so far as relates to power to make order under the Employment Rights Act 1996, s 43F; to be appointed, otherwise.

Sections omitted (ss 43K, 43L, as inserted by this section): outside the scope of this work.

2 Right not to suffer detriment

After section 47A of the 1996 Act there is inserted—

"47B Protected disclosures

(1) A worker has the right not to be subjected to any detriment by any act, or any deliberate failure to act, by his employer done on the ground that the worker has made a protected disclosure.

(2) Except where the worker is an employee who is dismissed in circumstances in which, by virtue of section 197, Part X does not apply to the dismissal, this section does not apply where—

(a) the worker is an employee, and

(b) the detriment in question amounts to dismissal (within the meaning of that Part).

(3) For the purposes of this section, and of sections 48 and 49 so far as relating to this section, "worker", "worker's contract", "employment" and "employer" have the extended meaning given by section 43K."

NOTES

Commencement: to be appointed.

3 Complaints to employment tribunal

In section 48 of the 1996 Act (complaints to employment tribunals), after subsection (1) there is inserted—

"(1A) A worker may present a complaint to an employment tribunal that he has been subjected to a detriment in contravention of section 47B."

NOTES

Commencement: to be appointed.

5 Unfair dismissal

After section 103 of the 1996 Act there is inserted—

"103A Protected disclosure

An employee who is dismissed shall be regarded for the purposes of this Part as unfairly dismissed if the reason (or, if more than one, the principal reason) for the dismissal is that the employee made a protected disclosure."

NOTES

Commencement: to be appointed.

6 Redundancy

After subsection (6) of section 105 of the 1996 Act (redundancy) there is inserted—

"(6A) This subsection applies if the reason (or, if more than one, the principal reason) for which the employee was selected for dismissal was that specified in section 103A."

NOTES

Commencement: to be appointed.

7 Exclusion of restrictions on right not to be unfairly dismissed

(1) In subsection (3) of section 108 of the 1996 Act (cases where qualifying period of employment not required), after paragraph (f) there is inserted—

"(ff) section 103A applies,"

(2) In subsection (2) of section 109 of the 1996 Act (disapplication of upper age limit), after paragraph (f) there is inserted—

"(ff) section 103A applies,".

NOTES

Commencement: to be appointed.

8 Compensation for unfair dismissal

(1)–(3) . . .

(4) After section 127A of the 1996 Act there is inserted—

"127B Dismissal as a result of protected disclosure

(1) This section applies where the reason (or, if more than one, the principal reason)—

(a) in a redundancy case, for selecting the employee for dismissal, or
(b) otherwise, for the dismissal,

is that specified in section 103A.

(2), (3) . . ."

NOTES

Commencement: 2 July 1998, so far as relates to power to make regulations under the Employment Rights Act 1996, s 127B; to be appointed, otherwise.

Sub-ss (1)–(3): outside the scope of this work.

Sub-s (4): s 127B(2), (3): outside the scope of this work.

18 Short title, interpretation, commencement and extent

(1) This Act may be cited as the Public Interest Disclosure Act 1998.

(2) In this Act "the 1996 Act" means the Employment Rights Act 1996.

(3) Subject to subsection (4), this Act shall come into force on such day or days as the Secretary of State may by order made by statutory instrument appoint, and different days may be appointed for different purposes.

(4) The following provisions shall come into force on the passing of this Act—

(a) section 1 so far as relating to the power to make an order under section 43F of the 1996 Act,
(b) section 8 so far as relating to the power to make regulations under section 127B of the 1996 Act,
(c) section 17, and
(d) this section.

(5) This Act, except section 17, does not extend to Northern Ireland.

NOTES

Commencement: 2 July 1998.

DATA PROTECTION ACT 1998

(c 29)

An Act to make new provision for the regulation of the processing of information relating to individuals, including the obtaining, holding, use or disclosure of such information.

[16 July 1998]

PART I
PRELIMINARY

1 Basic interpretative provisions

(1) In this Act, unless the context otherwise requires—

"data" means information which—

(a) is being processed by means of equipment operating automatically in response to instructions given for that purpose,

(b) is recorded with the intention that it should be processed by means of such equipment,

(c) is recorded as part of a relevant filing system or with the intention that it should form part of a relevant filing system, or

(d) does not fall within paragraph (a), (b) or (c) but forms part of an accessible record as defined by section 68;

"data controller" means, subject to subsection (4), a person who (either alone or jointly or in common with other persons) determines the purposes for which and the manner in which any personal data are, or are to be, processed;

"data processor", in relation to personal data, means any person (other than an employee of the data controller) who processes the data on behalf of the data controller;

"data subject" means an individual who is the subject of personal data;

"personal data" means data which relate to a living individual who can be identified—

(a) from those data, or

(b) from those data and other information which is in the possession of, or is likely to come into the possession of, the data controller,

and includes any expression of opinion about the individual and any indication of the intentions of the data controller or any other person in respect of the individual;

"processing", in relation to information or data, means obtaining, recording or holding the information or data or carrying out any operation or set of operations on the information or data, including—

(a) organisation, adaptation or alteration of the information or data,

(b) retrieval, consultation or use of the information or data,

(c) disclosure of the information or data by transmission, dissemination or otherwise making available, or

(d) alignment, combination, blocking, erasure or destruction of the information or data;

"relevant filing system" means any set of information relating to individuals to the extent that, although the information is not processed by means of equipment operating automatically in response to instructions given for that purpose, the set is structured, either by reference to individuals or by reference to criteria relating to individuals, in such a way that specific information relating to a particular individual is readily accessible.

(2) In this Act, unless the context otherwise requires—

(a) "obtaining" or "recording", in relation to personal data, includes obtaining or recording the information to be contained in the data, and

(b) "using" or "disclosing", in relation to personal data, includes using or disclosing the information contained in the data.

(3) In determining for the purposes of this Act whether any information is recorded with the intention—

(a) that it should be processed by means of equipment operating automatically in response to instructions given for that purpose, or

(b) that it should form part of a relevant filing system,

it is immaterial that it is intended to be so processed or to form part of such a system only after being transferred to a country or territory outside the European Economic Area.

(4) Where personal data are processed only for purposes for which they are required by or under any enactment to be processed, the person on whom the obligation to process the data is imposed by or under that enactment is for the purposes of this Act the data controller.

NOTES

Commencement: 16 July 1998.

2 Sensitive personal data

In this Act "sensitive personal data" means personal data consisting of information as to—

(a) the racial or ethnic origin of the data subject,

(b) his political opinions,

(c) his religious beliefs or other beliefs of a similar nature,

(d) whether he is a member of a trade union (within the meaning of the Trade Union and Labour Relations (Consolidation) Act 1992,

(e) his physical or mental health or condition,

(f) his sexual life,

(g) the commission or alleged commission by him of any offence, or

(h) any proceedings for any offence committed or alleged to have been committed by him, the disposal of such proceedings or the sentence of any court in such proceedings.

NOTES

Commencement: 16 July 1998.

3 The special purposes

In this Act "the special purposes" means any one or more of the following—

(a) the purposes of journalism,

(b) artistic purposes, and

(c) literary purposes.

NOTES

Commencement: 16 July 1998.

4 The data protection principles

(1) References in this Act to the data protection principles are to the principles set out in Part I of Schedule 1.

(2) Those principles are to be interpreted in accordance with Part II of Schedule 1.

(3) Schedule 2 (which applies to all personal data) and Schedule 3 (which applies only to sensitive personal data) set out conditions applying for the purposes of the first principle; and Schedule 4 sets out cases in which the eighth principle does not apply.

(4) Subject to section 27(1), it shall be the duty of a data controller to comply with the data protection principles in relation to all personal data with respect to which he is the data controller.

NOTES

Commencement: to be appointed.

5 Application of Act

(1) Except as otherwise provided by or under section 54, this Act applies to a data controller in respect of any data only if—

(a) the data controller is established in the United Kingdom and the data are processed in the context of that establishment, or

(b) the data controller is established neither in the United Kingdom nor in any other EEA State but uses equipment in the United Kingdom for processing the data otherwise than for the purposes of transit through the United Kingdom.

(2) (3) . . .

NOTES

Commencement: to be appointed.

Sub-ss (2), (3): outside the scope of this work.

6 The Commissioner and the Tribunal

(1) The office originally established by section 3(1)(a) of the Data Protection Act 1984 as the office of Data Protection Registrar shall continue to exist for the purposes of this Act but shall be known as the office of Data Protection Commissioner; and in this Act the Data Protection Commissioner is referred to as "the Commissioner".

(2) The Commissioner shall be appointed by Her Majesty by Letters Patent.

(3) For the purposes of this Act there shall continue to be a Data Protection Tribunal (in this Act referred to as "the Tribunal").

(4) The Tribunal shall consist of—

(a) a chairman appointed by the Lord Chancellor after consultation with the Lord Advocate,

(b) such number of deputy chairmen so appointed as the Lord Chancellor may determine, and

(c) such number of other members appointed by the Secretary of State as he may determine.

(5) The members of the Tribunal appointed under subsection (4)(a) and (b) shall be—

(a) persons who have a 7 year general qualification, within the meaning of section 71 of the Courts and Legal Services Act 1990,

(b) advocates or solicitors in Scotland of at least 7 years' standing, or

(c) members of the bar of Northern Ireland or solicitors of the Supreme Court of Northern Ireland of at least 7 years' standing.

(6) The members of the Tribunal appointed under subsection (4)(c) shall be—

(a) persons to represent the interests of data subjects, and

(b) persons to represent the interests of data controllers.

(7) Schedule 5 has effect in relation to the Commissioner and the Tribunal.

NOTES

Commencement: to be appointed.

PART II
RIGHTS OF DATA SUBJECTS AND OTHERS

7 Right of access to personal data

(1) Subject to the following provisions of this section and to sections 8 and 9, an individual is entitled—

(a) to be informed by any data controller whether personal data of which that individual is the data subject are being processed by or on behalf of that data controller,

(b) if that is the case, to be given by the data controller a description of—

(i) the personal data of which that individual is the data subject,

(ii) the purposes for which they are being or are to be processed, and

(iii) the recipients or classes of recipients to whom they are or may be disclosed,

(c) to have communicated to him in an intelligible form—

(i) the information constituting any personal data of which that individual is the data subject, and

(ii) any information available to the data controller as to the source of those data, and

(d) where the processing by automatic means of personal data of which that individual is the data subject for the purpose of evaluating matters relating to him such as, for example, his performance at work, his creditworthiness, his reliability or his conduct, has constituted or is likely to constitute the sole basis for any decision significantly affecting him, to be informed by the data controller of the logic involved in that decision-taking.

(2)–(7) . . .

(8) Subject to subsection (4), a data controller shall comply with a request under this section promptly and in any event before the end of the prescribed period beginning with the relevant day.

(9) If a court is satisfied on the application of any person who has made a request under the foregoing provisions of this section that the data controller in question has

failed to comply with the request in contravention of those provisions, the court may order him to comply with the request.

(10) In this section—

"prescribed" means prescribed by the Secretary of State by regulations;

"the prescribed maximum" means such amount as may be prescribed;

"the prescribed period" means forty days or such other period as may be prescribed;

"the relevant day", in relation to a request under this section, means the day on which the data controller receives the request or, if later, the first day on which the data controller has both the required fee and the information referred to in subsection (3).

(11) Different amounts or periods may be prescribed under this section in relation to different cases.

NOTES

Commencement: 16 July 1998 (sub-s (10), in so far as conferring the power to make subordinate legislation); to be appointed (otherwise).

Sub-ss (2)–(7): outside the scope of this work.

10 Right to prevent processing likely to cause damage or distress

(1) Subject to subsection (2), an individual is entitled at any time by notice in writing to a data controller to require the data controller at the end of such period as is reasonable in the circumstances to cease, or not to begin, processing, or processing for a specified purpose or in a specified manner, any personal data in respect of which he is the data subject, on the ground that, for specified reasons—

(a) the processing of those data or their processing for that purpose or in that manner is causing or is likely to cause substantial damage or substantial distress to him or to another, and

(b) that damage or distress is or would be unwarranted.

(2) Subsection (1) does not apply—

(a) in a case where any of the conditions in paragraphs 1 to 4 of Schedule 2 is met, or

(b) in such other cases as may be prescribed by the Secretary of State by order.

(3) The data controller must within twenty-one days of receiving a notice under subsection (1) ("the data subject notice") give the individual who gave it a written notice—

(a) stating that he has complied or intends to comply with the data subject notice, or

(b) stating his reasons for regarding the data subject notice as to any extent unjustified and the extent (if any) to which he has complied or intends to comply with it.

(4) If a court is satisfied, on the application of any person who has given a notice under subsection (1) which appears to the court to be justified (or to be justified to any extent), that the data controller in question has failed to comply with the notice, the court may order him to take such steps for complying with the notice (or for complying with it to that extent) as the court thinks fit.

(5) The failure by a data subject to exercise the right conferred by subsection (1) or section 11(1) does not affect any other right conferred on him by this Part.

NOTES

Commencement: 16 July 1998 (sub-s (2), in so far as conferring the power to make subordinate legislation); to be appointed (otherwise).

13 Compensation for failure to comply with certain requirements

(1) An individual who suffers damage by reason of any contravention by a data controller of any of the requirements of this Act is entitled to compensation from the data controller for that damage.

(2) An individual who suffers distress by reason of any contravention by a data controller of any of the requirements of this Act is entitled to compensation from the data controller for that distress if—

(a) the individual also suffers damage by reason of the contravention, or

(b) the contravention relates to the processing of personal data for the special purposes.

(3) In proceedings brought against a person by virtue of this section it is a defence to prove that he had taken such care as in all the circumstances was reasonably required to comply with the requirement concerned.

NOTES

Commencement: to be appointed.

14 Rectification, blocking, erasure and destruction

(1) If a court is satisfied on the application of a data subject that personal data of which the applicant is the subject are inaccurate, the court may order the data controller to rectify, block, erase or destroy those data and any other personal data in respect of which he is the data controller and which contain an expression of opinion which appears to the court to be based on the inaccurate data.

(2) Subsection (1) applies whether or not the data accurately record information received or obtained by the data controller from the data subject or a third party but where the data accurately record such information, then—

(a) if the requirements mentioned in paragraph 7 of Part II of Schedule 1 have been complied with, the court may, instead of making an order under subsection (1), make an order requiring the data to be supplemented by such statement of the true facts relating to the matters dealt with by the data as the court may approve, and

(b) if all or any of those requirements have not been complied with, the court may, instead of making an order under that subsection, make such order as it thinks fit for securing compliance with those requirements with or without a further order requiring the data to be supplemented by such a statement as is mentioned in paragraph (a).

(3) . . .

(4) If a court is satisfied on the application of a data subject—

(a) that he has suffered damage by reason of any contravention by a data controller of any of the requirements of this Act in respect of any personal data, in circumstances entitling him to compensation under section 13, and

(b) that there is a substantial risk of further contravention in respect of those data in such circumstances, the court may order the rectification, blocking, erasure or destruction of any of those data.

(5), (6). . . .

NOTES

Commencement: to be appointed.

Sub-ss (3), (5), (6): outside the scope of this work.

PART III
NOTIFICATION BY DATA CONTROLLERS

17 Prohibition on processing without registration

(1) Subject to the following provisions of this section, personal data must not be processed unless an entry in respect of the data controller is included in the register maintained by the Commissioner under section 19 (or is treated by notification regulations made by virtue of section 19(3) as being so included).

(2) Except where the processing is assessable processing for the purposes of section 22, subsection (1) does not apply in relation to personal data consisting of information which falls neither within paragraph (a) of the definition of "data" in section 1(1) nor within paragraph (b) of that definition.

(3) If it appears to the Secretary of State that processing of a particular description is unlikely to prejudice the rights and freedoms of data subjects, notification regulations may provide that, in such cases as may be prescribed, subsection (1) is not to apply in relation to processing of that description.

(4) Subsection (1) does not apply in relation to any processing whose sole purpose is the maintenance of a public register.

NOTES

Commencement: 16 July 1998 (sub-s (3), in so far as conferring the power to make subordinate legislation); to be appointed (otherwise).

PART IV
EXEMPTIONS

27 Preliminary

(1) References in any of the data protection principles or any provision of Parts II and III to personal data or to the processing of personal data do not include references to data or processing which by virtue of this Part are exempt from that principle or other provision.

(2) In this Part "the subject information provisions" means—

(a) the first data protection principle to the extent to which it requires compliance with paragraph 2 of Part II of Schedule 1, and

(b) section 7.

(3) In this Part "the non-disclosure provisions" means the provisions specified in subsection (4) to the extent to which they are inconsistent with the disclosure in question.

(4) The provisions referred to in subsection (3) are—

(a) the first data protection principle, except to the extent to which it requires compliance with the conditions in Schedules 2 and 3,
(b) the second, third, fourth and fifth data protection principles, and
(c) sections 10 and 14(1) to (3).

(5) Except as provided by this Part, the subject information provisions shall have effect notwithstanding any enactment or rule of law prohibiting or restricting the disclosure, or authorising the withholding, of information.

NOTES
Commencement: to be appointed.

28 National security

(1) Personal data are exempt from any of the provisions of—
(a) the data protection principles,
(b) Parts II, III and V, and
(c) section 55,

if the exemption from that provision is required for the purpose of safeguarding national security.

(2) Subject to subsection (4), a certificate signed by a Minister of the Crown certifying that exemption from all or any of the provisions mentioned in subsection (1) is or at any time was required for the purpose there mentioned in respect of any personal data shall be conclusive evidence of that fact.

(3) A certificate under subsection (2) may identify the personal data to which it applies by means of a general description and may be expressed to have prospective effect.

(4) Any person directly affected by the issuing of a certificate under subsection (2) may appeal to the Tribunal against the certificate.

(5) If on an appeal under subsection (4), the Tribunal finds that, applying the principles applied by the court on an application for judicial review, the Minister did not have reasonable grounds for issuing the certificate, the Tribunal may allow the appeal and quash the certificate.

(6) Where in any proceedings under or by virtue of this Act it is claimed by a data controller that a certificate under subsection (2) which identifies the personal data to which it applies by means of a general description applies to any personal data, any other party to the proceedings may appeal to the Tribunal on the ground that the certificate does not apply to the personal data in question and, subject to any determination under subsection (7), the certificate shall be conclusively presumed so to apply.

(7) On any appeal under subsection (6), the Tribunal may determine that the certificate does not so apply.

(8)–(10) . . .

(11) No power conferred by any provision of Part V may be exercised in relation to personal data which by virtue of this section are exempt from that provision.

(12) . . .

NOTES

Commencement: to be appointed.

Sub-ss (8)–(10), (12): outside the scope of this work.

29 Crime and taxation

(1) Personal data processed for any of the following purposes—

(a) the prevention or detection of crime,

(b) the apprehension or prosecution of offenders, or

(c) the assessment or collection of any tax or duty or of any imposition of a similar nature,

are exempt from the first data protection principle (except to the extent to which it requires compliance with the conditions in Schedules 2 and 3) and section 7 in any case to the extent to which the application of those provisions to the data would be likely to prejudice any of the matters mentioned in this subsection.

(2) Personal data which—

(a) are processed for the purpose of discharging statutory functions, and

(b) consist of information obtained for such a purpose from a person who had it in his possession for any of the purposes mentioned in subsection (1),

are exempt from the subject information provisions to the same extent as personal data processed for any of the purposes mentioned in that subsection.

(3) Personal data are exempt from the non-disclosure provisions in any case in which—

(a) the disclosure is for any of the purposes mentioned in subsection (1), and

(b) the application of those provisions in relation to the disclosure would be likely to prejudice any of the matters mentioned in that subsection.

(4) Personal data in respect of which the data controller is a relevant authority and which—

(a) consist of a classification applied to the data subject as part of a system of risk assessment which is operated by that authority for either of the following purposes—

(i) the assessment or collection of any tax or duty or any imposition of a similar nature, or

(ii) the prevention or detection of crime, or apprehension or prosecution of offenders, where the offence concerned involves any unlawful claim for any payment out of, or any unlawful application of, public funds, and

(b) are processed for either of those purposes,

are exempt from section 7 to the extent to which the exemption is required in the interests of the operation of the system.

(5) In subsection (4)—

"public funds" includes funds provided by any Community institution;

"relevant authority" means—

(a) a government department,

(b) a local authority, or

(c) any other authority administering housing benefit or council tax benefit.

NOTES

Commencement: to be appointed.

30 Health, education and social work

(1) The Secretary of State may by order exempt from the subject information provisions, or modify those provisions in relation to, personal data consisting of information as to the physical or mental health or condition of the data subject.

(2) The Secretary of State may by order exempt from the subject information provisions, or modify those provisions in relation to—

(a) personal data in respect of which the data controller is the proprietor of, or a teacher at, a school, and which consist of information relating to persons who are or have been pupils at the school, or

(b) personal data in respect of which the data controller is an education authority in Scotland, and which consist of information relating to persons who are receiving, or have received, further education provided by the authority.

(3) The Secretary of State may by order exempt from the subject information provisions, or modify those provisions in relation to, personal data of such other descriptions as may be specified in the order, being information—

(a) processed by government departments or local authorities or by voluntary organisations or other bodies designated by or under the order, and

(b) appearing to him to be processed in the course of, or for the purposes of, carrying out social work in relation to the data subject or other individuals;

but the Secretary of State shall not under this subsection confer any exemption or make any modification except so far as he considers that the application to the data of those provisions (or of those provisions without modification) would be likely to prejudice the carrying out of social work.

(4), (5) . . .

NOTES

Commencement: 16 July 1998 (sub-ss (1)–(3), in so far as conferring the power to make subordinate legislation); to be appointed (otherwise).

Sub-ss (4), (5): outside the scope of this work.

31 Regulatory activity

(1) Personal data processed for the purposes of discharging functions to which this subsection applies are exempt from the subject information provisions in any case to the extent to which the application of those provisions to the data would be likely to prejudice the proper discharge of those functions.

(2) Subsection (1) applies to any relevant function which is designed—

(a) for protecting members of the public against—

(i) financial loss due to dishonesty, malpractice or other seriously improper conduct by, or the unfitness or incompetence of, persons concerned in the provision of banking, insurance, investment or other financial services or in the management of bodies corporate,

(ii) financial loss due to the conduct of discharged or undischarged bankrupts, or

(iii) dishonesty, malpractice or other seriously improper conduct by, or the unfitness or incompetence of, persons authorised to carry on any profession or other activity,

(b) for protecting charities against misconduct or mismanagement (whether by trustees or other persons) in their administration,
(c) for protecting the property of charities from loss or misapplication,
(d) for the recovery of the property of charities,
(e) for securing the health, safety and welfare of persons at work, or
(f) for protecting persons other than persons at work against risk to health or safety arising out of or in connection with the actions of persons at work.

(3) In subsection (2) "relevant function" means—
(a) any function conferred on any person by or under any enactment,
(b) any function of the Crown, a Minister of the Crown or a government department, or
(c) any other function which is of a public nature and is exercised in the public interest.

(4) Personal data processed for the purpose of discharging any function which—
(a) is conferred by or under any enactment on—
(i) the Parliamentary Commissioner for Administration,
(ii) the Commission for Local Administration in England, the Commission for Local Administration in Wales or the Commissioner for Local Administration in Scotland,
(iii) the Health Service Commissioner for England, the Health Service Commissioner for Wales or the Health Service Commissioner for Scotland,
(iv) the Welsh Administration Ombudsman,
(v) the Assembly Ombudsman for Northern Ireland, or
(vi) the Northern Ireland Commissioner for Complaints, and
(b) is designed for protecting members of the public against—
(i) maladministration by public bodies,
(ii) failures in services provided by public bodies, or
(iii) a failure of a public body to provide a service which it was a function of the body to provide,

are exempt from the subject information provisions in any case to the extent to which the application of those provisions to the data would be likely to prejudice the proper discharge of that function.

(5) Personal data processed for the purpose of discharging any function which—
(a) is conferred by or under any enactment on the Director General of Fair Trading, and
(b) is designed—
(i) for protecting members of the public against conduct which may adversely affect their interests by persons carrying on a business,
(ii) for regulating agreements or conduct which have as their object or effect the prevention, restriction or distortion of competition in connection with any commercial activity, or
(iii) for regulating conduct on the part of one or more undertakings which amounts to the abuse of a dominant position in a market,

are exempt from the subject information provisions in any case to the extent to which the application of those provisions to the data would be likely to prejudice the proper discharge of that function.

NOTES

Commencement: to be appointed.

32 Journalism, literature and art

(1) Personal data which are processed only for the special purposes are exempt from any provision to which this subsection relates if—

(a) the processing is undertaken with a view to the publication by any person of any journalistic, literary or artistic material,

(b) the data controller reasonably believes that, having regard in particular to the special importance of the public interest in freedom of expression, publication would be in the public interest, and

(c) the data controller reasonably believes that, in all the circumstances, compliance with that provision is incompatible with the special purposes.

(2) Subsection (1) relates to the provisions of—

(a) the data protection principles except the seventh data protection principle,

(b) section 7,

(c) section 10,

(d) section 12, and

[(dd) section 12A,]

(e) section 14(1) to (3).

(3) In considering for the purposes of subsection (1)(b) whether the belief of a data controller that publication would be in the public interest was or is a reasonable one, regard may be had to his compliance with any code of practice which—

(a) is relevant to the publication in question, and

(b) is designated by the Secretary of State by order for the purposes of this subsection.

(4) Where at any time ("the relevant time") in any proceedings against a data controller under section 7(9), 10(4), 12(8)[, 12A(3)] or 14 or by virtue of section 13 the data controller claims, or it appears to the court, that any personal data to which the proceedings relate are being processed—

(a) only for the special purposes, and

(b) with a view to the publication by any person of any journalistic, literary or artistic material which, at the time twenty-four hours immediately before the relevant time, had not previously been published by the data controller,

the court shall stay the proceedings until either of the conditions in subsection (5) is met.

(5) Those conditions are—

(a) that a determination of the Commissioner under section 45 with respect to the data in question takes effect, or

(b) in a case where the proceedings were stayed on the making of a claim, that the claim is withdrawn.

(6) For the purposes of this Act "publish", in relation to journalistic, literary or artistic material, means make available to the public or any section of the public.

NOTES

Commencement: 16 July 1998 (sub-s (3), in so far as conferring the power to make subordinate legislation); to be appointed (otherwise).

Modification: during the period beginning with the commencement of s 72 and ending with 23 October 2007, sub-s (2)(dd) inserted and words in square brackets in sub-s (4) inserted by s 72, Sch 13, para 2.

33 Research, history and statistics

(1) In this section—

"research purposes" includes statistical or historical purposes;

"the relevant conditions", in relation to any processing of personal data, means the conditions—

(a) that the data are not processed to support measures or decisions with respect to particular individuals, and

(b) that the data are not processed in such a way that substantial damage or substantial distress is, or is likely to be, caused to any data subject.

(2) For the purposes of the second data protection principle, the further processing of personal data only for research purposes in compliance with the relevant conditions is not to be regarded as incompatible with the purposes for which they were obtained.

(3) Personal data which are processed only for research purposes in compliance with the relevant conditions may, notwithstanding the fifth data protection principle, be kept indefinitely.

(4) Personal data which are processed only for research purposes are exempt from section 7 if—

(a) they are processed in compliance with the relevant conditions, and

(b) the results of the research or any resulting statistics are not made available in a form which identifies data subjects or any of them.

(5) . . .

NOTES

Commencement: to be appointed.

Sub-s (5): outside the scope of this work.

38 Powers to make further exemptions by order

(1) The Secretary of State may by order exempt from the subject information provisions personal data consisting of information the disclosure of which is prohibited or restricted by or under any enactment if and to the extent that he considers it necessary for the safeguarding of the interests of the data subject or the rights and freedoms of any other individual that the prohibition or restriction ought to prevail over those provisions.

(2) The Secretary of State may by order exempt from the non-disclosure provisions any disclosures of personal data made in circumstances specified in the order, if he considers the exemption is necessary for the safeguarding of the interests of the data subject or the rights and freedoms of any other individual.

NOTES

Commencement: 16 July 1998 (in so far as conferring the power to make subordinate legislation); to be appointed (otherwise).

PART V
ENFORCEMENT

40 Enforcement notices

(1) If the Commissioner is satisfied that a data controller has contravened or is contravening any of the data protection principles, the Commissioner may serve him

with a notice (in this Act referred to as "an enforcement notice") requiring him, for complying with the principle or principles in question, to do either or both of the following—

(a) to take within such time as may be specified in the notice, or to refrain from taking after such time as may be so specified, such steps as are so specified, or

(b) to refrain from processing any personal data, or any personal data of a description specified in the notice, or to refrain from processing them for a purpose so specified or in a manner so specified, after such time as may be so specified.

(2) In deciding whether to serve an enforcement notice, the Commissioner shall consider whether the contravention has caused or is likely to cause any person damage or distress.

(3)–(9) . . .

(10) This section has effect subject to section 46(1).

NOTES

Commencement: to be appointed.

Sub-ss (3)–(9): outside the scope of this work.

41 Cancellation of enforcement notice

(1) If the Commissioner considers that all or any of the provisions of an enforcement notice need not be complied with in order to ensure compliance with the data protection principle or principles to which it relates, he may cancel or vary the notice by written notice to the person on whom it was served.

(2) A person on whom an enforcement notice has been served may, at any time after the expiry of the period during which an appeal can be brought against that notice, apply in writing to the Commissioner for the cancellation or variation of that notice on the ground that, by reason of a change of circumstances, all or any of the provisions of that notice need not be complied with in order to ensure compliance with the data protection principle or principles to which that notice relates.

NOTES

Commencement: to be appointed.

45 Determination by Commissioner as to the special purposes

(1) Where at any time it appears to the Commissioner (whether as a result of the service of a special information notice or otherwise) that any personal data—

(a) are not being processed only for the special purposes, or

(b) are not being processed with a view to the publication by any person of any journalistic, literary or artistic material which has not previously been published by the data controller,

he may make a determination in writing to that effect.

(2), (3) . . .

NOTES

Commencement: to be appointed.

Sub-ss (2), (3): outside the scope of this work.

46 Restriction on enforcement in case of processing for the special purposes

(1) The Commissioner may not at any time serve an enforcement notice on a data controller with respect to the processing of personal data for the special purposes unless—

- (a) a determination under section 45(1) with respect to those data has taken effect, and
- (b) the court has granted leave for the notice to be served.

(2) The court shall not grant leave for the purposes of subsection (1)(b) unless it is satisfied—

- (a) that the Commissioner has reason to suspect a contravention of the data protection principles which is of substantial public importance, and
- (b) except where the case is one of urgency, that the data controller has been given notice, in accordance with rules of court, of the application for leave.

(3) The Commissioner may not serve an information notice on a data controller with respect to the processing of personal data for the special purposes unless a determination under section 45(1) with respect to those data has taken effect.

NOTES

Commencement: to be appointed.

47 Failure to comply with notice

(1) A person who fails to comply with an enforcement notice, an information notice or a special information notice is guilty of an offence.

(2) A person who, in purported compliance with an information notice or a special information notice—

- (a) makes a statement which he knows to be false in a material respect, or
- (b) recklessly makes a statement which is false in a material respect,

is guilty of an offence.

(3) It is a defence for a person charged with an offence under subsection (1) to prove that he exercised all due diligence to comply with the notice in question.

NOTES

Commencement: to be appointed.

48 Rights of appeal

(1) A person on whom an enforcement notice, an information notice or a special information notice has been served may appeal to the Tribunal against the notice.

(2) A person on whom an enforcement notice has been served may appeal to the Tribunal against the refusal of an application under section 41(2) for cancellation or variation of the notice.

(3) Where an enforcement notice, an information notice or a special information notice contains a statement by the Commissioner in accordance with section 40(8), 43(5) or 44(6) then, whether or not the person appeals against the notice, he may appeal against—

(a) the Commissioner's decision to include the statement in the notice, or
(b) the effect of the inclusion of the statement as respects any part of the notice.

(4) A data controller in respect of whom a determination has been made under section 45 may appeal to the Tribunal against the determination.

(5) . . .

NOTES
Commencement: to be appointed.
Sub-s (5): outside the scope of this work.

49 Determination of appeals

(1) If on an appeal under section 48(1) the Tribunal considers—
(a) that the notice against which the appeal is brought is not in accordance with the law, or
(b) to the extent that the notice involved an exercise of discretion by the Commissioner, that he ought to have exercised his discretion differently,

the Tribunal shall allow the appeal or substitute such other notice or decision as could have been served or made by the Commissioner; and in any other case the Tribunal shall dismiss the appeal.

(2) On such an appeal, the Tribunal may review any determination of fact on which the notice in question was based.

(3) If on an appeal under section 48(2) the Tribunal considers that the enforcement notice ought to be cancelled or varied by reason of a change in circumstances, the Tribunal shall cancel or vary the notice.

(4) On an appeal under subsection (3) of section 48 the Tribunal may direct—
(a) that the notice in question shall have effect as if it did not contain any such statement as is mentioned in that subsection, or
(b) that the inclusion of the statement shall not have effect in relation to any part of the notice,

and may make such modifications in the notice as may be required for giving effect to the direction.

(5) On an appeal under section 48(4), the Tribunal may cancel the determination of the Commissioner.

(6) Any party to an appeal to the Tribunal under section 48 may appeal from the decision of the Tribunal on a point of law to the appropriate court; and that court shall be—
(a) the High Court of Justice in England if the address of the person who was the appellant before the Tribunal is in England or Wales,
(b) the Court of Session if that address is in Scotland, and
(c) the High Court of Justice in Northern Ireland if that address is in Northern Ireland.

(7) . . .

NOTES
Commencement: to be appointed.
Sub-s (7): outside the scope of this work.

Unlawful obtaining etc of personal data

55 Unlawful obtaining etc of personal data

(1) A person must not knowingly or recklessly, without the consent of the data controller—

(a) obtain or disclose personal data or the information contained in personal data, or

(b) procure the disclosure to another person of the information contained in personal data.

(2) Subsection (1) does not apply to a person who shows—

(a) that the obtaining, disclosing or procuring—

(i) was necessary for the purpose of preventing or detecting crime, or

(ii) was required or authorised by or under any enactment, by any rule of law or by the order of a court,

(b) that he acted in the reasonable belief that he had in law the right to obtain or disclose the data or information or, as the case may be, to procure the disclosure of the information to the other person,

(c) that he acted in the reasonable belief that he would have had the consent of the data controller if the data controller had known of the obtaining, disclosing or procuring and the circumstances of it, or

(d) that in the particular circumstances the obtaining, disclosing or procuring was justified as being in the public interest.

(3) A person who contravenes subsection (1) is guilty of an offence.

(4) A person who sells personal data is guilty of an offence if he has obtained the data in contravention of subsection (1).

(5) A person who offers to sell personal data is guilty of an offence if—

(a) he has obtained the data in contravention of subsection (1), or

(b) he subsequently obtains the data in contravention of that subsection.

(6) . . .

(7) Section 1(2) does not apply for the purposes of this section; and for the purposes of subsections (4) to (6), "personal data" includes information extracted from personal data.

(8) References in this section to personal data do not include references to personal data which by virtue of section 28 are exempt from this section.

NOTES

Commencement: to be appointed.

Sub-s (6): outside the scope of this work.

General

63 Application to Crown

(1) This Act binds the Crown.

(2)–(4) . . .

(5) Neither a government department nor a person who is a data controller by virtue of subsection (3) shall be liable to prosecution under this Act, but section 55

and paragraph 12 of Schedule 9 shall apply to a person in the service of the Crown as they apply to any other person.

NOTES

Commencement: to be appointed.

Sub-ss (2)–(4): outside the scope of this work.

72 Modifications of Act

During the period beginning with the commencement of this section and ending with 23rd October 2007, the provisions of this Act shall have effect subject to the modifications set out in Schedule 13.

NOTES

Commencement: to be appointed.

73 Transitional provisions and savings

Schedule 14 (which contains transitional provisions and savings) has effect.

NOTES

Commencement: to be appointed.

75 Short title, commencement and extent

(1) This Act may be cited as the Data Protection Act 1998.

(2) The following provisions of this Act—

- (a) sections 1 to 3,
- (b) section 25(1) and (4),
- (c) section 26,
- (d) sections 67 to 71,
- (e) this section,
- (f) paragraph 17 of Schedule 5,
- (g) Schedule 11,
- (h) Schedule 12, and
- (i) so much of any other provision of this Act as confers any power to make subordinate legislation,

shall come into force on the day on which this Act is passed.

(3) The remaining provisions of this Act shall come into force on such day as the Secretary of State may by order appoint; and different days may be appointed for different purposes.

(4) The day appointed under subsection (3) for the coming into force of section 56 must not be earlier than the first day on which sections 112, 113 and 115 of the Police Act 1997 (which provide for the issue by the Secretary of State of criminal conviction certificates, criminal record certificates and enhanced criminal record certificates) are all in force.

(5) Subject to subsection (6), this Act extends to Northern Ireland.

(6) Any amendment, repeal or revocation made by Schedule 15 or 16 has the same extent as that of the enactment or instrument to which it relates.

NOTES
Commencement: 16 July 1998.

SCHEDULES

SCHEDULE 1

Section 4(1) and (2)

THE DATA PROTECTION PRINCIPLES

PART I
THE PRINCIPLES

1. Personal data shall be processed fairly and lawfully and, in particular, shall not be processed unless—
   (a) at least one of the conditions in Schedule 2 is met, and
   (b) in the case of sensitive personal data, at least one of the conditions in Schedule 3 is also met.

2. Personal data shall be obtained only for one or more specified and lawful purposes, and shall not be further processed in any manner incompatible with that purpose or those purposes.

3. Personal data shall be adequate, relevant and not excessive in relation to the purpose or purposes for which they are processed.

4. Personal data shall be accurate and, where necessary, kept up to date.

5. Personal data processed for any purpose or purposes shall not be kept for longer than is necessary for that purpose or those purposes.

6. Personal data shall be processed in accordance with the rights of data subjects under this Act.

7. Appropriate technical and organisational measures shall be taken against unauthorised or unlawful processing of personal data and against accidental loss or destruction of, or damage to, personal data.

8. Personal data shall not be transferred to a country or territory outside the European Economic Area unless that country or territory ensures an adequate level of protection for the rights and freedoms of data subjects in relation to the processing of personal data.

NOTES
Commencement: to be appointed.

PART II
INTERPRETATION OF THE PRINCIPLES IN PART I

The first principle

1.—(1) In determining for the purposes of the first principle whether personal data are processed fairly, regard is to be had to the method by which they are obtained, including in particular whether any person from whom they are obtained is deceived or misled as to the purpose or purposes for which they are to be processed.

(2) Subject to paragraph 2, for the purposes of the first principle data are to be treated as obtained fairly if they consist of information obtained from a person who—
   (a) is authorised by or under any enactment to supply it, or
   (b) is required to supply it by or under any enactment or by any convention or other instrument imposing an international obligation on the United Kingdom.

2.—(1) Subject to paragraph 3, for the purposes of the first principle personal data are not to be treated as processed fairly unless—

(a) in the case of data obtained from the data subject, the data controller ensures so far as practicable that the data subject has, is provided with, or has made readily available to him, the information specified in sub-paragraph (3), and

(b) in any other case, the data controller ensures so far as practicable that, before the relevant time or as soon as practicable after that time, the data subject has, is provided with, or has made readily available to him, the information specified in sub-paragraph (3).

(2) . . .

(3) The information referred to in sub-paragraph (1) is as follows, namely—

(a) the identity of the data controller,

(b) if he has nominated a representative for the purposes of this Act, the identity of that representative,

(c) the purpose or purposes for which the data are intended to be processed, and

(d) any further information which is necessary, having regard to the specific circumstances in which the data are or are to be processed, to enable processing in respect of the data subject to be fair.

3.—(1) Paragraph 2(1)(b) does not apply where either of the primary conditions in sub-paragraph (2), together with such further conditions as may be prescribed by the Secretary of State by order, are met.

(2) The primary conditions referred to in sub-paragraph (1) are—

(a) that the provision of that information would involve a disproportionate effort, or

(b) that the recording of the information to be contained in the data by, or the disclosure of the data by, the data controller is necessary for compliance with any legal obligation to which the data controller is subject, other than an obligation imposed by contract.

4.–7. . . .

The sixth principle

8. A person is to be regarded as contravening the sixth principle if, but only if—

(a) he contravenes section 7 by failing to supply information in accordance with that section,

(b) he contravenes section 10 by failing to comply with a notice given under subsection (1) of that section to the extent that the notice is justified or by failing to give a notice under subsection (3) of that section,

(c) he contravenes section 11 by failing to comply with a notice given under subsection (1) of that section, *or*

(d) he contravenes section 12 by failing to comply with a notice given under subsection (1) or (2)(b) of that section or by failing to give a notification under subsection (2)(a) of that section or a notice under subsection (3) of that section, [or

(e) he contravenes section 12A by failing to comply with a notice given under subsection (1) of that section to the extent that the notice is justified.]

The seventh principle

9.–14. . . .

15.—(1) Where—

(a) in any proceedings under this Act any question arises as to whether the requirement of the eighth principle as to an adequate level of protection is met in relation to the transfer of any personal data to a country or territory outside the European Economic Area, and

(b) a Community finding has been made in relation to transfers of the kind in question,

that question is to be determined in accordance with that finding.

(2) In sub-paragraph (1) "Community finding" means a finding of the European Commission, under the procedure provided for in Article 31(2) of the Data Protection

Directive, that a country or territory outside the European Economic Area does, or does not, ensure an adequate level of protection within the meaning of Article 25(2) of the Directive.

NOTES

Commencement: to be appointed.

Para 2: sub-para (2) outside the scope of this work.

Paras 4–7, 9–14: outside the scope of this work.

Modification: during the period beginning with the commencement of s 72 and ending with 23 October 2007, word "or" at the end of para 8(c) repealed and para 8(e) and preceding word "or" inserted by s 72, Sch 13, para 5.

SCHEDULE 2

Section 4(3)

CONDITIONS RELEVANT FOR PURPOSES OF THE FIRST PRINCIPLE: PROCESSING OF ANY PERSONAL DATA

1. The data subject has given his consent to the processing.

2. The processing is necessary—
   (a) for the performance of a contract to which the data subject is a party, or
   (b) for the taking of steps at the request of the data subject with a view to entering into a contract.

3. The processing is necessary for compliance with any legal obligation to which the data controller is subject, other than an obligation imposed by contract.

4. The processing is necessary in order to protect the vital interests of the data subject.

5. The processing is necessary—
   (a) for the administration of justice,
   (b) for the exercise of any functions conferred on any person by or under any enactment,
   (c) for the exercise of any functions of the Crown, a Minister of the Crown or a government department, or
   (d) for the exercise of any other functions of a public nature exercised in the public interest by any person.

6.—(1) The processing is necessary for the purposes of legitimate interests pursued by the data controller or by the third party or parties to whom the data are disclosed, except where the processing is unwarranted in any particular case by reason of prejudice to the rights and freedoms or legitimate interests of the data subject.

(2) The Secretary of State may by order specify particular circumstances in which this condition is, or is not, to be taken to be satisfied.

NOTES

Commencement: 16 July 1998 (in so far as conferring the power to make subordinate legislation); to be appointed (otherwise).

SCHEDULE 3

Section 4(3)

CONDITIONS RELEVANT FOR PURPOSES OF THE FIRST PRINCIPLE: PROCESSING OF SENSITIVE PERSONAL DATA

1. The data subject has given his explicit consent to the processing of the personal data.

2.—(1) The processing is necessary for the purposes of exercising or performing any right or obligation which is conferred or imposed by law on the data controller in connection with employment.

(2) The Secretary of State may by order—

(a) exclude the application of sub-paragraph (1) in such cases as may be specified, or

(b) provide that, in such cases as may be specified, the condition in subparagraph (1) is not to be regarded as satisfied unless such further conditions as may be specified in the order are also satisfied.

3. The processing is necessary—

(a) in order to protect the vital interests of the data subject or another person, in a case where—

(i) consent cannot be given by or on behalf of the data subject, or

(ii) the data controller cannot reasonably be expected to obtain the consent of the data subject, or

(b) in order to protect the vital interests of another person, in a case where consent by or on behalf of the data subject has been unreasonably withheld.

4. The processing—

(a) is carried out in the course of its legitimate activities by any body or association which—

(i) is not established or conducted for profit, and

(ii) exists for political, philosophical religious or trade-union purposes,

(b) is carried out with appropriate safeguards for the rights and freedoms of data subjects,

(c) relates only to individuals who either are members of the body or association or have regular contact with it in connection with its purposes, and

(d) does not involve disclosure of the personal data to a third party without the consent of the data subject.

5. The information contained in the personal data has been made public as a result of steps deliberately taken by the data subject.

6. The processing—

(a) is necessary for the purpose of, or in connection with, any legal proceedings (including prospective legal proceedings),

(b) is necessary for the purpose of obtaining legal advice, or

(c) is otherwise necessary for the purposes of establishing, exercising or defending legal rights.

7.—(1) The processing is necessary—

(a) for the administration of justice,

(b) for the exercise of any functions conferred on any person by or under an enactment, or

(c) for the exercise of any functions of the Crown, a Minister of the Crown or a government department.

(2) . . .

8.—(1) The processing is necessary for medical purposes and is undertaken by—

(a) a health professional, or

(b) a person who in the circumstances owes a duty of confidentiality which is equivalent to that which would arise if that person were a health professional.

(2) . . .

9.—(1) The processing—

(a) is of sensitive personal data consisting of information as to racial or ethnic origin,

(b) is necessary for the purpose of identifying or keeping under review the existence or absence of equality of opportunity or treatment between persons of different racial or ethnic origins, with a view to enabling such equality to be promoted or maintained, and

(c) is carried out with appropriate safeguards for the rights and freedoms of data subjects.

(2) The Secretary of State may by order specify circumstances in which processing falling within sub-paragraph (1)(a) and (b) is, or is not, to be taken for the purposes of sub-

paragraph (1)(c) to be carried out with appropriate safeguards for the rights and freedoms of data subjects.

10. The personal data are processed in circumstances specified in an order made by the Secretary of State for the purposes of this paragraph.

NOTES

Commencement: 16 July 1998 (in so far as conferring the power to make subordinate legislation); to be appointed (otherwise).

Para 7: sub-para (2) outside the scope of this work.

Para 8: sub-para (2) outside the scope of this work.

SCHEDULE 4

Section 4(3)

CASES WHERE THE EIGHTH PRINCIPLE DOES NOT APPLY

1. The data subject has given his consent to the transfer.

2. The transfer is necessary—
   (a) for the performance of a contract between the data subject and the data controller, or
   (b) for the taking of steps at the request of the data subject with a view to his entering into a contract with the data controller.

3. The transfer is necessary—
   (a) for the conclusion of a contract between the data controller and a person other than the data subject which—
      (i) is entered into at the request of the data subject, or
      (ii) is in the interests of the data subject, or
   (b) for the performance of such a contract.

4.—(1) The transfer is necessary for reasons of substantial public interest.

(2) The Secretary of State may by order specify—
   (a) circumstances in which a transfer is to be taken for the purposes of subparagraph (1) to be necessary for reasons of substantial public interest, and
   (b) circumstances in which a transfer which is not required by or under an enactment is not to be taken for the purpose of sub-paragraph (1) to be necessary for reasons of substantial public interest.

5. The transfer—
   (a) is necessary for the purpose of, or in connection with, any legal proceedings (including prospective legal proceedings),
   (b) is necessary for the purpose of obtaining legal advice, or
   (c) is otherwise necessary for the purposes of establishing, exercising or defending legal rights.

6. The transfer is necessary in order to protect the vital interests of the data subject.

7. The transfer is of part of the personal data on a public register and any conditions subject to which the register is open to inspection are complied with by any person to whom the data are or may be disclosed after the transfer.

8. The transfer is made on terms which are of a kind approved by the Commissioner as ensuring adequate safeguards for the rights and freedoms of data subjects.

9. The transfer has been authorised by the Commissioner as being made in such a manner as to ensure adequate safeguards for the rights and freedoms of data subjects.

NOTES

Commencement: 16 July 1998 (in so far as conferring the power to make subordinate legislation); to be appointed (otherwise).

SCHEDULE 5

Section 6(7)

THE DATA PROTECTION COMMISSIONER AND THE DATA PROTECTION TRIBUNAL

PART I
THE COMMISSIONER

Status and capacity

1.—(1) The corporation sole by the name of the Data Protection Registrar established by the Data Protection Act 1984 shall continue in existence by the name of the Data Protection Commissioner.

(2) The Commissioner and his officers and staff are not to be regarded as servants or agents of the Crown.

Tenure of office

2.—(1) Subject to the provisions of this paragraph, the Commissioner shall hold office for such term not exceeding five years as may be determined at the time of his appointment.

(2) The Commissioner may be relieved of his office by Her Majesty at his own request.

(3) The Commissioner may be removed from office by Her Majesty in pursuance of an Address from both Houses of Parliament.

(4) The Commissioner shall in any case vacate his office—

(a) on completing the year of service in which he attains the age of sixty-five years, or

(b) if earlier, on completing his fifteenth year of service.

(5) Subject to sub-paragraph (4), a person who ceases to be Commissioner on the expiration of his term of office shall be eligible for re-appointment, but a person may not be re-appointed for a third or subsequent term as Commissioner unless, by reason of special circumstances, the person's re-appointment for such a term is desirable in the public interest.

3–17 . . .

NOTES

Commencement: to be appointed.

Paras 3–17: outside the scope of this work.

HUMAN RIGHTS ACT 1998

(C 42)

An Act to give further effect to rights and freedoms guaranteed under the European Convention on Human Rights; to make provision with respect to holders of certain judicial offices who become judges of the European Court of Human Rights; and for connected purposes.

[9 November 1998]

NOTES

For commencement, see s 22.

Introduction

1 The Convention Rights

(1) In this Act "the Convention rights" means the rights and fundamental freedoms set out in—

(a) Articles 2 to 12 and 14 of the Convention,

(b) Articles 1 to 3 of the First Protocol, and

(c) Articles 1 and 2 of the Sixth Protocol,

as read with Articles 16 to 18 of the Convention.

(2) Those Articles are to have effect for the purposes of this Act subject to any designated derogation or reservation (as to which see sections 14 and 15).

(3) The Articles are set out in Schedule 1.

(4) The Secretary of State may by order make such amendments to this Act as he considers appropriate to reflect the effect, in relation to the United Kingdom, of a protocol.

(5) In subsection (4) "protocol" means a protocol to the Convention—
- (a) which the United Kingdom has ratified; or
- (b) which the United Kingdom has signed with a view to ratification.

(6) No amendment may be made by an order under subsection (4) so as to come into force before the protocol concerned is in force in relation to the United Kingdom.

2 Interpretation of Convention rights

(1) A court or tribunal determining a question which has arisen in connection with a Convention right must take into account any—
- (a) judgment, decision, declaration or advisory opinion of the European Court of Human Rights,
- (b) opinion of the Commission given in a report adopted under Article 31 of the Convention,
- (c) decision of the Commission in connection with Article 26 or 27(2) of the Convention, or
- (d) decision of the Committee of Ministers taken under Article 46 of the Convention,

whenever made or given, so far as, in the opinion of the court or tribunal, it is relevant to the proceedings in which that question has arisen.

(2) Evidence of any judgment, decision, declaration or opinion of which account may have to be taken under this section is to be given in proceedings before any court or tribunal in such manner as may be provided by rules.

(3) In this section "rules" means rules of court or, in the case of proceedings before a tribunal, rules made for the purposes of this section—
- (a) by the Lord Chancellor or the Secretary of State, in relation to any proceedings outside Scotland;
- (b) by the Secretary of State, in relation to proceedings in Scotland; or
- (c) by a Northern Ireland department, in relation to proceedings before a tribunal in Northern Ireland—
  - (i) which deals with transferred matters; and
  - (ii) for which no rules made under paragraph (a) are in force.

Legislation

3 Interpretation of legislation

(1) So far as it is possible to do so, primary legislation and subordinate legislation must be read and given effect in a way which is compatible with the Convention rights.

(2) This section—
- (a) applies to primary legislation and subordinate legislation whenever enacted;
- (b) does not affect the validity, continuing operation or enforcement of any incompatible primary legislation; and

(c) does not affect the validity, continuing operation or enforcement of any incompatible subordinate legislation if (disregarding any possibility of revocation) primary legislation prevents removal of the incompatibility.

4 Declaration of incompatibility

(1) Subsection (2) applies in any proceedings in which a court determines whether a provision of primary legislation is compatible with a Convention right.

(2) If the court is satisfied that the provision is incompatible with a Convention right, it may make a declaration of that incompatibility.

(3) Subsection (4) applies in any proceedings in which a court determines whether a provision of subordinate legislation, made in the exercise of a power conferred by primary legislation, is compatible with a Convention right.

(4) If the court is satisfied—

(a) that the provision is incompatible with a Convention right, and

(b) that (disregarding any possibility of revocation) the primary legislation concerned prevents removal of the incompatibility,

it may make a declaration of that incompatibility.

(5) In this section "court" means—

(a) the House of Lords;

(b) the Judicial Committee of the Privy Council;

(c) the Courts-Martial Appeal Court;

(d) in Scotland, the High Court of Justiciary sitting otherwise than as a trial court or the Court of Session;

(e) in England and Wales or Northern Ireland, the High Court or the Court of Appeal.

(6) A declaration under this section ("a declaration of incompatibility")—

(a) does not affect the validity, continuing operation or enforcement of the provision in respect of which it is given; and

(b) is not binding on the parties to the proceedings in which it is made.

5 Right of Crown to intervene

(1) Where a court is considering whether to make a declaration of incompatibility, the Crown is entitled to notice in accordance with rules of court.

(2) In any case to which subsection (1) applies—

(a) a Minister of the Crown (or a person nominated by him),

(b) a member of the Scottish Executive,

(c) a Northern Ireland Minister,

(d) a Northern Ireland department,

is entitled, on giving notice in accordance with rules of court, to be joined as a party to the proceedings.

(3) Notice under subsection (2) may be given at any time during the proceedings.

(4) A person who has been made a party to criminal proceedings (other than in Scotland) as the result of a notice under subsection (2) may, with leave, appeal to the House of Lords against any declaration of incompatibility made in the proceedings.

(5) In subsection (4)—

"criminal proceedings" includes all proceedings before the Courts-Martial Appeal Court; and "leave" means leave granted by the court making the declaration of incompatibility or by the House of Lords.

Public authorities

6 Acts of public authorities

(1) It is unlawful for a public authority to act in a way which is incompatible with a Convention right.

(2) Subsection (1) does not apply to an act if—

(a) as the result of one or more provisions of primary legislation, the authority could not have acted differently; or

(b) in the case of one or more provisions of, or made under, primary legislation which cannot be read or given effect in a way which is compatible with the Convention rights, the authority was acting so as to give effect to or enforce those provisions.

(3) In this section "public authority" includes—

(a) a court or tribunal, and

(b) any person certain of whose functions are functions of a public nature,

but does not include either House of Parliament or a person exercising functions in connection with proceedings in Parliament.

(4) In subsection (3) "Parliament" does not include the House of Lords in its judicial capacity.

(5) In relation to a particular act, a person is not a public authority by virtue only of subsection (3)(b) if the nature of the act is private.

(6) "An act" includes a failure to act but does not include a failure to—

(a) introduce in, or lay before, Parliament a proposal for legislation; or

(b) make any primary legislation or remedial order.

7 Proceedings

(1) A person who claims that a public authority has acted (or proposes to act) in a way which is made unlawful by section 6(1) may—

(a) bring proceedings against the authority under this Act in the appropriate court or tribunal, or

(b) rely on the Convention right or rights concerned in any legal proceedings,

but only if he is (or would be) a victim of the unlawful act.

(2) In subsection (1)(a) "appropriate court or tribunal" means such court or tribunal as may be determined in accordance with rules; and proceedings against an authority include a counterclaim or similar proceeding.

(3) If the proceedings are brought on an application for judicial review, the applicant is to be taken to have a sufficient interest in relation to the unlawful act only if he is, or would be, a victim of that act.

(4) If the proceedings are made by way of a petition for judicial review in Scotland, the applicant shall be taken to have title and interest to sue in relation to the unlawful act only if he is, or would be, a victim of that act.

(5) Proceedings under subsection (1)(a) must be brought before the end of—

(a) the period of one year beginning with the date on which the act complained of took place; or

(b) such longer period as the court or tribunal considers equitable having regard to all the circumstances,

but that is subject to any rule imposing a stricter time limit in relation to the procedure in question.

(6) In subsection (1)(b) "legal proceedings" includes—

(a) proceedings brought by or at the instigation of a public authority; and

(b) an appeal against the decision of a court or tribunal.

(7) For the purposes of this section, a person is a victim of an unlawful act only if he would be a victim for the purposes of Article 34 of the Convention if proceedings were brought in the European Court of Human Rights in respect of that act.

(8) Nothing in this Act creates a criminal offence.

(9) In this section "rules" means—

(a) in relation to proceedings before a court or tribunal outside Scotland, rules made by the Lord Chancellor or the Secretary of State for the purposes of this section or rules of court,

(b) in relation to proceedings before a court or tribunal in Scotland, rules made by the Secretary of State for those purposes,

(c) in relation to proceedings before a tribunal in Northern Ireland—

(i) which deals with transferred matters; and

(ii) for which no rules made under paragraph (a) are in force,

rules made by a Northern Ireland department for those purposes,

and includes provision made by order under section 1 of the Courts and Legal Services Act 1990.

(10) In making rules, regard must be had to section 9.

(11) The Minister who has power to make rules in relation to a particular tribunal may, to the extent he considers it necessary to ensure that the tribunal can provide an appropriate remedy in relation to an act (or proposed act) of a public authority which is (or would be) unlawful as a result of section 6(1), by order add to—

(a) the relief or remedies which the tribunal may grant; or

(b) the grounds on which it may grant any of them.

(12) An order made under subsection (11) may contain such incidental, supplemental, consequential or transitional provision as the Minister making it considers appropriate.

(13) "The Minister" includes the Northern Ireland department concerned.

8 Judicial remedies

(1) In relation to any act (or proposed act) of a public authority which the court finds is (or would be) unlawful, it may grant such relief or remedy, or make such order, within its powers as it considers just and appropriate.

(2) But damages may be awarded only by a court which has power to award damages, or to order the payment of compensation, in civil proceedings.

(3) No award of damages is to be made unless, taking account of all the circumstances of the case, including—

(a) any other relief or remedy granted, or order made, in relation to the act in question (by that or any other court), and

(b) the consequences of any decision (of that or any other court) in respect of that act,

the court is satisfied that the award is necessary to afford just satisfaction to the person in whose favour it is made.

(4) In determining—

(a) whether to award damages, or

(b) the amount of an award,

the court must take into account the principles applied by the European Court of Human Rights in relation to the award of compensation under Article 41 of the Convention.

(5) A public authority against which damages are awarded is to be treated—

(a) in Scotland, for the purposes of section 3 of the Law Reform (Miscellaneous Provisions) (Scotland) Act 1940 as if the award were made in an action of damages in which the authority has been found liable in respect of loss or damage to the person to whom the award is made;

(b) for the purposes of the Civil Liability (Contribution) Act 1978 as liable in respect of damage suffered by the person to whom the award is made.

(6) In this section—

"court" includes a tribunal;

"damages" means damages for an unlawful act of a public authority; and

"unlawful" means unlawful under section 6(1).

9 Judicial acts

(1) Proceedings under section 7(1)(a) in respect of a judicial act may be brought only—

(a) by exercising a right of appeal;

(b) on an application (in Scotland a petition) for judicial review; or

(c) in such other forum as may be prescribed by rules.

(2) That does not affect any rule of law which prevents a court from being the subject of judicial review.

(3) In proceedings under this Act in respect of a judicial act done in good faith, damages may not be awarded otherwise than to compensate a person to the extent required by Article 5(5) of the Convention.

(4) An award of damages permitted by subsection (3) is to be made against the Crown; but no award may be made unless the appropriate person, if not a party to the proceedings, is joined.

(5) In this section—

"appropriate person" means the Minister responsible for the court concerned, or a person or government department nominated by him;

"court" includes a tribunal;

"judge" includes a member of a tribunal, a justice of the peace and a clerk or other officer entitled to exercise the jurisdiction of a court;

"judicial act" means a judicial act of a court and includes an act done on the instructions, or on behalf, of a judge; and

"rules" has the same meaning as in section 7(9).

Remedial action

10 Power to take remedial action

(1) This section applies if—

(a) a provision of legislation has been declared under section 4 to be incompatible with a Convention right and, if an appeal lies—

(i) all persons who may appeal have stated in writing that they do not intend to do so;

(ii) the time for bringing an appeal has expired and no appeal has been brought within that time; or

(iii) an appeal brought within that time has been determined or abandoned; or

(b) it appears to a Minister of the Crown or Her Majesty in Council that, having regard to a finding of the European Court of Human Rights made after the coming into force of this section in proceedings against the United Kingdom, a provision of legislation is incompatible with an obligation of the United Kingdom arising from the Convention.

(2) If a Minister of the Crown considers that there are compelling reasons for proceeding under this section, he may by order make such amendments to the legislation as he considers necessary to remove the incompatibility.

(3) If, in the case of subordinate legislation, a Minister of the Crown considers—

(a) that it is necessary to amend the primary legislation under which the subordinate legislation in question was made, in order to enable the incompatibility to be removed, and

(b) that there are compelling reasons for proceeding under this section,

he may by order make such amendments to the primary legislation as he considers necessary.

(4) This section also applies where the provision in question is in subordinate legislation and has been quashed, or declared invalid, by reason of incompatibility with a Convention right and the Minister proposes to proceed under paragraph 2(b) of Schedule 2.

(5) If the legislation is an Order in Council, the power conferred by subsection (2) or (3) is exercisable by Her Majesty in Council.

(6) In this section "legislation" does not include a Measure of the Church Assembly or of the General Synod of the Church of England.

(7) Schedule 2 makes further provision about remedial orders.

Other rights and proceedings

11 Safeguard for existing human rights

A person's reliance on a Convention right does not restrict—

(a) any other right or freedom conferred on him by or under any law having effect in any part of the United Kingdom; or

(b) his right to make any claim or bring any proceedings which he could make or bring apart from sections 7 to 9.

12 Freedom of expression

(1) This section applies if a court is considering whether to grant any relief which, if granted, might affect the exercise of the Convention right to freedom of expression.

(2) If the person against whom the application for relief is made ("the respondent") is neither present nor represented, no such relief is to be granted unless the court is satisfied—

(a) that the applicant has taken all practicable steps to notify the respondent; or

(b) that there are compelling reasons why the respondent should not be notified.

(3) No such relief is to be granted so as to restrain publication before trial unless the court is satisfied that the applicant is likely to establish that publication should not be allowed.

(4) The court must have particular regard to the importance of the Convention right to freedom of expression and, where the proceedings relate to material which the respondent claims, or which appears to the court, to be journalistic, literary or artistic material (or to conduct connected with such material), to—

(a) the extent to which—

(i) the material has, or is about to, become available to the public; or

(ii) it is, or would be, in the public interest for the material to be published;

(b) any relevant privacy code.

(5) In this section—

"court" includes a tribunal; and

"relief" includes any remedy or order (other than in criminal proceedings).

13 Freedom of thought, conscience and religion

(1) If a court's determination of any question arising under this Act might affect the exercise by a religious organisation (itself or its members collectively) of the Convention right to freedom of thought, conscience and religion, it must have particular regard to the importance of that right.

(2) In this section "court" includes a tribunal.

Derogations and reservations

14 Derogations

(1) In this Act "designated derogation" means—

(a) the United Kingdom's derogation from Article 5(3) of the Convention; and

(b) any derogation by the United Kingdom from an Article of the Convention, or of any protocol to the Convention, which is designated for the purposes of this Act in an order made by the Secretary of State.

(2) The derogation referred to in subsection (1)(a) is set out in Part I of Schedule 3.

(3) If a designated derogation is amended or replaced it ceases to be a designated derogation.

(4) But subsection (3) does not prevent the Secretary of State from exercising his power under subsection (1)(b) to make a fresh designation order in respect of the Article concerned.

(5) The Secretary of State must by order make such amendments to Schedule 3 as he considers appropriate to reflect—

(a) any designation order; or

(b) the effect of subsection (3).

(6) A designation order may be made in anticipation of the making by the United Kingdom of a proposed derogation.

15 Reservations

(1) In this Act "designated reservation" means—
  (a) the United Kingdom's reservation to Article 2 of the First Protocol to the Convention; and
  (b) any other reservation by the United Kingdom to an Article of the Convention, or of any protocol to the Convention, which is designated for the purposes of this Act in an order made by the Secretary of State.

(2) The text of the reservation referred to in subsection (1)(a) is set out in Part II of Schedule 3.

(3) If a designated reservation is withdrawn wholly or in part it ceases to be a designated reservation.

(4) But subsection (3) does not prevent the Secretary of State from exercising his power under subsection (1)(b) to make a fresh designation order in respect of the Article concerned.

(5) The Secretary of State must by order make such amendments to this Act as he considers appropriate to reflect—
  (a) any designation order; or
  (b) the effect of subsection (3).

16 Period for which designated derogations have effect

(1) If it has not already been withdrawn by the United Kingdom, a designated derogation ceases to have effect for the purposes of this Act—
  (a) in the case of the derogation referred to in section 14(1)(a), at the end of the period of five years beginning with the date on which section 1(2) came into force;
  (b) in the case of any other derogation, at the end of the period of five years beginning with the date on which the order designating it was made.

(2) At any time before the period—
  (a) fixed by subsection (1)(a) or (b), or
  (b) extended by an order under this subsection,

comes to an end, the Secretary of State may by order extend it by a further period of five years.

(3) An order under section 14(1)(b) ceases to have effect at the end of the period for consideration, unless a resolution has been passed by each House approving the order.

(4) Subsection (3) does not affect—
  (a) anything done in reliance on the order; or
  (b) the power to make a fresh order under section 14(1)(b).

(5) In subsection (3) "period for consideration" means the period of forty days beginning with the day on which the order was made.

(6) In calculating the period for consideration, no account is to be taken of any time during which—
  (a) Parliament is dissolved or prorogued; or
  (b) both Houses are adjourned for more than four days.

(7) If a designated derogation is withdrawn by the United Kingdom, the Secretary of State must by order make such amendments to this Act as he considers are required to reflect that withdrawal.

Parliamentary procedure

19 Statements of compatibility

(1) A Minister of the Crown in charge of a Bill in either House of Parliament must, before Second Reading of the Bill—

- (a) make a statement to the effect that in his view the provisions of the Bill are compatible with the Convention rights ("a statement of compatibility"); or
- (b) make a statement to the effect that although he is unable to make a statement of compatibility the government nevertheless wishes the House to proceed with the Bill.

(2) The statement must be in writing and be published in such manner as the Minister making it considers appropriate.

Supplemental

20 Orders etc under this Act

(1) Any power of a Minister of the Crown to make an order under this Act is exercisable by statutory instrument.

(2) The power of the Lord Chancellor or the Secretary of State to make rules (other than rules of court) under section 2(3) or 7(9) is exercisable by statutory instrument.

(3) Any statutory instrument made under section 14, 15 or 16(7) must be laid before Parliament.

(4) No order may be made by the Lord Chancellor or the Secretary of State under section 1(4), 7(11) or 16(2) unless a draft of the order has been laid before, and approved by, each House of Parliament.

(5) Any statutory instrument made under section 18(7) or Schedule 4, or to which subsection (2) applies, shall be subject to annulment in pursuance of a resolution of either House of Parliament.

(6) The power of a Northern Ireland department to make—

- (a) rules under section 2(3)(c) or 7(9)(c), or
- (b) an order under section 7(11),

is exercisable by statutory rule for the purposes of the Statutory Rules (Northern Ireland) Order 1979.

(7) Any rules made under section 2(3)(c) or 7(9)(c) shall be subject to negative resolution; and section 41(6) of the Interpretation Act (Northern Ireland) 1954 (meaning of "subject to negative resolution") shall apply as if the power to make the rules were conferred by an Act of the Northern Ireland Assembly.

(8) No order may be made by a Northern Ireland department under section 7(11) unless a draft of the order has been laid before, and approved by, the Northern Ireland Assembly.

21 Interpretation, etc

(1) In this Act—

"amend" includes repeal and apply (with or without modifications);

"the appropriate Minister" means the Minister of the Crown having charge of the appropriate authorised government department (within the meaning of the Crown Proceedings Act 1947);

"the Commission" means the European Commission of Human Rights;

"the Convention" means the Convention for the Protection of Human Rights and Fundamental Freedoms, agreed by the Council of Europe at Rome on 4th November 1950 as it has effect for the time being in relation to the United Kingdom;

"declaration of incompatibility" means a declaration under section 4;

"Minister of the Crown" has the same meaning as in the Ministers of the Crown Act 1975;

"Northern Ireland Minister" includes the First Minister and the deputy First Minister in Northern Ireland;

"primary legislation" means any—

(a) public general Act;
(b) local and personal Act;
(c) private Act;
(d) Measure of the Church Assembly;
(e) Measure of the General Synod of the Church of England;
(f) Order in Council—
  (i) made in exercise of Her Majesty's Royal Prerogative;
  (ii) made under section 38(1)(a) of the Northern Ireland Constitution Act 1973 or the corresponding provision of the Northern Ireland Act 1998; or
  (iii) amending an Act of a kind mentioned in paragraph (a), (b) or (c);

and includes an order or other instrument made under primary legislation (otherwise than by the National Assembly for Wales, a member of the Scottish Executive, a Northern Ireland Minister or a Northern Ireland department) to the extent to which it operates to bring one or more provisions of that legislation into force or amends any primary legislation;

"the First Protocol" means the protocol to the Convention agreed at Paris on 20th March 1952;

"the Sixth Protocol" means the protocol to the Convention agreed at Strasbourg on 28th April 1983;

"the Eleventh Protocol" means the protocol to the Convention (restructuring the control machinery established by the Convention) agreed at Strasbourg on 11th May 1994;

"remedial order" means an order under section 10;

"subordinate legislation" means any—

(a) Order in Council other than one—
  (i) made in exercise of Her Majesty's Royal Prerogative;
  (ii) made under section 38(1)(a) of the Northern Ireland Constitution Act 1973 or the corresponding provision of the Northern Ireland Act 1998; or
  (iii) amending an Act of a kind mentioned in the definition of primary legislation;
(b) Act of the Scottish Parliament;
(c) Act of the Parliament of Northern Ireland;
(d) Measure of the Assembly established under section 1 of the Northern Ireland Assembly Act 1973;

(e) Act of the Northern Ireland Assembly;
(f) order, rules, regulations, scheme, warrant, byelaw or other instrument made under primary legislation (except to the extent to which it operates to bring one or more provisions of that legislation into force or amends any primary legislation);
(g) order, rules, regulations, scheme, warrant, byelaw or other instrument made under legislation mentioned in paragraph (b), (c), (d) or (e) or made under an Order in Council applying only to Northern Ireland;
(h) order, rules, regulations, scheme, warrant, byelaw or other instrument made by a member of the Scottish Executive, a Northern Ireland Minister or a Northern Ireland department in exercise of prerogative or other executive functions of Her Majesty which are exercisable by such a person on behalf of Her Majesty;

"transferred matters" has the same meaning as in the Northern Ireland Act 1998; and

"tribunal" means any tribunal in which legal proceedings may be brought.

(2) The references in paragraphs (b) and (c) of section 2(1) to Articles are to Articles of the Convention as they had effect immediately before the coming into force of the Eleventh Protocol.

(3) The reference in paragraph (d) of section 2(1) to Article 46 includes a reference to Articles 32 and 54 of the Convention as they had effect immediately before the coming into force of the Eleventh Protocol.

(4) The references in section 2(1) to a report or decision of the Commission or a decision of the Committee of Ministers include references to a report or decision made as provided by paragraphs 3, 4 and 6 of Article 5 of the Eleventh Protocol (transitional provisions).

(5) Any liability under the Army Act 1955, the Air Force Act 1955 or the Naval Discipline Act 1957 to suffer death for an offence is replaced by a liability to imprisonment for life or any less punishment authorised by those Acts; and those Acts shall accordingly have effect with the necessary modifications.

22 Short title, commencement, application and extent

(1) This Act may be cited as the Human Rights Act 1998.

(2) Sections 18, 20 and 21(5) and this section come into force on the passing of this Act.

(3) The other provisions of this Act come into force on such day as the Secretary of State may by order appoint; and different days may be appointed for different purposes.

(4) Paragraph (b) of subsection (1) of section 7 applies to proceedings brought by or at the instigation of a public authority whenever the act in question took place; but otherwise that subsection does not apply to an act taking place before the coming into force of that section.

(5) This Act binds the Crown.

(6) This Act extends to Northern Ireland.

(7) Section 21(5), so far as it relates to any provision contained in the Army Act 1955, the Air Force Act 1955 or the Naval Discipline Act 1957, extends to any place to which that provision extends.

SCHEDULE 1

Section 1(3)

THE ARTICLES

(Part I (The Convention) not reproduced; see p 670 for extracts from the European Convention on Human Rights.)

PART II
THE FIRST PROTOCOL

Article 1
Protection of property

Every natural or legal person is entitled to the peaceful enjoyment of his possessions. No one shall be deprived of his possessions except in the public interest and subject to the conditions provided for by law and by the general principles of international law.

The preceding provisions shall not, however, in any way impair the right of a State to enforce such laws as it deems necessary to control the use of property in accordance with the general interest or to secure the payment of taxes or other contributions or penalties.

Article 2
Right to education

No person shall be denied the right to education. In the exercise of any functions which it assumes in relation to education and to teaching, the State shall respect the right of parents to ensure such education and teaching in conformity with their own religious and philosophical convictions.

Article 3
Right to free elections

The High Contracting Parties undertake to hold free elections at reasonable intervals by secret ballot, under conditions which will ensure the free expression of the opinion of the people in the choice of the legislature.

SCHEDULE 2

Section 10

REMEDIAL ORDERS

Orders

1.— (1) A remedial order may—

- (a) contain such incidental, supplemental, consequential or transitional provision as the person making it considers appropriate;
- (b) be made so as to have effect from a date earlier than that on which it is made;
- (c) make provision for the delegation of specific functions;
- (d) make different provision for different cases.

(2) The power conferred by sub-paragraph (1)(a) includes—

- (a) power to amend primary legislation (including primary legislation other than that which contains the incompatible provision); and
- (b) power to amend or revoke subordinate legislation (including subordinate legislation other than that which contains the incompatible provision).

(3) A remedial order may be made so as to have the same extent as the legislation which it affects.

(4) No person is to be guilty of an offence solely as a result of the retrospective effect of a remedial order.

Procedure

2. No remedial order may be made unless—

(a) a draft of the order has been approved by a resolution of each House of Parliament made after the end of the period of 60 days beginning with the day on which the draft was laid; or
(b) it is declared in the order that it appears to the person making it that, because of the urgency of the matter, it is necessary to make the order without a draft being so approved.

Orders laid in draft

3.—(1) No draft may be laid under paragraph 2(a) unless—
(a) the person proposing to make the order has laid before Parliament a document which contains a draft of the proposed order and the required information; and
(b) the period of 60 days, beginning with the day on which the document required by this sub-paragraph was laid, has ended.

(2) If representations have been made during that period, the draft laid under paragraph 2(a) must be accompanied by a statement containing—
(a) a summary of the representations; and
(b) if, as a result of the representations, the proposed order has been changed, details of the changes.

Urgent cases

4.— (1) If a remedial order ("the original order") is made without being approved in draft, the person making it must lay it before Parliament, accompanied by the required information, after it is made.

(2) If representations have been made during the period of 60 days beginning with the day on which the original order was made, the person making it must (after the end of that period) lay before Parliament a statement containing—
(a) a summary of the representations; and
(b) if, as a result of the representations, he considers it appropriate to make changes to the original order, details of the changes.

(3) If sub-paragraph (2)(b) applies, the person making the statement must—
(a) make a further remedial order replacing the original order; and
(b) lay the replacement order before Parliament.

(4) If, at the end of the period of 120 days beginning with the day on which the original order was made, a resolution has not been passed by each House approving the original or replacement order, the order ceases to have effect (but without that affecting anything previously done under either order or the power to make a fresh remedial order).

Definitions

5. In this Schedule—
"representations" means representations about a remedial order (or proposed remedial order) made to the person making (or proposing to make) it and includes any relevant Parliamentary report or resolution; and
"required information" means—
(a) an explanation of the incompatibility which the order (or proposed order) seeks to remove, including particulars of the relevant declaration, finding or order; and
(b) a statement of the reasons for proceeding under section 10 and for making an order in those terms.

Calculating periods

6. In calculating any period for the purposes of this Schedule, no account is to be taken of any time during which—
(a) Parliament is dissolved or prorogued; or
(b) both Houses are adjourned for more than four days.

PART II
INTERNATIONAL AND NON-STATUTORY MATERIALS

A: CONVENTIONS, TREATIES AND EC DIRECTIVES

CONSOLIDATED VERSION OF THE TREATY ESTABLISHING THE EUROPEAN COMMUNITY

NOTES

Consolidated version of the EC Treaty as amended by the Treaty of Amsterdam. Date of publication in the OJ: OJ C340, 10.11.97, p 1.

Preamble

His Majesty the King of the Belgians, the President of the Federal Republic of Germany, the President of the French Republic, the President of the Italian Republic, her Royal Highness the Grand Duchess of Luxembourg, her Majesty the Queen of the Netherlands,[1]

Determined to lay the foundations of an ever closer union among the peoples of Europe,

Resolved to ensure the economic and social progress of their countries by common action to eliminate the barriers which divide Europe,

Affirming as the essential objective of their efforts the constant improvements of the living and working conditions of their peoples,

Recognising that the removal of existing obstacles calls for concerted action in order to guarantee steady expansion, balanced trade and fair competition,

Anxious to strengthen the unity of their economies and to ensure their harmonious development by reducing the differences existing between the various regions and the backwardness of the less-favoured regions,

Desiring to contribute, by means of a common commercial policy, to the progressive abolition of restrictions on international trade,

Intending to confirm the solidarity which binds Europe and the overseas countries and desiring to ensure the development of their prosperity, in accordance with the principles of the Charter of the United Nations,

Resolved by thus pooling their resources to preserve and strengthen peace and liberty, and calling upon the other peoples of Europe who share their ideal to join in their efforts,

Determined to promote the development of the highest possible level of knowledge for their peoples through a wide access to education and through its continuous updating,

Have decided to create a European Community and to this end have designated as their Plenipotentiaries:

. . . Who, having exchanged their full powers, found in good and due form, have agreed as follows.

NOTES

[1] The Kingdom of Denmark, the Hellenic Republic, the Kingdom of Spain, Ireland, the Republic of Austria, the Portuguese Republic, the Republic of Finland, the Kingdom of Sweden and the United Kingdom of Great Britain and Northern Ireland have since become members of the European Community

PART ONE
PRINCIPLES

Article 1 (ex Article 1)

By this Treaty, the High Contracting Parties establish among themselves a European Community.

Article 2 (ex Article 2)

The Community shall have as its task, by establishing a common market and an economic and monetary union and by implementing common policies or activities referred to in Articles 3 and 4, to promote throughout the Community a harmonious, balanced and sustainable development of economic activities, a high level of employment and of social protection, equality between men and women, sustainable and non-inflationary growth, a high degree of competitiveness and convergence of economic performance, a high level of protection and improvement of the quality of the environment, the raising of the standard of living and quality of life, and economic and social cohesion and solidarity among Member States.

Article 3 (ex Article 3)

1. For the purposes set out in Article 2, the activities of the Community shall include, as provided in this Treaty and in accordance with the timetable set out therein—

(a) the prohibition, as between Member States, of customs duties and quantitative restrictions on the import and export of goods, and of all other measures having equivalent effect;
(b) a common commercial policy;
(c) an internal market characterised by the abolition, as between Member States, of obstacles to the free movement of goods, persons, services and capital;
(d) measures concerning the entry and movement of persons as provided for in Title IV;
(e) a common policy in the sphere of agriculture and fisheries;
(f) a common policy in the sphere of transport;
(g) a system ensuring that competition in the internal market is not distorted;
(h) the approximation of the laws of Member States to the extent required for the functioning of the common market;
(i) the promotion of co-ordination between employment policies of the Member States with a view to enhancing their effectiveness by developing a co-ordinated strategy for employment;
(j) a policy in the social sphere comprising a European Social Fund;
(k) the strengthening of economic and social cohesion;
(l) a policy in the sphere of the environment;
(m) the strengthening of the competitiveness of Community industry;
(n) the promotion of research and technological development;
(o) encouragement for the establishment and development of trans-European networks;
(p) a contribution to the attainment of a high level of health protection;
(q) a contribution to education and training of quality and to the flowering of the cultures of the Member States;
(r) a policy in the sphere of development co-operation;
(s) the association of the overseas countries and territories in order to increase trade and promote jointly economic and social development;
(t) a contribution to the strengthening of consumer protection;
(u) measures in the spheres of energy, civil protection and tourism.

2. In all the activities referred to in this Article, the Community shall aim to eliminate inequalities, and to promote equality, between men and women.

Article 4 (ex Article 3a)

1. For the purposes set out in Article 2, the activities of the Member States and the Community shall include, as provided in this Treaty and in accordance with the timetable set out therein, the adoption of an economic policy which is based on the close co-ordination of Member States' economic policies, on the internal market and on the definition of common objectives, and conducted in accordance with the principle of an open market economy with free competition.

2. Concurrently with the foregoing, and as provided in this Treaty and in accordance with the timetable and the procedures set out therein, these activities shall include the irrevocable fixing of exchange rates leading to the introduction of a single currency, the ECU, and the definition and conduct of a single monetary policy and exchange-rate policy the primary objective of both of which shall be to maintain price stability and, without prejudice to this objective, to support the general economic policies in the Community, in accordance with the principle of an open market economy with free competition.

3. These activities of the Member States and the Community shall entail compliance with the following guiding principles: stable prices, sound public finances and monetary conditions and a sustainable balance of payments.

Article 5 (ex Article 3b)

The Community shall act within the limits of the powers conferred upon it by this Treaty and of the objectives assigned to it therein.

In areas which do not fall within its exclusive competence, the Community shall take action, in accordance with the principle of subsidiarity, only if and insofar as the objectives of the proposed action cannot be sufficiently achieved by the Member States and can therefore, by reason of the scale or effects of the proposed action, be better achieved by the Community.

Any action by the Community shall not go beyond what is necessary to achieve the objectives of this Treaty.

Article 6 (ex Article 3c)

Environmental protection requirements must be integrated into the definition and implementation of the Community policies and activities referred to in Article 3, in particular with a view to promoting sustainable development.

Article 7 (ex Article 4)

1. The tasks entrusted to the Community shall be carried out by the following institutions—

— a European Parliament,
— a Council,
— a Commission,
— a Court of Justice,
— a Court of Auditors.

Each institution shall act within the limits of the powers conferred upon it by this Treaty.

2. The Council and the Commission shall be assisted by an Economic and Social Committee and a Committee of the Regions acting in an advisory capacity.

Article 8 (ex Article 4a)

A European System of Central Banks (hereinafter referred to as 'ESCB') and a European Central Bank (hereinafter referred to as 'ECB') shall be established in accordance with the procedures laid down in this Treaty; they shall act within the limits of the powers conferred upon them by this Treaty and by the Statute of the ESCB and of the ECB (hereinafter referred to as 'Statute of the ESCB') annexed thereto.

Article 9 (ex Article 4b)

A European Investment Bank is hereby established, which shall act within the limits of the powers conferred upon it by this Treaty and the Statute annexed thereto.

Article 10 (ex Article 5)

Member States shall take all appropriate measures, whether general or particular, to ensure fulfilment of the obligations arising out of this Treaty or resulting from action taken by the institutions of the Community. They shall facilitate the achievement of the Community's tasks.

They shall abstain from any measure which could jeopardise the attainment of the objectives of this Treaty.

Article 11 (ex Article 5a)

1. Member States which intend to establish closer co-operation between themselves may be authorised, subject to Articles 43 and 44 of the Treaty on European Union, to make use of the institutions, procedures and mechanisms laid down by this Treaty, provided that the co-operation proposed—

(a) does not concern areas which fall within the exclusive competence of the Community;
(b) does not affect Community policies, actions or programmes;
(c) does not concern the citizenship of the Union or discriminate between nationals of Member States;
(d) remains within the limits of the powers conferred upon the Community by this Treaty; and
(e) does not constitute a discrimination or a restriction of trade between Member States and does not distort the conditions of competition between the latter.

2. The authorisation referred to in paragraph 1 shall be granted by the Council, acting by a qualified majority on a proposal from the Commission and after consulting the European Parliament.

If a member of the Council declares that, for important and stated reasons of national policy, it intends to oppose the granting of an authorisation by qualified majority, a vote shall not be taken. The Council may, acting by a qualified majority, request that the matter be referred to the Council, meeting in the composition of the Heads of State or Government, for decision by unanimity.

Member States which intend to establish closer co-operation as referred to in paragraph 1 may address a request to the Commission, which may submit a proposal to the Council to that effect. In the event of the Commission not submitting a proposal, it shall inform the Member States concerned of the reasons for not doing so.

3. Any Member State which wishes to become a party to co-operation set up in accordance with this Article shall notify its intention to the Council and to the Commission, which shall give an opinion to the Council within three months of receipt of that notification. Within four months of the date of that notification, the Commission shall decide on it and on such specific arrangements as it may deem necessary.

4. The acts and decisions necessary for the implementation of co-operation activities shall be subject to all the relevant provisions of this Treaty, save as otherwise provided for in this Article and in Articles 43 and 44 of the Treaty on European Union.

5. This Article is without prejudice to the provisions of the Protocol integrating the Schengen acquis into the framework of the European Union.

Article 12 (ex Article 6)

Within the scope of application of this Treaty, and without prejudice to any special provisions contained therein, any discrimination on grounds of nationality shall be prohibited.

The Council, acting in accordance with the procedure referred to in Article 251, may adopt rules designed to prohibit such discrimination.

Article 13 (ex Article 6a)

Without prejudice to the other provisions of this Treaty and within the limits of the powers conferred by it upon the Community, the Council, acting unanimously on a proposal from the Commission and after consulting the European Parliament, may take appropriate action to combat discrimination based on sex, racial or ethnic origin, religion or belief, disability, age or sexual orientation.

Article 14 (ex Article 7a)

1. The Community shall adopt measures with the aim of progressively establishing the internal market over a period expiring on 31 December 1992, in accordance with the provisions of this Article and of Articles 15, 26, 47(2), 49, 80, 93 and 95 and without prejudice to the other provisions of this Treaty.

2. The internal market shall comprise an area without internal frontiers in which the free movement of goods, persons, services and capital is ensured in accordance with the provisions of this Treaty.

3. The Council, acting by a qualified majority on a proposal from the Commission, shall determine the guidelines and conditions necessary to ensure balanced progress in all the sectors concerned.

Article 15 (ex Article 7c)

When drawing up its proposals with a view to achieving the objectives set out in Article 14, the Commission shall take into account the extent of the effort that certain economies showing differences in development will have to sustain during the period of establishment of the internal market and it may propose appropriate provisions.

If these provisions take the form of derogations, they must be of a temporary nature and must cause the least possible disturbance to the functioning of the common market.

Article 16 (ex Article 7d)

Without prejudice to Articles 73, 86 and 87, and given the place occupied by services of general economic interest in the shared values of the Union as well as their role in promoting social and territorial cohesion, the Community and the Member States, each within their respective powers and within the scope of application of this Treaty, shall take care that such services operate on the basis of principles and conditions which enable them to fulfil their missions.

PART TWO
CITIZENSHIP OF THE UNION

Article 17 (ex Article 8)

1. Citizenship of the Union is hereby established. Every person holding the nationality of a Member State shall be a citizen of the Union. Citizenship of the Union shall complement and not replace national citizenship.

2. Citizens of the Union shall enjoy the rights conferred by this Treaty and shall be subject to the duties imposed thereby.

Article 18 (ex Article 8a)

1. Every citizen of the Union shall have the right to move and reside freely within the territory of the Member States, subject to the limitations and conditions laid down in this Treaty and by the measures adopted to give it effect.

2. The Council may adopt provisions with a view to facilitating the exercise of the rights referred to in paragraph 1; save as otherwise provided in this Treaty, the Council shall act in accordance with the procedure referred to in Article 251. The Council shall act unanimously throughout this procedure.

Article 19 (ex Article 8b)

1. Every citizen of the Union residing in a Member State of which he is not a national shall have the right to vote and to stand as a candidate at municipal elections in the Member State in which he resides, under the same conditions as nationals of that State. This right shall be exercised subject to detailed arrangements adopted by the Council, acting unanimously on a proposal from the Commission and after consulting the European Parliament; these arrangements may provide for derogations where warranted by problems specific to a Member State.

2. Without prejudice to Article 190(4) and to the provisions adopted for its implementation, every citizen of the Union residing in a Member State of which he is not a national shall have the right to vote and to stand as a candidate in elections to the European Parliament in the Member State in which he resides, under the same conditions as nationals of that State. This right shall be exercised subject to detailed arrangements adopted by the Council, acting unanimously on a proposal from the Commission and after consulting the European Parliament; these arrangements may provide for derogations where warranted by problems specific to a Member State.

Article 20 (ex Article 8c)

Every citizen of the Union shall, in the territory of a third country in which the Member State of which he is a national is not represented, be entitled to protection by the diplomatic or consular authorities of any Member State, on the same conditions as the nationals of that State. Member States shall establish the necessary rules among themselves and start the international negotiations required to secure this protection.

Article 21 (ex Article 8d)

Every citizen of the Union shall have the right to petition the European Parliament in accordance with Article 194.

Every citizen of the Union may apply to the Ombudsman established in accordance with Article 195.

Every citizen of the Union may write to any of the institutions or bodies referred to in this Article or in Article 7 in one of the languages mentioned in Article 314 and have an answer in the same language.

Article 22 (ex Article 8e)

The Commission shall report to the European Parliament, to the Council and to the Economic and Social Committee every three years on the application of the provisions of this Part. This report shall take account of the development of the Union.

On this basis, and without prejudice to the other provisions of this Treaty, the Council, acting unanimously on a proposal from the Commission and after consulting the European Parliament, may adopt provisions to strengthen or to add to the rights laid down in this Part, which it shall recommend to the Member States for adoption in accordance with their respective constitutional requirements.

PART THREE
COMMUNITY POLICIES

TITLE I
FREE MOVEMENT OF GOODS

Article 23 (ex Article 9)

1. The Community shall be based upon a customs union which shall cover all trade in goods and which shall involve the prohibition between Member States of customs duties on imports and exports and of all charges having equivalent effect, and the adoption of a common customs tariff in their relations with third countries.

2. The provisions of Article 25 and of Chapter 2 of this Title shall apply to products originating in Member States and to products coming from third countries which are in free circulation in Member States.

Article 24 (ex Article 10)

Products coming from a third country shall be considered to be in free circulation in a Member State if the import formalities have been complied with and any customs duties or charges having equivalent effect which are payable have been levied in that Member State, and if they have not benefited from a total or partial drawback of such duties or charges.

CHAPTER 1
THE CUSTOMS UNION

Article 25 (ex Article 12)

Customs duties on imports and exports and charges having equivalent effect shall be prohibited between Member States. This prohibition shall also apply to customs duties of a fiscal nature.

Article 26 (ex Article 28)

Common Customs Tariff duties shall be fixed by the Council acting by a qualified majority on a proposal from the Commission.

Article 27 (ex Article 29)

In carrying out the tasks entrusted to it under this Chapter the Commission shall be guided by—

(a) the need to promote trade between Member States and third countries;
(b) developments in conditions of competition within the Community insofar as they lead to an improvement in the competitive capacity of undertakings;
(c) the requirements of the Community as regards the supply of raw materials and semi-finished goods; in this connection the Commission shall take care to avoid distorting conditions of competition between Member States in respect of finished goods;
(d) the need to avoid serious disturbances in the economies of Member States and to ensure rational development of production and an expansion of consumption within the Community.

CHAPTER 2
PROHIBITION OF QUANTITATIVE RESTRICTIONS BETWEEN MEMBER STATES

Article 28 (ex Article 30)

Quantitative restrictions on imports and all measures having equivalent effect shall be prohibited between Member States.

Article 29 (ex Article 34)

Quantitative restrictions on exports, and all measures having equivalent effect, shall be prohibited between Member States.

Article 30 (ex Article 36)

The provisions of Articles 28 and 29 shall not preclude prohibitions or restrictions on imports, exports or goods in transit justified on grounds of public morality, public policy or public security; the protection of health and life of humans, animals or plants; the protection of national treasures possessing artistic, historic or archaeological value; or the protection of industrial and commercial property. Such prohibitions or restrictions shall not, however, constitute a means of arbitrary discrimination or a disguised restriction on trade between Member States.

Article 31 (ex Article 37)

1. Member States shall adjust any State monopolies of a commercial character so as to ensure that no discrimination regarding the conditions under which goods are procured and marketed exists between nationals of Member States.

The provisions of this Article shall apply to any body through which a Member State, in law or in fact, either directly or indirectly supervises, determines or appreciably influences imports or exports between Member States. These provisions shall likewise apply to monopolies delegated by the State to others.

2. Member States shall refrain from introducing any new measure which is contrary to the principles laid down in paragraph 1 or which restricts the scope of the Articles dealing with the prohibition of customs duties and quantitative restrictions between Member States.

3. If a State monopoly of a commercial character has rules which are designed to make it easier to dispose of agricultural products or obtain for them the best return, steps should be taken in applying the rules contained in this Article to ensure equivalent safeguards for the employment and standard of living of the producers concerned.

TITLE II
AGRICULTURE

Article 32 (ex Article 38)

1. The common market shall extend to agriculture and trade in agricultural products. 'Agricultural products' means the products of the soil, of stockfarming and of fisheries and products of first-stage processing directly related to these products.

2, 3 . . .

4. The operation and development of the common market for agricultural products must be accompanied by the establishment of a common agricultural policy.

NOTES

Paras (2), (3): outside the scope of this work.

TITLE III
FREE MOVEMENT OF PERSONS, SERVICES AND CAPITAL

CHAPTER 1
WORKERS

Article 39 (ex Article 48)

1. Freedom of movement for workers shall be secured within the Community.

2. Such freedom of movement shall entail the abolition of any discrimination based on nationality between workers of the Member States as regards employment, remuneration and other conditions of work and employment.

3. It shall entail the right, subject to limitations justified on grounds of public policy, public security or public health—

(a) to accept offers of employment actually made;

(b) to move freely within the territory of Member States for this purpose;

(c) to stay in a Member State for the purpose of employment in accordance with the provisions governing the employment of nationals of that State laid down by law, regulation or administrative action;
(d) to remain in the territory of a Member State after having been employed in that State, subject to conditions which shall be embodied in implementing regulations to be drawn up by the Commission.

4. The provisions of this Article shall not apply to employment in the public service.

CHAPTER 2
RIGHT OF ESTABLISHMENT

Article 43 (ex Article 52)

Within the framework of the provisions set out below, restrictions on the freedom of establishment of nationals of a Member State in the territory of another Member State shall be prohibited. Such prohibition shall also apply to restrictions on the setting-up of agencies, branches or subsidiaries by nationals of any Member State established in the territory of any Member State.

Freedom of establishment shall include the right to take up and pursue activities as self-employed persons and to set up and manage undertakings, in particular companies or firms within the meaning of the second paragraph of Article 48, under the conditions laid down for its own nationals by the law of the country where such establishment is effected, subject to the provisions of the Chapter relating to capital.

Article 45 (ex Article 55)

The provisions of this Chapter shall not apply, so far as any given Member State is concerned, to activities which in that State are connected, even occasionally, with the exercise of official authority.

The Council may, acting by a qualified majority on a proposal from the Commission, rule that the provisions of this Chapter shall not apply to certain activities.

Article 46 (ex Article 56)

1. The provisions of this Chapter and measures taken in pursuance thereof shall not prejudice the applicability of provisions laid down by law, regulation or administrative action providing for special treatment for foreign nationals on grounds of public policy, public security or public health.

2. The Council shall, acting in accordance with the procedure referred to in Article 251, issue directives for the co-ordination of the abovementioned provisions.

Article 47 (ex Article 57)

1. In order to make it easier for persons to take up and pursue activities as self-employed persons, the Council shall, acting in accordance with the procedure referred to in Article 251, issue directives for the mutual recognition of diplomas, certificates and other evidence of formal qualifications.

2, 3 . . .

NOTES

Paras (2), (3): outside the scope of this work.

CHAPTER 3
SERVICES

Article 49 (ex Article 59)

Within the framework of the provisions set out below, restrictions on freedom to provide services within the Community shall be prohibited in respect of nationals of Member States who are established in a State of the Community other than that of the person for whom the services are intended.

The Council may, acting by a qualified majority on a proposal from the Commission, extend the provisions of the Chapter to nationals of a third country who provide services and who are established within the Community.

Article 50 (ex Article 60)

Services shall be considered to be 'services' within the meaning of this Treaty where they are normally provided for remuneration, insofar as they are not governed by the provisions relating to freedom of movement for goods, capital and persons.

'Services' shall in particular include—

(a) activities of an industrial character;
(b) activities of a commercial character;
(c) activities of craftsmen;
(d) activities of the professions.

Without prejudice to the provisions of the Chapter relating to the right of establishment, the person providing a service may, in order to do so, temporarily pursue his activity in the State where the service is provided, under the same conditions as are imposed by that State on its own nationals.

CHAPTER 4
CAPITAL AND PAYMENTS

Article 56 (ex Article 73b)

1. Within the framework of the provisions set out in this Chapter, all restrictions on the movement of capital between Member States and between Member States and third countries shall be prohibited.

2. Within the framework of the provisions set out in this Chapter, all restrictions on payments between Member States and between Member States and third countries shall be prohibited.

Article 58 (ex Article 73d)

1. The provisions of Article 56 shall be without prejudice to the right of Member States—

(a) to apply the relevant provisions of their tax law which distinguish between taxpayers who are not in the same situation with regard to their place of residence or with regard to the place where their capital is invested;
(b) to take all requisite measures to prevent infringements of national law and regulations, in particular in the field of taxation and the prudential supervision of financial institutions, or to lay down procedures for the declaration of capital movements for purposes of administrative or statistical information, or to take measures which are justified on grounds of public policy or public security.

2. The provisions of this Chapter shall be without prejudice to the applicability of restrictions on the right of establishment which are compatible with this Treaty.

3. The measures and procedures referred to in paragraphs 1 and 2 shall not constitute a means of arbitrary discrimination or a disguised restriction on the free movement of capital and payments as defined in Article 56.

TITLE IV (ex Title IIIA)
VISAS, ASYLUM, IMMIGRATION AND OTHER POLICIES RELATED TO FREE MOVEMENT OF PERSONS

Article 61 (ex Article 73i)

In order to establish progressively an area of freedom, security and justice, the Council shall adopt—

(a) within a period of five years after the entry into force of the Treaty of Amsterdam, measures aimed at ensuring the free movement of persons in accordance with Article 14, in conjunction with directly related flanking measures with respect to external border controls, asylum and immigration, in accordance with the provisions of Article 62(2) and (3) and Article 63(1)(a) and (2)(a), and measures to prevent and combat crime in accordance with the provisions of Article 31(e) of the Treaty on European Union;

(b) other measures in the fields of asylum, immigration and safeguarding the rights of nationals of third countries, in accordance with the provisions of Article 63;

(c) measures in the field of judicial co-operation in civil matters as provided for in Article 65;

(d) appropriate measures to encourage and strengthen administrative co-operation, as provided for in Article 66;

(e) measures in the field of police and judicial co-operation in criminal matters aimed at a high level of security by preventing and combating crime within the Union in accordance with the provisions of the Treaty on European Union.

Article 62 (ex Article 73j)

The Council, acting in accordance with the procedure referred to in Article 67, shall, within a period of five years after the entry into force of the Treaty of Amsterdam, adopt—

(1) measures with a view to ensuring, in compliance with Article 14, the absence of any controls on persons, be they citizens of the Union or nationals of third countries, when crossing internal borders;

(2) measures on the crossing of the external borders of the Member States which shall establish—

   (a) standards and procedures to be followed by Member States in carrying out checks on persons at such borders;

   (b) rules on visas for intended stays of no more than three months, including—

      (i) the list of third countries whose nationals must be in possession of visas when crossing the external borders and those whose nationals are exempt from that requirement;

      (ii) the procedures and conditions for issuing visas by Member States;

      (iii) a uniform format for visas;

      (iv) rules on a uniform visa;

(3) measures setting out the conditions under which nationals of third countries shall have the freedom to travel within the territory of the Member States during a period of no more than three months.

Article 63 (ex Article 73k)

The Council, acting in accordance with the procedure referred to in Article 67, shall, within a period of five years after the entry into force of the Treaty of Amsterdam, adopt—

(1) measures on asylum, in accordance with the Geneva Convention of 28 July 1951 and the Protocol of 31 January 1967 relating to the status of refugees and other relevant treaties, within the following areas—
  (a) criteria and mechanisms for determining which Member State is responsible for considering an application for asylum submitted by a national of a third country in one of the Member States,
  (b) minimum standards on the reception of asylum seekers in Member States,
  (c) minimum standards with respect to the qualification of nationals of third countries as refugees,
  (d) minimum standards on procedures in Member States for granting or withdrawing refugee status;

(2) measures on refugees and displaced persons within the following areas—
  (a) minimum standards for giving temporary protection to displaced persons from third countries who cannot return to their country of origin and for persons who otherwise need international protection,
  (b) promoting a balance of effort between Member States in receiving and bearing the consequences of receiving refugees and displaced persons;

(3) measures on immigration policy within the following areas—
  (a) conditions of entry and residence, and standards on procedures for the issue by Member States of long term visas and residence permits, including those for the purpose of family reunion,
  (b) illegal immigration and illegal residence, including repatriation of illegal residents;

(4) measures defining the rights and conditions under which nationals of third countries who are legally resident in a Member State may reside in other Member States.

Measures adopted by the Council pursuant to points 3 and 4 shall not prevent any Member State from maintaining or introducing in the areas concerned national provisions which are compatible with this Treaty and with international agreements.

Measures to be adopted pursuant to points 2(b), 3(a) and 4 shall not be subject to the five year period referred to above.

Article 64 (ex Article 73l)

1. This Title shall not affect the exercise of the responsibilities incumbent upon Member States with regard to the maintenance of law and order and the safeguarding of internal security.

2. In the event of one or more Member States being confronted with an emergency situation characterised by a sudden inflow of nationals of third countries and without prejudice to paragraph 1, the Council may, acting by qualified majority on a proposal from the Commission, adopt provisional measures of a duration not exceeding six months for the benefit of the Member States concerned.

Article 65 (ex Article 73m)

Measures in the field of judicial co-operation in civil matters having cross-border implications, to be taken in accordance with Article 67 and insofar as necessary for the proper functioning of the internal market, shall include—

(a) improving and simplifying—
- — the system for cross-border service of judicial and extrajudicial documents;
- — co-operation in the taking of evidence;
- — the recognition and enforcement of decisions in civil and commercial cases, including decisions in extrajudicial cases;

(b) promoting the compatibility of the rules applicable in the Member States concerning the conflict of laws and of jurisdiction;

(c) eliminating obstacles to the good functioning of civil proceedings, if necessary by promoting the compatibility of the rules on civil procedure applicable in the Member States.

Article 66 (ex Article 73n)

The Council, acting in accordance with the procedure referred to in Article 67, shall take measures to ensure co-operation between the relevant departments of the administrations of the Member States in the areas covered by this Title, as well as between those departments and the Commission.

Article 67 (ex Article 73o)

1. During a transitional period of five years following the entry into force of the Treaty of Amsterdam, the Council shall act unanimously on a proposal from the Commission or on the initiative of a Member State and after consulting the European Parliament.

2. After this period of five years—
- — the Council shall act on proposals from the Commission; the Commission shall examine any request made by a Member State that it submit a proposal to the Council;
- — the Council, acting unanimously after consulting the European Parliament, shall take a decision with a view to providing for all or parts of the areas covered by this Title to be governed by the procedure referred to in Article 251 and adapting the provisions relating to the powers of the Court of Justice.

3. By derogation from paragraphs 1 and 2, measures referred to in Article 62(2)(b)(i) and (iii) shall, from the entry into force of the Treaty of Amsterdam, be adopted by the Council acting by a qualified majority on a proposal from the Commission and after consulting the European Parliament.

4. By derogation from paragraph 2, measures referred to in Article 62(2)(b)(ii) and (iv) shall, after a period of five years following the entry into force of the Treaty of Amsterdam, be adopted by the Council acting in accordance with the procedure referred to in Article 251.

Article 68 (ex Article 73p)

1. Article 234 shall apply to this Title under the following circumstances and conditions: where a question on the interpretation of this Title or on the validity or

interpretation of acts of the institutions of the Community based on this Title is raised in a case pending before a court or a tribunal of a Member State against whose decisions there is no judicial remedy under national law, that court or tribunal shall, if it considers that a decision on the question is necessary to enable it to give judgment, request the Court of Justice to give a ruling thereon.

2. In any event, the Court of Justice shall not have jurisdiction to rule on any measure or decision taken pursuant to Article 62(1) relating to the maintenance of law and order and the safeguarding of internal security.

3. The Council, the Commission or a Member State may request the Court of Justice to give a ruling on a question of interpretation of this Title or of acts of the institutions of the Community based on this Title. The ruling given by the Court of Justice in response to such a request shall not apply to judgments of courts or tribunals of the Member States which have become res judicata.

Article 69 (ex Article 73q)

The application of this Title shall be subject to the provisions of the Protocol on the position of the United Kingdom and Ireland and to the Protocol on the position of Denmark and without prejudice to the Protocol on the application of certain aspects of Article 14 of the Treaty establishing the European Community to the United Kingdom and to Ireland.

TITLE V (ex Title IV) TRANSPORT

Article 70 (ex Article 74)

The objectives of this Treaty shall, in matters governed by this Title, be pursued by Member States within the framework of a common transport policy.

Article 80 (ex Article 84)

1. The provisions of this Title shall apply to transport by rail, road and inland waterway.

2. The Council may, acting by a qualified majority, decide whether, to what extent and by what procedure appropriate provisions may be laid down for sea and air transport.

The procedural provisions of Article 71 shall apply.

TITLE VI (ex Title V) COMMON RULES ON COMPETITION, TAXATION AND APPROXIMATION OF LAWS

CHAPTER 1 RULES ON COMPETITION

SECTION 1 RULES APPLYING TO UNDERTAKINGS

Article 81 (ex Article 85)

1. The following shall be prohibited as incompatible with the common market: all agreements between undertakings, decisions by associations of undertakings and

concerted practices which may affect trade between Member States and which have as their object or effect the prevention, restriction or distortion of competition within the common market, and in particular those which—

(a) directly or indirectly fix purchase or selling prices or any other trading conditions;
(b) limit or control production, markets, technical development, or investment;
(c) share markets or sources of supply;
(d) apply dissimilar conditions to equivalent transactions with other trading parties, thereby placing them at a competitive disadvantage;
(e) make the conclusion of contracts subject to acceptance by the other parties of supplementary obligations which, by their nature or according to commercial usage, have no connection with the subject of such contracts.

2. Any agreements or decisions prohibited pursuant to this Article shall be automatically void.

3. The provisions of paragraph 1 may, however, be declared inapplicable in the case of—

— any agreement or category of agreements between undertakings;
— any decision or category of decisions by associations of undertakings;
— any concerted practice or category of concerted practices,

which contributes to improving the production or distribution of goods or to promoting technical or economic progress, while allowing consumers a fair share of the resulting benefit, and which does not—

(a) impose on the undertakings concerned restrictions which are not indispensable to the attainment of these objectives;
(b) afford such undertakings the possibility of eliminating competition in respect of a substantial part of the products in question.

Article 82 (ex Article 86)

Any abuse by one or more undertakings of a dominant position within the common market or in a substantial part of it shall be prohibited as incompatible with the common market insofar as it may affect trade between Member States.

. . .

NOTES

Words omitted outside the scope of this work.

Article 83 (ex Article 87)

1. The appropriate regulations or directives to give effect to the principles set out in Articles 81 and 82 shall be laid down by the Council, acting by a qualified majority on a proposal from the Commission and after consulting the European Parliament.

2. . . .

NOTES

Para (2): outside the scope of this work.

Article 86 (ex Article 90)

1. In the case of public undertakings and undertakings to which Member States grant special or exclusive rights, Member States shall neither enact nor maintain in

force any measure contrary to the rules contained in this Treaty, in particular to those rules provided for in Article 12 and Articles 81 to 89.

2, 3 . . .

NOTES

Paras (2), (3): outside the scope of this work.

CHAPTER 2
TAX PROVISIONS

Article 90 (ex Article 95)

No Member State shall impose, directly or indirectly, on the products of other Member States any internal taxation of any kind in excess of that imposed directly or indirectly on similar domestic products.

Furthermore, no Member State shall impose on the products of other Member States any internal taxation of such a nature as to afford indirect protection to other products.

CHAPTER 3
APPROXIMATION OF LAWS

Article 94 (ex Article 100)

The Council shall, acting unanimously on a proposal from the Commission and after consulting the European Parliament and the Economic and Social Committee, issue directives for the approximation of such laws, regulations or administrative provisions of the Member States as directly affect the establishment or functioning of the common market.

Article 95 (ex Article 100a)

1. By way of derogation from Article 94 and save where otherwise provided in this Treaty, the following provisions shall apply for the achievement of the objectives set out in Article 14. The Council shall, acting in accordance with the procedure referred to in Article 251 and after consulting the Economic and Social Committee, adopt the measures for the approximation of the provisions laid down by law, regulation or administrative action in Member States which have as their object the establishment and functioning of the internal market.

2. Paragraph 1 shall not apply to fiscal provisions, to those relating to the free movement of persons nor to those relating to the rights and interests of employed persons.

3. The Commission, in its proposals envisaged in paragraph 1 concerning health, safety, environmental protection and consumer protection, will take as a base a high level of protection, taking account in particular of any new development based on scientific facts. Within their respective powers, the European Parliament and the Council will also seek to achieve this objective.

4. If, after the adoption by the Council or by the Commission of a harmonisation measure, a Member State deems it necessary to maintain national provisions on grounds of major needs referred to in Article 30, or relating to the protection of the environment or the working environment, it shall notify the Commission of these provisions as well as the grounds for maintaining them.

5. Moreover, without prejudice to paragraph 4, if, after the adoption by the Council or by the Commission of a harmonisation measure, a Member State deems it necessary to introduce national provisions based on new scientific evidence relating to the protection of the environment or the working environment on grounds of a problem specific to that Member State arising after the adoption of the harmonisation measure, it shall notify the Commission of the envisaged provisions as well as the grounds for introducing them.

6. The Commission shall, within six months of the notifications as referred to in paragraphs 4 and 5, approve or reject the national provisions involved after having verified whether or not they are a means of arbitrary discrimination or a disguised restriction on trade between Member States and whether or not they shall constitute an obstacle to the functioning of the internal market.

In the absence of a decision by the Commission within this period the national provisions referred to in paragraphs 4 and 5 shall be deemed to have been approved.

When justified by the complexity of the matter and in the absence of danger for human health, the Commission may notify the Member State concerned that the period referred to in this paragraph may be extended for a further period of up to six months.

7, 8 . . .

9. By way of derogation from the procedure laid down in Articles 226 and 227, the Commission and any Member State may bring the matter directly before the Court of Justice if it considers that another Member State is making improper use of the powers provided for in this Article.

10. . . .

NOTES

Paras (7), (8), (10): outside the scope of this work.

TITLE VII (ex Title VI)
ECONOMIC AND MONETARY POLICY

CHAPTER 1
ECONOMIC POLICY

Article 98 (ex Article 102a)

Member States shall conduct their economic policies with a view to contributing to the achievement of the objectives of the Community, as defined in Article 2, and in the context of the broad guidelines referred to in Article 99(2). The Member States and the Community shall act in accordance with the principle of an open market economy with free competition, favouring an efficient allocation of resources, and in compliance with the principles set out in Article 4.

Article 99 (ex Article 103)

1. Member States shall regard their economic policies as a matter of common concern and shall co-ordinate them within the Council, in accordance with the provisions of Article 98.

2. The Council shall, acting by a qualified majority on a recommendation from the Commission, formulate a draft for the broad guidelines of the economic policies of the Member States and of the Community, and shall report its findings to the European Council.

The European Council shall, acting on the basis of the report from the Council, discuss a conclusion on the broad guidelines of the economic policies of the Member States and of the Community.

On the basis of this conclusion, the Council shall, acting by a qualified majority, adopt a recommendation setting out these broad guidelines. The Council shall inform the European Parliament of its recommendation.

3. In order to ensure closer co-ordination of economic policies and sustained convergence of the economic performances of the Member States, the Council shall, on the basis of reports submitted by the Commission, monitor economic developments in each of the Member States and in the Community as well as the consistency of economic policies with the broad guidelines referred to in paragraph 2, and regularly carry out an overall assessment.

For the purpose of this multilateral surveillance, Member States shall forward information to the Commission about important measures taken by them in the field of their economic policy and such other information as they deem necessary.

4. Where it is established, under the procedure referred to in paragraph 3, that the economic policies of a Member State are not consistent with the broad guidelines referred to in paragraph 2 or that they risk jeopardising the proper functioning of economic and monetary union, the Council may, acting by a qualified majority on a recommendation from the Commission, make the necessary recommendations to the Member State concerned. The Council may, acting by a qualified majority on a proposal from the Commission, decide to make its recommendations public.

The President of the Council and the Commission shall report to the European Parliament on the results of multilateral surveillance. The President of the Council may be invited to appear before the competent committee of the European Parliament if the Council has made its recommendations public.

5. The Council, acting in accordance with the procedure referred to in Article 252, may adopt detailed rules for the multilateral surveillance procedure referred to in paragraphs 3 and 4 of this Article.

Article 100 (ex Article 103a)

1. Without prejudice to any other procedures provided for in this Treaty, the Council may, acting unanimously on a proposal from the Commission, decide upon the measures appropriate to the economic situation, in particular if severe difficulties arise in the supply of certain products.

2. Where a Member State is in difficulties or is seriously threatened with severe difficulties caused by exceptional occurrences beyond its control, the Council may, acting unanimously on a proposal from the Commission, grant, under certain conditions, Community financial assistance to the Member State concerned. Where the severe difficulties are caused by natural disasters, the Council shall act by qualified majority. The President of the Council shall inform the European Parliament of the decision taken.

Article 103

1. The Community shall not be liable for or assume the commitments of central governments, regional, local or other public authorities, other bodies governed by public law, or public undertakings of any Member State, without prejudice to mutual financial guarantees for the joint execution of a specific project. A Member State shall not be liable for or assume the commitments of central governments, regional, local or other public authorities, other bodies governed by public law, or public undertakings of another Member State, without prejudice to mutual financial guarantees for the joint execution of a specific project.

2. . . .

NOTES

Para (2): outside the scope of this work.

Article 104 (ex Article 104c)

1. Member States shall avoid excessive government deficits.

2. The Commission shall monitor the development of the budgetary situation and of the stock of government debt in the Member States with a view to identifying gross errors . . .

3–14 . . .

NOTES

Words omitted from para (2) and paras (3)–(14) outside the scope of this work.

CHAPTER 2
MONETARY POLICY

Article 105 (ex Article 105)

1. The primary objective of the ESCB shall be to maintain price stability. Without prejudice to the objective of price stability, the ESCB shall support the general economic policies in the Community with a view to contributing to the achievement of the objectives of the Community as laid down in Article 2. The ESCB shall act in accordance with the principle of an open market economy with free competition, favouring an efficient allocation of resources, and in compliance with the principles set out in Article 4.

2–6 . . .

NOTES

Paras (2)–(6): outside the scope of this work.

Article 106 (ex Article 105a)

1. The ECB shall have the exclusive right to authorise the issue of banknotes within the Community. The ECB and the national central banks may issue such notes. The banknotes issued by the ECB and the national central banks shall be the only such notes to have the status of legal tender within the Community.

2. Member States may issue coins subject to approval by the ECB of the volume of the issue. The Council may, acting in accordance with the procedure referred to in

Article 252 and after consulting the ECB, adopt measures to harmonise the denominations and technical specifications of all coins intended for circulation to the extent necessary to permit their smooth circulation within the Community.

Article 107 (ex Article 106)

1. The ESCB shall be composed of the ECB and of the national central banks.

2. The ECB shall have legal personality.

3–6 . . .

NOTES

Paras (3)–(6): outside the scope of this work.

CHAPTER 4
TRANSITIONAL PROVISIONS

Article 116 (ex Article 109e)

1. The second stage for achieving economic and monetary union shall begin on 1 January 1994.

2. Before that date—

(a) each Member State shall—

— adopt, where necessary, appropriate measures to comply with the prohibitions laid down in Article 56 and in Articles 101 and 102(1);

— adopt, if necessary, with a view to permitting the assessment provided for in subparagraph (b), multiannual programmes intended to ensure the lasting convergence necessary for the achievement of economic and monetary union, in particular with regard to price stability and sound public finances;

(b) the Council shall, on the basis of a report from the Commission, assess the progress made with regard to economic and monetary convergence, in particular with regard to price stability and sound public finances, and the progress made with the implementation of Community law concerning the internal market.

3. The provisions of Articles 101, 102(1), 103(1) and 104 with the exception of paragraphs 1, 9, 11 and 14 shall apply from the beginning of the second stage.

The provisions of Articles 100(2), 104(1), (9) and (11), 105, 106, 108, 111, 112, 113 and 114(2) and (4) shall apply from the beginning of the third stage.

4. In the second stage, Member States shall endeavour to avoid excessive government deficits.

5. During the second stage, each Member State shall, as appropriate, start the process leading to the independence of its central bank, in accordance with Article 109.

Article 117 (ex Article 109f)

1. At the start of the second stage, a European Monetary Institute (hereinafter referred to as 'EMI') shall be established and take up its duties; it shall have legal personality and be directed and managed by a Council, consisting of a President and the Governors of the national central banks, one of whom shall be Vice-President.

The President shall be appointed by common accord of the governments of the Member States at the level of Heads of State or Government, on a recommendation from the Council of the EMI, and after consulting the European Parliament and the Council. The President shall be selected from among persons of recognised standing and professional experience in monetary or banking matters. Only nationals of Member States may be President of the EMI. The Council of the EMI shall appoint the Vice-President.

The Statute of the EMI is laid down in a Protocol annexed to this Treaty.

2. The EMI shall—
- — strengthen co-operation between the national central banks;
- — strengthen the co-ordination of the monetary policies of the Member States, with the aim of ensuring price stability;
- — monitor the functioning of the European Monetary System;
- — hold consultations concerning issues falling within the competence of the national central banks and affecting the stability of financial institutions and markets;
- — take over the tasks of the European Monetary Co-operation Fund, which shall be dissolved; the modalities of dissolution are laid down in the Statute of the EMI;
- — facilitate the use of the ECU and oversee its development, including the smooth functioning of the ECU clearing system.

3. For the preparation of the third stage, the EMI shall—
- — prepare the instruments and the procedures necessary for carrying out a single monetary policy in the third stage;
- — promote the harmonisation, where necessary, of the rules and practices governing the collection, compilation and distribution of statistics in the areas within its field of competence;
- — prepare the rules for operations to be undertaken by the national central banks within the framework of the ESCB;
- — promote the efficiency of cross-border payments;
- — supervise the technical preparation of ECU banknotes.

At the latest by 31 December 1996, the EMI shall specify the regulatory, organisational and logistical framework necessary for the ESCB to perform its tasks in the third stage. This framework shall be submitted for decision to the ECB at the date of its establishment.

4, 5 . . .

6. The EMI shall be consulted by the Council regarding any proposed Community act within its field of competence.

Within the limits and under the conditions set out by the Council, acting by a qualified majority on a proposal from the Commission and after consulting the European Parliament and the EMI, the EMI shall be consulted by the authorities of the Member States on any draft legislative provision within its field of competence.

7. The Council may, acting unanimously on a proposal from the Commission and after consulting the European Parliament and the EMI, confer upon the EMI other tasks for the preparation of the third stage.

8. Where this Treaty provides for a consultative role for the ECB, references to the ECB shall be read as referring to the EMI before the establishment of the ECB.

9. During the second stage, the term 'ECB' used in Articles 230, 232, 233, 234, 237 and 288 shall be read as referring to the EMI.

NOTES

Paras (4), (5): outside the scope of this work.

Article 118 (ex Article 109g)

The currency composition of the ECU basket shall not be changed.

From the start of the third stage, the value of the ECU shall be irrevocably fixed in accordance with Article 123(4).

Article 119 (ex Article 109h)

1. Where a Member State is in difficulties or is seriously threatened with difficulties as regards its balance of payments either as a result of an overall disequilibrium in its balance of payments, or as a result of the type of currency at its disposal, and where such difficulties are liable in particular to jeopardise the functioning of the common market or the progressive implementation of the common commercial policy, the Commission shall immediately investigate the position of the State in question and the action which, making use of all the means at its disposal, that State has taken or may take in accordance with the provisions of this Treaty. The Commission shall state what measures it recommends the State concerned to take.

If the action taken by a Member State and the measures suggested by the Commission do not prove sufficient to overcome the difficulties which have arisen or which threaten, the Commission shall, after consulting the Committee referred to in Article 114, recommend to the Council the granting of mutual assistance and appropriate methods therefor.

The Commission shall keep the Council regularly informed of the situation and of how it is developing.

2. The Council, acting by a qualified majority, shall grant such mutual assistance; it shall adopt directives or decisions laying down the conditions and details of such assistance, . . .

3. If the mutual assistance recommended by the Commission is not granted by the Council or if the mutual assistance granted and the measures taken are insufficient, the Commission shall authorise the State which is in difficulties to take protective measures, the conditions and details of which the Commission shall determine.

Such authorisation may be revoked and such conditions and details may be changed by the Council acting by a qualified majority.

4. Subject to Article 122(6), this Article shall cease to apply from the beginning of the third stage.

NOTES

Para (2): words omitted outside the scope of this work.

Article 120 (ex Article 109i)

1. Where a sudden crisis in the balance of payments occurs and a decision within the meaning of Article 119(2) is not immediately taken, the Member State concerned

may, as a precaution, take the necessary protective measures. Such measures must cause the least possible disturbance in the functioning of the common market and must not be wider in scope than is strictly necessary to remedy the sudden difficulties which have arisen.

2–4 . . .

NOTES

Paras (2)–(4): outside the scope of this work.

Article 121 (ex Article 109j)

1. The Commission and the EMI shall report to the Council on the progress made in the fulfilment by the Member States of their obligations regarding the achievement of economic and monetary union . . .

2–3 . . .

4. If by the end of 1997 the date for the beginning of the third stage has not been set, the third stage shall start on 1 January 1999. Before 1 July 1998, the Council, meeting in the composition of the Heads of State or Government, after a repetition of the procedure provided for in paragraphs 1 and 2, with the exception of the second indent of paragraph 2, taking into account the reports referred to in paragraph 1 and the opinion of the European Parliament, shall, acting by a qualified majority and on the basis of the recommendations of the Council referred to in paragraph 2, confirm which Member States fulfil the necessary conditions for the adoption of a single currency.

NOTES

Words omitted from para (1) and paras (2), (3) outside the scope of this work.

TITLE VIII (ex Title VIA)
EMPLOYMENT

Article 125 (ex Article 109n)

Member States and the Community shall, in accordance with this Title, work towards developing a co-ordinated strategy for employment and particularly for promoting a skilled, trained and adaptable workforce and labour markets responsive to economic change with a view to achieving the objectives defined in Article 2 of the Treaty on European Union and in Article 2 of this Treaty.

TITLE IX (ex Title VII)
COMMON COMMERCIAL POLICY

Article 131 (ex Article 110)

By establishing a customs union between themselves Member States aim to contribute, in the common interest, to the harmonious development of world trade, the progressive abolition of restrictions on international trade and the lowering of customs barriers.

The common commercial policy shall take into account the favourable effect which the abolition of customs duties between Member States may have on the increase in the competitive strength of undertakings in those States.

Article 133 (ex Article 113)

1. The common commercial policy shall be based on uniform principles, particularly in regard to changes in tariff rates, the conclusion of tariff and trade agreements, the achievement of uniformity in measures of liberalisation, export policy and measures to protect trade such as those to be taken in the event of dumping or subsidies.

2–5 . . .

NOTES

Paras (2)–(5): outside the scope of this work.

TITLE X (ex Title VIIA) CUSTOMS CO-OPERATION

Article 135 (ex Article 116)

Within the scope of application of this Treaty, the Council, acting in accordance with the procedure referred to in Article 251, shall take measures in order to strengthen customs co-operation between Member States and between the latter and the Commission. These measures shall not concern the application of national criminal law or the national administration of justice.

TITLE XI (ex Title VIII) SOCIAL POLICY, EDUCATION, VOCATIONAL TRAINING AND YOUTH

CHAPTER 1 SOCIAL PROVISIONS

Article 136 (ex Article 117)

The Community and the Member States, having in mind fundamental social rights such as those set out in the European Social Charter signed at Turin on 18 October 1961 and in the 1989 Community Charter of the Fundamental Social Rights of Workers, shall have as their objectives the promotion of employment, improved living and working conditions, so as to make possible their harmonisation while the improvement is being maintained, proper social protection, dialogue between management and labour, the development of human resources with a view to lasting high employment and the combating of exclusion.

To this end the Community and the Member States shall implement measures which take account of the diverse forms of national practices, in particular in the field of contractual relations, and the need to maintain the competitiveness of the Community economy.

They believe that such a development will ensue not only from the functioning of the common market, which will favour the harmonisation of social systems, but also from the procedures provided for in this Treaty and from the approximation of provisions laid down by law, regulation or administrative action.

Article 137 (ex Article 118)

1. With a view to achieving the objectives of Article 136, the Community shall support and complement the activities of the Member States in the following fields—
   - — improvement in particular of the working environment to protect workers' health and safety;
   - — working conditions;
   - — the information and consultation of workers;
   - — the integration of persons excluded from the labour market, without prejudice to Article 150;
   - — equality between men and women with regard to labour market opportunities and treatment at work.

2. To this end, the Council may adopt, by means of directives, minimum requirements for gradual implementation, having regard to the conditions and technical rules obtaining in each of the Member States. Such directives shall avoid imposing administrative, financial and legal constraints in a way which would hold back the creation and development of small and medium-sized undertakings.

The Council shall act in accordance with the procedure referred to in Article 251 after consulting the Economic and Social Committee and the Committee of the Regions.

The Council, acting in accordance with the same procedure, may adopt measures designed to encourage co-operation between Member States through initiatives aimed at improving knowledge, developing exchanges of information and best practices, promoting innovative approaches and evaluating experiences in order to combat social exclusion.

3. However, the Council shall act unanimously on a proposal from the Commission, after consulting the European Parliament, the Economic and Social Committee and the Committee of the Regions in the following areas—
   - — social security and social protection of workers;
   - — protection of workers where their employment contract is terminated;
   - — representation and collective defence of the interests of workers and employers, including co-determination, subject to paragraph 6;
   - — conditions of employment for third-country nationals legally residing in Community territory;
   - — financial contributions for promotion of employment and job-creation, without prejudice to the provisions relating to the Social Fund.

4. A Member State may entrust management and labour, at their joint request, with the implementation of directives adopted pursuant to paragraphs 2 and 3.

In this case, it shall ensure that, no later than the date on which a directive must be transposed in accordance with Article 249, management and labour have introduced the necessary measures by agreement, the Member State concerned being required to take any necessary measure enabling it at any time to be in a position to guarantee the results imposed by that directive.

5. The provisions adopted pursuant to this Article shall not prevent any Member State from maintaining or introducing more stringent protective measures compatible with this Treaty.

6. The provisions of this Article shall not apply to pay, the right of association, the right to strike or the right to impose lock-outs.

Article 141 (ex Article 119)

1. Each Member State shall ensure that the principle of equal pay for male and female workers for equal work or work of equal value is applied.

2. For the purpose of this Article, 'pay' means the ordinary basic or minimum wage or salary and any other consideration, whether in cash or in kind, which the worker receives directly or indirectly, in respect of his employment, from his employer.

Equal pay without discrimination based on sex means—

(a) that pay for the same work at piece rates shall be calculated on the basis of the same unit of measurement;

(b) that pay for work at time rates shall be the same for the same job.

3. The Council, acting in accordance with the procedure referred to in Article 251, and after consulting the Economic and Social Committee, shall adopt measures to ensure the application of the principle of equal opportunities and equal treatment of men and women in matters of employment and occupation, including the principle of equal pay for equal work or work of equal value.

4. With a view to ensuring full equality in practice between men and women in working life, the principle of equal treatment shall not prevent any Member State from maintaining or adopting measures providing for specific advantages in order to make it easier for the under-represented sex to pursue a vocational activity or to prevent or compensate for disadvantages in professional careers.

Article 142 (ex Article 119a)

Member States shall endeavour to maintain the existing equivalence between paid holiday schemes.

Article 143 (ex Article 120)

The Commission shall draw up a report each year on progress in achieving the objectives of Article 136, including the demographic situation in the Community. It shall forward the report to the European Parliament, the Council and the Economic and Social Committee.

The European Parliament may invite the Commission to draw up reports on particular problems concerning the social situation.

Article 144 (ex Article 121)

The Council may, acting unanimously and after consulting the Economic and Social Committee, assign to the Commission tasks in connection with the implementation of common measures, particularly as regards social security for the migrant workers referred to in Articles 39 to 42.

Article 145 (ex Article 122)

The Commission shall include a separate chapter on social developments within the Community in its annual report to the European Parliament.

The European Parliament may invite the Commission to draw up reports on any particular problems concerning social conditions.

CHAPTER 2
THE EUROPEAN SOCIAL FUND

Article 146 (ex Article 123)

In order to improve employment opportunities for workers in the internal market and to contribute thereby to raising the standard of living, a European Social Fund is hereby established in accordance with the provisions set out below; it shall aim to render the employment of workers easier and to increase their geographical and occupational mobility within the Community, and to facilitate their adaptation to industrial changes and to changes in production systems, in particular through vocational training and retraining.

Article 147 (ex Article 124)

The Fund shall be administered by the Commission.

The Commission shall be assisted in this task by a Committee presided over by a Member of the Commission and composed of representatives of governments, trade unions and employers' organisations.

Article 148 (ex Article 125)

The Council, acting in accordance with the procedure referred to in Article 251 and after consulting the Economic and Social Committee and the Committee of the Regions, shall adopt implementing decisions relating to the European Social Fund.

CHAPTER 3
EDUCATION, VOCATIONAL TRAINING AND YOUTH

Article 149 (ex Article 126)

1. The Community shall contribute to the development of quality education by encouraging co-operation between Member States and, if necessary, by supporting and supplementing their action, while fully respecting the responsibility of the Member States for the content of teaching and the organisation of education systems and their cultural and linguistic diversity.

2. Community action shall be aimed at—
   - — developing the European dimension in education, particularly through the teaching and dissemination of the languages of the Member States;
   - — encouraging mobility of students and teachers, inter alia by encouraging the academic recognition of diplomas and periods of study;
   - — promoting co-operation between educational establishments;
   - — developing exchanges of information and experience on issues common to the education systems of the Member States;
   - — encouraging the development of youth exchanges and of exchanges of socio-educational instructors;
   - — encouraging the development of distance education.

3, 4 . . .

NOTES

Paras (3), (4): outside the scope of this work.

TITLE XII (ex Title IX)
CULTURE

Article 151 (ex Article 128)

1. The Community shall contribute to the flowering of the cultures of the Member States, while respecting their national and regional diversity and at the same time bringing the common cultural heritage to the fore.

2. Action by the Community shall be aimed at encouraging co-operation between Member States and, if necessary, supporting and supplementing their action in the following areas—
- — improvement of the knowledge and dissemination of the culture and history of the European peoples;
- — conservation and safeguarding of cultural heritage of European significance;
- — non-commercial cultural exchanges;
- — artistic and literary creation, including in the audiovisual sector.

3. The Community and the Member States shall foster co-operation with third countries and the competent international organisations in the sphere of culture, in particular the Council of Europe.

4. The Community shall take cultural aspects into account in its action under other provisions of this Treaty, in particular in order to respect and to promote the diversity of its cultures.

5 . . .

NOTES
Para (5): outside the scope of this work.

TITLE XIII (ex Title X)
PUBLIC HEALTH

Article 152 (ex Article 129)

1. A high level of human health protection shall be ensured in the definition and implementation of all Community policies and activities.

Community action, which shall complement national policies, shall be directed towards improving public health, preventing human illness and diseases, and obviating sources of danger to human health. Such action shall cover the fight against the major health scourges, by promoting research into their causes, their transmission and their prevention, as well as health information and education.

The Community shall complement the Member States' action in reducing drugs-related health damage, including information and prevention.

2. The Community shall encourage co-operation between the Member States in the areas referred to in this Article and, if necessary, lend support to their action.

Member States shall, in liaison with the Commission, co-ordinate among themselves their policies and programmes in the areas referred to in paragraph 1. The

Commission may, in close contact with the Member States, take any useful initiative to promote such co-ordination.

3–5 . . .

NOTES

Paras (3)–(5): outside the scope of this work.

TITLE XIV (ex Title XI)
CONSUMER PROTECTION

Article 153 (ex Article 129a)

1. In order to promote the interests of consumers and to ensure a high level of consumer protection, the Community shall contribute to protecting the health, safety and economic interests of consumers, as well as to promoting their right to information, education and to organise themselves in order to safeguard their interests.

2. Consumer protection requirements shall be taken into account in defining and implementing other Community policies and activities.

3–5 . . .

NOTES

Paras (3)–(5): outside the scope of this work.

TITLE XVI (ex Title XIII)
INDUSTRY

Article 157 (ex Article 130)

1. The Community and the Member States shall ensure that the conditions necessary for the competitiveness of the Community's industry exist.

2, 3 . . .

NOTES

Paras (2), (3): outside the scope of this work.

TITLE XVII (ex Title XIV)
ECONOMIC AND SOCIAL COHESION

Article 158 (ex Article 130a)

In order to promote its overall harmonious development, the Community shall develop and pursue its actions leading to the strengthening of its economic and social cohesion.

In particular, the Community shall aim at reducing disparities between the levels of development of the various regions and the backwardness of the least favoured regions or islands, including rural areas.

Article 160 (ex Article 130c)

The European Regional Development Fund is intended to help to redress the main regional imbalances in the Community through participation in the development and structural adjustment of regions whose development is lagging behind and in the conversion of declining industrial regions.

TITLE XIX (ex Title XVI) ENVIRONMENT

Article 174 (ex Article 130r)

1. Community policy on the environment shall contribute to pursuit of the following objectives—

- — preserving, protecting and improving the quality of the environment;
- — protecting human health;
- — prudent and rational utilisation of natural resources;
- — promoting measures at international level to deal with regional or worldwide environmental problems.

2. Community policy on the environment shall aim at a high level of protection taking into account the diversity of situations in the various regions of the Community. It shall be based on the precautionary principle and on the principles that preventive action should be taken, that environmental damage should as a priority be rectified at source and that the polluter should pay.

In this context, harmonisation measures answering environmental protection requirements shall include, where appropriate, a safeguard clause allowing Member States to take provisional measures, for non-economic environmental reasons, subject to a Community inspection procedure.

3, 4 . . .

NOTES

Paras (3), (4): outside the scope of this work.

TITLE XX (ex Title XVII) DEVELOPMENT CO-OPERATION

Article 177 (ex Article 130u)

1. Community policy in the sphere of development co-operation, which shall be complementary to the policies pursued by the Member States, shall foster—

- — the sustainable economic and social development of the developing countries, and more particularly the most disadvantaged among them;
- — the smooth and gradual integration of the developing countries into the world economy;
- — the campaign against poverty in the developing countries.

2. Community policy in this area shall contribute to the general objective of developing and consolidating democracy and the rule of law, and to that of respecting human rights and fundamental freedoms.

3. The Community and the Member States shall comply with the commitments and take account of the objectives they have approved in the context of the United Nations and other competent international organisations.

PART FIVE
INSTITUTIONS OF THE COMMUNITY

TITLE I
PROVISIONS GOVERNING THE INSTITUTIONS

CHAPTER 1
THE INSTITUTIONS

SECTION 1
THE EUROPEAN PARLIAMENT

Article 189 (ex Article 137)

The European Parliament, which shall consist of representatives of the peoples of the States brought together in the Community, shall exercise the powers conferred upon it by this Treaty.

The number of Members of the European Parliament shall not exceed seven hundred.

Article 190 (ex Article 138)

1. The representatives in the European Parliament of the peoples of the States brought together in the Community shall be elected by direct universal suffrage.

2. The number of representatives elected in each Member State shall be as follows—

Belgium	25
Denmark	16
Germany	99
Greece	25
Spain	64
France	87
Ireland	15
Italy	87
Luxembourg	6
Netherlands	31
Austria	21
Portugal	25
Finland	16
Sweden	22
United Kingdom	87.

In the event of amendments to this paragraph, the number of representatives elected in each Member State must ensure appropriate representation of the peoples of the States brought together in the Community.

3. Representatives shall be elected for a term of five years.

4. The European Parliament shall draw up a proposal for elections by direct universal suffrage in accordance with a uniform procedure in all Member States or in accordance with principles common to all Member States.

The Council shall, acting unanimously after obtaining the assent of the European Parliament, which shall act by a majority of its component members, lay down the appropriate provisions, which it shall recommend to Member States for adoption in accordance with their respective constitutional requirements.

5. The European Parliament shall, after seeking an opinion from the Commission and with the approval of the Council acting unanimously, lay down the regulations and general conditions governing the performance of the duties of its Members.

Article 191 (ex Article 138a)

Political parties at European level are important as a factor for integration within the Union. They contribute to forming a European awareness and to expressing the political will of the citizens of the Union.

Article 192 (ex Article 138b)

Insofar as provided in this Treaty, the European Parliament shall participate in the process leading up to the adoption of Community acts by exercising its powers under the procedures laid down in Articles 251 and 252 and by giving its assent or delivering advisory opinions.

The European Parliament may, acting by a majority of its Members, request the Commission to submit any appropriate proposal on matters on which it considers that a Community act is required for the purpose of implementing this Treaty.

Article 193 (ex Article 138c)

In the course of its duties, the European Parliament may, at the request of a quarter of its Members, set up a temporary Committee of Inquiry to investigate, without prejudice to the powers conferred by this Treaty on other institutions or bodies, alleged contraventions or maladministration in the implementation of Community law, except where the alleged facts are being examined before a court and while the case is still subject to legal proceedings.

The temporary Committee of Inquiry shall cease to exist on the submission of its report.

The detailed provisions governing the exercise of the right of inquiry shall be determined by common accord of the European Parliament, the Council and the Commission.

Article 194 (ex Article 138d)

Any citizen of the Union, and any natural or legal person residing or having its registered office in a Member State, shall have the right to address, individually or in association with other citizens or persons, a petition to the European Parliament on a matter which comes within the Community's fields of activity and which affects him, her or it directly.

Article 195 (ex Article 138e)

1. The European Parliament shall appoint an Ombudsman empowered to receive complaints from any citizen of the Union or any natural or legal person residing or having its registered office in a Member State concerning instances of maladministration in the activities of the Community institutions or bodies, with the exception of the Court of Justice and the Court of First Instance acting in their judicial role.

In accordance with his duties, the Ombudsman shall conduct inquiries for which he finds grounds, either on his own initiative or on the basis of complaints submitted to him direct or through a Member of the European Parliament, except where the alleged facts are or have been the subject of legal proceedings. Where the Ombudsman establishes an instance of maladministration, he shall refer the matter to the institution concerned, which shall have a period of three months in which to inform him of its views. The Ombudsman shall then forward a report to the European Parliament and the institution concerned. The person lodging the complaint shall be informed of the outcome of such inquiries.

The Ombudsman shall submit an annual report to the European Parliament on the outcome of his inquiries.

2. The Ombudsman shall be appointed after each election of the European Parliament for the duration of its term of office. The Ombudsman shall be eligible for reappointment.

The Ombudsman may be dismissed by the Court of Justice at the request of the European Parliament if he no longer fulfils the conditions required for the performance of his duties or if he is guilty of serious misconduct.

3. The Ombudsman shall be completely independent in the performance of his duties. In the performance of those duties he shall neither seek nor take instructions from any body. The Ombudsman may not, during his term of office, engage in any other occupation, whether gainful or not.

4. The European Parliament shall, after seeking an opinion from the Commission and with the approval of the Council acting by a qualified majority, lay down the regulations and general conditions governing the performance of the Ombudsman's duties.

Article 196 (ex Article 139)

The European Parliament shall hold an annual session. It shall meet, without requiring to be convened, on the second Tuesday in March.

The European Parliament may meet in extraordinary session at the request of a majority of its Members or at the request of the Council or of the Commission.

Article 197 (ex Article 140)

The European Parliament shall elect its President and its officers from among its Members.

Members of the Commission may attend all meetings and shall, at their request, be heard on behalf of the Commission.

The Commission shall reply orally or in writing to questions put to it by the European Parliament or by its Members.

The Council shall be heard by the European Parliament in accordance with the conditions laid down by the Council in its Rules of Procedure.

Article 198 (ex Article 141)

Save as otherwise provided in this Treaty, the European Parliament shall act by an absolute majority of the votes cast.

The Rules of Procedure shall determine the quorum.

Article 199 (ex Article 142)

The European Parliament shall adopt its Rules of Procedure, acting by a majority of its Members.

The proceedings of the European Parliament shall be published in the manner laid down in its Rules of Procedure.

Article 200 (ex Article 143)

The European Parliament shall discuss in open session the annual general report submitted to it by the Commission.

Article 201 (ex Article 144)

If a motion of censure on the activities of the Commission is tabled before it, the European Parliament shall not vote thereon until at least three days after the motion has been tabled and only by open vote.

If the motion of censure is carried by a two-thirds majority of the votes cast, representing a majority of the Members of the European Parliament, the Members of the Commission shall resign as a body. They shall continue to deal with current business until they are replaced in accordance with Article 214. In this case, the term of office of the Members of the Commission appointed to replace them shall expire on the date on which the term of office of the Members of the Commission obliged to resign as a body would have expired.

SECTION 2
THE COUNCIL

Article 202 (ex Article 145)

To ensure that the objectives set out in this Treaty are attained the Council shall, in accordance with the provisions of this Treaty—

— ensure co-ordination of the general economic policies of the Member States;
— have power to take decisions;
— confer on the Commission, in the acts which the Council adopts, powers for the implementation of the rules which the Council lays down. The Council may impose certain requirements in respect of the exercise of these powers. The Council may also reserve the right, in specific cases, to exercise directly implementing powers itself. The procedures referred to above must be consonant with principles and rules to be laid down in advance by the Council, acting unanimously on a proposal from the Commission and after obtaining the Opinion of the European Parliament.

Article 203 (ex Article 146)

The Council shall consist of a representative of each Member State at ministerial level, authorised to commit the government of that Member State.

The office of President shall be held in turn by each Member State in the Council for a term of six months in the order decided by the Council acting unanimously.

Article 204 (ex Article 147)

The Council shall meet when convened by its President on his own initiative or at the request of one of its members or of the Commission.

Article 205 (ex Article 148)

1. Save as otherwise provided in this Treaty, the Council shall act by a majority of its members.

2. Where the Council is required to act by a qualified majority, the votes of its members shall be weighted as follows—

Belgium	5
Denmark	3
Germany	10
Greece	5
Spain	8
France	10
Ireland	3
Italy	10
Luxembourg	2
Netherlands	5
Austria	4
Portugal	5
Finland	3
Sweden	4
United Kingdom	10.

For their adoption, acts of the Council shall require at least—

— 62 votes in favour where this Treaty requires them to be adopted on a proposal from the Commission,

— 62 votes in favour, cast by at least 10 members, in other cases.

3. Abstentions by members present in person or represented shall not prevent the adoption by the Council of acts which require unanimity.

Article 206 (ex Article 150)

Where a vote is taken, any member of the Council may also act on behalf of not more than one other member.

Article 207 (ex Article 151)

1. A committee consisting of the Permanent Representatives of the Member States shall be responsible for preparing the work of the Council and for carrying out the tasks assigned to it by the Council. The Committee may adopt procedural decisions in cases provided for in the Council's Rules of Procedure.

2. The Council shall be assisted by a General Secretariat, under the responsibility of a Secretary-General, High Representative for the common foreign and security policy, who shall be assisted by a Deputy Secretary-General responsible for the running of the General Secretariat. The Secretary-General and the Deputy Secretary-General shall be appointed by the Council acting unanimously.

The Council shall decide on the organisation of the General Secretariat.

3. The Council shall adopt its Rules of Procedure.

For the purpose of applying Article 255(3), the Council shall elaborate in these Rules the conditions under which the public shall have access to Council documents. For the purpose of this paragraph, the Council shall define the cases in which it is to be regarded as acting in its legislative capacity, with a view to allowing greater access to documents in those cases, while at the same time preserving the effectiveness of its decision-making process. In any event, when the Council acts in its legislative capacity, the results of votes and explanations of vote as well as statements in the minutes shall be made public.

Article 208 (ex Article 152)

The Council may request the Commission to undertake any studies the Council considers desirable for the attainment of the common objectives, and to submit to it any appropriate proposals.

Article 209 (ex Article 153)

The Council shall, after receiving an opinion from the Commission, determine the rules governing the committees provided for in this Treaty.

Article 210 (ex Article 154)

The Council shall, acting by a qualified majority, determine the salaries, allowances and pensions of the President and Members of the Commission, and of the President, Judges, Advocates-General and Registrar of the Court of Justice. It shall also, again by a qualified majority, determine any payment to be made instead of remuneration.

SECTION 3
THE COMMISSION

Article 211 (ex Article 155)

In order to ensure the proper functioning and development of the common market, the Commission shall—

- ensure that the provisions of this Treaty and the measures taken by the institutions pursuant thereto are applied;
- formulate recommendations or deliver opinions on matters dealt with in this Treaty, if it expressly so provides or if the Commission considers it necessary;
- have its own power of decision and participate in the shaping of measures taken by the Council and by the European Parliament in the manner provided for in this Treaty;
- exercise the powers conferred on it by the Council for the implementation of the rules laid down by the latter.

Article 212 (ex Article 156)

The Commission shall publish annually, not later than one month before the opening of the session of the European Parliament, a general report on the activities of the Community.

Article 213 (ex Article 157)

1. The Commission shall consist of 20 Members, who shall be chosen on the grounds of their general competence and whose independence is beyond doubt.

The number of Members of the Commission may be altered by the Council, acting unanimously.

Only nationals of Member States may be Members of the Commission.

The Commission must include at least one national of each of the Member States, but may not include more than two Members having the nationality of the same State.

2. The Members of the Commission shall, in the general interest of the Community, be completely independent in the performance of their duties.

In the performance of these duties, they shall neither seek nor take instructions from any government or from any other body. They shall refrain from any action incompatible with their duties. Each Member State undertakes to respect this principle and not to seek to influence the Members of the Commission in the performance of their tasks.

The Members of the Commission may not, during their term of office, engage in any other occupation, whether gainful or not. When entering upon their duties they shall give a solemn undertaking that, both during and after their term of office, they will respect the obligations arising therefrom and in particular their duty to behave with integrity and discretion as regards the acceptance, after they have ceased to hold office, of certain appointments or benefits. In the event of any breach of these obligations, the Court of Justice may, on application by the Council or the Commission, rule that the Member concerned be, according to the circumstances, either compulsorily retired in accordance with Article 216 or deprived of his right to a pension or other benefits in its stead.

Article 214 (ex Article 158)

1. The Members of the Commission shall be appointed, in accordance with the procedure referred to in paragraph 2, for a period of five years, subject, if need be, to Article 201.

Their term of office shall be renewable.

2. The governments of the Member States shall nominate by common accord the person they intend to appoint as President of the Commission; the nomination shall be approved by the European Parliament.

The governments of the Member States shall, by common accord with the nominee for President, nominate the other persons whom they intend to appoint as Members of the Commission.

The President and the other Members of the Commission thus nominated shall be subject as a body to a vote of approval by the European Parliament. After approval by the European Parliament, the President and the other Members of the Commission shall be appointed by common accord of the governments of the Member States.

Article 215 (ex Article 159)

Apart from normal replacement, or death, the duties of a Member of the Commission shall end when he resigns or is compulsorily retired.

The vacancy thus caused shall be filled for the remainder of the Member's term of office by a new Member appointed by common accord of the governments of the Member States. The Council may, acting unanimously, decide that such a vacancy need not be filled.

In the event of resignation, compulsory retirement or death, the President shall be replaced for the remainder of his term of office. The procedure laid down in Article 214(2) shall be applicable for the replacement of the President.

Save in the case of compulsory retirement under Article 216, Members of the Commission shall remain in office until they have been replaced.

Article 216 (ex Article 160)

If any Member of the Commission no longer fulfils the conditions required for the performance of his duties or if he has been guilty of serious misconduct, the Court of Justice may, on application by the Council or the Commission, compulsorily retire him.

Article 217 (ex Article 161)

The Commission may appoint a Vice-President or two Vice-Presidents from among its Members.

Article 218 (ex Article 162)

1. The Council and the Commission shall consult each other and shall settle by common accord their methods of co-operation.

2. The Commission shall adopt its Rules of Procedure so as to ensure that both it and its departments operate in accordance with the provisions of this Treaty. It shall ensure that these rules are published.

Article 219 (ex Article 163)

The Commission shall work under the political guidance of its President.

The Commission shall act by a majority of the number of Members provided for in Article 213.

A meeting of the Commission shall be valid only if the number of Members laid down in its Rules of Procedure is present.

SECTION 4
THE COURT OF JUSTICE

Article 220 (ex Article 164)

The Court of Justice shall ensure that in the interpretation and application of this Treaty the law is observed.

Article 221 (ex Article 165)

The Court of Justice shall consist of 15 Judges.

The Court of Justice shall sit in plenary session. It may, however, form chambers, each consisting of three, five or seven Judges, either to undertake certain preparatory inquiries or to adjudicate on particular categories of cases in accordance with rules laid down for these purposes.

The Court of Justice shall sit in plenary session when a Member State or a Community institution that is a party to the proceedings so requests.

Should the Court of Justice so request, the Council may, acting unanimously, increase the number of Judges and make the necessary adjustments to the second and third paragraphs of this Article and to the second paragraph of Article 223.

Article 222 (ex Article 166)

The Court of Justice shall be assisted by eight Advocates-General. However, a ninth Advocate-General shall be appointed as from 1 January 1995 until 6 October 2000.

It shall be the duty of the Advocate-General, acting with complete impartiality and independence, to make, in open court, reasoned submissions on cases brought before the Court of Justice, in order to assist the Court in the performance of the task assigned to it in Article 220.

Should the Court of Justice so request, the Council may, acting unanimously, increase the number of Advocates-General and make the necessary adjustments to the third paragraph of Article 223.

Article 223 (ex Article 167)

The Judges and Advocates-General shall be chosen from persons whose independence is beyond doubt and who possess the qualifications required for appointment to the highest judicial offices in their respective countries or who are jurisconsults of recognised competence; they shall be appointed by common accord of the governments of the Member States for a term of six years.

Every three years there shall be a partial replacement of the Judges. Eight and seven Judges shall be replaced alternately.

Every three years there shall be a partial replacement of the Advocates-General. Four Advocates-General shall be replaced on each occasion.

Retiring Judges and Advocates-General shall be eligible for reappointment.

The Judges shall elect the President of the Court of Justice from among their number for a term of three years. He may be re-elected.

Article 224 (ex Article 168)

The Court of Justice shall appoint its Registrar and lay down the rules governing his service.

Article 225 (ex Article 168a)

1. A Court of First Instance shall be attached to the Court of Justice with jurisdiction to hear and determine at first instance, subject to a right of appeal to the Court of Justice on points of law only and in accordance with the conditions laid down by the Statute, certain classes of action or proceeding defined in accordance with the conditions laid down in paragraph 2. The Court of First Instance shall not be competent to hear and determine questions referred for a preliminary ruling under Article 234.

2. At the request of the Court of Justice and after consulting the European Parliament and the Commission, the Council, acting unanimously, shall determine the classes of action or proceeding referred to in paragraph 1 and the composition of the Court of First Instance and shall adopt the necessary adjustments and additional provisions to the Statute of the Court of Justice. Unless the Council decides otherwise, the provisions of this Treaty relating to the Court of Justice, in particular the provisions of the Protocol on the Statute of the Court of Justice, shall apply to the Court of First Instance.

3. The members of the Court of First Instance shall be chosen from persons whose independence is beyond doubt and who possess the ability required for appointment to judicial office; they shall be appointed by common accord of the governments of the Member States for a term of six years. The membership shall be partially renewed every three years. Retiring members shall be eligible for reappointment.

4. The Court of First Instance shall establish its Rules of Procedure in agreement with the Court of Justice. Those rules shall require the unanimous approval of the Council.

Article 226 (ex Article 169)

If the Commission considers that a Member State has failed to fulfil an obligation under this Treaty, it shall deliver a reasoned opinion on the matter after giving the State concerned the opportunity to submit its observations.

If the State concerned does not comply with the opinion within the period laid down by the Commission, the latter may bring the matter before the Court of Justice.

Article 227 (ex Article 170)

A Member State which considers that another Member State has failed to fulfil an obligation under this Treaty may bring the matter before the Court of Justice.

Before a Member State brings an action against another Member State for an alleged infringement of an obligation under this Treaty, it shall bring the matter before the Commission.

The Commission shall deliver a reasoned opinion after each of the States concerned has been given the opportunity to submit its own case and its observations on the other party's case both orally and in writing.

If the Commission has not delivered an opinion within three months of the date on which the matter was brought before it, the absence of such opinion shall not prevent the matter from being brought before the Court of Justice.

Article 228 (ex Article 171)

1. If the Court of Justice finds that a Member State has failed to fulfil an obligation under this Treaty, the State shall be required to take the necessary measures to comply with the judgment of the Court of Justice.

2. If the Commission considers that the Member State concerned has not taken such measures it shall, after giving that State the opportunity to submit its observations, issue a reasoned opinion specifying the points on which the Member State concerned has not complied with the judgment of the Court of Justice.

If the Member State concerned fails to take the necessary measures to comply with the Court's judgment within the time-limit laid down by the Commission, the latter may bring the case before the Court of Justice. In so doing it shall specify the amount of the lump sum or penalty payment to be paid by the Member State concerned which it considers appropriate in the circumstances.

If the Court of Justice finds that the Member State concerned has not complied with its judgment it may impose a lump sum or penalty payment on it.

This procedure shall be without prejudice to Article 227.

Article 229 (ex Article 172)

Regulations adopted jointly by the European Parliament and the Council, and by the Council, pursuant to the provisions of this Treaty, may give the Court of Justice unlimited jurisdiction with regard to the penalties provided for in such regulations.

Article 230 (ex Article 173)

The Court of Justice shall review the legality of acts adopted jointly by the European Parliament and the Council, of acts of the Council, of the Commission and of the ECB, other than recommendations and opinions, and of acts of the European Parliament intended to produce legal effects vis-à-vis third parties.

It shall for this purpose have jurisdiction in actions brought by a Member State, the Council or the Commission on grounds of lack of competence, infringement of an essential procedural requirement, infringement of this Treaty or of any rule of law relating to its application, or misuse of powers.

The Court of Justice shall have jurisdiction under the same conditions in actions brought by the European Parliament, by the Court of Auditors and by the ECB for the purpose of protecting their prerogatives.

Any natural or legal person may, under the same conditions, institute proceedings against a decision addressed to that person or against a decision which, although in the form of a regulation or a decision addressed to another person, is of direct and individual concern to the former.

The proceedings provided for in this Article shall be instituted within two months of the publication of the measure, or of its notification to the plaintiff, or, in the absence thereof, of the day on which it came to the knowledge of the latter, as the case may be.

Article 231 (ex Article 174)

If the action is well founded, the Court of Justice shall declare the act concerned to be void.

In the case of a regulation, however, the Court of Justice shall, if it considers this necessary, state which of the effects of the regulation which it has declared void shall be considered as definitive.

Article 232 (ex Article 175)

Should the European Parliament, the Council or the Commission, in infringement of this Treaty, fail to act, the Member States and the other institutions of the Community may bring an action before the Court of Justice to have the infringement established.

The action shall be admissible only if the institution concerned has first been called upon to act. If, within two months of being so called upon, the institution concerned has not defined its position, the action may be brought within a further period of two months.

Any natural or legal person may, under the conditions laid down in the preceding paragraphs, complain to the Court of Justice that an institution of the Community has failed to address to that person any act other than a recommendation or an opinion.

The Court of Justice shall have jurisdiction, under the same conditions, in actions or proceedings brought by the ECB in the areas falling within the latter's field of competence and in actions or proceedings brought against the latter.

Article 233 (ex Article 176)

The institution or institutions whose act has been declared void or whose failure to act has been declared contrary to this Treaty shall be required to take the necessary measures to comply with the judgment of the Court of Justice.

This obligation shall not affect any obligation which may result from the application of the second paragraph of Article 288.

This Article shall also apply to the ECB.

Article 234 (ex Article 177)

The Court of Justice shall have jurisdiction to give preliminary rulings concerning—

(a) the interpretation of this Treaty;

(b) the validity and interpretation of acts of the institutions of the Community and of the ECB;

(c) the interpretation of the statutes of bodies established by an act of the Council, where those statutes so provide.

Where such a question is raised before any court or tribunal of a Member State, that court or tribunal may, if it considers that a decision on the question is necessary to enable it to give judgment, request the Court of Justice to give a ruling thereon.

Where any such question is raised in a case pending before a court or tribunal of a Member State against whose decisions there is no judicial remedy under national law, that court or tribunal shall bring the matter before the Court of Justice.

Article 235 (ex Article 178)

The Court of Justice shall have jurisdiction in disputes relating to compensation for damage provided for in the second paragraph of Article 288.

Article 236 (ex Article 179)

The Court of Justice shall have jurisdiction in any dispute between the Community and its servants within the limits and under the conditions laid down in the Staff Regulations or the Conditions of Employment.

Article 237 (ex Article 180)

The Court of Justice shall, within the limits hereinafter laid down, have jurisdiction in disputes concerning—

(a) the fulfilment by Member States of obligations under the Statute of the European Investment Bank. In this connection, the Board of Directors of the Bank shall enjoy the powers conferred upon the Commission by Article 226;

(b) measures adopted by the Board of Governors of the European Investment Bank. In this connection, any Member State, the Commission or the Board of Directors of the Bank may institute proceedings under the conditions laid down in Article 230;

(c) measures adopted by the Board of Directors of the European Investment Bank. Proceedings against such measures may be instituted only by Member States or by the Commission, under the conditions laid down in Article 230, and solely on the grounds of non-compliance with the procedure provided for in Article 21(2), (5), (6) and (7) of the Statute of the Bank;

(d) the fulfilment by national central banks of obligations under this Treaty and the Statute of the ESCB. In this connection the powers of the Council of the ECB in respect of national central banks shall be the same as those conferred upon the Commission in respect of Member States by Article 226. If the Court of Justice finds that a national central bank has failed to fulfil an obligation under this Treaty, that bank shall be required to take the necessary measures to comply with the judgment of the Court of Justice.

Article 238 (ex Article 181)

The Court of Justice shall have jurisdiction to give judgment pursuant to any arbitration clause contained in a contract concluded by or on behalf of the Community, whether that contract be governed by public or private law.

Article 239 (ex Article 182)

The Court of Justice shall have jurisdiction in any dispute between Member States which relates to the subject matter of this Treaty if the dispute is submitted to it under a special agreement between the parties.

Article 240 (ex Article 183)

Save where jurisdiction is conferred on the Court of Justice by this Treaty, disputes to which the Community is a party shall not on that ground be excluded from the jurisdiction of the courts or tribunals of the Member States.

Article 241 (ex Article 184)

Notwithstanding the expiry of the period laid down in the fifth paragraph of Article 230, any party may, in proceedings in which a regulation adopted jointly by the European Parliament and the Council, or a regulation of the Council, of the Commission, or of the ECB is at issue, plead the grounds specified in the second paragraph of Article 230 in order to invoke before the Court of Justice the inapplicability of that regulation.

Article 242 (ex Article 185)

Actions brought before the Court of Justice shall not have suspensory effect. The Court of Justice may, however, if it considers that circumstances so require, order that application of the contested act be suspended.

Article 243 (ex Article 186)

The Court of Justice may in any cases before it prescribe any necessary interim measures.

Article 244 (ex Article 187)

The judgments of the Court of Justice shall be enforceable under the conditions laid down in Article 256.

Article 245 (ex Article 188)

The Statute of the Court of Justice is laid down in a separate Protocol.

The Council may, acting unanimously at the request of the Court of Justice and after consulting the Commission and the European Parliament, amend the provisions of Title III of the Statute.

The Court of Justice shall adopt its Rules of Procedure. These shall require the unanimous approval of the Council.

SECTION 5
THE COURT OF AUDITORS

Article 246 (ex Article 188a)

The Court of Auditors shall carry out the audit.

Article 247 (ex Article 188b)

1. The Court of Auditors shall consist of 15 Members.

2. The Members of the Court of Auditors shall be chosen from among persons who belong or have belonged in their respective countries to external audit bodies or who are especially qualified for this office. Their independence must be beyond doubt.

3. The Members of the Court of Auditors shall be appointed for a term of six years by the Council, acting unanimously after consulting the European Parliament.

The Members of the Court of Auditors shall be eligible for reappointment.

They shall elect the President of the Court of Auditors from among their number for a term of three years. The President may be re-elected.

4. The Members of the Court of Auditors shall, in the general interest of the Community, be completely independent in the performance of their duties.

In the performance of these duties, they shall neither seek nor take instructions from any government or from any other body. They shall refrain from any action incompatible with their duties.

5. The Members of the Court of Auditors may not, during their term of office, engage in any other occupation, whether gainful or not. When entering upon their duties they shall give a solemn undertaking that, both during and after their term of office, they will respect the obligations arising therefrom and in particular their duty to behave with integrity and discretion as regards the acceptance, after they have ceased to hold office, of certain appointments or benefits.

6. Apart from normal replacement, or death, the duties of a Member of the Court of Auditors shall end when he resigns, or is compulsorily retired by a ruling of the Court of Justice pursuant to paragraph 7.

The vacancy thus caused shall be filled for the remainder of the Member's term of office.

Save in the case of compulsory retirement, Members of the Court of Auditors shall remain in office until they have been replaced.

7. A Member of the Court of Auditors may be deprived of his office or of his right to a pension or other benefits in its stead only if the Court of Justice, at the request of the Court of Auditors, finds that he no longer fulfils the requisite conditions or meets the obligations arising from his office.

8. The Council, acting by a qualified majority, shall determine the conditions of employment of the President and the Members of the Court of Auditors and in particular their salaries, allowances and pensions. It shall also, by the same majority, determine any payment to be made instead of remuneration.

9. The provisions of the Protocol on the privileges and immunities of the European Communities applicable to the Judges of the Court of Justice shall also apply to the Members of the Court of Auditors.

Article 248 (ex Article 188c)

1. The Court of Auditors shall examine the accounts of all revenue and expenditure of the Community. It shall also examine the accounts of all revenue and expenditure of all bodies set up by the Community insofar as the relevant constituent instrument does not preclude such examination.

The Court of Auditors shall provide the European Parliament and the Council with a statement of assurance as to the reliability of the accounts and the legality and regularity of the underlying transactions which shall be published in the *Official Journal of the European Communities.*

2. The Court of Auditors shall examine whether all revenue has been received and all expenditure incurred in a lawful and regular manner and whether the financial management has been sound. In doing so, it shall report in particular on any cases of irregularity.

. . .

3. The audit shall be based on records and, if necessary, performed on the spot in the other institutions of the Community, on the premises of any body which manages revenue or expenditure on behalf of the Community and in the Member States, including on the premises of any natural or legal person in receipt of payments from the budget. In the Member States the audit shall be carried out in liaison with national audit bodies or, if these do not have the necessary powers, with the competent national departments. The Court of Auditors and the national audit bodies of the Member States shall co-operate in a spirit of trust while maintaining their independence. These bodies or departments shall inform the Court of Auditors whether they intend to take part in the audit.

. . .

4. The Court of Auditors shall draw up an annual report after the close of each financial year. It shall be forwarded to the other institutions of the Community and shall be published, together with the replies of these institutions to the observations of the Court of Auditors, in the *Official Journal of the European Communities.*

The Court of Auditors may also, at any time, submit observations, particularly in the form of special reports, on specific questions and deliver opinions at the request of one of the other institutions of the Community.

It shall adopt its annual reports, special reports or opinions by a majority of its Members.

It shall assist the European Parliament and the Council in exercising their powers of control over the implementation of the budget.

NOTES

Paras (2), (3): words omitted outside the scope of this work.

CHAPTER 2
PROVISIONS COMMON TO SEVERAL INSTITUTIONS

Article 249 (ex Article 189)

In order to carry out their task and in accordance with the provisions of this Treaty, the European Parliament acting jointly with the Council, the Council and the Commission shall make regulations and issue directives, take decisions, make recommendations or deliver opinions.

A regulation shall have general application. It shall be binding in its entirety and directly applicable in all Member States.

A directive shall be binding, as to the result to be achieved, upon each Member State to which it is addressed, but shall leave to the national authorities the choice of form and methods.

A decision shall be binding in its entirety upon those to whom it is addressed.

Recommendations and opinions shall have no binding force.

Article 250 (ex Article 189a)

1. Where, in pursuance of this Treaty, the Council acts on a proposal from the Commission, unanimity shall be required for an act constituting an amendment to that proposal, subject to Article 251(4) and (5).

2. As long as the Council has not acted, the Commission may alter its proposal at any time during the procedures leading to the adoption of a Community act.

Article 251 (ex Article 189b)

1. Where reference is made in this Treaty to this Article for the adoption of an act, the following procedure shall apply.

2. The Commission shall submit a proposal to the European Parliament and the Council.

The Council, acting by a qualified majority after obtaining the opinion of the European Parliament,

— if it approves all the amendments contained in the European Parliament's opinion, may adopt the proposed act thus amended;
— if the European Parliament does not propose any amendments, may adopt the proposed act;
— shall otherwise adopt a common position and communicate it to the European Parliament. The Council shall inform the European Parliament fully of the reasons which led it to adopt its common position. The Commission shall inform the European Parliament fully of its position.

If, within three months of such communication, the European Parliament—

(a) approves the common position or has not taken a decision, the act in question shall be deemed to have been adopted in accordance with that common position;
(b) rejects, by an absolute majority of its component members, the common position, the proposed act shall be deemed not to have been adopted;
(c) proposes amendments to the common position by an absolute majority of its component members, the amended text shall be forwarded to the Council and to the Commission, which shall deliver an opinion on those amendments.

3. If, within three months of the matter being referred to it, the Council, acting by a qualified majority, approves all the amendments of the European Parliament, the act in question shall be deemed to have been adopted in the form of the common position thus amended; however, the Council shall act unanimously on the amendments on which the Commission has delivered a negative opinion. If the Council does not approve all the amendments, the President of the Council, in agreement with the President of the European Parliament, shall within six weeks convene a meeting of the Conciliation Committee.

4. The Conciliation Committee, which shall be composed of the members of the Council or their representatives and an equal number of representatives of the European Parliament, shall have the task of reaching agreement on a joint text, by a qualified majority of the members of the Council or their representatives and by a majority of the representatives of the European Parliament. The Commission shall take part in the Conciliation Committee's proceedings and shall take all the necessary initiatives with a view to reconciling the positions of the European Parliament and the Council. In fulfilling this task, the Conciliation Committee shall address the common position on the basis of the amendments proposed by the European Parliament.

5. If, within six weeks of its being convened, the Conciliation Committee approves a joint text, the European Parliament, acting by an absolute majority of the votes cast, and the Council, acting by a qualified majority, shall each have a period of six weeks from that approval in which to adopt the act in question in accordance with the joint text. If either of the two institutions fails to approve the proposed act within that period, it shall be deemed not to have been adopted.

6. Where the Conciliation Committee does not approve a joint text, the proposed act shall be deemed not to have been adopted.

7. The periods of three months and six weeks referred to in this Article shall be extended by a maximum of one month and two weeks respectively at the initiative of the European Parliament or the Council.

Article 252 (ex Article 189c)

Where reference is made in this Treaty to this Article for the adoption of an act, the following procedure shall apply—

(a) The Council, acting by a qualified majority on a proposal from the Commission and after obtaining the opinion of the European Parliament, shall adopt a common position.

(b) The Council's common position shall be communicated to the European Parliament. The Council and the Commission shall inform the European Parliament fully of the reasons which led the Council to adopt its common position and also of the Commission's position.

 If, within three months of such communication, the European Parliament approves this common position or has not taken a decision within that period, the Council shall definitively adopt the act in question in accordance with the common position.

(c) The European Parliament may, within the period of three months referred to in point (b), by an absolute majority of its component Members, propose amendments to the Council's common position. The European Parliament may also, by the same majority, reject the Council's common position. The result of the proceedings shall be transmitted to the Council and the Commission.

If the European Parliament has rejected the Council's common position, unanimity shall be required for the Council to act on a second reading.

(d) The Commission shall, within a period of one month, re-examine the proposal on the basis of which the Council adopted its common position, by taking into account the amendments proposed by the European Parliament.

The Commission shall forward to the Council, at the same time as its re-examined proposal, the amendments of the European Parliament which it has not accepted, and shall express its opinion on them. The Council may adopt these amendments unanimously.

(e) The Council, acting by a qualified majority, shall adopt the proposal as re-examined by the Commission.

Unanimity shall be required for the Council to amend the proposal as re-examined by the Commission.

(f) In the cases referred to in points (c), (d) and (e), the Council shall be required to act within a period of three months. If no decision is taken within this period, the Commission proposal shall be deemed not to have been adopted.

(g) The periods referred to in points (b) and (f) may be extended by a maximum of one month by common accord between the Council and the European Parliament.

Article 253 (ex Article 190)

Regulations, directives and decisions adopted jointly by the European Parliament and the Council, and such acts adopted by the Council or the Commission, shall state the reasons on which they are based and shall refer to any proposals or opinions which were required to be obtained pursuant to this Treaty.

Article 254 (ex Article 191)

1. Regulations, directives and decisions adopted in accordance with the procedure referred to in Article 251 shall be signed by the President of the European Parliament and by the President of the Council and published in the *Official Journal of the European Communities*. They shall enter into force on the date specified in them or, in the absence thereof, on the twentieth day following that of their publication.

2. Regulations of the Council and of the Commission, as well as directives of those institutions which are addressed to all Member States, shall be published in the *Official Journal of the European Communities*. They shall enter into force on the date specified in them or, in the absence thereof, on the twentieth day following that of their publication.

3. Other directives, and decisions, shall be notified to those to whom they are addressed and shall take effect upon such notification.

Article 255 (ex Article 191a)

1. Any citizen of the Union, and any natural or legal person residing or having its registered office in a Member State, shall have a right of access to European Parliament, Council and Commission documents, subject to the principles and the conditions to be defined in accordance with paragraphs 2 and 3.

2. General principles and limits on grounds of public or private interest governing this right of access to documents shall be determined by the Council, acting in accordance with the procedure referred to in Article 251 within two years of the entry into force of the Treaty of Amsterdam.

3. Each institution referred to above shall elaborate in its own Rules of Procedure specific provisions regarding access to its documents.

Article 256 (ex Article 192)

Decisions of the Council or of the Commission which impose a pecuniary obligation on persons other than States, shall be enforceable.

Enforcement shall be governed by the rules of civil procedure in force in the State in the territory of which it is carried out . . .

NOTES

Words omitted outside the scope of this work.

CHAPTER 3
THE ECONOMIC AND SOCIAL COMMITTEE

Article 257 (ex Article 193)

An Economic and Social Committee is hereby established. It shall have advisory status.

The Committee shall consist of representatives of the various categories of economic and social activity, in particular, representatives of producers, farmers, carriers, workers, dealers, craftsmen, professional occupations and representatives of the general public.

Article 258 (ex Article 194)

The number of members of the Economic and Social Committee shall be as follows—

Belgium	12
Denmark	9
Germany	24
Greece	12
Spain	21
France	24
Ireland	9
Italy	24
Luxembourg	6
Netherlands	12
Austria	12
Portugal	12
Finland	9
Sweden	12
United Kingdom	24

The members of the Committee shall be appointed by the Council, acting unanimously, for four years. Their appointments shall be renewable.

The members of the Committee may not be bound by any mandatory instructions. They shall be completely independent in the performance of their duties, in the general interest of the Community.

The Council, acting by a qualified majority, shall determine the allowances of members of the Committee.

Article 259 (ex Article 195)

1. For the appointment of the members of the Committee, each Member State shall provide the Council with a list containing twice as many candidates as there are seats allotted to its nationals.

The composition of the Committee shall take account of the need to ensure adequate representation of the various categories of economic and social activity.

2. The Council shall consult the Commission. It may obtain the opinion of European bodies which are representative of the various economic and social sectors to which the activities of the Community are of concern.

Article 260 (ex Article 196)

The Committee shall elect its chairman and officers from among its members for a term of two years.

It shall adopt its Rules of Procedure.

The Committee shall be convened by its chairman at the request of the Council or of the Commission. It may also meet on its own initiative.

Article 261 (ex Article 197)

The Committee shall include specialised sections for the principal fields covered by this Treaty.

. . .

NOTES

Words omitted outside the scope of this work.

Article 262 (ex Article 198)

The Committee must be consulted by the Council or by the Commission where this Treaty so provides. The Committee may be consulted by these institutions in all cases in which they consider it appropriate. It may issue an opinion on its own initiative in cases in which it considers such action appropriate.

. . .

The Committee may be consulted by the European Parliament.

NOTES

Words omitted outside the scope of this work.

CHAPTER 4
THE COMMITTEE OF THE REGIONS

Article 263 (ex Article 198a)

A Committee consisting of representatives of regional and local bodies, hereinafter referred to as 'the Committee of the Regions', is hereby established with advisory status.

The number of members of the Committee of the Regions shall be as follows—

Belgium	12
Denmark	9
Germany	24
Greece	12
Spain	21
France	24
Ireland	9
Italy	24
Luxembourg	6
Netherlands	12
Austria	12
Portugal	12
Finland	9
Sweden	12
United Kingdom	24

The members of the Committee and an equal number of alternate members shall be appointed for four years by the Council acting unanimously on proposals from the respective Member States. Their term of office shall be renewable. No member of the Committee shall at the same time be a Member of the European Parliament.

The members of the Committee may not be bound by any mandatory instructions. They shall be completely independent in the performance of their duties, in the general interest of Community.

Article 265 (ex Article 198c)

The Committee of the Regions shall be consulted by the Council or by the Commission where this Treaty so provides and in all other cases, in particular those which concern cross-border co-operation, in which one of these two institutions considers it appropriate.

. . .

The Committee of the Regions may be consulted by the European Parliament.

It may issue an opinion on its own initiative in cases in which it considers such action appropriate.

The opinion of the Committee, together with a record of the proceedings, shall be forwarded to the Council and to the Commission.

NOTES

Words omitted outside the scope of this work.

CHAPTER 5
THE EUROPEAN INVESTMENT BANK

Article 266 (ex Article 198d)

The European Investment Bank shall have legal personality.

The members of the European Investment Bank shall be the Member States.

The Statute of the European Investment Bank is laid down in a Protocol annexed to this Treaty.

Article 267 (ex Article 198e)

The task of the European Investment Bank shall be to contribute, by having recourse to the capital market and utilising its own resources, to the balanced and steady development of the common market in the interest of the Community . . .

In carrying out its task, the Bank shall facilitate the financing of investment programmes in conjunction with assistance from the Structural Funds and other Community financial instruments.

2. Member States shall take the same measures to counter fraud affecting the financial interests of the Community as they take to counter fraud affecting their own financial interests.

NOTES

Para (1): words omitted outside the scope of this work.

PART SIX
GENERAL AND FINAL PROVISIONS

Article 281 (ex Article 210)

The Community shall have legal personality.

Article 282 (ex Article 211)

In each of the Member States, the Community shall enjoy the most extensive legal capacity accorded to legal persons under their laws; it may, in particular, acquire or dispose of movable and immovable property and may be a party to legal proceedings. To this end, the Community shall be represented by the Commission.

Article 284 (ex Article 213)

The Commission may, within the limits and under conditions laid down by the Council in accordance with the provisions of this Treaty, collect any information and carry out any checks required for the performance of the tasks entrusted to it.

Article 286 (ex Article 213b)

1. From 1 January 1999, Community acts on the protection of individuals with regard to the processing of personal data and the free movement of such data shall apply to the institutions and bodies set up by, or on the basis of, this Treaty.

2. Before the date referred to in paragraph 1, the Council, acting in accordance with the procedure referred to in Article 251, shall establish an independent supervisory body responsible for monitoring the application of such Community acts to Community institutions and bodies and shall adopt any other relevant provisions as appropriate.

Article 287 (ex Article 214)

The members of the institutions of the Community, the members of committees, and the officials and other servants of the Community shall be required, even after their duties have ceased, not to disclose information of the kind covered by the obligation of professional secrecy, in particular information about undertakings, their business relations or their cost components.

Article 290 (ex Article 217)

The rules governing the languages of the institutions of the Community shall, without prejudice to the provisions contained in the Rules of Procedure of the Court of Justice, be determined by the Council, acting unanimously.

Article 291 (ex Article 218)

The Community shall enjoy in the territories of the Member States such privileges and immunities as are necessary for the performance of its tasks, under the conditions laid down in the Protocol of 8 April 1965 on the privileges and immunities of the European Communities. The same shall apply to the European Central Bank, the European Monetary Institute, and the European Investment Bank.

Article 292 (ex Article 219)

Member States undertake not to submit a dispute concerning the interpretation or application of this Treaty to any method of settlement other than those provided for therein.

Article 294 (ex Article 221)

Member States shall accord nationals of the other Member States the same treatment as their own nationals as regards participation in the capital of companies or firms within the meaning of Article 48, without prejudice to the application of the other provisions of this Treaty.

Article 295 (ex Article 222)

This Treaty shall in no way prejudice the rules in Member States governing the system of property ownership.

Article 296 (ex Article 223)

1. The provisions of this Treaty shall not preclude the application of the following rules—

(a) no Member State shall be obliged to supply information the disclosure of which it considers contrary to the essential interests of its security;

(b) any Member State may take such measures as it considers necessary for the protection of the essential interests of its security which are connected with the production of or trade in arms, munitions and war material; such measures shall not adversely affect the conditions of competition in the common market regarding products which are not intended for specifically military purposes.

2. The Council may, acting unanimously on a proposal from the Commission, make changes to the list, which it drew up on 15 April 1958, of the products to which the provisions of paragraph 1(b) apply.

Article 297 (ex Article 224)

Member States shall consult each other with a view to taking together the steps needed to prevent the functioning of the common market being affected by measures which a Member State may be called upon to take in the event of serious internal disturbances affecting the maintenance of law and order, in the event of war, serious international tension constituting a threat of war, or in order to carry out obligations it has accepted for the purpose of maintaining peace and international security.

Article 298 (ex Article 225)

If measures taken in the circumstances referred to in Articles 296 and 297 have the effect of distorting the conditions of competition in the common market, the Commission shall, together with the State concerned, examine how these measures can be adjusted to the rules laid down in the Treaty.

By way of derogation from the procedure laid down in Articles 226 and 227, the Commission or any Member State may bring the matter directly before the Court of Justice if it considers that another Member State is making improper use of the powers provided for in Articles 296 and 297. The Court of Justice shall give its ruling in camera.

Article 308 (ex Article 235)

If action by the Community should prove necessary to attain, in the course of the operation of the common market, one of the objectives of the Community and this Treaty has not provided the necessary powers, the Council shall, acting unanimously on a proposal from the Commission and after consulting the European Parliament, take the appropriate measures.

Article 309 (ex Article 236)

1. Where a decision has been taken to suspend the voting rights of the representative of the government of a Member State in accordance with Article 7(2) of the Treaty on European Union, these voting rights shall also be suspended with regard to this Treaty.

2. Moreover, where the existence of a serious and persistent breach by a Member State of principles mentioned in Article 6(1) of the Treaty on European Union has been determined in accordance with Article 7(1) of that Treaty, the Council, acting by a qualified majority, may decide to suspend certain of the rights deriving from the application of this Treaty to the Member State in question. In doing so, the Council shall take into account the possible consequences of such a suspension on the rights and obligations of natural and legal persons.

The obligations of the Member State in question under this Treaty shall in any case continue to be binding on that State.

3. The Council, acting by a qualified majority, may decide subsequently to vary or revoke measures taken in accordance with paragraph 2 in response to changes in the situation which led to their being imposed.

4. When taking decisions referred to in paragraphs 2 and 3, the Council shall act without taking into account the votes of the representative of the government of the Member State in question. By way of derogation from Article 205(2) a qualified majority shall be defined as the same proportion of the weighted votes of the members of the Council concerned as laid down in Article 205(2).

This paragraph shall also apply in the event of voting rights being suspended in accordance with paragraph 1. In such cases, a decision requiring unanimity shall be taken without the vote of the representative of the government of the Member State in question.

Article 310 (ex Article 238)

The Community may conclude with one or more States or international organisations agreements establishing an association involving reciprocal rights and obligations, common action and special procedure.

Article 311 (ex Article 239)

The protocols annexed to this Treaty by common accord of the Member States shall form an integral part thereof.

Article 312 (ex Article 240)

This Treaty is concluded for an unlimited period.

FINAL PROVISIONS

Article 313 (ex Article 247)

This Treaty shall be ratified by the High Contracting Parties in accordance with their respective constitutional requirements. The instruments of ratification shall be deposited with the Government of the Italian Republic.

This Treaty shall enter into force on the first day of the month following the deposit of the instrument of ratification by the last signatory State to take this step. If, however, such deposit is made less than 15 days before the beginning of the following month, this Treaty shall not enter into force until the first day of the second month after the date of such deposit.

Article 314 (ex Article 248)

This Treaty, drawn up in a single original in the Dutch, French, German, and Italian languages, all four texts being equally authentic, shall be deposited in the archives of the Government of the Italian Republic, which shall transmit a certified copy to each of the Governments of the other signatory States.

Pursuant to the Accession Treaties, the Danish, English, Finnish, Greek, Irish, Portuguese, Spanish and Swedish versions of this Treaty shall also be authentic.

CONSOLIDATED VERSION OF THE TREATY ON EUROPEAN UNION

NOTES

Consolidated version of the Treaty on European Union as amended by the Treaty of Amsterdam. Date of publication in the OJ: OJ C340, 10.11.97, p 1.

Preamble

His Majesty the King of the Belgians, her Majesty the Queen of Denmark, the President of the Federal Republic of Germany, the President of the Hellenic Republic, his Majesty the King of Spain, the President of the French Republic, the President of Ireland, the President of the Italian Republic, his Royal Highness the Grand Duke of Luxembourg, her Majesty the Queen of the Netherlands, the President of the Portuguese Republic, her Majesty the Queen of the United Kingdom of Great Britain and Northern Ireland,

Resolved to mark a new stage in the process of European integration undertaken with the establishment of the European Communities,

Recalling the historic importance of the ending of the division of the European continent and the need to create firm bases for the construction of the future Europe,

Confirming their attachment to the principles of liberty, democracy and respect for human rights and fundamental freedoms and of the rule of law,

Confirming their attachment to fundamental social rights as defined in the European Social Charter signed at Turin on 18 October 1961 and in the 1989 Community Charter of the Fundamental Social Rights of Workers,

Desiring to deepen the solidarity between their peoples while respecting their history, their culture and their traditions,

Desiring to enhance further the democratic and efficient functioning of the institutions so as to enable them better to carry out, within a single institutional framework, the tasks entrusted to them,

Resolved to achieve the strengthening and the convergence of their economies and to establish an economic and monetary union including, in accordance with the provisions of this Treaty, a single and stable currency,

Determined to promote economic and social progress for their peoples, taking into account the principle of sustainable development and within the context of the accomplishment of the internal market and of reinforced cohesion and environmental protection, and to implement policies ensuring that advances in economic integration are accompanied by parallel progress in other fields,

Resolved to establish a citizenship common to nationals of their countries,

Resolved to implement a common foreign and security policy including the progressive framing of a common defence policy, which might lead to a common defence in accordance with the provisions of Article 17, thereby reinforcing the European identity and its independence in order to promote peace, security and progress in Europe and in the world,

Resolved to facilitate the free movement of persons, while ensuring the safety and security of their peoples, by establishing an area of freedom, security and justice, in accordance with the provisions of this Treaty,

Resolved to continue the process of creating an ever closer union among the peoples of Europe, in which decisions are taken as closely as possible to the citizen in accordance with the principle of subsidiarity,

In view of further steps to be taken in order to advance European integration,

Have decided to establish a European Union and . . . have agreed as follows

TITLE I
COMMON PROVISIONS

Article 1 (ex Article A)

By this Treaty, the High Contracting Parties establish among themselves a European Union, hereinafter called 'the Union'.

This Treaty marks a new stage in the process of creating an ever closer union among the peoples of Europe, in which decisions are taken as openly as possible and as closely as possible to the citizen.

The Union shall be founded on the European Communities, supplemented by the policies and forms of co-operation established by this Treaty. Its task shall be to organise, in a manner demonstrating consistency and solidarity, relations between the Member States and between their peoples.

Article 2 (ex Article B)

The Union shall set itself the following objectives—

— to promote economic and social progress and a high level of employment and to achieve balanced and sustainable development, in particular through the creation of an area without internal frontiers, through the strengthening of economic and social cohesion and through the establishment of economic and monetary union, ultimately including a single currency in accordance with the provisions of this Treaty;

— to assert its identity on the international scene, in particular through the implementation of a common foreign and security policy including the progressive framing of a common defence policy, which might lead to a common defence, in accordance with the provisions of Article 17;

- to strengthen the protection of the rights and interests of the nationals of its Member States through the introduction of a citizenship of the Union;
- to maintain and develop the Union as an area of freedom, security and justice, in which the free movement of persons is assured in conjunction with appropriate measures with respect to external border controls, asylum, immigration and the prevention and combating of crime;
- to maintain in full the acquis communautaire and build on it with a view to considering to what extent the policies and forms of co-operation introduced by this Treaty may need to be revised with the aim of ensuring the effectiveness of the mechanisms and the institutions of the Community.

The objectives of the Union shall be achieved as provided in this Treaty and in accordance with the conditions and the timetable set out therein while respecting the principle of subsidiarity as defined in Article 5 of the Treaty establishing the European Community.

Article 3 (ex Article C)

The Union shall be served by a single institutional framework which shall ensure the consistency and the continuity of the activities carried out in order to attain its objectives while respecting and building upon the acquis communautaire.

The Union shall in particular ensure the consistency of its external activities as a whole in the context of its external relations, security, economic and development policies. The Council and the Commission shall be responsible for ensuring such consistency and shall co-operate to this end. They shall ensure the implementation of these policies, each in accordance with its respective powers.

Article 4 (ex Article D)

The European Council shall provide the Union with the necessary impetus for its development and shall define the general political guidelines thereof.

The European Council shall bring together the Heads of State or Government of the Member States and the President of the Commission. They shall be assisted by the Ministers for Foreign Affairs of the Member States and by a Member of the Commission. The European Council shall meet at least twice a year, under the chairmanship of the Head of State or Government of the Member State which holds the Presidency of the Council.

The European Council shall submit to the European Parliament a report after each of its meetings and a yearly written report on the progress achieved by the Union.

Article 5 (ex Article E)

The European Parliament, the Council, the Commission, the Court of Justice and the Court of Auditors shall exercise their powers under the conditions and for the purposes provided for, on the one hand, by the provisions of the Treaties establishing the European Communities and of the subsequent Treaties and Acts modifying and supplementing them and, on the other hand, by the other provisions of this Treaty.

Article 6 (ex Article F)

1. The Union is founded on the principles of liberty, democracy, respect for human rights and fundamental freedoms, and the rule of law, principles which are common to the Member States.

2. The Union shall respect fundamental rights, as guaranteed by the European Convention for the Protection of Human Rights and Fundamental Freedoms signed in Rome on 4 November 1950 and as they result from the constitutional traditions common to the Member States, as general principles of Community law.

3. The Union shall respect the national identities of its Member States.

4. The Union shall provide itself with the means necessary to attain its objectives and carry through its policies.

Article 7 (ex Article F.1)

1. The Council, meeting in the composition of the Heads of State or Government and acting by unanimity on a proposal by one third of the Member States or by the Commission and after obtaining the assent of the European Parliament, may determine the existence of a serious and persistent breach by a Member State of principles mentioned in Article 6(1), after inviting the government of the Member State in question to submit its observations.

2. Where such a determination has been made, the Council, acting by a qualified majority, may decide to suspend certain of the rights deriving from the application of this Treaty to the Member State in question, including the voting rights of the representative of the government of that Member State in the Council. In doing so, the Council shall take into account the possible consequences of such a suspension on the rights and obligations of natural and legal persons.

The obligations of the Member State in question under this Treaty shall in any case continue to be binding on that State.

3. The Council, acting by a qualified majority, may decide subsequently to vary or revoke measures taken under paragraph 2 in response to changes in the situation which led to their being imposed.

4. For the purposes of this Article, the Council shall act without taking into account the vote of the representative of the government of the Member State in question. Abstentions by members present in person or represented shall not prevent the adoption of decisions referred to in paragraph 1. A qualified majority shall be defined as the same proportion of the weighted votes of the members of the Council concerned as laid down in Article 205(2) of the Treaty establishing the European Community.

This paragraph shall also apply in the event of voting rights being suspended pursuant to paragraph 2.

5. For the purposes of this Article, the European Parliament shall act by a two-thirds majority of the votes cast, representing a majority of its members.

TITLE V
PROVISIONS ON A COMMON FOREIGN AND SECURITY POLICY

Article 11 (ex Article J.1)

1. The Union shall define and implement a common foreign and security policy covering all areas of foreign and security policy, the objectives of which shall be—

— to safeguard the common values, fundamental interests, independence and integrity of the Union in conformity with the principles of the United Nations Charter;

— to strengthen the security of the Union in all ways;
— to preserve peace and strengthen international security, in accordance with the principles of the United Nations Charter, as well as the principles of the Helsinki Final Act and the objectives of the Paris Charter, including those on external borders;
— to promote international co-operation;
— to develop and consolidate democracy and the rule of law, and respect for human rights and fundamental freedoms.

2. The Member States shall support the Union's external and security policy actively and unreservedly in a spirit of loyalty and mutual solidarity.

The Member States shall work together to enhance and develop their mutual political solidarity. They shall refrain from any action which is contrary to the interests of the Union or likely to impair its effectiveness as a cohesive force in international relations.

The Council shall ensure that these principles are complied with.

Article 12 (ex Article J.2)

The Union shall pursue the objectives set out in Article 11 by—
— defining the principles of and general guidelines for the common foreign and security policy;
— deciding on common strategies;
— adopting joint actions;
— adopting common positions;
— strengthening systematic co-operation between Member States in the conduct of policy.

Article 13 (ex Article J.3)

1. The European Council shall define the principles of and general guidelines for the common foreign and security policy, including for matters with defence implications.

2. The European Council shall decide on common strategies to be implemented by the Union in areas where the Member States have important interests in common.

Common strategies shall set out their objectives, duration and the means to be made available by the Union and the Member States.

3. The Council shall take the decisions necessary for defining and implementing the common foreign and security policy on the basis of the general guidelines defined by the European Council.

The Council shall recommend common strategies to the European Council and shall implement them, in particular by adopting joint actions and common positions.

The Council shall ensure the unity, consistency and effectiveness of action by the Union.

Article 14 (ex Article J.4)

1. The Council shall adopt joint actions. Joint actions shall address specific situations where operational action by the Union is deemed to be required. They

shall lay down their objectives, scope, the means to be made available to the Union, if necessary their duration, and the conditions for their implementation.

2. . . .

3. Joint actions shall commit the Member States in the positions they adopt and in the conduct of their activity.

4–7 . . .

NOTES

Paras (2), (4)–(7): outside the scope of this work.

Article 15 (ex Article J.5)

The Council shall adopt common positions. Common positions shall define the approach of the Union to a particular matter of a geographical or thematic nature. Member States shall ensure that their national policies conform to the common positions.

Article 16 (ex Article J.6)

Member States shall inform and consult one another within the Council on any matter of foreign and security policy of general interest in order to ensure that the Union's influence is exerted as effectively as possible by means of concerted and convergent action.

Article 17 (ex Article J.7)

1. The common foreign and security policy shall include all questions relating to the security of the Union, including the progressive framing of a common defence policy, in accordance with the second subparagraph, which might lead to a common defence, should the European Council so decide. It shall in that case recommend to the Member States the adoption of such a decision in accordance with their respective constitutional requirements.

The Western European Union (WEU) is an integral part of the development of the Union providing the Union with access to an operational capability notably in the context of paragraph 2. It supports the Union in framing the defence aspects of the common foreign and security policy as set out in this Article. The Union shall accordingly foster closer institutional relations with the WEU with a view to the possibility of the integration of the WEU into the Union, should the European Council so decide. It shall in that case recommend to the Member States the adoption of such a decision in accordance with their respective constitutional requirements.

The policy of the Union in accordance with this Article shall not prejudice the specific character of the security and defence policy of certain Member States and shall respect the obligations of certain Member States, which see their common defence realised in the North Atlantic Treaty Organisation (NATO), under the North Atlantic Treaty and be compatible with the common security and defence policy established within that framework.

The progressive framing of a common defence policy will be supported, as Member States consider appropriate, by co-operation between them in the field of armaments.

2. Questions referred to in this Article shall include humanitarian and rescue tasks, peacekeeping tasks and tasks of combat forces in crisis management, including peacemaking.

3. . . .

4. The provisions of this Article shall not prevent the development of closer co-operation between two or more Member States on a bilateral level, in the framework of the WEU and the Atlantic Alliance, provided such co-operation does not run counter to or impede that provided for in this Title.

5. . . .

NOTES

Paras (3), (5): outside the scope of this work.

Article 18 (ex Article J.8)

1. The Presidency shall represent the Union in matters coming within the common foreign and security policy.

2. The Presidency shall be responsible for the implementation of decisions taken under this Title; in that capacity it shall in principle express the position of the Union in international organisations and international conferences.

3. The Presidency shall be assisted by the Secretary-General of the Council who shall exercise the function of High Representative for the common foreign and security policy.

4. The Commission shall be fully associated in the tasks referred to in paragraphs 1 and 2. The Presidency shall be assisted in those tasks if need be by the next Member State to hold the Presidency.

5. The Council may, whenever it deems it necessary, appoint a special representative with a mandate in relation to particular policy issues.

Article 19 (ex Article J.9)

1. Member States shall co-ordinate their action in international organisations and at international conferences. They shall uphold the common positions in such fora.

In international organisations and at international conferences where not all the Member States participate, those which do take part shall uphold the common positions.

2. Without prejudice to paragraph 1 and Article 14(3), Member States represented in international organisations or international conferences where not all the Member States participate shall keep the latter informed of any matter of common interest.

Member States which are also members of the United Nations Security Council will concert and keep the other Member States fully informed. Member States which are permanent members of the Security Council will, in the execution of their functions, ensure the defence of the positions and the interests of the Union, without prejudice to their responsibilities under the provisions of the United Nations Charter.

Article 20 (ex Article J.10)

The diplomatic and consular missions of the Member States and the Commission Delegations in third countries and international conferences, and their representations to international organisations, shall co-operate in ensuring that the common positions and joint actions adopted by the Council are complied with and implemented.

They shall step up co-operation by exchanging information, carrying out joint assessments and contributing to the implementation of the provisions referred to in Article 20 of the Treaty establishing the European Community.

Article 21 (ex Article J.11)

The Presidency shall consult the European Parliament on the main aspects and the basic choices of the common foreign and security policy and shall ensure that the views of the European Parliament are duly taken into consideration. The European Parliament shall be kept regularly informed by the Presidency and the Commission of the development of the Union's foreign and security policy.

The European Parliament may ask questions of the Council or make recommendations to it. It shall hold an annual debate on progress in implementing the common foreign and security policy.

Article 22 (ex Article J.12)

1. Any Member State or the Commission may refer to the Council any question relating to the common foreign and security policy and may submit proposals to the Council.

2. In cases requiring a rapid decision, the Presidency, of its own motion, or at the request of the Commission or a Member State, shall convene an extraordinary Council meeting within forty-eight hours or, in an emergency, within a shorter period.

Article 23 (ex Article J.13)

1. Decisions under this Title shall be taken by the Council acting unanimously. Abstentions by members present in person or represented shall not prevent the adoption of such decisions.

When abstaining in a vote, any member of the Council may qualify its abstention by making a formal declaration under the present subparagraph. In that case, it shall not be obliged to apply the decision, but shall accept that the decision commits the Union. In a spirit of mutual solidarity, the Member State concerned shall refrain from any action likely to conflict with or impede Union action based on that decision and the other Member States shall respect its position. If the members of the Council qualifying their abstention in this way represent more than one third of the votes weighted in accordance with Article 205(2) of the Treaty establishing the European Community, the decision shall not be adopted.

2. By derogation from the provisions of paragraph 1, the Council shall act by qualified majority—

- when adopting joint actions, common positions or taking any other decision on the basis of a common strategy;
- when adopting any decision implementing a joint action or a common position.

If a member of the Council declares that, for important and stated reasons of national policy, it intends to oppose the adoption of a decision to be taken by qualified majority, a vote shall not be taken. The Council may, acting by a qualified majority, request that the matter be referred to the European Council for decision by unanimity.

The votes of the members of the Council shall be weighted in accordance with Article 205(2) of the Treaty establishing the European Community. For their adoption, decisions shall require at least 62 votes in favour, cast by at least 10 members.

This paragraph shall not apply to decisions having military or defence implications.

3. For procedural questions, the Council shall act by a majority of its members.

TITLE VI
PROVISIONS ON POLICE AND JUDICIAL CO-OPERATION IN CRIMINAL MATTERS

Article 29 (ex Article K.1)

Without prejudice to the powers of the European Community, the Union's objective shall be to provide citizens with a high level of safety within an area of freedom, security and justice by developing common action among the Member States in the fields of police and judicial co-operation in criminal matters and by preventing and combating racism and xenophobia.

That objective shall be achieved by preventing and combating crime, organised or otherwise, in particular terrorism, trafficking in persons and offences against children, illicit drug trafficking and illicit arms trafficking, corruption and fraud, through—

— closer co-operation between police forces, customs authorities and other competent authorities in the Member States, both directly and through the European Police Office (Europol), in accordance with the provisions of Articles 30 and 32;

— closer co-operation between judicial and other competent authorities of the Member States in accordance with the provisions of Articles 31(a) to (d) and 32;

— approximation, where necessary, of rules on criminal matters in the Member States, in accordance with the provisions of Article 31(e).

Article 30 (ex Article K.2)

1. Common action in the field of police co-operation shall include—

(a) operational co-operation between the competent authorities, including the police, customs and other specialised law enforcement services of the Member States in relation to the prevention, detection and investigation of criminal offences;

(b) the collection, storage, processing, analysis and exchange of relevant information, including information held by law enforcement services on reports on suspicious financial transactions, in particular through Europol, subject to appropriate provisions on the protection of personal data;

(c) co-operation and joint initiatives in training, the exchange of liaison officers, secondments, the use of equipment, and forensic research;

(d) the common evaluation of particular investigative techniques in relation to the detection of serious forms of organised crime.

2. . . .

NOTES

Para (2): outside the scope of this work.

Article 31 (ex Article K.3)

Common action on judicial co-operation in criminal matters shall include—

(a) facilitating and accelerating co-operation between competent ministries and judicial or equivalent authorities of the Member States in relation to proceedings and the enforcement of decisions;

(b) facilitating extradition between Member States;

(c) ensuring compatibility in rules applicable in the Member States, as may be necessary to improve such co-operation;

(d) preventing conflicts of jurisdiction between Member States;

(e) progressively adopting measures establishing minimum rules relating to the constituent elements of criminal acts and to penalties in the fields of organised crime, terrorism and illicit drug trafficking.

Article 33 (ex Article K.5)

This Title shall not affect the exercise of the responsibilities incumbent upon Member States with regard to the maintenance of law and order and the safeguarding of internal security.

TITLE VIII (ex Title VII)
FINAL PROVISIONS

Article 49 (ex Article O)

Any European State which respects the principles set out in Article 6(1) may apply to become a member of the Union. It shall address its application to the Council, which shall act unanimously after consulting the Commission and after receiving the assent of the European Parliament, which shall act by an absolute majority of its component members.

The conditions of admission and the adjustments to the Treaties on which the Union is founded which such admission entails shall be the subject of an agreement between the Member States and the applicant State. This agreement shall be submitted for ratification by all the contracting States in accordance with their respective constitutional requirements.

Article 51 (ex Article Q)

This Treaty is concluded for an unlimited period.

Article 52 (ex Article R)

1. This Treaty shall be ratified by the High Contracting Parties in accordance with their respective constitutional requirements. The instruments of ratification shall be deposited with the Government of the Italian Republic.

2. This Treaty shall enter into force on 1 January 1993, provided that all the instruments of ratification have been deposited, or, failing that, on the first day of the month following the deposit of the instrument of ratification by the last signatory State to take this step.

Article 53 (ex Article S)

This Treaty, drawn up in a single original in the Danish, Dutch, English, French, German, Greek, Irish, Italian, Portuguese and Spanish languages, the texts in each of these languages being equally authentic, shall be deposited in the archives of the government of the Italian Republic, which will transmit a certified copy to each of the governments of the other signatory States.

Pursuant to the Accession Treaty of 1994, the Finnish and Swedish versions of this Treaty shall also be authentic.

COUNCIL DIRECTIVE

of 9 February 1976

on the implementation of the principle of equal treatment for men and women as regards access to employment, vocational training and promotion, and working conditions

(76/207/EEC)

NOTES

Date of publication in OJ: OJ L39, 14.2.76, p 40.

Article 1

1. The purpose of this Directive is to put into effect in the Member States the principle of equal treatment for men and women as regards access to employment, including promotion, and to vocational training and as regards working conditions and, on the conditions referred to in paragraph 2, social security. This principle is hereinafter referred to as "the principle of equal treatment".

2. . . .

NOTES

Para (2): outside the scope of this work.

Article 2

1. For the purposes of the following provisions, the principle of equal treatment shall mean that there shall be no discrimination whatsoever on grounds of sex either directly or indirectly by reference in particular to marital or family status.

2. This Directive shall be without prejudice to the right of Member States to exclude from its field of application those occupational activities and, where appropriate, the training leading thereto, for which, by reason of their nature of the context in which they are carried out, the sex of the worker constitutes a determining factor.

3. This Directive shall be without prejudice to provisions concerning the protection of women, particularly as regards pregnancy and maternity.

4. This Directive shall be without prejudice to measures to promote equal opportunity for men and women, in particular by removing existing inequalities which affect women's opportunities in the areas referred to in Article 1(1).

Article 3

1. Application of the principle of equal treatment means that there shall be no discrimination whatsoever on grounds of sex in the conditions, including selection criteria, for access to all jobs or posts, whatever the sector or branch of activity, and to all levels of the occupational hierarchy—

2. To this end, Member States shall take the measures necessary to ensure that—
   (a) any laws, regulations and administrative provisions contrary to the principle of equal treatment shall be abolished;
   (b) any provisions contrary to the principle of equal treatment which are included in collective agreements, individual contracts of employment, internal rules of undertakings, or in rules governing the independent occupations and professions shall be, or may be declared, null and void or may be amended;
   (c) those laws, regulations and administrative provisions contrary to the principle of equal treatment when the concern for protection which originally inspired them is no longer well founded shall be revised; and that where similar provisions are included in collective agreements labour and management shall be requested to undertake the desired revision.

Article 4

Application of the principle of equal treatment with regard to access to all types and to all levels, of vocational guidance, vocational training, advanced vocational training and retraining . . .

NOTES
Words omitted outside the scope of this work.

Article 5

1. Application of the principle of equal treatment with regard to working conditions, including the conditions governing dismissal, means that men and women shall be guaranteed the same conditions without discrimination on grounds of sex.

2. To this end, Member States shall take the measures necessary to ensure that—
   (a) any laws, regulations and administrative provisions contrary to the principle of equal treatment shall be abolished;
   (b) any provisions contrary to the principle of equal treatment which are included in collective agreements, individual contracts of employment, internal rules of undertakings or in rules governing the independents occupations and professions shall be, or may be declared, null and void or may be amended;
   (c) those laws, regulations and administrative provisions contrary to the principle of equal treatment when the concern for protection which originally inspired them is no longer well founded shall be revised; and that where similar provisions are included in collective agreements labour and management shall be requested to undertake the desired revision.

Article 6

Member States shall introduce into their national legal systems such measures as are necessary to enable all persons who consider themselves wronged by failure to apply to them the principle of equal treatment within the meaning of Articles 3, 4 and 5 to pursue their claims by judicial process after possible recourse to other competent authorities.

Article 7

Member States shall take the necessary measures to protect employees against dismissal by the employer as a reaction to a complaint within the undertaking or to any legal proceedings aimed at enforcing compliance with the principle of equal treatment.

EUROPEAN CONVENTION FOR THE PROTECTION OF HUMAN RIGHTS AND FUNDAMENTAL FREEDOMS

Rome, 4 November 1950

Entry into force: 3 September 1953, in accordance with Article 66.

The governments signatory hereto, being members of the Council of Europe,

Considering the Universal Declaration of Human Rights proclaimed by the General Assembly of the United Nations on 10 December 1948;

Considering that this Declaration aims at securing the universal and effective recognition and observance of the rights therein declared;

Considering that the aim of the Council of Europe is the achievement of greater unity between its members and that one of the methods by which that aim is to be pursued is the maintenance and further realisation of human rights and fundamental freedoms;

Reaffirming their profound belief in those fundamental freedoms which are the foundation of justice and peace in the world and are best maintained on the one hand by an effective political democracy and on the other by a common understanding and observance of the human rights upon which they depend;

Being resolved, as the governments of European countries which are like-minded and have a common heritage of political traditions, ideals, freedom and the rule of law, to take the first steps for the collective enforcement of certain of the rights stated in the Universal Declaration,

Have agreed as follows—

Article 1

Obligation to respect human rights

The High Contracting Parties shall secure to everyone within their jurisdiction the rights and freedoms defined in Section I of this Convention.

SECTION I
RIGHTS AND FREEDOMS

Article 2

Right to life

1. Everyone's right to life shall be protected by law. No one shall be deprived of his life intentionally save in the execution of a sentence of court following his conviction of a crime for which this penalty is provided by law.

2. Deprivation of life shall not be regarded as inflicted in contravention of this Article when it results from the use of force which is no more than absolutely necessary—

(a) in defence of any person from unlawful violence;

(b) in order to effect a lawful arrest or to prevent the escape of a person lawfully detained;

(c) in action lawfully taken for the purpose of quelling a riot or insurrection.

Article 3

Prohibition of torture

No one shall be subjected to torture or to inhuman or degrading treatment or punishment.

Article 4

Prohibition of slavery and forced labour

1. No one shall be held in slavery or servitude.

2. No one shall be required to perform forced or compulsory labour.

3. For the purpose of this article the term "forced or compulsory labour" shall not include—

(a) any work required to be done in the ordinary course of detention imposed according to the provisions of Article 5 of this Convention or during conditional release from such detention;

(b) any service of a military character or, in case of conscientious objectors in countries where they are recognised, service exacted instead of compulsory military service;

(c) any service exacted in case of an emergency or calamity threatening the life or well-being of the community;

(d) any work or service which forms part of normal civic obligations.

Article 5

Right to liberty and security

1. Everyone has the right to liberty and security of person. No one shall be deprived of his liberty save in the following cases and in accordance with a procedure prescribed by law—

(a) the lawful detention of a person after conviction by a competent court;

(b) the lawful arrest or detention of a person for non-compliance with the lawful order of a court or in order to secure the fulfilment of any obligation prescribed by law;

(c) the lawful arrest or detention of a person effected for the purpose of bringing him before the competent legal authority on reasonable suspicion of having committed an offence or when it is reasonably considered necessary to prevent his committing an offence or fleeing after having done so;

(d) the detention of a minor by lawful order for the purpose of educational supervision or his lawful detention for the purpose of bringing him before the competent legal authority;

(e) the lawful detention of persons for the prevention of the spreading of infectious diseases, of persons of unsound mind, alcoholics or drug addicts or vagrants;

(f) the lawful arrest or detention of a person to prevent his effecting an unauthorised entry into the country or of a person against whom action is being taken with a view to deportation or extradition.

2. Everyone who is arrested shall be informed promptly, in a language which he understands, of the reasons for his arrest and of any charge against him.

3. Everyone arrested or detained in accordance with the provisions of paragraph 1(c) of this article shall be brought promptly before a judge or other officer authorised by law to exercise judicial power and shall be entitled to trial within a reasonable time or to release pending trial. Release may be conditioned by guarantees to appear for trial.

4. Everyone who is deprived of his liberty by arrest or detention shall be entitled to take proceedings by which the lawfulness of his detention shall be decided speedily by a court and his release ordered if the detention is not lawful.

5. Everyone who has been the victim of arrest or detention in contravention of the provisions of this article shall have an enforceable right to compensation.

Article 6

Right to a fair trial

1. In the determination of his civil rights and obligations or of any criminal charge against him, everyone is entitled to a fair and public hearing within a reasonable time by an independent and impartial tribunal established by law. Judgment shall be pronounced publicly but the press and public may be excluded from all or part of the trial in the interests of morals, public order or national security in a democratic society, where the interests of juveniles or the protection of the private life of the parties so require, or to the extent strictly necessary in the opinion of the court in special circumstances where publicity would prejudice the interests of justice.

2. Everyone charged with a criminal offence shall be presumed innocent until proved guilty according to law.

3. Everyone charged with a criminal offence has the following minimum rights—

(a) to be informed promptly, in a language which he understands and in detail, of the nature and cause of the accusation against him;

(b) to have adequate time and facilities for the preparation of his defence;

(c) to defend himself in person or through legal assistance of his own choosing or, if he has not sufficient means to pay for legal assistance, to be given it free when the interests of justice so require;

(d) to examine or have examined witnesses against him and to obtain the attendance and examination of witnesses on his behalf under the same conditions as witnesses against him;

(e) to have the free assistance of an interpreter if he cannot understand or speak the language used in court.

Article 7

No punishment without law

1. No one shall be held guilty of any criminal offence on account of any act or omission which did not constitute a criminal offence under national or international

law at the time when it was committed. Nor shall a heavier penalty be imposed than the one that was applicable at the time the criminal offence was committed.

2. This article shall not prejudice the trial and punishment of any person for any act or omission which, at the time when it was committed, was criminal according to the general principles of law recognised by civilised nations.

Article 8

Right to respect for private and family life

1. Everyone has the right to respect for his private and family life, his home and his correspondence.

2. There shall be no interference by a public authority with the exercise of this right except such as is in accordance with the law and is necessary in a democratic society in the interests of national security, public safety or the economic well-being of the country, for the prevention of disorder or crime, for the protection of health or morals, or for the protection of the rights and freedoms of others.

Article 9

Freedom of thought, conscience and religion

1. Everyone has the right to freedom of thought, conscience and religion; this right includes freedom to change his religion or belief and freedom, either alone or in community with others and in public or private, to manifest his religion or belief, in worship, teaching, practice and observance.

2. Freedom to manifest one's religion or beliefs shall be subject only to such limitations as are prescribed by law and are necessary in a democratic society in the interests of public safety, for the protection of public order, health or morals, or for the protection of the rights and freedoms of others.

Article 10

Freedom of expression

1. Everyone has the right to freedom of expression. This right shall include freedom to hold opinions and to receive and impart information and ideas without interference by public authority and regardless of frontiers. This article shall not prevent States from requiring the licensing of broadcasting, television or cinema enterprises.

2. The exercise of these freedoms, since it carries with it duties and responsibilities, may be subject to such formalities, conditions, restrictions or penalties as are prescribed by law and are necessary in a democratic society, in the interests of national security, territorial integrity or public safety, for the prevention of disorder or crime, for the protection of health or morals, for the protection of the reputation or rights of others, for preventing the disclosure of information received in confidence, or for maintaining the authority and impartiality of the judiciary.

Article 11

Freedom of assembly and association

1. Everyone has the right to freedom of peaceful assembly and to freedom of association with others, including the right to form and to join trade unions for the protection of his interests.

2. No restrictions shall be placed on the exercise of these rights other than such as are prescribed by law and are necessary in a democratic society in the interests of national security or public safety, for the prevention of disorder or crime, for the protection of health or morals or for the protection of the rights and freedoms of others. This article shall not prevent the imposition of lawful restrictions on the exercise of these rights by members of the armed forces, of the police or of the administration of the State.

Article 12

Right to marry

Men and women of marriageable age have the right to marry and to found a family, according to the national laws governing the exercise of this right.

Article 13

Right to an effective remedy

Everyone whose rights and freedoms as set forth in this Convention are violated shall have an effective remedy before a national authority notwithstanding that the violation has been committed by persons acting in an official capacity.

Article 14

Prohibition of discrimination

The enjoyment of the rights and freedoms set forth in this Convention shall be secured without discrimination on any ground such as sex, race, colour, language, religion, political or other opinion, national or social origin, association with a national minority, property, birth or other status.

Article 15

Derogation in time of emergency

1. In time of war or other public emergency threatening the life of the nation any High Contracting Party may take measures derogating from its obligations under this Convention to the extent strictly required by the exigencies of the situation, provided that such measures are not inconsistent with its other obligations under international law.

2. No derogation from Article 2, except in respect of deaths resulting from lawful acts of war, or from Articles 3, 4 (paragraph 1) and 7 shall be made under this provision.

3. Any High Contracting Party availing itself of this right of derogation shall keep the Secretary General of the Council of Europe fully informed of the measures which it has taken and the reasons therefor. It shall also inform the Secretary General of the Council of Europe when such measures have ceased to operate and the provisions of the Convention are again being fully executed.

Article 16

Restrictions on political activity of aliens

Nothing in Articles 10, 11 and 14 shall be regarded as preventing the High Contracting Parties from imposing restrictions on the political activity of aliens.

Article 17

Prohibition of abuse of rights

Nothing in this Convention may be interpreted as implying for any State, group or person any right to engage in any activity or perform any act aimed at the destruction of any of the rights and freedoms set forth herein or at their limitation to a greater extent than is provided for in the Convention.

Article 18

Limitation on use of restrictions on rights

The restrictions permitted under this Convention to the said rights and freedoms shall not be applied for any purpose other than those for which they have been prescribed.

SECTION II
EUROPEAN COURT OF HUMAN RIGHTS

Article 19

Establishment of the Court

To ensure the observance of the engagements undertaken by the High Contracting Parties in the Convention and the Protocols thereto, there shall be set up a European Court of Human Rights, hereinafter referred to as "the Court". It shall function on a permanent basis.

Article 20

Number of judges

The Court shall consist of a number of judges equal to that of the High Contracting Parties.

Article 21

Criteria for office

1. The judges shall be of high moral character and must either possess the qualifications required for appointment to high judicial office or be jurisconsults of recognised competence.

2. The judges shall sit on the Court in their individual capacity.

3. During their term of office the judges shall not engage in any activity which is incompatible with their independence, impartiality or with the demands of a full-time office; all questions arising from the application of this paragraph shall be decided by the Court.

Article 22

Election of judges

1. The judges shall be elected by the Parliamentary Assembly with respect to each High Contracting Party by a majority of votes cast from a list of three candidates nominated by the High Contracting Party.

2. The same procedure shall be followed to complete the Court in the event of the accession of new High Contracting Parties and in filling casual vacancies.

Article 23

Terms of office

1. The judges shall be elected for a period of six years. They may be re-elected. However, the terms of office of one-half of the judges elected at the first election shall expire at the end of three years.

2–7 . . .

NOTES

Paras (2)–(7): outside the scope of this work.

Article 24

Dismissal

No judge may be dismissed from his office unless the other judges decide by a majority of two-thirds that he has ceased to fulfil the required conditions.

Article 33

Inter-State cases

Any High Contracting Party may refer to the Court any alleged breach of the provisions of the Convention and the protocols thereto by another High Contracting Party.

Article 34

Individual applications

The Court may receive applications from any person, non-governmental organisation or group of individuals claiming to be the victim of a violation by one of the High Contracting Parties of the rights set forth in the Convention or the protocols thereto. The High Contracting Parties undertake not to hinder in any way the effective exercise of this right.

Article 35

Admissibility criteria

1. The Court may only deal with the matter after all domestic remedies have been exhausted, according to the generally recognised rules of international law, and within a period of six months from the date on which the final decision was taken.

2. The Court shall not deal with any application submitted under Article 34 that
   - (a) is anonymous; or
   - (b) is substantially the same as a matter that has already been examined by the Court or has already been submitted to another procedure of international investigation or settlement and contains no relevant new information.

3. The Court shall declare inadmissible any individual application submitted under Article 34 which it considers incompatible with the provisions of the Convention or the protocols thereto, manifestly ill-founded, or an abuse of the right of application.

4. The Court shall reject any application which it considers inadmissible under this Article. It may do so at any stage of the proceedings.

Article 40

Public hearings and access to documents

1. Hearings shall be in public unless the Court in exceptional circumstances decides otherwise.

2. Documents deposited with the Registrar shall be accessible to the public unless the President of the Court decides otherwise.

Article 41

Just satisfaction

If the Court finds that there has been a violation of the Convention or the protocols thereto, and if the internal law of the High Contracting Party concerned allows only partial reparation to be made, the Court shall, if necessary, afford just satisfaction to the injured party.

Article 46

Binding force and execution of judgments

1. The High Contracting Parties undertake to abide by the final judgment of the Court in any case to which they are parties.

2. The final judgment of the Court shall be transmitted to the Committee of Ministers, which shall supervise its execution.

B: FOREIGN CONSTITUTIONS AND BILLS OF RIGHT

THE CONSTITUTION OF THE UNITED STATES OF AMERICA

Articles I–VII (*Outside the scope of this work.*)

AMENDMENTS TO THE CONSTITUTION OF THE UNITED STATES

Articles in addition to, and amendment of the Constitution of the United States of America, proposed by Congress, and ratified by the several states, pursuant to the fifth article of the original Constitution.

AMENDMENT I

Congress shall make no law respecting an establishment of religion, or prohibiting the free exercise thereof; or abridging the freedom of speech, or of the press, or the right to the people peaceably to assemble. and to petition the Government for a redress of grievances.

NOTES
Ratified: 15 December 1791.

AMENDMENT II

A well-regulated Militia, being necessary to the security of a free State, the right of the people to keep and bear Arms, shall not be infringed.

NOTES
Ratified: 15 December 1791.

AMENDMENT III

No soldier shall, in time of peace be quartered in any house, without the consent of the Owner, nor in time of war, but in a manner to be prescribed by law.

NOTES
Ratified: 15 December 1791.

AMENDMENT IV

The right of the people to be secure in their persons, houses, papers, and effects, against unreasonable searches and seizures, shall not be violated, and no warrants shall issue, but upon probable cause, supported by oath or affirmation, and particularly describing the place to be searched, and the persons or things to be seized.

NOTES
Ratified: 15 December 1791.

AMENDMENT V

No person shall be held to answer for a capital, or otherwise infamous crime, unless on a presentment or indictment of a Grand Jury, except in cases arising in the land or naval forces, or in the Militia, when in actual service in time of war or public danger; nor shall any person be subject for the same offence to be twice put in jeopardy of life or limb, nor shall be compelled in any criminal case to be a witness against himself, nor be deprived of life, liberty, or property, without due process of law; nor shall private property be taken for public use without just compensation.

NOTES

Ratified: 15 December 1791.

AMENDMENT VI

In all criminal prosecutions, the accused shall enjoy the right to a speedy and public trial, by an impartial jury of the State and district wherein the crime shall have been committed; which district shall have been previously ascertained by law, and to be informed of the nature and cause of the accusation; to be confronted with the witnesses against him; to have compulsory process for obtaining witnesses in his favour, and to have the assistance of counsel for his defence.

NOTES

Ratified: 15 December 1791.

AMENDMENT VII

In suits at common law, where the value in controversy shall exceed twenty dollars, the right of trial by jury shall be preserved, and no fact tried by a jury shall be otherwise re-examined in any Court of the United States, than according to the rules of the common law.

NOTES

Ratified: 15 December 1791.

AMENDMENT VIII

Excessive bail shall not be required, nor excessive fines imposed, nor cruel and unusual punishments inflicted.

NOTES

Ratified: 15 December 1791.

AMENDMENT IX

The enumeration in the Constitution of certain rights shall not be construed to deny or disparage others retained by the people.

NOTES

Ratified: 15 December 1791.

AMENDMENT X

The powers not delegated to the United States by the Constitution, nor prohibited by it to the States, are reserved to the States respectively, or to the people.

NOTES
Ratified: 15 December 1791.

(Amendments XI–XIII outside the scope of this work.)

AMENDMENT XIV

Section 1. All persons born or naturalized in the United States and subject to the jurisdiction thereof, are citizens of the United States and of the State wherein they reside. No State shall make or enforce any law which shall abridge the privileges or immunities of citizens of the United States; nor shall any State deprive any person of life, liberty, or property, without due process of law; nor deny to any person within its jurisdiction the equal protection of the laws.

Sections 2–4. . . .

Section 5. The Congress shall have power to enforce, by appropriate legislation, the provisions of this article.

NOTES
Ratified: 9 July 1868.
Sections 2–4: outside the scope of this work.

(Amendments XV–XXVII outside the scope of this work.)

CONSTITUTION OF THE REPUBLIC OF SOUTH AFRICA 1996

As adopted by the Constitutional Assembly on 8 May 1996 and as amended on 11 October 1996.

NOTES
Chapter 1, paras 2, 3 and Chapter 2 (Bill of Rights) are reproduced.

CHAPTER 1
FOUNDING PROVISIONS

2 Supremacy of Constitution

This Constitution is the supreme law of the Republic; law or conduct inconsistent with it is invalid, and the obligations imposed by it must be fulfilled.

3 Citizenship

(1) There is a common South African citizenship.

(2) All citizens are—
- (a) equally entitled to the rights, privileges and benefits of citizenship; and
- (b) equally subject to the duties and responsibilities of citizenship.

(3) National legislation must provide for the acquisition, loss and restoration of citizenship.

CHAPTER 2
BILL OF RIGHTS

7 Rights

(1) This Bill of Rights is a cornerstone of democracy in South Africa. It enshrines the rights of all people in our country and affirms the democratic values of human dignity, equality and freedom.

(2) The state must respect, protect, promote and fulfil the rights in the Bill of Rights.

(3) The rights in the Bill of Rights are subject to the limitations contained or referred to in section 36, or elsewhere in the Bill.

8 Application

(1) The Bill of Rights applies to all law, and binds the legislature, the executive, the judiciary and all organs of state.

(2) A provision of the Bill of Rights binds a natural or a juristic person if, and to the extent that, it is applicable, taking into account the nature of the right and the nature of any duty imposed by the right.

(3) When applying a provision of the Bill of Rights to a natural or juristic person in terms of subsection (2), a court—

(a) in order to give effect to a right in the Bill, must apply, or if necessary develop, the common law to the extent that legislation does not give effect to that right; and

(b) may develop rules of the common law to limit the right, provided that the limitation is in accordance with section 36(1).

(4) A juristic person is entitled to the rights in the Bill of Rights to the extent required by the nature of the rights and the nature of that juristic person.

9 Equality

(1) Everyone is equal before the law and has the right to equal protection and benefit of the law.

(2) Equality includes the full and equal enjoyment of all rights and freedoms. To promote the achievement of equality, legislative and other measures designed to protect or advance persons, or categories of persons, disadvantaged by unfair discrimination may be taken.

(3) The state may not unfairly discriminate directly or indirectly against anyone on one or more grounds, including race, gender, sex, pregnancy, marital status, ethnic or social origin, colour, sexual orientation, age, disability, religion, conscience, belief, culture, language and birth.

(4) No person may unfairly discriminate directly or indirectly against anyone on one or more grounds in terms of subsection (3). National legislation must be enacted to prevent or prohibit unfair discrimination.

(5) Discrimination on one or more of the grounds listed in subsection (3) is unfair unless it is established that the discrimination is fair.

10 Human dignity

Everyone has inherent dignity and the right to have their dignity respected and protected.

11 Life

Everyone has the right to life.

12 Freedom and security of the person

(1) Everyone has the right to freedom and security of the person, which includes the right—

(a) not to be deprived of freedom arbitrarily or without just cause;
(b) not to be detained without trial;
(c) to be free from all forms of violence from either public or private sources;
(d) not to be tortured in any way; and
(e) not to be treated or punished in a cruel, inhuman or degrading way.

(2) Everyone has the right to bodily and psychological integrity, which includes the right—

(a) to make decisions concerning reproduction;
(b) to security in and control over their body; and
(c) not to be subjected to medical or scientific experiments without their informed consent.

13 Slavery, servitude and forced labour

No one may be subjected to slavery, servitude or forced labour.

14 Privacy

Everyone has the right to privacy, which includes the right not to have—

(a) their person or home searched;
(b) their property searched;
(c) their possessions seized; or
(d) the privacy of their communications infringed.

15 Freedom of religion, belief and opinion

(1) Everyone has the right to freedom of conscience, religion, thought, belief and opinion.

(2) Religious observances may be conducted at state or state-aided institutions, provided that—

(a) those observances follow rules made by the appropriate public authorities;
(b) they are conducted on an equitable basis; and
(c) attendance at them is free and voluntary.

(3) (a) This section does not prevent legislation recognising—

(i) marriages concluded under any tradition, or a system of religious, personal or family law; or
(ii) systems of personal and family law under any tradition, or adhered to by persons professing a particular religion.

(b) Recognition in terms of paragraph (a) must be consistent with this section and the other provisions of the Constitution.

16 Freedom of expression

(1) Everyone has the right to freedom of expression, which includes—
- (a) freedom of the press and other media;
- (b) freedom to receive or impart information or ideas;
- (c) freedom of artistic creativity; and
- (d) academic freedom and freedom of scientific research.

(2) The right in subsection (1) does not extend to—
- (a) propaganda for war;
- (b) incitement of imminent violence; or
- (c) advocacy of hatred that is based on race, ethnicity, gender or religion, and that constitutes incitement to cause harm.

17 Assembly, demonstration, picket and petition

Everyone has the right, peacefully and unarmed, to assemble, to demonstrate, to picket and to present petitions.

18 Freedom of association

Everyone has the right to freedom of association.

19 Political rights

(1) Every citizen is free to make political choices, which includes the right—
- (a) to form a political party;
- (b) to participate in the activities of, or recruit members for, a political party; and
- (c) to campaign for a political party or cause.

(2) Every citizen has the right to free, fair and regular elections for any legislative body established in terms of the Constitution.

(3) Every adult citizen has the right—
- (a) to vote in elections for any legislative body established in terms of the Constitution, and to do so in secret; and
- (b) to stand for public office and, if elected, to hold office.

20 Citizenship

No citizen may be deprived of citizenship.

21 Freedom of movement and residence

(1) Everyone has the right to freedom of movement.

(2) Everyone has the right to leave the Republic.

(3) Every citizen has the right to enter, to remain in and to reside anywhere in, the Republic.

(4) Every citizen has the right to a passport.

22 Freedom of trade, occupation and profession

Every citizen has the right to choose their trade, occupation or profession freely. The practice of a trade, occupation or profession may be regulated by law.

23 Labour relations

(1) Everyone has the right to fair labour practices.

(2) Every worker has the right—
- (a) to form and join a trade union;
- (b) to participate in the activities and programmes of a trade union; and
- (c) to strike.

(3) Every employer has the right—
- (a) to form and join an employers' organisation; and
- (b) to participate in the activities and programmes of an employers' organisation.

(4) Every trade union and every employers' organisation has the right—
- (a) to determine its own administration, programmes and activities;
- (b) to organise; and
- (c) to form and join a federation.

(5) Every trade union, employers' organisation and employer has the right to engage in collective bargaining. National legislation may be enacted to regulate collective bargaining. To the extent that the legislation may limit a right in this Chapter, the limitation must comply with section 36(1).

(6) National legislation may recognise union security arrangements contained in collective agreements. To the extent that the legislation may limit a right in this Chapter, the limitation must comply with section 36(1).

24 Environment

Everyone has the right—
- (a) to an environment that is not harmful to their health or well-being; and
- (b) to have the environment protected, for the benefit of present and future generations, through reasonable legislative and other measures that—
  - (i) prevent pollution and ecological degradation;
  - (ii) promote conservation; and
  - (iii) secure ecologically sustainable development and use of natural resources while promoting justifiable economic and social development.

25 Property

(1) No one may be deprived of property except in terms of law of general application, and no law may permit arbitrary deprivation of property.

(2) Property may be expropriated only in terms of law of general application—
- (a) for a public purpose or in the public interest; and
- (b) subject to compensation, the amount of which and the time and manner of payment of which have either been agreed to by those affected or decided or approved by a court.

(3) The amount of the compensation and the time and manner of payment must be just and equitable, reflecting an equitable balance between the public interest and the interests of those affected, having regard to all relevant circumstances, including—
- (a) the current use of the property;
- (b) the history of the acquisition and use of the property;
- (c) the market value of the property;

(d) the extent of direct state investment and subsidy in the acquisition and beneficial capital improvement of the property; and
(e) the purpose of the expropriation.

(4) For the purposes of this section—
(a) the public interest includes the nation's commitment to land reform, and to reforms to bring about equitable access to all South Africa's natural resources; and
(b) property is not limited to land.

(5) The state must take reasonable legislative and other measures, within its available resources, to foster conditions which enable citizens to gain access to land on an equitable basis.

(6) A person or community whose tenure of land is legally insecure as a result of past racially discriminatory laws or practices is entitled, to the extent provided by an Act of Parliament, either to tenure which is legally secure or to comparable redress.

(7) A person or community dispossessed of property after 19 June 1913 as a result of past racially discriminatory laws or practices is entitled, to the extent provided by an Act of Parliament, either to restitution of that property or to equitable redress.

(8) No provision of this section may impede the state from taking legislative and other measures to achieve land, water and related reform, in order to redress the results of past racial discrimination, provided that any departure from the provisions of this section is in accordance with the provisions of section 36(1).

(9) Parliament must enact the legislation referred to in subsection (6).

26 Housing

(1) Everyone has the right to have access to adequate housing.

(2) The state must take reasonable legislative and other measures, within its available resources, to achieve the progressive realisation of this right.

(3) No one may be evicted from their home, or have their home demolished, without an order of court made after considering all the relevant circumstances. No legislation may permit arbitrary evictions.

27 Health care, food, water and social security

(1) Everyone has the right to have access to—
(a) health care services, including reproductive health care;
(b) sufficient food and water; and
(c) social security, including, if they are unable to support themselves and their dependants, appropriate social assistance.

(2) The state must take reasonable legislative and other measures, within its available resources, to achieve the progressive realisation of each of these rights.

(3) No one may be refused emergency medical treatment.

28 Children

(1) Every child has the right—
(a) to a name and a nationality from birth;
(b) to family care or parental care, or to appropriate alternative care when removed from the family environment;

(c) to basic nutrition, shelter, basic health care services and social services;
(d) to be protected from maltreatment, neglect, abuse or degradation;
(e) to be protected from exploitative labour practices;
(f) not to be required or permitted to perform work or provide services that—
  (i) are inappropriate for a person of that child's age; or
  (ii) place at risk the child's well-being, education, physical or mental health or spiritual, moral or social development;
(g) not to be detained except as a measure of last resort, in which case, in addition to the rights a child enjoys under sections 12 and 35, the child may be detained only for the shortest appropriate period of time, and has the right to be—
  (i) kept separately from detained persons over the age of 18 years; and
  (ii) treated in a manner, and kept in conditions, that take account of the child's age;
(h) to have a legal practitioner assigned to the child by the state, and at state expense, in civil proceedings affecting the child, if substantial injustice would otherwise result; and
(i) not to be used directly in armed conflict, and to be protected in times of armed conflict.

(2) A child's best interests are of paramount importance in every matter concerning the child.

(3) In this section "child" means a person under the age of 18 years.

29 Education

(1) Everyone has the right—
  (a) to a basic education, including adult basic education; and
  (b) to further education, which the state, through reasonable measures, must make progressively available and accessible.

(2) Everyone has the right to receive education in the official language or languages of their choice in public educational institutions where that education is reasonably practicable. In order to ensure the effective access to, and implementation of, this right, the state must consider all reasonable educational alternatives, including single medium institutions, taking into account—
  (a) equity;
  (b) practicability; and
  (c) the need to redress the results of past racially discriminatory laws and practices.

(3) Everyone has the right to establish and maintain, at their own expense, independent educational institutions that—
  (a) do not discriminate on the basis of race;
  (b) are registered with the state; and
  (c) maintain standards that are not inferior to standards at comparable public educational institutions.

(4) Subsection (3) does not preclude state subsidies for independent educational institutions.

30 Language and culture

Everyone has the right to use the language and to participate in the cultural life of their choice, but no one exercising these rights may do so in a manner inconsistent with any provision of the Bill of Rights.

31 Cultural, religious and linguistic communities

(1) Persons belonging to a cultural, religious or linguistic community may not be denied the right, with other members of that community—

- (a) to enjoy their culture, practise their religion and use their language; and
- (b) to form, join and maintain cultural, religious and linguistic associations and other organs of civil society.

(2) The rights in subsection (1) may not be exercised in a manner inconsistent with any provision of the Bill of Rights.

32 Access to information

(1) Everyone has the right of access to—

- (a) any information held by the state; and
- (b) any information that is held by another person and that is required for the exercise or protection of any rights.

(2) National legislation must be enacted to give effect to this right, and may provide for reasonable measures to alleviate the administrative and financial burden on the state.

33 Just administrative action

(1) Everyone has the right to administrative action that is lawful, reasonable and procedurally fair.

(2) Everyone whose rights have been adversely affected by administrative action has the right to be given written reasons.

(3) National legislation must be enacted to give effect to these rights, and must—

- (a) provide for the review of administrative action by a court or, where appropriate, an independent and impartial tribunal;
- (b) impose a duty on the state to give effect to the rights in subsections (1) and (2); and
- (c) promote an efficient administration.

34 Access to courts

Everyone has the right to have any dispute that can be resolved by the application of law decided in a fair public hearing before a court or, where appropriate, another independent and impartial tribunal or forum.

35 Arrested, detained and accused persons

(1) Everyone who is arrested for allegedly committing an offence has the right—

- (a) to remain silent;
- (b) to be informed promptly—
  - (i) of the right to remain silent; and
  - (ii) of the consequences of not remaining silent;
- (c) not to be compelled to make any confession or admission that could be used in evidence against that person;

(d) to be brought before a court as soon as reasonably possible, but not later than—
  (i) 48 hours after the arrest; or
  (ii) the end of the first court day after the expiry of the 48 hours, if the 48 hours expire outside ordinary court hours or on a day which is not an ordinary court day;

(e) at the first court appearance after being arrested, to be charged or to be informed of the reason for the detention to continue, or to be released; and

(f) to be released from detention if the interests of justice permit, subject to reasonable conditions.

(2) Everyone who is detained, including every sentenced prisoner, has the right—
  (a) to be informed promptly of the reason for being detained;
  (b) to choose, and to consult with, a legal practitioner, and to be informed of this right promptly;
  (c) to have a legal practitioner assigned to the detained person by the state and at state expense, if substantial injustice would otherwise result, and to be informed of this right promptly;
  (d) to challenge the lawfulness of the detention in person before a court and, if the detention is unlawful, to be released;
  (e) to conditions of detention that are consistent with human dignity, including at least exercise and the provision, at state expense, of adequate accommodation, nutrition, reading material and medical treatment; and
  (f) to communicate with, and be visited by, that person's—
    (i) spouse or partner;
    (ii) next of kin;
    (iii) chosen religious counsellor; and
    (iv) chosen medical practitioner.

(3) Every accused person has a right to a fair trial, which includes the right—
  (a) to be informed of the charge with sufficient detail to answer it;
  (b) to have adequate time and facilities to prepare a defence;
  (c) to a public trial before an ordinary court;
  (d) to have their trial begin and conclude without unreasonable delay;
  (e) to be present when being tried;
  (f) to choose, and be represented by, a legal practitioner, and to be informed of this right promptly;
  (g) to have a legal practitioner assigned to the accused person by the state and at state expense, if substantial injustice would otherwise result, and to be informed of this right promptly;
  (h) to be presumed innocent, to remain silent, and not to testify during the proceedings;
  (i) to adduce and challenge evidence;
  (j) not to be compelled to give self-incriminating evidence;
  (k) to be tried in a language that the accused person understands or, if that is not practicable, to have the proceedings interpreted in that language;
  (l) not to be convicted for an act or omission that was not an offence under either national or international law at the time it was committed or omitted;
  (m) not to be tried for an offence in respect of an act or omission for which that person has previously been either acquitted or convicted;

(n) to the benefit of the least severe of the prescribed punishments if the prescribed punishment for the offence has been changed between the time that the offence was committed and the time of sentencing; and

(o) of appeal to, or review by, a higher court.

(4) Whenever this section requires information to be given to a person, that information must be given in a language that the person understands.

(5) Evidence obtained in a manner that violates any right in the Bill of Rights must be excluded if the admission of that evidence would render the trial unfair or otherwise be detrimental to the administration of justice.

36 Limitation of rights

(1) The rights in the Bill of Rights may be limited only in terms of law of general application to the extent that the limitation is reasonable and justifiable in an open and democratic society based on human dignity, equality and freedom, taking into account all relevant factors, including—

(a) the nature of the right;

(b) the importance of the purpose of the limitation;

(c) the nature and extent of the limitation;

(d) the relation between the limitation and its purpose; and

(e) less restrictive means to achieve the purpose.

(2) Except as provided in subsection (1) or in any other provision of the Constitution, no law may limit any right entrenched in the Bill of Rights.

37 States of emergency

(1) A state of emergency may be declared only in terms of an Act of Parliament, and only when—

(a) the life of the nation is threatened by war, invasion, general insurrection, disorder, natural disaster or other public emergency; and

(b) the declaration is necessary to restore peace and order.

(2) A declaration of a state of emergency, and any legislation enacted or other action taken in consequence of that declaration, may be effective only—

(a) prospectively; and

(b) for no more than 21 days from the date of the declaration, unless the National Assembly resolves to extend the declaration. The Assembly may extend a declaration of a state of emergency for no more than three months at a time. The first extension of the state of emergency must be by a resolution adopted with a supporting vote of a majority of the members of the Assembly. Any subsequent extension must be by a resolution adopted with a supporting vote of at least 60 per cent of the members of the Assembly. A resolution in terms of this paragraph may be adopted only following a public debate in the Assembly.

(3) Any competent court may decide on the validity of—

(a) a declaration of a state of emergency;

(b) any extension of a declaration of a state of emergency; or

(c) any legislation enacted, or other action taken, in consequence of a declaration of a state of emergency.

(4) Any legislation enacted in consequence of a declaration of a state of emergency may derogate from the Bill of Rights only to the extent that—

(a) the derogation is strictly required by the emergency; and

(b) the legislation—

(i) is consistent with the Republic's obligations under international law applicable to states of emergency;

(ii) conforms to subsection (5); and

(iii) is published in the national Government Gazette as soon as reasonably possible after being enacted.

(5) No Act of Parliament that authorises a declaration of a state of emergency, and no legislation enacted or other action taken in consequence of a declaration, may permit or authorise—

(a) indemnifying the state, or any person, in respect of any unlawful act;

(b) any derogation from this section; or

(c) any derogation from a section mentioned in column 1 of the Table of Non-Derogable Rights, to the extent indicated opposite that section in column 3 of the Table.

Table of Non-Derogable Rights

Section number	*Section title*	*Extent to which the right is protected*
9	Equality	With respect to unfair discrimination solely on the grounds of race, colour, ethnic or social origin, sex religion or language
10	Human Dignity	Entirely
11	Life	Entirely
12	Freedom and Security of the person	With respect to subsections (1)(d) and (e) and (2)(c).
13	Slavery, servitude and forced labour	With respect to slavery and servitude
28	Children	With respect to: — subsection (1)(d) and (e); — the rights in subparagraphs (i) and (ii) of subsection (1)(g); and — subsection 1(i) in respect of children of 15 years and younger
35	Arrested, detained and accused persons	With respect to: — subsections (1)(a), (b) and (c) and (2)(d); — the rights in paragraphs (a) to (o) of subsection (3), excluding paragraph (d) — subsection (4); and — subsection (5) with respect to the exclusion of evidence if the admission of that evidence would render the trial unfair.

(6) Whenever anyone is detained without trial in consequence of a derogation of rights resulting from a declaration of a state of emergency, the following conditions must be observed—

(a) An adult family member or friend of the detainee must be contacted as soon as reasonably possible, and informed that the person has been detained.

(b) A notice must be published in the national Government Gazette within five days of the person being detained, stating the detainee's name and place of detention and referring to the emergency measure in terms of which that person has been detained.

(c) The detainee must be allowed to choose, and be visited at any reasonable time by, a medical practitioner.

(d) The detainee must be allowed to choose, and be visited at any reasonable time by, a legal representative.

(e) A court must review the detention as soon as reasonably possible, but no later than 10 days after the date the person was detained, and the court must release the detainee unless it is necessary to continue the detention to restore peace and order.

(f) A detainee who is not released in terms of a review under paragraph (e), or who is not released in terms of a review under this paragraph, may apply to a court for a further review of the detention at any time after 10 days have passed since the previous review, and the court must release the detainee unless it is still necessary to continue the detention to restore peace and order.

(g) The detainee must be allowed to appear in person before any court considering the detention, to be represented by a legal practitioner at those hearings, and to make representations against continued detention.

(h) The state must present written reasons to the court to justify the continued detention of the detainee, and must give a copy of those reasons to the detainee at least two days before the court reviews the detention.

(7) If a court releases a detainee, that person may not be detained again on the same grounds unless the state first shows a court good cause for re-detaining that person.

(8) Subsections (6) and (7) do not apply to persons who are not South African citizens and who are detained in consequence of an international armed conflict. Instead, the state must comply with the standards binding on the Republic under international humanitarian law in respect of the detention of such persons.

38 Enforcement of rights

Anyone listed in this section has the right to approach a competent court, alleging that a right in the Bill of Rights has been infringed or threatened, and the court may grant appropriate relief, including a declaration of rights. The persons who may approach a court are:

(a) Anyone acting in their own interest;

(b) anyone acting on behalf of another person who cannot act in their own name;

(c) anyone acting as a member of, or in the interest of, a group or class of persons;

(d) anyone acting in the public interest; and

(e) an association acting in the interest of its members.

39 Interpretation of Bill of Rights

(1) When interpreting the Bill of Rights, a court, tribunal or forum—
- (a) must promote the values that underlie an open and democratic society based on human dignity, equality and freedom;
- (b) must consider international law; and
- (c) may consider foreign law.

(2) When interpreting any legislation, and when developing the common law or customary law, every court, tribunal or forum must promote the spirit, purport and objects of the Bill of Rights.

(3) The Bill of Rights does not deny the existence of any other rights or freedoms that are recognised or conferred by common law, customary law or legislation, to the extent that they are consistent with the Bill.

CANADIAN CHARTER OF RIGHTS AND FREEDOMS

NOTES

Enacted as Schedule B to the Canada Act 1982 (UK), which came into force on 17 April 1982.

PART I
CANADIAN CHARTER OF RIGHTS AND FREEDOMS

Whereas Canada is founded upon principles that recognize the supremacy of God and the rule of law—

Guarantee of Rights and Freedoms

1 Rights and freedoms in Canada.

The *Canadian Charter of Rights and Freedoms* guarantees the rights and freedoms set out in it subject only to such reasonable limits prescribed by law as can be demonstrably justified in a free and democratic society.

Fundamental Freedoms

2 Fundamental freedoms

Everyone has the following fundamental freedoms—
- (a) freedom of conscience and religion;
- (b) freedom of thought, belief, opinion and expression, including freedom of the press and other media of communication;
- (c) freedom of peaceful assembly; and
- (d) freedom of association.

Democratic Rights

3 Democratic rights of citizens

Every citizen of Canada has the right to vote in an election of members of the House of Commons or of a legislative assembly and to be qualified for membership therein.

4 Maximum duration of legislative bodies

(1) No House of Commons and no legislative assembly shall continue for longer than five years from the date fixed for the return of the writs of a general election of its members.

Continuation in special circumstances

(2) In time of real or apprehended war, invasion or insurrection, a House of Commons may be continued by Parliament and a legislative assembly may be continued by the legislature beyond five years if such continuation is not opposed by the votes of more than one-third of the members of the House of Commons or the legislative assembly, as the case may be.

5 Annual sitting of legislative bodies

There shall be a sitting of Parliament and of each legislature at least once every twelve months

Mobility Rights

6 Mobility of citizens

(1) Every citizen of Canada has the right to enter, remain in and leave Canada.

Rights to move and gain livelihood

(2) Every citizen of Canada and every person who has the status of a permanent resident of Canada has the right

(a) to move to and take up residence in any province; and
(b) to pursue the gaining of a livelihood in any province.

Limitation

(3) The rights specified in subsection (2) are subject to

(a) any laws or practices of general application in force in a province other than those that discriminate among persons primarily on the basis of province of present or previous residence; and
(b) any laws providing for reasonable residency requirements as a qualification for the receipt of publicly provided social services.

Affirmative action programs

(4) Subsections (2) and (3) do not preclude any law, program or activity that has as its object the amelioration in a province of conditions of individuals in that province who are socially or economically disadvantaged if the rate of employment in that province is below the rate of employment in Canada.

Legal Rights

7 Life, liberty and security of person

Everyone has the right to life, liberty and security of the person and the right not to be deprived thereof except in accordance with the principles of fundamental justice.

8 Search or seizure

Everyone has the right to be secure against unreasonable search or seizure.

9 Detention or imprisonment

Everyone has the right not to be arbitrarily detained or imprisoned.

10 Arrest or detention

Everyone has the right on arrest or detention

(a) to be informed promptly of the reasons therefor;
(b) to retain and instruct counsel without delay and to be informed of that right; and
(c) to have the validity of the detention determined by way of habeas corpus and to be released if the detention is not lawful.

11 Proceedings in criminal and penal matters

Any person charged with an offence has the right

(a) to be informed without unreasonable delay of the specific offence;
(b) to be tried within a reasonable time;
(c) not to be compelled to be a witness in proceedings against that person in respect of the offence;
(d) to be presumed innocent until proven guilty according to law in a fair and public hearing by an independent and impartial tribunal;
(e) not to be denied reasonable bail without just cause;
(f) except in the case of an offence under military law tried before a military tribunal, to the benefit of trial by jury where the maximum punishment for the offence is imprisonment for five years or a more severe punishment;
(g) not to be found guilty on account of any act or omission unless, at the time of the act or omission, it constituted an offence under Canadian or international law or was criminal according to the general principles of law recognized by the community of nations;
(h) if finally acquitted of the offence, not to be tried for it again and, if finally found guilty and punished for the offence, not to be tried or punished for it again; and
(i) if found guilty of the offence and if the punishment for the offence has been varied between the time of commission and the time of sentencing, to the benefit of the lesser punishment.

12 Treatment or punishment

Everyone has the right not to be subjected to any cruel and unusual treatment or punishment.

13 Self-crimination

A witness who testifies in any proceedings has the right not to have any incriminating evidence so given used to incriminate that witness in any other proceedings, except in a prosecution for perjury or for the giving of contradictory evidence.

14 Interpreter

A party or witness in any proceedings who does not understand or speak the language in which the proceedings are conducted or who is deaf has the right to the assistance of an interpreter.

Equality Rights

15 Equality before and under law and equal protection and benefit of law

(1) Every individual is equal before and under the law and has the right to the equal protection and equal benefit of the law without discrimination and, in particular, without discrimination based on race, national or ethnic origin, colour, religion, sex, age or mental or physical disability.

Affirmative action programs

(2) Subsection (1) does not preclude any law, program or activity that has as its object the amelioration of conditions of disadvantaged individuals or groups including those that are disadvantaged because of race, national or ethnic origin, colour, religion, sex, age or mental or physical disability.

Enforcement

24 Enforcement of guaranteed rights and freedoms

(1) Anyone whose rights or freedoms, as guaranteed by this Charter, have been infringed or denied may apply to a court of competent jurisdiction to obtain such remedy as the court considers appropriate and just in the circumstances.

Exclusion of evidence bringing administration of justice into disrepute

(2) Where, in proceedings under subsection (1), a court concludes that evidence was obtained in a manner that infringed or denied any rights or freedoms guaranteed by this Charter, the evidence shall be excluded if it is established that, having regard to all the circumstances, the admission of it in the proceedings would bring the administration of justice into disrepute.

General

25 Aboriginal rights and freedoms not affected by Charter

The guarantee in this Charter of certain rights and freedoms shall not be construed so as to abrogate or derogate from any aboriginal, treaty or other rights or freedoms that pertain to the aboriginal peoples of Canada including

- (a) any rights or freedoms that have been recognized by the Royal Proclamation of October 7, 1763; and
- (b) any rights or freedoms that now exist by way of land claims agreements or may be so acquired.

26 Other rights and freedoms not affected by Charter

The guarantee in this Charter of certain rights and freedoms shall not be construed as denying the existence of any other rights or freedoms that exist in Canada.

27 Multicultural heritage

This Charter shall be interpreted in a manner consistent with the preservation and enhancement of the multicultural heritage of Canadians.

28 Rights guaranteed equally to both sexes

Notwithstanding anything in this Charter, the rights and freedoms referred to in it are guaranteed equally to male and female persons.

29 Rights respecting certain schools preserved

Nothing in this Charter abrogates or derogates from any rights or privileges guaranteed by or under the Constitution of Canada in respect of denominational, separate or dissentient schools.

Application of Charter

32 Application of Charter

(1) This Charter applies

(a) to the Parliament and government of Canada in respect of all matters within the authority of Parliament including all matters relating to the Yukon Territory and Northwest Territories; and

(b) to the legislature and government of each province in respect of all matters within the authority of the legislature of each province.

Exception

(2) Notwithstanding subsection (1), section 15 shall not have effect until three years after this section comes into force.

33 Exception where express declaration

(1) Parliament or the legislature of a province may expressly declare in an Act of Parliament or of the legislature, as the case may be, that the Act or a provision thereof shall operate notwithstanding a provision included in section 2 or sections 7 to 15 of this Charter.

Operation of exception

(2) An Act or a provision of an Act in respect of which a declaration made under this section is in effect shall have such operation as it would have but for the provision of this Charter referred to in the declaration.

Five year limitation

(3) A declaration made under subsection (1) shall cease to have effect five years after it comes into force or on such earlier date as may be specified in the declaration.

Re-enactment

(4) Parliament or the legislature of a province may re-enact a declaration made under subsection (1).

Five year limitation

(5) Subsection (3) applies in respect of a re-enactment made under subsection (4).

Citation

34 Citation

This Part may be cited as the *Canadian Charter of Rights and Freedoms.*

C: NON-STATUTORY MATERIAL

MINISTERIAL CODE

(EXTRACT)

(Cabinet Office, July 1997)

1. MINISTERS OF THE CROWN

1. Ministers of the Crown are expected to behave according to the highest standards of constitutional and personal conduct in the performance of their duties. In particular, they must observe the following principles of Ministerial conduct:

(i) Ministers must uphold the principle of collective responsibility;

(ii) Ministers have a duty to Parliament to account, and be held to account, for the policies, decisions and actions of their Departments and Next Steps Agencies;

(iii) It is of paramount importance that Ministers give accurate and truthful information to Parliament, correcting any inadvertent error at the earliest opportunity. Ministers who knowingly mislead Parliament will be expected to offer their resignation to the Prime Minister;

(iv) Ministers should be as open as possible with Parliament and the public, refusing to provide information only when disclosure would not be in the public interest, which should be decided in accordance with relevant statute and the Government's Code of Practice on Access to Government Information (Second Edition, January 1997);

(v) Similarly, Ministers should require civil servants who give evidence before Parliamentary Committees on their behalf and under their directions to be as helpful as possible in providing accurate, truthful and full information in accordance with the duties and responsibilities of civil servants as set out in the Civil Service Code (January 1996).

(vi) Ministers must ensure that no conflict arises, or appears to arise, between their public duties and their private interests;

(vii) Ministers should avoid accepting any gift or hospitality which might, or might reasonably appear to, compromise their judgement or place them under an improper obligation;

(viii) Ministers in the House of Commons must keep separate their role as Minister and constituency Member;

(ix) Ministers must not use resources for party political purposes. They must uphold the political impartiality of the Civil Service, and not ask civil servants to act in any way which would conflict with the Civil Service Code.

These notes detail the arrangements for the conduct of affairs by Ministers. They are intended to give guidance by listing the principles and the precedents which may apply. They apply to all Members of the Government (the position of Parliamentary Private Secretaries is described separately in Section 4.) The notes should be read against the background of the duty of Ministers to comply with the law, including international law and treaty obligations, and to uphold the administration of justice, the general obligations listed above; and in the context of protecting the integrity of public life. Ministers must also, of course, adhere at all times to the requirements Parliament has itself laid down. For Ministers in the Commons, these are set by the Resolution carried on 19 March 1997 (Official Report, cols 1946–47): the terms of the Resolution are repeated at ii to v above. For Ministers in the Lords, Official Report col 1057. It will be for individual Ministers to judge how best to act in order to uphold the highest standards. They are responsible for justifying their conduct to Parliament. And they can only remain in office for so long as they retain the Prime Minister's confidence.

CODE OF PRACTICE ON ACCESS TO GOVERNMENT INFORMATION

(EXTRACTS)

(Second Edition (1997))

PART I

Information the Government will release

3. Subject to the exemptions in Part II, the Code commits departments and public bodies under the jurisdiction of the Parliamentary Commissioner for Administration (the Ombudsman)—

(i) to publish the facts and analysis of the facts which the Government considers relevant and important in framing major policy proposals and decisions; such information will normally be made available when policies and decisions are announced;

(ii) to publish or otherwise make available, as soon as practicable after the Code becomes operational, explanatory material on departments' dealings with the public (including such rules, procedures, internal guidance to officials, and similar administrative manuals as will assist better understanding of departmental action in dealing with the public) except where publication could prejudice any matter which should properly be kept confidential under Part II of the Code;

(iii) to give reasons for administrative decisions to those affected;[1]

(iv) to publish in accordance with the Citizen's Charter—

— full information about how public services are run, how much they cost, who is in charge, and what complaints and redress procedures are available;

— full and, where possible, comparable information about what services are being provided, what targets are set, what standards of service are expected and the results achieved.

(v) to release, in response to specific requests, information relating to their policies, actions and decisions and other matters related to their areas of responsibility.

NOTES

[1] There will be a few areas where well-established convention or legal authority limits the commitment to give reasons, for example certain decisions on merger and monopoly cases or on whether to take enforcement action.

4. There is no commitment that pre-existing documents, as distinct from information, will be made available in response to requests. The Code does not require departments to acquire information they do not possess, to provide information which is already published, or to provide information which is provided as part of an existing charged service other than through that service.

Responses to requests for information

5. Information will be provided as soon as practicable. The target for response to simple requests for information is 20 working days from the date of receipt. This target may need to be extended when significant search or collation of material is required. Where information cannot be provided under the terms of the Code, an explanation will normally be given.

Scope

6. The Code applies to those Government departments and other bodies within the jurisdiction of the Ombudsman (as listed in Schedule 2 to the Parliamentary Commissioner Act 1967). The Code applies to agencies within departments and to functions carried out on behalf of a department or public body by contractors. The Security and Intelligence Services are not within the scope of the Code, nor is information obtained from or relating to them.

Relationship to statutory access nghts

8. This Code is non-statutory and cannot override provisions contained in statutory rights of access to information or records (nor can it override statutory prohibitions on disclosure). Where the information could be sought under an existing statutory right, the terms of the right of access takes precedence over the Code. There are already certain access rights to health, medical and educational records, to personal files held by local authority housing and social services departments, and to personal data held on computer. There is also a right of access to environmental information. It is not envisaged that the Ombudsman will become involved in supervising these statutory rights.

. . .

NOTES

Words omitted outside the scope of this work.

Public records

9. The Code is not intended to override statutory provisions on access to public records, whether over or under thirty years old. Under s 12(3) of the Parliamentary Commissioner Act 1967, the Ombudsman is not required to question the merits of a decision if it is taken without maladministration by a Government department or other body in the exercise of a discretion vested in it. Decisions on public records made in England and Wales by the Lord Chancellor, or in Scotland and Northern Ireland by the Secretary of State, are such discretionary decisions.

Investigation of complaints

11. Complaints that information which should have been provided under the Code has not been provided, or that unreasonable charges have been demanded, should be made first to the department or body concerned. If the applicant remains dissatisfied, complaints may be made through a Member of Parliament to the Ombudsman. Complaints will be investigated at the Ombudsman's discretion in accordance with the procedures provided in the 1967 Act.

PART II

Reasons for confidentiality

The following categories of information are exempt from the commitments to provide information in this Code. In those categories which refer to harm or prejudice, the presumption remains that information should be disclosed unless the harm likely to arise from disclosure would outweigh the public interest in making the information available.

References to harm or prejudice include both actual harm or prejudice and risk or reasonable expectation of harm or prejudice. In such cases it should be considered whether any harm or prejudice arising from disclosure is outweighed by the public interest in making information available.

The exemptions will not be interpreted in a way which causes injustice to individuals.

1. Defence, security and international relations

(a) Information whose disclosure would harm national security or defence.

(b) Information whose disclosure would harm the conduct of international relations or affairs.

(c) Information received in confidence from foreign governments, foreign courts or international organisations.

2. Internal discussion and advice

Information whose disclosure would harm the frankness and candour of internal discussion, including—

— proceedings of Cabinet and Cabinet committees;

— internal opinion, advice, recommendation, consultation and deliberation;

— projections and assumptions relating to internal policy analysis; analysis of alternative policy options and information relating to rejected policy options;

— confidential communications between departments, public bodies and regulatory bodies.

3. Communications with the Royal Household

Information relating to confidential communications between Ministers and Her Majesty the Queen or other Members of the Royal Household, or relating to confidential proceedings of the Privy Council.

4. Law enforcement and legal proceedings

(a) Information whose disclosure could prejudice the administration of justice (including fair trial), legal proceedings or the proceedings of any tribunal, public inquiry or other formal investigations (whether actual or likely) or whose disclosure is, has been, or is likely to be addressed in the context of such proceedings.

(b) Information whose disclosure could prejudice the enforcement or proper administration of the law, including the prevention, investigation or detection of crime, or the apprehension or prosecution of offenders.

(c) Information relating to legal proceedings or the proceedings of any tribunal, public inquiry or other formal investigation which have been completed or terminated, or relating to investigations which have or might have resulted in proceedings.

(d) Information covered by legal professional privilege.

(e) Information whose disclosure would harm public safety or public order; or would prejudice the security of any building or penal institution.

(f) Information whose disclosure could endanger the life or physical safety of any person, or identify the source of information or assistance given in confidence for law enforcement or security purposes.

(g) Information whose disclosure would increase the likelihood of damage to the environment, or rare or endangered species and their habitats.

5. Immigration and nationality

Information relating to immigration, nationality, consular and entry clearance cases. However, information will be provided, though not through access to personal records, where there is no risk that disclosure would prejudice the effective administration of immigration controls or other statutory provisions.

6. Effective management of the economy and collection of tax

(a) Information whose disclosure would harm the ability of the Government to manage the economy, prejudice the conduct of official market operations, or could lead to improper gain or advantage.

(b) Information whose disclosure would prejudice the assessment or collection of tax, duties or National Insurance contributions, or assist tax avoidance or evasion.

7. Effective management and operations of the public service

(a) Information whose disclosure could lead to improper gain or advantage or would prejudice—

— the competitive position of a department or other public body or authority;

— negotiations or the effective conduct of personnel management, or commercial or contractual activities;

— the awarding of discretionary grants.

(b) Information whose disclosure would harm the proper and efficient conduct of the operations of a department or other public body or authority, including NHS organisations, or of any regulatory body.

8. Public employment, public appointments and honours

(a) Personnel records (relating to public appointments as well as employees of public authorities) including those relating to recruitment, promotion and security vetting.

(b) Information, opinions and assessments given in confidence in relation to public employment and public appointments made by Ministers of the Crown, by the Crown on the advice of Ministers or by statutory office holders.

(c) Information, opinions and assessments given in relation to recommendations for honours.

9. Voluminous or vexatious requests

Requests for information which are vexatious or manifestly unreasonable or are formulated in too general a manner, or which (because of the amount of information to be processed or the need to retrieve information from files not in current use) would require unreasonable diversion of resources.

10. Publication and prematurity in relation to publication

Information which is or will soon be published, or whose disclosure, where the material relates to a planned or potential announcement or publication, could cause harm (for example, of a physical or financial nature).

11. Research, statistics and analysis

(a) Information relating to incomplete analysis, research or statistics, where disclosure could be misleading or deprive the holder of priority of publication or commercial value.

(b) Information held only for preparing statistics or carrying out research, or for surveillance for health and safety purposes (including food safety), and which relates to individuals, companies or products which will not be identified in reports of that research or surveillance, or in published statistics.

12. Privacy of an individual

Unwarranted disclosure to a third party of personal information about any person (including a deceased person) or any other disclosure which would constitute or could facilitate an unwarranted invasion of privacy.

13. Third party's commercial confidences

Information including commercial confidences, trade secrets or intellectual property whose unwarranted disclosure would harm the competitive position of a third party.

14. Information given in confidence

(a) Information held in consequence of having been supplied in confidence by a person who—
- — gave the information under a statutory guarantee that its confidentiality would be protected; or
- — was not under any legal obligation, whether actual or implied, to supply it, and has not consented to its disclosure.

(b) Information whose disclosure without the consent of the supplier would prejudice the future supply of such information.

(c) Medical information provided in confidence if disclosure to the subject would harm their physical or mental health, or should only be made by a medical practitioner.

15. Statutory and other restrictions

(a) Information whose disclosure is prohibited by or under any enactment, regulation, European Community law or international agreement.

(b) Information whose release would constitute a breach of Parliamentary Privilege.